A Guide Book of

QUARTER EAGLE GOLD COINS

A Complete History and Price Guide

Q. Davi

Foreword by

Mike Fuljenz

Whitman Publishing, LLC
Publishing since 1934
Whitman.com

A Guide Book of

QUARTER EAGLE GOLD COINS

Whitman Publishing, LLC
PUBLISHING SINCE 1934
Whitman.com

1974 Chandalar Drive, Suite D, Pelham, AL 35124

Correspondence concerning this book may be directed to Whitman Publishing, Attn: Quarter Eagles, at the address above.

ISBN: 0794847331
Printed in China

Disclaimer: Expert opinion should be sought in any significant numismatic purchase. This book is presented as a guide only. No warranty or representation of any kind is made concerning the completeness of the information presented. The author, a professional numismatist, regularly buys, sells, and holds certain of the items discussed in this book.

Caveat: The value estimates given are subject to variation and differences of opinion. Before making decisions to buy or sell, consult the latest information. Past performance of the rare-coin market or any coin or series within that market is not necessarily an indication of future performance, as the future is unknown. Such factors as changing demand, popularity, grading interpretations, strength of the overall coin market, and economic conditions will continue to be influences.

Other books in the Bowers Series include: *A Guide Book of Morgan Silver Dollars; A Guide Book of Double Eagle Gold Coins; A Guide Book of United States Type Coins; A Guide Book of Modern United States Proof Coin Sets; A Guide Book of Shield and Liberty Head Nickels; A Guide Book of Flying Eagle and Indian Head Cents; A Guide Book of Washington Quarters; A Guide Book of Buffalo and Jefferson Nickels; A Guide Book of Lincoln Cents; A Guide Book of United States Commemorative Coins; A Guide Book of United States Tokens and Medals; A Guide Book of Gold Dollars; A Guide Book of Peace Dollars; A Guide Book of the Official Red Book of United States Coins; A Guide Book of Franklin and Kennedy Half Dollars; A Guide Book of Civil War Tokens; A Guide Book of Hard Times Tokens; A Guide Book of Mercury Dimes, Standing Liberty Quarters, and Liberty Walking Half Dollars; A Guide Book of Half Cents and Large Cents; A Guide Book of Barber Silver Coins; A Guide Book of Liberty Seated Silver Coins; A Guide Book of Modern United States Dollar Coins; A Guide Book of the United States Mint; A Guide Book of Gold Eagle Coins;* and *A Guide Book of Continental Currency and Coins.*

Whitman®

Contents

Foreword

Whenever Q. David Bowers releases a new book, numismatists everywhere smile. His literary contributions are legendary. Long before I received a Clemy, Bowers's excellence was recognized by the Numismatic Literary Guild when he too was awarded the Clemy, their top award for long-term literary excellence.

What is less known, perhaps, is David's wonderful leadership qualities, which were on display when he served as president of the American Numismatic Association in the early 1980s.

When I first met Dave, I was a young (27) grader/authenticator for the American Numismatic Association Certification Service (ANACS), joining David at an ANA board meeting in Colorado Springs. At the time, the board of ANA luminaries was debating whether to change the way our grading service described coins from numbers to adjectival grading. We graders pointed out that the hobby and our customers preferred numerical grading. Many of the elder statesmen (and stateswomen) on the board preferred adjectives like "Choice Uncirculated" to a numerical grade like "MS-63." With 20/20 hindsight, I think we graders not only had a better crystal ball for the future, but we also understood what the majority of our members wanted.

To his credit, President Bowers agreed with us younger graders and adroitly led the board to a decision to forego changing our grading methodology to an adjectival system. I will never forget his respectful command and leadership in that important board meeting. As the newest grader—just six weeks on the job—he may have saved my job (as last-in, first-out). Thanks, Dave!

Forty years later, Dave continues to provide invaluable insights throughout this book on quarter eagles, including counterfeit and altered coin dangers. For example, he wisely notes that the 1911-D quarter eagle is often produced by adding a "D" to a 1911 Philadelphia Mint coin. Dave also reminds us that while the lettering and motifs on the Indian quarter eagle are incused or recessed, a departure from the normal relief style, curiously the mintmark is raised above the field on the branch-mint coins struck in Denver in 1911, 1914, and 1925. Dave also importantly points out that collectors should look for strong "D" mintmarks on the rare 1911-D coins. That tip alone to the beginner is worth the price of admission to Dave's quarter eagle world.

Like Dave, I had to work odd jobs to buy coins in my teen years. Neither of us could afford the rarities we dreamed about owning. Many yards were mowed to be able to buy silver coins, but my first gold coins were the incused quarter and half eagle I bought after winning $50 playing bingo with my grandmother. Thus, I truly appreciate Dave writing a book about one of the first gold coins I was so proud to call my own.

Like many in the day, I had to get a special Capital plastic holder to display and protect my first precious rarity, and I had to carefully put all the plastic screws in place with my favorite small screwdriver. I am sure Dave had similar holder experiences. Dealers back then sometimes provided a four- or eight-piece type set plastic holder with the purchase of one coin, in order to encourage set building. This was an old-time form of a "continuity marketing" program.

This superb book, *A Guide Book of Quarter Eagle Gold Coins*, is subtitled as a "Complete History and Price Guide," and it is indeed complete. Every design and coin in the series is covered in depth, from 1796 to 1929, including circulation strikes, Proofs, patterns, and all varieties.

The first quarter eagle was struck in 1796, a year after the U.S. Mint first released the half eagle and eagle. The eagle represented $10, hence a quarter eagle was the $2.50 denomination. The double eagle ($20) gold coin would not be minted for over 50 years, in 1849.

America's quarter eagles were minted in years when the country's "hard dollar" was backed by the gold standard. Dave not only addresses the beginning of this denomination but also includes information about what brought an end to this popular collector coin. He includes excerpts from the March 1930 *Numismatist* that speculates about a strain on our gold reserves caused by European withdrawals or, more likely, the Treasury trying to maintain its gold supply at preferred levels.

Dave includes several interesting tidbits throughout the book. For example, he points out that quarter eagles were popular with the more affluent for gift giving, so banks carried extra of those coins at Christmas. Similarly, today banks often order extra $2 bills at Christmas time. These $2 Thomas Jefferson bills are their most requested note for holiday gift giving. The director of the Bureau of Engraving and Printing told me the bills are also the most popular seller on their website.

While this book is enjoyable, it also serves as a useful reference guide. If you want to review selected auction results, they are right at your fingertips. If you are a student of varieties, this book is for you, too. If you like date-by-date analyses, this book is also for you. If you like Proof coins, you need this book. If you are interested in the opinion of our country's foremost numismatist on of how many quarter eagles were melted, you need this book. If you want to know what Bowers thinks about grading and survival rates in various coin grades, you need this book. If you find striking characteristics interesting, here's your source. If patterns are your cup of tea, this book is a must. If you like the latest information on die and planchet preparation by mint, this book is for you. If you want information on important quarter eagle collections, hoards, and treasure finds, you need this book. If you want helpful distribution information by mint, get this book. If you want helpful numismatic morsels—like Proof mintages from the 1840s to the 1870s in the *Red Book* and elsewhere being overstated or just speculations, as those coins would be struck and sold, but if buyers failed to materialize, the leftovers were melted—this book is for you. If you want to know more about why there were quarter eagle shortages over the years, you need this book.

For these reasons and more, every gold coin enthusiast needs this book. This book truly lives up to its subtitle as "A Complete History and Price Guide."

Inside this important book, Q. David Bowers takes the reader on a fascinating journey through history utilizing the quarter eagle as his "time machine." His life experiences, knowledge, and immeasurable skills provides money-saving and money-making insights into this denomination like no other book on quarter eagles. Most importantly, his contribution will be the foundation for many new enthusiasts to begin their lifelong journey enjoying and collecting this important denomination. Having this book on your shelf is a must. and I will be referring to it periodically forever—and always with a smile.

Mike Fuljenz
Beaumont, Texas

Publisher's Preface

In the sixty-plus years Q. David Bowers has been studying the gold coins of the United States, he has examined countless related periodicals, read more than 5,000 numismatic catalogs, and consumed every available reference on the subject. Beyond this "book learning" he has personally studied hundreds of thousands of gold coins and has cataloged many of the most famous coin collections ever sold.

Dave became a professional numismatist and coin dealer in the 1950s, when he was a young teenager. Back then gold coins weren't often seen in the hobby community; in his local coin club, even the older members rarely brought them in for show-and-tell, or to sell. Since the 1930s, Great Depression–era orders had legally restricted "hoarding" of such precious-metal coins (although collectors could keep gold pieces of numismatic significance, and personal exemptions allowed any American to own a small face-value amount). Those federal restrictions would abide until the early 1970s. Starting with the Bicentennial gold-medal program, Congress and the Treasury Department would tinker with mass-market distribution of federal gold products, including the trial-and-error exploration embodied by the American Arts Gold Medallions and, finally, the debut of the nation's first widely successful gold-bullion program, the American Eagle coinage of 1986 to date. Today Americans find it easier than ever to buy, sell, and trade gold coins. This includes numismatic offerings such as Proofs and Reverse Proofs, high-relief gold medals, and other collectibles.

Classic pre-1934 U.S. gold coins, too, are now easy to study and collect. Many factors contribute to this.

- Since the late 1940s, the *Guide Book of United States Coins* (the popular *Red Book*) has given numismatics a strong boost, making the hobby accessible to more than just wealthy and leisured intellectuals;
- starting in the 1950s, global economic conditions repatriated a flood of old U.S. gold coins, mainly from European bank holdings;
- in the 1980s, the development of modern professional third-party coin certification brought seemingly scientific stability to the art of grading, and gave birth to a robust sight-unseen market;
- since the 1990s, the communications boom and modern technology have made U.S. gold coins widely accessible for any collector with an Internet connection; and
- since the early 2000s, the modern renaissance of American numismatic book publishing has brought dozens of new books featuring U.S. gold coins into the hands of collectors and researchers.

When Dave Bowers started in the hobby in the 1950s, books about gold coins were even rarer than the coins themselves. Researcher Walter Breen wrote a 24-page monograph on gold dollars in 1964. In 1975 numismatist David W. Akers, after spending more than 20 years researching gold coins (dollars in particular), published *United States Gold Coins: An Analysis of Auction Records, Gold Dollars*. Over the next seven years, Akers compiled volumes covering every U.S. gold coin series. In the meantime Breen, too, continued to write monographs on other gold coins (up to the $10 denomination, published in 1967), and included gold coins in his two encyclopedias published in 1977 and 1988.

Other writers over time added to the hobby community's knowledge of U.S. gold coins. Researchers published their work in *Numismatic Scrapbook Magazine*, *Numismatic News*, *Coin World*, *The Numismatist*, *Coins Magazine*, and other periodicals. Historian Cornelius Vermeule explored the aesthetics of U.S. coinage, including gold, in *Numismatic Art in America* (1971). *Coin World* published its *Almanac* in several editions starting in 1975, providing much technical information and data. Kenneth Bressett and others codified the grading of U.S. coins, including gold, in the *Official American Numismatic Association Grading Standards for United States Coins* (first edition, 1978). Later, Richard Doty, curator of the Smithsonian Institution's National Numismatic Collection, wrote his broad-ranging *America's Money, America's Story*, and Roger W. Burdette crafted his award-winning *Renaissance of American Coinage* books from deep study of the National Archives, Treasury records, and other primary sources. The gold coins of individual mints were covered by specialists including Rusty Goe (Carson City) and Douglas Winter (Carson City, Charlotte, Dahlonega, and New Orleans).

In the midst of this activity, Q. David Bowers emerged as the preeminent author on U.S. gold coinage—a position he holds to this day.

Bowers's *History of United States Coinage, As Illustrated by the Garrett Collection*, published in 1979, included his analysis of the nation's gold coins. In 1982 he published *United States Gold Coins: An Illustrated History*. His numismatic history of collecting U.S. gold coins was released as part of the proceedings of the 1989 Coinage of the Americas Conference. In various other books of the 1990s and early 2000s, plus hundreds of articles and columns before and since, he's shared stories and insight on U.S. gold coins.

In 2003 Bowers joined forces with Whitman Publishing, longtime publisher of the *Red Book* and other hobby books, signing on as the company's numismatic director. This collaboration has led to a boom in American book-publishing in the field of numismatics. Whitman publishes an average of one new book either entirely or substantially about gold coins every year, ranging from popular single-denomination guidebooks to (also popular) 650-page encyclopedias. The first came out in 2004: Bowers's *Guide Book of Double Eagle Gold Coins* was the first book to cover the entire spectrum of the $20 denomination since David Akers's 1982 volume on the subject. Among the more recent are *Gold: Everything You Need to Know to Buy and Sell Today* (Bowers and Garrett, first edition 2010); my own *American Gold and Silver: U.S. Mint Collector and Investor Coins and Medals, Bicentennial to Date* (2016); *1849: The Philadelphia Mint Strikes Gold* (Moran and Garrett, 2016); and *Lost and Found Coin Hoards and Treasures* (Bowers, second edition 2019).

David W. Akers, who in the 1970s and 1980s broke new ground publishing his numismatic research, has said, "If one had a library consisting only of books and auction catalogs that Dave Bowers has written, the field of U.S. numismatics would be quite thoroughly and satisfactorily covered. Such a claim could not be made about any other person, past or present."

The *Guide Book of Quarter Eagle Gold Coins*—the 26th volume in the Bowers Series, and the 20th of those volumes written by Bowers himself—expands and confirms that distinction.

Dennis Tucker
Publisher, Whitman Publishing, LLC

Introduction

Research for this and other of my Whitman books began in the 1950s, although I did not know it at the time. As a young teenager I studied and read all I could about rare coins. By 1954 I had a good working library and was keeping notes of interesting things I learned. Fast forward to adulthood, a highly successful rare-coin business, and other activities and pleasures. One of my greatest satisfactions continues to be research followed by writing on subjects ranging from the esoteric to the popular.

The present book adds to the roster of gold studies in the Bowers Series, which now has more than two dozen titles. Among the different denominations of American gold coins, the $2.50 gold quarter eagles have always been among the most popular with numismatists. The series divides itself into early issues from 1796 to early 1834, skipping many years in which there was no coinage. Today, all range from rare to very rare. Classic Head quarter eagles from 1834 to 1839 introduce in the last year that coins from the three new (as of 1838) branch mints at Charlotte, Dahlonega, and New Orleans. All dates and mintmarks in the Classic Head series are readily collectible, although the mintmarked issues are scarcer. Liberty Head quarter eagles were struck continuously at the Philadelphia Mint from 1840 to 1907. Of particular numismatic interest is the exceedingly rare 1841 issue, nicknamed the Little Princess. The Proof-only 1863 and the low-mintage 1875 are two other landmark rarities.

Charlotte and Dahlonega coins, with C and D mintmarks, were made in the 1840s and 1850s (plus 1860-C) and range from scarce to rare, but all are collectible. The first San Francisco Mint quarter eagles were struck in 1854 and only to the extent of 246 coins, adding another rarity to the series. The other issues from 1840 to 1907 are collectible, but there are many scarce and rare issues. Indian Head quarter eagles of 1908 to 1929 are easily enough found, but the 1911-D, while not rarer, is scarcer than the others.

Over a long course of years I have assembled many thousands of auction listings and other citations. I have selected a small percentage of these for inclusion in the present book, nearly all from the nineteenth and twentieth centuries to about 1960, as later descriptions are widely available on the Internet (many at the Newman Numismatic Portal or at PCGS Coin Facts). As a special feature in this book I have given expanded pre-2000 listings for one coin—the 1797 quarter eagle. This reflects that many historical descriptions are interesting to read and also show changing philosophies concerning rarity. My presentation of the 1841 "Little Princess" quarter eagle (pages 162–170) would make a monograph in itself.

At the turn of the twenty-first century Mark R. Borckardt worked with me on the Classic Head series, and for chapter 10 of the present book he updated his research. Accordingly, he is the coauthor of that chapter. The population reports published by the Professional Coin Grading Service (PCGS) and Numismatic Guaranty Company of America (NGC) give much information about the rarity and values of certified coins and can be viewed on the Internet.

As you read this book you will learn many details involving politics, gold prices, designs, mintages, the mints themselves, and numismatic information. If you have a good memory, by the time you turn the last page you should be an expert!

In the meantime, enjoy the experience!

1

Overview of $2.50 Gold Coins

The Early Years

Various proposals for a federal Mint were made in 1783 and at other times. The 1787-dated Fugio pieces—copper coins the size of the later cent—were produced under federal contract.

The Mint Act of April 2, 1792, provided for the establishment of a federal coining facility that became a reality. The legislation also established a monetary system based on dollars and the decimal system, and gave weights and finenesses for various issues from the copper half-cent to the $10 gold coin, or eagle. The $2.50 gold coin, being one-fourth the denomination of the eagle, was called the quarter eagle.

Artist Edwin Lamasure's concept of the Philadelphia Mint as painted in 1914. The front part on the street consisted of two old buildings joined. New facilities were added to the rear. This facility was used from autumn 1792 until early 1833.

On July 31, 1792, in Philadelphia (then the seat of the federal government), the cornerstone was laid for the Mint, which consisted of two main buildings. It is thought that President George Washington, whose temporary residence was nearby, led the ceremony, with various dignitaries in attendance, including Mint Director David Rittenhouse, a well-known scientist of many talents, including interests in philosophy and clock making.[1]

In the meantime, in July, silver five-cent pieces called *half dismes* were struck for the government at the workshop of John Harper, a local saw-maker and machinist. (The *disme* designation, used at first, was later changed to *dime*, the term used today.) It is believed that about 1,500 were made. The Mint was in operation by early autumn and produced pattern coins as well as additional half dismes.

The 1792 silver half disme.

In 1793, copper cents and half cents were coined. Silver coins in quantity were first made in 1794 with half dollars and dollars. Half dimes from dies dated 1794 were first made in 1795. The first gold coins were $5 half eagles struck in late July 1795, followed later in the year by eagles. The first quarter eagles were not issued until 1796. For many years afterward the quarter eagle remained the smallest-denomination federal gold coin, a status it enjoyed until the advent of the gold dollar in 1849.

In America in the late eighteenth and early nineteenth centuries, most domestic commerce was conducted by credit, drafts, and currency. Gold coins seem to have played a relatively minor part, especially in districts away from the larger cities. Although foreign commerce was dominated by silver coins, especially Spanish-American eight-real "dollars," much trade, especially with Europe, was conducted with gold coins. Gold eagles were the export coins of choice from 1795 to 1804, but after that date, when $10 mintage was suspended (not to resume until 1838), the $5 half eagle became the largest gold coin of the realm. These were produced to the extent of many hundreds of thousands of coins. Beginning in late 1820 and continuing through the summer of 1834, no gold coins of any kind were seen in domestic circulation. Those that were distributed, such as in the pay of congressmen, were worth a premium, and were not exchanged at par.

The first copper cents for circulation were made in March 1793 and had a linked chain on the reverse and the abbreviation AMERI. This type was made for only a short time.

In American commerce, the quarter eagle denomination was betwixt and between. Too small for convenient use in the maritime and export trade (except for a very limited number of coins in the early years to summer 1834), and not needed for everyday domestic transactions normally serviced by silver coins or paper obligations, the quarter eagle denomination was made intermittently and only in small quantities. Thus, we have coinage dated from 1796 to 1798 and again from 1802 to 1808 (except 1803), but never made in substantial numbers.

1807 quarter eagle.

1807 half eagle, the first of two types coined this year.

As a handy comparison, the largest-mintage early quarter eagle is the 1807, of which 6,812 were struck, containing $17,030 face value in gold. In the same year, the largest gold denomination currently being struck was the $5, of which 84,093 pieces were struck, amounting to $420,465, or over 24 times as much!

It is likely that most of the 1796–1808 quarter eagles were used stateside, for the larger $5 and $10 coins were more convenient for international trade. The reason was simple arithmetic: it would take twice as long to count $1,000 in $2.50 coins than in $5 coins, and four times as long compared to counting $10 pieces.

The entire $2.50 coinage of 1796–1808 amounted to only 22,199 coins (no further $2.50 coins were made until years later in 1821). In 1810 the third Federal Census listed the population of the United States at 7,239,881, including 1,211,364 slaves, 186,746 free Negroes, and 60,000 persons designated as immigrants. By calculation, this amounted to one $2.50 coin for every 326 people! It is likely that there were many Americans who were born, grew to adulthood, and died without ever seeing a 1796–1808 quarter eagle.

The War of 1812 and Later

The War of 1812 conducted against England was perhaps the war that never should have been. A complicated dispute involving maritime trade and British aggression toward American interests, combined with the tail-end of the Napoleonic Wars, created an encounter concerning which the average American citizen knew little. The situation changed dramatically later in the conflict when British troops set fire to Washington and threatened other cities. Which side won the war has been a matter of debate ever since. Most agree it was a draw. Peace was declared on December 24, 1814, but it took months before the settlement was generally known. The Battle of New Orleans, which eventually propelled Gen. Andrew Jackson into the White House, was fought with the British in January 1815, after the war had officially ended.

After the War of 1812 most coined money in American circulation was composed of copper cents and silver half dollars (silver dollars had not been struck since 1804) plus a large quantity of foreign silver issues, most notably Spanish-American issues such as the two-real or "two-bit" coin worth 25 cents. However, quantities of copper and silver coins paled into insignificance in relation to untold millions of dollars in paper notes issued by private banks. Mostly made in denominations of $1, $2, $3, $5, and $10, such currency circulated far and wide. While some notes were worth face value or close to it, many others were completely worthless.

In time, the economic situation became chaotic. Certainly, if any citizen had a gold coin or two, he or she would hold on to it tightly and would not dream of exchanging it for a paper note. From time to time, depending on economic cycles, gold coins traded at *more than face value* domestically, and were not obtainable at par from banks in exchange for paper money or bank drafts. They could be purchased from specie dealers, who made markets in gold and silver coins of the United States and various European, Central American, and South American nations. Silver and gold coins traded by *weight*. For this reason, it was not found necessary to put the denomination on the obverse or reverse of the first U.S. gold and silver coins struck in the 1790s. On the quarter eagle there was no mark of value until 1808, when "2½ D." was incorporated into the reverse design.

The Capped Bust half dollar, type of 1807 to 1836 with lettered edge, was the largest federal coin in general circulation from 1821 to late 1834.

Today, some of the quarter eagles minted during the 1796–1808 years still exist, perhaps 3% to 6% of the original mintages. After 1808, quarter eagles were not made for a long time. Then from 1821 through the first half of 1834, a small number of the coins were made, amounting to 42,065 pieces in total—not enough that citizens had a realistic chance of seeing one, as not a single gold coin was used in circulation. It seems that nearly all were hoarded or exported. During this period, Missouri Senator Thomas Hart Benton and certain of his fellow legislators insisted on receiving their salaries in gold coins. One can imagine Benton having a little bag of quarter eagles and half eagles. As noted, the larger part of the needs of international commerce was taken care of neatly by immense mintages of $5 gold coins, which remained the largest current denomination.

As gold coins were not available for everyday trade, the burden fell upon silver coins of various types, including Spanish-American silver reales and their parts, and the Capped Bust half dollar. Many commercial contracts of the 1820s and 1830s were drawn to be payable in silver.

Most bank notes issued during and after the War of 1812 became worthless, this $5 note from Owl Creek Bank of Mount Vernon, Ohio, being an example.

William Gouge on Gold Coins (1833)

An 1833 text, *History of Paper Money and Banking in the United States*, by William M. Gouge, describes an exposition of problems surrounding the ratio of silver and gold at the time (excerpts):

> The money unit of the United States is the [silver] dollar, consisting of 416 grains of standard silver, or 371¼ grains of pure silver and 34¾ grains of alloy. All our contracts are to pay and receive dollars; all our accounts are kept in dollars. The dollar is thus our money of both account and contract, and its legal value is fixed by our having a coin of the same name, containing the quantity of pure silver and alloy which has just been mentioned.
>
> The market rate of gold to silver, as determined by sales of gold bullion and silver bullion, in a series of years past, is about 15.8 to 1. Consequently, if the Mint rate corresponded with the market rate, the quantity of pure gold contained in an eagle and a half eagle ought to be estimated at the mint at about $15.80.
>
> The undervaluation of gold at the Mint is not the reason that it has disappeared from circulation. Eagles have disappeared for the same reason that dollars have disappeared. Whenever bank notes are used, no more specie is retained in a country than is necessary for transactions of a smaller amount than the least denomination of paper, and is necessary for meeting the few stray notes that may be presented to the banks for payment. It has been found impossible in England to make sovereigns and one pound notes circulate currently; and we all know that small notes in the United States have not only driven away gold coins, but also such silver coins as are of a higher denomination than a half dollar.
>
> If bank notes had never been introduced, eagles, half-eagles, and quarter-eagles would have continued in circulation, notwithstanding the undervaluation of gold at the Mint. The eagle would not have been current at the rate of $10.00; but at the rate of $10.50, $10.75—or whatever else it would have been worth [indication of gold coins being worth more than face value, in exchange for silver coins]. The calculation of the fraction would have been productive of some inconvenience; but the utility of gold coins, in large transactions, would have made them current at a rate probably a little above that which they have borne in the bullion market.
>
> A new gold coinage is desirable; but the proposition to coin eagles of a less weight than the eagles of former times, is not entirely free from objection. As all our contracts are to pay in dollars, and as there is no gold at present in circulation, an issue of a new coin, called an eagle, which should be of the exact value of ten dollars, would cause no practical injustice. But the issue of a new coin of different weight from the old, and yet bearing the same name, might give countenance to the idea that money is something which owes its value to the authority of government, and lead, perhaps, at some future time, to an alteration in the dollar—an alteration in our true standard of value.
>
> Overvalued forms of money circulate in preference to undervalued. The public has always preferred to hoard specie [silver and gold coins] and spend paper; the latter was often traded at a sharp discount in terms of specie. Two equivalent values of money, one of silver and of full weight of a dollar and the other of paper and of no intrinsic value, could not each circulate at par.

The second
Philadelphia Mint.

In 1833 the idea of a fiduciary coinage—coins worth less than intrinsic value than the face value stamped upon them—was not acceptable in the silver and gold series. And, yet, to mint coins of full weight and value meant that the slightest upward change in the market value of either gold or silver would result in the withdrawal from circulation and the melting of coins made of the metal affected. The Mint could not at the same time serve these two conflicting considerations: coins of full value and coins with the ability to remain in circulation over a protracted period of time despite bullion fluctuations.

In the meantime a new Philadelphia Mint building, designed in the Greek Revival style, was constructed. Completed by 1832, it remained in use through 1901.

THE "CLASSIC HEAD" COINAGE OF 1834–1839

To remedy the situation of melting and exporting current gold coins, Congress passed the Act of June 28, 1834, which reduced the authorized weight of American gold coins. The leading exponent of the legislation was Senator Thomas Hart Benton, nicknamed "Old Bullion"—the previously mentioned legislator who insisted that his salary be paid in gold coins.

Gold coins made after the Coinage Act of August 1, 1834—the effective date of implementation of the act—were of lighter weight and thus stayed in circulation. To enable quick visual differentiation of the new from the old, the obverse and reverse designs were modified, and the motto E PLURIBUS UNUM was deleted from the reverse. The motif, by Engraver William Kneass, is known today as the Classic Head design and is a modification of the Classic Head created by John Reich for use on half cents of 1809–1836 and cents of 1808–1814. Quarter eagles of this type were made from 1834 to 1839. In financial and banking circles, the earlier, heavier gold coins were often called *old tenor*, and the lighter ones, *new tenor*. For many years after 1834, old-style gold coins were listed with bid and ask prices in bullion exchanges and always sold at a premium.

For all its efforts with the Coinage Act of 1834, the U.S. government did not achieve success with the monetary system. Immediately, silver coins became especially desirable, and soon they were preferred to gold! To remedy this, the authorized weights of silver coins were reduced by the Coinage Act of January 18, 1837. From that time until the end of 1861, silver and gold were at par.

Classic economic theory held that a country should have silver as the monetary standard, or it should have gold instead, but if it tried to have both simultaneously there would be problems if each was minted to full value of the bullion contained. Despite the best intentions of the U.S. government as well as foreign entities, the values of these precious metals could not be regulated effectively. Thus, worldwide the prices of gold and silver, usually computed in London, rose and fell constantly, a veritable see-saw.

The With Motto quarter eagles were discontinued by the Act of June 28, 1834. Today, such coins are rarities.

In addition to having differences in the portrait, the lighter-weight Classic Head quarter eagle lacked the motto on the reverse, to permit quick identification. Mintage of these began in the summer of 1834, and by late in the year they were plentiful in the channels of commerce. The design was continued through 1839. Shown is a Proof 1835.

During the 1830s, and continuing through the Civil War, bullion traders, securities houses, and bankers did an active business in buying and selling gold and silver coins—American issues as well as the multitudinous varieties from foreign countries—by weight. Because of their premium value, any stray old-tenor gold coin that came to light in the 1840s or 1850s was apt to be taken to a bullion dealer and melted. It is no wonder that all were scarce and many were very rare by the time numismatics became popular in a significant way in America, beginning circa 1857, following widespread public interest when the old "large" copper cent was discontinued.

However, many thousands of old-tenor gold coins remained in the hands of the public. Each year, many would be sold to bullion dealers or redeemed at the Mint or other depositories. As the interest in numismatics spread, bullion dealers sold old-tenor coins to collectors and dealers. In this way many coins were saved that might have been melted otherwise. W. Elliot Woodward told of an 1815 half eagle—today one of America's most famous gold coin rarities—that was found in a bag of old gold coins in the mid-nineteenth century. Harlan P. Smith told of a precious 1822 half eagle, of which just three are known today, being purchased for a nominal premium from a bullion dealer. Reminiscing in 1867, old-time collector William Sumner Appleton related that dealers in silver and gold were his prime source of supply for desired specimens of the early dates.

As an example of the premium paid for old gold coins, *The Financial Register* reported that on January 4, 1837, American gold coins minted prior to August 1, 1834, traded in New York City at a 6½% premium in terms of current (August 1, 1834, and later) gold. This meant that to buy $100 face value of early gold coins, it took $106.50 worth of the new lighter-weight Classic Head pieces. By June 16, 1838, the premium on old-tenor U.S. gold coins increased to 7%.

The Classic Head gold coinage, consisting of $2.50 and $5 coins, was an immediate commercial success. From summer 1834 through 1839, the unprecedented quantity of 968,228 $2.50 pieces was made for circulation, a figure nearly 15 times greater than the combined total of all previous quarter eagle coinage, 1796–1834! The Panic of 1837, which resulted in banks' suspending payment of specie (silver and gold coins) at par in exchange for bank notes, spread across the country beginning on March 10, 1837. Copper half cents and cents and paper currency constituted the American financial system. Many banks failed. In time, the stronger banks reopened, and by 1840 some were again paying and receiving specie. Beginning around the spring of 1843, the national economy took an upward trend.

Classic Head Quarter Eagles in the News

As gold coins had not been in circulation for many years, the appearance of the new Classic Head quarter eagles and half eagles in 1834 created a lot of interest, such as in the following accounts. From the August 20, 1834, *Evening Post* (New York City):

> **Quarter Eagles**
>
> The half eagles are circulating extensively, and are eagerly sought after and received by all classes. There is not, we verily believe, a word of truth in any of the stories got up by the mercenary tools of the bank in relation to the coinage.
>
> Our correspondents are inquiring for quarter eagles. They ask us why coin of this denomination is not issued. All we have been able to discover is, that, as we are informed, the die sinker of the mint has been industriously employed upon the dies, but without being able yet to complete the quarter eagle die. It is again demanded by the public why, if one artist cannot do the necessary business in time, another is not immediately employed? We are unable to give a satisfactory reply. *Philad. Paper.*

September 25, 1834, *Macon* (Georgia) *Weekly Telegraph:*

> **Quarter Eagles**
>
> This beautiful coin, fresh from the mint, made its appearance among us some days since. It will constitute the most important, and far the most convenient part of our circulating medium. We have been fortunate enough to get hold of some dozen of them, and any bank partisan who *really* wishes a sight of them, and who will call on us, and promise not to get into a *furious* passion, shall be gratified. *Delaware Watchman.*

September 26, 1834, *Gloucester* (Massachusetts) *Democrat:*

> **Gold Quarter Eagles**
>
> We have been much gratified to see some of the new gold quarter eagles, in this city yesterday. They are broader than the old ones, and hence more convenient—and are well calculated, in their flight over land, to carry terror and panic into the hearts of the Bank editors and Bank partisans—while their yellow harvest and solid worth, will cheer and delight the honest farmer and mechanic. *Globe.*

October 10, 1834, *Painesville* (Ohio) *Telegraph*, exchange item, taking issue with the Jackson administration's financial policies:

The Gold Humbug

The *Washington Globe* expresses its gratification at *seeing* some of the new gold quarter Eagles in that city, and observes in relation to them, that "They are broader than the old one, and hence more convenient, and are well calculated, in their flight over the land, to carry panic and terror into the hearts of the Bank editors and bank partisans; while their yellow harvest hue and solid worth will cheer with delight the honest farmer and mechanic."

This is a fair specimen of the *fustian* with which the Jackson papers throughout the country regale their readers on the subject of the new gold coin. From a perusal of their papers one would be led to believe that gold was to be had in abundance for the mere asking, and without an equivalent being required for it. Now the truth is, that so very few of these new quarter eagles "in their flight over the land" have found a resting place in this section of the Union, we should be inclined to doubt their existence altogether if we did not occasionally hear of one being seen perched on the finger of some lucky office-holder, who exhibited it as a decoy to catch the gulls of the party.

A person from this county called at the Commonwealth Bank, one of the Government pets in Boston, a few days since, to obtain the money due on several pension certificates. His request for a little gold could not be granted! The Administration, which we are told has created such a profusion of gold that it "flows upon the Mississippi in a stream," could not spare the poor Revolutionary pensioner a few quarter eagles, the "yellow harvest hue" of which would have "cheered with delight" the war worn veteran, and caused him to thank his stars that he had been spared to witness the return of the "golden age!!"

Of all the *humbugs* invented by the Jackson party to delude the people, and sustain themselves in power, this golden humbug is certainly the most ridiculous. The idea of the General Government attempting to introduce a hard money currency to the exclusion of paper is perfectly absurd, so long as each of the 24 states of the Union can establish Banks and create paper money to an unlimited extent without asking leave of Congress.

Notwithstanding the golden streams that flow in other parts of the country, about which we *learn* so much, it is certain that but little of the new coin is found in this state—excepting in the columns of the Jackson papers. A small supply may be expected previous to the election in November The *panic* and *terror* it will *carry into the hearts* of the Whigs will no doubt be pro-di-gious!

Branch Mints

In 1835, Congress realized the need for branch mints to service the needs of the expanding American population and territory. In 1838, the New Orleans, Charlotte (North Carolina), and Dahlonega (Georgia) Mints opened their doors and started their coining presses. New Orleans was a maritime trading hub and located at the entrance to the Mississippi River Valley, while Charlotte and Dahlonega were situated close to native gold deposits, and were set up as a convenience to miners and tradesmen. Mintmarks

O, C, and D were used to identify the coinage from these branches, while Philadelphia, known as the "mother mint," used no mint letter. The first branch-mint quarter eagles were 1838-C, followed the next year by 1839-C, D, and O.

The 1834–1839 Classic Head quarter eagles remained a staple in circulation for a long time afterward, and although they disappeared from circulation for the interval from 1862 to 1878 (to be explained shortly), at the turn of the twentieth century a sharp-eyed bank teller might spot an occasional piece in a cash drawer. By that time, most such coins were worn down to the grade of Very Fine.

The Charlotte Mint.

The Dahlonega Mint.

The New Orleans Mint.

Early Liberty Head Coinage (1840–1861)

Christian Gobrecht joined the Mint as an engraver in 1835 and remained until his passing in 1844.

In 1840 a new quarter eagle design was produced, the Liberty Head or Coronet Head style by Christian Gobrecht. *Liberty Head* is the preferred numismatic term, but in recent years *Coronet Head* has been viewed as being more descriptive by some scholars, for any portrait of Miss Liberty could be called a Liberty Head. On the Liberty Head quarter eagle Miss Liberty is wearing a coronet—or a diadem.

At the Mint, Gobrecht, who had signed on as *second* (he did not like the term "assistant") engraver in 1835, had done nearly all of the creative work since that time, when engraver William Kneass suffered a debilitating stroke. The various later Classic Head portraits were his work. After Kneass's death in 1840, Gobrecht became the first engraver, a position he held until his passing in 1844 (at which time he was succeeded by James B. Longacre, who seems to have been the first to be called *chief* engraver).

The Liberty Head was one of several portrait styles that Gobrecht had created during the general period from 1837 to 1839, as part of experimentation that reached its zenith in the copper cent series in the latter year (when portraits included what collectors know today as the *Head of 1838*, *Booby Head*, *Silly Head*, and *Head of 1840* styles).

The Liberty Head was first used in the gold series on the revivified $10 gold denomination, which appeared in 1838, followed by the $5 in 1839. Thus, by 1840 the debut of the Liberty Head on the $2.50 was somewhat late.

During the 1840s, coinage of quarter eagles took place at the Philadelphia, Charlotte, Dahlonega, and New Orleans Mints. Quantities were typically small in comparison to the $5 and $10 coins, but there were exceptions. As a rule, $2.50 coins were used domestically, while the larger denominations were popular in the export trade.

On January 24, 1848, precious yellow flakes were discovered by James Marshall in the tailrace at Sutter's Mill on the American River in California, igniting the Gold Rush that would galvanize the world. Within several years, the borders of America extended from coast to coast, and the westward course of empire had been achieved. Vast quantities of gold were brought forth from the streams and earth, with the result that by 1850, the year when California achieved statehood, gold became "common" in relation to silver, and *silver* coins rose to become worth more than face value—the latest variation in the gold-silver see-saw of prices.

By early 1851, silver was worth a 3½% premium in terms of gold. Silver was hoarded, a situation that stripped commercial and banking channels of half dimes, dimes, quarter dollars, half dollars, and silver dollars. Mintages of gold coins increased to take up the slack for the missing silver coins. The Act of February 21, 1853, reduced the authorized weight of new silver coins from the half dime through the half dollar, but left the silver dollar untouched. In one of those interesting footnotes in American financial history, silver dollars remained off the market and were no longer seen in circulation (until

1873, when the price of silver metal fell sharply), while half dimes, dimes, quarters, and halves circulated readily.

Mention is also made of the silver three-cent piece, officially called a *trime*. Introduced in 1851, it contained less silver in relation to its face value than did other silver denominations and circulated effectively until the summer of 1853, when its use was superseded by a flood of the new lighter-weight half dimes, dimes, quarter dollars, and half dollars.

In 1854 the San Francisco Mint opened for business, making it possible to convert gold bullion into federal coins without having to ship it by sea to Philadelphia or one of the other distant mints. In the first year of operation a quarter eagle rarity was created when just 246 of this denomination were minted!

Gold Coins Disappear (1862–1878)

In April 1861, troops of the newly formed Confederate States of America fired upon Fort Sumter, the federal outpost in the harbor of Charleston, South Carolina. A small force of Union soldiers held out for several days, while the ramparts fell to dust around them, finally surrendering to the inevitable—remarkably without loss of life. The Civil War had begun, the culmination of internecine wrangling that had dominated Congress for three decades.

At the outset, hopes were high in both the North and the South. In the Southern states citizens looked forward to a new era of self-government, and to a new nation in which slaves could be held without interference and the "wealth of the South"—natural products such as corn, cotton, rice, and tobacco—would bring great prosperity to the inhabitants (slaves excepted). The resources of the South were permanent, it was said, while those of the North—such as manufacturing, commerce, and related activities—were subject to many vagaries. The Charlotte, Dahlonega, and New Orleans Mints fell to the Confederacy in spring 1861 and were soon closed. The Confederacy issued its own paper money and a few coins (including 1861-D gold dollars struck at Dahlonega before it closed in the spring).

The bombardment of Fort Sumter on April 12, 1861.

In the Union in 1861, the war was viewed as an easy win. The South had been itching for a fight for a long time, and now it would get its comeuppance. In a matter of months, Union soldiers would devastate the ill-prepared Southerners, it was thought. Many adventurers sought to take part in the action and signed on as soldiers. Hopes and enthusiasm ran high. Victory, if not actually in sight, was just around the corner. President Abraham Lincoln called for men to enlist for three months, by which time the conflict would surely be over.

Reality proved to be quite different.

Although there were engagements, the first important battle between the North and South did not take place until the third week of July. As armies from both sides drew close to Manassas, Virginia, a short distance from Washington, the impending clash was reported in newspapers. Crowds of onlookers rode from Washington to see the Rebels (as they were called) fall in defeat. At the outset this seemed to be the case, but by the afternoon the Confederates had the upper hand. The Union forces broke apart in scattered retreat. The summer and autumn of 1861 came and went, and after several bloody battles there was no clear indication as to the outcome. It was anything but an easy win for either side. Soldiers died by the thousands.

The public became alarmed and set about hoarding "hard assets," as had been done in times of war and economic uncertainty in earlier times. By December 1861, newly issued Union paper money notes were readily available at banks, but gold and silver coins were becoming scarce. On December 28, 1861, certain banks stopped paying out gold coins, followed in the spring by the cessation of silver coin disbursements. By mid-July 1862, not a single silver or gold coin was to be found in general commerce anywhere in the East or Midwest, and even the low-value copper-nickel Flying Eagle and Indian Head cents were being hoarded. The financial chaos was eased to an extent by a flood of federal paper money, including Legal Tender Notes from the $1 denomination upward and paper Fractional Currency notes from 3 cents to 50 cents. These were redeemable at par with other notes, but not specie. Private entrepreneurs got into the act and turned out millions of little copper-cent-sized tokens bearing portraits ranging from George Washington to Indians, and inscribed with mottoes and advertisements. Others issued encased postage stamps consisting of a mica-fronted brass frame enclosing a stamp, private paper money notes, or other substitutes.

Postage Currency was introduced in the summer of 1862 to facilitate commerce at a time when no coins were in circulation.

Federal gold and silver coins sold at a premium, which at one time was more than twice face value. The Treasury Department continued to strike gold coins in Philadelphia, but in reduced quantities. These were made available to citizens and merchants, but only at a sharp premium in terms of paper money. Bullion

Encased postage stamps were another monetary substitute. Issued in denominations from 1 to 90 cents, they used regular stamps in a mica-faced brass frame with an advertisement on the back.

Well over 10,000 different varieties of cent-sized Civil War tokens were issued in copper and brass, with patriotic motifs as well as advertisements.

dealers prospered, and every large city had a number of shops where notes could be exchanged for federal gold coins including quarter eagles. Alfred Robinson, who in the early 1860s was a rare-coin dealer, stock broker, and banker, by 1870 had styled himself as a gold broker, apparently finding the profits greatest in that specialty. The U.S. Treasury kept track of the considerable profits it made in this manner—it, too, sold federal gold coins at large markups in terms of paper money—a very curious situation when viewed in hindsight.

Silver coins and federal paper money achieved parity around April 1876, at which time long-hoarded early coins appeared in vast quantities in the marketplace. Gold coins remained off the market until December 17, 1878, when, at long last, gold coins and paper money were exchangeable at par.

THE CALIFORNIA SCENE

Meanwhile, in distant California, gold and silver coins remained in circulation during the Civil War and traded with each other at par. However, there were no paper notes in general circulation there, and whenever a Legal Tender Note was presented—as by a soldier or federal government employee who'd received it in a pay envelope—it traded at a discount in terms of gold. Thus, if in New York City it cost $200 in Legal Tender Notes to buy $100 in gold coins, at the same time in San Francisco, someone with $200 in Legal Tender Notes could buy only $100 worth of merchandise at prices posted in this "gold city." There was no way to win!

This had the unusual result that newly minted San Francisco gold coins reached general circulation quickly and soon became worn. The Mint there opened in March 1854. The 1854-S quarter eagle was struck only to the extent of 246 pieces, creating what would later become a numismatic rarity.

In contrast, most quarter eagles minted in Philadelphia during the Civil War, continuing to December 1878, were kept in storage, or were sold domestically at a premium in terms of paper money; they tended to be better preserved than those used in active commerce in the West. Thus, an understanding of monetary history is necessary to realize today why, for example, a Philadelphia Mint gold coin of 1868 is likely to be found in a high grade such as Extremely Fine or About Uncirculated, while its San Francisco Mint counterpart might be worn down to the Very Fine level.

The San Francisco Mint opened for business in March 1854 in a building earlier used by private coiner Moffat & Co. During the Civil War, coins struck there were widely circulated, while in the East silver and gold coins were hoarded.

In 1874 the second San Francisco Mint replaced the first and was fitted with modern equipment.

Meanwhile, in the South, just about anyone who was fortunate to own a handful of "local" gold coins—made at Dahlonega or Charlotte in the days before the Civil War—hoarded them carefully. Later, this would account for a higher survival ratio than for the quarter eagles of other mints.

It is relevant to note that the private mint of Christopher Bechtler and his family, operated in Rutherfordton, North Carolina, from 1830 to 1852, produced $2.50 gold coins, but they were not known as quarter eagles. They bore no eagle or other motif but displayed only letters and numbers. The gold came from regional mines in North Carolina and Georgia.

Bechtler $2.50 gold coin.

The Late Liberty Head Era (1879–1907)

In 1879, quarter eagles and other gold denominations again circulated freely in commerce in the East and Midwest. However, by this time the general public was quite accustomed to paper money. Thus, when gold coins became available, they were not widely used except in certain areas of the West—particularly in the Rocky Mountain states—where "hard money" was still preferred.

The San Francisco Mint struck its last quarter eagle in 1879, after which Liberty Head $2.50 coinage was limited to the Philadelphia Mint. From this point onward, with paper money in the forefront in domestic American commerce, most gold coinage was in the form of $20 double eagles, easy to count and ship to foreign countries. Quarter eagles were made in relatively small quantities, primarily to avoid creating rarities

The third Philadelphia Mint opened in 1901 and was used until 1967.

The Denver Mint opened in 1906, but the first quarter eagles were not struck there until 1911.

for speculators or collectors (this per the *Annual Report of the Director of the Mint*, 1887). The same thing was done with $1 and $3 gold coins. While investors were drawn to the gold dollars, it seems that few purchased quarter eagles. Thus, in Mint State many of the low-mintage quarter eagles of the 1880s and early 1890s are rare today.

The Liberty Head motif continued to be used year after year until 1907, when it was retired at last. By that time it had been employed continuously since 1840, the longest time any American coin design was used without a major change.

THE INDIAN HEAD COINAGE (1908–1929)

In 1908, a new quarter eagle design was inaugurated—the Indian Head motif by Massachusetts artist Bela Lyon Pratt, a student of famous sculptor Augustus Saint-Gaudens. On the new design the lettering and motifs were incuse or recessed in the coin, a departure from the normal relief style. Curiously, on branch-mint issues struck at Denver in 1911, 1914, and 1925, the mintmark was *raised*, becoming the only feature to rise above the level field!

Indian Head quarter eagles were made from 1908 to 1915, and then again from 1925 to 1929. In 1911 the Denver Mint, which had opened for business in 1906, struck its first coins of this denomination. Mintage was quite low for this particular issue, and in time the 1911-D became the key numismatic date in the series.

Quarter eagles were scarce in circulation in the 1920s, even as new issues continued to be minted. None were minted after 1929.

QUARTER EAGLES IN DEMAND

After the production of quarter eagles ceased in 1915 (not to be resumed until 1925) quarter eagles were available only at a premium. The December 12, 1926, *Los Angeles Times* told this:

> **Christmastide "Gold Rush" On**
>
> NEW YORK, Dec. 11 (AP)—Wall street's annual "gold rush" has begun.
>
> Stacks of gold pieces in the $2.50, $5, $10 and $20 denominations are now leaving the vaults of the New York Federal Reserve Bank by the truckload, bound for country and city banks which will supply the stream of gold coins that pour into Christmas stockings and gift envelopes.

Every year at this time the New York and other Federal Reserve banks have watched a growing flood of gold pieces pour forth, and then suddenly, after the holidays, pour back and become a part of the bank reserves until another Christmas rolls around.

Officials at the Chase National Bank estimate that between $80,000,000 and $90,000,000 in gold coins will be withdrawn from the banks of the country this year, probably setting a new high record. Last year it was estimated that $75,000,000 in gold was put into circulation at this time. In New York alone, it is expected that between $15,000,000 and $20,000,000 will be distributed this year.

For the first time in years the United States Treasury has minted a limited amount of new $2.50 gold pieces as its contribution to the holiday movement. In former years the demand for these coins was so great that they commanded a premium of 25 and 50 cents. They are rarely seen in circulation except around the holiday season. Despite the addition of newly minted gold, the New York Federal Reserve Bank has less than 100,000 of these "quarter eagles" available to meet the demand of the banks in this district and will be obliged to make allotments in order to insure their equitable distribution.

The peak of the public demand for gold coins will be reached in the three days immediately preceding Christmas, when tellers in the banks of the country will be kept busy passing them out, along with other money in the form of Christmas bonuses. Most of the gold, as well as the currency, will be returned by the middle of January, but bank officials have noted that the number of coins coming back is always smaller and that only a few of the quarter eagles get back into circulation. Even the savings banks, which are the first banking destination of many Christmas gold pieces, handle few of the $2.50 pieces.

The Twilight of Quarter Eagles

Returning to quarter eagles in American commerce, beginning about 1920, these mostly disappeared from circulation. The situation generated many news articles as well as comments in numismatic circles, examples of which are given here.

In his February 1921 catalog of the M.K. McMullin and H.C. Whipple Collections, Thomas L. Elder commented concerning these:

> The entire coinage of this denomination has been discontinued, and all quarter eagles command a premium. So these quarter eagles bid fair to be selling in the near future at the same premiums as the gold dollars and will be regarded in the same way as premium U.S. gold coins. ["Premium" issues were all $1 and $3 coins.] The banks report no more of this denomination offered, while the government does not allow them to be passed out at the Sub Treasuries, and has ordered *any on hand to be melted up.* They are good coins for investment.

The story was further told by Theodore J. Venn in *The Numismatist*, February 1922:

> Nearly all coin dealers and the majority of the collectors are familiar with the history of the $1 and $3 gold pieces and how the commercial demand for these coins—for ornamentation and presentation purposes—caused all dates to be placed at a

> premium a few years after the discontinuation of their coinage. This was the primary factor, although the numismatic demand also cut a large figure as a contributory one. And the same causes are now, and have been for nearly two years, at work on the quarter eagles.
>
> Have you gone to a bank lately and tried to get a $2.50 gold piece? If not, make the attempt and see what a revelation awaits you. Should you know the paying teller well, he probably will give you a knowing smile and inform you that he is looking for some himself, 'the Liberty Head variety preferred.' Up to about 18 months ago you could occasionally get a few pieces from a friendly cashier, but that day has now passed. This holds good to a great degree with gold of any denomination. At no time since the close of the Civil War, when gold went to a heavy premium, have the banking institutions seemed as anxious to add the yellow metal to their reserves as within the past year or two.

In his November 1925 catalog of the Brevoort, Stoddard, Orcutt, and Witherspoon Collections, Thomas L. Elder stated, "Quarter eagles. No more being coined. In greatest demand at the present time. Dealers offer us $3.50 for the commonest dates."

Soon, 1925-D $2.50 coins would become available, but, apparently, not at face value.

Elder continued to monitor the market. This appeared in his February 1926 catalog of the Havemeyer, McMurray, Gallagher, and Reeves Collections, regarding earlier Liberty Head coins: "New York brokers have been offering $3.80 each for Liberty Head quarter eagles for some time. These are exported to the Orient."

The March 1930 issue of *The Numismatist* related this concerning the smallest current United States gold denomination:

> Efforts to abolish the coinage of the $2.50 gold piece have been revived in Washington, and Secretary Mellon has requested Congress to enact legislation to provide for the discontinuance of the coin. He said the gold was needed for credit purposes and that the pieces disappeared from circulation, especially after being given away as Christmas presents. His reason for wishing for authority to end the coinage of the piece, namely, that the gold used in minting it is needed by the government for credit purposes, may be indicative of the strain that is being put on our gold reserve by European withdrawals, or, what is more likely, that the Treasury is merely taking a precautionary measure to keep up its gold supply.
>
> The number of $2.50 pieces turned out by the mints in a year is small. In the 140 years the coin has been minted some $50 million worth of them has been minted in all, and for a number of years they have been struck only to supply a Christmas demand. This amounts to $1 million. But small though the sum is, it represents an appreciable drain from year to year on the gold supply, as a great many of the pieces only get back into circulation by necessity. They go often into children's banks and remain there as nest eggs.
>
> The $2.50 gold piece has been a popular one with collectors, and they will regret to see the coin discontinued. The design adopted in 1908 has been much less popular than the Liberty Head type. All dates of the Liberty Head type in Fine condition have been selling for some time at varying prices over face value. If the coin is discontinued it will not rob the series of any of its attractions, but, on the contrary, will add to them.

As it turned out, no additional quarter eagles were coined after 1929. By that year, quarter eagles were not regularly seen in circulation, and all were considered to be somewhat scarce.

The following Associated Press newspaper item is datelined Chicago, November 25, 1930:

> There will be no more $2.50 gold pieces in Yuletide hosiery. The Federal Reserve Bank of Chicago today advised banks of the Seventh Reserve District that no supply of the old coins is available. An act of Congress, April 11, 1930, abolished the die of the tiny coin, so no new ones can be made.

The scarcity of the denomination was reflected by Orangeville, Illinois, dealer M.H. Bolender in his 68th Public Sale, June 26, 1932:

> Gold quarter eagles are fast becoming rare. Coinage has been discontinued, and none are in banks or circulation. Because of the steady demand, it will be useless for collectors to make bids of less than $3 each for any of the following quarter eagles.

The April 15, 1933, *Register-Republic* (Rockford, Illinois) included this:

> Quarter eagles had the queer faculty of disappearing. Each year banks would put in great stocks of them for men and women who wished to give gold for Christmas—gold in minimum quantity. Bright young nephews and nieces with shining faces would receive them with thanks. And that would be the end of the quarter eagles. The banks would never get them back. Where they went, no one knows. Disappearing quarter eagles is one of the minor mysteries of American economics.

In 1933–1934, when President Franklin Delano Roosevelt issued a mandate that the public turn in gold coins to banks and to the Treasury Department, all quarter eagles were exempt from the edict on the grounds that they all had numismatic value. Nevertheless, untold quantities went to the melting pot.

2

Mints and Minting

Mintage Totals

The following figures are cumulative and are from the *Annual Report of the Director of the Mint*, 1934, by which time U.S. gold coinage had ceased. Totals are for various denominations from 1795 to 1933.[1]

Grand Totals for All U.S. Gold Denominations

$1 gold coins: $19,499,337 face value (19,499,337 coins). If commemoratives are added: $19,874,754 (19,874,754 coins).

$2.50 gold quarter eagles: $50,541,475 face value (20,216,590 coins). If commemoratives are added: $51,067,082.50 (20,426,833 coins).

$3 gold coins: $1,619,376 face value (539,792 coins).

$5 gold half eagles: $397,684,345 face value (79,536,869 coins).

$10 gold eagles: $582,619,850 face value (58,261,985 coins).

$20 gold double eagles: $3,473,202,120 face value (173,660,106 coins).

Gold $2.50 Coinage by Mints

Philadelphia Mint: 16,765,329 regular issues (face value of $41,913,322.50) plus 200,226 commemoratives coined (face value of $500,565), for a grand total of 16,965,555 pieces coined, and a face value of $42,413,887.50.

Charlotte Mint: 217,966 pieces coined, for a face value of $544,915.

Dahlonega Mint: 197,850 pieces coined, for a face value of $494,625.

Denver Mint: 1,081,680 pieces coined, for a face value of $2,704,200.

New Orleans Mint: 1,209,263 pieces coined, for a face value of $3,023,157.50.

San Francisco Mint: 744,502 regular issues (face value of $1,861,255) plus 10,017 commemoratives coined (face value of $25,042.50) for a grand total of 754,519 pieces coined, and a face value of $1,886,297.50.

Calendar Year Mintage Figures (Early Years, 1796–1808)

The following are *calendar-year* mintages for $2.50 gold coins from the annual *Report of the Director of the Mint*, with modern commentary added (these bear only an indirect relationship to the actual quantities minted with those dates, as little attention was paid to using dies in the calendar year they were dated).

1796: 963

1797: 859 (As 1797 quarter eagles are much rarer than those dated 1796, it is conventional numismatic wisdom that much of the mintage figure for this year consisted of coins dated 1796.)

1798: 614

1799: 480 (As no $2.50 coins dated 1799 are known to exist, this figure consists of mintage from earlier-dated dies.)

1800: 0

1801: 0

1802: 2,612

1803: 423 (As no $2.50 coins dated 1803 are known to exist, this figure consists of mintage from earlier-dated dies.)

1804: 3,327

1805: 1,781

1806: 1,616

1807: 6,812

1808: 2,710 (New design introduced this year.)

Characteristics of Mints, Dies, and Striking

Quarter eagles struck during the same era, but at different mints (branch-mint coinage began in 1838), can have widely varying characteristics. Further, coins struck from the same dies at the same mint, but at different times, can have different characteristics.

The following are general observations relevant to quarter eagles and lend to their understanding. There are exceptions, but these comments apply to most of the issues of a given design, mint, and time and explain the "personality" that various coins display, those from the Charlotte and Dahlonega mints being the most "rustic."

Planchet-Preparation Processes

Planchets were prepared by taking gold ingots and running them between two steel rollers. Several pass-throughs were done, each time with the rollers spaced more closely together. Finally, by use of the drawing bench, the planchet strip was pulled through the rollers at its desired thickness.

As the strip grew ever longer during this process, small inclusions of carbon or foreign material, or imperfectly mixed copper added to the ingot as an alloy, or air bubbles, became distended or lengthened. Sometimes, flakes or distended pieces of the planchet metal would separate, causing a recess or depression in the planchet surface.

Planchets would then be cut from the strip by the use of metal punches, in the manner of a cookie cutter. While the above processes were common to all mints, there were differences in their execution.

Philadelphia Mint: Planchet preparation was excellent with regard to smooth surfaces. In the 1880s in particular, there was imperfect mixing of the copper alloy, causing "copper toning" or "copper spots" on the finished coins, including Proofs. In the early days (1796–1808), planchets were often made slightly overweight, then dressed or reduced to the correct weight by filing; this created *adjustment marks*, which remained visible on the finished coins (particularly on the higher areas at the centers and the rims).

Charlotte Mint: Planchet preparation was poor, often with flaking and laminations. Quality deteriorated further after the mid-1850s. The Charlotte Mint operated only from 1838 to 1861, with quarter eagles being minted for most but not all of these years.

Dahlonega Mint: Planchet preparation was poor, often with flaking and laminations, but was generally better than at Charlotte. Quality deteriorated further after the mid-1850s. The Dahlonega Mint operated only from 1838 to 1861, with quarter eagles being minted for most but not all of these years.

New Orleans Mint: Planchet preparation was excellent with regard to smooth surfaces. The New Orleans Mint, opened in 1838, did not strike quarter eagles after the Civil War (although it produced other gold denominations intermittently in later years, with the final issue being the 1909-O half eagle).

San Francisco Mint: Planchet preparation was excellent with regard to smooth surfaces. Quarter eagles were struck for nearly all years from 1854 through 1879.

Denver Mint: Planchet preparation was excellent. A latecomer to the quarter eagle series, the Denver Mint, opened in 1906 and outfitted with the most modern equipment, struck its first quarter eagles in 1911, of the Indian head type.

Die Preparation and Use

All dies, including for the branch mints (1838 and later), were prepared at the Philadelphia Mint. Each die was "basined," or given a gentle curve to the fields, curving upward toward the border. In the early days, the dies sent to the branch mints were not hardened for use, but were sent "raw." Upon arrival at the branch mints, the dies often showed light rust. It was the job of the coining department at each branch mint to harden the dies by rapid quenching in cold water or oil. After this was done, the die face had scale and roughness. The die was then dressed or prepared for use by a machinist. The final preparation varied from mint to mint.

Philadelphia Mint: Final die preparation of a high order of excellence. Die surfaces were made smooth and ready for coinage.

Charlotte and Dahlonega Mints: Surfaces on the dies received from Philadelphia were not fully finished. At the branch mint they were dressed or finished by rough grinding, with the result that there were many irregularities. In some instances, the die was pressed against a flat grinding device, removing the basining of the die and creating a flat field, this being most noticeable at the center, but not as prominent on quarter eagles as on certain gold dollars.

New Orleans Mint: Final preparation of a high order of excellence. Die surfaces were made smooth and ready for coinage. Sometimes during storage in the miasmic lowland in which the New Orleans Mint was situated, the dies would acquire light rust or pitting.

San Francisco Mint: Final preparation of a high order of excellence. Die surfaces were made smooth and ready for coinage.

Denver Mint: Final preparation was probably done at the Philadelphia Mint by the late time that the Denver Mint first struck quarter eagles (the 1911-D).

Design Types and Striking Sharpness

The sharpness of details and the general appearance of a given coin were due to a combination of many factors, including the design type.

Early types, 1796–1808: The relief of the head is somewhat high at the center, sometimes causing incomplete striking of details, particularly in the hair of Miss Liberty. Stars and borders are often weak. Planchet adjustment marks are the *rule*, not the exception, and are most noticeable at the highest-relief areas of the centers (where the metal from the original planchet did not completely fill the die recesses, thus revealing the marks on the planchet) and the rims. The lighter the strike, the more prominent the planchet-adjustment marks are apt to be. These adjustment marks are taken for granted and are not usually mentioned in catalog descriptions, nor do numismatic certification services make reference to them.

1821–1827 type, regular diameter: Striking was usually excellent except for some hair details at the center of the obverse. Planchet-adjustment marks are infrequent.

1829–1834 type, reduced diameter: Sometimes the deepest recesses of the obverse die would not fill completely, causing a hardly noticeable weakening of certain hair details. Planchet-adjustment marks are infrequent.

1834–1839 Classic Head type: The relief of the head higher was than optimal, resulting in incomplete metal flow into the deepest portions of the die. Several varieties of portraits were made, with slightly different characteristics to each.

1840–1907 Liberty Head type: The highest portion of the head of Miss Liberty was opposite in the coining press from the eagle's right leg (to observer's left). This caused problems for many if not most issues, particularly for the era from 1840 to about 1880, including all branch-mint issues.

1908–1929 Indian Head type: Recessed designs. Weakness sometimes occurred at the highest part of the Indian's portrait and/or the highest area of the eagle's wing. Mintmarks sometimes were weakly impressed into the working die, or filled during use, creating incomplete detailing.

Coining Processes

After the dies were readied for use, and a supply of planchets was on hand, the dies were placed into a steam-powered coining press (hand-powered at the Philadelphia Mint prior to 1836). A technician adjusted the obverse and reverse dies as the press went through its cycle. As the hammer (top) die came toward the anvil (bottom) die, it would travel far enough down to strike the quarter eagle, but not too far. If the dies were placed too close together, metal would be squeezed out of the collar (creating a "wire" or "knife" rim), and the dies would wear more rapidly.[2] On the other hand, if the dies were spaced too far apart, they would last longer, but the planchet metal would not completely fill the deepest recesses of the dies. Adjustments varied each time a new die or pair of dies was put into the coining press, and sometimes during the process of a given press run.

Philadelphia Mint: Hand-powered press adjustment varied, especially for the early years (1796–1808). Steam presses (initiated in 1836) were adjusted in various spacings, sometimes slightly too far apart, creating weakness on the high points of the portrait and on one leg of the eagle. Better spacing is evident on coins struck after the Civil War. Dies were usually replaced soon after significant cracks developed.

Charlotte and Dahlonega Mints: Presses were casually adjusted, with dies too far apart, resulting in lightness of design details on most issues. Dies were kept in service long after significant cracks developed.

New Orleans Mint: Presses were adjusted in various spacings, often slightly too far apart, creating weakness on the high points of the portrait and on one leg of the eagle. Dies were usually replaced soon after significant cracks developed.

San Francisco Mint: Presses were adjusted in various spacings, usually slightly too far apart, creating weakness on the high points of the portrait and on one leg of the eagle. Dies were kept in service long after significant cracks developed.

Denver Mint: Indian Head design only. Adjustment was generally excellent for 1911-D and 1914-D, casual or poor for 1925-D.

Edge-Reeding Characteristics

The grooved or "reeded" metal collar into which the edges of coins were squeezed varied in certain eras and locations. Dr. John McCloskey commented:[3] "The edge reeding on all early Charlotte and Dahlonega quarter eagles is much wider than the reeding for Philadelphia and New Orleans coins. The wide reeding can be used to authenticate coins from both of these Southern branch mints."

The unusual wide reeding was used on all Dahlonega quarter eagles from the 1839-D to the 1859-D. Any Dahlonega quarter eagle without the wide reeding would be a counterfeit in my opinion."

The early Charlotte quarter eagles had slightly wider reeding than the Dahlonega coins, with slightly fewer reeds. This wide reeding was used to strike 1838-C to 1844-C quarter eagles.

The Charlotte Mint was destroyed by fire during the summer of 1844. When Charlotte quarter eagles were again struck in 1846 a narrow reeding was used. All Charlotte quarter eagles from the 1846-C to the 1860-C have the narrow reeding.

3

Circulation and Distribution

Distribution Procedures

Quarter eagles of different eras and from different mints were distributed in different ways. A knowledge of these procedures is valuable in regard to analyzing the rarity of certain coins today and the degrees of wear that they have received.

Philadelphia Mint: Quarter eagles from 1796 through 1808 were nearly all used domestically, where it was not at all unusual for the pieces to wear down to such numismatic grades as Fine and, in particular, Very Fine. There was no collecting interest in saving such pieces. The Capped Head style of 1821 to 1834 did not circulate domestically. Most were saved by their recipients, or found their way to bullion dealers or to the mints, where they were melted. As such coins were not used in hand-to-hand commerce, they exist today in higher grades such as Extremely Fine and About Uncirculated, and occasionally in Mint State. The Classic Head style of 1834 to 1839 as well as early issues of Liberty Head quarter eagles, 1840–1861, were primarily used in domestic commerce, where they circulated widely. Beginning in late 1861, such coins were hoarded, thus fixing in time the wear the coins had received to that point—with early issues being in such numismatic grades as Fine and Very Fine, and issues of the late 1850s and early 1860s in Extremely Fine and About Uncirculated grades. From 1862 to 1878 quarter eagles were available from the Treasury only upon payment of a premium. None circulated, except a few which were taken to the West. During and after this time, coins of this denomination did not receive extensive wear (circulating coins in the West excepted). From 1879 to 1920 quarter eagles were available for face value at banks, were widely used as gifts and souvenirs (a favorite with those who stopped at the Mint in the early twentieth century), and saw circulation in the West. After 1920, quarter eagles were not readily available at par and did not circulate.

Charlotte Mint: Coinage was placed into circulation, where the pieces received wear. Many remained in banks and in the hands of the public in the Southeast. Circa 1860–1861, most of the available coins still in the South were hoarded, by which time most early dates were well worn; but issues of the 1850s often ranged up to high-level Extremely Fine or About Uncirculated. Proportionally, more Charlotte and Dahlonega coins were saved than were those of the other mints.

Dahlonega Mint: Same situation as for Charlotte: coinage was placed into circulation, where the pieces received wear. Many remained in banks and in the hands of the public in the Southeast. Circa 1860–1861, most of the available coins still in the South were hoarded, by which time most early dates were well worn, but issues of the 1850s often ranged up to high-level Extremely Fine or About Uncirculated. Proportionally, more Charlotte and Dahlonega coins were saved than were those of the other mints.

New Orleans Mint: Mintages from 1839 through the 1850s were placed into circulation, where they were dispersed far and wide and received extensive wear. During the Civil War, those that remained in the South and East were hoarded, but many others were in circulation in the West. Few were saved. In time, most were melted. The survival ratio was very low, and those that did remain were apt to be well worn.

San Francisco Mint: From the first year of quarter eagle coinage, 1854, to the last, 1879, coins were placed into circulation, where they saw continuous, extensive use. By the turn of the twentieth century, the average San Francisco Mint quarter eagle was worn down to the Very Fine level, a lower grade than the average coin from the Charlotte, Dahlonega, or Philadelphia Mint.

Denver Mint: While the 1911-D and 1914-D quarter eagles circulated and became worn down to the Extremely Fine level (on average), the 1925-D did not. Thus, of the three quarter eagles struck at the Denver Mint, the first two are rare today in Mint State, while the third is common in that grade.

4

Proofs for Collectors

Proof Quarter Eagles

The reverse die used to strike this Proof 1831 quarter eagle was in use from 1830 through early 1834.

Regarding Proofs, the determination of whether certain coins of the 1821–1834 years are Proofs or prooflike circulation strikes is often a matter of opinion. In nearly all instances, the same die pairs used to make Proofs were also employed to make circulation strikes. The writer is aware of only two instances from 1821 to 1834 for which there is documentation or incontrovertible evidence that actual specimen or "special finish" coins were made. The first is for 1821, as evidenced by a full set of Proof coins of this year that was given to the Mint Cabinet and that today is in the Smithsonian Institution; and the second is for at least two, possibly four, specimens made in 1834 to be included in sets of coins to be presented to the Sultan of Muscat and the King of Siam. All other "facts" concerning Proofs are conjectural, ranging from wildly so to highly probable.

Writing of the 1830 quarter eagle, which used the same die that made all Proofs and circulation strikes from 1830 through 1834 inclusive, Walter Breen stated: "The reverse die introduced for this year . . . was repolished at the beginning of each year to make a few Proofs . . . then put into the regular press to make business strikes."[1]

It seems obvious that the ensuing circulation strikes would closely resemble Proofs, or might even completely resemble Proofs (and thus *be* Proofs). The status of certain specimens—Proof vs. circulation strike—may never be determined, and it seems that neither a given certification service nor any expert has all the answers. From a financial viewpoint, the controversy may be moot, for a gem prooflike circulation strike would likely sell for about as much—or possibly even more—than a gem Proof.

Adding to the confusion, coins that were in high grades such as About Uncirculated or Mint State were sometimes called "Proof" in the nineteenth century, to emphasize a combination of rarity and excellent preservation, even though a coin may have lacked a prooflike surface. This practice extended for a long time thereafter. In 1950 when B. Max Mehl offered the Jerome Kern Collection for sale at auction he noted that *most* of the Uncirculated quarter eagles in the Kern Collection were bought as "Proof"! As a perusal of old-time auction citations will quickly reveal, many quarter eagles in the 1820s and 1830s were described as Proofs in the last century, this in an era before Kern began collecting, so the era of Kern's purchases hardly marked the beginning of the practice. Thus, the policy of calling prooflike Mint State coins *Proofs* was long-enduring. Probably, most of these would be called *prooflike Mint State*, not *Proof*, today.

For the Classic Head quarter eagles of 1834 to 1839, a few Proofs exist—mainly of the 1834 date—and are very rare. Most if not all Proofs can be identified by close study of their die variety and the mirror quality of their surface.

Liberty Head quarter eagle Proofs exist for some, but not all, of the early dates from 1840 to 1857, and in all instances are formidable rarities. Beginning in 1858, Proofs were distributed with some regularity to numismatists, although quantities were very small through the 1870s. For nearly all of these dates, actual Proof mintages are unknown. Published figures in the *Red Book* and elsewhere are mainly guesses or, in some cases, estimates made by Walter Breen. Moreover, in many instances Proofs were made on speculation that they would be sold, but when buyers failed to materialize in the quantities hoped for, the undistributed Proofs were placed into circulation or melted. Thus, we have a combination of unknown mintages for many issues, and for all issues, unknown total distribution. The 1910 Satin Finish Proof with a record-high mintage is a special situation (see chapter 12).

Concerning Indian Head quarter eagles, Proofs were minted from 1908 to 1915, inclusive. All were of the Sandblast Proof finish (today popularly called *Matte Proof*), except for 1909 and 1910, which were given a special Satin Proof finish. Sand Blast Proofs were made individually by an operator blasting tiny sand particles onto the surface of a circulation strike coin. The finishes are not uniform and vary in brightness. All Indian Head quarter eagles are rare in Proof format, and most are very rare.

Proof 1834 quarter eagle, the first year of the 1834 to 1839 Classic Head type.

Proof 1840 quarter eagle, the first year of a design that was continued through 1907.

Sand Blast Proof quarter eagle, 1908. Sand Blast Proofs were made in 1908 and again from 1910 to 1915.

Satin Finish Proof quarter eagle, 1909. This finish was used in 1909 and 1910.

5

Quarter Eagles on the Numismatic Scene

The Mitchelson Collection in 1908

Quarter eagles have been a favorite series for many numismatists over the years. An early paean to the series appeared in the *Minneapolis Star Tribune* on December 14, 1908:

Has Rare Collection of Quarter Eagles

HARTFORD, Conn.—One might expect to find the most complete collection of United States $2.50 gold pieces in the Mint, but the fact is that a private citizen, Joseph F. Mitchelson of Tariffville, Conn., has not only a greater variety of these coins than the government, but in addition several specimens of which the Mint has no record.

Mr. Mitchelson is a collector of all sorts of curiosities, but his favorite subject is coins and quarter eagles in particular. For 25 years he has ransacked the United States for additional specimens of this piece. There are fully 172 different varieties, taking into account the coins made at the various mints—Philadelphia, Charlotte, Dahlonega, New Orleans and San Francisco. The Carson City mint so far as is known has never made a coin of this denomination.

Mr. Mitchelson believes that he has looked over at least three-fourths of the present supply of quarter eagles in circulation in the United States. He is well known among bankers, being himself a retired banker, and has examined the stock of quarter eagles owned by such banks in this city as the Chemical, the Mechanics, the Yorkville, the Garfield and other national banks for new specimens. One day a cashier of a bank in this city let him have a bag of $1,800 worth of quarter eagles upon his promise not to bring them back, as the little coins were a nuisance to the bank. In the lot he discovered several desirable specimens, and when the bag of gold finally reached the New York assay office he received a bill for $18, which represented the shortage in weight.

One year he bought more than $100,000 worth of quarter eagles in different parts of the country and looked through the supply of coins in this denomination in the vaults of about every bank in New England. His custom was to buy the coins in thousand dollar lots and then, after looking them over, to exchange them with a money broker for bills, paying a small commission. There was nearly always a loss of several dollars on the transaction, but the collector felt himself well repaid if occasionally he secured a new variety.

Of the 172 varieties issued since 1796 Mr. Mitchelson has 169. The first of the three specimens that he lacks is the one known to collectors as the "six over five." In 1806 no new dies were made for the quarter eagles so far as is known. The dies of 1805 were used, the figure "5" being cut out and the figure "6" substituted. The alteration was executed in such a way that traces of the original figure "5" can easily be distinguished under the figure "6." In the same year the dies used in 1804 for the quarter eagles were similarly altered, producing a variety known as the "six over four." Both varieties are very rare, the "six over five" exceedingly so. A specimen of "six over four" variety in fine condition brought $43 at the Stickney sale. The "six over five" variety would bring a very much higher price.

The other two varieties missing from Mr. Mitchelson's collection were struck at the San Francisco mint in 1854 and 1858 and bear the mint letter S. The records show that 246 pieces were struck in 1854 and 1,200 in 1858 at this branch mint, the limited number being due to the trouble the authorities had in obtaining refining acids, which had to be brought around from the Atlantic states on board ship.

Not a single specimen of the quarter eagle of either of these dates is known to be in existence, and if one should come to light it would command a handsome premium.

Mr. Mitchelson has at least two varieties of the $2.50 gold piece of which the Mint has no record. One of these is dated 1845, and was struck at the New Orleans mint, showing the letter O. Of this variety Mr. Mitchelson has two specimens.

Another unlisted variety owned by him was struck at the Philadelphia mint in 1841. Only two specimens are known, the one owned by Mr. Mitchelson and another in the coin collection of the Philadelphia Mint.

Perhaps the highest priced coin in the collection of quarter eagles is the variety issued in 1834, with the motto "E Pluribus Unum" on a band over the head of the eagle on the reverse. In 1834, when the fineness of the gold in the United States coins was reduced from 916 2–3 to 899.25, the design was changed by removing the liberty cap from the Goddess of Liberty, on the obverse, and representing the hair as confined by a band on which was inscribed the word "Liberty." The reverse was the same as in previous issues save that the motto, "E Pluribus Unum," was omitted. A few coins were struck with the motto and of these only five or six are now known to exist. One of these, in a high state of preservation, brought $320 at the Stickney sale in 1906.

The next rarest variety is that of 1797. The obverse dies was cracked when the coin was struck and a line reaches across the surface of the piece. There are said to be only 10 specimens of this variety in existence, one of which brought $210 at the Smith sale, held a few years ago.

Only seven specimens of the quarter eagle struck in 1826 are known to exist. A very fine specimen brought $190 when recently sold.

Among the most difficult quarter eagles to get are the proof $2.50 pieces issued at the Philadelphia mint from 1862 to 1866. During this period gold was quoted as high as $280, and the average collector did not think it advisable to purchase from the Mint these specially struck coins, as the premium on the gold was sure to fall, and it would then be difficult to sell save at a loss. Consequently, these coins now are scarce.

The Proof quarter eagle of 1863 is extremely rare. Only 30 Proof specimens were struck at the Philadelphia mint, and owing to the lack of demand for them some were remelted at the mint.

In 1801 dies were made for the quarter eagle, as is evident by the specimen of 1802 struck over 1801, but no coin of the denomination bearing a perfect date is on record.

Mitchelson Retrospective

Remarkably, today there is little to correct in this article from well over a century ago. "Retired banker" is incorrect, at least regarding his primary business activity. Further, more is known about the rarity of certain varieties today, as will be explained under the various issues in the present text. Regarding the missing 1858-S, today it is thought that none were struck of this variety, and any published numbers referred to the well-known 1857-S mintage.

Born in Tariffville, Connecticut, on May 22, 1856, Joseph C. Mitchelson developed a keen interest in the world around him. After completing his education at Dr. Nash's Institute for Boys in Amherst, Massachusetts, and at the Eastman Business College in Poughkeepsie, New York, he entered the family tobacco business, which included a farm of more than one thousand acres in nearby Simsbury. At the time there were many tobacco farms in the lowland areas of the state, and his family was the major wholesaler. The firm had branches in Kansas City and San Francisco. For many years, Kansas City was Joseph's primary residence. While there he married Emma Wilson, of Genesee, Illinois. The couple had no children. With the Midwest as his base, Joseph was in charge of marketing and traveled widely, including to Europe and Asia, and along the way pursued his favorite pastime, numismatics. In June 1900 *The Numismatist* reported that he had recently spent much time in San Francisco, and while there picked a numismatic plum, a rare 1894-S dime. "The mint authorities there informed him that while 24 were originally struck, only 14 went into circulation."[1]

At the turn of the century, Mitchelson returned to his native state and made plans for his collection to be stored in a large vault at the Aetna National Bank in Hartford. This was a temporary measure, and he arranged to have it exhibited in a vault in the Connecticut State Library, to be especially constructed. In time he provided funds so that the collection could be continued and expanded by adding new issues as they were minted. Several years later he retired, his traveling days coming to an end. One can imagine that he spent a lot of time with his coins. In January 1906 the ANA published his comment, "I cannot live without *The Numismatist*. It is the cream of my reading matter." He was also a member of the American Numismatic Society, the Chicago Coin Club, the New York Numismatic Club, and the British Numismatic Society. Although quarter eagles were his first love, his collection was one of the finest ever formed in the colonial and early American series and extended to include rarities in the federal series as well as private and territorial gold.

Mitchelson passed to his final reward on September 25, 1911. His collection, bequeathed to the state, has been maintained ever since, with the exception of coins added after 1911, many of which were sold. Today the Mitchelson Collection can be viewed and studied by special appointment.

COLLECTING CONSIDERATIONS

One of the most desired quarter eagles in the Liberty Head series is the 1848 with CAL. counterstamped on the reverse. Just 1,389 pieces were struck from the first Gold Rush metal to be sent to the Philadelphia Mint.

Today, as you read these words, the quarter eagle denomination is very appealing to numismatists, for while it contains some landmark rarities, these elusive dates are not completely *impossible*—just difficult. With the exception of a handful of major rarities, the completion of a full set of quarter eagles from 1796 to 1929 is a challenge that can be mounted by nearly any serious collector. Along the way much enjoyment will be derived in tracking down issues that have nominal catalog value but that in reality are rarities in disguise.

No important collection of quarter eagles was ever formed in a short time. However, with patience—and some good fortune—a beautiful cabinet can be gathered. Quarter eagles form a very pleasing denomination to collect. They are small enough to be "cute" and cameo-like, and yet large enough to permit study of the interesting design details that many possess. Moreover, quarter eagles are the only gold series that can be realistically collected over the span of years from the 1790s into the twentieth century. Half eagles were minted more continuously, but there are so many formidable rarities that only the well-financed, stout-hearted, patient numismatist can aspire to obtain the dates 1819–1834. Eagles were not minted from 1805 to 1837, and thus continuity was lost (no pieces of John Reich's Capped Head design or Kneass's Classic Head are to be found in the $10 series).

Some collectors aspire to acquire one of each major quarter eagle design type. Front-row center in numismatic interest are the 1796, No Stars on Obverse, and the 1808, as both are of designs that were produced only in their respective, single years. The 1821 to early 1834 coins range from rare to very rare.

Particularly notable among specialized collections of early quarter eagles from 1796 to the late 1830s are those of Harry W. Bass Jr. and D. Brent Pogue. Both were gathered over a long period of years and combine rarity with high quality.

A Basic Type Set

A *basic* type set of quarter eagles, 1796–1929, includes one of each of the following issues.

Type I: Capped Bust to Right, No Stars on Obverse (1796). These are very rare, and the most difficult type to acquire.

Type II: Capped Bust to Right, Stars on Obverse (1796–1807). While it is popular to assign all Stars on Obverse quarter eagles minted from 1796 to 1807 under the heading of a single type, it would be more accurate to have multiple designations within this range. The number of stars and their placement vary from issue to issue. Stars on Obverse quarter eagles of 1796 have eight stars to the left and eight to the right, for a total of 16, while those of the years 1797 through 1807 have 13 stars arranged in various ways. The 1797 quarter eagles have seven stars to the left and six to the right, while 1798 quarter eagles have six to the left and seven to the right. Quarter eagles of 1802 (often called 1802, 2 Over 1) have eight left and five right. The year 1806 comes in two varieties: eight left and five right as well as seven left and six right.

Type III: Draped Bust to Left (1808). These were struck in one year only and are the second most difficult type to acquire.

Type IV: Capped Head to Left, Large Diameter (1821–1827). All dates are rare, much more so than is generally realized. This is the third-rarest type. Some numismatists combine this and the next into a single type, easing the financial aspect of collecting.

Type V: Capped Head to Left, Reduced Diameter (1829–1834). All dates are rare.

Type VI: Classic Head (1834–1839). The Classic Head is easily available in grades up to and including About Uncirculated. In Mint State the 1834 is the date seen most often.

Type VII: Liberty Head (1840–1907). These are easily available in Mint State (this being true for issues of the last decade of production).

Type VIII: Indian Head (1908–1929). The Indian Head style, too, is easily available in Mint State, especially for those dated in the 1920s.

Numismatic Challenges

The quarter eagle series from the first year of issue, 1796, to the last, 1929, has as many challenges as any in American numismatics. Many dates and mintmarks are plentiful enough if Very Fine or Extremely Fine in grade, but are world-class rarities if MS-60 or finer. Nearly all of the early issues from 1796 to 1834 are rare in any grade, but especially so at higher levels. The 1796, No Stars on Obverse, and the 1808 are in special demand for inclusion in type sets because of their one-year-of-issue status. Among early die varieties there are a number of very elusive issues, including one reverse die of the 1796, No Stars on Obverse; the 1804, 13-Star Reverse; and the 1806, 6 Over 5.

There are no world-class rarities among basic Classic Head quarter eagle dates and mintmarks of 1834 to 1839, although the 1838-C, with its low mintage of 7,880 pieces, must be counted as an especially hard-to-find issue, especially as contrasted to the most prolific quarter eagle of the era, the 1836 Philadelphia Mint version, which posted a production of 547,986. Records from the early twentieth century reveal that Classic Head quarter eagles were still in circulation as of that time, although often worn down to Fine or Very Fine grades. The Philadelphia Mint varieties are readily available in worn grades, but are rare in Mint State and exceedingly rare in gem Mint State, this being especially true for the dates toward the end of the series. Certain 1834–1839 die varieties, first studied in depth by Dr. John W. McCloskey and finessed by Mark R. Borckardt, are very elusive.

The 1838-C quarter eagle is the rarest basic date and mintmark issue in the 1834 to 1839 Classic Head series.

Later, for a whole string of Coronet design dates in the 1860s and 1870s, choice and gem circulation strikes are harder to find than Proofs—and the Proofs themselves are great rarities. In the Liberty Head series the prime rarities are the 1841, 1854-S, and 1863. Indeed, in the entire series of major quarter eagle varieties (dates, mintmarks, and types; but not star counts), these are the "big three." The 1848 with CAL. counterstamped on the reverse is one of the most popular of all gold coins because of its status as a candidate for the first U.S. commemorative, and because of its scarcity.

The 1854-S quarter eagle is the key San Francisco Mint rarity and was struck in small numbers in the first year of the Mint's operation.

Charlotte and Dahlonega quarter eagles are all scarce, and some are major rarities, especially in high grades such as About Uncirculated or Mint State, although in general these low-mintage C and D issues are easier to find in high grades than are their New Orleans and San Francisco branch-mint counterparts. Coins of the Charlotte and Dahlonega mints have an especially strong numismatic following, and the demand for them has always been great.

The Charlotte Mint (drawn by George Osborn).

The Dahlonega Mint (drawn by George Osborn).

The 1911-D quarter eagle, while not a rarity, is the key issue in the 1908–1929 Indian Head series.

There are two curious situations contributing to more "C" and "D" mint coins being saved, proportionally, than those of other mints. First, as noted earlier, at the advent of the Civil War many Charlotte and Dahlonega quarter eagles, which were still in regional circulation in the Southeast, were hoarded, with the result that high-grade coins of the 1850s were preserved. Second, in the 1890s the Charlotte and Dahlonega coins were recognized for their scarcity, and specimens still in bank holdings were found by alert tellers and cashiers and were saved; at the same time, little or no attention was paid to Philadelphia, New Orleans, and San Francisco quarter eagles.

New Orleans coins are among the quarter eagles that were often made in fairly large quantities, but since few if any collectors bothered to save them, they are great rarities in high grades today. The same can be said for nearly all of the San Francisco Mint quarter eagles, first struck in 1854 and last in 1879. As noted, San Francisco Mint coins were intensively used in circulation during the 1860s and 1870s—at a time when gold coins were not seen in commerce in the East and Midwest. Thus, for many San Francisco quarter eagles Very Fine is the typical grade encountered, an Extremely Fine specimen would be unusual, and an About Uncirculated coin might be a rarity. At the same time, for a Philadelphia Mint quarter eagle the grades Extremely Fine and About Uncirculated would be what to expect. No numismatist has ever completed a collection of Philadelphia, New Orleans, or San Francisco Mint quarter eagles in Mint State, or, so far as I know, has even come close.

Later Philadelphia Mint quarter eagles in the Liberty Head series, 1879 to 1907, include many low-mintage dates, but most are available with a modicum of searching. Most of the issues of the 1880s have remarkably low mintages and are elusive in all grades, especially Mint State. The reason for this is that collectors of that era bought Proofs and ignored circulation strikes. Beginning in the late 1890s and continuing to the last year of the Liberty Head design, 1907, many Mint State coins exist for each date.

Among the fifteen different date and mintmark varieties made of Indian Head quarter eagles from 1908 to 1929, the only scarce issue is the 1911-D. The design of the Indian Head quarter eagle is such—with the field being the highest area—that even a small amount of handling would create an appearance of wear. Many of the early issues in the Indian Head series—1908 through 1915—are common enough in grades such as Extremely Fine or About Uncirculated but are very rare in gem Mint State. Coins of the later era of the series, 1925–1929 (none were minted 1916–1924), are normally seen in Mint State, as coins minted in the 1920s did not actively circulate.

6

Using This Book to Understand the Market

The information given under the individual listings in each catalog incorporates the essentials to understanding the market. Each date and mintmark quarter eagle issued from 1796 to 1929 is given a separate analysis, as are several major varieties. The title photographs are of actual coins of that variety, obverse and reverse (not composites).

The market value of a quarter eagle is determined by many factors. Before making significant purchases it is advisable to learn as much as you can and to consult other sources for opinions as to grade, rarity, desirability, and market value. Often, a trustworthy professional numismatist can be of great assistance.

In the field of quarter eagles the traditional estimates of rarity within a specific grade have changed greatly and continue to change, mainly due to gradeflation. Nearly all quarter eagles of the late eighteenth century and nineteenth century that were graded in high About Uncirculated levels several decades ago are now certified as MS-60 to MS-62. For the latest population-report figures check the PCGS and NGC websites. This important factor is reiterated on pages 38–39.

Rarities

Rarity figures, which are used most frequently with the copious die varieties in chapter 10, follow the scale devised by Dr. William H. Sheldon in 1949:

Rarity-1 = common
Rarity-2 = not so common
Rarity-3 = scarce
Rarity-4 = very scarce (population estimated at 76–200)
Rarity-5 = rare (31–75)
Rarity-6 = very rare (13–30)
Rarity-7 = extremely rare (4–12)
Rarity-8 = unique or very nearly so (1, 2, or 3)

Circulation Strikes

Circulation-Strike Mintage

This figure is the quantity minted for general circulation in commerce. For quarter eagles from 1796 through 1808 the figures are largely guesswork, as dies from earlier years were sometimes kept on hand and used later, until they cracked or broke. The mintage figures thus represent the quarter eagles struck during a given calendar year and not necessarily the quantity of coins bearing that specific date. From the 1830s onward the mintages of a calendar year represent coins struck during that year. There are some isolated mysteries, such as for 1841—a rarity with no official mintage figures. Where the reported mintages differ from those that are commonly published, a discussion is provided in the subsequent text.

Estimated Total Population (Mint State)

This reflects *modern grading interpretations.* As noted previously, countless coins that were graded AU–50 to AU-58 years ago are now certified as MS-60 to MS-62, sometimes even higher. If this book had been compiled and published in, say, 1980, the range would be much smaller, although it would reference the exact same coins—just with less-elevated grades. Taking the listings at face value, many quarter eagles that were great rarities or even unknown in Mint State now exist with several or more certified in that state. This number is based on auction appearances, research, and the study of certified populations as published by PCGS and NGC, plus an element of guesswork. Many certified coins, especially those that are valuable, have been resubmitted many times. Accordingly, ten listings or events in a population report may represent just two or three different coins.

Both PCGS and NGC have Registry Sets—competitions in which thousands of participants strive to have the greatest number of points possible. Each service gives instructions on how these numbers are compiled. As a general rule, for the PCGS Registry a coin that is the finest of its kind or is tied for the finest wins many points. Ditto for the NGC competition. Such coins can be exceedingly expensive. A quarter eagle that is as common as can be in MS-65 can be inexpensive and very desirable to the traditional specialist. If just a few are known in, say, MS-67, the price for a Registry Set player can be many multiples of the MS-65 valuation. High valuations for ultra-grade quarter eagles can be risky, as two dangers are present: (1) More coins will be certified from repatriations and other sources, and (2) coins will graduate a point or more in certified grade.

The velocity of coin movement in the market has gone from very slow in early times to a rapid pace today. It is not unusual for the same quarter eagle to appear in a half dozen different auctions during a span of a decade or two, often with different grades each time.

In modern times PCGS and NGC have added + marks to certain Mint State listings. Such listings with + marks, such as MS-64+, are incorporated into the regular listings and in this book are given simply as, for example, MS-64. As it is, population reports suggest that coins with + marks are of great rarity, but it is a reality that many earlier coins, if regraded now, would also have plus marks. Probably more than 90% of quarter eagles certified by PCGS and NGC were done before + marks were invented as additions. For current certified-coin information see the PCGS and NGC websites.

As is evident, grading as practiced by NGC and PCGS today does not conform to the traditional American Numismatic Association standards. With the addition of + signs there are now 20 different Mint State grades between 60 and 70. These have never been defined in print, and no one can consistently apply them.

Adding to the above, it is the author's view that a beautiful MS-63 quarter eagle, well struck and lustrous and with great eye appeal, is much more desirable to own than an MS-65 that is dull and unattractive.

The operative advice here is: *Be careful! Numbers are only a part of the desirability of a coin and are often not the most important part.*

Estimated Total Population (Circulated Grades)

This is the author's estimate or educated (hopefully!) guess of the number of coins in numismatic hands in grades below MS-60.

Die Data

Details regarding the known dies may appear under each individual listing or as part of the introductory narrative in each chapter. The location of this text depends on the amount of information known about each quarter eagle type, the number of known die combinations within that type, and other factors. For example, Classic Head quarter eagles are exceedingly complex; the known dies and die combinations for 1836 alone fill more than three pages. Thus the die information for all years is in the general introduction, under "Dies and Known Die Combinations, 1821–1827." The Liberty Head coinage, on the other hand, is more straightforward, often with little to be said about the dies apart from a description of the date logotype. This information is placed under "Die Data" in the individual listings.

Selected Auction Records

As a special feature of this book I offer a wide selection of auction citations, including representative early auction appearances and selected higher-grade later offerings. These give a flavor of cataloging styles of the period, show how elements of rarity and publicity have changed over the years, and reveal other transitions that have taken place. These are *not* the latest listings, nor do they capture the highest grades and prices to date. For that information consult the websites of the auction companies. Many twenty-first-century listings can be found elsewhere on the Internet.

Among auction citations, emphasis has been placed on early listings as these often include comments and theories from an era in which factual information was lacking. In modern times auction listings have often been recitations of population reports published by PCGS and NGC, with little emphasis on numismatic history. For expanded information many auction catalogs are available for free on the Newman Numismatic Portal website.

PROOFS

Proof Mintage

This figure is estimated for early issues through the 1850s and is taken from the *Mint Report* for the years from the 1860s onward.

Estimated Total Population (Proof)

This number is an estimate of the number of Proofs known to exist today. The National Numismatic Collection in the Smithsonian Institution has many Proofs from 1821 into the 1850s and a full run of all dates after that time. The American Numismatic Society has gold Proof sets from the 1860s into the early 1900s, as does the Joseph Mitchelson Collection preserved by the Connecticut State Library. These are included in the estimates. For most Proofs a significant number of any given mintage has been lost by having been spent when they had little resale value.

Selected Proof Auction Records

As with the circulation strikes, Proof coins have a section on selected auction records, where relevant.

MARKET VALUES

Average market values as of press time have been provided by Whitman Publishing using information from more than 100 different professionals and others who have contributed to *A Guide Book of United States Coins* and the *Guide Book of United States Coins: Expanded Deluxe Edition*.

These are suggested typical market values for *average-quality* examples of the grade indicated. As gradeflation or liberalized interpretation has been practiced by the third-party services in recent decades, a coin certified as, for example, MS-65 might be of the same quality as one certified as MS-63 or MS-64 in 1990, when certified grades were viewed by many as conservative. Many of yesteryear's About Uncirculated coins are today's Mint State selections. For that reason it is not possible to use historic *Red Book* or other prices to formulate accurate market trends or performance.

The prices herein are intended to reflect what an informed buyer will pay to an established and reputable seller, at the time this book goes to press. Market prices can and do vary among sellers and buyers at any given time. As a study of auction prices reveals, it is often the case that in a given year multiple examples of a particular variety in a given grade and certified by the same service can vary widely. It is wise to check multiple sources before making purchases.

7

Capped Bust to Right $2.50 Gold Coins (1796–1807)

Capped Bust to Right, No Stars on Obverse (1796)

Designer: *Robert Scot.* **Weight:** *4.37 grams.* **Composition:** *.9167 gold, .0833 silver and copper.* **Diameter:** *Approximately 20 mm.* **Edge:** *Reeded.* **Mint:** *Philadelphia.*

Inaugural Design

The first quarter eagles minted bear the date 1796. The inaugural design is distinguished from the later motif by having no stars on the obverse. The engraver is believed to have been Robert Scot.[1]

Designated as the Capped Bust to Right style, the first quarter eagle type of 1796 (called Type I by Walter Breen) features the head and shoulder portrait of Miss Liberty facing right, wearing a cloth cap, with LIBERTY above and the date below. There are no stars in the field, giving the obverse a cameo-like aspect. To me, Conical Cap, Bust to Right would be more descriptive. The reason for the omission of the stars is not known. Perhaps the engraver believed that the die would be more attractive without them, in view that there were stars on the reverse.

The reverse is of the Heraldic Eagle design similar to that used on gold and silver denominations of the era, this being its first known appearance in coinage. It was adopted on the $5 gold half eagle in 1797 (although, as noted on page 43, a 1795-dated die still on hand was used at that time to make 1795-dated coins), and on the $10 gold eagle the same year. The other denominations adopted the motif in the following order: in 1798, the silver dime and half dollar; in 1800, the silver half dime; in 1801, the silver half dollar; and in 1804, the silver quarter dollar. The engraver may have been Scot or else his assistant, John Smith Gardner.

Adapted from the Great Seal of the United States, the center motif depicts an eagle with a shield on its breast, holding an olive branch and arrows in its talons, and in its beak a ribbon inscribed E PLURIBUS UNUM. Above the eagle is a galaxy of sixteen stars is above (the number of stars was reduced to 13 in 1798) with a group of clouds in an arc extending from one wing to the other. On the shield are eight vertical solid stripes, a style continued through 1797, after which six multi-element stripes were used. The inscription UNITED STATES OF AMERICA surrounds. There is no mark indicating the denomination. Two reverse dies, each differing slightly from the other, combined with the No Stars obverse, creating varieties BD-1 and BD-2.

Certain numeral and letter punches used on early $2.50 dies were also used on silver dime dies of like diameter.

Although the Heraldic Eagle device first appeared in federal coinage on the 1796 quarter eagle, it had been used earlier elsewhere, including for the 1791-dated Washington Small Eagle copper cents struck in England and the Getz silver Washington half dollar of 1792.

The diameter of the early quarter eagles was standardized at 13/16" (20.6 mm), which was used for the entire coinage of the 1796–1808 era.

In *Description of Ancient and Modern Coins, in the Cabinet Collection at the Mint of the United States*, 1860, Mint Director James Ross Snowden described the first issues of the denomination, the two different styles of 1796:

> 1796. The gold coins of this year have sixteen stars upon the obverse, eight upon each side of the effigy. The first coinage of quarter eagles took place in this year. The first issue, which was made on the twenty first of September, was of the same type as the eagle. The amount, however, was very small, being only 66 pieces. Subsequently the die was altered, and on the eighth of November there was a coinage of 897 pieces of the following type: Obverse same as the eagle. (A portion, and probably a small one, had no stars upon the obverse.) Rev. An eagle with raised wings, holding in its beak a scroll, inscribed "E PLURIBUS UNUM," and grasping in the right talon a bundle of arrows, and in the left an olive branch. Upon its breast is the United States shield. Above the eagle are clouds, and sixteen stars. Legend. "UNITED STATES OF AMERICA."

MINTAGE FIGURES FOR 1796

During calendar year 1796 the mintage of the $2.50 denomination amounted to 1,395 pieces, which Walter Breen (*Encyclopedia*, 1988, and elsewhere) divided into 963 coins of the No Stars on Obverse type and 432 of the Stars on Obverse style. In actuality, no such neat separation is recorded officially, and this is simply a guess based upon deliveries. Coins struck under Warrant 76, September 22, 1796, amounted to just 66 coins, while Warrant 77 of December 8 involved 897 coins. Toward the end of the latter month, 432 additional quarter eagles were struck (but were delivered on January 14, 1797).

It is convenient to combine the first two groups, 66+897, to create a mintage of 963 for No Stars on Obverse coins and assign the third group, 432, to the Stars on Obverse strikes, but, as noted, this is simply a guess. Nor is it by any means certain that 1796-dated dies were discarded at the end of 1796. They may have been used later, in 1797, 1798, or thereafter. The evidence of keeping earlier-dated obverses on hand is dramatically shown by the use of a 1795 *half eagle* die in 1798, when it was combined with the new Heraldic Eagle design. The same guesswork or—better, estimation—is found throughout Walter Breen's texts and has been adapted without question into many popular references including *A Guide Book of United States Coins.* It is likely that more accurate numbers could be obtained with a modern re-study of the issues. In any and all instances, information in the Bass-Dannreuther text (*Early U.S. Gold Coin Varieties: A Study of Die States 1795–1834*, by Harry W. Bass Jr. and John W. Dannreuther; hereafter Bass-Dannreuther or BD) supersedes all other information, including the Breen studies.

During this era the calendar-year mintage figures (never mind the separation of these figures into estimated quantities for different varieties) for early gold coins must be taken with a large grain of salt. They are interesting to contemplate, but do not necessarily represent the number of coins struck bearing that particular year date. During the years 1796–1808, the Mint concentrated on the economy of using dies until they cracked or were otherwise rendered useless. The inquiries of future generations of numismatists, yet unborn, were not even considered.

Collecting Considerations

The number of surviving specimens of the 1796, No Stars on Obverse, quarter eagle has been subject to many guesses, ranging from as low as a dozen or so to something over the 100 mark. Bass-Dannreuther suggests four to six for BD-1 and 100 to 125 for BD-2.

Irrespective of which estimate you choose the 1796 quarter eagle is famous as one of the most elusive and highly sought-after early American gold coins. The vast majority of historical auction prices do not identify the two die varieties. It can be assumed that the vast majority have been BD-2.

Most extant specimens are in grades from Very Fine to Extremely Fine, although a few higher-condition examples exist. One of the most important presentations of this issue was in Stack's catalog of the John Whitney Walter Collection, 1999, which featured specimens acquired and studied over many years by a dedicated numismatist with an ample budget. An appendix to that catalog lists several *hundred* sale appearances for the 1796, No Stars on Obverse, quarter eagle over a long period of years.

Curiously, the starless obverse field and the cameo-like effect it gave to the portrait of Miss Liberty resulted in an inordinate number of these pieces' being used as jewelry. Thus, today it is not unusual to find examples that once had loops attached to the edge, or that have been burnished.

Nearly all specimens show some Mint-caused planchet-adjustment marks in the form of grooves or file marks, these being particularly evident along the border, but sometimes appearing on the portrait of Miss Liberty and among the reverse motifs.

It was not known until Edgar H. Adams studied a coin in the 1914 sale of the William F. Gable Collection that the 1796, No Stars on Obverse, quarter eagle was mated with *two different* reverses. However, this discovery was not widely mentioned in auction listings until modern times.

Dies and Known Die Combinations, 1796, No Stars on Obverse

1796, No Stars, Obverse Die 1. The 1, 7, and 9 in 1796 lean right while 6 is upright. The digits 17 are farthest apart, 79 is close, and 96 is in between. The 6 is closer to the denticles than are the first three digits; the top of the 6 and ball overlap the details of the neck truncation. LIBERTY is widely spaced, with LI and BE wider than IB; B is entirely over the upper part of the cap; and the bases of E and R are on the same level.

1796, No Stars, Reverse Die A. Sixteen stars; *the star ray points to left upright of the second U in UNUM*; this is definitive. *The tip of the lowest outside arrowhead is opposite the right upright of N in UNITED.* Star 15 (under the eagle's beak) is to the right of and slightly *above* star 8.

1796, No Stars, Reverse Die B. Sixteen stars; *the star rays point to either side of the second U in UNUM* and, on the other side of the eagle, *the star ray points to R in PLURIBUS;* this is definitive. *The tip of the longest arrowhead is opposite the space between N and I in UNITED.* Star 15 (under the eagle's beak) is to the right of and slightly *below* star 8.

1796, No Stars, BD-1: Dies 1-A. 4 to 6 known. *Commentary:* This is a very rare variety, not described in the literature until recent decades, but known to Edgar H. Adams. In his commentary printed in Stack's 1999 sale of his collection of 1796-dated coins of all denominations, John Whitney Walter stated that of the dozens of die varieties and combinations known of 1796 issues, from half cents to $10 gold eagles, the only one he was not able to obtain in two decades of searching was what is now known as BD-1.

1796, No Stars, BD-2: Dies 1-B. 100 to 125 known. *Commentary:* This is the usually seen variety of this type. One of three in the National Coin Collection, the specimen from the Mint Cabinet, is perhaps Very Fine to Extremely Fine, evidence that the Mint did not save specimens of its own coinage in this year.

Grading Standards

Note: Grading Standards are identical for Capped Bust to Right, No Stars on Obverse, quarter eagles and Capped Bust to Right, Stars on Obverse, quarter eagles.

MS-60 to 70 (Mint State). ***Obverse:*** At MS-60, some abrasion and contact marks are evident, most noticeably on the hair to the left of Miss Liberty's forehead and on the higher-relief areas of the cap. On the No Stars on Obverse quarter eagles, there is some abrasion in the field—more so than on the Stars

1802, 2 Over 1. Graded MS-61.

on Obverse coins, whose field is more protected. Luster is present, but may be dull or lifeless, and interrupted in patches. At MS-63, contact marks are few, and abrasion is very light. An MS-65 coin will have hardly any abrasion, and contact marks are so minute as to require magnification. Luster should be full and rich. Coins grading above MS-65 exist more in theory than in reality for this type—but they do exist, and are defined by having fewer marks as perfection is approached. ***Reverse:*** Comments apply as for the obverse, except that abrasion and contact marks are most noticeable on the upper part of the eagle and the clouds. The field area is complex; there is not much open space, with stars above the eagle, the arrows and olive branch, and other features. Accordingly, marks are not as noticeable as on the obverse.

AU-50, 53, 55, 58 (About Uncirculated). ***Obverse:*** Light wear is seen on the cheek, the hair immediately to the left of the face, and the cap, more so at AU-50 than at AU–53 or 55. An AU-58 coin has minimal traces of wear. An AU-50 coin has luster in protected areas among the stars and letters, with little in the open fields or on the portrait. At AU-58 most luster is present in the fields, but is worn away on the highest parts of the motifs. The 1796, No Stars on Obverse, type has less luster in any given grade. ***Reverse:*** Comments as for Mint State, except that the eagle's neck, the tips and top of the wings, the clouds, and the tail now show noticeable wear, as do other features. Luster ranges from perhaps 40% remaining in protected areas at AU-50 to nearly full mint bloom at AU-58. Often the reverse of this type retains much more luster than does the obverse.

1796, No Stars; BD-2. Graded AU-58.

EF-40, 45 (Extremely Fine). ***Obverse:*** Wear is evident all over the portrait, with some loss of detail in the hair to the left of Miss Liberty's face. Excellent detail remains in low-relief areas of the hair, such as the front curl and the back of the head. The stars show wear, as do the date and letters. Luster, if present at all, is minimal and in protected areas. ***Reverse:*** Wear is greater than at the About Uncirculated level. The neck lacks feather detail on its highest points. Feathers have lost some detail near the edges of the wings, and some areas of the horizontal lines in the shield may be blended together. Some traces of luster may be seen, more so at EF-45 than at EF-40. Overall, the reverse appears to be in a slightly higher grade than the obverse.

1802; BD-1. Graded EF-45.

VF-20, 30 (Very Fine). ***Obverse:*** The higher-relief areas of hair are well worn at VF-20, less so at VF-30. The stars are flat at their centers. ***Reverse:*** Wear is greater, including on the shield and wing feathers. The star centers are flat. Other areas have lost detail as well. E PLURIBUS UNUM is easy to read.

1802, 2 Over 1. Graded MS-61.

The Capped Bust to Right quarter eagle is seldom collected in grades lower than VF-20.

1796, No Stars on Obverse

Circulation-Strike Mintage:
963 (estimated by Walter Breen)

Rarest U.S. gold design.
Only year of design type.
First U.S. quarter eagle.

The first U.S. quarter eagle gold coin, the 1796, No Stars on Obverse, is a one-year design type. It is also the rarest U.S. gold design.

Estimated Total Population (Mint State). 5 to 8. The dividing line between a truly Mint State 1796, No Stars on Obverse, quarter eagle and one that is About Uncirculated is fuzzy in the literature. A number of high-grade coins that have been called Mint State (or, years ago, the equivalent *Uncirculated*) seem to be no better than AU-55 or AU-58 today. Conversely, some that have been called About Uncirculated before are now graded Mint State. High-grade coins are very attractive and usually are prooflike.

Estimated Total Population (Circulated Grades). 100 to 120. Among surviving circulated 1796, No Stars on Obverse, quarter eagles, Very Fine and Extremely Fine examples are the norm, but there are at least 15 that are About Uncirculated, usually with prooflike surfaces; some of these were probably called Extremely Fine years ago. Grading is a moving target in many areas of numismatics, and the 1796, No Stars on Obverse, quarter eagle is a study in this regard.

Selected Auction Records

Note: Hundreds of offerings have reached print over the years. Those cited here are a combination of early listings, citations that have die-state descriptions, and later listings describing pieces of exceptional grade or provenance.

In September 1863, lot 454 in the George F. Seavey Collection was described by W.H. Strobridge: "1796 No stars, Very Fine, very rare." Realized $20. In May 1864, W. Elliot Woodward's John F. McCoy Collection sale included lot 1961: "1796 Without stars, Uncirculated, a fine impression, extremely rare." Realized $15. In March 1863, Woodward described lot 2789 in the Bache, Bertsch, Lightbody, Lilliendahl, Vinton, and Watson Collections: "1796 Without stars; Extremely Fine, nearly Proof, very rare." Realized $13.50. *Nearly Proof*, meaning a high grade, was a common term at the time and does not relate to today's definition of *Proof*.

In January 1884 Woodward offered lot 880 in the Heman Ely Collection: "1796 Without stars; Uncirculated, exceedingly rare." Realized $24.50. Moving into the twentieth century, in June 1906 the Chapman brothers described Lot 97 in the Major W.B. Wetmore Collection: "1796 Bust of Liberty right, draped, wearing cap; LIBERTY above, date beneath. Reverse, UNITED STATES OF AMERICA. Heraldic Eagle. Very Fine. Rare." By implication this was the variety without stars. Realized $40. The Peter Mougey Collection offered by Thomas L. Elder in September 1910 included lot 1144: "1796. Bust of Liberty to right with cap. Heraldic Eagle. Planchet marks across the obverse rim, otherwise a brilliant Uncirculated specimen with Proof surface. Very rare." Realized $200. No doubt the "planchet marks" are what would be called *adjustment marks* today. In his *Encyclopedia* (1988), Walter Breen called this particular specimen a "presentation piece," apparently an assumption based upon his reading of the catalog description. Breen assumed many things that had little or no evidence.

In his April 1956 sale of the Melish and Hester Collections, Abe Kosoff offered two examples, one from a later (lapped) state of the obverse, both being the BD-2 variety of today. Lot 1096: "1796. Without stars on obverse. A splendid coin, acquired as Uncirculated, and it is just about that. Undoubtedly one of the finest available examples of our first quarter eagle, it should bring well over its catalog price of $450. It should bring closer to $750." Realized $650. Lot 1097: "Another 1796 without obverse stars, from a different die.[2] The lower hairs were not completed. Not often do we find two specimens of this rare date—only when collections such as this one are marketed does the collector have an opportunity to choose. Very Fine. In my November 1955 auction a similar specimen went for over $500." Realized $460.

Prices were rising. In Stack's May 1964 sale of the Philip H. Ward Jr. Collection lot 1660 was offered: "1796 The first year of issue and the only year of its type. Obverse: Bust of draped Liberty left, NO STARS in the field. Reverse: Heraldic eagle. BRILLIANT UNCIRCULATED with full frosty mint luster. A gem coin with some die adjustment marks on the right obverse edge and correspondingly on the reverse which obliterates the tops of 'AMER.' Otherwise the coin is as sharp a specimen as we have ever handled or seen. The Wolfson coin which was Very Fine realized $4,250.00. We feel this specimen could easily approach $6,000.00. This coin is the highlight of the US Section of this fine collection." Realized $7,750.

For this and other quarter eagles, many later offerings can be found on the Internet. Across the board, later prices are much higher.

F-12	VF-20	EF-40	AU-50	AU-55	MS-60	MS-63
$60,000	$80,000	$100,000	$130,000	$165,000	$260,000	$850,000

Capped Bust to Right, Stars on Obverse (1796–1807)

Designer: *Robert Scot.* **Weight:** *4.37 grams.* **Composition:** *.9167 gold, .0833 silver and copper.* **Diameter:** *Approximately 20 mm.* **Edge:** *Reeded.* **Mint:** *Philadelphia.*

Revised Design

Following a brief emission of 1796 quarter eagles without obverse stars, the design was modified to add stars to the left and right of Liberty's head. This was done by making a new die (not by adding stars to the No Stars die).

The reverse continued the Heraldic Eagle design adopted from the Great Seal; sixteen stars were used on the reverse in 1797 (for the admission of Tennessee as the sixteenth state, June 1, 1796; apparently, this was a leftover unused 1796 reverse), changed to thirteen (for the original thirteen states) in 1798, lest the design become too crowded as more states were added. Later anomalous star counts resulted from error or inattention in die making (examples in the gold series include the 1804 quarter eagle with fourteen stars on the reverse and the 1832 half eagle with twelve stars on the obverse).

The quarter eagles of 1796–1797 with sixteen stars on the reverse have eight solid vertical stripes on the shield, while those of 1798–1807 have six vertical stripes (pale gules), each composed of several finely spaced lines. Walter Breen called this design Type II.

Based upon the estimates of Breen (who set aside 963 coins for the earlier-studied 1796, No Stars on Obverse, coinage), the total mintage of the 1796–1807, Stars on Obverse, quarter eagle aggregated 18,524 pieces. While this number may not be the precise total, it must be approximately correct.

Numismatic Considerations

While a few Uncirculated examples are known of scattered dates, most quarter eagles within the 1796–1807 span grade from Very Fine to Extremely Fine, with Very Fine being the norm. In keeping with other gold coins, Mint-caused planchet-adjustment marks are often seen, as are areas of light striking, especially at the border. Each and every quarter eagle in the 1796–1807 type is considered a rarity today, with the 1807 being the least difficult to locate, but still worthy of the rarity designation.

Most numismatists who form type sets of gold coins elect to have but a single piece to illustrate the 1796–1807, Stars on Obverse, type. However, the technically minded collector may want to take note of these seven subtypes within the range:

Subtype A (1796): The obverse has sixteen stars arranged 8x8; the reverse has eight solid vertical shield stripes and sixteen reverse stars. LIBERTY extends over the top of the cap.

Subtype B (1797): The obverse has thirteen stars arranged 7x6; the reverse has eight solid vertical shield stripes and sixteen reverse stars. LIBERTY extends over the top of the cap.

Subtype C (1798): The obverse has thirteen stars arranged 6x7; the reverse has six multi-element vertical shield stripes and thirteen stars. This stripe format and reverse star count was standard for the rest of the series through 1807. LIBERTY extends over the top of the cap.

Subtype D (1802 and 1806, 6 Over 4): The obverse has thirteen stars arranged 8x5. LIBERTY begins at the upper right of the cap (also true of all later dies of this type).

Subtype E (1804; 1805; 1806, 6 Over 5; and 1807): The obverse has thirteen stars arranged 7x6.

Subtype F (1804): The obverse has thirteen stars arranged 7x6; the reverse has anomalous fourteen stars.

Quarter eagles of this era are so appealing that anyone aspiring to collect all six subtypes would probably expand his or her horizons to collect all of the major dates, overdates, and star arrangements.

The rarest *date* by far is 1797, although the 1796, Stars on Obverse, gets more publicity and is listed at higher prices. This is due to the very low mintage figure assigned to it by Walter Breen, just 432 pieces (which may or may not be correct). The rarest *major variety* is the 1804 with thirteen reverse stars, with the 1806, 6 Over 5, right on its heels. Both of these rarities are poorly documented in the literature, as early catalogs often failed to distinguish the varieties of 1804 and 1806.

Certain reverse dies used to coin quarter eagles of this type were also used to strike *dimes*. In the following text such correlations are noted. These are the only such instances in regular-issue American coinage in which two different denominations shared common reverse dies. There was no mark of value or denomination on the die, and the diameters of the quarter eagle and dime were the same, so the interchange was easy to do. In theory, a similar interchange could have taken place with certain half dollar dies and $10 gold eagles of the early nineteenth century, but no correlations have ever been found.

Dies and Known Die Combinations, 1796–1807

Quarter Eagles of 1796, Stars on Obverse

1796, Obverse Die 2. *Stars are present in the field;* this is definitive. This is the second die for the year, and is not the earlier 1796, No Stars on Obverse, die with stars added to it.

1796, Reverse Die C. Sixteen stars are present; *the star ray points to the right upright of the second U in UNUM;* this is definitive. *The tip of the longest arrowhead on the left is opposite the center of N in UNITED.*

1796, BD-3: Dies 2-C. As a date and type the 1796, Stars on Obverse, all of which are BD-3, is rarer than the two combined varieties of 1796, No Stars on Obverse.

Quarter Eagles of 1797

1797, Obverse Die 1. The stars are arranged 7 left and 6 right. The base of the 1 in 1797 is high. *Details:* The upper-left serif of 1 is close to the curl; 97 is closely spaced; the upper right of the second 7 touches the drapery. The bases of LIB in LIBERTY are lower than ERTY. On the left, star pairs 3-4 and 6-7 are more closely spaced than the others. The ray of star 9 points to a double-cut denticle.

1797, Reverse Die A. Sixteen stars are present; *the star ray points to the right upright of the second U in UNUM* and, on the other side of the eagle, *the star rays point to either side of R* in PLURIBUS; this is definitive (with relation to the other three sixteen-star reverse dies, those three being used in 1796).

First used to strike 1797 quarter eagle variety BD-1 (see the next paragraph), this die was later used to strike the 1798, 8 Over 7 dime variety JR-1,[3] creating a 1798 dime with sixteen stars on the reverse two years after the sixteen-star format had been abandoned in other series. As there was no mark of value on the die, it could be interchanged. In its use on the dime a crack is seen from star 10, extending horizontally for a short distance to the right, to over eagle's head. Some late strikes show a diagonal die line from the left tail feather to the border. Some late strikes show clash marks. This is the only sixteen-star reverse die used to strike dimes.

1797, BD-1: Dies 1-A. In the quarter eagle series both dies were used only in this combination.

Quarter Eagles of 1798

Both obverse dies of the 1798 quarter eagle have the stars arranged 6 left and 7 right, the only use of this configuration on any quarter eagle of the 1796–1807 type.

On both of the following dies the final digit (8) of the 1798 date is a tiny numeral compared to the first three digits (179). This situation, which occurs among several late-eighteenth-century and early-nineteenth-century American issues of various denominations, was caused by the practice of preparing the dies in advance with the first three digits of the date. Then, at the actual time of use the remaining digit was punched in. It was easy at that time to use a wrong-size punch.

1798, Obverse Die 1. *Low Close Date.* The stars are arranged 6 left and 7 right (on both dies of this year). *Details:* The 1 in 1798 is close to the hair; 98 is separated from the drapery; 8 is too small (true of both 1798 dies). LIB in LIBERTY is widely spaced; TY is very close; Y is close to star 7. Star pairs 7-8, 8-9, and 12-13 are more widely spaced than are any of the others.

1798, Obverse Die 2. *High Wide Date.* The stars are arranged 6 left and 7 right (on both dies of this year). *Details:* The tops of both the 9 and the 8 touch the drapery, with the latter digit slightly overlapping the lower drapery edge. The IB in LIBERTY and ER are more widely spaced than are any other letter pairs; the base of the Y is high. On the left, star pairs 1-2 and 2-3 are more widely spaced than are any of the others. On the right, star pairs 9-10 and 12-13 are more widely spaced than are any of the others.

1798, Reverse Die A (used on BD-1). *Four* berries appear on the branch. *This is the only thirteen-star reverse die of the Capped Bust to Right, Stars on Obverse, quarter eagle with no star near U in PLURIBUS and with no star close to the rightmost cloud. Details:* D in

UNITED is far from the wing. The O in OF is over the right part of the cloud. The left foot of the first A in AMERICA rests on the feather; the bases of AMERI are close or touch; the leaf does not touch the I. The lowest outside left arrowhead tip is below the left upright of N in UNITED. The Melish Collection example (Abe Kosoff, 1956) had a large "cud" break on the obverse rim encompassing most of the 1 in 1798, stars 1-3, and part of star 4, and must be among the final impressions from this obverse die.

1798, Reverse Die B (used on BD-2). *Five* berries appear on the branch. *Details:* The D in UNITED is much closer to the wing than on other the reverse die of this year. The O in OF is over the space between two clouds. There is a space between the feather and the left foot of the first A in AMERICA; the bases of AMERI are distinctly separated; and the leaf touches the I. The lowest outside left arrowhead tip is below the right upright of U in UNITED. *The star ray pierces the rightmost cloud.*

First used to strike 1798 quarter eagle variety BD-2, this die was then used to strike 1798 dime variety JR-4 and then 1800 dime variety JR-1.[4] On the 1798 JR-4 dime, a crack runs from the tip of the second feather of the left wing to the rim. The rim begins to crumble over the E in STATES, continuing to the right over the F in OF. On very late strikes of the 1800 JR-1 dime, a vertically bisecting crack was reported but was not confirmed by the authors. During the 1800 use the rim-crumbling expands.

1798, BD-1: Dies 1-A. This is generally considered to be the rarer of the two varieties, although expert opinions vary. Bass-Dannreuther rates it R-5+ on the Sheldon scale.

1798, BD-2: Dies 2-B. Bass-Dannreuther rates this R-5 on the Sheldon scale.

Quarter Eagles of 1802

1802, Obverse Die 1 (used on BD-1, 2, and 3). The 1 is medium, the 80 large, and the 2 very small.[5] The stars are arranged 8 left and 5 right. *Details:* The 1 in 1802 is close to and nearly touches the hair; 18 is spaced widely; the 8 is heavy; the 0 is thin and open; and the 2 is very small. RTY in LIBERTY is spaced widely; the lower left serif of the L is very close to the cap; the upper right serif of Y is fairly close to the ray of the star. The stars are fairly evenly spaced, but pair 7-8 is more widely spaced than any of the others. Two rays of star 1 are close to the lower left curl and point to either side of it; star 9 is closer to Y than star 13 is to the bust. This single obverse die has sometimes been cataloged as 1802, 2 Over 1, but the under-digit 1 has never been confirmed. In his 1988 *Encyclopedia* Walter Breen commented: "Any trace of 1 within 2 requires a microscope," which does not directly address the question. Further, Breen thought there were two different obverse dies, but this has been discredited. There is just one, and it is not an overdate.

Each of the following three reverse dies was used to strike one or more dime varieties as well:

1802, Reverse Die A (used on BD-1). *The ray of star 5 pierces the cloud; a horizontal die scratch is seen at the upper left shield tip;* definitive. *Details:* All three E's are missing the upper left serif and were extended by hand. No letter touches another letter. The leaf is solidly joined to the base of the I in AMERICA; the I leans slightly right. The upper inside berry is stemless; the branch stem is much thicker on this die than on any others of the year. The lowest left outside arrow point is slightly left of the left base of the N. Of the five topmost stars, only star 4 *does not* touch a cloud. Star 12 touches both the ribbon and the upper beak; star 13 touches neither device.

This die was also used to strike 1802 dime variety BD-1, then 1802 dime variety JR-3, and finally 1803 dime variety JR-2.[6] On the 1802 JR-3 dime, a crack is seen from the rim to the second A in AMERICA and C; and a crack runs from cloud 6 to the tip of star 6 and on to star 11, star 13, the shield, the claw and arrows, and the rim. On its use with the 1803 JR-2 dime the crack that runs from the rim to the second A in AMERICA and C now extends to the adjacent I. The aforementioned crack from cloud 6 to the tips of stars 6, 11, and 13 and thence to the shield, claw and arrows, and rim is, of course, present; late strikings show a crack from the rim at D in UNITED in an arc through the stars and right side of second S in STATES to the rim.

1802, Reverse Die B (used on BD-2). *The O in OF is completely (including the right side of the O) over a cloud;* definitive. The bases of ME in AMERICA and RI are extremely close and may touch. Five berries appear on the branch, with the three lowest berries being free of leaves. The lowest left outside arrow point is below the right edge of U in UNITED.

First used to strike 1802 quarter eagle variety BD-2, this die was then used for 1802 dime variety JR-4, the 1804 quarter eagle variety BD-1; and finally the 1804 dime variety JR-1.[7] On the 1802 JR-4 dimes, no die cracks have been seen; on the 1804 JR-1 dime, a crack extends from the rim over the wing tip at left, toward the first S in STATES. A study of the peregrinations of this single die would make interesting reading!

1802, Reverse Die C (used on BD-3). *A vertical die scratch is visible at the upper left shield tip;* definitive. *Details:* The U in UNITED is very close to the lowest left outside arrow, which is simply a pointed shaft (without distinct arrowhead). The bases of TA in STATES are widely separated, with the lower left base of the A higher than the base of the T; the upright of E is over the right side of cloud 4 (on the other two dies the upright is over the junction of two clouds). Five berries are present on the branch, with four of these touching leaves; only the lowest outside berry is separated from the leaves. One leaf joins the right foot of the I in AMERICA and another is extremely close to the left base of the second A. Star 1 is sharply double-punched and has at least nine points; one of these lightly joins cloud 1. The remaining stars in the top row touch the clouds or are extremely close. Star 12 touches the upper beak but does not touch the ribbon.

This die was first used to strike the 1802 dime variety JR-1, which is exceedingly rare. Its next use was to strike the 1802 quarter eagle variety BD-3; its final use was to strike the 1803 dime variety JR-1. On the 1802 JR-1 dime the vertical die scratch at the upper left shield tip is visible; a tiny crack extends from the border to the tip of the wing at upper right. On the 1803 JR-1 dime use, the aforementioned crack from the tip of the eagle's wing to the border at upper right is still visible; a crack is seen from the left rim to N in UNITED, to the third feather above the shield, through the left wing, through the first U in PLURIBUS.

1802, BD-1: Dies 1-A. Bass-Dannreuther estimates 90 to 120 known.

1802, BD-2: Dies 1-B. Bass-Dannreuther estimates 30 to 35 known, the rarest variety of the year.

1802, BD-3: Dies 1-C. Bass-Dannreuther estimates 60 to 75 known.

Quarter Eagles of 1804, 13-Star Reverse

1804, Obverse Die 1 (used on BD-1 and 2). *The 8 is large and heavy.* The stars are arranged with eight to the left and five to the right; there is only one obverse this year. *Details:* The 1, 0, and 4 in 1804 are medium-sized; the 8 is heavy and slightly larger; the digits 80 are more widely separated than other digits; the 0 is large and open; the 4 is plain (with no serif on the crossbar); the 1 and 4 are each close to the bust and about the same distance from it. The upper left serif of E in LIBERTY is mostly missing. On the left, star pairs 2-3, 4-5, and 5-6 are more closely spaced than the others. On the right, star pairs 9-10 and 10-11 are closer than the others. Stars 1 and 8 are equally spaced from the hair curl and cap. The upper point of star 9 is extremely close to the top right of Y. Star 13 is quite close to the bust.

1802, Reverse Die B (reused for BD-1). Reverse Die B from 1802 was reused for the 1804 strikings. *The O in OF is completely (including the right side of the O) over a cloud;* definitive. The bases of ME in AMERICA and RI are extremely close together and may touch. There are five berries on the branch, with the three lowest berries free of leaves. The lowest left outside arrow point is below the right edge of U in UNITED.

This die was used for dimes as well as quarter eagles: first the 1802 quarter eagle variety BD-2, then the 1802 dime variety JR-4, followed by the 1804 quarter eagle variety BD-1, and finally the 1804 dime variety JR-1.[8] On the 1802 JR-4 dimes, no die cracks have been seen; on the 1804 JR-1 dime, a crack extends from the rim over the wing tip at the left, toward the first S in STATES.

1804, BD-1: Dies 1-1802 B.

Quarter Eagles of 1804, 14-Star Reverse

1804, Obverse Die 1. *The 8 is large and heavy.* The stars are arranged 8 left and 5 right. There is only one obverse this year, which was used on thirteen-star (BD-1) and fourteen-star (BD-2) reverse combinations. *Details:* The 1, 0, and 4 in 1804 are medium-sized; the 8 is heavy and slightly larger; the digits 80 more widely separated than the other digits; and the 0 is large and open. The die has a "plain 4" (i.e., there is no serif on the crossbar). The 1 and 4 are each close to the bust and about the same distance from it. The upper left serif of the E in LIBERTY is mostly missing. On the left, star pairs 2-3, 4-5, and 5-6 are more closely spaced than the others. On the right, star pairs 9-10 and 10-11 are closer than the others. Stars 1 and 8 are equally spaced from the hair curl and cap. The upper point of star 9 is extremely close to the top right of the Y. Star 13 is quite close to the bust.

1804, Reverse Die A. *Fourteen stars are present;* definitive. *Details:* The reverse has fourteen stars arranged in lines or rows (Breen: "cross pattern"), quite unlike on any other die used in the quarter eagle series. No letters in the border inscription touch each other, and all letters are separated from the designs except the I in AMERICA, which touches a leaf. STATES OF is higher above the clouds than on any other $2.50 die. Star 1 has two points embedded in the eagle's wing, which is unique among early quarter eagle dies. The branch has four berries, with the center outside berry merged with a leaf tip. The lowest outside left arrow point is below the center of the left base of the N.

First used to strike 1804 quarter eagle variety BD-2, in a later die state this reverse was used to strike 1804 dimes with fourteen-star reverses (JR-2).[9] No die cracks have been reported on this die in use in the dime series.

1804, BD-2: Dies 1-A. This is the 1804 variety most commonly seen; the reverse was also used on dimes of this year.

Quarter Eagles of 1805

1805, Obverse Die 1. The date was formed from mismatched punches, with a very small 5 (similar to that used on the half cent of 1805 with Small 5 obverse). The stars are arranged 7 left and 8 right. *Details:* The upper left serif of the 1 in 1805 nearly touches the hair curl. The 1 is medium-sized, the 8 larger, the 0 large and open; the 5 is the smallest numeral of all. The bases of IB in LIBERTY are the most closely spaced of letters; the upper left serif of E mostly missing. Star 1 is distant from the hair; star 13 is distant from the bust; star 7 is fairly close to the cap; and star 8 closer yet to the Y. Star pairs 8-9 and 10-11 are slightly closer than the others. A prominent "spur" or distended denticle is present at the border near star 9. This obverse die, after being used to coin 1805-dated quarter eagles, was overstamped with the *entire date* 1806 and used to make 1806, 6 Over 5, issues—a very unusual procedure, as overdates usually were made from previously unused dies.

1805, Reverse Die A. *Star 12 is repunched and has 10 rays. Details:* All E's have their upper left serif mostly missing. The base of the first S in STATES is lower than other letters; the base of A is high; the upright of E is over the junction of clouds 4 and 5. The first A in AMERICA is close to but distinctly separated from the feathers; the bases of AME and RI are closer than are the bases of other letters; one leaf touches the I and another touches the C; the second A touches the claw. Five berries are on the branch, with one stemless, two having short stems, and two having long stems. The group of arrow points extends barely past the right side of U in UNITED, with the lowest left outside arrow point below the center of U. Of the six stars in the top row, all but star 5 touch a cloud. Star 12 has a ray between the lower and upper beak with another ray touching the ribbon.

This reverse proved to be durable and was used to strike quarter eagles dated 1805, 1806 (combined with two different obverses), and 1807, then *dimes* dated 1807 (variety JR-1).[10] In its use to strike dimes, "E in motto is weak or missing on all specimens, including gems."

1805, BD-1: Dies 1-A. There is only one die combination this year. As noted above, this obverse die was overdated and used again in 1806—a very unusual situation.

Quarter Eagles of 1806, 6 Over 4, 8 Stars Left, 5 Right

1806, 6 Over 4, Obverse Die 1. *Overdate, over 1804; the stars are arranged 8 left and 5 right. Details:* On this overdate the 4 is visible beneath the left side of the 6. The 1 in 1806 is very close to the hair; the top of the 6 extends into the drapery. The 1 is slightly smaller than the 806; this is the first time the numerals were more or less the same size since 1797! The bases of LIB in LIBERTY are closely spaced; the L is very close to the cap. Star 1 touches the hair; star 8 touches the cap. Stars 9 and 13 are distant from Y and the bust. A long triangular denticle is at the border above star 12. This obverse die was overdated from an unused 1804 die with the standard 8x5 star configuration for the 1804 date.

1805, Reverse Die A. *Star 12 is repunched and has 10 rays. Details:* All E's have their upper left serif mostly missing. The base of the first S in STATES is lower than the other letters; the base of the A is high; the upright of the E is over the junction of clouds 4 and 5. The first A in AMERICA is close to but distinctly separated from the feathers; the bases of

AME and RI are closer than are the bases of the other letters. One leaf touches the I and another touches the C; the second A touches the claw. Five berries are on the branch, with one stemless, two having short stems, and two having long stems. The group of arrow points extends barely past right side of U in UNITED, with the lowest left outside arrow point below the center of U. Of the six stars in the top row, all but star 5 touch a cloud. Star 12 has a ray between the lower and upper beak with another ray touching the ribbon.

This reverse proved to be durable and was used to strike quarter eagles dated 1805, 1806 (combined with two different obverses), and 1807, followed by *dimes* dated 1807 (JR-1).[11] In its use to strike dimes, "E in motto is weak or missing on all specimens, including gems."

1806, 6 Over 4, BD-1: Dies 1-A. This variety is the more readily available of the two overdates this year. The Mint Cabinet specimen (now in the Smithsonian, *Sylloge* no. 116), is perhaps Very Good grade with graffiti in the field; it is mentioned here to dispel the idea that the Mint saved specimens for numismatic purposes in the early years. Many other examples could be cited.

Quarter Eagles of 1806, 6 Over 5, 7 Stars Left, 6 Right

1806, 6 Over 5, Obverse Die 2 (1805, Obverse Die 1). *Overdate, over 1805; the stars are arranged 7 left and 6 right. Details:* The entire date 1806 was overpunched on the date 1805, with the 180 in the same register, thus making the figures bolder and appearing slightly closer together, but in the same relative position. The final 6, a large digit, was punched over the very small 5. The digits 80 are very close and on some specimens seem to touch. *Other details of the die are the same as for 1805 obverse die 1.*

The present obverse die, 1806, 6 Over 5, was made by overpunching the date 1806 on the 1805 die previously used to strike 1805-dated quarter eagles. (In contrast the 1806, 6 Over 4, quarter eagle was made by overdating an unused 1804 die.) This obverse die in overdated form displays a large digit 6 punched over the left side of the 5, so that 0 and 6 almost touch. The reverse die is also the same as that used for 1805 coinage; *thus, this variety is technically the same die marriage as the 1805 quarter eagle!* As such, this is one of the most curious of all early gold coin varieties.

1805, Reverse Die A. *Star 12 is repunched and has 10 rays. Details:* All E's have their upper left serif mostly missing. The base of the first S in STATES is lower than the other letters; the base of A is high; the upright of E is over the junction of clouds 4 and 5. The first A in AMERICA is close to but distinctly separated from the feathers; the bases of AME and RI are closer than are the bases of other letters. One leaf touches the I and another touches the C; the second A touches a claw. Five berries are on the branch, with one stemless, two having short stems, and two having long stems. The group of arrow points extends barely past the right side of U in UNITED, with the lowest left outside arrow point below the center of U. Of the six stars in the top row, all but star 5 touch a cloud. Star 12 has a ray between the lower and upper beak with another ray touching the ribbon.

This reverse proved to be durable and was used to strike quarter eagles dated 1805, 1806 (combined with two different obverses), and 1807, followed by *dimes* dated 1807 (JR-1).[12] In its use to strike dimes, "E in motto is weak or missing on all specimens, including gems."

1806, 6 Over 5, BD-2: Dies 2-A. This is the rarer of the two overdates this year.

Quarter Eagles of 1807

1807, Obverse Die 1. *The numeral 1 touches* the *hair; 7 touches* the *drapery.* Stars are arranged 7 left and 6 right. *Details:* The date is fairly high on the die; 07 barely touch. The bases of LIB in LIBERTY are close. Stars 1, 7, and 13 are distant from the central motif; star 8 is close to Y. At the right border, stars 11, 12, and 13 are more closely spaced than are the others.

1805, Reverse Die A. *Star 12 is repunched and has 10 rays. Details:* All E's have their upper left serif mostly missing. The base of the first S in STATES is lower than the other letters; the base of A is high; the upright of E is over the junction of clouds 4 and 5. The first A in AMERICA is close to but distinctly separated from the feathers; the bases of AME and RI are closer than are the bases of the other letters. One leaf touches the I and another touches the C; the second A touches a claw. Five berries are on the branch, with one stemless, two having short stems, and two having long stems. The group of arrow points extends barely past the right side of U in UNITED, with the lowest left outside arrow point below the center of U. Of the six stars in the top row, all but star 5 touch a cloud. Star 12 has a ray between the lower and upper beak with another ray touching the ribbon.

This reverse proved to be durable and was used to strike quarter eagles dated 1805, 1806 (combined with two different obverses), and 1807, followed by *dimes* dated 1807.[13] In its use to strike dimes, "E in motto is weak or missing on all specimens, including gems."

1807, BD-1: Dies 1-A. There is only one die combination this year.

Grading Standards

Note: Please see the grading standards given for Capped Bust to Right, No Stars, quarter eagles (page 44).

1796, Stars on Obverse

Circulation-Strike Mintage: 432

Stars 8x8 on obverse. Rarer of the two major 1796 types.

The 1796, Stars on Obverse, design is the rarer of the two major types of the year. The sixteen stars are arranged with eight to the left and eight to the right.

Estimated Total Population (Mint State). 3 to 5. An extreme rarity, although there are multiple listings in the literature. The John Whitney Walter Collection (Stack's, 1999) featured two remarkable Mint State coins. In the nineteenth century, some prooflike Mint State coins were called *Proof.*

Estimated Total Population (Circulated Grades). 35 to 50. Very Fine is the norm, followed by Extremely Fine and the occasional About Uncirculated. Probably up to a dozen have been described as having been cleaned or polished. By all accounts the 1796, Stars on Obverse, is considerably rarer than its No Stars on Obverse cousin.

Characteristics of Striking and Die Notes. Weakness of strike is evident at the lower part of the obverse, including the date, and at the stars on the left. Sometimes

ER in LIBERTY is light. Sometimes the tail of the eagle is weak. Again, these qualities are rarely described, but can be ascertained from photographs.

Some have obverse and reverse clash marks, sometimes very prominent, but these are rarely described in print. Many if not most have Mint-caused planchet-adjustment marks.

Selected Auction Records

Note: Many dozens of offerings of this coin have reached print over the years—fewer than for the No Stars on Obverse type, but still enough that if all were to be quoted here, a decent-size monograph could be created. Thus, those cited here represent a selection from these—a combination of early listings, citations that have die-state descriptions, and later listings describing pieces of exceptional grade or provenance.

In March 1865, lot 2790 in W. Elliot Woodward's sale of the Bache, Bertsch, Lightbody, Lilliendahl, Vinton, and Watson Collections was described: "1796 With stars; perfectly Uncirculated, almost Proof impression, undoubtedly the finest existing specimen of this variety, *excessively rare.*" Realized $40 to Mendes I. Cohen, the Baltimore collector. The same coin was sold in by Edward Cogan as lot 182 in the Cohen Collection auction: "1796 With stars. Proof. Very rare." Realized $16. This is an interesting instance in which a coin Woodward described as "Uncirculated," but with some Proof characteristics, was described by Cogan as a full Proof. The term *Proof* was used very casually by nearly all catalogers of the era—and generally described a specimen that today would be called *prooflike.*

Lot 881 in Woodward's January 1884 sale of the Ely Collection was described: "1796 With stars; Uncirculated, exceedingly rare. Without doubt one of the very rarest of the entire gold series, and far less common than the 1797 quarter eagle, which is generally thought to be the scarcest of all. I trace this piece in but three sales—first in the McCoy Coll., next in Sale No. 6, and the same piece catalogued in the Cohen Sale. This is the McCoy specimen. There was none in the Mickley Collection, and I know of only two mentioned." Realized $50 to Lancaster, Pennsylvania, dealer Charles Steigerwalt, his only gold coin purchase in the sale.

In June 1886, H.P. Smith offered lot 12 in his sale of the Dr. Edward Maris Collection: "1796 Quarter eagle. With stars. In beautiful Proof condition, showing, as they all do, slight drift marks. With one exception, believed to be the finest known. Extremely rare in any condition and exceptionally desirable in this. Valued by its former owner at $100." Realized $45.50.

In December 1921, Henry Chapman's sale of lot 5785 in the John Story Jenks Collection was described: "1796. Eight stars before and behind bust, otherwise as last; same design on reverse, but not same die as last. Extremely Fine. The tips of the hair in center not struck up, and this central weakness shows also on neck of the eagle on reverse where it did eliminate the file marks in the planchet. Scratch from forehead to edge between first and second star. Excessively rare." Realized $150. The same coin was offered years later in the November 1956 New Netherlands sale of the Thomas L. Gaskill Collection as Lot 179: "1796 With stars; 8 before, 8 behind head. . . . Strictly Extremely Fine. Almost free of handling marks, but with a long obverse scratch from first star to forelock [quite the "but" here!] The unusually bold reverse could be called About Uncirculated, despite some unevenness of striking, and numerous adjustment (file) marks as commonly seen on early gold. Both dies badly injured and cracked perhaps accounting for the infinitesimal mintage of 432 pieces (after November 24, 1796, when the Director's *Report* had already been made; formerly included in the 1797 coinage figure). Rarer than the last; it is doubtful if more than a dozen now survive. Should easily bring from $550 to $600 today—the recently sold Melish piece commanded $675. A definite 'type' coin. From Henry Chapman's famous Jenks sale (1921), lot 5785." Realized $475.

The Jerome Kern coin was sold by B. Max Mehl in May 1950. Lot 2: "1796. First year of issue but second type. Variety with sixteen stars on obverse, eight stars to right and eight to left of bust. Magnificent Uncirculated specimen with full mint lustre; in fact it is a semi-Proof. An imperceptible pinpoint nick on upper obverse edge, hardly noticeable, and only mentioned here for the sake of accuracy. Only 66 specimens said to have been struck of both varieties of the quarter eagles of 1796.[14] Record well over $400, and if a 1796 quarter eagle was ever worthy of making a new record, this is certainly the specimen." Realized $325.

In the sale of the Melish Collection (actually the R.E. Naftzger Jr. Collection) in March 1956 this was included as lot 1098: "1796. With obverse stars. Acquired as 'Uncirculated with full brilliant Proof surface.' Well, it has claims to justify such a superlative. I will say it's the nicest piece I can recall, and I have been lucky enough to see some of the best. I predict a record price for this gem to exceed $750." Realized $675.

F-12	VF-20	EF-40	AU-50	AU-55	MS-60	MS-63
$55,000	$70,000	$95,000	$115,000	$135,000	$200,000	$450,000

1797

Circulation-Strike Mintage:
427 (calendar-year mintage)

Stars 7x6 on obverse. Rarest early quarter eagle date. All known pieces have a massive obverse die crack.

The present-day rarity of the 1797 quarter eagle suggests that the mintage was very low. The figure of 427 given for the calendar year may include some pieces dated 1796; if so, this would account for the fact that the 1797 is at least 50% rarer than the 1796, Stars on Obverse, although both have been listed with about equal mintages (432 for the 1796, Stars on Obverse; 427 for the 1797).

The difficulty arising in the quest for information concerning the *grades* of coins as given in the literature is exemplified by a 1797 quarter eagle described by Carl W.A. Carlson in his 1991 article, "Tracker: An Introduction to Pedigree Research in the Field of Rare American Coins," which appeared in *The American Numismatic Association Centennial Anthology:*

> In the spring of 1883, Harold P. Newlin, of Philadelphia, visited [W. Elliot] Woodward in his home in Roxbury, Massachusetts, and saw there, among other rarities, a prooflike Uncirculated 1797 quarter eagle (this later passed through Newlin to Garrett).

This is the same coin that was sold in March 1980 in the Bowers and Ruddy sale (for the Johns Hopkins University) of the Garrett Collection, lot 734. The coin was described:

"AU-50, with prooflike surface. Just the tiniest whisper of a file or adjustment mark appears at the left obverse border. A bold die break. The sharpness of the piece is particularly excellent, with all areas being quite well defined. From Harold P. Newlin on October 31, 1884; earlier the property of W. Elliot Woodward; William Sumner Appleton John C. Schayer (owner or intermediary), and America's pioneer numismatist, Joseph J. Mickley."

In 1859, Dr. Montroville W. Dickeson *(American Numismatical Manual)* wrote, "One type and two varieties. They are seldom met with, except in cabinet collections, and hence are extremely rare." This is an early numismatic recognition of this highly important quarter eagle rarity. The notation "two varieties" is incorrect; or at least no second variety is known today. In 1883, the lead article in *Steigerwalt's Coin Journal*, "Early Gold," by "An Old Collector," included this: "1797 Very rare. Said to be the rarest [of all early quarter eagles], but I think more plenty than the '96 with stars and the 1826." And in 1968, in *New Varieties of $1, $2.50, and $5.00 U.S. Gold*, Walter Breen commented that "at least nine different [specimens of the 1797] are now traceable." In 1988 in his *Encyclopedia*, Breen upped his estimate to "possibly 20 survive," adding, "mostly VF."

Estimated Total Population (Circulated Grades). 20 to 30. The 1797 quarter eagle is one of the rarest *dates* in the American gold series. Although in the mid-nineteenth century the 1797 was widely recognized as a classic, in modern times the issue has been more-or-less overlooked—no doubt because there are few if any high grades of so-called "investment quality" to entice the well-moneyed but only superficially knowledgeable buyer. Typical grades seen for the 1797 are Very Fine or Extremely Fine, rarely finer. At the About Uncirculated level the 1797 is truly a formidable rarity.

The above estimate does not include perhaps a half-dozen pieces that have been mounted or used as jewelry.

Characteristics of Striking and Die Notes: All known examples have a die crack extending from just left of the top of the Y in LIBERTY, grazing the innermost point of star 8, downward through the field to stars 12 and 13, to the border below. On some impressions, the crack begins later and/or ends earlier than the description just given.

Most 1797 quarter eagles are decently struck, albeit with some lightness on the higher points. Some have traces of a prooflike surface. Many if not most have Mint-caused adjustment marks.

Selected Auction Records

In March 1865, W. Elliot Woodward, in the sale of the Bache, Bertsch, Lightbody, Lilliendahl, Vinton, and Watson Collections, offered lot 2791: "1797 In Fair or Very Good condition, the rarest of the entire series of quarter eagles." Realized $47.50. But did it sell? In May of the same year Woodward described lot 1963 in the John F. McCoy Collection: "1797 In Fair or Very Good condition, of the highest rarity; probably the rarest of the series of quarter eagles." Could it have been the earlier coin? Realized $75.25, a very high, indeed *extraordinary* price for the time. In January 1884 this coin reappeared as lot 882 in Woodward's sale of the Heman Ely Collection: "1797 In Very Good condition and exceedingly rare; from the McCoy Sale, No. 1963." Realized $40 to Bell. The grade seems to have improved slightly, and "Fair" is no longer a part of the description. Throughout the corpus of Woodward catalogs there are many instances, some conjectural and others verifiable, that certain items were "bought in," but listed as being sold. It could have been that at the sale the bought-in price was announced as "passed," or with some other indication, but if so, this is not known today.

In October 1875 in the Col. Mendes I. Cohen Collection sale Edward Cogan offered lot 183: "1797 Uncirculated. Extremely rare. Cracked die." Realized $14. Seemingly, this was one of the finest preserved specimens of this rare date, and yet the listed price was very low. The cracked die is characteristic of the 1797, and the obverse die state is not known otherwise. However, as is seen from various citations, it is mentioned only occasionally in auction catalogs. Among catalogers of the era, Cogan was one of the least knowledgeable.

In November 1880 in his 15th Sale, S.K. Harzfeld referenced the McCoy coin under lot 615: "1797 Broken die, *excessively rare*, the rarest of the quarter eagles. Sold in the McCoy sale for $75.25. *Fine.*" Realized $7. (The coin must not have been all that *fine* to observers!)

In June 1883 John W. Haseltine described lot 421 in his sale of the William J. Jenks Collection: "1797 Broken die. The rarest of the quarter eagles. A beautiful impression with Proof surface, and believed to be the finest known. This date is most difficult to obtain in any state of preservation, and one in McCoy sale in only fair condition brought $75.25." Realized $40. Ed. Frossard in the sale of his own collection in October 1884 offered the same coin as lot 327: "1797 Head of Liberty with cap; six stars facing. Reverse, Heraldic Eagle. Die cracked from Y in LIBERTY to lower star. Very Fine and extremely rare; the same piece that sold in W.E. Woodward's Jenks sale, June 1883, at $49.50." Realized $27.25. Frossard lost a few dollars on this one. The $49.50 price vis-à-vis the $40 announced at the Jenks sale may have represented some sort of a buying fee or commission added to the $40 purchase at the time (although the normal commission was just 10%).

Another high-grade example was offered by H.P. Smith in April 1887 in his sale of the Charles White Collection, Part II, lot 472: "1797 Die cracked before face as usual. A strong, sharp impression, marred only by the planchet cutter having been misplaced on the metal before striking. Nevertheless, one of the finest known specimens of this very desirable date." Realized $40 to J. Colvin Randall, who was the largest buyer of gold coins at the White Collection sale. Randall, a dealer and investor from Philadelphia, was always trading in and out of coins.

In 1907 in a fixed-price list Elmer S. Sears offered this: "1797 Die cracked from 'Y' of Liberty to lower right star as is the case with all known quarter eagles of this date. One of the rarest of this denomination. I have yet to see one in better condition. $250."

Wayte Raymond in his fixed-price list of March 1911 offered this: "1797 About Uncirculated, brilliant Proof surface, excessively rare. $300."

In May 1915 B. Max Mehl in his sale of the B.W. Smith Collection described lot 239: "1797 Thirteen stars, 6 before and 7 behind bust. The Obv. Die is cracked from the letter Y to the last star, as are all known specimens of this date. Well centered and struck, strictly Very Good, Fine for coin. Excessively rare. One of the very rarest quarter eagles and classed among the rarest U.S. gold coins. Auction record over $300." Realized $78. Perhaps Mehl should have asserted that the "over $300" was for a much nicer coin. (Also see the 1941 Dunham listing on page 61.)

Mehl in his May 1922 sale of the James Ten Eyck Collection described lot 46: "1797 Six stars to right and seven to left of Liberty. Stars on obverse larger and on reverse smaller. Usual die break on obverse from Y down to first star on right. Few, hardly noticeable light nicks on obverse. Extremely Fine, with considerable Proof surface on reverse. Excessively rare. Seldom offered. One of the really rare U.S. gold coins." Realized $175.

An exceptional coin was offered by Henry Chapman as lot 832 in his July 1922 sale of the Reimers, Jenkins, Preston, and Bardeen Collections: "1797 Die broken down from Y to edge below last star; every specimen known is so. Extremely Fine. Much stronger impression than usual. The obverse shows the slightest abrasion, while the reverse is brilliant. The finest specimen of this excessively rare coin that has ever passed through my hands, and should command a record-breaking figure." Realized $375.

In June 1941 in the William Forrester Dunham Collection sale Mehl offered lot 1906: "1797 The usual die break on obverse, as found on all the specimens of this rarity. Extremely Fine, with considerable luster. Very light hairline marks on left obverse; the reverse is sharp and beautiful. One of the very rarest of the early quarter eagles with record up to $300." Mehl forgot that in the B.W. Smith sale (May 1915) he had said that the record was *over* $300. Realized $195.

The Numismatic Gallery in its January 1946 sale of the "World's Greatest Collection" (F.C.C. Boyd Collection) included lot 81: "1797 The usual die break on obverse as found in all specimens of this very rare date. Extremely Fine with an exceptionally beautiful reverse. Very Fine condition." Realized $450.[15]

In June 1946 Mehl offered the Cutler Atwater Collection with lot 1918, described as: "1797. Die break on right obverse as on all the quarter eagles of this date. Practically Uncirculated with full mint luster. The reverse is almost a brilliant Proof. Undoubtedly as choice a specimen of this rarity as exists. Valued above $500. Recent record $450." Realized $350.

Mehl again overestimated the value of a 1797 quarter eagle in his description of lot 3 in the Jerome Kern Collection sold in May 1950: "1797 Same type as the 1796, with stars on obverse, but with six stars to right and seven to left of bust. As usual, die break on obverse from Y to first lower star. Practically Uncirculated with mint luster; in fact the coin is Uncirculated but shows just slight cabinet friction. Record $450.00 for a similar specimen." Realized $215.

F-12	VF-20	EF-40	AU-50	AU-55	MS-60	MS-63
$13,500	$20,000	$40,000	$65,000	$115,000	$200,000	$350,000

1798

Circulation-Strike Mintage:
1,094 (calendar-year mintage)

Stars 6x7 on obverse.
Seldom seen date.

Estimated Total Population (Mint State). 5 to 7. The literature describes more (and also includes some called "Proofs"). Today, certain of these past listings would be better called About Uncirculated. Any true Mint State coin is a truly great rarity. Bass-Dannreuther-1 is somewhat rarer than BD-2. Until relatively recent times, listings have not differentiated the two varieties.

Among the true Mint State coins at least one is in the gem category (once owned by Stack's; cited by Akers, 1975). Others are in the citations below.

Estimated Total Population (Circulated Grades). 70 to 90. Estimates vary widely. Very rare, one of the most elusive of all eighteenth-century American gold coin dates. Most pieces are well worn. At the About Uncirculated level the 1798 is very rare. At one time Virgil M. Brand had three specimens.

Characteristics of Striking and Die Notes: These usually have slight evidence of weak striking at the centers, in particular on the higher areas of the obverse. Many if not most 1798 quarter eagles have Mint-caused adjustment marks.

Over the years a few pieces have been called *Proof*, but a more conservative description might be *Mint State, prooflike*. Walter Breen describes his Proof coin in his *Encyclopedia* (1987) thusly: "Close date. 7th star very close to Y, four berries, Breen-1. Not seen. Reported in presentation piece state by Ronnie Carr, who saw it in the possession of Leo A. Young about 1959; 1959 ANA sale, Lot 956." That coin is now on display at the ANA Money Museum as part of the Harry W. Bass Jr. Collection. The Breen book, which the cover states is about *Proof* coins, includes many "presentation pieces" based on casual examination or second-hand reports, and without serious credentials.

Selected Auction Records

In September 1863 W.H. Strobridge described lot 455 in the George F. Seavey Collection: "1798 Very Fine, very rare." Realized $32.

In May 1864 W. Elliot Woodward's sale of the John F. McCoy Collection included lot 1964: "1798 Very Fine, almost Proof. In this year the coinage of this denomination amounted to only about 600 pieces. In any condition they are of extreme rarity, and are scarcely ever met with so fine as this." Realized $35. A generation later, in January 1884, the coin reappeared as lot 883 in Woodward's sale of the Heman Ely Collection: "1798 Brilliant, sharp Proof impression; extremely rare, only 600 coined. McCoy Collection." Realized $16 to Peters. Note that the grade has improved to "Sharp, a Proof impression," from the "Very Fine, almost Proof" quality described by the same cataloger 20 years earlier. As was true of some other Ely coins, it came back on the market soon after, in June 1885, as lot 960 in Woodward's sale of the J. Colvin Randall Collection: "1798 Sharp; a Proof impression; only six hundred coined; cost in the McCoy sale $35." Realized $10. The transition of ownership from Ely (1884) to Peters (at the Ely sale, 1884), to Randall (1885) is not explained. Many situations found in nineteenth-century catalogs are beyond understanding today.

Skipping over time, in June 1941 B. Max Mehl described lot 1907 in the William Forrester Dunham Collection: "1798 Beautiful Uncirculated specimen with semi-Proof surface; highest portions show slight cabinet friction and upper center of reverse is not as bold as the balance of the coin. A magnificent specimen of this rarity. Seldom offered. Listed at $150 and seldom obtainable at that price." Realized $157.50.

A trio of 1798 quarter eagles was offered by Abe Kosoff in his April 1956 sale of the Melish and Hester Collections. Lot 1101: "1798. A Proof! See this one—it's a beauty! Should bring a runaway price." Realized $375. Lot 1102: "1798. A most unusual die variety with a very strong break which obliterates most of the 1 in date, and all but two and a half stars on the left. The same break obliterates ED and ST on reverse. A sharp,

Uncirculated rarity. $350." Realized $285. Lot 1103: "1798. From still another die; the 8 touches the bust, no such die break as described above; all stars, lettering, etc. are clear. Very Fine. $175." Realized $175.

F-12	VF-20	EF-40	AU-50	AU-55	MS-60	MS-63
			$27,500	$35,000	$90,000	$220,000

Note: Close Date and Wide Date varieties exist. Values are for the more common Wide Date variety.

1802

Stars 8x5 on obverse. Sometimes called "1802, 2 Over 1."

Circulation-Strike Mintage: 3,035 (calendar-year mintage; not all necessarily have this date)

Estimated Total Population (Mint State). 15 to 25, mostly in the lower range of the category.

Estimated Total Population (Circulated Grades). 150 to 250, although estimates vary widely. Typical grades are Very Fine and Extremely Fine, rarely higher or lower.

Characteristics of Striking and Die Notes: These are usually lightly struck at the centers, although there are infrequent exceptions. Many if not most have Mint-caused adjustment marks, these being standard for all gold coins of this era.

Selected Auction Records

A very early listing is for lot 77 of the sale in June 1859 of the John K. Curtis Collection by Bangs, Merwin & Co.: "Proof ¼ eagle or $2½ piece. 1802."[16] Realized $2.75. Curtis was an active coin dealer at the time, and this was more likely inventory than a personal collection. In January 1861 the same auction house sold the Benjamin Haines Collection. Lot 334: "1802 Almost Proof, very rare." Sold for $5.25. The buyer was J.K. Wiggin, Boston numismatist and bookseller.

In his April 1937 sale of the George M. Agurs Collection, B. Max Mehl described lot 674: "1802 Beautiful Uncirculated specimen. The field on obverse shows the slightest cabinet friction, but every star and letter is well struck up and the coin is perfectly centered. A truly beautiful specimen, and as such, rare and valuable." Realized $35.25. In May 1950, in his Jerome Kern Collection sale, B. Max Mehl described lot 5: "1802 Uncirculated with frosty mint surfaces. Not a rarity, but very rare so choice. Catalogs at $70 in only Very Fine. A specimen not quite as choice brought $100.00 four years ago." Realized $87.50.

For lot 182 in Walter Breen's cataloging of the November 1956 New Netherlands Coin Co. sale, he stated this: "1802/1 Stars 8x5. Rev. Leaf joins right half of base of 1. Fully Extremely Fine; a few minute handling marks, mainly at the rims. Though not in a class with the earlier dates, still rare and underrated in any condition. Only a few hundred struck from each of the four [*sic*] reverse dies used this year; 3,035 in all. Cheap at $100." Realized $140. The next lot in the sale: "1802 No sign of overdate. Evidently from the same obverse as last, but the die now well worn down. Rev. Leaf joins corner of I; the four upper berries merged into leaves. Unknown to Adams, Clapp and Newcomer. Barely Extremely Fine; very much like the last. Traces of granularity; faint adjustment marks and evidence of handling. Some proof-like lustre upon the reverse, as with many of these. Rarer than the last, and easily salable as an unpublished 'type.' Neither the *Guide Book* nor *Standard Catalogue* lists 1802 except as an overdate." Realized $125.

The overdate listings continued in many catalogs until the Bass-Dannreuther study was published.

F-12	VF-20	EF-40	AU-50	AU-55	MS-60	MS-63
$5,000	$8,500	$16,500	$20,000	$22,500	$32,500	$70,000

1804, 13-Star Reverse

Circulation-Strike Mintage:
200 to 230 (estimated)

Stars 8x5 on obverse
Unknown in Mint State.
Rarest major popular variety of 1796–1807.

The mintage for the 1804, 13-Star Reverse, was not recorded; the above figure is an estimate based upon the number of surviving pieces today. The total mintage of 3,327 for the calendar year was divided into 1,003 thirteen-star and 2,324 fourteen-star coins by Walter Breen (*Encyclopedia*, 1988, and elsewhere), but this seems far off the mark. Today it seems that the thirteen-star reverse is about 15 times rarer than the second variety.

Estimated Total Population (Mint State). None.

Estimated Total Population (Circulated Grades). 12 to 14. Most major collections have lacked an example, and *years* can pass between auction offerings. Among those that do exist, grades are listed as Very Fine, Extremely Fine, and About Uncirculated.

This is *the* great rarity among widely published *obvious* varieties in the early quarter eagle series. The number known has been subject to varying opinions over the years. However, with the information explosion of recent years, and with increased attention paid to early die varieties, is seems quite likely that a dozen or slightly more different pieces are known. It is interesting that although the thirteen-star and fourteen-star varieties were recognized at the turn of the twentieth century, they were not listed in popular catalogs or checklists, and several generations of numismatists came and went without having these varieties on their want lists; one 1804 quarter eagle was sufficient.

In the 1970s the author remarked to Michael G. Brownlee, the Dallas dealer, that he had never had the privilege of including a specimen of the thirteen-star variety in an auction sale, whereupon Brownlee stated that in Dallas there were three examples that he had sold to as many different clients—Messrs. Browning, Murrell, and Bass.

Characteristics of Striking and Die Notes: These coins are usually well struck. Many if not most have Mint-caused adjustment marks.

Selected Auction Records

Note: These citations include pieces specifically cataloged or otherwise identified as having the thirteen-star reverse (citations that do not mention the reverse star count are listed under the much more plentiful fourteen-star reverse and may include a few with the thirteen-star reverse).

An early authoritative listing by Lyman H. Low in his June 1903 offering of the John Hurd Comstock Collection was lot 459: "1804 13 stars on reverse. Fine." Realized $8. In the Comstock sale a related fourteen-star 1804 quarter eagle, lot 460, also described as "Fine" but with planchet file marks mentioned, realized $7. This would indicate that to bidders at the time, the thirteen- and fourteen-star varieties were valued about the same.

The New Netherlands sale of the Cicero Collection, December 1960, included this lot 259: "1804. Thirteen reverse stars. . . . Probably R-7. Very Fine, clean; reverse weakly struck, apparently as always on this type. The thirteen stars coin has been a major sleeper apparently ever since the difference was discovered. The present one is, if anything, nicer than the Gaskill example, which is the only other one we have handled. Mintage 1,003 of this type. The Neumoyer Collection had one of these, impaired, which (though not cataloged as a 13-star coin) was bid up to $620 on the floor; there were three of the 14-star variety in that collection. This variety was altogether lacking in such important collections as W.G.C., Atwater, Memorable, Dr. Green, Graves, Dr. Smith, and Melish, among many others. One of the high points of this auction!" Sold for $550.

In later years the thirteen-stars variety was widely recognized and showcased in auction offerings.

F-12	VF-20	EF-40	AU-50	AU-55
$60,000	$95,000	$150,000	$185,000	$350,000

1804, 14-Star Reverse

Circulation-Strike Mintage: 3,000 (or slightly more)

Estimated Total Population (Circulated Grades). 150 to 200. Very Fine and Extremely Fine are usual grades.

The 1804 variety usually seen. Stars 8x5 on obverse. Reverse die also used for 1804 dimes.

Characteristics of Striking and Die Notes: Sometimes these are seen lightly struck in areas, especially around the borders. Stars 1–3, sometimes 1–4, are usually weaker than the others. Evidence of die clashing is often present, and many if not most have Mint-caused adjustment marks.

Selected Auction Records

Note: These citations include pieces that do not mention the reverse star count; some of these may be the much rarer thirteen-star reverse.

Lot 78 in a consignment from John K. Curtis was described in the June 1859 catalog of Bangs, Merwin & Co.: "Proof ¼ eagle or $2½ piece. 1804."[17] Realized $2.62½. In his sale of April 1860, Edward Cogan described lot 698: "1804 Quarter eagle, in Fine condition, and scarce." Realized $3.62½. We reiterate that in the early days *Fine* often meant *nice, choice,* or *a pleasing example*, not necessarily equivalent to the F-12 numerical grading used today. Similarly, *Very Fine, Extremely Fine,* and other early adjectival descriptions cannot be directly correlated with modern adjectival or numerical grading. Another was offered as lot 857 in W.H. Strobridge's May 1862 sale of the William A. Lilliendahl

Collection: "1804 Quarter eagle. Very Fine." Realized $4.25. Lot 457 in Strobridge's September 1863 sale of the George F. Seavey Collection: "1804 Fine, rare." Realized $5.

Cogan's May 1871 sale of the Emil Cauffman Collection included lot 248: "1804 *Very* Fine impression. Scarce." Realized $3.50. W. Elliott Woodward described lot 2018 in his May 1883 sale of the Winslow Lewis Collection: "1804 A Proof impression, Very Fine; scarce." Realized $8.25. The October 1897 sale of the F.S. Winston Collection by J.W. Scott Co. included lot 253: "1804 Fine." Realized $5.35. The William H. Woodin Collection sold by Thomas L. Elder in March 1911 included lot 933: "1804. Sharp, beautiful, even impression. Uncirculated, mint luster. No recent sale contained one so fine; in this state very rare." Realized $35.25.

B. Max Mehl's May 1922 sale of the James Ten Eyck Collection included lot 49: "1804 A magnificent Uncirculated specimen, beautiful impression, every letter and star stands out; broad milled borders and with considerable Proof surface, nearly equal to a perfect brilliant Proof. A very scarce date, and in this beautiful condition I consider a great rarity." Realized $31. The same coin appeared years later in the November 1956 New Netherlands sale of the Thomas L. Gaskill Collection as lot 185: "1804 Fourteen stars; the identical reverse used on the dime of this year, after the other die had worn down or been broken. A superb example, with just about full mint sharpness and considerable proof-like gloss. Evenly centered; the strike exceptionally bold and clear. This variety, even more so than the dime with the same reverse, is a great rarity just beginning to come into its own. It deserves the attention alike of specialists and type collectors, as a clearly defined 'type.' Potentially worth to $350, so fine. From Mehl's Ten Eyck sale (1922), lot 49." Realized $175.

The William B. Hale Collection sold by Mehl in November 1939 included this description of lot 744: "1804 Extremely Fine. Rare. Purchased from the old famous dealer Ben. G. Green of Chicago in 1909. Listed up to $40." Realized $31.50. Stack's December 1944 auction of the J.F. Bell Collection included lot 84: "1804 Brilliant Uncirculated. Really scarce in this condition." Realized $67.50. In April 1956 Abe Kosoff's sale of the Melish and Hester Collections included lot 1105: "1804 None minted in 1803. Extremely Fine." Realized $110.

F-12	VF-20	EF-40	AU-50	AU-55	MS-60	MS-63
$6,750	$9,000	$14,000	$17,000	$22,500	$32,500	$165,000

1805

Stars 7x6 on obverse.

Circulation-Strike Mintage:
1,781 (calendar-year mintage)

Estimated Total Population (Mint State). 6 to 9, mostly toward the lower end of the Mint State grade range. A rarity by any evaluation.

David Akers (1975) located eighteen historical citations for Mint State coins, which he found to be "a bit surprising since I have found the 1805 to be just as rare in Uncirculated as the 1802, 2 Over 1 or 1804 and certainly more rare than the 1807."

Estimated Total Population (Circulated Grades). 125 to 175. Quite scarce. A perusal of "name" collection sale catalogs reveals that About Uncirculated coins appear with some frequency and seem to be the standard for those numismatists who could both find and afford to buy one.

Characteristics of Striking and Die Notes: The reverse is often highly prooflike, especially in protected areas of the surface. It is sometimes lightly struck, seemingly more so at the center of the reverse than anywhere else. Many if not most have Mint-caused adjustment marks, seemingly more so than for other quarter eagles of the era.

Selected Auction Records

The June 1859 sale of coins from the inventory of John K. Curtis included lot 79, which, like others from the consignment, was called *Proof*—probably by an amateur cataloger, as the auction firm had no in-house expert. "Proof ¼ eagle or $2½ piece. 1805." Realized $2.75. Buyers in auction sales of this era nearly always examined the coins in person, as descriptions were often wildly erratic. Collectors at a distance usually placed bids with someone attending a sale. Lot 458 in W. H. Strobridge's sale of the George F. Seavey Collection was described as: "1805 Very good, rare." Realized $10. In his sale of the John F. McCoy Collection in May 1864, W. Elliot Woodward offered lot 1967: "1805 Very Fine indeed, and very rare." Realized $7.50.

Edward Cogan in his sale of April 1877 described lot 351: "1805 But little circulated." Realized $3.75. Forty years later, in 1907, Elmer S. Sears offered in his fixed-price list lot 144: "1805 Extremely Fine specimen, Almost Uncirculated. Rare, when so fine. $25." Lot 145: "1805 Another, almost as fine. $20." In April 1931 in his sale of the Morris Collection, B. Max Mehl described lot 496: "1805 Practically Uncirculated, sharp, with full mint luster. Nearly as choice as the specimen in my last sale which brought $62.50. This is not a rare date, but unusually rare in choice condition." Realized $35. Mehl in his November 1939 sale of the William B. Hale Collection described lot 745: "1805 Uncirculated, with frosty mint luster. A little gem. Rare so choice. Listed at $45 in Very Fine condition." Realized $43.25. At the time, most numismatists were content to have a "nice" specimen of a given early gold variety, and strong premiums were not paid for Uncirculated pieces. That would soon change. By this time grades were more consistent (although with no definition) than they were in the nineteenth century, and many collectors bid by mail.

Mehl in his February 1944 sale of the Belden E. Roach Collection described lot 853: "1805 Uncirculated with mint luster. A beautiful quarter eagle. Although not a rare date it is quite rare so choice and is in great demand." Realized $52.50. In December of the same year in the Stack's sale of the J.F. Bell Collection lot 85 was described: "1805 Brilliant Uncirculated, semi-Proof Surface. A desirable and choice gem." Realized $100. In Mehl's May 1950 auction of the Jerome Kern Collection he mentioned wide variances in prices in his description of lot 7: "1805 Uncirculated with brilliant mint luster; the reverse is a brilliant semi-Proof. Just the very slightest touch of cabinet friction on obverse. Not a very rare date, but truly very rare in this beautiful condition. Even such a great collection as the Atwater had a specimen only in fine to Very Fine condition which brought $68.50. Record for an equal specimen over $180." Realized $105.

In November 1956, New Netherlands' sale of the Thomas L. Gaskill Collection included lot 186: "1805 Stars 7x6, unlike the coins of 1802–04. Only the one variety of this date. On the obverse, spur almost runs into 9th star; ICA (of AMERICA) upon the rev. touching leaves and claw. Just Very Fine; the reverse as usual, sharper and more attractive. Desirable; the only apparent flaws minute, and located upon the right obverse rim. Only 1,781 coined." Realized $120.

F-12	VF-20	EF-40	AU-50	AU-55	MS-60	MS-63
$5,000	$8,000	$13,000	$16,500	$20,000	$35,000	$135,000

1806, 6 Over 4, 8 Stars Left, 5 Right

Stars 8x5 on obverse.
Reverse die of 1805.

Circulation-Strike Mintage:
1,136 (estimated by Walter Breen)

Estimated Total Population (Mint State). 5 to 8. As is the case with most quarter eagles of this era, grading is sometimes optimistic, and it is more likely that an About Uncirculated coin will be graded Mint State than vice versa. What few Mint State coins do exist are in lower numerical ranges.

Estimated Total Population (Circulated Grades). 80 to 100, making it scarce by any standard, but more readily available than its 1806, 6 Over 5 cousin.

Characteristics of Striking and Die Notes: The obverse center is typically lightly struck, as is the center of the reverse, due to metal-flow requirements when the dies were in the coining press. A raised dot is seen in the obverse field between the portrait and star 6. Many if not most have Mint-caused adjustment marks.

Usually, the obverse die is cracked through the top of LIBERTY. A unique example in the Harry W. Bass Jr. Core Collection on display at the ANA Money Museum has a rim break joining the tops of LI in LIBERTY.

Selected Auction Records

Note: These citations include several identified as 1806, 6 Over 4 or simply listed as "1806," although some of the latter may represent the scarcer 1806, 6 Over 5 variety.

An early listing of the 1806 quarter eagles lacks information about the overdate or star arrangement and was given by Edward Cogan for lot 699 in his April 1860 sale: "1806 Quarter eagle, in Fine condition, and scarce." Realized $3.62½. No description of overdate or star arrangement. Similarly, W. Elliot Woodward, in his May 1864 sale of the John F. McCoy Collection, gave this for lot 1968: "1806 Splendid, nearly Proof. No record exists of the coinage of this piece, and it is of the highest rarity, only four or five known." Realized $90. This same coin was offered by Woodard as lot 887 in his January 1884 sale of the Heman Ely Collection: "1806 Sharp Proof impression; extremely rare. The Mint has no record of the coinage of this piece. Purchased at the McCoy Sale." Realized $18.25 to Bell.[18] No description of overdate or star arrangement. Other listings simply as 1806 could be given. Today it is not known which of the two varieties these are.

By the 1880s the overdate was recognized, as with lot 964 in Woodward's June 1885 sale of the J. Colvin Randall Collection: "1806 Five stars facing; struck over 1804; Very

Fine indeed; there is no Mint record existing of the coinage of this piece. McCoy's brought $90." Realized $40. The buyer was T. Harrison Garrett of Baltimore. In November 1888 the Scott Stamp & Coin Co. offering of the Rev. W. Foster Ely Collection included lot 55: "1806 (over 04). 13 stars (5 facing). Fine and very rare; not in U.S. Mint collection." Realized $22. Two years later, in January 1890, the competing New York Coin & Stamp Co. in its sale of the R. Coulton Davis Collection offered lot 851, pointing out the Scott error. Lot 851: "1806/4: 5 stars on right: barely touched by circulation. The statement made in the Ely catalogue that this variety was not in the Mint Cabinet was erroneous and misleading." Sold for $14. There was very little camaraderie among dealers of the era.

In his fixed-price list of 1907, Elmer S. Sears offered this: "1806 Over 1804, 5 stars before Bust, 8 behind it. Uncirculated specimen with Proof surface. Probably the finest known. Extremely rare. $75." In June 1941 B. Max Mehl's sale of the William Forrester Dunham Collection included lot 1911: "1806/4. Practically Uncirculated, with considerable luster. A hardly noticeable nick at O in OF. This does not affect the appearance nor value of the coin, but due to its rarity, it should be mentioned. Recent record of $85." Realized $55.25. Numismatic Gallery's December 1944 of the "World's Greatest Collection" included lot 86: "1806/4 A beautiful coin with considerable luster and slight cabinet friction on the higher portions. In 1944, the Bell specimen sold for $182.50. Uncirculated." Realized $150. An exceptionally nice example appeared in Mehl's June 1947 sale of the W. Neil Collection, lot 2399: "1806 over 1804, Beautiful semi-proof, almost equal to a Proof. Sharp and perfect in every respect. A gem and of the greatest rarity in this beautiful state. Note accompanying this coin states that it is as beautiful a specimen as can possibly exist. Record over $200. Should bring much more today." Realized $175.

In November 1956, New Netherlands' sale of the Thomas L. Gaskill Collection included lot 187: "1806 over 4. Stars 8x5, as in 1804, but from a different obverse die. Very Fine plus; die weakness in the centre of the reverse. File or adjustment marks at Liberty's head; two minor obv. nicks above T (of LIBERTY) and at 9th star. Abrasions from contact with other coins almost entirely about the obverse rim. The reverse from the same die as last, now somewhat worn down. Despite the minor imperfections named, an attractive item and a rare one. Only 1,136 struck." Realized $150.

F-12	VF-20	EF-40	AU-50	AU-55	MS-60	MS-63
$5,000	$8,250	$14,000	$18,000	$25,000	$37,000	$150,000

1806, 6 Over 5, 7 Stars Left, 6 Right

Stars 7x6 on obverse. Obverse and reverse die of 1805. A classic rarity unknown in Mint State.

Circulation-Strike Mintage:
480 (estimated by Walter Breen)

Estimated Total Population (Mint State). None.

Estimated Total Population (Circulated Grades). 25 to 35. The 1806, 6 Over 5, is a great rarity, one of the greatest objects of desire in the entire early quarter eagle series.

Characteristics of Striking and Die Notes: The 1806, 6 Over 5, is always seen with a crack at LIB in LIBERTY, perhaps explaining the rarity, if the die failed after a few pieces were struck. Many if not most have Mint-caused adjustment marks.

Selected Auction Records

Note: In the early years (generally, prior to the 1880s) quarter eagles of 1806 were not classified by overdate or star arrangement; some of these listings are given earlier under the 1806, 6 Over 4, entry, and may include a few 1806, 6 Over 5, examples.

In his June 1885 sale of the J. Colvin Randall Collection, W. Elliot Woodward speculated as to the rarity of the overdate. Lot 965: "1806 Six stars facing; Very Fine and excessively rare. I know not if it exists in any other collection." Realized $20. In his 1907 fixed-price list Elmer S. Sears offered lot 147: "1806 Over 1805, 6 stars before Bust, 7 behind it. Uncirculated, with semi-Proof surface. The rarest of the early quarter eagles and the finest specimen known of the date and variety. $350." In his February 1921 sale of the Dr. G.F.E. Wilharm Collection, B. Max Mehl offered lot 64: "1806 over '05. Extremely Fine, sharp, with considerable Mint luster. One of the best known of this excessively rare variety. Cost $150." Realized $330.

In June 1946 Mehl's sale of the William Cutler Atwater Collection included lot 1924: "1806 over '05. The usual light die break connecting 806 of date. Uncirculated, just the barest touch of cabinet friction on highest portion. Full brilliant mint luster; the reverse almost equal to a brilliant Proof. The rarest variety of this date and one of the finest specimens known. Recent record $300 for an inferior specimen." Realized $285. In April 1956 in his sale of the Melish and Hester Collections Abe Kosoff described lot 1108: "1806/5. About Extremely Fine; small edge bruise at bottom. A rare coin seldom offered so nice. The W.G.C. equal realized $300 in 1946. Should exceed $350." Realized $300.

F-12	VF-20	EF-40	AU-50	AU-55	MS-60	MS-63
$7,500	$11,500	$20,000	$35,000	$50,000	$90,000	$300,000

1807

Circulation-Strike Mintage:
6,812 (calendar-year mintage)

Stars 7x6 on obverse.
Reverse die of 1805.
Most readily available date of type.

Estimated Total Population (Mint State). 20 to 30, making this the most available Mint State issue in the early series.

Estimated Total Population (Circulated Grades). 300 to 400, making this far and away the most plentiful early quarter eagle, although in absolute terms any coin of which only a few hundred exist can be called *rare.* Typical grades encountered are Very Fine and Extremely Fine, not often About Uncirculated.

Characteristics of Striking and Die Notes: Most are lightly struck in areas, especially at the center, but sometimes at the border as well, although some sharply struck pieces exist. Many if not most have Mint-caused adjustment marks.

Selected Auction Records

Note: Over the years there have been hundreds of other 1807 quarter eagle listings in auction catalogs, mainly Very Good to Very Fine or Extremely Fine. This is the date usually chosen for a type set to represent the reverse used on quarter eagles of 1796–1807.

Among early auction listings are these: February 1859, lot 1212 in the Henry Bogert Collection, cataloged by his friend and sometimes partner Augustus B. Sage: "1807 *Very Fine.*" Realized $3. Lot 700 in Edward Cogan's sale of April 1860: "1807 Fine condition, and scarce." Realized $3.50. April 1863, W. Elliot Woodward's sale of the Brooks, Colburn, Finotti, Field, and Shurtleff Collections, lot 371: "1807 Very Fine order and extra rare." Realized $5.50. May 1864, Woodward's sale of the John F. McCoy Collection, lot 1969: "1807 Very fine, Uncirculated, scarce." Realized $6.

Going into the twentieth century, in his 1907 fixed-price list Elmer S. Sears offered lot 148: "1807 Sharp, Uncirculated specimen with Proof surface. The handsomest example of the coin that I have ever seen. $25." Lot 149: "1807 Another, Very Fine. $12.50." In May 1913 the U.S. Coin Co.'s sale of the Malcolm N. Jackson Collection included lot 103: "1807 Extremely Fine, sharp, well struck impression, rare." Realized $12. B. Max Mehl in his April 1937 sale of the George M. Agurs collection offered two. Lot 75: "1807 Just a shade from Uncirculated; considerable mint luster. Very scarce." Realized $21.50. Lot 1686: "1807 A perfect Uncirculated specimen, with frosty mint surface. These early Quarter-Eagles, especially in choice condition are getting very rare." Realized $26. In June 1941 Mehl's sale of the William Forrester Dunham Collection included lot 1912: "1807 Just About Uncirculated, with frosty mint surface. An infinitesimal nick on edge at Y. Not a rare date, but quite rare so choice. Lists at $30 only in Very Fine condition." Realized $16.75. As can be seen from the various auction listings for quarter eagles up to this time, there is very little consistency in prices.

Stack's October 1947 sale of the H.R. Lee Collection (Louis E. Eliasberg duplicates) offered lot 993: "1807 Minute nick on edge, otherwise Brilliant Uncirculated with full mint bloom." Realized $87.50. In November 1956, New Netherlands' sale of the Thomas L. Gaskill Collection included lot 189: "1807 Last year of the Liberty Cap type; only the one variety. Choice Uncirculated with proof-like lustre. This piece is separated from perfection by a very few unimportant faults, the most serious of them a reverse rim mark at the eagle's right wing tip and a tiny surface scratch near the claw. One of the most beautiful early quarter eagles we have seen and although not one of the rarer dates, worth a high price as a 'gem' quality coin. From the WGC sale, ten years ago, whereas lot 88 (no defects mentioned) this piece brought full estimate of $110. The 'Cap' quarter eagles, 1797–1807 constitute a highly interesting series for the conscientious collector of types. Six basic alterations of design were made, as follows: I, No Obverse Stars, 1796; II, 16 Obverse Stars, 8x8, 1796 III, 13 Obverse Stars, 7x6, 1797, 1805, 1806/5, 1807; IV 13 Obverse Stars, 6x7, 1798; V, 13 Obverse Stars, 8x5, 1802/1, 1804, 1806/4; VI Same, 14 Reverse Stars, 1804. Sub-type designations would include allowance for the 4 and 5 berry (on branch) reverses, which put 1805, 06/5, 07 in a IIIa (5 berry) classification; the rarer 1798 (with 5 berries) as IVa. Complicated as this may appear here, all U.S. coins will be so broken down in the eventual publication of a greatly revised *Standard Catalogue.*" Realized $150.[19]

F-12	VF-20	EF-40	AU-50	AU-55	MS-60	MS-63
$5,000	$7,500	$13,000	$17,500	$23,500	$31,500	$85,000

8

Draped Bust to Left, Large Size, $2.50 Gold Coins (1808)

Draped Bust to Left, Large Size (1808)

Designer: *John Reich.* **Weight:** *4.37 grams.* **Composition:** *.9167 gold, .0833 silver and copper.* **Diameter:** *Approximately 20 mm.* **Edge:** *Reeded.* **Mint:** *Philadelphia.*

A Short-Lived Design

In 1808 John Reich redesigned the quarter eagle. In the previous year he had restyled the motif for the half dollar, creating what numismatists of a later generation would call the Capped Bust design. Now it was the quarter eagle's turn. The diameter and authorized weight remained the same as earlier, but the obverse and reverse motifs were changed.

Miss Liberty now faces left, wearing a loose cloth cap secured by a band inscribed LIBERTY. Seven stars are to the left and six are to the right, and the date 1808 appears below. This design is often called *Draped Bust to Left*, for the garment across Liberty's bust.

The reverse depicts an eagle perched on an olive branch and holding three arrows. The motto E PLURIBUS UNUM is on a band or ribbon above. The inscription UNITED STATES OF AMERICA is around the border, along with 2½ D.—the first time the denomination is stated on a quarter eagle. This same general reverse style would be used on the subsequent quarter eagle type (1821–1834) as well.

In *Description of Ancient and Modern Coins, in the Cabinet Collection at the Mint of the United States*, 1860, Mint director James Ross Snowden described the 1807 change of design for the $5 coin, and noted that the new motif had not been used that year on quarter eagles:

> No further changes were made in the devices on the gold coins until the year 1807. In this year it became apparent to the Director of the Mint (Robert Patterson) that the gentleman who was then engraver, Mr. Robert Scot, "though indeed a meritorious and faithful officer, was yet so far advanced in life that he could not very long be expected to continue his labors;" and, in anticipation of such a contingency, he employed Mr. John Reich, with the approbation of the President, to act as assistant engraver, and under date of April 2nd, 1807, wrote to the President as follows:
>
> "Mr. Reich is now preparing a set of new dies, in which some improvements in the devices will be introduced, (adhering, however, to the strict letter of the law,) which, it is hoped, will meet with public approbation."
>
> Half and quarter eagles had already been issued of the old type. At precisely what time the new dies were put in use we cannot ascertain, but judge that it could not have been before the latter part of summer, consequently there was issued from the Mint about 33,496 half eagles, and 6,812 quarter eagles, bearing the old devices. If our conclusions be correct, the first issue of coins of the new type took place on the 30th of September, and consisted of 15,967 half-eagles, after which there were five other deliveries of the same denomination.

No quarter eagles of the new design were issued in 1807, as there was only one delivery of this denomination (on February 15) during the year. The new quarter eagle appeared in the year 1808.

The Mint reported that 2,710 quarter eagles were struck in calendar year 1808. There is no way of knowing whether all were dated 1808, or if earlier-dated dies were also used. However, it seems logical from the foregoing account that Reich's new design was used.

Numismatic Considerations

The mintage figure of 2,710 on its own would suggest a rarity, but the demand for the coin as the only year of its design type has projected it into the forefront of popular rarities among American gold coins. It has been available in all grades over the years, with Mint State coins being rarities. Its status as a type coin has placed it in the limelight when examples are offered at auction.

Dies and Known Die Combinations, 1808

1808, Obverse Die 1. *The portrait of Miss Liberty faces right; stars are arranged 7 left, 6 right. Details:* The date digits are widely separated. The first 8 is low; the second 8 is high. The 1 is thick; the 8's are heavy, with small interior spaces, while the 0 has a large opening at center. There is ample space above and below the date. The bases of BE in LIBERTY on the headband are slightly high. The lower inside ray of star 7 points to the hair curl below the headband. Star 13 has a chip or notch in one of the rays, believed to have been the "signature" of engraver John Reich.

1808, Reverse Die A. *The reverse letters are large. Details:* The letters in the border inscriptions are significantly larger than on the later use of the same basic design on the type of 1821–1834. The top of the O in OF is low. The numerator in the fraction ½ is to the left of center over the horizontal fraction bar, with its serif close to but not touching the arrow feather above. The branch has six leaves and a split bud (or berry). The point of the middle arrow is below the I in AMERICA. The I in PLURIBUS is below the right foot of the T in STATES. The large 2 in 2½ has the top left curiously curved down, with the ball of the 2 touching the diagonal.

1808, BD-1: Dies 1-A. There is only one die combination this year.

GRADING STANDARDS

MS-60 to 70 (Mint State). ***Obverse:*** At MS-60, some abrasion and contact marks are seen on the cheek, on the hair below the LIBERTY inscription, and on the highest-relief folds of the cap. Luster is present, but may be dull or lifeless, and interrupted in patches. At MS-63, contact marks are few, and abrasion is very light. Abrasion is even less at MS-64. (Discussion of such high grades in these early coins starts to enter the realm of theory.) Quarter eagles of this type are almost, but not quite, non-existent in a combination of high grade and nice eye appeal. ***Reverse:*** Comments apply as for the obverse, except that abrasion is most noticeable on the eagle's neck and highest area of the wings.

1808; BD-1. Graded MS-63.

AU-50, 53, 55, 58 (About Uncirculated). ***Obverse:*** Light wear is seen on the cheek and higher-relief areas of the hair and cap. Friction and scattered marks are in the field, ranging from extensive at AU-50 to minimal at AU-58. The low rim affords little protection to the field of this coin, but the stars in relief help. Luster may be seen in protected areas, minimal at AU-50, but less so at AU-58. At AU-58 the field retains some luster as well. ***Reverse:*** Comments are as for a Mint State coin, except that the eagle's neck, the top of the wings, the leaves, and the arrowheads now show noticeable wear, as do other features. Luster ranges from perhaps 40% remaining in protected areas at AU-50 to nearly full mint bloom at AU-58. Often the reverse of this type retains much more luster than does the obverse, as on this type the motto, eagle, and lettering protect the surrounding flat areas.

1808. Graded AU-50.

EF-40, 45 (Extremely Fine). ***Obverse:*** More wear is seen on the portrait, the hair, the cap, and the drapery near the clasp. Luster is likely to be absent on the obverse due to the low rim. ***Reverse:*** Wear is more extensive on the eagle, including the top of the wings, the head, the top of the shield, and the claws. Some traces of luster may be seen in protected areas, more so at EF-45 than at EF-40.

1808. Graded EF-40.

VF-20, 30 (Very Fine). ***Obverse:*** Wear on the portrait has reduced the hair detail, especially to the right of the face and the top of the head, but much can still be seen. ***Reverse:*** Wear on the eagle is greater, and details of feathers near the shield and near the top of the wings are weak or missing. All other features show wear, but most are fairly sharp. Generally, Draped Bust gold coins at this grade level lack eye appeal.

1808. Graded VF-20.

The Draped Bust to Left, Large Size, quarter eagle is seldom collected in grades lower than VF-20.

1808

Circulation-Strike Mintage: 2,710

The entire mintage for this year was delivered on February 26, 1808, probably all dated 1808 and of the new type.

Only year of design type.

After 1808, quarter eagles were not minted for a long span of years, until 1821. At the time, gold coins were struck to the order of depositors. As there was little domestic call for the denomination, and as most gold coins were used in the export trade, the largest current denomination, the $5 half eagle, was preferred (the $10 eagle having been discontinued in 1804).

In 1859 Dr. Montroville W. Dickeson wrote in the *American Numismatical Manual,* "Designs the same [as on the $5 of this year]. One type and three varieties. They are scarce." The multiple varieties he mentions cannot be confirmed today. Throughout the gold series, Dickeson made many errors with regard to the *varieties* designation.

Estimated Total Population (Mint State). 8 to 12, most of which are in lower numerical ranges, MS-60 or so, with a few likely being more properly in the About Uncirculated category—the result of gradeflation. A fair number of coins described as Mint State have appeared in sales over the years, often moving from one notable collection to another and reappearing in the auction venue. The author has seen two high-level choice or gem specimens over the years.

Estimated Total Population (Circulated Grades). 125 to 175. The 1808 is not a great rarity in the context of early quarter eagles, but as an American "type" coin needed by everyone completing a type set, it is in *incredible* demand. Opinions as to the number of extant 1808 quarter eagles have varied widely, with Walter Breen (1988) suggesting between 35 and 40.

Characteristics of Striking and Die Notes. On all known specimens of the 1808 quarter eagle some or most of the border denticles are missing, although the central motifs are usually fairly sharply struck.

All specimens seen are from a die that has a crack extending from Miss Liberty's cap. Apparently, the die broke very early during the striking process. However, only a few catalog descriptions mention the crack.

Many if not most 1808 quarter eagles have Mint-caused adjustment marks, these being particularly evident at the border due to the usual indistinct striking of the denticles there.

Selected Auction Records

Among early listings are Edward Cogan's sale of April 1860, lot 701: "1808 Quarter eagle, in Fine condition, and scarce." Realized $4.12½. W.H. Strobridge's September 1863 sale of the George F. Seavey Collection, lot 460: "1808 Fine for this date, very scarce." Realized $7. W. Elliot Woodward's May 1865 sale of the John F. McCoy Collection, lot 1970: "1808 Uncirculated, and very scarce." Realized $5. Cogan's October 1875 sale of the Col. Mendes I. Cohen Collection, lot 190: "1808 Very Fine." Realized $3.25. This particular sale did rather poorly across the board, for reasons not clear today.

Woodward's January 1884 sale of the Heman Ely Collection mentioned the design type under lot 889: "1808 New type. Very Fine, scarce." Realized $5.30. For lot 16 in the June 1886 sale of the Dr. Edward Maris Collection, H.P. Smith stated this about lot 16: "1808 Quarter eagle. Uncirculated, and the best I have seen. This piece is rare, and generally found in rather poor condition." Realized $5. Over a period of time the 1808 gained traction in the marketplace, as evidenced in 1907 when in his fixed-price list Elmer S. Sears offered lot 150: "1808 A Very Fine example of a very rare coin. All specimens of this date are weakly struck, but this specimen is unusually nice. $40." Still, prices were hardly consistent. In May 1913 the U.S. Coin Co.'s sale of the Malcolm N. Jackson Collection included lot 104: "1808 Extremely Fine. Stars on right and one or two on left not struck up, but the head is very sharp. Very rare." Realized $41. In February 1921 the catalog of B. Max Mehl's sale of the Dr. G.F.E. Wilharm Collection described lot 66: "1808 Large bust of Liberty with cap inscribed Liberty, 7 stars to left and 6 to right, date below. Rev. small eagle with upraised wings, on olive branch in his right talon and three arrows in left, E. Pluribus Unum incused on scroll above, 2½ d. below; United States Of America around, milled edge. Practically Uncirculated with Mint luster. Very rare and a most difficult date to find so choice. Valued at $50." Realized $52.

In June 1941 Mehl's sale of the William Forrester Dunham Collection included lot 1913: "1808 First year of the new type, with bust to left. Very light nick on obverse right stars. Extremely Fine. Rare. A most difficult date to find choice. A similar specimen in my Sale of the Hale Collection brought $55.50. This date seems to be in great demand, as I notice that I had twenty-one bids for the specimen in the Hale Sale." Realized $57.50. For lot 2401 in his June 1947 sale of the Will W. Neil Collection, Mehl gave this: "1808. . . . Very Fine obverse with Extremely Fine reverse. This is another coin the rarity of which was not appreciated until just recently. Only in 1944 the coin cataloged at $100. Today it catalogs at $200 in only Very Fine, but a specimen in my Atwater Sale in similar condition brought $235 and have noticed it advertised at retail at $325. This specimen here offered is just about as choice as is possible to obtain of this rarity." Realized $200. Mehl gave an expanded description of an 1808 under lot 11 of his March 1950 sale of the Jerome Kern Collection: "1808. New type. Larger bust of Liberty facing left, in turban the band of which is inscribed LIBERTY, date below. Thirteen stars. Reverse, new design of eagle, with outstretched wings and shield on breast; motto above, and value, 2-1/2 below. Legend. Milled edge. Uncirculated with practically full brilliant mint luster. Another pleasing feature of this specimen is that the stars are struck up which is quite unusual for this date quarter eagle. A beautiful gold coin of this age, although never having been in circulation, must show just a slight touch of cabinet friction. For the sake of accuracy I also mention that on the obverse edge at the second star from bottom there is what appears to be an infinitesimal pinpoint nick, but what I think it is, is a tiny die defect which, of course, does not in the slightest degree affect the appearance or value of this coin. Even the great Atwater Collection only had a very fine to extremely fine specimen which brought $235. I have never seen a more beautiful specimen of this date quarter eagle. The Atwater specimen was not struck up boldly as this one is. Very rare and valuable. The Atwater specimen brought $235. This one is worth much more." Realized $242.50.

F-12	VF-20	EF-40	AU-50	AU-55	MS-60	MS-63
$30,000	$42,500	$72,500	$115,000	$145,000	$200,000	$500,000

9

Capped Head to Left $2.50 Gold Coins (1821–1834)

Capped Head to Left, Large Diameter (1821–1827)

Designer: *John Reich, possibly modified by Robert Scot.*
Weight: *4.37 grams.* **Composition:** *.9167 gold, .0833 silver and copper.*
Diameter: *Approximately 18.5 mm.* **Edge:** *Reeded.* **Mint:** *Philadelphia.*

New Design

In 1821 quarter eagles were again struck, following a hiatus since 1808. A new obverse motif, possibly by engraver Robert Scot, was used in 1821, replacing the Reich design of 1808. However, as Reich had left the Mint and Scot was in declining health, the engraver may have been someone else.

The diameter was reduced from the 20.6 mm standard used from 1796 to 1808 to just 19 mm. This diameter was used through 1827. The coins were made very slightly thicker than they were previously, so as to maintain the standard weight.

The design features the Capped Head adapted from John Reich's 1808 motif, presumably by chief engraver Robert Scot. The portrait is now smaller, with modifications to the cap, Miss Liberty's neckline, and other features. Stars encircle the portrait except for the date area. The quarter eagles dated 1826 and 1827 have larger stars than do the other obverse dies of this type. The stars were punched into each die by hand and thus vary slightly in their relation to each other, to the denticles, and so on. Dates were entered into the working dies by hand, one digit at a time. The headband has the letters in LIB in LIBERTY progressively lower and ER slightly higher, with R tilted slightly left; this inscription is in the portrait punch and is common to all dies.

The reverse is similar in general design to that of 1808 by John Reich, with a perched eagle, the motto E PLURIBUS UNUM above, and UNITED STATES OF AMERICA and 2½ D. at the border. The letters are smaller than on the 1808 issue, and the dies are more finely cut. The letter punches for the reverse were done by Henry Starr. The denticles on the 1821–1827 quarter eagles are in the form of extended tabs.

Mintages in all instances were low, with the production of one variety, the 1826, estimated at just 760 pieces, although this is probably incorrect and represents calendar-year coinage rather than quarter eagles actually minted with the date 1826. Likely, 1826 quarter eagles were also coined later, perhaps in 1827.

The Coins That Never Were

The quarter eagles of this and the following type, covering the era from 1821 to 1834, are the coins that never were, at least from the standpoint of anyone ever seeing them in circulation! After the War of 1812 ended (in 1814 by treaty, but in 1815 in reality), gold coins were no longer used in regular domestic American commerce. Examples of all three denominations—$2.50, $5, and $10—were worth more than their face value in terms of contemporary American silver coins or paper bills and exchange.

Capped Head to Left quarter eagles were primarily minted for limited distribution in the United States, such as part of the salaries of certain federal legislators (e.g., Sen. Thomas Hart Benton of Missouri) who requested and received their stipends in gold. Unlike the situation with contemporary half eagles, nearly all of which were shipped abroad, it is probable that most quarter eagles of 1821–1827 and also 1829–1834 remained in the United States. In later years, many went into the hands of bullion dealers and were melted, and thousands of other pieces were redeemed at the several mints.

Numismatic Considerations

All quarter eagles of 1821–1827 are rare today, with, perhaps, 1827 being the very rarest, although the 1826 receives more publicity in this regard. The most frequently encountered date—and that is not very often—is the 1824, 4 Over 1. Most are found in worn grades. In contrast, the 1825 is seen less often in terms of total specimens, but Mint State coins are more readily available for this particular date than for any others of the 1821–1827 type.

Most examples of this design are seen in grades from Very Fine through About Uncirculated, although scattered Uncirculated pieces have appeared at auction, as have a very few Proofs. It is not unusual for an Uncirculated piece to have a prooflike surface.

One obverse die was used for 1821, 1824/1, 1826, and 1827, while two obverse dies were used in 1825. Two reverse dies were used: BD reverse 1821A for all 1821, 1824/1, and some 1825 quarter eagles; and reverse 1825A for some 1825 and all 1826 and 1827 quarter eagles. There is one die variety for each year except for 1825, which has three die varieties for the specialist to contemplate.

DIES AND KNOWN DIE COMBINATIONS, 1821–1827

Quarter Eagles of 1821

1821, Obverse Die 1. *The bases of the 1's are high. Details:* The date is wide; the bases of the 1's are high. Star 1 points to a place slightly above the leftmost area of the neck. The 2 has a square base with knob, as for all quarter eagle dies this decade. The lowest part of the curl is above the space between 2 and 1 and closer to 2. Each of stars 3, 4, 5 (slightly right of center), 8, 9, 11, 12, and 13 (slightly right of center) has a ray pointing to the center of a denticle or close to center.[1] The border denticles are usually bold, long, and prominent, "framing" the coin and giving it a very pleasing impression.

1821, Reverse Die A. Reverse die 1821A was used to coin all quarter eagles of 1821 and 1824, 4 Over 1, and some of 1825. *The branch ends over the upright of D in the denomination;* definitive. *Details:* The U and D in UNITED are slightly low; the point of the highest left leaf is below and slightly to the left of the lower left base of the N. The base of the first S in STATES is slightly low. The horizontal fraction bar is very long, and the numerator, 1, is very small. The left upright of the first U in UNUM is below the right side of the second S in STATES. Quick reference point: The large 2 in 2½ is far from the leaf.

1821, BD-1: Dies 1-A. This is the only known die combination.

Quarter Eagles of 1824

1824, 4 Over 1, Obverse Die 1. *The 4 in the date is placed over a previous 1; the serif of that 1 is visible as a small projection from the diagonal of the 4. Details:* This die was overdated 1824 on an *unused* 1821 die; on the obverse the first 1 is slightly closer to the portrait than to the denticles, whereas on the "perfect date" 1821 die that is known to have been used for coinage in 1821, the first 1 is much closer to the denticles. The 1, 8, and 2 in the date are widely spaced; the 2 and 4 are closer. The bottom of the lowest curl is over the left side of the 4. Each of stars 1, 8, 9, 11, and 12 has a ray pointing more or less at the center of a denticle.

1821, Reverse Die A. Reverse die 1821A was used to coin all quarter eagles of 1821 and 1824, 4 Over 1, and some of 1825. It is described in detail above, with the other die of that year. Quick reference point: The large 2 in 2½ is far from the leaf.

1824, 4 Over 1, BD-1: Dies 1-1821A. This is the only known die combination.

Quarter Eagles of 1825

1825, Obverse Die 1 (used only on BD-1). *In the date, all four digits are equally distant from the border, although the 5 appears slightly high. Details:* Star 1 is slightly closer to the bust than on obverse die 2. Each of stars 6, 7, 9, and 13 has a ray pointing to the center of a denticle. The flag on the 5 is small and tapers to a point at the right end. This variety was discovered by Harry W. Bass Jr. and so listed in his unpublished (before BD) notes. The die was first published after Mark Borckardt discovered another example while examining the plate for lot 298 in the January 2000 Rarities Sale by Bowers and

Merena Galleries. This led to close examination of other 1825 quarter eagles. Bass-Dannreuther suggests a population of 12 to 15 coins. The Bass coin is double-struck, with the first striking about 50% off center—an extraordinary rare Mint error.

1825, Obverse Die 2 (used on BD-2 and 3). *In the date, the 2 is high, and the 5 leans left. Details:* The upright of 5, if extended, would touch lowest part of the hair curl. Star 1 is closer to the bust than to the denticles. Each of stars 3, 7, and 11 has a ray pointing to the center of a denticle; the ray of star 13 points slightly to the right of center of a denticle.

1821, Reverse Die A (used on BD-1 and 2). Reverse die 1821A was used to coin all quarter eagles of 1821 and 1824, 4 Over 1, and some of 1825. It is described in detail on page 80, with the other die of that year. Quick reference point: The large 2 in 2½ is far from the leaf.

1825, Reverse Die A (used only on BD-3). Reverse die A was used to coin some quarter eagles of 1825 and all of 1826 and 1827. *The 1 in the numerator of ½ leans left. The 2 touches the fraction bar, which extends far to the left of the tip of the lowest arrow feather;* definitive. *Details:* The base of the second T in STATES is higher above the ribbon than the other letters in the word. The top of the O in OF is higher than the top of the F. The M in AMERICA is in a taller font than adjacent E. Quick reference point: The large 2 in 2½ is close to the leaf. Walter Breen credits the discovery of this die to Waldo C. Newcomer, circa 1915.[2]

1825, BD-1: Dies 1-1821A. Rarity-7. This variety was discovered by Harry W. Bass Jr. As of early 2000 it was believed to be unique, but by 2002 two others had been identified. The Bass coin is double-struck, ex 1890 Cleneay Sale but not described there as a distinct die variety. This is the rarest of the three die combinations this year.

1825, BD-2: Dies 2-1821A. This is far and away the most readily available of the three die combinations of this year.

1825, BD-3: Dies 2-A. Rare in all grades.

Quarter Eagles of 1826

The "Close Denomination" reverse die, first used in 1825, was used to coin all quarter eagles dated 1826 and 1827. The 1826 is often called 1826, 6 Over 5, including in the *Red Book*, but it is more likely a "perfect date" with slight repunching. The obverse stars are overly large on this die.

1826, Obverse Die 1. *In the date, the 8 and 6 are slightly larger than the 1 and 2. The 6 is repunched (making this an "overdate" in the view of some observers, but called "1826, 6 Over 6" or "recut" by BD, with detailed discussion). Details:* The stars are large (as also in 1827). Star 1 is closer to the bust than on any other Capped Head to Left, Large Diameter, quarter eagle die. The date, 1826, has the digits in 18 most widely spaced, 82 closest, and 26 in between. Digits 8 and 6 are larger than the other numerals. The 1 is closer to the neck truncation than to the denticle and is positioned directly over a denticle; the 2 has a prominent knob and a straight base. The 6 has a small knob distant from the curve below. The following obverse stars point at or near the center of a denticle: 5 (slightly left of center), 7 (slightly left of center), 8, and 9 (slightly left of center).

1825, Reverse Die A. Reverse die 1825A was used to coin some quarter eagles of 1825 and all those of 1826 and 1827. It is described in detail on page 81, with the other dies of that year. Quick reference point: The large 2 in 2½ is close to the leaf.

1826, BD-1: Dies 1-1825A. This is the only known die combination.

Quarter Eagles of 1827

1827, Obverse Die 1. *The date is widely spaced; the base of the 7 is directly above a denticle and closer to border than any other digit. The stars are large. Details:* Large stars (as also in 1826). Stars 1, 2, and 6–11 have rays that point to the center of a denticle or nearly to the center.

1825, Reverse Die A. Reverse die 1825A was used to coin some quarter eagles of 1825 and all those of 1826 and 1827. It is described in detail on page 81, with the other die of that year. Quick reference point: The large 2 in 2½ is close to a leaf.

1827, BD-1: Dies 1-1825A. This is the only known die combination.

Grading Standards

Note: The grading standards are identical for Capped Head to Left, Large Diameter, and Capped Head to Left, Reduced Diameter, quarter eagles.

1827, BD-1. Graded MS-65.

MS-60 to 70 (Mint State). ***Obverse:*** At MS-60, some abrasion and contact marks are seen on the cheek, on the hair below the LIBERTY inscription, and on the highest-relief folds of the cap. Luster is present, but may be dull or lifeless, and interrupted in patches. At MS-63, contact marks are few, and abrasion is very light. Abrasion is even less at MS-64. (Discussion of such high grades in these early coins starts to enter the realm of theory.) Quarter eagles of this type are almost, but not quite, non-existent in a combination of high grade and nice eye appeal. ***Reverse:*** Comments apply as for the obverse, except that abrasion is most noticeable on the eagle's neck and highest area of the wings.

1833; BD-1. Graded AU-53.

AU-50, 53, 55, 58 (About Uncirculated). ***Obverse:*** Light wear is seen on the cheek and higher-relief areas of the hair and cap. Friction and scattered marks are in the field, ranging from extensive at AU-50 to minimal at AU-58. The low rim affords little protection to the field of this coin, but the stars in relief help. Luster may be seen in protected areas, minimal at AU-50, but less so at AU-58. At AU-58 the field retains some luster as well. ***Reverse:*** Comments are as for a Mint State coin, except that the eagle's neck, the top of the wings, the leaves, and the arrowheads now show noticeable wear, as do other features. Luster ranges from perhaps 40% remaining in protected areas at AU-50 to nearly full mint bloom at AU-58. Often the reverse of this type retains much more luster than does the obverse, as on this type the motto, eagle, and lettering protect the surrounding flat areas.

EF-40, 45 (Extremely Fine). ***Obverse:*** More wear is seen on the portrait, the hair, the cap, and the drapery near the clasp. Luster is likely to be absent on the obverse due to the low rim. ***Reverse:*** Wear is more extensive on the eagle, including the top of the wings, the head, the top of the shield, and the claws. Some traces of luster may be seen in protected areas, more so at EF-45 than at EF-40.

1821; BD-1. Graded EF-40.

The Capped Head to Left quarter eagle is seldom collected in grades lower than EF-40.

PF-60 to 70 (Proof). ***Obverse and Reverse:*** PF–60 to 62 coins have extensive hairlines and may have nicks and contact marks. At PF-63, hairlines are prominent, but the mirror surface is very reflective. PF-64 coins have fewer hairlines. At PF-65, hairlines should be minimal and mostly seen only under magnification. There should be no nicks or marks. PF-66 and higher coins should have no marks or hairlines visible to the unaided eye.

1824, 4 Over 1. Proof.

1821

Circulation-Strike Mintage: 6,448

Proof Mintage: Unknown, but small

First year of new design.
Rare date.

The mintage of the 1821 quarter eagle is far and away the largest among the Capped Head to Left, Large Diameter, issues. As it is exceedingly unlikely that any earlier-dated (e.g., 1808) dies were held over to this late date, the mintage no doubt represents pieces bearing the 1821 date.

Regarding how many 1821 quarter eagles exist in circulated grades versus Mint State, the following two publications offer information.

David W. Akers (1975) located 34 auction appearances, including five Very Fine coins, twelve Extremely Fine, five About Uncirculated, nine Mint State, and three Proof. This represented the spread of grades across collections as they came to the auction block. As important collections tend to have higher-than-average-grade coins, there is a slight bias toward multiple appearances of high-grade pieces. A choice or gem Mint State 1821 would gravitate toward a "name" collector, while a damaged or well-worn coin might be ignored and not purchased. This writer believes the bias in the instance of the 1821 quarter eagle is not great but does tend to slightly overstate the availability of Mint State coins as opposed to those in a lower grade, such as Very Fine.

The *PCGS Population Report* (August 1999) included one Extremely Fine, five About Uncirculated, seven Mint State, and two Proof.

A reading of the Akers book, based upon auction appearances of 1821 quarter eagles prior to 1975, suggests that the ratio of circulated coins to Mint State pieces is 22 to 9, with circulated pieces outnumbering Mint State coins about 2.5 to 1. The PCGS data suggest a ratio of 6 to 7, giving the *completely opposite* view that Mint State coins are more readily available. Both sources include duplicate appearances of certain specimens.

Estimates in the present work are based upon a combination of many factors, with the added opinion that PCGS, NGC, and other certified-population numbers tend to be too high for rare and valuable coins, as coins that are in or near Mint State are much more likely to be resubmitted for grading than are Very Fine, Extremely Fine, or lower-level About Uncirculated coins. Conversely, for low-grade, inexpensive coins the certification data are too low. In the writer's view the Akers data give a more realistic view of the true distribution of grades. As earlier noted, many high-level circulated coins are now certified as Mint State.

Estimated Total Population (Mint State). 8 to 12, mostly in the range of MS-60 to MS-62 by traditional grading, higher in recent decades due to gradeflation. The typical Mint State coin is prooflike. Certification data and publicity would seem to indicate that the 1821 is as readily available in Mint State as it is in circulated grades. However, a perusal of a long run of auction appearances demonstrates that Mint State coins are distinctly in the minority. Many About Uncirculated coins of earlier times have been regraded as Mint State. As coins of this era did not circulate, *most* are About Uncirculated by traditional grading, with gradeflation putting them in the majority today, as noted.

Estimated Total Population (Circulated Grades). 50 to 60. Typical grades are Extremely Fine and About Uncirculated. Many of the Very Fine and Extremely Fine coins of early times would have been called About Uncirculated by 1975, when David W. Akers studied quarter eagles. By that year grading was more or less standardized, without great fluctuations. The mintage figure suggests that this should be the most plentiful of all Capped Head to Left, Large Diameter, quarter eagles, but reality is different. The 1821 is quite rare, and the lower-mintage 1824, 4 Over 1, and 1825 are more often seen.

Characteristics of Striking and Die Notes. On many if not most specimens there is a small recessed area on the cheek, probably from a piece of lint or metal adhering to the obverse die. Some show lightness of striking on the eagle at the upper left of the shield.

On very early impressions, raised compass arcs—the guide references for lettering—are seen at the border of the *reverse;* these gradually wear away on later impressions.

Only one die pair was used this year. A second obverse die was made but was kept on the shelf (ultimately used in 1824, and overdated 1824, 4 Over 1). The 1821 reverse die was also used in 1824 and again in 1825. Circulation strikes as well as Proofs were made from this die pair.

Selected Auction Records

W. Elliot Woodward's 1864 sale of the John F. McCoy Collection catalog described lot 1971: "1821 Almost Proof, extremely rare. To the *especial* rarity of this, particular attention is requested." Realized $87.50, one of the highest prices in the sale. Prices recorded in the McCoy Sale were in some instances higher than any that would be seen elsewhere for many years. The coin described by Edward Cogan in his October 1875 sale of the Col. Mendes I. Cohen Collection was likely Extremely Fine or Mint Sate. "Very Good" probably meant very nice or very choice. "1821 Very Good. Scarce." Realized $3.50. Lot 1942 in Woodward's sale of October 1884 was described: "1821 Uncirculated; reverse, the feathers of the eagle's wings barely touched; extremely rare." Realized $19.

The Chapman brothers in December 1890 offered the Thomas Cleneay Collection coin: "1821 Head of Liberty left, 13 stars and date. R. as last. Type 1821 to 1834. Extremely Fine. Slight dent on edge below date. Very rare." Realized $10. In June 1900, Lyman H. Low described lot 676 in his Parcel Sale: "1821 Only the most trifling indication of circulation; sharp and brilliant, and the equal of the one in my sale of April 21, which brought $30. Constantly increasing in value, like many of the gold coins." Realized $29. The Chapmans offered this as lot 247 in their June 1906 sale of the Major W.B. Wetmore Collection: "1821 Head of Liberty l., surrounded by 13 stars and date. Rev., same type. Very Fine. Proof surface. Very rare." Realized $28.

In June 1946 B. Max Mehl's sale of the William Cutler Atwater Collection included lot 1927: "1821 (No quarter-eagles were minted from 1809 to 1820 inclusive.) Same type as last, but the Liberty head is much smaller and the entire coin is slightly reduced in diameter. Uncirculated with brilliant luster. Highest portions show just the slightest cabinet friction. Very rare. Record $185." Realized $115. In 1950, in his sale of the Jerome Kern Collection, Mehl described lot 12: "1821 (No quarter-eagles minted from 1809 to 1820 inclusive). Same type as the 1808 but the Liberty head is much smaller and the coin as a whole is slightly reduced in size. Brilliant Uncirculated with semi-Proof surface. Some may call this a Proof. Catalogs $150." Realized $142.50. In November 1956 New Netherlands' sale of the Thomas L. Gaskill Collection included lot 191: "1821 First year of the reduced size—next to the 1808 the most difficult type of quarter eagle to find choice. A splendid proof-like 'first strike.' Evidently never in circulation for more than a few minutes, this piece was struck from dies retaining polish, immediately after the few Proofs of this date were made. The similar Melish specimen brought $235. Apparently the Harrie Price example, sold by Wayte Raymond in 1935." Realized $200.

Proofs

Estimated Total Population (Proof). 5 to 7. A Proof is in the Mint Collection (now in the Smithsonian; *Sylloge* no. 187), this being the earliest-dated quarter eagle of any variety that seems to have been deliberately saved for numismatic purposes at the Mint.[3]

Proof Die Data and Notes. For the first time in the quarter eagle series, Proof impressions were made. The distribution of these was probably single as well as in a few sets. The Smithsonian Institution has a full set of Proofs of this year, cent to half eagle, this being its earliest-dated set.

Selected Proof Auction Records

W. Elliot Woodward described lot 2021 in his May 1883 sale of the Lewis Collection: "1821 Proof, excessively rare." Realized $21. The Chapman brothers in their October 1883 sale of the Haines Collection described lot 138: "Proof, sharp, even impression. Very rare. Realized $21.50." Woodward's June 1885 sale of the J. Colvin Randall Collection included lot 968: "1821 Sharp; a Proof impression, extremely rare. McCoy's brought $87.50." Realized $16, perhaps indicating there was a major problem with the coin. In the April 1904 sale of the John G. Mills Collection the Chapmans offered lot 537: "1821 Head of Liberty l. wearing cap similar to above; around 13 stars, beneath date. Reverse, same design. Brilliant Proof. Very rare." Realized $37. This coin later appeared the Eliasberg Collection of U.S. Gold Coins in 1982, still later in other sales.

Lot 939 in Thomas L. Elder's March 1911 sale of the William H. Woodin Collection was described: "1821. Brilliant Proof. Slightest planchet defect on jaw. Almost unique in this state. Parmelee Collection." Realized $63.50. The buyer was Virgil Brand (Brand journal item 57041).[4] In December 1944 lot 90 in the J.F. Bell Collection was described by Stack's: "1821 Reduced in size from the 1808, this is a beautiful perfect and Brilliant Proof which is a gem." Realized $185. In the Memorable Collection sold in March 1948, in the depth of a coin-market slump, Abe Kosoff of the Numismatic Gallery described lot 86: "1821. None minted between 1808 and 1821. First year of reduced size. A superb brilliant Proof. Extremely rare and valuable. Only one we have seen in this condition and sold by us into this collection." Realized $190.

F-12	VF-20	EF-40	AU-50	AU-55	MS-60	MS-63	PF-63	PF-64
$6,250	$9,000	$14,500	$16,000	$17,500	$35,000	$85,000	$275,000	$500,000

1824, 4 Over 1

Circulation-Strike Mintage: 2,600

Proof Mintage: Unknown, but small (calendar-year mintage; some could have been dated 1821)

Rare date.
Only overdate of the type.

Niles' Weekly Register, May 15, 1824, had this: "The Bank of the United States has lately put into circulation an unusual quantity of half and quarter eagles, in payments to members of Congress." Congressional delegates who wanted their salaries in gold—Thomas Hart Benton among them—may have accounted for certain of the other mintages of the quarter eagle denomination through 1834, as half eagles were more popular for export. These were not put into circulation, but if disposed of, were sold at a premium to bullion brokers and exchange houses.

Estimated Total Population (Mint State). 10 to 14. Mint State specimens are very rare, although published information is often contradictory. However, over a long span of decades most "name" collections have *not* included a Mint State coin.

Estimated Total Population (Circulated Grades). 45 to 65. Typical grades are Extremely Fine and About Uncirculated, many upgraded to Mint State (not included in the above estimate) due to gradeflation in modern times. This is the second most available date (1825 is the most available) of the design type, but in absolute terms a population of 100 or fewer proclaims 1824, 4 Over 1, as a first-class rarity.

Characteristics of Striking and Die Notes. These are usually seen somewhat lightly struck at the centers, due to inadequate die spacing. This lightness is most evident on the obverse. On the reverse, areas of the eagle to the left of the shield are usually softly defined.

Selected Auction Records

Note: The overdate feature was not mentioned in early listings.

In his sale of April 1860 Edward Cogan described lot 702: "1824 Fine condition, and scarce." Realized $3.50. W. Elliot Woodward's description of lot 377 in his April 1863 sale of the Brooks, Colburn, Finotti, Field, and Shurtleff Collections: "1824 Very Good and extremely rare." "Very Good" meant "very nice" and bears no relation to the VG-8 used in today's grading system. In May 1864 as lot 1972 Woodward described this: "1824 Very Fine, rare." Realized $10. In his September 1869 sale of the Edward B. Taylor Collection, Woodward described lot 437: "1824 Quarter eagle Very Fine; Uncirculated condition." Realized $7.25. In October 1875 as lot 192 Cogan offered this in the Col. Mendes I. Cohen Collection sale, another of the great bargains in this sale with below-market results: "1824 Almost Proof." Realized $3.25.

In the Chapman brothers' sale of the Thomas Cleneay Collection in December 1890 this was included: Lot 712: "1824 over 1821. Extremely Fine. Very rare." Realized $8.75. This is an early description of the overdate feature of the variety; most often the variety was simply designated as 1824. The same coin was sold as lot 940 by Thomas L. Elder in his March 1911 sale of the William H. Woodin Collection: "1824, over '21. Uncirculated, with luster, the obverse is Proof. Extremely rare in this condition. Cleneay Collection. Record $50." Realized $51. The Chapmans described lot 538 in April 1904 in their sale of the John G. Mills Collection: "1824 Over 1821. Uncirculated. Proof surface. Very rare." Realized $27. Fifteen years later Henry Chapman offered the Mills coin as lot 5794 in his December 1921 sale of the John Story Jenks Collection: "1824 over 1821. Semi Proof, Uncirculated. Sharp even impression. A most beautiful specimen. Extremely rare so fine. From Mills Collection, 1904." Realized $125.

In June 1941 B. Max Mehl's sale of the William Forrester Dunham Collection included lot 1915: "1824/21. As all are. An imperceptible pin-point nick in field of reverse. Extremely Fine, with considerable mint luster. Very rare. Listed up to $100." Realized $92.50. In June 1946 Mehl's sale of the William Cutler Atwater Collection included lot 1928: "1824 over '21, as all are. (None minted in 1822 and 1823.) About Uncirculated with mint luster. Rare. Record $140." Realized $130.

PROOFS

Estimated Total Population (Proof). 2 or 3, one of which is a hybrid or semi-proof, the Cleneay-Woodin coin, called by Breen (1988) a one-sided Proof, "mirror obverse field, frosty reverse field." Whether such a coin should be included in the Proof roster is a matter of debate; for the present it is included on page 87 under circulation strikes. A Proof is in the Mint Collection (now in the Smithsonian; *Sylloge* no. 195).[5]

Proof Die Data and Notes. The same dies used to produce circulation strikes were used to make Proofs.

Selected Proof Auction Records

In January 1884 in his sale of the Heman Ely Collection, W. Elliot Woodward described lot 891: "1824 Proof, very rare." Realized $8.75. As to whether this was the same coin is not known: Lot 1943 in Woodward's sale in October later in the same year: "1824 Proof impression, very rare." Realized $9.10. In June 1885 in his J. Colvin Randall Collection sale lot 969 was offered: "1824 Proof; rare." Realized $8.50.

F-12	VF-20	EF-40	AU-50	AU-55	MS-60	MS-63
$6,250	$9,500	$14,000	$16,500	$18,750	$32,500	$80,000

1825

Circulation-Strike Mintage: 4,434 (calendar-year mintage; not all necessarily have this date)

Proof Mintage: Unknown, but small

Three die combinations.

In 1859, Dr. Montroville W. Dickeson wrote (probably without knowledge, but presciently) in the *American Numismatical Manual:* "One type and three varieties. Scarce."

Estimated Total Population (Mint State). 15 to 25.

Estimated Total Population (Circulated Grades). 100 to 125. Very Fine, Extremely Fine, and About Uncirculated coins represent the most available issue of the Capped Head to Left, Large Diameter, quarter eagle, although the quantity is so small that by any account the 1825 is a rarity.

BD gives these estimated populations: BD-1, 12 to 15; BD-2, 80 to 100; BD-3, 12 to 15.

Characteristics of Striking and Die Notes. The quality of strike varies from slightly struck at the centers to boldly struck. Partway through the year, reverse die 1821A cracked vertically on the reverse, in effect bisecting the die. The crack extends from the border between TA in STATES, down to the scroll, to the eagle's wing and body to the left of the shield, to the right side of the large numeral 2, and on to the border below. This rendered the die unfit for further use and is the reason for employing die A for the rest of the year's coinage.

Selected Auction Records

Note: The present BD varieties were not known or described by early catalogers.

An early offering was lot 703 in Edward Cogan's April 1860 sale: "1825 Fine condition, and scarce." Realized $3.87½. The George F. Seavey Collection lot 462, cataloged by W.H. Strobridge, was sold in September 1863: "1825 Very Fine, rare." Realized $7. Cogan offered lot 438 in his September 1869 sale of the Edward B. Taylor Collection: "1825 Very Fine; Uncirculated condition." Realized $5.50. The December 1871 offering of the Dr. Charles Clay Collection by W.H. Strobridge included lot 1108: "1825 Uncirculated, nearly Proof; in this condition, rare." Realized $5. As might be expected from reading the present narrative to this point, lot 193 in Cogan's October 1875 sale of the Col. Mendes I. Cohen Collection laid an egg: "1825 About as good." Realized $3. The preceding lot, an 1824 $2.50, had been described as "Almost Proof."

Scott & Co.'s 40th sale, March 1882, included lot 116: "1825 Small stars; Very Fine and very rare." Realized $5.10. Mention of the star size was unusual; although all 1825 half eagles have the same size stars, the stars on the 1821, 1824/1, and 1825 are smaller than on the 1826 and 1827. The auction house of Bangs & Co. offered lot 667 in October 1884: "1825 Quarter eagle Very Fine. Has been Proof. Rare." Realized $6.50. In his 1907 fixed-price list Elmer S. Sears offered two: Lot 154: "1825 A beautiful Uncirculated example with bright yellow mint bloom. Perfectly centered, sharp, and a gem of the highest order. $30." Lot 155: "1825 Another Extremely Fine, with Proof surface. $25." In May 1913 the U.S. Coin Co.'s sale of the Malcolm N. Jackson Collection included lot 107: "1825 Extremely Fine, barely touched by circulation; sharp, well struck piece. Very rare." Realized $26.

In June 1941 B. Max Mehl's sale of the William Forrester Dunham Collection included lot 1916: "1825 Beautiful Uncirculated specimen; sharp, with brilliant semi-Proof luster. Extremely rare so choice." Realized $105. In June 1946 Mehl's sale of the William Cutler Atwater Collection included lot 1929: "1825. Beautiful brilliant Uncirculated specimen, almost equal to a Proof. A little gem. I won't say that this is the finest specimen known, but I certainly feel justified in saying that I believe that a better specimen does not exist. Record up to $180.00." Realized $115. In November 1956 New Netherlands' sale of the Thomas L. Gaskill Collection included lot 193: "1825 First variety; reverse of 1821, 2 (on rev.) away from leaf. Extremely Fine; desirable proof-like lustre. A nicely centered coin with well-defined borders, showing only a few hundred more struck than of 1824/1. From H. Chapman's huge Earle sale of 1912, lot 2512; the WGC sale, lot 92. The second variety of 1825 has the reverse later used in 1826–7, with the 2 much closer to the leaf. It generally occurs in Proof, and is of extreme rarity." Realized $105.

Proofs

Estimated Total Population (Proof). 2 or 3.

Proof Die Data and Notes. Bass-Dannreuther suggests that all Proofs are of the BD-2 variety.

Selected Proof Auction Records

W. Elliot Woodward's May 1864 sale of the John F. McCoy Collection included lot 1973: "1825 Splendid Proof; as Proof, very rare." Realized $8.50. Woodward described lot 892 in his January 1884 sale of the Heman Ely Collection: "1825 Proof, very rare." Realized $8.50, possibly to Chapman.

F-12	VF-20	EF-40	AU-50	AU-55	MS-60	MS-63
$6,250	$7,750	$14,000	$16,500	$17,500	$30,000	$65,000

1826

Circulation-Strike Mintage: 760 (calendar-year mintage)

Proof Mintage: Unknown, but small

Earlier sometimes called "1826, 6 Over 5." Large obverse stars. Rarest Mint State Capped Head to Left, Large Diameter, quarter eagle.

The number of extant specimens of the 1826 suggests that the published mintage of 760—delivered on February 19, 1836—may not represent the total number made of this *date.* Perhaps the obverse die was used in 1827 as well; this seems likely, considering that today the 1826 is only slightly less rare than the 1827. The calendar-year mintage for 1826 (760) plus the calendar-year mintage for 1827 (2,800) totals 3,560.

In 1859, Dr. Montroville W. Dickeson wrote in the *American Numismatical Manual:* "One type and two varieties. Very rare." If Dickeson actually studied and observed two die varieties, this represents their first confirmation in print. However, much of Dickeson's other die information for quarter eagles of the era is guesswork and is often far off the mark.

Estimated Total Population (Mint State). 4 to 6. The 1826 wins the rarity sweepstakes for the Capped Head to Left, Large Diameter, quarter eagle. Exceedingly rare.

Estimated Total Population (Circulated Grades). 25 to 35. The 1826 quarter eagle, while very rare, is more readily available than the mintage figure of 760 would indicate.

The certification data suggest that circulated 1826 quarter eagles are more plentiful than those dated 1821 and 1824, but appearances in old-time collections and other auction events do not substantiate this. Often, even large collections have lacked an 1826.

Characteristics of Striking and Die Notes. These coins are usually seen well struck. In addition, the dies clashed during the coinage, so some specimens show light impressions of the obverse die on the reverse of the coin, and vice versa.

Selected Auction Records

Note: Compared to earlier quarter eagles the 1826 brought high prices in most early sales. This is because the published mintage was viewed as the precise mintage for this date—in an era before researchers studied and analyzed Mint records.

Lot 463 in W.H. Strobridge's September 1863 sale of the George A. Seavey Collection: "1826 Good, rare." Realized $12. W. Elliot Woodward's description of lot 1668 in his October 1864 sale of the Levick, Emery, Ilsley, Abbey Collections: "1826 Nearly Proof, rare." Realized $26, one of the higher prices for quarter eagles in the sale. As might be expected by numismatic historians, the coin in Edward Cogan's October 1875 sale of the Col. Mendes I. Cohen Collection brought below market: "1826 Fine." Realized $8. Lot 62 in the Scott Stamp & Coin Co.'s November 1888 sale of the Rev. W. Foster Ely Collection: "1826 Very Fine, extremely rare." Realized $50.

In his 1907 fixed-price list Elmer S. Sears offered lot 156: "1826 Extremely Fine, with much Proof surface. Of excessive rarity and but few collectors have, or ever will have a specimen. $225." In March of the same year S.H. Chapman offered lot 169 in his sale of the David S. Wilson Collection: "1826 Very Fine. Excessively rare." Realized $190. Chapman's description of lot 370 in his May 1914 sale of the William F. Gable Collection: "1826 Border broader and heavier. Extremely Fine, with slight Proof surface. Minute nick on nose. Excessively rare, the rarest date of quarter eagles, and one of the finest known. Note:—The collection lacks 1827, very rare. None struck in 1828." Sold for $220. This coin reappeared in B. Max Mehl's November 1939 sale of the William B. Hale Collection as lot 751: "1826 Just a shade from Uncirculated, with semi-proof surface. From the Gable Sale in 1915 [*sic*]. (Cost $220.) Catalogs up to $350. One of the real rarities of the American gold series." Realized $315.

In June 1941 Mehl's sale of the William Forrester Dunham Collection included lot 1917: "1826/25 as all are. Practically Uncirculated; in fact the coin is Uncirculated with just the slightest cabinet friction, as it has full bright mint luster. Excessively rare. One of the rarest of American gold coins. A similar specimen in my Sale of the Hale Collection brought $315." Realized $195. Mehl's June 1946 sale of the William Cutler Atwater Collection included lot 1930: "1826 over '25, as all are. Practically Uncirculated with almost full mint luster. Originally purchased by Mr. Atwater as Uncirculated. One of the rarest of our early quarter-eagles. Only 760 minted. Record of $350.00." Mehl's May 1950 sale of the Jerome Kern Collection included lot 15: "1826 Uncirculated; brilliant mint luster, slightly frosty. Just the barest evidence of cabinet friction. Only a total of 760 specimens minted and of which number undoubted only an infinitesimal number exist today. Auction record $350. Priced at private sale for much more. This specimen from the famous Colonel Green Collection." Realized $315.

New Netherlands' June 1957 sale of Eliasberg duplicates included lot 571: "1826/5. Large stars as in 1827; just the single variety. High rarity 6, only 760 coined. Extremely Fine, with much original proof-like luster, a sharp, vivid impression. Neatly centered and definitely attractive, but careful examination reveals several minute handling nicks and scratches. Comparable to the Judge Gaskill piece in our last sale at $245. Likewise on a par with the Dunham, Atwater, Kern and Menjou offerings (which probably represented only three different coins). More desirable than the extensively scratched Melish lot for $225. From the Mehl sold Curtis coll. (Jan 1942), later 'Lee' 998. The high records for this year, William B. Hale (Mehl, 1939) $315., Bell $350., Kern $315., are above what the coin has been bringing as of late, but will appear low when collectors take seriously the tiny mintages. At least one hundred times rarer than a 1936 Proof Set!" Realized $260.

Proofs

Estimated Total Population (Proof). 2 or 3. Data are sketchy. A Proof is in the Mint Collection (now in the Smithsonian; *Sylloge* no. 204).

Proof Die Data and Notes. From the same dies used to make circulation strikes.

Selected Proof Auction Records

In May 1864 W. Elliot Woodward described lot 1974 in the John F. McCoy Collection: "1826 Proof, very scarce in any condition, and scarcely ever met with so fine as this." Realized the impressive sum of $81. As noted, for many coins the McCoy sale was the high-water mark in prices of the decade. What seems to have been the same coin slept as lot 893 in Woodward's January 1884 sale of the Ely Collection: "1826 Proof, scarce in any condition, and as Proof, very rare. McCoy Sale." Realized $14.25 to Chapman.

F-12	VF-20	EF-40	AU-50	AU-55	MS-60
$10,000	$12,500	$16,500	$25,000	$35,000	$62,500

1827

Circulation-Strike Mintage: 2,800 (calendar-year mintage)

Proof Mintage: Small, if any

Large obverse stars. Second-rarest Capped Head to Left, Large Diameter, date.

In calendar year 1827, some 2,800 quarter eagles were delivered in one batch on February 19. It seems likely that some of the pieces were from the 1826 obverse die (see notes under the "Circulation strike mintage" for 1826).

Estimated Total Population (Mint State). 6 to 9. Data are inconclusive, but in any event there are very few Mint State coins in existence.

In 1975 David W. Akers considered the 1827 to be very rare, challenging the 1826 in this regard. Moreover, "Choice specimens of this date are extremely rare and are, in my opinion, less available than for any other date of this type." However, at a later point in time, as reflected by the August 1999 *PCGS Population Report*, there was just one certification of a Mint State 1826 as compared to a remarkable 16 for 1827! While hyper-activity in the resubmission department could be a factor, it does seem likely that more Mint State coins are known today than were evident in 1975. Perhaps a small group was found. Certainly, the auction catalogs of "name" collections do not reflect such availability!

Estimated Total Population (Circulated Grades). 40 to 50, mostly in About Uncirculated grades. A prime American gold coin rarity, but not widely recognized as such, these are seldom offered for sale in any grade. This is more readily available than the 1826, but only slightly so.

Characteristics of Striking and Die Notes. Usually these are well struck except for certain details below the word LIBERTY. Some or all 1827 quarter eagles have a faint trace of clashed dies in the reverse field, below the left side of the scroll, from contact with the *1826* obverse die during the 1826 coinage.

Selected Auction Records

Note: Prices are generally much lower than for 1826. The guiding star was the calendar mintage figure for 1826, which was much larger than for 1827.

William H. Strobridge's September 1863 George F. Seavey Collection had this description for lot 464: "1827 Uncirculated, scarce." Realized $11. In May 1864 W. Elliot Woodward's John F. McCoy Collection sale included lot 1975: "1827 Splendid, almost Proof, rare." Realized $8.50. Edward Cogan's September 1869 sale of the Edward B. Taylor Collection included lot 439: "1827 Quarter eagle Very Fine; Uncirculated condition." Realized $5.50.

Over the years a number of auction listings have described a Proof *obverse* (also see the Proof notes below). Two samples are as follows. Woodward's May 1883 sale of the Winslow Lewis Collection included lot 2024: "1827 Splendid, obverse Proof." Realized $7.20. John W. Haseltine's 69th sale, June 1883, described lot 432: "1827 A beautiful piece. Obverse proof. Very rare." Realized $8.12½. In the same month Haseltine's 70th sale had a coin with, seemingly, a regular or non-Proof obverse: "1827 Quarter eagle. Uncirculated. Very handsome." Realized $7. B. Max Mehl's November 1939 sale of the William B. Hale Collection included lot 752: "1827 Uncirculated; highest portions show slight cabinet friction; full milled borders with sharp stars. Excessively rare. Seldom offered. Listed up to $175." Realized $157.50. *Cabinet friction* was a very popular numismatic term until the 1980s, when modifying the term *Uncirculated* described a coin equal to today's high-level About Uncirculated (AU-55 or AU-58). In June 1941 Mehl's sale of the William Forrester Dunham Collection had lot 1918: "1827 Uncirculated, with frosty mint surface. The highest portions show just the slightest cabinet friction, but every star is bold and full. Another great rarity. Catalogs at $175. A specimen not quite as choice in my Sale of the Hale Collection brought $157.50." Realized $100.

In June 1946 Mehl's sale of the William Cutler Atwater Collection included lot 1931: "1827 About Uncirculated, strong impression with frosty mint surface. Just the very slightest cabinet friction. Rare and valuable. Record over $200." Realized $175.

Proofs

Estimated Total Population (Proof). None confirmed.

Walter Breen in his monograph (1964) commented, "None seen in Proof; only one reported so, and the report is unverified." In his *New Varieties of $1, $2.50 and $5.00 United States Gold* (1968), an expansion appeared: "The Proof reported is Woodside 943, ex Cleneay [at the 1890 Cleneay sale it was simply called "Fine. Rare" by the Chapman brothers], and also one-sided, the reverse being of Proof sharpness but with mint bloom (unpolished die). On all genuine 'one-sided Proofs' the obverse is perfection with mirror surfaces, the reverse with mint bloom; this holds for all denominations in which they are known."

David W. Akers knew of no Proofs of this year. No confirmation found of their existence. None is in the Mint Collection (which has two circulation strikes).

F-12	VF-20	EF-40	AU-50	AU-55	MS-60	MS-63
$6,500	$9,000	$13,100	$17,500	$19,500	$35,000	$65,000

Capped Head to Left, Reduced Diameter (1829–1834)

Designer: *John Reich, modified by William Kneass.* **Weight:** *4.37 grams.* **Composition:** *.9167 gold, .0833 silver and copper.* **Diameter:** *18.2 mm.* **Edge:** *Reeded.* **Mint:** *Philadelphia.*

Design Modification

In 1829, engraver William Kneass made slight modifications to the quarter eagle dies, including reducing the diameter further, to 18.2 mm.

On the obverse the stars are closer to the border as a result of the narrower diameter, with the spacing appearing especially tight above Miss Liberty's head. The stars were punched into each die by hand and thus vary slightly in their relation to each other, to the denticles, etc. Dates were entered into the working dies by hand, one digit at a time.

On the reverse the letters are closer to the border. On both obverse and reverse the denticles are shorter and differently formed than on the pre-1829 issues, which have beadlike denticles (sometimes described as a "beaded" border, although this is a misnomer). The rim appears more prominent than on the earlier issues. The entire effect is less delicate than on quarter eagles of the 1821–1827 years. Certain punches may have been cut by Christian Gobrecht, who at the time performed work under contract to the Mint (he later joined the Mint staff, in 1835).

In 1832, William Kneass modified the portrait very slightly. The details of certain hair curls (such as below LIBERTY, especially below the B, and at the bottom of the portrait) are different, and the relief of the head appears to be more "solid." The obverse border is more prominent. This portrait was employed through early 1834.

Mintages were low for each year. Perhaps a few dozen Proofs were struck, but original information is virtually nonexistent except for pieces made in 1834 for presentation sets. Complicating the question is the use of polished dies to create prooflike circulation strikes.

Numismatic Considerations

All quarter eagles of 1829–1834 are rare today. Most examples seen are in grades of Extremely Fine and About Uncirculated, although scattered Uncirculated pieces have appeared at auction, as have a few Proofs. Today, many if not most coins certified as lower-level Mint State are what David Akers and others would have called About Uncirculated decades ago. It is not unusual for an Uncirculated piece to have a prooflike surface, this being truer for this type than for the earlier dates (1821–1827).

Although each and every Capped Head to Left, Reduced Diameter, quarter eagle is a rarity, the winner for the very rarest goes to the 1834. Apparently, most of these were melted at the Mint. In 1860, Mint Director Snowden, commenting on the 1834 coinage, observed that no official record could be located of *any* being released.

From 1829 to 1834, just over 25,000 coins were struck. Many if not most were melted as soon as they fell into the hands of specie and bullion dealers. Probably no more than 400 to 500 coins, at best, survive today, this quantity being distributed among six different die combinations.

For each year only one obverse die was used. Two reverse dies were used, one in 1829 and the other from 1830 through 1834.

Dies and Known Die Combinations, 1829–1834

Quarter Eagles of 1829

1829, Obverse Die 1. Details can be found in Bass-Dannreuther.

1829, Reverse Die A. *The large 2 in the denominator has a straight base;* definitive. *Details:* The tip of the leaf at upper left is under the right upright and right side of U in UNITED. The O in OF is over the space between the N and U in UNUM. The lowest arrowhead, which is also the shortest of the three arrowheads, has its tip under the left side of C in AMERICA. This die was used only in 1829. As no specimen has been recorded with a "fatal break," it is unknown why its use was not continued into later years.

1829, BD-1: Dies 1-A. This is the only known die combination.

Quarter Eagles of 1830

1830, Obverse Die 1. *The date is high, with 83 close. Details:* The lowest part of the curl is over the left side of 0 in 1830.

1830, Reverse Die A. *The 2 in the denominator is large and has a curved base;* definitive. *Details:* The tip of the leaf at upper left is under the center of U in UNITED; the U is sharply repunched. The O in OF is over the right upright of the N in UNUM. The lowest arrowhead, which is also the shortest of the three arrowheads, has its tip under the lower right side of C in AMERICA. A prominent center dot is in the horizontal stripes of the shield high above and slightly to the left of the second vertical stripe element. This is the final die of the type and was continued in use from 1829 through the first part of 1834.

1830, BD-1: Dies 1-A. This is the only known die combination.

Quarter Eagles of 1831

1831, Obverse Die 1. *The date is evenly spaced; the bases of 83 are low. Details:* The center of the curl is over tip of upper left serif of the final 1.

1830, Reverse Die A. The final die of the type, this reverse die was continued in use from 1830 through the first part of 1834. It is described in detail above, with the other die of that year.

1831, BD-1: Dies 1-1830A. Although this is the only known die combination, there is a possibility of another variety being known for this year. In his April 1886 sale of the J.S. Twining Collection, W. Elliot Woodward offered lot 950, a Proof 1831, followed by lot 951, described as: "1831 Different die; nearly equal to the last, scarce." The relevant auction record is cited in the 1831 listing.

Quarter Eagles of 1832

1832, Obverse Die 1. *The 1 in 1832 is high and close to the bust. The 2 has a curled base. Details:* The center of the curl is over the ball of the 2. In 1832, engraver William Kneass modified the portrait very slightly. The detail of certain hair curls is very slightly different, and the relief of the head appears to be more "solid." The obverse border is more prominent. This portrait was employed through 1834.

1830, Reverse Die A. The final die of the type, this reverse die was continued in use from 1830 through the first part of 1834. It is described in detail on page 95, with the other die of that year.

1832, BD-1: Dies 1-1830A. This is the only known die combination.

Quarter Eagles of 1833

1833, Obverse Die 1. *The date is high; the 1 is close to the bust; the top of the 8 is high. Details:* The bottom of the curl is quite close to the top of the second 3. There is a small gap in the denticles slightly past star 10.

1830, Reverse Die A. The final die of the type, this reverse die was continued in use from 1830 through the first part of 1834. It is described in detail on page 95, with the other die of that year.

1833, BD-1: Dies 1-1830A. This is the only known die combination.

Quarter Eagles of 1834

1834, With Motto, Obverse Die 1: *The 1 in 1834 is close to the bust. Details:* The bottom of the curl is about on a level with the top of the upright of the 4 and to the left of it. The denticles are small and irregular, indicating that either the master die was impressed shallowly into the working die, or that the working die was relapped. However, as the star rays are bold, relapping does not seem probable.

1830, Reverse Die A: The final die of the type, this reverse die was continued in use from 1830 through the first part of 1834. It is described in detail on page 95, with the other die of that year.

1834, BD-1: Dies 1-1830A. Only one die combination of the With Motto reverse has been confirmed for this year, but in the early twentieth century Edgar H. Adams and John H. Clapp mentioned a second; see Bass-Dannreuther for details.

GRADING STANDARDS

Note: Please see the grading standards given for Capped Head to Left, Large Diameter, quarter eagles (page 82).

1829

Circulation-Strike Mintage: 3,403

Proof Mintage: Unknown, but small

First year of reduced diameter. Only use of this reverse die.

The entire production was delivered on February 9, 1829, probably all dated 1829 and of the new type.

Walter Breen, who would become very prominent in numismatic research during the 1950s, was near the beginning of his numismatic career when he wrote "How Our Coinage Became Mechanized," which was published in the March 1951 edition of *The Numismatist.* The following excerpt is relevant to the quarter eagles and half eagles of 1829:

> Returning to the mechanization of our coinage, we see that the next step came with some improvements the engraver Kneass initiated in 1828 and afterwards. The principal features of these are the resumption for the first time since 1793 of beads in the borders instead of serrations or radial lines, and a much cleaner execution and finish in the devices. In 1828 the dimes with small date exhibit this new technique; the following year Kneass used it on the quarter-eagles and the Small Date "type of 1830" half-eagles, and when half-dime coinage was resumed July 4, 1829 (the same day on which construction of the new Mint building and its machinery began) these also bore the same improvements. After a short lapse, the half-cents and quarter dollars appeared in 1831 with the same techniques, and by 1834 all the coined denominations had benefited to some extent thereby. These techniques in part seem to have coincided with the 1833 removal of the Mint to larger quarters at Juniper and Chestnut streets, with still further (but only vaguely indicated) improvements in the machinery.

Estimated Total Population (Mint State). 15 to 25. Although this is the lowest-mintage issue of the modified 1829–1834 type, it is more often seen in high grades than the typical coin of this design.

Estimated Total Population (Circulated Grades). 55 to 70. Most are in the Extremely Fine and About Uncirculated categories, typically with prooflike areas.

Characteristics of Striking and Die Notes. These are usually seen with light striking at the center of the reverse, in the areas near the shield. Many if not most have at least some prooflike surface in the fields. Some have prooflike surface on the obverse but not on the reverse, equal to or at least resembling the so-called "one-sided Proofs" of this era.

Selected Auction Records

W. Elliott Woodward's September 1879 sale of the George W. Pratt Collection included lot 1203: "1829 Sharp, nearly Proof impression, scarce." Realized $3.10. The June 1890 New York Coin & Stamp Co. sale of the Lorin Parmelee Collection included lot 990 under the coinage of 1829: "Quarter Eagle: sharp, perfect proof; rare." Realized $11.50. The same coin appeared as lot 944 in Thomas L. Elder's March 1911 sale of the William H. Woodin Collection: "1829. Perfect, sharp impression, Uncirculated, brilliant, with Proof surface. A gem in every particular. Rare. Parmelee Collection." Realized $66. In May 1913 the U.S. Coin Co.'s sale of the Malcolm N. Jackson Collection included lot 110: "1829 About Uncirculated. Sharp, beautiful impression with Proof surface. Very rare." Realized $35. In June 1941 B. Max Mehl's sale of the William Forrester Dunham Collection included lot 1919: "1829 Brilliant Uncirculated; obverse is equal to a Proof. The highest portions show just the barest touch of cabinet friction. Last record, $62.50." Realized $58.50.

In June 1946 Mehl's sale of the William Cutler Atwater Collection included lot 1932: "1829. (None minted in 1828.) Listed in Mr. Atwater's private catalog as a Proof, and I have seen specimens listed as brilliant Proof which were no better than this. I would rather play safe and describe this coin as a brilliant semi-proof, nearly equal to a brilliant Proof. Record $125 and certainly this specimen is worthy of its highest record." Realized $85. Mehl's May 1950 sale of the Jerome Kern Collection included lot 17: "1829. Brilliant semi-Proof. A beautiful specimen, and as such, quite rare. Originally purchased as a Proof. Record $125." Realized $115. In April 1956 Abe Kosoff's sale of the Melish and Hester Collections described lot 1116: "1829 Uncirculated." Realized $90.

PROOFS

Estimated Total Population (Proof). 4 to 7. Walter Breen (1988) suggested that "at least 8, possibly 12" Proofs are known. However, if this is the case, they certainly are elusive in the marketplace today. Most are impaired, suggesting that some may have been issued as souvenirs to mark the first year of the modified design or, perhaps, in connection with the inauguration of President Andrew Jackson (the quarter eagle being the smallest gold coin issued at the time, and thus ideal for presentation or gift purposes, similar to the situation years later when certain 1848 quarter eagles were struck as souvenirs from California gold). A Proof is in the Mint Collection (now in the Smithsonian; *Sylloge* no. 215). The citations given below reflect extensive offerings of Proofs over a long period of time. How many would qualify as Proofs if reexamined today is not known. The historical record is inconclusive—the Winsor Collection coin (1895), cited below, being an example.

Proof Die Data and Notes. Over the years a number of pieces have been described as having Proof obverses and lustrous (Mint State) reverses; some have called these one-sided Proofs. The same die pair was used for circulation strikes.

Selected Proof Auction Records

In May 1864 W. Elliot Woodward's John F. McCoy Collection sale included lot 1976: "1829 Proof, scarce." Realized $8.50. In October 1875 sale of the Col. Mendes I. Cohen Collection by Edward Cogan lot 196 joined many other coins selling at basement prices, for reasons not known today: "1829 Fine Proof." Realized $3. Another coin, also seemingly a bargain, was offered by Cogan in his April 1877 sale: Lot 354: "1829 Fine Proof, and scarce." Realized $3.50. Woodward's sale of lot 2025 in his May 1882 sale of the Winslow Lewis Collection reached a high spot in the market: "1829 Splendid Proof, rare." Realized $12. In contrast was lot 1417 in Woodward's sale of the German Collection in October 1883: "1829 Splendid Proof, scarce." Realized $4.75.

The grade and format of this coin from the December 1895 sale of the Richard B. Winsor Collection by the Chapman brothers is hard to determine today. Lot 330: "1829. . . . Extremely Fine, brilliant. Three small nicks on edge of reverse. Rare." The same coin was offered decades later by New Netherlands Coin Co. as lot 196 in its November 1956 sale of the Thomas L. Gaskill Collection: "1829 New type, with beaded border within raised rim, like that on the dime and half dime of the year; Kneass's improved design. Extremely Fine, considerable Proof surface; minor rubbing in fields, a wire edge with two or three almost microscopic nicks on it. Undoubtedly an impaired Proof; only one pair of dies known for this date, and Proofs were struck from them. Just 3,404 made in all, Richard B. Winsor collection, lot 330." Realized $80.

In his 1907 fixed-price list Elmer S. Sears offered lot 158: "1829 A perfect Brilliant Proof. As rare in this condition as any of the foregoing. $50." In June 1941 B. Max Mehl's sale of the William Forrester Dunham Collection included lot 1919: "1829 Brilliant Uncirculated; obverse is equal to a Proof. The highest portions show just the barest touch of cabinet friction. Last record, $62.50." Realized $58.50. In June 1957 New Netherlands described lot 573 in its sale of Eliasberg duplicates: "1829. New type, with beaded border within raised rim; Kneass's improved design, as on the Half Dimes, Dimes and late half eagles of this year. Only one variety of the date. High rarity 4 (as a date); only 3,404 coined (in all). Brilliant, but slightly imperfect Proof. This coin, which retains practically is full original surface, got into circulation just long enough to acquire slight rubbing in the fields, faint evidence of contact with other coins, one or two infinitesimal nicks upon the high obverse border. Rarity 7 as a Proof. Besides this piece and the impaired Winsor-Gaskill example, we can trace but three others: Eliasberg, W.G.C.-Memorable, Menjou (impaired), or only five specimens in all. Ex 'Lee' 1000 as 'A beautiful Brilliant Proof with high wire edge, just like it left the Mint.'" Realized $137.

F-12	VF-20	EF-40	AU-50	AU-55	MS-60	MS-63
$6,000	$7,250	$9,500	$14,000	$17,500	$22,500	$35,000

1830

Circulation-Strike Mintage: 4,540 (calendar-year mintage)

Proof Mintage: Unknown, but tiny

Estimated Total Population (Mint State). 40 to 55. Of the quarter eagles of the modified type (1829–1834), this is the most commonly available in Mint State, including in gem preservation, with many appearing in the PCGS and NGC reports. However, at any given time a Mint State example may be very hard to find. Moreover, on a historical basis—as reflected by auction appearances years ago—gems are very rare.

Most have handling marks, ranging from a few to many, the appearance of which is made all the more obvious by the prooflike character of the fields of most specimens.

Estimated Total Population (Circulated Grades). 40 to 55. Most are in the About Uncirculated category. The 1830 is often seen with marks and nicks (not unexpected for these grades, but such marks are mentioned more than usual in past auction citations, a small sample of which follows).

Characteristics of Striking and Die Notes. Most are well struck and with prooflike surfaces. Some are more prooflike on the obverse than on the reverse.

Selected Auction Records

Augustus B. Sage in February 1859 offered the Henry Bogert Collection with lot 1212: "1830 Curious head. *Very Fine.*" Realized $3.25 to Thompson. William H. Strobridge's September 1863 George F. Seavey Collection had this description for lot 466: "1830 Very Fine, scarce." Realized $5. In May 1864 W. Elliot Woodward's John F. McCoy Collection sale included lot 1977: "1830 Very fine indeed, Uncirculated, scarce." Realized $6.50. Lot 624 was described by S.K. Harzfeld in his 15th sale, November 1880: "1830 Uncirculated." Realized $4.10, the same price realized for several other dates in the early 1830s. In his 25th sale, December 1884, Dr. George W. Massamore described lot 943: "1830 Uncirculated, rare." Realized $4.60. The 1830 quarter eagle was not gaining much traction on the marketplace.

Into the twentieth century, in his 1907 fixed-price list Elmer S. Sears offered lot 160: "1830 Uncirculated, with Proof surface. Rare. $25." In May 1913 the U.S. Coin Co.'s sale of the Malcolm N. Jackson Collection included lot 111: "1830 Uncirculated. Fields very slightly rubbed, Proof surface. Very rare." Realized $20.50. In June 1941 B. Max Mehl's sale of the William Forrester Dunham Collection included lot 1920: "1830 Brilliant semi-proof; equal in every respect to a perfect Proof, with raised borders. Not a particularly rare date, but very rare so choice. Seldom found better than Very Fine." Realized $31. In November 1956 New Netherlands' sale of the Thomas L. Gaskill Collection included lot 197: "1830 Very similar to last; new reverse die, used until the change of type in 1834; U in UNITED recut. Choice Uncirculated. Highly lustrous." Realized $95.

Proofs

Estimated Total Population (Proof). 3 to 5. There are dozens of auction listings over the years, many of which were probably prooflike Mint State. A Proof is in the Mint Collection (now in the Smithsonian; *Sylloge* no. 221).

Proof Die Data and Notes. The same dies were used for Proofs and circulation strikes. Walter Breen (monograph, 1964) wrote, "The reverse die introduced for this year . . . was repolished at the beginning of each year to make a few Proofs . . . then put into the regular press to make business strikes. This process occurred also on half cents of 1833–4-5."

Selected Proof Auction Records

In the early days W. Elliot Woodward's offerings of Proofs included the following. September 1879, George W. Pratt Collection, lot 1204: "1830 Splendid, a Proof, scarce." Realized $4. May 1883, Winslow Lewis Collection, lot 2026: "1830 Splendid Proof, rare." Realized $7.50. June 1885, J. Colvin Randall Collection, lot 974: "1830 Uncirculated; a Proof impression; very scarce." Realized $4.60. This description is excellently representative of the highly subjective attribution of coins as *Proofs* during the nineteenth century. This coin could have been a prooflike Uncirculated coin, or it could have been a Proof that bore no marks of handling (circulation), thus an "Uncirculated Proof." Who knows?

F-12	VF-20	EF-40	AU-50	AU-55	MS-60	MS-63
$6,000	$7,250	$9,500	$14,000	$17,500	$22,500	$35,000

1831

Circulation-Strike Mintage: 4,520 (calendar-year mintage)

Proof Mintage: Unknown, but tiny

Estimated Total Population (Mint State). 30 to 45. Rare on an absolute basis, but one of the more readily available issues of this type, with many auction citations.

Estimated Total Population (Circulated Grades). 50 to 65. Most are in the About Uncirculated category.

Characteristics of Striking and Die Notes. These are usually well struck. The character of the fields ranges from frosty to somewhat prooflike, to nearly fully prooflike.

Selected Auction Records

In September 1869 Edward Cogan described lot 441 in his sale of the Edward B. Taylor Collection: "1831 Quarter eagle Very Fine; almost Proof and scarce." Realized $4. In Scott & Company's 40th Auction Sale, March 1882, lot 119 was offered: "1831 Head to left; Very Fine, rare." Realized $5.10. There was not much interest in this or other contemporary quarter eagles at the time (market interest was led by large copper cents). H.P. Smith's April 1887 sale of the Charles White Collection Part II included lot 479: "1831 Few light nicks. Fine." Realized $2.60 to Charles Steigerwalt, of Lancaster, Pennsylvania, who had traveled to New York City to attend the sale.

The John G. Mills Collection offered by the Chapman brothers in April 1904 included this lot 544: "1831 Uncirculated. Proof surface. Rare state." Realized $8.50. Advancing to February 1921, B. Max Mehl described lot 67 in the Dr. G.F.E. Wilharm Collection: "1831 Uncirculated, with Proof surface, nearly equal to a brilliant Proof. Rare, especially so choice." Realized $35. More than two decades later in June 1946 Mehl's sale of the William Cutler Atwater Collection included lot 1934: "1831 Brilliant Uncirculated with Proof surface; slight wear or cabinet friction on highest portions. Record up to $100." Realized $65. In November 1956 New Netherlands' sale of the Thomas L. Gaskill Collection included lot 198: "1831 'gem' Uncirculated. Impaired by two or three minute face scratches, visible only in a certain light. Also an early strike from dies which had lately made Proofs. A truly lovely piece, hampered perhaps (like so many of these), by our ultra-conservative descriptions. Slightly rarer than 1830." Realized $130. It seems questionable that a "gem" coin could have face scratches.

Proofs

Estimated Total Population (Proof). 6 to 10. Breen (1988) states "at least 8." Quality is better than, for example, the Proofs of 1829, with several pieces being in the choice and gem categories. A Proof is in the Mint Collection (now in the Smithsonian; *Sylloge* no. 227).

Proof Die Data and Notes. Proofs and circulation strikes were made from the same dies. As is true of many other quarter eagles of this type, the dividing line between a full Proof and a highly prooflike Mint State coin is not defined with precision, and various professional numismatists have had legitimate differences of opinion concerning the status of certain specimens.

Selected Proof Auction Records

In May 1864 W. Elliot Woodward's John F. McCoy Collection sale included lot 1978: "1831 Splendid Proof. As Proof, very rare." Realized $9.50. As is generally true of other McCoy prices, the realization was high for the time. George W. Cogan's sale of coins consigned by J. Colvin Randall in March 1882 offered lot 584: "1831 Proof" Realized $4.20. Woodward offered lot 2027 in his May 1883 sale of the Winslow Lewis Collection: "1831 Splendid Proof, rare." Realized $14. Repeating a previous citation, in April 1886 Woodward described the following two lots in the J.S. Twining Collection. First, lot 950: "1831 Proof, rare." Realized $3.60. Lot 951: "1831 Different die; nearly equal to the last, scarce." Realized $3.90. Under the coinage of 1831 in the Parmelee Collection catalog, New York Coin & Stamp Co. described lot 1004: "Quarter Eagle; sharp and perfect proof; rare." Realized $11.

Into the twentieth century, in his March 1911 sale of the William H. Woodin Collection, Thomas L. Elder offered lot 946: "1831. Brilliant, perfect Proof. The Stickney specimen sold for $31, which, judging by the subsequent advances in gold, was a low price. Excessively rare. Parmelee Collection." Realized $47. In May 1922 B. Max Mehl described lot 61 in the James Ten Eyck Collection: "1831. Proof, sharp. Very rare so choice. As perfect a specimen of this coin as I have ever seen." Realized $42. Lot 1118 of the April 1956 Thomas G. Melish Collection was described by Abe Kosoff: "1831. Brilliant Proof." Realized $130.

F-12	VF-20	EF-40	AU-50	AU-55	MS-60	MS-63	PF-63	PF-64
$6,000	$7,250	$9,500	$14,000	$17,500	$22,500	$35,000	$100,000	$150,000

1832

Circulation-Strike Mintage: 4,400 (calendar-year mintage)

Proof Mintage: Unknown, but tiny

Portrait slightly modified.

Estimated Total Population (Mint State). 15 to 20. In Mint State the 1832 is very scarce.

Estimated Total Population (Circulated Grades). 60 to 80. Most are in the About Uncirculated category.

Characteristics of Striking and Die Notes. The field surfaces vary from slightly prooflike to nearly fully prooflike. The date is usually found well struck, although some may have a lightness in the hair below the word LIBERTY.

Selected Auction Records

W.H. Strobridge's September 1863 George F. Seavey Collection had this description for lot 468: "1832 Very Fine, scarce." Realized $6. In May 1864 W. Elliot Woodward's John F. McCoy Collection sale included lot 1979: "1832 Very Fine, scarce." Realized $7.50. Lot 626 in S.K. Harzfeld's 15th Sale, November 1880: "1832 Uncirculated." Realized $4.10, the same price realized for several other dates in the early 1830s. W. Elliot Woodward's September 1885 sale of the J. Colvin Randall Collection included this lot 1052: "1832 Nearly Proof." Realized $3.80.

In June 1907 Henry Chapman offered the Matthew Adams Stickney Collection, which included lot 741: "1832 Extremely Fine. Scarce." Realized $11. In May 1913 the U.S. Coin Co.'s sale of the Malcolm N. Jackson Collection included lot 113: "1832 Extremely Fine, only faint traces of circulation, very rare." Realized $20.25. In June 1941 B. Max Mehl's sale of the William Forrester Dunham Collection included lot 1922: "1832 Beautiful Uncirculated specimen with frosty mint surface; raised borders. Very rare so choice." Realized $34.25. In November 1956 New Netherlands' sale of the Thomas L. Gaskill Collection included lot 199: "1832 Mostly brilliant Uncirculated. Infinitesimal evidence of 'bag handling.' In a class with the last; 4,400 pieces made. The Melish coin realized $100 against an $85. estimate. This was lot 741 in the fabulous 1907 Stickney sale." Realized $115.

Proofs

Estimated Total Population (Proof). 4 to 6. No Proof is in the Mint Collection (which has two circulation strikes).

Proof Die Data and Notes. Proof quarter eagles of 1832 were struck from the same dies used to make circulation strikes.

Selected Proof Auction Records

In May 1883, W. Elliot Woodward's Sale of the Winslow Lewis Collection included lot 2028: "1832 Splendid Proof, rare." Realized $11. Woodward's December 1885 sale of the Matthews, Randall, and Levick Collections included lot 1043: "1832 Sharp, Proof impression." Realized $3. Lot 1044: "1832 Another; Proof, slightly haymarked." Realized $3. Thomas L. Elder's March 1911 sale of the William H. Woodin Collection included lot 947: "1832. Proof, with slight nick. Very rare so fine. Wilson specimen, Uncirculated, sold for $28. Davis Collection." Realized $25. Decades later in March 1948, in a slump period in the coin market, Numismatic Gallery's sale of the Memorable Collection included lot 92: "1832. Brilliant Proof. Faint cheek lines." Realized $40.

F-12	VF-20	EF-40	AU-50	AU-55	MS-60	MS-63
$6,000	$7,250	$9,500	$14,000	$17,500	$22,500	$37,500

1833

Circulation-Strike Mintage:
4,160 (calendar-year mintage)
Proof Mintage: Unknown, but tiny

Especially rare in Mint State.

Estimated Total Population (Mint State). 6 to 9, including a few gems. The 1833 is especially rare in Mint State, and only a few seem to have survived.

Estimated Total Population (Circulated Grades). 50 to 70. Most are in the Extremely Fine and About Uncirculated categories.

Characteristics of Striking and Die Notes. On many, if not most, the die was polished at Miss Liberty's chin and, especially, on the neck below the ear; this is noticeable on high-grade pieces. The date is usually found well struck.

Selected Auction Records

In May 1864 W. Elliot Woodward's John F. McCoy Collection sale included lot 1980: "1833 Fine and very scarce." Realized $7.50. S.K. Harzfeld's 15th sale, November 1880, included lot 627: "1830 Uncirculated." Realized $4.10, the same price realized for several other dates in the early 1830s. Moving to the twentieth century, in March 1913 Thomas L. Elder's sale of the William H. Woodin Collection included lot 948: "1833. Uncirculated, Proof surface. Rare. Record about $14." Realized $17.

In June 1941 B. Max Mehl's sale of the William Forrester Dunham Collection included lot 1923: "1833 About Uncirculated; the highest portions show very slight cabinet friction and the surface has considerable Proof luster. Quite rare." Realized $35. Stack's sale of the H.R. Lee Collection, October 1947, included lot 1004: "1833 Brilliant Uncirculated. Deep raised borders." Realized $65. In November 1956 New Netherlands' sale of the Thomas L. Gaskill Collection included lot 200: "1833 Imperfect 3's in date, as on the dimes of the year. Strictly Very Fine, with the usual light handling marks. Rarer than the '32; desirable as a type in any condition. Actually, a bargain at anything under $100, regardless of catalog listings." Realized $75.

Proofs

Estimated Total Population (Proof). 4 to 6. A Proof is in the Mint Collection (now in the Smithsonian; *Sylloge* no. 236).

Proof Die Data and Notes. Proofs of 1833 were struck from the same dies used to make circulation strikes.

Selected Proof Auction Records

New York Coin & Stamp Co. offered the Lorin Parmelee Collection in June 1890, including lot 1022, under the coinage of 1833: "Quarter Eagle: sharp and perfect proof; rare to excess." Realized $17. The Chapman brothers' April 1904 sale of the John G. Mills Collection included lot 546: "1833 Brilliant Proof. Superb impression. Parmelee Collection 1022. Very rare state of preservation." Realized $18. Stack's description of lot 99 in the December 1944 sale of the J.F. Bell Collection read as follows: "1833 Perfect brilliant Proof gem, with high wire edge." Realized $127.50. In the Numismatic Gallery's offering of the Memorable Collection in March 1948, lot 93 was described as: "1833. Brilliant Proof. Rubbing in field." Realized $55.

F-12	VF-20	EF-40	AU-50	AU-55	MS-60	MS-63
$6,000	$7,250	$9,500	$11,000	$17,500	$22,500	$35,000

1834, With Motto

Circulation-Strike Mintage: 4,000 (calendar-year mintage)

Proof Mintage: Unknown, but very small

Most were melted. Famous rarity.

In *Description of Ancient and Modern Coins, in the Cabinet Collection at the Mint of the United States*, 1860, Mint director James Ross Snowden furnished a scenario which seems to explain the great rarity of the 1834, With Motto, type:

> The act reducing the standard was passed on the 28th of June [1834]. Up to this time there had already been coined 74,709 half-eagles, and 4,000 quarter eagles; 50,141 of the half-eagles had been issued from the Mint on the thirty-first of March, the remainder, including the quarter eagles, were in the hands of the Chief Coiner at the time the act passed, and were returned by him to the Treasurer two days after, on the thirteenth. This fact makes it extremely doubtful whether there was any issue of quarter eagles of the old standard; as it is probable that the last return would be immediately re-coined at the reduced standard, as they would yield a considerable profit.

However, at the time, most gold coins were struck specifically to the order of depositors, and thus the Mint did not make pieces on speculation. It must have been the case that quarter eagles, the smaller of the two gold denominations being made at the time, were made for the account of the government, since certain federal debts—including some salaries (including that of Senator Thomas Hart Benton, father of the Coinage Act of June 28, 1834)—were paid in gold. Thus, while the Mint may have had its own stock of quarter eagles, this scenario seems less likely for the related 1834, With Motto, *half* eagle.

On November 26, 1884, Harold P. Newlin included mention of the 1834 old-type quarter eagle in a letter to Baltimore numismatist T. Harrison Garrett, who by that time had purchased many items from Newlin.[6]

> One of the rarest quarter eagles in brilliant Proof condition. In regard to its rarity, you will find in Snowden's Mint Manual of Coins, page 115, that he says the act reducing the standard (weight) was passed June 28, 1834, and there were coined 4,000 quarter eagles of the old type. "These were in the hands of the chief coiner at the time the act was passed and were returned by him to the treasurer two days after,

on the 30th. This fact makes extremely doubtful whether there was any issue of quarter eagles of the old standard, as it is probable that the last return would be immediately recoined at the reduced standard, as they would yield a considerable profit. . . ."

I believe but few of these coins got into circulation. I bought the piece that McCoy had (Mickley never had one), which was described as Fine but is only Very Good. There was also one sold in the Jenks Collection sold in Haseltine's 69th sale in January. It was only Good and brought $22. I think the piece rarer than the 1797 quarter eagle or 1796, and I believe that a really Fine specimen has never been offered.

I value the piece at $50 and think it worth that amount in rarity and point of condition. Should you desire the piece for your cabinet it is at your service and should you think the price I ask is too high, you can send me a check for any amount you may deem the piece to be worth. I doubt if you ever again have the opportunity of getting a piece in such condition.

Estimated Total Population (Mint State). 3 to 5. If pieces called *Proof* in the past are included now, the population swells to, say, 5 to 8. Specimens have a prooflike surface.

Estimated Total Population (Circulated Grades). 10 to 15. By any evaluation, the 1834, With Motto, quarter eagle is the rarest of any early date up to this time.

Characteristics of Striking and Die Notes. These are usually seen well struck, and always with partially or fully prooflike surfaces. As noted, the differentiation between circulation strikes and Proofs has been muddled in the literature.

Selected Auction Records

Note: As this is the rarity within the type, more citations are given than for other quarter eagles of the era.

William H. Strobridge's September 1863 George F. Seavey Collection had this description for lot 470: "1834 Old type, Very Fine, very scarce." Realized $18. In May 1864 W. Elliot Woodward's John F. McCoy Collection sale included lot 1981: "The old variety, with motto; very fine indeed, and rare." Realized $20. The same coin later appeared in Woodward's January 1884 sale of the Heman Ely Collection, lot 900: "1834 The old type; Very Fine indeed, almost Proof, rare. From the McCoy Sale." Realized $10.25 to Heath. It did not stay off the market for long, as it reappeared in December 1885 as lot 576 in H.G. Sampson's sale of that date: "1834 Quarter eagle Old style. In Very Fine condition. From the McCoy sale, where it brought $20. Extremely rare. Limited at $10." Realized $10.25. This is a very unusual instance of stating a reserve price. S.K. Harzfeld's 15th sale, November 1880, included lot 628: "1834 [presumably With Motto, but not stated]. Uncirculated." Realized $4.10, the same price realized for several other dates of the With Motto type in the early 1830s.

The price advanced sharply. In Thomas L. Elder's September 1910 sale of the Peter Mougey Collection it was offered as lot 1160: "1834. With the Motto! Excessively rare. Uncirculated with nearly full Proof surface." Realized $310. Elder on March 1911 included an example as lot 949 in his sale of the William H. Woodin Collection: "1834. Old type with motto 'E. Pluribus Unum' on band over head of eagle. Uncirculated, Proof surface. Records of $310 (Mougey) and $320 (Stickney) have been made for this notable coin, of which probably not over six specimens are known, so a new record may be expected for this." Realized $300. The rarity of the variety was showcased by B. Max Mehl in his February 1922 sale of the Dr. G.F.E. Wilharm Collection, lot 70: "1834 Same type as last, with E. Pluribus Unum on scroll above eagle. Extremely Fine. Excessively rare. One of the rarest of all U.S. gold coins. The first that I have ever offered at Auction. Record well over $300. And according to the great demand for all rare gold this specimen should bring well above its record." Realized $390. As luck would have it, a few months later in May, in his sale of the James Ten Eyck Collection, Mehl would offer another—lot 64: "1834. The Excessively Rare 1834 quarter eagle With Motto, E. PLURIBUS UNUM on scroll above eagle. Uncirculated, with considerable Proof surface, raised borders. Excessively rare, only about six known, and one of the rarest of all American coins. Of the few known specimens of this rarity I doubt if any of them excels this one in condition." Realized $400.

Years later, in December 1944, Stack's sold the J.F. Bell Collection, which included lot 100: "1834 With motto over eagle. A brilliant Uncirculated coin, said to be one of the rarest and most sought after coins, as rare as that of 1863." Realized $510. Stack's offered another in October 1947 in the H.R. Lee Collection as lot 1005: "1834 With motto over Eagle. Probably not more than 10 or 12 pieces are known. This is a brilliant semi Proof with raised borders. $700 was paid for this coin, should bring in nearer to the 4 figures. Possibly the finest known." Realized $750.

Proofs

Estimated Total Population (Proof). 3 to 5. Proof specimens were struck to the extent of at least four pieces for inclusion in as many presentation sets, including one each for the Sultan of Muscat and King of Siam; these sets also included Proof strikes of the Classic Head quarter eagle of the same year. A Proof is in the Mint Collection (now in the Smithsonian; *Sylloge* no. 241).

Proof Die Data and Notes. Proofs and circulation strikes are from the same die pair. Experts are sometimes of divided opinions as to the differentiation between a Proof and a highly prooflike circulation strike.

Selected Proof Auction Records

In May 1913 the U.S. Coin Co.'s sale of the Malcolm N. Jackson Collection included lot 115: "1834 With motto. Brilliant Proof, very slightly rubbed on obverse field. Excessively rare and possibly the finest known specimen of this coin." Realized $200.

F-12	VF-20	EF-40	AU-50	AU-55	MS-60	MS-63
$22,500	$30,000	$55,000	$90,000	$135,000	$200,000	$300,000

10

Classic Head, No Motto on Reverse, $2.50 Gold Coins (1834–1839)

With Mark R. Borckardt

Classic Head, No Motto on Reverse (1834–1839)

Designer: *William Kneass.* **Weight:** *4.18 grams.* **Composition:** *.8992 gold, .1008 silver and copper.* **Diameter:** *18.2 mm.* **Edge:** *Reeded.* **Mints:** *Philadelphia, Charlotte, Dahlonega, New Orleans.*

New Design

To permit gold coins to circulate at par, which had not happened since late 1820, Congress reduced the authorized weight of the various denominations through the Act of June 28, 1834. Senator Thomas Hart Benton, nicknamed "Old Bullion," spearheaded the movement. For the quarter eagle the weight was reduced from 67.5 grains to 64.5 grains. On August 1, 1834, the new standard went into effect.

The design was changed to better adhere to the law for the design of U.S. coins, for taste and classic authority, and to ease the manufacturing process. The public could also more readily differentiate the new coins from the old. Engraver William Kneass created what is today called the Classic Head design. The head of Miss Liberty faces left, her hair secured by a band inscribed LIBERTY; stars encircle the bust, below which is the date. The motif was adapted from that created by John Reich for the copper cent of 1808 and used on the half cent of 1809.

The reverse depicts an eagle with a shield on its breast, perched on an olive branch and holding three arrows. The inscriptions UNITED STATES OF AMERICA and

2½ D. surround. One proposal contemplated that the new coins would bear the date AUG. 1, 1834 on the reverse to make them easy to differentiate, but in practice this was not done. It is interesting to observe that certain coins minted by Christopher Bechtler in North Carolina did adhere to that proposal and included the full date. The motto E PLURIBUS UNUM, used on quarter eagles since 1796, was omitted, making it easy even at a casual glance to distinguish the new reverse from the one of somewhat similar design in general use from 1808 to 1834. The diameter remained 18.2 mm, the standard adopted in 1829.

Mint Director Moore Explains the New Portrait

Director of the Mint Samuel Moore wrote to Secretary of the Treasury Levi Woodbury, explaining the changes:

> [To] Hon. LEVI WOODBURY, Secretary of the Treasury[1]
>
> [From] MINT OF THE UNITED STATES,
>
> Philadelphia, 9th July, 1834.
>
> SIR:—The certified copy of the Act relative to the Gold Coins of the United States, forwarded with your letter of the 7th, has been received.
>
> In regard to your suggestion of affixing to the gold coinage, after the 31st inst. The date of the month, to designate the new coins from others of the current year, I have respectfully to observe, that for the purpose of such designation, the engraver has been directed to execute new dies, in which two improvements, contemplated for some years past, shall be introduced; one is, the omission of the words "E pluribus unum" on the reverse; the other is, the substitution of a new Head of Liberty without the dress-cap—the hair being only restrained by the cincture bearing the inscription "Liberty."
>
> The cap has by many been regarded as intended for the classic cap of liberty, and under this idea has received favor, as proper to be retained, even with some who have not been insensible that it impaired the beauty of the coin. I have, however, to remark, that the cap on our coins was not designed as the Liberty Cap. It was not introduced on the silver coins until about the year 1806, and was then copied from what was considered handsome specimen of the female head dress of that day. On the gold coins a cap had been introduced from the first, which has certainly some resemblance to the usual form of the Cap of Liberty. I am, however, satisfied, from several considerations, and indeed have the direct assurance of Mr. Eckfeldt, the chief coiner, who has been familiar with the whole subject from the first, that it was not so intended. When a cap was introduced, as before stated, on the silver coin, that on the gold was conformed thereto.
>
> It is wholly at variance with classic authority to place the Pileus, or Liberty Cap, on the head of the figure representing Liberty. When it is introduced in statuary, or on a medal, or a coin, it is found borne by Liberty herself on a wand, or in her hand, or appears at her feet, and indicates her as the beneficial being through whose influence the blessings of freedom are conferred on others; and such a cap, placed on a freed man, we know from the Roman annals, was the insignium of his freedom.

This view of classic propriety was, no doubt, very familiar to those under whose authority the first coinage of the United States commenced.—The early copper coins bear the Cap of Liberty, but never on the head of the figure. The coinage of France of that period, presents also various pertinent examples in point.

It may be satisfactory further to remark, that soon after my appointment to the charge of the Mint, I addressed to Mr. Jefferson, who at the commencement of the Mint was a member of the Government, then resident in this city, an inquiry in regard to the authority on which the devices of our coins had been originally adopted, and particularly presented the question as it regards the cap on the head of Liberty. His recollection, he informed me, did not reach the subject, and no notes had been preserved in regard to it; but he was direct and explicit as to the unfitness of placing the Pileus or Cap of Liberty on the head of the figure—adding, "for we are not emancipated slaves."

I have the honor to be, with great respect, &c.

SAMUEL MOORE.

Mint Director Moore Gives Further Details

The *Saturday Courier*, Philadelphia, August 9, 1834, further explained the reasons for the design change and told of the commencement of the new coinage, quoting a letter sent by Mint Director Moore to Secretary of the Treasury Woodbury:

NEW GOLD COIN: Treasury Department, August 2d, 1834. The annexed letter will enable the public readily to distinguish the new from the old coins.

As the date could not by law, be altered, but the cap and motto might be legally omitted, and would serve plainly to distinguish the new impression, that course has been adopted at the mint till the commencement of the next year, when the motto will probably be restored, and the date of the new year, instead of the omission of the motto, will be found sufficient to indicate the change in the coin.

Mint of the United States,

Philadelphia, 1st Aug., 1834.

Sir—I have the honor to inform the Department, that the coinage of Gold, according to the new ratio of gold to silver, commenced this morning, being the earliest day permitted by the provisions of the act.

In making this communication, it may be satisfactory to recur to the peculiarities by which the new gold coins are to be distinguished from those of former issues. They are the following:

On the face, the new coins will be readily distinguished by a head of Liberty disencumbered of a cap.

On the reverse, the surplus motto, "E Pluribus Unum," which for many years has occupied a portion of the disk above the figure of the eagle, is now omitted.

These changes, independent of the facility to be derived from them in distinguishing the future from the past emissions of our gold coins, are recommended by a nearer adherence to the provisions of the law, as well as by the rules of taste and classic authority. The views, in these respects, presented in my communication of the 9th ult., having met your approbation, will, I doubt not, be sustained by the judgment of the public.

In regard to the omission of the motto above referred to, the same improvement was introduced in the quarter dollar in 1831; the subject having, by communication of the 28th January, of that year, been submitted to the President, through the Department, and approved.

The Eagle of the former issues weighs 270 grains, the half eagle 135 grains, and the Quarter 67 1/2 grains. The Eagle, under the present law will weigh 258 grains, the half eagle 129 grains, and the Quarter 64-1/2 grains. These weights are recited, because desirable to be kept in mind, rather than as affording a further criterion of distinction between the two classes of coins—since an inspection, much more cursory than that of weighing, will distinguish them by the preceding characteristics.

The Eagle and Half Eagle of the new coinage will be less in diameter than those of the former emissions, and that in a greater proportion than the diminution of weight would indicate. This however, though a decided amendment in our coinage, is of less value as a distinctive mark, since the comparison would require the presence of coin of both classes.

I have the honor to be, with great respect, your obedient servant,

SAMUEL MOORE, Director of the Mint.

[Letter addressed to] Hon. Levi Woodbury,

Secretary of the Treasury.

In his *Description of Ancient and Modern Coins, in the Cabinet Collection at the Mint of the United States*, 1860, Mint Director James Ross Snowden described the new No Motto coins, including their popular nickname, "Benton Mint Drops."[2] He noted that the first delivery of half eagles included 98,075 pieces, and the first delivery of quarter eagles included 18,400 pieces. In total, Snowden said, "the entire coinage of the new standard consisted of 658,028 half eagles, and 112,234 quarter eagles—there being no eagles."

Mintage of the New Quarter Eagle

Mintage quantities were large in the earliest years of the Classic Head coinage span, with the high-water mark being 1836, when 547,986 were struck. In 1838 quarter eagles were struck at Charlotte for the first time, followed the next year by supplementary coinage at Charlotte, Dahlonega, and New Orleans. By far, the greatest number of 1834–1839 Classic Head quarter eagles was produced at Philadelphia.

The Classic Head quarter eagles circulated effectively and were seen in the channels of commerce until the early years of the twentieth century, except for the years 1862–1878, when these and other gold coins were replaced in circulation by paper notes (see chapter 1). However, after 1878, while some pieces circulated in the West, in the East and Midwest such quarter eagles were usually encountered only in bank holdings. This longevity in circulation accounts for the existence today of many examples worn down to such grades as Very Fine.

The total circulation-strike mintage for 1834–1839 Classic Head quarter eagles amounted to 968,228 pieces. Probably fewer than 40 Proofs were struck. Interestingly, the presentation coin sets made in 1834 for the Sultan of Muscat and the King of Siam each contained two Proof quarter eagles, one of the old style and one of the new. The Siam coins survive today.

Numismatic Considerations

Examples of the Classic Head quarter eagle can be obtained readily in grades from Fine through Extremely Fine. About Uncirculated pieces are scarce, and Uncirculated pieces are scarcer yet, the two exceptions of note being the first year of issue, 1834, and the high-mintage year of 1836. Of these two dates, the 1834 can be found in choice and gem preservation, but all other dates and issues in the series—including the 1836—are rare at such high levels. Mint State 1834 coins often display prooflike surfaces. Later Mint State coins often have a creamy, satiny finish that can be of exquisite beauty. As is true of many if not most quarter eagles of the various types, many coins that were called About Uncirculated decades ago have been certified in low Mint State grades today. David W. Akers's 1975 study of quarter eagles gives a view that is useful for comparison.

The lowest mintage of the type was registered by the first mintmarked issue, the 1838-C, of which only 7,880 were struck. Today, this variety is very scarce in any grade and very rare at the About Uncirculated level. The mintmarked issues of the next year—1839-C, 1839-D, and 1839-O—are all scarce, with the typically encountered example grading Very Fine to About Uncirculated. (See the individual listings for more details.) Any 1839 coin in Mint State or finer grade is a rarity, with the possible exception of 1839-O, for which a few specimens of stunning beauty have survived, probably by chance. At the time, the numismatic community—consisting of no more than a couple hundred widely scattered enthusiasts—took no note of mintmarks, and not even the Mint Cabinet saved examples.

In Mint State the 1835, 1837, 1838, and 1839-O are elusive, but are available to the extent that examples can be acquired with some patience, although choice and gem pieces are few and far between. The 1838-C (most elusive), 1839, 1839-C, and 1839-D are extreme rarities.

Classic Head quarter eagles were struck from handmade dies, with the portrait, stars, and date numerals entered separately on the obverse and the eagle, denomination numbers, and lettering added separately on the reverse. Thus, die varieties can be recognized from positional differences. The carefully compiled study of Dr. John W. McCloskey was sent to me in the year 2000, after which I incorporated much information and sent the manuscript back to him for editing. He did this and made some further suggestions. His working notes were made available for the present work, and numerous references are made to them. McCloskey's research has been incorporated into the book *United States Classic Gold Coins of 1834-1839* by author Daryl J. Haynor. Additional observations were made by Mark R. Borckardt, then on the staff of Bowers and Merena Galleries.

The present writers have minimized using certain *low-relief* characteristics of dies—such as the eagle's tongue (present or absent), size of the berry (a.k.a. "bud") on the stem, etc., as these features can change appearance or even disappear on relapped dies or certain other die states. Borckardt assisted greatly with this series at the turn of the twenty-first century and has added more for the present text. McCloskey's notes have been helpful as well.

Portrait Variations

For the Classic Head quarter eagle coinage of 1834–1839 several different types of portraits were employed, each representing the use of a differently styled punch that was entered into the working die. The creators of the portraits have not been differentiated with certainty. It is likely that those used on the 1834–1836 coinage were by engraver William Kneass, with some of the 1836 dies being made in advance, completed except for the date. After Kneass suffered a stroke on August 27, 1835, much of the further creative work was done by Christian Gobrecht (who joined the Mint staff as second engraver a few weeks later). Gobrecht performed many experiments with portraits, not only in the quarter eagle series, but most familiarly with the copper cents of 1839 (resulting in the Booby Head, Silly Head, and other cent variations).

This portrait series is fascinating and, to the specialist, very interesting to study.

Observation points for differentiating the portraits including the outline of the curls at the top and bottom of the head, the configuration of the lower curls, the size and separation of the two ribbons behind the head, and the angle of the front of the neck from the chin downward. Working dies were touched-up, so that even though the same portrait was used between years, they appear slightly different. In his 1964 monograph on quarter eagles, Walter Breen gave extensive narrative, quoted below. In 2000, John W. McCloskey suggested to me that it is much easier just to use the dates and mintmarks, except for 1834, than observations of differences.

Small Head: This portrait was used in 1834 only, on the first No Motto coins. It is smaller than on any other die of the 1834–1839 series (see the individual die descriptions to follow). Breen wrote in his monograph: "Small head . . . Outlines of curls atop head less pronounced than on other obv. type; the roll of curls at back of head above the ribbon forms an almost unbroken straight line—that is, along with the low date, possibly the easiest identifying feature."

Head of 1835: Used on the single known 1835-dated die, this portrait is also one of the six known obverse dies of 1836. In his monograph, Breen suggested the head might be taller, but it is doubtful that he measured them: "Obv. taller head . . . upper ribbon end almost concealed by a curl; bust point much narrower than in 1834."

Head of 1837: Attributed to Christian Gobrecht (as are later dies of this type), the Head of 1837 was used on three of the six known obverse dies of 1836, then re-engraved and used on both dies of 1837. Breen wrote in his 1964 monograph: "Somewhat similar to last, but a trifle more of upper ribbon end visible past protruding curl, and hair slopes back abruptly above head band."

Head of 1838-C and 1839-D: This style appeared on the 1838-C and 1839-D quarter eagles. The Breen monograph contains no additional portrait information for 1838-C; and for 1839-D, which he incorrectly identified as an overdate, he wrote that it had "the same head as on the 1838 C and mintmark above date."

Head of 1839: Philadelphia quarter eagles of 1839 received this obverse portrait, which Breen discussed briefly in his monograph: "Not from the head of 1838; the design is slightly smaller with noticeable differences in the back curls."

Head of 1839-C: This portrait was used on 1839 Charlotte Mint quarter eagles. Breen did not discuss Miss Liberty's appearance on the 1839-C and 1839-O obverse dies in his monograph.

Head of 1839-O: New Orleans Mint quarter eagles of 1839 were the recipients of this portrait.

Dies and Known Die Combinations, 1834–1839

The 19 obverse dies are numbered from 1 to 19, and the 16 reverse dies are lettered from A to Q (skipping I and O to avoid confusion). This system is a modification of the classification system devised by Mark R. Borckardt, and enables instant identification of an early reverse that was used at a later time, as, for example, in 1839 when an 1836 reverse was used.

Bowers and Borckardt (BB) numbers are added. Permission is granted for use of these numbers in numismatic media. BB numbers have become standard for use in describing early silver dollars of 1794 to 1804.

Quarter Eagles of 1834

1834, Obverse Die 1. *The portrait is the Small Head style (with a straight vertical line of curls at the back of the head). The 4 in the date is very slightly closer to the denticles than to the curl;* definitive.

1834, Obverse Die 2. *The portrait is the Large Head style (with an indented vertical line of curls at the back of the head), a.k.a. Head of 1834. The 4 in the date is close to the curl and distant from the denticles;* definitive.

1834, Reverse Die A. *The tip of the lowest arrow touches the base of the right foot of the second A in AMERICA; the tip of the branch is over the inner right side of the upright of D in 2½ D.;* definitive for 1834. This reverse was used in 1834 and again in 1837. *Details:* The S and T in STATES are widely spaced at the bases; the top of the second T is about on the same level as the top of the E. The base of O in OF is lower than base of F. The lower left of the first A in AMERICA is close to but does not touch the wing; the bases of A, M, and E as well as those of R and I touch. The tip of the branch is over the right side of the upright of D in 2½ D. The shaft of the lowest arrow feather at the left, if extended, would intersect the upper left of the large 2. This reverse die was used in 1834 and again in 1837; see its description under "Quarter Eagles of 1837" (page 121) for additional details.

1834, Reverse Die B. *The A and M in AMERICA are widely separated at the bases;* definitive for 1834. *Details:* The base of the first T in STATES is below the base of the A. The first A in AMERICA is slightly high, is close to the wing, and is widely separated from the M; the tip of the lowest arrow ends below the right serif of the left foot of the second A. On some high-grade pieces, upon very close examination, three lines in each of the two right-side pales (vertical stripes) extend upward into the horizontal lines and are evident as high as the point between the lowest and next-lowest horizontal lines.[3] This reverse die was combined with obverses dated 1834, 1835, and 1836.

1834, Reverse Die C. *The denticle at 6:00 extends nearly to the bottom of the diagonal fraction bar;* definitive for 1834. This reverse was used only in 1834.

1834, Reverse Die D. *The M in AMERICA is missing its upper inside right diagonal;* definitive for 1834. *Details:* The letters in STATES are widely spaced; the A and T are widest, and the second S is low. The F in OF is high. The tip of the lowest arrow is below the second A and has its point below the tip of the left serif of the right foot of the A. Three lines in each of the two right-side pales (vertical stripes) extend upward into the horizontal lines and are evident as high as the point between the lowest and next-lowest horizontal lines.[4] This reverse die was combined with obverse dies dated 1834 and 1835.

1834, BB-201: Dies 1-A. Rarity-1. This is the only die combination with the Small Head portrait. This variety, from a monogamous die pair, is considered the first 1834 variety, although that is not known with certainty. The other 1834-dated obverse die was used with three reverse dies in 1834, and two of those reverse dies were used in 1835 and/or 1836. Nearly 60% (56.6%) of all 1834 quarter eagles appearing in recent auctions are from this die pair.[5] *Equivalents:* Breen (monograph) II-1 (State A); Breen (monograph) II-1 (State B; the dies are "worn down"; the arrow point now seems to run into the A); Breen *(Encyclopedia)* 6138; McCloskey-1; Dannreuther JD-1; Haynor HM-1.[6] *McCloskey Notes:* This is the most common variety of this date. It is available in all grades through Mint State. Proof examples have been offered at auction over the years.

Breen (monograph) included his variety II-2, not otherwise traced: "Obv. as last. Rev. small arrows; arrow near center of base of final A, but not touching." Also listed in Breen's 1988 *Encyclopedia*, B-6139. McCloskey was able to confirm only one die combination with obverse 1, the 1-A variety.

1834, BB-202: Dies 2-B. Rarity-2. The Borckardt auction survey indicates that a fourth of 1834 quarter eagles appearing at auction are from this die pair. *Equivalents:* Breen (monograph) II-3; Breen *(Encyclopedia)* 6140; McCloskey-2; Haynor HM-2. *McCloskey Notes:* This is the most common of the three Large Head varieties of 1834. It is available in all grades through Mint State.

1834, BB-203: Dies 2-C. Rarity-5. On well-worn specimens the repunching at D in UNITED simply gives that letter an overly heavy appearance. The Borckardt auction survey indicates that about one of every twenty 1834 quarter eagles appearing at auction are from this die pair. *Equivalents:* Breen (monograph) II-5; Breen *(Encyclopedia)* 6140; McCloskey-3; Haynor HM-3. *McCloskey Notes:* This is a very scarce 1834 variety. A strong die break develops from the rim through the tip of the right wing; on still later states, it extends through the bases of the letters AMER and up through the I to the rim. This variety is very seldom offered at auction.

1834, BB-204: Dies 2-D. Rarity-4. The Borckardt auction survey indicates that slightly more than 10% of 1834 quarter eagles appearing at auction are from this die pair. *Equivalents:* Breen (monograph) II-4; Breen *(Encyclopedia)* 6140; McCloskey-4; Dannreuther JD-2; Haynor HM-4. *McCloskey Notes:* The BB-204 pairing is not nearly as readily available as BB-202, but About Uncirculated examples can be obtained with patience. A Proof example of this variety is in the Smithsonian Institution.

Quarter Eagles of 1835

1835, Obverse Die 3. *The portrait is the Large Head of 1835.* This is the only 1835 obverse die, and the only 1834–1839 die with the fourth date digit to the left of the curl. *Details:* The 1 in 1835 is slightly closer to the denticles than to the bust; the 1 was punched more deeply into the working die than were other numerals; the 8 is in the "block" (normal) style but with the center element very thin; the 3 is wide with knobs closely spaced; and the flag of the 5 does not extend as far as the lower right curve of the numeral. The entire date is oriented farther to the left than on any other Classic Head obverse die; no part of the date is below the lowest curl.

1834, Reverse Die B. This reverse die was combined with obverses dated 1834, 1835, and 1836. It is described in detail on page 115, with the other dies of 1834.

1834, Reverse Die D. This reverse die was combined with obverse dies dated 1834 and 1835. It is described in detail on page 115, with the other dies of 1834.

1835, Reverse Die E. *The A and M in AMERICA are close, and the M is perfect;* definitive for 1835. *Details:* The ST and AT in STATES are wider apart at the bases than are the other letters in the word. The first A in AMERICA seems to lightly touch the eagle's wing (but on sharp, early impressions is very slightly separated); the tip of the middle arrow is below the heavy left side of the C; the tip of the lowest arrowhead touches the tip of the right serif of the left foot of the second A in AMERICA. The numerator is closer to the fraction bar than is the denominator. No berry is present on the branch (although the branch's other features are well defined). Each shield stripe has three vertical lines, and the third line of stripe 6 extends into the horizontal lines, reaching the second line above.[7] This reverse die was also combined with an obverse dated 1836.

1835, BB-211: Dies 3-D. Rarity-6. The Borckardt auction survey indicates that 1.5% of 1835 quarter eagles appearing at auction are from this die pair. *Equivalents:* Breen (monograph) 2; Breen *(Encyclopedia)* 6141; McCloskey-1; Dannreuther JD-1; Haynor HM-1. *McCloskey Notes:* Circulation strikes of this pairing are scarce. Proofs include the Smithsonian, Eliasberg, and Pittman specimens.

1835, BB-212: Dies 3-B. Rarity-2. During the striking of this combination the die was relapped later in the production sequence; relapping completely removed the stem from the berry and removed much of the lowest leaf in the middle pair. The Borckardt auction survey indicates that more than 90% of 1835 quarter eagles appearing at auction are from this die pair. *Equivalents:* Breen (monograph) 1; Breen *(Encyclopedia)* 6141; McCloskey-2; Haynor HM-2. *McCloskey Notes:* This is the most common variety of the year and is readily available in all grades through Mint State.

1835, BB-213: Dies 3-E. Rarity-6. The Borckardt auction survey indicates that slightly more than 5% of 1835 quarter eagles appearing at auction are from this die pair. *Equivalents:* Breen (monograph) 3; Breen *(Encyclopedia)* 6141; McCloskey-3; Haynor HM-3. *McCloskey Notes:* This pairing is scarce and is seldom offered for sale. A light die crack develops from the rim, through star 6 and the hair to the ear. This combination represents the final use of the only known obverse die of the year.

Quarter Eagles of 1836

The first obverse die used this year, the Head of 1835, is known with three different reverse dies. Each of the remaining five obverse dies is known in a single die pairing. Memorizing the obverse die characteristics will allow the variety collector to identify many 1836 varieties without examining the reverse. That said, in the determination of die combinations for 1836 quarter eagles it is often easiest to begin with the reverse, with the position of the lowest arrow point being a good first observation.

1836, Obverse Die 4. *The portrait is the Large Head of 1834 (with an indented vertical line of curls at the back of the head);* definitive for 1836. *Details:* The date has a Block 8 with a thin center element. The date is about centered with the serif of 1 and the base of 1 equally distant from the bust and the border. The top of the 6 is slightly closer to the curl than to the denticles. The 3 leans left, with its top much closer to the 8 and its bottom equally spaced between the 8 and 6. The first hair curl above the L in LIBERTY protrudes above the headband with a gap between this and the second hair curl. The upper hair ribbon is long and extends farther into the field than does the bottom. The ray of star 6 points to the lower corner of the headband and is far from the curl. The ray of star 7 points slightly to the left of center at the top of the second curl.

1836, Obverse Die 5. *The portrait is the Small Head of 1834 (with a straight vertical line of curls at the back of the head);* definitive for 1836. *Details:* The 8 in 1836 is a Script (or Fancy) 8. The point of the upper left serif of the 1 is about the same distance from the neck as the base of the upright is from the denticles; the date is about evenly spaced left to right; the top of 3 is low; the 3 leans left, toward the 8; the left edge of the curl is above the thick left side of the 6. Star 1 is about the same distance from the tip of the bust and the denticles. The ray of star 6 points to the front center of the headband; the ray of star 7 points to the top of the second curl. The denticle at 1:30 is doubled, and there is a gap in the denticles above star 3, slightly past 9:00.

1836, Obverse Die 6. *The portrait is the Head of 1837; the date has a Script 8 (a.k.a.* Fancy 8*);* definitive for 1836. *Details:* The upper and lower loops of the 8 and 3 are equally spaced. The left edge of the curl is over the inner left curve of the 6. Digit 6 is closer to the curl than to the denticles. Star 1 is far from the bust, and star 6 is far from the curl.

1836, Obverse Die 7. *The portrait is the Head of 1835; the date has a Script 8 (a.k.a.* Fancy 8*);* definitive for 1836. *Details:* The date is low. The upright of the 1 is over a denticle; the base of the 3 is lower than other digits; the tops of 8 and 3 are close; the 6 is large, high, and about twice as close to the curl as to the denticles; the left side of the curl is above the inside of the left side of the 6. The ray of star 6 points to the curl just above the headband; the ray of star 7 points to the lower left side of the crevice between the second and third curls (counting the first low curl).

1836, Obverse Die 8. *The portrait is the Head of 1837; the date has a Block 8; star 7 points between curls;* definitive for 1836. *Details:* The Block 8 has a thin center element. Each digit is slightly farther from the denticles. The left edge of the curl is between the inner and outer left curves of the 6. Star 1 is far from the bust. Star 6 points to the top corner of the headband and is equally spaced between the head and the denticles. Star 13 has two points close to the curl and one point farther from the denticles.

1836, Obverse Die 9. *The portrait is the Head of 1837; the date has a Block 8; star 7 points about to the center of the curl;* definitive for 1836. *Details:* The date is low; the upright of

1 is over a denticle; the top of the 6 is close to the curl; the left edge of the curl is above the thick left side of the 6. The ray of star 6 points to the top of the forelock just below the headband; the ray of star 7 points to the closest part of the first prominent curl above the headband.

1834, Reverse Die B. This reverse die was combined with obverses dated 1834, 1835, and 1836. It is described in detail on page 115, with the other dies of 1834.

1835, Reverse Die E. This reverse die was combined with obverses dated 1835 and 1836. It is described in detail on page 117, with the other dies of 1835.

1836, Reverse Die F. *Details:* The U in UNITED leans slightly right; the bases of I and T are on the same level. All letters in STATES are fairly widely spaced; ST is especially widely spaced. The base of O in OF is slightly lower than the base of F. The first A in AMERICA is close to but not touching the eagle's wing; the bases of A, M, and E are close but do not touch; the base of E is about on the same level as the base of R; *the tip of the middle arrow is below the center of C; the tip of the lowest arrow is under the inside of the right foot of the second A.* The diagonal fraction bar is extremely close to the right base of the numerator and lightly joins the left top of the denominator. Each vertical shield stripe has three lines. This reverse die was combined with obverses dated 1836, 1837, and 1839.

1836, Reverse Die G. *Details:* The U in UNITED leans slightly left; the base of T is higher than the base of I but on the same level as the base of E. The first five letters in STATES are widely spaced; the second S is low and leans left. The bases of O and F are on the same level. The first A in AMERICA lightly touches the eagle's wing; the bases of A and M have space between them, about the same distance as the space between the bases of E and R; the right base of E is higher than the left base of R; *the tip of the middle arrow is close to and points to the lower right serif of I;* the tip of the lowest arrow is under the left serif of the left foot of the second A. This reverse was combined only with obverse die 4 of 1836.

1836, BB-221: Dies 4-F. *Large Head of 1834 (with indented vertical line of curls at the back of the head).* Rarity-3. The Borckardt auction survey indicates that 14.1% of 1836 quarter eagles appearing at auction are from this die pair. *Equivalents:* Breen *(Encyclopedia)* 6142; McCloskey-6; Haynor HM-1. *McCloskey Notes:* This common variety is available in circulated grades as well as Mint State. It usually comes well struck on obverse and reverse.

1836, BB-222: Dies 5-B. *Small Head of 1834 (with straight vertical line of curls at the back of the head).* Rarity-8. This is apparently a Proof-only variety. *Equivalents:* Breen *(Encyclopedia)* 6144; McCloskey-8; Dannreuther JD-2; Haynor HM-2. *McCloskey Notes:* The Pittman Collection Proof was an example of this variety, as was another Proof McCloskey saw at a convention in the late 1990s. He stated that he was not aware of any circulation-strike examples of this variety.

1836, BB-223: Dies 6-E. *Head of 1837.* Rarity-7. John W. McCloskey discovered this variety a number of years ago. A second example appeared in a Heritage sale in February 2011, reappearing in the August 2014 Stack's Bowers sale of the Farrendelli Collection.

Equivalents: Breen *(Encyclopedia)* 6144; McCloskey-4; Haynor HM-3. *McCloskey Notes:* This is a very rare variety. An obverse die crack proceeds from the rim, through the right side of star 6, through the hair and the field, to the rim between stars 11 and 12. McCloskey stated he'd seen only one example of this variety in a ten-year search.

1836, BB-224: Dies 7-E. *Head of 1835.* Rarity-2. Heavy diagonal die striae from upper left to lower right are present on some obverse impressions. The Borckardt auction survey indicates that more than 40% of 1836 quarter eagles appearing at auction are from this die pair. *Equivalents:* Breen (monograph) II-1; Breen *(Encyclopedia)* 6143; McCloskey-2; Dannreuther JD-3; Haynor HM-4. *McCloskey Notes:* This is the most common variety of the 1836 quarter eagle; it is readily available in all grades through Mint State. An obverse die crack develops from the rim over star 6, running through the left side of star 6, through the curls and the ear, and out toward the rim between stars 12 and 13. On later states the crack from the rim to star 6 divides into two segments; the crack is heavier at the top of the coin and grows progressively lighter as it continues to the lower right rim. Examples exist with and without this crack. This establishes that BB-222 was struck after BB-221 (and, as seen below, before BB-223).

1836, BB-225: Dies 7-B. *Head of 1835.* Rarity-5. The Borckardt auction survey indicates that 3.2% of 1836 quarter eagles appearing at auction are from this die pair. *Equivalents:* Breen (monograph) II-3; Breen *(Encyclopedia)* 6143; McCloskey-1; Haynor HM-5. *McCloskey Notes:* This pairing is scarce and seldom offered at auctions. No obverse die cracks have been observed on this variety.

1836, BB-226: Dies 7-G. *Head of 1835.* Rarity-3. The Borckardt auction survey indicates that 7.7% of 1836 quarter eagles appearing at auction are from this die pair. *Equivalents:* Breen (monograph) II-3; Breen *(Encyclopedia)* 6143; McCloskey-3; Haynor HM-6. *McCloskey Notes:* Although this is a scarce variety, a number of Mint State specimens have been offered at auction over the years. It is always seen with an obverse die crack from the rim over star 6, through the left side of star 6, through the curls, and out toward the rim between stars 12 and 13; this establishes that BB-223 was struck after BB-222. The crack is doubled between the border and star 6.

1836, BB-227: Dies 8-E. *Head of 1837.* Rarity-6. The Borckardt auction survey indicates that 1.1% of 1836 quarter eagles appearing at auction are from this die pair. *Equivalents:* Breen *(Encyclopedia)* 6144; McCloskey-7; Haynor HM-7. *McCloskey Notes:* This very scarce variety is seldom offered at auction. A die crack runs from the rim upward through the *right side* of the 6 in 1836; it later expands and continues up through the curls to Y in LIBERTY on the headband. A crack from the rim runs between stars 3 and 4, through the tip of nose to the ear, connecting with the earlier crack. Another crack runs from the rim between stars 11 and 12 to the curls over Y on the headband. McCloskey stated that most he encountered had multiple obverse cracks; the Bass Collection had two examples with the crack just beginning at the bottom, and extending upward through the 6 to the curl.

1836, BB-228: Dies 9-F. *Head of 1837.* Rarity-2. On late circulation-strike impressions there is a crack from the denticles through the *left side* of the 6 in 1836 to the left element of the lowest curl. The Borckardt auction survey indicates that 31.8% of 1836 quarter eagles appearing at auction are from this die pair. *Equivalents:* Breen (monograph) III-1; Breen *(Encyclopedia)* 6144; McCloskey-5; Dannreuther JD-1; Haynor HM-8. *McCloskey Notes:* This is a very common variety. Circulation strikes are readily available in all grades through Mint State. Proofs include examples in the Smithsonian Institution, the Eliasberg Collection, and Stack's 55th Anniversary Sale.

Quarter Eagles of 1837

1837, Obverse Die 10. *The portrait is the Large Head of 1837; the ray of star 7 points to the right side of the curl near the crevice;* definitive. *Details:* The 7 in the date is at least twice as close to the curl as to the denticle. The ray of star 8 points to the upper left of the top of the curl.

1837, Obverse Die 11. *The portrait is the Large Head of 1837; the ray of star 7 points to the top of the curl;* definitive. *Details:* The 7 in the date is slightly closer to the curl than to the denticles; the 7 is double-punched at upper right. The ray of star 8 points to the crevice between the second and third large curls. Stars 8 and 9 are repunched.

1834, Reverse Die A. *Each vertical shield stripe has three lines; the second A in AMERICA and the lowest arrowhead are joined;* definitive for a reverse die combined with an 1837 obverse. Reverse die A of 1834 was combined with obverses dated 1834 and 1837; it is described in further detail on page 115, with the other dies of 1834.

1836, Reverse Die F. *Details:* This reverse die was combined with obverses dated 1836, 1837, and 1839. It is described in detail on page 119, with the other dies of 1836.

1837, Reverse Die H. *Each vertical shield stripe has two lines;* definitive for a reverse die combined with an 1837 obverse. *Details:* The left upright of U in UNITED is double-punched; the N and I are closely spaced; two tiny "islands" are seen to the right of T. The S and T in STATES are closely spaced at the bases; ST is low; minute traces of double-punching are visible on the right side of the upright of the first T; the top of the second T is higher than the top of E. The base of O in OF is about on the same level as the base of F. The lower left of the first A in AMERICA is exceedingly close to but does not touch the wing; A is slightly lower than M; a small gap is present in the denticles immediately past the upper right serif of C; the tip of the middle arrow touches C at the bottom and slightly to the left of center;[8] the tip of the lowest arrow is below the tip of the left serif of the right foot of the second A. The tip of the branch is over the upper left serif of the upright of D in 2½ D; the period after D is high. The shaft of the lowest arrow feather at left, if extended, would pass far above the large 2. This die was also used with an obverse dated 1838.

1837, BB-231: Dies 10-A. *Large Head of 1837.* Rarity-3. The Borckardt auction survey found 284 examples of this variety and one each of the other two varieties. *Equivalents:* Breen (monograph) 1; Breen *(Encyclopedia)* 6145; McCloskey-1; Haynor HM-1. *McCloskey Notes:* Nearly all 1837 quarter eagles are of this die combination. Obverse has a die crack from the rim through star 9 and the curls, extending down to the right side of 8 in the date. Although the 1837 date is scarce, a Mint State example of this variety can be obtained with some patience.

1837, BB-232: Dies 10-F. *Large Head of 1837; different dies.* Rarity-7. A single example of this variety appeared in the Heritage Permanent Auction Archives. *Equivalents:* Breen (monograph) 2; Breen *(Encyclopedia)* 6145; McCloskey-2; Haynor HM-2. *McCloskey Notes:* This is a very rare variety. An obverse die crack runs from the rim through star 9 and the curls, extending down to the right side of the 8 in the date. Additional cracks appear from the right side of the 8 to the denticles and from the upright of the 1 to the denticles. McCloskey stated he'd seen only one example of this variety.

1837, BB-233: Dies 11-H. *Large Head of 1837; different dies.* Rarity-7. This is apparently a Proof-only variety. *Equivalents:* Breen *(Encyclopedia)* 6145; McCloskey-3; Dannreuther JD-1; Haynor HM-3. *McCloskey Notes:* An obverse die crack proceeds from the rim through star 8 and the curls, through TY in LIBERTY, to the edge of the bust, to the upper left serif of 7 in the date.[9] McCloskey knew of only two pieces, the Smithsonian Institution and Eliasberg Collection examples, both Proofs. All known pieces have the die crack.

Quarter Eagles of 1838

1838, Obverse Die 12. *The portrait is the Head of 1838. This is the only die of the year; coins have a flat, "broad-mill" rim. Details:* The 1 and 8 in the date are low and close to the border; the second 8 is high, and its upper right is very close to the curl. The lowest part of the curl is to the right of 8. The stars are small and not close to the denticles; the ray of star 6 points to the top of the forelock below the headband. All stars except 2, 3, and 6 show signs of repunching, which is most noticeable on stars 8, 9, and 10.[10]

1837, Reverse Die H. This die was used with obverses dated 1837 and 1838. It is described in detail on page 121, with the other dies of 1837.

1838, BB-241: Dies 12-H. *Head of 1838.* Rarity-3. *Equivalents:* Breen (monograph) 1; Breen *(Encyclopedia)* 6146; McCloskey-1; Dannreuther JD-1; Haynor HM-1. *McCloskey Notes:* This is a scarce date, but examples appear on the market, including at auctions, on a regular basis. Some beautiful high-grade specimens have been offered for sale in recent years.

In his 1964 monograph, Walter Breen listed two varieties, each with a different 1837 reverse. Today, only one is confirmed.

Quarter Eagles of 1838-C

Two obverse and reverse dies were shipped from the Philadelphia Mint to Charlotte, but it seems that only one pair of dies actually saw use. All of these dies were apparently destroyed in 1843.

1838-C, Obverse Die 13. *The portrait is the Head of 1838-C and 1839-D. This is the only obverse die of the year; coins have a flat, "broad-mill" rim. Details:* The 8's in the date are in a script or "fancy" style. The digits in the date are closely spaced, but 8 and 3 are farther apart than the other digits; 1 and 3 are high; 1 is about the same distance from the bust as from the denticles; the top right of 1 is very slightly double-punched; the

8's are low, with the first 8 being lowest; the second 8 is very close to the curl. The C mintmark is to the left of center of 3 and about halfway between the top of 3 and the bust; C is double-punched, with the original C still visible (including partially below it) but lightly defined, and touching the top of 3. The ray of star 6 points to the junction of the headband and the forelock below; the ray of star 7 points to the nearby curve of a hair curl; star 8 points to the right side of the hair curl near the crevice. Stars 1, 5, 8, 9, 10, and 13 are each doubled. This portrait punch was used on the 1838-C and 1839-D quarter eagle dies.

1838-C, Reverse Die J. *Details:* The top of T in UNITED is lower than the tops of the adjacent letters. The letters STAT in STATES are widely spaced, with T, E, and S closer. The left foot of the first A in AMERICA touches the wing; the A leans slightly left and is distant from M; the M and E touch at the bases; the middle arrow point is very close to or lightly touches the bottom of C; the bottom arrow point is very close to or touches the left serif of the right foot of A. The 1 in the fraction is close to the feather; the lower right of 1 touches the fraction bar; the small 2 is clear of the fraction bar. The tip of the branch is over the inside right of the upright of D. Each vertical shield stripe has two lines. This die was used on all 1838-C and some 1839-C quarter eagles.

1838-C, BB-251: Dies 13-J. Rarity-3. This die was also used to coin part of the 1839-C mintage. The 1838-C Classic Head quarter eagle represents 3% of all quarter eagles of this type appearing at auction. *Equivalents:* Breen (monograph) C-1; Breen *(Encyclopedia)* 6147; McCloskey-1; Winter 1-A; Haynor HM-1. *McCloskey Notes:* Most of those seen are Very Fine to Extremely Fine; the variety is quite scarce in About Uncirculated and very rare in Mint State. A die crack develops from the denticles over the left wing to the top of the left wing. Another crack runs from the upper left edge of the shield to the eagle's beak.

Quarter Eagles of 1839

1839, Obverse Die 14. *This is the only die of the year. Details:* The 8 in the date is the script or "fancy" style. Due to the evidence of repunching, this is sometimes called "1839, 9 Over 8," although there is no reasonable possibility that the under-digit is an 8.[11] The 9 and 1 are about the same distance from the denticles, while the two central digits are higher above the denticles; the tops of 1 and 3 slightly lower than the other digits; the 1 is about as close to the bust as to the denticles; the 8 and 3 are more closely spaced than the other numerals; the top of 9 is close to the curl; the left edge of the curl is over the upper left part of 9. The ray of star 6 points to the base of the headband where it joins the forelock; the ray of star 7 points to the curve of the second curl; the ray of star 8 points to the upper right of the third curl; star 9 points to the upper right edge of the fourth curl. Star 8 is repunched.

1836, Reverse Die F. This reverse die was combined with obverses dated 1836, 1837, and 1839. It is described in detail on page 119, with the other dies of 1836.

1839, BB-261: Dies 14-F. *The reverse die, which has three lines in each vertical shield stripe, was first used in 1836.* Rarity-3. Slightly less than 3% of all Classic Head quarter eagles appearing at auction are from this coinage date. The denticles are much more prominent on the obverse die than on the reverse. As mentioned, the reverse die has three lines in each vertical shield stripe as used in 1836; this is somewhat anachronistic in the present 1839 use of the same die. *Equivalents:* Breen (monograph) 1; Breen *(Encyclopedia)* 6148; McCloskey-1; Dannreuther JD-1; Haynor HM-1. *McCloskey Notes:* McCloskey stated that he'd always found it surprising that an old three-pale-gule reverse would be used in 1839 after the two-pale-gule reverses had already been in use for two years in Philadelphia.

Quarter Eagles of 1839-C

On January 10, 1839, two obverse dies were shipped to Charlotte from Philadelphia. A reverse die already on hand from 1838 was employed, to which two reverse dies, shipped on May 3, 1839, were added.

1839-C, Obverse Die 15. *Mintmark C is over and slightly to the left of the center of 3 in the date and about equidistant from the 8 and the curl;* definitive. *Details:* The 8 in the date is the script or "fancy" style. Digits 1 and 8 are lower than the others, and each leans slightly right. The ray of star 6 points to the junction of the headband and the forelock below. Stars 6, 8, and 11 show evidence of repunching; this die is often called an overdate, although the interior spaces of the 8 and 9 would not match in the manner shown here (see the description of the 1839 Philadelphia obverse die on the previous page).

1839-C, Obverse Die 16. *The C mintmark is centered over the left side of 3 in the date and is much closer to the 8 than to the curl;* definitive. *Details:* The 8 in the date is of the script or "fancy" style. Digits 3 and 9 are repunched; their final-position tops are slightly higher than the tops of 1 and 8. The ray of star 6 points to the forelock below the headband. This is often called the *Repunched Date* or *Recut Date.*

1838-C, Reverse Die J. This die was used on all 1838-C and some 1839-C quarter eagles. It is described in detail on page 123, with the other 1838-C dies.

1839-C, Reverse Die K. *Details:* The A and M in AMERICA are separated at the bases; the M and E are joined. The tip of the branch stem is over the right upright of D in denomination. Each vertical shield stripe has two lines.

1839-C, Reverse Die L. *Details:* The second S in STATES is repunched (visible only on the early die state, before relapping). The first A in AMERICA leans slightly left; the tip of the middle arrowhead touches the bottom of C; the tip of the lowest arrowhead touches the inner right foot of the second A. The 1 in the fraction is far from the fraction bar. The tip of the branch stem is over the upper left serif of D in the denomination. Each vertical shield stripe has two lines.

1839-C, BB-271: Dies 15-K. Rarity-6. The Borckardt auction survey indicates that 7.5% of 1839-C quarter eagles appearing at auction are from this die pair. *Equivalents:* Breen (monograph) 1; Breen *(Encyclopedia)* 6149; McCloskey-1; Winter 2-A; Haynor HM-2. *McCloskey Notes:* This very scarce variety is very rare in Mint State. A die crack on the reverse runs from the right rim through the tip of the wing and along the top of the wing, through the field to the eagle's neck.

1839-C, BB-272: Dies 15-L. Rarity-5. The Borckardt auction survey indicates that slightly more than one-fourth of 1839-C quarter eagles appearing at auction are from this die pair. *Equivalents:* Breen (monograph) 2; Breen *(Encyclopedia)* 6149; McCloskey-2; Winter 2-B; Haynor HM-3. *McCloskey Notes:* This scarce variety is usually seen in circulated grades. The obverse has a die defect on the cheek. On the reverse, the second S in STATES is visibly repunched in early die states, but this feature fades after the die is relapped; relapping also created weakness through the leaves on the branch. A die crack develops on the reverse from the rim through the E in STATES and continues to the top of the eagle's head.

1839-C, BB-273: Dies 16-J. *Repunched Date.* Rarity-3. Light clash marks are often seen on both dies. The Borckardt auction survey indicates that nearly two-thirds of 1839-C quarter eagles appearing at auction are from this die pair. *Equivalents:* Breen (monograph) 3; Breen *(Encyclopedia)* 6150; McCloskey-3; Winter 3-C; Haynor HM-1. *McCloskey Notes:* This is the 1839-C variety seen most often, but only in circulated grades. It is a great rarity in Mint State. A crack on the reverse runs from the left tip of the shield through the eagle's beak, through the field to the right side of A in STATES, to the rim. Another crack extends from the rim through the field over the wing at left, to the top of wing, through the field, to the earlier crack. The first crack now extends down along the left side of the shield, through the eagle's talons to the left side of the large 2, to the rim. In McCloskey's observation, in combination with the 1839-C obverse this die always has some cracks. However, the very late state, with cracked *obverse,* is very rare; on these coins a crack runs from the rim through star 2 to the chin, through the ear and the curls, to star 9, to the rim.

Quarter Eagles of 1839-D

Two obverse and two reverse dies were sent from Philadelphia on January 10,[12] 1839, and arrived in Dahlonega on February 1, 1839. Philadelphia Mint director Robert Maskell Patterson requested that the Dahlonega Mint "sink some coins" of the denomination. These dies were defaced on February 8, 1840, indicating that no old dies were on hand after that time.[13]

1839-D, Obverse Die 17. *The upright of the D mintmark is over left part of the 3 in the date;* this is the only obverse die for this year and Mint. *Details:* The 1 in the date is closer to the denticles than to the 9; the top of 9 touches the curl. The digits 39 are slightly repunched, suggesting an overdate to some observers in the past, but this is highly improbable (see the description of the 1839 Philadelphia obverse die on page 123). Stars 1 and 8 are lightly repunched. The denticles on this die are very prominent—more so than on either of the two reverses combined with it. This portrait punch was used on the 1838-C and 1839-D quarter eagle dies.

1839-D, Reverse Die M. *The tip of the light stem is over the upright of D in 2½ D;* definitive for a die used with the 1839-D obverse. *Details:* The tip of the leftmost upper leaf is between the U and N in UNITED. The base of A in STATES is too high; the bases of T, E, and S are close. The right serif of the foot of the second A in AMERICA is clear of the lowest arrowhead. The vertical shield stripes each have two lines (which is true of both reverse dies used with the 1839-D obverse). *No berry is present on the branch.*

1839-D, Reverse Die N. *The tip of* the *heavy stem is slightly to the left of D in 2½ D;* definitive for a die used with the 1839-D obverse. *Details:* The tip of the leftmost upper leaf is distant from U in UNITED and is close to lower left serif of N. The bases of T, E, and S in STATES are farther apart than on reverse die M. The right serif of the foot of the second A in AMERICA is joined to the edge of the lowest arrowhead. Each of the vertical shield stripes has two lines (which is true of both reverse dies used with the 1839-D obverse).

1839-D, BB-281: Dies 17-M. Rarity-4. The Borckardt auction survey indicates that about 60% of 1839-D quarter eagles appearing at auction are from this die pair. *Equivalents:* Breen (monograph) 1; Breen *(Encyclopedia)* 6151; McCloskey-1; Winter 1-A; Haynor HM-2. *McCloskey Notes:* This is the more often seen of the two varieties of 1839-D. Most are Very Fine or Extremely Fine; BB-281 is very rare in About Uncirculated or Mint State.

1839-D, BB-282: Dies 17-N. Rarity-5. The Borckardt auction survey indicates that about 40% of 1839-D quarter eagles appearing at auction are from this die pair. *Equivalents:* Breen (monograph) 1; Breen *(Encyclopedia)* 6151; McCloskey-2; Winter 1-B; Haynor HM-1. *McCloskey Notes:* This variety is very scarce. The reverse has a die crack from the tip of the wing on the left side to the denticles. Another crack runs along the bases of the letters in UNITED, connecting to the rim past D. A crack proceeds from the rim through the upright of the second T in STATES to the top of the eagle's head. This pairing is very rare in About Uncirculated or Mint State.

Quarter Eagles of 1839-O

Two pairs of dies were sent from Philadelphia to New Orleans on March 14, 1839. Both were used for coinage.

1839-O, Obverse Die 18. *The date is low; 9 is closer to the denticles than to the curl;* definitive. *Details:* The date is low and close to the denticles, with 1 and 9 being lowest; the upper insides of 3 and 9 are slightly double-punched. Stars 3, 4, and 5 are repunched.

1839-O, Obverse Die 19. *The date is high; 9 is closer to the curl than to the denticles;* definitive. *Details:* The date is high in the die; the upper left serif of 1 is longer than on obverse die 18; the base of 3 is low. Stars 11 and 12 are repunched.

1839-O, Reverse Die P. *The small 2 in the denomination touches the fraction bar;* definitive. *Details:* The U in UNITED is high and leans left. The E and S in STATES are close. The tip of the middle arrow touches the bottom of C in AMERICA; the tip of the lowest arrow touches the right base of the second A. *Close fraction:* The numerator is very close to the fraction bar, with the denominator touching. A small berry is present on a broken stem; the end of the stem is bold. Each vertical shield stripe has two lines; the second line of the third stripe and the first line of the sixth stripe pierce the horizontal line above.

1839-O, Reverse Die Q. *The small 2 in the denomination does not touch fraction bar;* definitive. *Details:* The D in UNITED is slightly low. The letters STAT in STATES are wide; T and E are close. The tips of the middle and lowest arrows end below CA in AMERICA. *Wide fraction:* Neither the numerator nor the denominator in ½ is close to the fraction bar. The end of the stem is weak. Each vertical shield stripe has two lines.

1839-O, BB-291: Dies 18-P. *Low date. Close fraction.* Rarity-4. On some examples the reverse die has been excessively polished, with many of the lower details weak or missing. The arrow shafts are weak, the lower one broken. The stem to the branch is almost entirely gone, leaving a branch tip isolated in the field above and to the left of D in the denomination and leaving three pairs of leaves isolated in the field. The berry and stem are also entirely missing. The Borckardt auction survey indicates that about one-third of 1839-O quarter eagles appearing at auction are from this die pair. *Equivalents:* Breen (monograph) 2; Breen *(Encyclopedia)* 6153; McCloskey-1; Winter-2; Haynor HM-2. This die combination is often seen with the obverse and reverse dies aligned in the same direction, rather than the normal 180° alignment. *McCloskey Notes:* This is the scarcer of the two varieties of 1839-O. A reverse die crack extends from the rim to the wing tip on the right, through the wing and into the field to the eagle's neck, from the tip of the eagle's beak, continuing left to the wing and along the wing to the denticles beyond the wing tip. Another crack runs from the denticles through the center of R in AMERICA, through the field to the upper arrowhead, through the eagle's talons and out into the field to the left of the eagle. A final crack goes from the rim through the left upright of the N, through the leaf tip, to the earlier crack.

1839-O, BB-292: Dies 19-Q. *High date. Wide fraction.* Rarity-3. On the reverse die the branch and certain related elements are weak or missing. The Borckardt auction survey indicates that about two-thirds of 1839-O quarter eagles appearing at auction are from this die pair. *Equivalents:* Breen (monograph) 1; Breen *(Encyclopedia)* 6152; McCloskey-2; Winter-1; Haynor HM-1. *McCloskey Notes:* A reverse die crack runs from the denticles through I in UNITED, into the field to the tip of the upper leaf, through the eagle's talons and down through the large 2 to the denticles. Another crack connects the bases of I and T in UNITED.

Grading Standards

MS-60 to 70 (Mint State). ***Obverse:*** At MS-60, some abrasion and contact marks are seen on the portrait, most noticeably on the cheek, as the hair details are complex on this type. Luster is present, but may be dull or lifeless, and interrupted in patches. Many low-level Mint State coins have grainy surfaces. At MS-63, contact marks are few, and abrasion is very light. Abrasion is even less at MS-64. An MS-65 coin has hardly any abrasion, and contact marks are minute. Luster should be full and rich and is often more intense on the obverse. Grades above MS-65 are defined by having fewer marks as perfection is approached. ***Reverse:*** Comments apply as for the obverse, except that abrasion is most noticeable on the eagle's neck and the highest area of the wings.

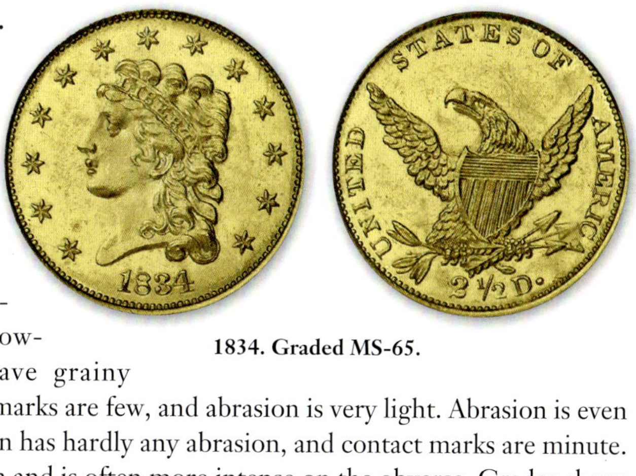

1834. Graded MS-65.

1837. Graded AU-55.

AU-50, 53, 55, 58 (About Uncirculated). ***Obverse:*** Friction is seen on the higher parts, particularly the cheek and hair (under magnification) of Miss Liberty. Friction and scattered marks are in the field, ranging from extensive at AU-50 to minimal at AU-58. Luster may be seen in protected areas, minimal at AU-50 but more visible at AU-58. On an AU-58 coin the field retains some luster as well. ***Reverse:*** Comments as for Mint State, except that the eagle's neck, the top of the wings, the leaves, and the arrowheads now show noticeable wear, as do other features. Luster ranges from perhaps 40% remaining in protected areas at AU-50 to nearly full mint bloom at AU-58. Often the reverse of this type retains much more luster than does the obverse.

1834. Graded EF-40.

EF-40, 45 (Extremely Fine). ***Obverse:*** Wear is seen on the portrait overall, with reduction or elimination of some separation of hair strands, especially in the area close to the face. The cheek shows light wear. Luster is minimal or nonexistent at EF-40, and may survive in among the letters of LIBERTY at EF-45. ***Reverse:*** Wear is greater than on an About Uncirculated coin. On most (but not all) coins the eagle's neck lacks some feather detail on its highest points. Feathers have lost some detail near the edges and tips of the wings. Some areas of the horizontal lines in the shield may be blended together. Some traces of luster may be seen, more so at EF-45 than at EF-40.

1836. Graded VF-30.

VF-20, 30 (Very Fine). ***Obverse:*** Wear on the portrait has reduced the hair detail, especially to the right of the face and the top of the head, but much can still be seen. ***Reverse:*** Wear is greater, including on the shield and wing feathers. Generally, Classic Head gold at this grade level lacks eye appeal.

The Classic Head quarter eagle is seldom collected in grades lower than VF-20.

1836. Graded PF-65 Cameo.

PF-60 to 70 (Proof). ***Obverse and Reverse:*** PF-60 to 62 coins have extensive hairlines and may have nicks and contact marks. At PF-63, hairlines are prominent, but the mirror surface is very reflective. PF-64 coins have fewer hairlines. At PF-65, hairlines should be minimal and mostly seen only under magnification. There should be no nicks or marks. PF-66 and higher coins should have no marks or hairlines visible to the unaided eye.

1834, Classic Head, No Motto

Circulation-Strike Mintage: 112,234

Proof Mintage: 12 (estimated by John Dannreuther)

First year of type.

Virtually all went into circulation, where they furnished the first quarter eagles to be seen in commercial channels in more than 20 years. Gold coins were a novelty to the contemporary generation of Americans, and a number of pieces were saved as souvenirs.

Estimated Total Population (Mint State). 200 to 300. Over a long period of years many Mint State coins have been cited in the literature. It is likely that these coins—representing, along with the gold $5 half eagle of the same style, the first gold coins to be seen in general circulation for more than a generation—were widely saved as souvenirs. The quality of the survivors ranges from MS-60 upward, often with handling marks, but occasionally of choice or gem quality, sometimes with prooflike surfaces.

Most Mint State specimens are of the Small Head obverse style and often are partly prooflike (Proofs were also struck from this die). Large Head examples are scarcer in all Mint State and other grades, and at the choice or gem level are especially hard to find. Large Head quarter eagles usually are lustrous and frosty, not prooflike.

Estimated Total Population (Circulated Grades). 2,200 to 2,800. The 1834, No Motto, coins are very plentiful and easily collectible; this is the most widely available date of the Classic Head type (although 1836 has a higher mintage). Extremely Fine seems to be about the norm for historical appearances at auctions, as reflected in David W. Akers's 1975 study. Very Fine and Extremely Fine coins abound, and About Uncirculated coins are seen with some frequency. As is pointed out in appendix A, these pieces circulated very extensively.

While Mint State coins are dominated by coins with the Small Head obverse, circulated specimens are most frequently seen with the Large Head portrait style.

Characteristics of Striking and Die Notes. Quality of strike varies from variety to variety—as multiple dies were used on several occasions, sharpness varies. Some show softness on the highest curls in Miss Liberty's hair, this being especially true of the Small Head pieces. Overall, however, most are quite well struck. The fields of the quarter eagle varieties of this year are on a flat plane (there is virtually no basining). See also McCloskey's notes on the known die combinations described on page 116 for this issue.

Selected Auction Records

In June 1864, lot 396 was described by an uninformed cataloger in the catalog of the George F. Seavey Collection sold by Bangs, Merwin & Co. (an auctioneer of many things with no numismatist on staff): "1834 New type, Uncirculated, very rare." Actually, this is not a rare date, and the description is representative of the disinformation given in many auction catalogs of this era. In his December 1875 sale of the Col. Mendes I. Cohen Collection, Edward Cogan described lot 202: "1834 Small head. New standard. Uncirculated." Realized $3. John W. Haseltine, in his 18th sale description of lot 1150, gave this early recognition of the Large Head style: "1834: head of 1835; Uncirculated."

W. Elliot Woodward's sixty-ninth sale, October 1884, included lot 1951: "1834 The new type; Very Fine or Uncirculated." Realized $2.50. That interesting description reflects the casual nature of grading! Years later in his 1907 fixed-price list Elmer S. Sears offered lot 167: "1834 Another from different dies. The head a shade larger and with a different expression to face. Uncirculated, Proof surface. $7." S.H. Chapman's June 1909 sale of the Henry L. Jewett Collection included lot 889: "1834 New, weaker style, with small head, without cap, and with hair in puffs on top of head; head bound with ribbon, on which LIBERTY. Reverse, same design smaller and without motto. Variety with smaller head. Scarce. Very Fine." Realized $3.75. Varieties were discussed by Thomas L. Elder in his March 1911 sale of the William H. Woodin Collection, which included lot 951: "1834. Variety with larger head, the date closer to the bust, and curl, just over the figure 4; second star at left is double-struck. On reverse the arrows are smaller, points are shorter and do not reach C or A. Slight nick or two on reverse. Very Fine." Realized $2.75. Lot 952: "1834. Small head of Liberty, date away from bust, the 4 more distant than lot 950; arrows thicker than in last, one touching A. Uncirculated, Proof surface." Realized $3.75.

Proofs

John Dannreuther's study *United States Proof Coins*, volume 4, is the prime source for Proof die data and notes and for estimated populations of Classic Head issues. In this chapter, JD numbers from that text are used in addition to BB numbers.

At least four Proof pieces were struck for inclusion in as many presentation sets, including one each for the Sultan of Muscat and King of Siam; these sets also included Proof strikes of the earlier With Motto quarter eagle of the same year. Additional Proofs were struck, possibly for distribution, as this represented the first time in many years that gold coins were being struck for general domestic circulation. The Act of June 28, 1834, attracted much attention, and perhaps some ceremonies were involved, although no records have been located in this regard.

Proof Die Data and Notes. Proofs have the Small Head style obverse, save for a solitary specimen in the Smithsonian Institution, which is of the Large Head style. The Small Head style is JD-1; the Large Head, JD-2.
Estimated Total Population (Proof). BB-201, JD-1: seven. BB-204, JD-2: one.

Selected Auction Records

Note: There have been many listings for Proof coins over the years. Probably, most represent prooflike circulation strikes.

In May 1864 W. Elliot Woodward's John F. McCoy Collection sale included lot 1982: "1834 The new type, splendid Proof, rare." Realized $7.50. Woodward's June 1885 sale of the J. Colvin Randall Collection had two. Lot 978: "1834 New type; brilliant Proof, very scarce." Realized $3. Lot 979: "1834 New Type; a variety; Proof, rare." Realized $2.60. In his 1907 fixed-price list Elmer S. Sears offered lot 166: "1834 New type. The small 'classic' head a perfect Proof. Excessively rare in this condition. $15." Thomas L. Elder's March 1911 sale of the William H. Woodin Collection included this description of lot 950 (BB-201): "1834. New type with small head of Liberty to left, and without motto. Variety with date distant from the bust, and curl between 3 and 4 in date; arrow points touch right foot of A. and C. Brilliant, glittering Proof. Finest known. Parmelee Collection." Realized $15. The same catalog included lot 953 (BB-204): "1834. Head, stars and lettering smaller than lot 950, and date distant from bust, curl between 3 and 4; arrows long, one touching A, differing from any of preceding. Proof. Rare." Realized $4.30.

In February 1921 the catalog of B. Max Mehl's sale of the Dr. G.F.E. Wilharm Collection described lot 71: "1834 The new type, small Liberty head to left, wavy hair, band inscribed Liberty; date below, 13 stars; reverse as last but without motto. Yellow gold. Magnificent perfect brilliant Proof, sharp. This is not a bright Uncirculated specimen but a really struck Proof and as perfect as is possible to obtain. And as such I consider it of excessive rarity." Realized $21. Stack's sale of the J.F. Bell Collection in December 1944 included lot 101: "1834 New type brilliant Proof with high wire edge." Realized $22.50. In April 1956 Abe Kosoff's sale of the Melish and Hester Collections included lot 1121: "1834 Without motto. Brilliant Proof, sharp." Realized $105.

F-12	VF-20	EF-40	AU-50	AU-55	MS-60	MS-63	PF-60	PF-63	PF-65
$425	$600	$800	$1,250	$1,650	$3,100	$7,000	$35,000	$100,000	$300,000

1835

Circulation-Strike Mintage: 131,402 (calendar year mintage; not necessarily all with this date)

Proof Mintage: 5 (estimated by John Dannreuther)

Rare in Mint State.

Walter Breen *(Encyclopedia)* writes, "Most of reported 1835 mintage was dated 1834." Some 1835-dated quarter eagles were also struck in calendar year 1836.

These quarter eagles circulated extensively in domestic commerce, as did all others of the Classic Head type.

Estimated Total Population (Mint State). 25 to 30. Mint State coins are much scarcer than for the lower-mintage 1834, since, by 1835, the novelty of seeing a gold coin had faded, and few were saved as souvenirs. Mint State coins, when found, are apt to be in lower ranges, quite unlike the situation for 1834. Published data are contradictory, but it is quite evident that very few Mint State coins have appeared in important collections over the years.

Estimated Total Population (Circulated Grades). 400 to 600. In circulated grades the 1835 is fairly scarce, at least in comparison to the preceding and following dates. Very Fine and Extremely Fine are the usual grades encountered, although About Uncirculated coins are sufficiently available that the collector will have no difficulty finding one. Circulated specimens could still be found in bank holdings as late as the early twentieth century.

In 1884, in the Hon. Heman Ely Collection catalog, W. Elliot Woodward expressed surprise to find that the 1835 was quite elusive (see citation below).

Characteristics of Striking and Die Notes. These usually show lightness of strike on the highest hair curls. The surfaces are usually lustrous, not prooflike. See also McCloskey's notes on the known die combinations described on page 117 for this issue.

Selected Auction Records

The October 1875 sale of the Col. Mendes I. Cohen Collection included Edward Cogan's description of lot 203: "1835 Good impression." Realized $3.50. "Good impression" probably meant "sharp strike." The catalog of John W. Haseltine's June 1883 sale of the William J. Jenks Collection described lot 440: "1835 Uncirculated. Very scarce." Realized $4. W. Elliot Woodward's description of lot 902 in his January 1884 sale of the Heman Ely Collection ran thusly: "1835 Fine. I find this piece in only one catalogue, which seems to indicate a high degree of rarity."[14] Realized $4.50 to Chapman. In his 1907 fixed-price list Elmer S. Sears offered lot 168: "1835 Uncirculated, Proof surface. $8."

In May 1915 B. Max Mehl's catalog of the B.W. Smith Collection included this description of lot 256: "1835 Variety with 'comma' above D in 2½ D. About Fine. Scarce." Realized $3.25. In his November 1939 sale of the William B. Hale Collection, Mehl described lot 759: "1835 About Uncirculated, sharp with mint luster." Realized $5. In April 1956 Abe Kosoff's sale of the Melish and Hester Collections included lot 1125: "1835 Proof-like; some rubbing." Realized $17.50.

PROOFS

The following are the examples known to David W. Akers,[15] later in the Dannreuther study:

1. National Numismatic Collection, Smithsonian Institution.
2. John Jay Pittman Collection Part II, lot 1719; "Memorable Collection," lot 96; "World's Greatest Collection," lot 102, this being the F.C.C. Boyd coin; William H. Woodin, lot 954; John G. Mills, lot 549; Lorin G. Parmelee, lot 1046.

3. Harry W. Bass Jr. Research Foundation; Louis Eliasberg, lot 102; George H. Earle, lot 2525.
4. Davis-Graves, lot 685; "J.F. Bell" Collection (Jake Shapiro), lot 102.

Proof Die Data and Notes. Proofs of this date were struck from a pair of dies also used to make circulating coinage. The reverse die appears on Proofs of 1834 and 1835.

Estimated Total Population (Proof). BB-211, JD-1: four.

Selected Auction Records

In June 1885, W. Elliot Woodward's sale of the J. Colvin Randall Collection included lot 980: "1835 Proof; very scarce." Realized $2.60. In September of the same year Woodward offered another coin from Randall, lot 1055: "1835 Very Fine, a Proof impression, scarce." Realized $2.80. Thomas L. Elder's March 1911 sale of the William H. Woodin Collection included this description of lot 954: "1835. Proof; rare." Realized $6. Stack's sale of the J.F. Bell Collection in December 1944 included lot 102: "1835 Brilliant Proof, very rare. High auction records." Realized $87.50. In April 1956 Abe Kosoff's sale of the Melish and Hester Collections included lot 1124: "1835 Proof, not brilliant. Small edge bruise." Realized $31.

F-12	VF-20	EF-40	AU-50	AU-55	MS-60	MS-63	PF-60	PF-63	PF-65
$425	$600	$800	$1,250	$1,650	$3,100	$8,500	$35,000	$100,000	$350,000

1836

Circulation-Strike Mintage: 547,986 (calendar-year mintage)

Proof Mintage: 10 (estimated total for three varieties by John Dannreuther)

The 1836 has the largest calendar-year mintage of the Classic Head type. The mintage figure includes some coins dated 1835.

In December 1836, the secretary of the Treasury reported that a record number of quarter eagles had been coined to provide an "active and convenient circulation."[16] At the time, the Treasury Department had a large amount of gold on hand as indemnification by the French, Spanish, and Neapolitan interests for spoliations upon American commerce in the era 1807 and later. Not having to deal with the specific requests of outside depositors—as the Mint usually had to do—it was free to coin more pieces than usual of the quarter eagle denomination. There was a great need for small gold coins in circulation, and the Treasury had recently petitioned Congress to authorize a new denomination, the gold dollar, although that denomination would not be made until years later in 1849.

Estimated Total Population (Mint State). 150 to 225. Despite the very high mintage of this date, Mint State specimens are equally as scarce as for the low-mintage 1834. Still, there are enough Mint State 1836 issues around that the specialist will not lack for an example.

Estimated Total Population (Circulated Grades). 1,800 to 2,200. The 1836 is most plentiful in circulated grades, in proportion to its original mintage. Typically seen conditions are Very Fine to About Uncirculated.

Characteristics of Striking and Die Notes. Walter Breen wrote, "Presumably the 1836s with Head of 1834 and Head of 1835 were from dies completed earlier [by engraver William Kneass before he had his stroke on August 27, 1835], but with final digit omitted."[17] See also McCloskey's notes on the known die combinations described on pages 119–121 for this issue.

Selected Auction Records

Note: The vast majority of listings in auction catalogs are for circulated pieces, often described tersely as "1836 Very Fine" or similar, and contribute little to knowledge, except to indicate that this is a common date in the Classic Head series. The following is an expanded selection, including descriptions of die varieties.

In May 1864 W. Elliot Woodward's John F. McCoy Collection sale included lot 1983, curiously described as rare: "1836 Very Fine and rare." Realized $5.50. October 1875 sale of the Col. Mendes I. Cohen Collection included Edward Cogan's description of lot 204: "1836 Good impression." Realized $3. J.W. Haseltine's eighteenth sale, December 1875, included lot 1152: "1836; Uncirculated." The catalog of John W. Haseltine's June 1883 sale of the William J. Jenks Collection described lot 441: "1836 Uncirculated. Very rare." Realized $3. In his 1907 fixed-price list Elmer S. Sears offered lot 170: "1836 Uncirculated. Mint bloom. $7.50." Thomas L. Elder's March 1911 sale of the William H. Woodin Collection included several. Lot 955 was described thusly: "1836. Straight 6; arrows do not touch lettering. Uncirculated." Realized $2.90. Lot 957: "1836. Crooked 6, figure 3 very low. Small leaves without berry; point of arrow touches left part of A, A touches wing. Uncirculated, Proof surface." Realized $2.90. Lot 958: "1836. Crooked, high 6; small leaves without berry, arrows barely touch C and A. Uncirculated." Realized $4. Lot 959: "1836. Crooked 6, date nearly straight; large leaves with berry; arrow points away from lettering; differs from any preceding. Uncirculated." Realized $3.90.

In May 1913 the U.S. Coin Co.'s sale of the Malcolm N. Jackson Collection included multiples. Lot 119: "1836 Even date. Arrow points to left foot of A. Very Fine." Realized $2.75. Lot 120: "1836 Uneven date. Arrow points to right foot of A. Extremely Fine." Realized $2.75. Lot 121: "1836 Same variety. Extremely Fine." Realized $2.75. "High 6; curved date. Rev. Variety with berry in olive branch. Very Fine." Realized $3.50. In February 1921 the catalog of B. Max Mehl's sale of the Dr. G.F.E. Wilharm Collection described lot 74: "1836 Brilliant Uncirculated, with frosty Mint surface. As perfect as the day it was minted. Rare so choice. Cost $9.50." Realized $6.10. The November 1932 sale of the R. Taylor Collection included Mehl's description of lot 123: "1836, Curl directly over 6. Fine." Realized $2.80. In his November 1939 sale of the William B. Hale Collection, Mehl described lot 760: "1836 Curl over and to right of 6. Very Fine." Realized $6. In April 1956 Abe Kosoff's sale of the Melish and Hester Collections included lot 1126: "1836 Extremely Fine. Arrow points to the left edge of right stand of A." Realized $12.50.

The November 1956 New Netherlands sale of the Thomas L. Gaskill Collection included lot 208: "1836 Head of 1837. Different from all preceding heads; smaller stars.

Brilliant Uncirculated. Not sharply struck, and barely perfect, but unusually attractive. Only one die variety seen, therefore apparently scarce or rare." Realized $26. In June 1957 the New Netherlands sale of Eliasberg duplicates had multiples. Lot 578: "1836. Head of '34 . . . . Obv. Clapp 1, rev. Clapp 5. Fully equal to the Gaskill coin, lot 206 in our Forty-Eighth sale, which was called 'Choice Unc. Dullish; unimportant traces of bag handling.' Rare, more than ten times so than the next." Realized $25. Lot 579: "1836. Head of '35. The usual type. Fine or better, rather flat struck upon the obverse like many of this date. Ex John H. Clapp." Realized $11. Lot 580: "1836. Head of '37. About Very Fine; nice, clean surface. Same die as the Gaskill coin, lot 208, which brought $26. Unc. Very scarce, almost rare. The three basic types of the 1836 were illustrated in our last (48th) catalog, the obverse enlarged for clear comparison." Realized $13.

Proofs

Proof Die Data and Notes. At least two die combinations were used to strike Proofs of this year, probably indicating that Proofs were made on at least two different occasions.

Estimated Total Population (Proof). BB-225, JD-1: three. BB-228, JD-2: two. BB-222, JD-3: two. See the Dannreuther study for a list of the known examples of the three varieties.

Selected Auction Records

In his May 1883 sale of the Winslow Lewis Collection, W. Elliot Woodward described lot 2033: "1836 Proof impression, Very Fine." Realized $8. In October of the year in this sale of the collection, Woodward may have offered the same coin as lot 1423: "1836 Fine Proof impression." Realized $3.85. Abe Kosoff, cataloger for the January 1946 sale of the "World's Greatest Collection" (F.C.C. Boyd Collection; Numismatic Gallery), described lot 103: "1836 brilliant Proof." Realized $80. The same cataloger and firm offered lot 97 from Jacob Shapiro, billed in March 1948 as the Memorable Collection: "1836. Brilliant Proof. Rare. W.G.C." Realized $45. B. Max Mehl's sale of the Jerome Kern Collection in May 1950 included lot 26: "1836. Perfect brilliant Proof gem. Extremely rare in this remarkable condition. Mr. Kern's notation states this is from the Green Collection, purchased at private sale, at $165."

F-12	VF-20	EF-40	AU-50	AU-55	MS-60	MS-63	PF-60	PF-63	PF-65
$425	$600	$800	$1,250	$1,650	$3,100	$7,000	$35,000	$125,000	$350,000

1837

Circulation-Strike Mintage: 45,080 (calendar-year mintage)

Proof Mintage: 5 (per John Dannreuther)

Rare in Mint State.

Estimated Total Population (Mint State). 20 to 30. Mint State specimens are fairly rare and come on the market only on widely spaced occasions. Nearly all are in lower grade ranges, MS-60 to MS-62 being typical.

Estimated Total Population (Circulated Grades). 300 to 500. Circulated examples of the 1837 are quite scarce. Very Fine and Extremely Fine are typical grades.

Characteristics of Striking and Die Notes. See McCloskey's notes on the known die combinations described on pages 121–122 for this issue.

Selected Auction Records

The October 1875 sale of the Col. Mendes I. Cohen Collection included Edward Cogan's description of lot 205: "1837 Good impression." Realized $2.85. In June 1885, W. Elliot Woodward's sale of the J. Colvin Randall Collection included lot 982: "1837 Sharp; nearly Proof, scarce." Realized $2.60. In his 1907 fixed-price list Elmer S. Sears offered lot 172: "1837 Uncirculated. Mint lustre. Rare, and especially so when as fine. $12." Thomas L. Elder's March 1911 sale of the William H. Woodin Collection included this description of lot 960: "1837 Wide date. Arrow touches A, but not C. Mint bloom." Realized $6.75. In May 1915 B. Max Mehl's catalog of the B.W. Smith Collection included this description of lot 258: "1837 Compact date. Extremely Fine, sharp impression." Realized $3.10. Lot 509 in Mehl's April 1931 sale of the Morris Collection was described thusly: "1837 Curl slightly over and to left of 7. Very Fine. Very scarce." Realized $3.75. It appears that Mehl was viewing this from inside the coin, as the two known dies have the curl slightly over and to the *right* of 7.

In June 1941 Mehl's sale of the William Forrester Dunham Collection included lot 1928: "1837 Uncirculated, with frosty mint surface. Slightest evidence of being handled with other coins. A scarce date in rare condition. Listed at $10 in only fine." Realized $7.90. Stack's sale of the J.F. Bell Collection in December 1944 included lot 104: "1837 Brilliant Uncirculated." Realized $20. Mehl's sale of the Jerome Kern Collection in May 1950 included lot 27: "1837 Practically Uncirculated with frosty mint surface. Very scarce date in scarce condition. Seldom equaled. Record $25." Realized $19. In April 1956 Abe Kosoff's sale of the Melish and Hester Collections included lot 1128: "1837 Uncirculated." Realized $23.50. In June 1957 the New Netherlands Coin Company's sale of Eliasberg duplicates had this for lot 581: "1837. First of only two varieties of the year; the same die as the Unc. one in our previous sale. Very Fine or so. Only 45,080 made. The W.G.C. lot, also VF, commanded $25 in 1946." Realized $11.50.

Proofs

Estimated Total Population (Proof). BB-233, JD-1: four. In the past it has been suggested that there are two die varieties of the 1837 Proof quarter eagle, but research by John Dannreuther has confirmed only one. See the Dannreuther study for the list of the four known examples of the single combination.

F-12	VF-20	EF-40	AU-50	AU-55	MS-60	MS-63	PF-60	PF-63	PF-65
$450	$750	$1,200	$1,750	$2,000	$4,500	$13,500	$32,500	$125,000	$400,000

1838

Circulation-Strike Mintage:
47,030 (calendar-year mintage)

Proof Mintage: 2 (per John Dannreuther)

Rare in Mint State.

Estimated Total Population (Mint State). 20 to 30. The 1838 is quite rare in Mint State. Most are in lower grades of MS-60 to MS-62.

Estimated Total Population (Circulated Grades). 400 to 600. In circulated grades the 1838 is quite scarce. Very Fine and Extremely Fine are typical grades.

Characteristics of Striking and Die Notes. See McCloskey's notes on the known die combination described on page 122 for this issue.

Selected Auction Records

The October 1875 sale of the Col. Mendes I. Cohen Collection included Edward Cogan's description of lot 206: "1838 Good impression." Realized $5. The catalog of John W. Haseltine's June 1883 sale of the William J. Jenks Collection described lot 444: "1838 Uncirculated. Proof surface. Rare." Realized $8. In his 1907 fixed-price list Elmer S. Sears offered lot 173: "1838 Uncirculated. (Copper alloy.) Handsome. Mint lustre. Sharp beautiful specimen. A gem. $15." Thomas L. Elder's March 1911 sale of the William H. Woodin Collection included this description of lot 961: "1838. Leaf ends at U. Extremely Fine." Realized $3.10. The May 1915 B. Max Mehl catalog of the B.W. Smith Collection included this description of lot 259: "1838 Wide date, broad borders. Arrows touch CA. Very Fine." Realized $3.50.

In his November 1939 sale of the William B. Hale Collection, Mehl described lot 763: "1838 Uncirculated with Proof surface." Realized $7.50. In June 1941 Mehl's sale of the William Forrester Dunham Collection included lot 1929: "1838 Uncirculated, with mint luster; broad borders. Rare so choice. Listed at $10 in Very Fine condition. This one certainly worth much more." Realized $7.35. The November 1956 New Netherlands sale of the Thomas L. Gaskill Collection included lot 210: "1838 New head, . . . seen on this date and 1839/8 Philadelphia coins only. Broad borders, narrow dentils, very small stars. Extremely Fine or so, even though bought as Uncirculated. About as rare as last; some 47,030 coined." Realized $17.50. In June 1957 the New Netherlands sale of Eliasberg duplicates had this for lot 582: "1838. New head, as on 1839/8 Philadelphia coins. Rev. of 1837; (another variety exists with the same obv., different rev.). Though bought as Unc. (understandably), this is just an unusually beautiful Ex. Fine. Broad obverse border; nicely struck. The W.G.C.-Memorable example realized $25., eleven years ago." Realized $13.50.

Proofs

Estimated Total Population (Proof). BB-241, JD-1: one. The only known example is in the Harry W. Bass Jr. Core Collection exhibit, on loan at the American Numismatic Association headquarters in Colorado Springs, Colorado.

Selected Auction Records

Note: It not known how many of these, if any, would qualify as Proof today; Elder's 1913 example does not match the reverse die of JD-1.

In November 1880 in S.K. Harzfeld's 15th Sale, lot 631 was offered: "1838 Philadelphia Mint. *Proof.* Rare." Realized $4.07. W. Elliot Woodward's May 1883 sale of the Winslow Lewis Collection included lot 2034: "1838 Proof impression, Very Fine." Realized $7.25. In October 1913 in his eighth sale Thomas L. Elder offered lot 967: "1838 Arrow under left foot of A. Brilliant Proof. Very rare in this condition."

F-12	VF-20	EF-40	AU-50	AU-55	MS-60	MS-63
$425	$625	$1,000	$1,500	$1,750	$4,250	$11,500

1838-C

Circulation-Strike Mintage: 7,894

Rarest Classic Head quarter eagle. Incredibly rare in Mint State.

The Charlotte Mint opened for business this year, and this is the first branch-mint coin of the quarter eagle denomination. It has the lowest mintage of the Classic Head series.

The deliveries were reported as follows:[18] July 27: 2,104; September 27: 3,506; November 8: 2,244 (these were struck in October); December 31: 40. These figures total 7,894, or slightly more than the 7,880 later published in the *Mint Report*.

Estimated Total Population (Mint State). 4 to 6. This issue is exceedingly rare in Mint State. It is traditionally considered to be *the* great Mint State rarity in the Classic Head series, but in recent times certification listings have expanded for various reasons—including resubmissions and optimism. To find a truly beautiful, truly choice specimen is no easy task.

The data on the 1838-C are quite confusing. In *Gold Coins of the Charlotte Mint: 1838–1861*, Douglas Winter suggests that the finest is an MS-63 (PCGS) specimen that is from the Melish Collection (1956). Another coin mentioned by Winter is described as "graded MS-63 by PCGS. It appears that this coin was salvaged, along with a group of Mint State 1840 quarter eagles, from a shipwreck off the coast of North Carolina." If this sea-salvaged coin has an etched surface, then it would seem that it would not be in the same class as the Stanley Elrod coin. The point of this is that grading numbers are seen here and there in the literature, but in-person examination is necessary to see which pieces are better than others.

Estimated Total Population (Circulated Grades). 100 to 150. The 1838-C is very elusive in all circulated grades. Very Fine and, in particular, Extremely Fine are the conditions normally seen. Examples that grade About Uncirculated or finer are very rare. As the first Charlotte Mint quarter eagle the 1838-C has been quite popular for a long time, and in any grade it is a highly sought-after issue.

Characteristics of Striking and Die Notes. The 1838-C is usually well struck, except, perhaps, for some insignificant lightness on the highest central hair strands. All known specimens have a raised area from die rust at the border below the lowest curl.

The edge reeding on Classic Head quarter eagles from the Charlotte and Dahlonega Mints "is much wider than the reeding for Philadelphia and New Orleans coins."[19]

See also McCloskey's notes on the known die combination described on page 123 for this issue.

Selected Auction Records

The catalog of John W. Haseltine's June 1883 sale of the William J. Jenks Collection described lot 443: "1838 C above date. Uncirculated. Rare." Realized $4.25. Thomas L. Elder's March 1911 sale of the William H. Woodin Collection included this description of lot 1115: "1838-C. Small head of Liberty to left, C over the date." Realized $5.25. No grade given. In May 1913 the U.S. Coin Co.'s sale of the Malcolm N. Jackson Collection included lot 269: "1838-C Fine." Realized $4. In his November 1939 sale of the William B. Hale Collection, Mehl described lot 832: "1838-C First year of issue. C. between date and bust. Strictly Fine. Rare. Catalogs at $20. Purchased by Mr. Hale in 1913." Realized $10.50. Stack's sale of the J.F. Bell Collection in December 1944 included lot 187: "1838-C Brilliant Uncirculated, mintmark above date." Realized $37.50. In June 1946 Mehl's sale of the William Cutler Atwater Collection included lot 2020: "1838-C. First year of issue. Mint letter C between bust and date. Uncirculated with unusually high raised borders, especially on obverse. Sharp with full mint luster. Very scarce so choice. Recent record $40." Realized $35.50.

Mehl's sale of the Jerome Kern Collection in May 1950 included lot 114: "1838 C. First year of issue. Mint letter C between bust and date. Practically Uncirculated with mint luster; high raised borders. Scarce so choice. A similar specimen in my Atwater Sale brought $35.50." Realized $30. In Abe Kosoff's sale of the Melish and Hester Collections, April 1956, this was the description of lot 1130: "1838-C. First issue of quarter eagles from the Charlotte Mint. Uncirculated, scarce. Cost $47.50 years ago." Realized $52.50. In November 1956 New Netherlands' sale of the Thomas L. Gaskill Collection included lot 211: "1838-C First year of issue; mintmark between date and bust, as on 1839 branch mint coins. Head different from last, seen on this and 1839/8-D coins only. Very Fine. Exceptionally bold upon the obverse; the weak reverse with a few defects, the most serious a tiny rim nick at bottom right. Very scarce. The head on the last shows differences in the upper and back curls. These differences acquire significance when one remembers that each new head, as in the cents, required the manufacture of a new hub from which working dies were made."

F-12	VF-20	EF-40	AU-50	AU-55	MS-60	MS-63
$3,000	$4,500	$7,500	$10,000	$13,500	$27,000	$50,000

1839

Circulation-Strike Mintage: 27,021 (calendar-year mintage)

Proof Mintage: 5 (estimated by John Dannreuther)

Date slightly repunched. Sometimes called "1839, 9 Over 8." Rarest 1839 quarter eagle. Incredibly rare in Mint State.

Estimated Total Population (Mint State). 3 to 5. An exceedingly rare issue in Mint State, the 1839 is far and away the most elusive Philadelphia Mint date at this grade level. Even the finest collections were apt to have a worn specimen.

Estimated Total Population (Circulated Grades). 150 to 250. Very Fine and Extremely Fine are the usual grades for this very scarce and somewhat underappreciated coin. It may come as a surprise for the reader to learn that the 1839 Philadelphia Mint quarter eagle is the rarest issue of the year.

Characteristics of Striking and Die Notes. Typical examples have sharp central details and weak stars on the obverse; see McCloskey's notes on the known die combination described on pages 123–124 for this issue.

Selected Auction Records

Note: Until modern times many listings called the 1839 an overdate.

In his 1907 fixed-price list Elmer S. Sears offered lot 176: "1839 Over 1838. Extremely fine and very rare. This date of the Philadelphia mintage is much rarer than most collectors or dealers are aware. $10." Thomas L. Elder's March 1911 sale of the William H. Woodin Collection included this description of lot 962: "1839. End of leaf between U and N. Very Fine." Realized $2.75. In May 1913 the U.S. Coin Co.'s sale of the Malcolm N. Jackson Collection included lot 124: "1839 Extremely Fine and rare." Realized $3.25. In his November 1939 sale of the William B. Hale Collection, B. Max Mehl described two offerings. Lot 762: "1839 over 38. Plain over-date. Extremely Fine. Rare." Realized $10. Lot 764: "1839 Perfect date. Very Fine, some luster." Realized $6.80. Stack's sale of the J.F. Bell Collection in December 1944 included lot 106: "1839 Brilliant Uncirculated." Realized $18.50.

Mehl's sale of the Jerome Kern Collection in May 1950 included lot 29: "1839 Uncirculated, frosty mint surface. Scarce so choice. Record $27.50." Realized $31. In October 1951 the Numismatic Gallery sale of the B.A. Talmadge collection included lot 1097: "1839 About Extremely Fine. Scarce. W.G.C." Realized $10. In April 1956 Abe Kosoff's sale of the Melish and Hester Collections included lot 1131: "1839 About Uncirculated, scarce." Realized $19. In November 1956 New Netherlands' sale of the Thomas L. Gaskill Collection included lot 212: "1839/8. Only the one variety of this year seen; head of 38. Extremely Fine or better, though obtained as Uncirculated, like most of these. Twenty times as rare as the 1836, twice as rare as 1837–8; only 27,021 coined, which is half as many as of the highly touted 1911-D. Definitely a $25 coin now; should increase in value." Realized $25. In June 1957 the New Netherlands sale of Eliasberg duplicates had this for lot 584: "1839/8. Only the one variety. Close to Extremely Fine, with some luster. In spite of a few picayune marks upon the obverse, this is a nice little coin. Just 27,021 issued, which is half as many as the overrated 1911-D. The EF one in our Forty-Eighth sale brought $25." Realized $22.50.

Proofs

Estimated Total Population (Proof). BB-261, JD-1: four. The Dannreuther study lists the four known examples, three of which were found by Marc Emory in Europe in 1981.

F-12	VF-20	EF-40	AU-50	AU-55	MS-60	MS-63
$650	$1,000	$1,650	$3,000	$4,000	$9,500	$35,000

1839-C

Circulation-Strike Mintage:
18,205 (calendar-year mintage)

Sometimes called "1839-C, 9 Over 8." Scarce in any grade. Incredibly rare in Mint State.

The high mintage figure includes nearly 6,000 struck in March 1839 from gold that had been intended to make half eagles, except that the half eagle dies were "unfit" for coinage. Deliveries were reported as follows:[20] March 16: 5,892 plus ten reserved for assay; May 16: 4,868 plus eight reserved for assay; July 10: 2,544 plus five for assay; October 7: 1,533 plus three for assay; December 9: 3,336 plus six for assay. These figures total 18,205,[21] which differs slightly from the usually published figure of 18,140.

Estimated Total Population (Mint State). 3 to 5. A formidable rarity, the 1839-C is a key issue in the series.

Estimated Total Population (Circulated Grades). 200 to 300. More have survived proportionally than might be expected, this being somewhat true of most Charlotte and Dahlonega Mint quarter eagles of various years. Many are in the Extremely Fine and About Uncirculated categories.

Characteristics of Striking and Die Notes. The edge reeding on Classic Head quarter eagles from the Charlotte and Dahlonega Mints "is much wider than the reeding for Philadelphia and New Orleans coins."[22] See also McCloskey's notes on the known die combinations described on pages 124–125 for this issue.

Selected Auction Records

In June 1885 W. Elliot Woodward's sale of the J. Colvin Randall Collection included lot 984: "1839-C Very Fine." Realized $2.60. Thomas L. Elder's March 1911 sale of the William H. Woodin Collection included this description of lot 1116: "1839-C. Break through obverse. Very Fine. Very scarce." Realized $4.75. In May 1913 the U.S. Coin

Co. sale of the Malcolm N. Jackson Collection included two listings. Lot 270: "1839-C Fine." Realized $3.50. Lot 271: "1839-C Broken dies. Fine." Realized $3.10. In May 1915 B. Max Mehl's catalog of the B.W. Smith Collection included this description of lot 289: "1839-C C between bust and date. Die break on reverse. Fine. Very scarce." Realized $4. In February 1921 the catalog of Mehl's sale of the Dr. G.F.E. Wilharm Collection described lot 170: "1839-C Small C between date and bust. Variety with faint die break. Extremely Fine, some Mint luster. Rare." Realized $4.50. The November 1932 sale of the R. Taylor Collection included Mehl's description of lot 165: "1839-C, C between date and bust. About Uncirculated; sharp with full mint luster. Very scarce." Realized $4.60. In June 1941 Mehl's sale of the William Forrester Dunham Collection included lot 1930: "1839-C Mint letter C between date and bust. Variety with faint die breaks on obverse and reverse. Nearly Uncirculated. Very scarce." Realized $5.

Mehl's February 1944 catalog of the sale of the Belden E. Roach Collection included these lot 954: "1839-C Mint letter C between bust and date. Variety with die break across reverse. Extremely Fine. Rare variety." Realized $11.75. It also included lot 955: "1839-C As last but with perfect die. Lightly scratched on obverse. Extremely Fine; bold impression." Realized $9.80. Stack's sale of the J.F. Bell Collection in December 1944 included lot 188: "1839-C Brilliant Uncirculated, with recut '39' in date, very scarce variety." Realized $35. In June 1946 B. Mehl's sale of the William Cutler Atwater Collection included lot 2021: "1839-C. Practically Uncirculated. Slight cabinet friction. Very scarce. Record for an Uncirculated specimen, $35.00." Realized $8.25. Mehl's sale of the Jerome Kern Collection in May 1950 included lot 115: "1839 C. Same type as last, with mint letter between bust and date. The 3 in date seems to be double-struck. Practically Uncirculated with mint luster. Catalogs $17.50 in only very fine." Realized $24.25. Abe Kosoff's sale of the Melish and Hester Collections, April 1956, featured multiples. Lot 1132: "1839-C. The mint mark is over the left part of 3. About Uncirculated." Realized $27.50. Lot 1134: "1839-C. The C is centered above 83. The 39 are re-cut. Extremely Fine." Realized $30. Lot 1135: "1839-C. An obverse die crack starts at rim, through 2nd star, head, 9th star to rim; strong reverse break through eagle's beak to shield. About Extremely Fine." Realized $27.50.

F-12	VF-20	EF-40	AU-50	AU-55	MS-60	MS-63
$2,500	$4,250	$5,500	$9,000	$10,000	$25,000	$65,000

1839-D

Circulation-Strike Mintage: 13,674

Inexplicably rare in Mint State. Sometimes called "1839-D, 9 Over 8."

Early in 1839 (in anticipation of the 1839-D coinage) and 1840 (for the 1840-D coinage), Superintendent Joseph J. Singleton wrote from Dahlonega to the Philadelphia Mint stating that coinage could not commence as current dies were not on hand.[23]

Mintage of the quarter eagle denomination commenced at Dahlonega in February 1839, during which month 5,487 were coined plus eleven for assay. Subsequent production during the year was as follows: March 30 delivery, 4,026 plus eight for assay; and April 3 delivery, 4,161 plus eight for assay. The yearly total given on the previous page does not include the assay coins.

During the first two years of coinage at Dahlonega, difficulties were experienced with the rollers used to reduce gold ingots into planchet strips, and correspondence was sent by coiner David Mason and Superintendent Joseph J. Singleton in Dahlonega to the Mint in Philadelphia, seeking better equipment.[24]

Estimated Total Population (Mint State). 7 to 10. Why this many exist, while the 1839-C of higher mintage is far rarer, is one of the little mysteries of numismatics.

Estimated Total Population (Circulated Grades). 200 to 300. Very Fine is the typically seen grade, followed in population by Extremely Fine.

Characteristics of Striking and Die Notes. These are often lightly struck on highest areas of hair above the ear. On the reverse there is usually some lightness on the eagle near the upper left of the shield. However, a few completely sharply struck pieces are mentioned in the literature.

The edge reeding on Classic Head quarter eagles from the Charlotte and Dahlonega Mints "is much wider than the reeding for Philadelphia and New Orleans coins."[25]

See also McCloskey's notes on the known die combinations described on pages 125–126 for this issue.

Selected Auction Records

The October 1875 sale of the Col. Mendes I. Cohen Collection included Edward Cogan's description of lot 207: "1839-D Denver [*sic*] Mint. Fine and scarce." Realized $5. Cogan misattributed the D mintmark to Denver, as he did on some other occasions as well. Regarding federal gold coinage, his knowledge was superficial at best. In his 1907 fixed-price list Elmer S. Sears offered lot 179: "1839 Dahlonega Mint. Uncirculated. Mint bloom. Very rare in this choice condition. $12." Thomas L. Elder's March 1911 sale of the William H. Woodin Collection included this description of lot 1091: "1839-D. Head of Liberty to left, D. over the date. Extremely Fine, and very scarce." Realized $4.75. In May 1913 the U.S. Coin Co. sale of the Malcolm N. Jackson Collection included lot 247: "1839-D Fine, scarce." Realized $4.75.

Elder's June 1935 sale of the Wendell C. Foster Collection included this description of lot 2786: "1839-D Ext. Fine. Rare." Realized $10.50. B. Max Mehl's November 1939 sale of the William B. Hale Collection included lot 845: "1839-D Mint Letter D between date and bust. About Uncirculated, sharp. A pin-point nick on obverse. From the great Jewett Sale, 1909." Realized $8. Stack's sale of the J.F. Bell Collection in December 1944 included lot 207: "1839-D First year of issue. Mint mark above date. Brilliant Uncirculated." Realized $42.50. Mehl's sale of the Jerome Kern Collection in May 1950 included lot 131: "1839-D. First Quarter Eagle of this Mint. Mint letter between date and bust. Uncirculated with frosty mint surface. Partly wire edge. Rare so choice. The Atwater specimen, which was not as choice as this, brought $41." Realized $42.50. In October 1951 the Numismatic Gallery sale of the B.A. Talmadge collection included lot 1212: "1839-D First year of issue. Mint mark above date. About Uncirculated. Very rare in this condition." Realized $40. In November 1956 New

Netherlands' sale of the Thomas L. Gaskill Collection included lot 214: "1839/8-D First year of issue. Same head as 1838-C. Strictly Extremely Fine, the obverse particularly bold. As with the two previous, numeral 9 in date cut over 8 on all seen. Rare." Realized $48. The overdate status was later discredited.

F-12	VF-20	EF-40	AU-50	AU-55	MS-60	MS-63
$3,000	$5,000	$7,500	$10,000	$14,000	$30,000	$55,000

1839-O

Circulation-Strike Mintage: 17,781

First New Orleans gold coin. Only New Orleans gold coin with obverse mintmark. Most often seen 1839 issue.

This represents the first gold issue of the New Orleans Mint ($5 gold coins were not struck at New Orleans until the next year, 1840). At the time, the New Orleans Mint received gold from various deposits consisting primarily of foreign coins. There was no significant regional source of native gold (later, small deposits in Alabama yielded some of this precious metal).

Information from New Orleans had not arrived in Philadelphia in time to be included by Robert Maskell Patterson in the 1839 *Mint Report*, dated January 30, 1840, but was printed in a supplemental statement on February 12, 1840:[26] "A communication just received from the superintendent of that Mint States that, from the recommencement of operations in November, to the end of the year, they coined $23,490 in gold, consisting of 9,396 quarter eagles."

Thus, the first coinage of gold from New Orleans took place late in the year. Coinage of silver coins had been suspended at New Orleans as of August 17, by which time no gold coins had been struck.[27]

Some additional 1839-O quarter eagles of the Classic Head may have been struck in early 1840 and included under the 1840-O mintage figure.[28]

Estimated Total Population (Mint State). 25 to 40. These are quite scarce in Mint State, and yet are the most readily available mintmarked Classic Head issue in this grade. Specimens often have beautiful, satiny, lustrous fields and are a visual treat. Most examples are in grades of MS-60 to 63, but occasionally a finer example appears on the market.

Estimated Total Population (Circulated Grades). 250 to 400. Very Fine is the usual grade for the 1839-O. The New Orleans coinage of this era circulated far and wide.

Characteristics of Striking and Die Notes. The obverse is usually fairly well struck. The reverse is usually sharp as well; if weakness exists, it is usually on the eagle near the upper left of the shield. It is not unusual for examples of BB-291 to have the obverse and reverse aligned in the same direction, instead of the normal 180° alignment.

Selected Auction Records

Thomas L. Elder's March 1911 sale of the William H. Woodin Collection included two Classic Head quarter eagles. Lot 1034: "1839-O. Variety with date farther from bust; reverse cracked die and with arrow touching C and A, and branch touching D. Fine; rare." Realized $2.60. Lot 1033: "1839-O. Small head of Liberty, O over date. Small eagle. Variety with date near bust; small arrow points do not touch lettering, and branch away from D. Fine; rare." Realized $3. In February 1921 the catalog of B. Max Mehl's sale of the Dr. G.F.E. Wilharm Collection described lot 184: "1839-O First year of issue. Small O between bust and date. A small scratch on reverse. Uncirculated, with bright Mint luster. Very scarce." Realized $4.10. The November 1932 sale of the R. Taylor Collection included Mehl's description of lot 170: "1839-O, O between bust and date. Variety with so-called large stars [on obverse] and large letters on reverse. Die break connecting legend and eagle. Extremely Fine. Scarce." Realized $4.10. This sale also included lot 171: "1839-O, Small O and small stars. Reverse, small letters and perfect die. Uncirculated. Rare." Realized $3.50. Thomas L. Elder's June 1935 sale of the Wendell C. Foster Collection included this description of lot 2785: "1839-O Ex. Fine, about Unc, first year at O. Mint Rare." Realized $5.75.

Mehl's February 1944 catalog of the sale of the Belden E. Roach Collection described lot 969: "1839-O First year of issue. Mint letter O between bust and date. Uncirculated with attractive frosty mint surface. Quite rare so choice." Realized $9.30. In October 1951 the Numismatic Gallery sale of the B.A. Talmadge collection included lot 1232: "1839-O First year of issue. Mint mark above date. Splendid and Uncirculated coin, scarce." Realized $22.50. In April 1956 Abe Kosoff's sale of the Melish and Hester Collections included lot 1137: "1839-O First year of issue at the New Orleans Mint. About Uncirculated." Realized $27.50. In November 1956 New Netherlands' sale of the Thomas L. Gaskill Collection included lot 216: "1839-O First year of issue. Last of the Classic Heads, most like that of the 1834, . . . but different in details. Perfect date. Close to Uncirculated, highly frosty reverse. Uncommon." Realized $33. In June 1957 the New Netherlands sale of Eliasberg duplicates had this for lot 586: "1839-O. The other variety. Low date in a straight line; a small berry detached from branch, closely spaced 1/2, and large arrows. Reverse die shattered. Very Fine plus, bold and clean. Ex 'Lee,' lot 1130. Rarer than the variety previously described. Only two pairs of dies made; they were sent to N.O. March 14, 1839." Realized $20.

F-12	VF-20	EF-40	AU-50	AU-55	MS-60	MS-63
$1,000	$1,650	$3,000	$4,250	$7,000	$11,000	$30,000

11

Liberty Head $2.50 Gold Coins (1840–1907)

Liberty Head (1840–1907)

Designer: *Christian Gobrecht.* **Weight:** *4.18 grams.* **Composition:** *.900 gold, .100 copper.* **Diameter:** *18 mm.* **Edge:** *Reeded.* **Mints:** *Philadelphia, Charlotte, Dahlonega, New Orleans, San Francisco.*

New Motif

The Liberty Head motif, also called the *Coronet Head* or *Braided Hair* style, designed and engraved by Christian Gobrecht, appeared on the quarter eagle in 1840 and continued uninterrupted through 1907, the longest span in American coinage history of a design in use without major change or alteration.

The obverse depicts Miss Liberty, her hair in a bun secured with a string of beads, wearing a coronet inscribed LIBERTY. She faces left, her portrait circled by stars, with the date below. This general design was used elsewhere on U.S. coinage including on half cents of 1840–1857, large copper cents of 1839–1857, $5 gold half eagles of 1839–1908, and $10 gold eagles of 1838–1907; it may have been inspired by the head of Venus in Benjamin West's painting *Omnia Vincit Amor*, although Gobrecht commented that it was "a female head resembling everybody and nobody."[1]

Thus, the Liberty Head motif was a latecomer to the quarter eagle denomination and had been used earlier on the other gold denominations. Often, among early American coinage, a given motif was introduced on larger denominations first. As an example, the various copper designs were usually seen first on cents, then on the smaller half cents: the Draped Bust motif appeared in 1796 on the cent, but not until 1800 on half cents; the Classic Head appeared on the cent in 1808, followed by the half cent a year later. In silver coinage, the Draped Bust obverse was first used on the silver dollar in 1795, but not until later on the lesser silver denominations; the Liberty Seated motif made its debut on the dollar in 1836, followed by other denominations from 1837 through 1839, and so on.

The reverse of the Liberty Head quarter eagle of 1840–1907 depicts an eagle with a shield on its breast, perched on an olive branch and holding three arrows. The inscription UNITED STATES OF AMERICA surrounds, with the denomination 2½ D. below. This design dated back many years and probably traced its origin at the Mint to that made by John Reich for use on the 1807 quarter eagle and half eagle gold coins. Afterward it enjoyed many incarnations, not only on later U.S. coin designs but as part of many token and store-card motifs.

The diameter of the 1840 quarter eagle is about 17/24 inch, or 18 mm, this being slightly smaller than the 18.2 mm diameter used for the Classic Head issues of 1834–1839. The alloy is 90% gold with the balance copper; silver was permitted to be no more than 5% of the alloy. Silver existed as an impurity in gold, although its percentage could be regulated during the refining process. Gold coins with a generous amount of silver, close to 5%, have a light yellow or brassy color.

Hub Change

Philadelphia Mint quarter eagles of the Liberty Head design minted during the early range of the series (1840–1858), plus some coins of 1859 and a few of 1860, have the so-called Old Reverse or early hub, with heavy arrowheads spaced closely together and slightly larger letters. This has also been called the Type I hub. Beginning in 1859, the hub was changed at the Philadelphia Mint, and from that time through 1861 both reverses were used interchangeably. The New Reverse, or Type II, hub is most easily identified by the arrowheads, which are lighter and differently spaced with regard to their closeness to the letters.

More details about the two hub varieties are given under the 1859 and 1860 entries.

At the San Francisco Mint the old-style reverse was used up to and including 1876, at which time the new reverse was employed (although Walter Breen mentions in passing that an 1862-S with the new type of reverse may be known).

These reverse styles have not been widely studied, but upon close inspection can provide interesting varieties that are quite collectible. No doubt the listing of these in *Walter Breen's Complete Encyclopedia of U.S. and Colonial Coins* could be modified by close study of many different pieces, particularly with respect to which dates and mintmarks of coins from 1859 through the 1870s exist with which reverses. In the present text, hub differences are not noted until 1859, as all before that date are of the Old Reverse variety.

Detail of heavy arrows on the 1840-style hub, the standard through 1858.

Detail of heavy arrows on the new hub introduced in 1859.

DIE VARIETIES

The dates on the various Liberty Head dies were entered with a four-digit logotype punch, this being a technological improvement from the single-digit punches used on earlier quarter eagle dies of 1796–1839. Usually just one logotype was employed for all dies and mints, but there were exceptions (beginning with two different date logotype styles for 1843).

Mintmarks were entered into the dies with individual punches. For low-mintage issues there is often only one variety (or combination of obverse and reverse die) for a given mint, but for some extensive issues there are multiple variations of position and sometimes of mintmark size. These are discussed in this chapter.

Four-digit date logotypes were entered into obverse dies in a variety of positions over the years. These can be distinguished by several reference points including the distance of the first digit (1) from the neck and from the denticles, and the distance of the final digit from the neck and the denticles and also its position (varying distances left) from the lower right neck point. Often, the space between the neck and the denticles was insufficient for artistic placing of the date logotype, and in such instances the date appears to be crowded into the area available.

Differences in date logotype positions range from subtle to dramatic. Nearly always, Proofs in the Liberty Head quarter series were from different dies than circulation strikes, this being a different procedure from that used in the 1820s and early 1830s, when the same die pairs were used first to strike Proofs, then to make circulation strikes.[2] The Philadelphia Mint quarter eagle dated 1841 is a puzzlement in this regard and is discussed at length under that heading.

"Heavy" and "light" dates and mintmarks were caused by impressing the punches either deeply or lightly into the working die or, if punched deeply, by later relapping or resurfacing the die so as to remove some of the details. On deeply punched date logotypes the numerals will seem to be closer together than on lightly punched or relapped dies. Relapping caused all features to become lighter, including the stars and certain details around the border of the obverse portrait. Some of these "heavy" and "light" variations are listed in the Breen *Encyclopedia*, but these constitute die *states*, not die *varieties*. If a four-digit date logotype was punched more heavily at one side or another, the digits will seem slightly larger in the area of the deepest punching.

MINTAGE AND CIRCULATION

Throughout the coinage span from 1840 to 1907 the Philadelphia Mint produced Liberty Head quarter eagles each year. Additional coinage was accomplished from time to time at branch mints in Charlotte, Dahlonega, and New Orleans during the 1840s and 1850s, and at San Francisco from 1854 to 1879.

Among Philadelphia issues early dates were usually struck in small quantities, with the 1841 in particular being a prime rarity. It is believed that Norman Stack first gave this issue the nickname *Little Princess*—nomenclature that has endured and seems to be used whenever a specimen is described in a catalog.

Particularly notable in another regard in the quarter eagle series is the 1848 CAL. quarter eagle. A total of 1,389 of these were produced using gold bullion brought to the Philadelphia Mint from California in one of the earliest shipments to the East from the Gold Rush. The distinguishing counterstamp, applied at the Mint while the coins were still in the die, served to hallmark the issue and at the same time to specifically create a souvenir for those desiring the same. In actuality, the 1848 CAL. quarter eagle is the first official U.S. commemorative coin, although few people recognize it as such. Only a few hundred pieces exist today. Interestingly, chief engraver James B. Longacre must have taken a special fancy to this variety, for the estate auction of his collection included *three* specimens.

The quarter eagle denomination was fairly popular in American commerce until the end of December 1861, when banks and the Treasury stopped paying out gold coins at par. After that time, until December 17, 1878, gold coins were available only at a premium in terms of paper money. Liberty Head quarter eagles of the 1840–1861 years circulated very extensively. By 1861, when circulation stopped, most extant pieces of the early dates had been worn down to such levels as Very Fine and Extremely Fine.

After 1861, the coinage scene changed. The Charlotte and Dahlonega Mints, now under the control of the Confederate States of America, lapsed into inactivity. The New Orleans Mint no longer struck coins and would remain dormant until 1879, at which time certain silver and gold coins were again struck—but no quarter eagles. The Carson City Mint, opened for business in 1870, also struck gold and silver coins, but no quarter eagles.

Thus, of the Liberty Head quarter eagles, only the Philadelphia and San Francisco Mints struck pieces after 1861. Curiously, the West Coast operated under a different monetary policy during the period from 1862 to 1878, and gold coins were extensively used in circulation. Today a survey of the literature will quickly reveal that a circulated quarter eagle from the Philadelphia Mint, dated in the 1860s or early 1870s, is apt to be in a grade such as Extremely Fine or About Uncirculated, for such coins circulated not at all during that time, and only on a limited basis afterward. In contrast, the average quarter eagle bearing an S mintmark is apt to be just Very Fine. It was a "hard money" society in the American West until the 1870s, and Legal Tender Notes, National Bank Notes, and other federal notes, including Fractional Currency, were not used.

Liberty Head quarter eagles were minted at San Francisco until 1879, after which time production was limited to Philadelphia. For the remainder of the nineteenth century, mintages tended to be small. Early in the twentieth century, a demand arose for the denomination, and more than 100,000 were made of each year from 1902 to 1907. However, quarter eagles never circulated widely after 1878 except in inland areas in the American West. Contemporary accounts reveal that there was a great demand for quarter eagles as gifts around the December holiday season, and banks usually laid in an extra supply of them. Similarly, many visitors to the Philadelphia Mint—usually several tens of thousands of tourists annually—purchased for face value the smallest American gold coin currently being minted, the quarter eagle, as a souvenir of their experience.

During the years 1840–1907 the total circulation-strike mintage of the Liberty Head quarter eagle totaled 11,921,171. Production hit a high point in 1853 (a year in which gold from California was particularly abundant) and registered 1,404,668 pieces at the Philadelphia Mint. Three other years accounted for production of more than a million coins at Philadelphia: 1851, 1852, and 1861.

Several other issues in addition to the aforementioned famous 1841 are remarkable for their extraordinarily low mintages, these being 1854-S (246 minted), 1856-D (874), 1863 (30, all Proofs), 1875 (420, of which 20 were Proofs), 1881 (691, of which 51 were Proofs), and 1885 (887, of which 87 were Proofs).

In general, Philadelphia Mint quarter eagles of the 1860s through the early 1890s are quite rare in Mint State and especially rare if in choice or gem preservation, for numismatists desiring examples of the dates were apt to buy Proofs at the time.

PROOFS

Proofs were made for presentation purposes in the 1840s and 1850s. Beginning circa 1858, they were generally available to collectors, but very few opted to specialize in gold coins. For a long time thereafter, distribution of Proofs hovered in the range of 20 to 30 per year, although most published figures through the 1880s are estimates, not factual. Toward the end of the series production increased, with the high-water mark reached in 1901 with 223 coins. All Proofs up to and including 1901 were of the Brilliant finish, with mirrorlike fields and frosted designs and devices. Beginning in 1902 and continuing to the end of the series in 1907, the portrait was polished in the die for most (but not all) issues, thus giving a shiny rather than frosty appearance to this feature.

A Proof for each year from 1840 forward is in the Mint Collection, except for the years 1849 to 1855 inclusive; they can be seen on loan to the National Numismatic Collection at the Smithsonian Institution. A solitary Proof 1850 quarter eagle is known, discovered by Marc Emory in Europe in the early 1980s. Accordingly, the Mint Collection Proofs are not individually cited in the listings herein. These are illustrated in John Dannreuther's study, *United States Proof Coins*, volume 4: *Gold*.

It is estimated that somewhat over 4,000 Proofs were struck from 1840 to 1907, with most being made after 1880. Probably no more than a third to half of these exist today, and many are impaired. As demonstrated by contemporary auction prices (selectively cited in the listings to follow), Proofs were little appreciated in their own era, and on the resale market in the 1870s and 1880s such coins were likely to realize just a slight amount over face value, incredible as this may seem today—when Proofs are highly prized. As examples the author need only point to W. Elliot Woodward's sale of the J. Colvin Randall Collection, June 1885, which offered these two Proof quarter eagles, each of the same date:

> Lot 998: 1862 Splendid Proof; very rare as Proof.
> Lot 999: 1862 Scarce; and, as Proof, very rare.

Both Proofs, offered 23 years after they were struck, brought *face value.*

Not much of an improvement was a complete 1864 gold Proof set containing the $1, $2.50, $3, $5, $10, and $20 denominations—a total face value of $41.50, which sold for $45.50.

Thus, many collectors found it expedient to spend Proofs after their numismatic interest waned.

All Proofs are rare today, this being particularly true of any date prior to the 1890s and, especially, before the 1880s. As will be seen under the individual listings, there are many dates in the 1860s and 1870s for which only 10 to 15 pieces can be traced today.

As a general rule of thumb, for Proofs of most dates one is represented in the National Numismatic Collection in the Smithsonian Institution and, for dates 1858 and later, the American Numismatic Society, thus reducing the available population most years by at least two.

Many Proof quarter eagles toward the end of the Liberty Head series, especially in the first decade of the twentieth century, have copper stains, toning, or spots, the result of improper mixing of the copper added to the alloy. Circulation strikes also show this characteristic.

Aspects of Collecting

The type-set collector will have no difficulty acquiring an inexpensive representative example of the Liberty Head quarter in any grade desired from Very Fine through About Uncirculated. Uncirculated pieces are encountered with frequency, particularly those of the type's final years in the early twentieth century. Superb Uncirculated pieces are available but are very scarce in relation to lower grades. Most numismatists select a readily available Mint State coin from the 1900s for type-set purposes.

Charlotte and Dahlonega quarter eagles minted during the 1840–1860 years are all elusive, although these seem to have been saved in a higher proportion to their mintages than were coins struck at the other mints. The writer suggests that many such pieces remained in regional circulation in the Southeast until the Civil War, and were plucked from circulation at that time. Although many if not most were later returned to circulation, others remained as mementos and souvenirs. The Charlotte and Dahlonega quarter eagles have formed a special collecting focus for many numismatists, with the result that C and D coins have had a large play or presence in the market and in catalog listings. As a result, certification-service data are skewed in some instances, giving indications that these particular branch-mint issues are more readily available than are related New Orleans coins. In reality, not many collectors specialize in O-Mint issues, and the typical piece is not as apt to be sent in for certification.

A curious aspect of Charlotte and Dahlonega Mint coins is that the later issues of the 1850s, when found, are apt be seen in higher grades, including About Uncirculated, probably the result of the aforementioned hoarding on the eve of the Civil War. In dramatic contrast, San Francisco Mint quarter eagles of the 1850s and 1860s were not hoarded at all but remained in circulation on the West Coast, where they became well worn. Thus, for example, it is not unusual at all for a Charlotte or Dahlonega quarter eagle of the late 1850s to be in lovely About Uncirculated preservation, while San Francisco Mint quarter eagles are hardly ever seen at that grade level.

In general, the date logotypes are more deeply impressed into the working dies of Charlotte and Dahlonega quarter eagles than in Philadelphia Mint dies. The writer believes this was a precaution to allow those distant, inland mints to keep their dies in service longer through relapping and regrinding, whereas at the Philadelphia Mint new dies could be procured on short notice.

The systematic collecting of Liberty Head quarter eagles by date and mintmark is a fascinating challenge, one that has attracted several dozen dedicated enthusiasts over the years. There are no "impossible" rarities, but the aforementioned 1841, 1854-S, 1863, and 1875 are difficult to find and expensive when located. And there are some surprises in store, as even a casual reading of the entries given in the text for 1864 and 1865 Philadelphia Mint coins will dramatically reveal. Thus, for the value-conscious buyer, there are many interesting opportunities to acquire major rarities for fairly low cost, in contrast to highly publicized condition rarities in certain other series.

No one has ever assembled a complete collection of Liberty Head quarter eagles in Mint State preservation, simply because certain early varieties are not known to exist at that level or are so rare that years will elapse between offerings. For the collector who can afford it, a reasonable goal for issues of 1840–1878 is Extremely Fine and About Uncirculated (Very Fine for most of the San Francisco issues), adding Mint State coins here and there as they become available. Certain Philadelphia Mint dates—1853 is an example—will be no problem in Mint State, but certain early Charlotte, Dahlonega, and New Orleans coins from the 1840s are next to impossible to find at this level. Charlotte and Dahlonega coins of the 1850s are often seen grading Extremely Fine and About Uncirculated, but New Orleans coins are quite elusive so fine. It seems that the O-Mint coins were scattered far and wide up and down the Mississippi River, in contrast with regional circulation of the C and D pieces.

To reiterate, as a general rule, all San Francisco quarter eagles of the design are either scarce, rare, or virtually nonexistent in Mint State, simply because no one collected them during the time of issue (1854–1879), and they were not stored by banks or the Treasury Department. Such S-Mint coins were used extensively in circulation in the West. Thus, in contrast to other branch-mint issues of the mid-nineteenth century, those bearing the mint letter S on the reverse are usually found in Very Fine grade, occasionally Extremely Fine, but almost never in Mint State, the only significant exceptions being at the tail end of the San Francisco Mint issues in the 1870s.

Quarter eagles of the 1880s and 1890s, struck only at the Philadelphia Mint, are obtainable in such high grades as Extremely Fine and About Uncirculated, and for some dates, Uncirculated, although some are major rarities in the latter preservation. After the early 1890s and continuing to the last year of issue, 1907, Mint State coins are fairly easy to find, this being particularly true of those minted after the turn of the century.

Unlike their larger counterparts such as the $5, $10, and, in particular, $20 gold coins, which were extensively exported to Europe, Central America, and South America, the $2.50 coins tended to stay at home. For purposes of international commerce it was far easier to count and ship a bag containing $5,000 in $20 pieces—amounting to just 250 coins—than a bag containing the same value in $2.50 pieces, which would have been 2,000 coins. Because of this, very few Mint State pieces have been found in overseas bank and government holdings. A survey of the holdings of American gold coins in the national treasury of Belgium in 1875 disclosed tens of thousands of double eagles but not a single coin of a lower denomination![3] Experiences of this author and conversations with large-scale gold importers (i.e., Ronald J. Gillio and Manfra, Tordella & Brookes) indicate that Liberty Head $2.50 coins were never exported in quantity. Those few scattered pieces that have been found abroad are believed to be the personal coins of various private depositors from different foreign countries, many of whom sent gold coins to Switzerland for safekeeping.

Large quantities of quarter eagles struck from the mid-1890s to the end of the design in 1907 were stored domestically in banks and Treasury reserves. Beginning about 1920, there was a popular demand for the denomination—a speculation—and it is likely that many thousands of long-stored pieces went into private hands and stayed there. Thus, as noted, late-date Liberty Head quarter eagles are readily available in Mint State today.

The Search for "Nice" Coins

Among Liberty Head quarter eagles of the branch mints, and for many Philadelphia coins as well (especially for issues before the Civil War), typical coins show light striking, particularly at the highest hair strands on the obverse and on the reverse (primarily outside the lower left of the shield, but sometimes elsewhere).

This light striking was caused by the normal minting practice of spacing the dies slightly wider apart in the coining press to prevent metal being squeezed up at the borders into a wire rim; it was also done to lessen die wear and breakage. Such quarter eagles were being made to serve in commerce, with no thought of making specimens for numismatic cabinets.

The certification services make no notation concerning lightness of strike, which in any event may be normal for a given issue and is not distracting. Accept the situation, or else your enthusiasm will be dampened and you will become quite frustrated. In building a set of quarter eagles, for the earlier dates the best method, in the author's opinion, is to study a coin as a complete entity—with *normal* striking characteristics (which may include lightness in some areas), a smooth planchet with pleasing fields, and the absence of bruises, scratches, or staining. None of these considerations are marked on certification holders, so you will need to look at several specimens in some instances to find one that is just right. Further, it is always better to buy an aesthetically pleasing AU-55 coin rather than an ugly certified MS-60. Not only is the former cheaper, but the AU-55 coin is more desirable from a numismatic viewpoint, at least in the opinion of the writer. The beauty part of this is that while you are searching for a coin of real quality, probably 90% of your competitors are looking only at the number printed on a plastic holder—and are perfectly content to buy coins of substandard appearance, as long as the number is right!

The frenetic chasing of the "finest known" or "Condition Census" specimen of a given variety is largely a waste of time, in the writer's opinion, *if based upon grading numbers*. Perhaps the explanation given by Douglas Winter in his book *Gold Coins of the Charlotte Mint: 1838–1861* tells the story best:

> **A Change in Grading Standards:**
>
> The most important thing to remember about grading is that, despite claims to the contrary, it remains highly subjective. It is hard enough to get a group of experts to agree on Mint State common date Morgan dollar grades, let alone complex issues such as Charlotte coins. In the late 1980s and early 1990s, PCGS and NGC began grading a significant amount of Charlotte gold coins. For the most part, the grading standards of that era tended to be very conservative.
>
> Today, standards have relaxed considerably. In my opinion, the EF-45 of the late 1980s is an AU-50 (or even an AU-53) today. And the AU-55 of the late 1980s is an MS-60 (or even an MS-61) today.
>
> The primary effect of this is to provide an unrealistic picture of availability for certain issues.

Moreover, as much fun as it may be to look through auction catalogs in the quest for which coins are fine, finer, and absolutely finest, even a cursory peek at several leading gold sales will show that a single coin can be graded several different ways. If such lack of clarity and definition is for you, then you have a very easy road ahead: simply buy any holder bearing the number you desire. However, just about every significant gold-coin collection ever formed was done the hard way—by considering the coins one at a time. Along the way of "the road not taken," at least not by many, the thrill of the chase will provide endless enjoyment and satisfaction.

PCGS and NGC maintain registry sets in which the owners of the highest numbers win, with no consideration of strike or eye appeal. This can be a dangerous game finance-wise, as the quantity of high-number coins continually increases. For a given coin, say a 1907 quarter eagle certified as MS-65, there are many more now than there were 20 years ago. If you do not care about resale value, then continue playing.

In the listings that follow, interesting and informative comments about die varieties, history, and so on have been selected, as well as notable specimens in high grades—generally from Extremely Fine or About Uncirculated upward for some of the scarcer early issues, and Mint State (or Proof) for later dates. For certain rarities such as 1841, 1854-S, 1863, and 1875, many citations have been preserved in order to reflect the esteem in which these pieces have been held and how they have been cataloged over the years.

For most of the later dates, particularly those of the 1890s and 1900s, citations have been proportionally fewer as there are thousands of such coins listed in catalogs, usually with little information besides grade and market information. There would be little point in listing hundreds of repetitive citations for a 1901 quarter eagle, as an example.

Listings are for earlier auction appearances from early days through the 1950s. Modern auction descriptions and prices can be found on the Internet.

GRADING STANDARDS

1859-S. Graded MS-65.

MS-60 to 70 (Mint State). ***Obverse:*** At MS-60, some abrasion and contact marks are evident, most noticeably on the hair to the right of Miss Liberty's forehead, and on the jaw. Luster is present, but may be dull or lifeless, and interrupted in patches. At MS-63, contact marks are few, and abrasion is very light. An MS-65 coin has hardly any abrasion, and contact marks are so minute as to require magnification. Luster should be full and rich. Grades above MS-65 are usually found late in the series and are defined by having fewer marks as perfection is approached. ***Reverse:*** Comments apply as for the obverse, except that abrasion and contact marks are most noticeable on the eagle's neck and to the lower left of the shield.

1855-D. Graded AU-55.

AU-50, 53, 55, 58 (About Uncirculated). ***Obverse:*** Light wear is seen on the face, the hair to the right of the face, and the highest area of the hair bun, more so at AU-50 than at AU–53 or 55. An AU-58 coin has minimal traces of wear. An AU-50 coin has luster in protected areas among the stars and letters, with little in the open fields or on the portrait. At AU-58, most luster is present in the fields, but is worn away on the highest parts of the motifs. ***Reverse:*** Comments apply as for the preceding, except that the eagle shows wear in all of the higher areas, as well as the leaves and arrowheads. Luster ranges from perhaps 40% remaining in protected areas at AU-50 to nearly full mint bloom at AU-58. Often the reverse of this type retains more luster than the obverse.

1860-C. Graded EF-40.

EF-40, 45 (Extremely Fine). ***Obverse:*** Wear is evident on all high areas of the portrait, including the hair to the right of the forehead, the tip of the coronet, and the hair bun. The stars show light wear at their centers. Luster, if present at all, is minimal and in protected areas such as between the star points. ***Reverse:*** Wear is greater than on an AU coin. The eagle's neck is nearly smooth, much detail is lost on the right wing, and there is flatness at the lower left of the shield, and on the leaves and arrowheads. Traces of luster may be seen, more so at EF-45 than at EF-40. Overall, the reverse appears to be in a slightly higher grade than the obverse.

1843-O, Small Date, Crosslet 4. Graded VF-20.

VF-20, 30 (Very Fine). ***Obverse:*** The higher-relief areas of hair are worn flat at VF-20, less so at VF-30. The hair to the right of the coronet is merged into heavy strands. The stars are flat at their centers. ***Reverse:*** Much of the eagle is flat, with less than 50% of the feather detail remaining. The vertical shield stripes, being deeply recessed, remain bold.

Liberty Head quarter eagles are seldom collected in grades lower than VF-20.

PF-60 to 70 (Proof). ***Obverse and Reverse:*** PF–60 to 62 coins have extensive hairlines and may have nicks and contact marks. At PF-63, hairlines are prominent, but the mirror surface is very reflective. PF-64 coins have fewer hairlines; PF-65, minimal hairlines mostly seen only under magnification, and no nicks or marks. PF-66 and higher coins should have no marks or hairlines visible to the unaided eye.

1895. Graded PF-66.

1840

Circulation-Strike Mintage: 18,859
Proof Mintage: 3 or 4

Exceedingly rare in Mint State.

The year 1840 sets the scene for a generation of quarter eagles for which Mint State coins are at the very least rare, and which in most instances are *extremely* rare.

Reader, be advised: current PCGS and NGC population reports list more Mint State coins than were thought to exist years ago. This seems to be the result of gradeflation raising former About Uncirculated coins to Mint State as well as of multiple submissions of the same coin. *This comment is true of all Liberty Head quarter eagles in population reports.*

Estimated Total Population (Circulated Grades). 50 to 80, equal to less than one-half of 1% of the mintage. The 1840 is exceptionally scarce, far more so than its mintage would indicate. Most examples are well worn, with Very Fine being typical. At the About Uncirculated level the 1840 quarter eagle is a rarity.

Die Data. *1840 four-digit date logotype:* This is a compact logotype with small numerals. The 1 and 8 are distinctly separated on just about all impressions; 8, 4, and 0 are more closely spaced, with 8 and 4 most closely spaced of all. The 4 leans slightly right and has a thick, fan-shaped serif on right. The 0 is slightly smaller than the other digits. This was used on all dies for all mints.

One obverse has the 1 in the date centered between the neck and denticles; another die has the 1 twice as close to the neck as to the denticles. A few strikings have a wide rim.

Characteristics of Striking and Die Notes. The 1840 is usually lightly struck at the portrait, the obverse stars (particularly star 6), and the eagle's leg on the left side of the reverse. Some are slightly better struck, but hardly sharp. On some high-grade specimens a prooflike surface is evident. A number have been reported with cracked or shattered reverse die.

Selected Auction Records

An early listing is lot 208 in Edward Cogan's sale of the Col. Mendes I. Cohen Collection: "1840 Good impression." Realized $2.80. The term *Good* probably meant *nice* or *pleasing* rather than referring to a specific grade level. Across the board, it is generally not possible to relate early auction grade commentaries to the modern numerical system. In June 1885, W. Elliot Woodward's 77th sale (the J. Colvin Randall Collection), included lot 985: "1840 Fine." Realized $2.50 (i.e., face value; a premium was probably added for this and similar sales).

Into the twentieth century, in March 1907 S.H. Chapman's sale of the David S. Wilson Collection included lot 187: "1840. . . . Extremely Fine. Rare state." Realized $12.50. As a further example of erratic results, in March 1911, Thomas L. Elder's sale of the William H. Woodin Collection included these lot 963: "1840. New type of head to left. Eagle smaller, and rim broader. Perfect die. Extremely Fine." Realized $3.90. The Elder sale also held lot 964: "1840. Same, but cracked die. Very Good; scarce." Realized $2.50 (face value).

Proofs

John Dannreuther's study, *United States Proof Coins*, volume 4: *Gold*, is the source for estimated populations of Liberty Head issues. Also see this chapter's introductory information about the Mint Collection (page 150).

Estimated Total Population (Proof). 2.

Selected Proof Auction Records

The 48th sale of the New Netherlands Coin Co., November 1956, described lot 217: "1840 Braided Hair, Coronet Type, continued until 1907. Ex. Fine. Cleaned. Apparently struck as a Proof. Square borders; partial wire edge. However, weak upon the obv. at 6th star; on the rev., at eagle's right leg. Should be seen." This was later confirmed as a Proof by John Dannreuther, who noted that it is now certified as PF-50 (PCGS).

VF-20	EF-40	AU-50	AU-55	MS-60	MS-62	MS-63
$850	$1,250	$2,100	$3,250	$6,500	$8,000	$16,500

1840-C

Circulation-Strike Mintage: 12,838

First Liberty Head coinage in Charlotte. Circular lathe marks on obverse die. Very rare in Mint State.

Deliveries of this issue were reported as follows:[4] June, 3,530; August, 3,390; fourth quarter, 5,918.[5] Total: 12,838. These figures are from the coiner's records and differ slightly from the 12,814 reported at the end of the year by coiner Bolton and 12,834 in the cumulative report of operations and branches given by Director R.M. Patterson on January 23, 1844. The oft-cited figure of 12,822 is given by Breen.

Estimated Total Population (Mint State). 4 to 7. Most are around the MS-60 to MS-62 level. A Mint State 1840-C quarter eagle is a first-class rarity. (See the "reader caution" note under 1840, page 156, about certification reports.)

Estimated Total Population (Circulated Grades). 100 to 150, this being the estimate of David W. Akers in the Pittman catalog. Grades in the Very Fine and Extremely Fine range are typical. For some unknown reason, 1840-C quarter eagles have always been more readily available than the higher-mintage 1840 Philadelphia Mint pieces.

Die Data. *1840 four-digit date logotype: See the Philadelphia Mint listing for this year.*

Two pairs of dies were shipped from Philadelphia to Charlotte on February 5 and 6. The mintmark C is very small, as also seen on 1841-C, 1842-C, and 1843-C, Small Date, Crosslet 4. The top of the C is embedded in an arrow feather.

Douglas Winter reports that only one die pair is known today.

The Bass Collection Part II coin lot 326, was in part described as follows (a situation observed on multiple 1840-C quarter eagles and apparently common to all specimens, but, incredibly, not known to have been described in detail prior to this 1999 commentary):

> Date logotype very boldly impressed into the die, and positioned slightly high. Reverse with small C mintmark high and with the upper right serif embedded in the arrow feather. Under high magnification many *circular raised lathe lines* are seen in the portrait of Miss Liberty, these being particular evident among the letters in the word LIBERTY and on the neck. This phenomenon is very rare in American coinage, although in the course of cataloguing the Liberty Head pieces in the Bass sale we have come across two different dies with it. The reader is referred to the present author's dissertation relating to circular lathe lines as given beginning on page 64 of *A Buyer's and Enthusiast's Guide to Flying Eagle and Indian Cents*, where an 1864 Indian cent with circular lathe lines is illustrated. Thus far, relatively few coins in American numismatics have been identified with such features, although in today's era of research and enlightenment we would not be a bit surprised to see others found.

To the aforementioned book Craig B. Sholley, a modern leading light in matters involving Mint processes, contributed the following commentary:

> On the question of which elements were in the model and which were entered at the master hub or master die stage, I think that the enclosed coins [1840 Liberty Seated half dollar and 1864 bronze Indian cent] and photos will assist in a rather straightforward analysis. On the 1840 Liberty Seated half dollar, note that the lathe lines can be seen within the letters of LIBERTY. Therefore LIBERTY was in the model, since any punching of the letters after the reduction would have destroyed the machining lines. Likewise, note that some lines can be seen going up the sides of the crossbars and stripes in the shield. This demonstrates that these lines were also in the model. However, note that the reverse shield lines on all Liberty Seated halves prior to 1858 are hand cut. This effectively demonstrates the limitation of the lathe's high aspect ratio (height to width) elements cannot be reproduced. In 1858 a new reduction was made to produce the Type II half dollar hub. The shield lines were cut into the new master die and reproduced by hubbing from that point on. On the

> 1864 bronze Indian cent, note that the lathe lines can be seen within the upper loop of B and between the middle and upper crossbar of E in LIBERTY. I also believe that the lines can be seen crossing the right lower serif of I and the left upper serif of E. However, note that I've only looked at this on my home 'scope (20x); this should be checked at higher magnification. Regardless, this still shows that LIBERTY was in the model for the same reason as with the 1840 Liberty Seated half dollar. Regarding the peripheral lettering UNITED STATES OF AMERICA, I believe that lettering was entered in the master dies. I have never seen lathe lines on this period coinage passing through the peripheral lettering. Also, Charles Hoskins and R.W. Julian have informed me that the lathe was not capable of reproducing the lettering unless the sides of the letters were raked 15° to allow the tool point to pass over. The first series to show lettering in the reduction is the Peace silver dollar series beginning years later in 1921 (note the beveled lettering on such silver dollars). As to the reverse of the Indian cent, I can only draw parallels from the Liberty Seated half dollar series. I have several pieces which show the lathe lines on the reverse passing over details in the feathers, arrows, claws, etc. From this and the obverse of both the 1840 Liberty Seated half dollar and the 1864 bronze Indian cent, I would conclude that the wreath and the entire shield, including lines, were in the model. The inscription ONE CENT was punched into the master die.

While the preceding discussion focuses upon the Indian cent series, it is relevant to the methodology by which the present 1840-C obverse die was created.

Characteristics of Striking and Die Notes. Examples are usually fairly well struck except for the higher details of the portrait. High-grade examples usually have prooflike surfaces. Some are seen with wire rims, not from the dies' being spaced too closely so as to force metal upward at the collar, but due to the collar's being slightly too large for the dies; thus, pieces can have wire rims and yet still be weakly struck at the centers.

Selected Auction Records

Emphasis is on higher-grade pieces and descriptions mentioning die characteristics. Many Very Good to Very Fine and other citations are to be found in the literature, but are not quoted here. Collecting gold by mintmarks was rarely done until the 1890s and did not become popular until well into the twentieth century.

Among early citations, John W. Haseltine's June 1883 sale of the William J. Jenks Collection included lot 446: "1840 C on reverse. Very Good." Realized $3.25. In January 1884, lot 907 in W. Elliot Woodward's sale of the Heman Ely Collection was described: "1840-C Fine." Realized $4.60 to Chapman. B. Max Mehl's November 1932 sale of the R. Taylor Collection included lot 166: "1840-C, C directly over fraction. Fine. Rare." Realized $4.20. After this point, numismatic interest in mintmarked gold increased dramatically. In June 1935, Thomas L. Elder's sale of the Wendell C. Foster Collection included lot 2788: "1840-C Extremely Fine, about Uncirculated and very rare. Mintmark on reverse." Realized $32.

VF-20	EF-40	AU-50	AU-55	MS-60	MS-62	MS-63
$1,750	$3,250	$4,000	$5,250	$10,000	$16,500	$27,500

1840-D

Circulation-Strike Mintage: 3,532

First Liberty Head coinage in Dahlonega. Incredibly rare in Mint State.

Early in 1839 and 1840, Superintendent Joseph J. Singleton wrote from Dahlonega to the Philadelphia Mint stating that coinage could not commence as current dies were not on hand.[6] Although two pairs of dies were shipped from Philadelphia on February 6, 1840, coinage of quarter eagles did not commence until November, apparently all on one day (November 23) from just a single die pair. Thus, for at least the quarter eagle denomination, the non-availability of dies early in the year was not a problem. Apparently, depositors had not requested quarter eagles before that time.

Estimated Total Population (Mint State). 0 or 1. Today's low-range Mint State was yesterday's About Uncirculated. The Bareford coin, sold by Stack's as About Uncirculated in 1978, had been raised in grade to Mint State by the time of its resale in January 1999. In his 1975 study David W. Akers was not able to find even a single Mint State coin in the hundreds of catalogs he examined, including most all of the "name" cabinets of the previous several decades. Accordingly he commented that the 1840-D is "an extremely rare coin in all grades and, as far as I know, unknown in full Mint State. I have, however, seen several About Uncirculated pieces, the finest of which is in a Connecticut collection [the Fairfield Collection]. . . . From the standpoint of number of auction appearances, this is one of the dozen rarest Coronet Head quarter eagles and it has actually appeared at auction fewer times than the highly regarded 1854-D and 1856-D."

In 2019 PCGS listed one MS-61 coin in its population report and NGC one each in MS-60, 61, and 62. (See the "reader caution" note under 1840, page 156. Such figures are certification *events* and do not necessarily involve different coins.)

Estimated Total Population (Circulated Grades). 40 to 60. Examples are very elusive in all circulated grades. Most are well worn, with Very Fine being the norm. At the About Uncirculated level the 1840-D is a rarity, approximately equal to the much more famous 1854-D.

Die Data. *1840 four-digit date logotype: See the Philadelphia Mint listing for this year.*

Two obverse and two reverse dies were sent from Philadelphia on February 6, 1840, and arrived in Dahlonega on February 18 or 25, 1840.[7] These dies were used in 1840 and were defaced on January 12, 1841, meaning that no old dies were on hand after that day. By that time, both quarter eagle reverse dies on hand were cracked. However, Douglas Winter, in *Gold Coins of the Dahlonega Mint 1838–1861*, stated that "only one die variety is known to exist," suggesting that another reverse variety awaits discovery.

The date logotype was deeply punched into the die and slightly high. Only one die variety has been identified. Presumably, all have this feature, as described of a Bass Collection coin:

> The horizontal shield lines are pierced by multiple extensions of the vertical stripes, an interesting but not necessarily unusual phenomenon of the era. Evidences of *circular lathe lines* are seen at the left and right open shield spaces, a characteristic

> which ties in nicely with the *obverse* die used to strike [the 1840-C]. The same process was used at the Mint. However, unlike the obverse where the lathe lines are prominent, we notice them on the *reverse* only in this small area—and, unlike the obverse of the 1840-C, the reverse of this 1840-D is not spectacular in its aspect.

Characteristics of Striking and Die Notes. The 1840-D is usually seen with some areas of light striking, particularly at the stars on the obverse and the eagle on the reverse. The dies cracked, then shattered. The planchets are often of irregular quality.

Selected Auction Records

As collecting branch-mint gold coins was not popular until into the twentieth century, little premium was attached to 1840-D quarter eagles until the 1930s. In June 1886, W. Elliot Woodward's sale of the J. Colvin Randall Collection offered lot 986: "1840-D; Very Fine, scarce." Realized $2.50 (face value). In October 1923, B. Max Mehl offered the Charles Wellinger Collection with lot 125: "Dahlonega Mint. 1840-D. The unusual cracked die on obverse. Very Good. Rare." Realized $7.35.

By 1944 there was much interest in branch-mint gold. The February 1944 sale by Mehl of the Belden E. Roach Collection included lot 983: "1840-D About Uncirculated with mint luster. Rare. Listed at $25 in only Very Fine." Realized $31.75.

VF-20	EF-40	AU-50	AU-55	MS-60	MS-62
$3,250	$8,500	$11,000	$18,500	$35,000	$85,000

1840-O

Circulation-Strike Mintage: 33,580

First Liberty Head coinage in New Orleans. Very rare in Mint State. Seemingly, some struck in 1841.

Some additional 1839-O quarter eagles of the Classic Head design may have been struck in early 1840 and included in the 1840-O mintage figure. The mintage situation is further complicated by the delivery of 3,580 quarter eagles (included in the above mintage) in August *1841*, although no 1841-O quarter eagles are known to exist today. The 1841 obverse dies are said to have been destroyed at New Orleans on February 27, 1841; if these were used, then the coins would have been struck prior to that time, but held until August.[8] Certainly, the situation is anything but simple!

Estimated Total Population (Mint State). 6 to 10. Examples are very rare in Mint State. The dividing line between high-grade About Uncirculated and low-grade Mint State is blurry. Paul Taglione, in his 1985 study of the series (p. 232), stated that he knew of just two Mint State coins in existence, and about nine at the About Uncirculated level. The finest may be the Eliasberg Collection coin, lot 115, MS-65 (later graded MS-64 by PCGS; Bass Collection Part II, lot 331). *Walter Breen's Complete Encyclopedia of U.S. and Colonial Coins* listed this particular example as its only citation in the Mint State category.

Estimated Total Population (Circulated Grades). 80 to 120. Very scarce.

The mintage of 1840-O quarter eagles quickly and quietly passed into the channels of commerce, where most pieces became worn down to the grade typically encountered today—Very Fine or, occasionally, Extremely Fine. There was no numismatic interest in mintmarks at the time, and not even the Mint Cabinet (formed in June 1838) desired branch-mint coins.

Die Data. *1840 four-digit date logotype: See the Philadelphia Mint listing for this year.*

Mint records reveal that a pair of dies for this coinage was shipped to New Orleans on February 6, 1840. Another pair was sent later.

The mintmark O is small (usually seen) or *slightly* large (very rare; e.g., Eliasberg lot 116), depending upon the die. In reality, while the "large" O is bigger than the "small" O, both are quite small.

Characteristics of Striking and Die Notes. Examples are usually lightly struck.

Selected Auction Records

Similar to other mintmarked quarter eagles of this era, the 1840-O was more or less ignored by collectors until into the early twentieth century and did not become widely popular until the 1930s.

In March 1907 in S.H. Chapman's sale of the David S. Wilson Collection, lot 188 was described: "1840-O Extremely Fine." Realized $5.50, a high price for the era. In May 1913 the U.S. Coin Co. sale of the Malcolm N. Jackson Collection included lot 201: "1840-O Small mint mark. Extremely Fine, scarce." Realized $3.50. The same sale included lot 202: "1840-O Small mint mark. Fine." Realized $3.25. What seems to have been an exceptional coin was offered in February 1921 as lot 185 by B. Max Mehl in the Dr. G.F.E. Wilharm Collection; "1840-O Small O over 2 of fraction. Uncirculated. Rare." Realized $4. In Mehl's February 1944 sale another high-quality coin was offered as lot 970: "1840-O Uncirculated with brilliant mint luster. A real little gem. Although not a rarity as far as the date is concerned, it is very rare in this unusually choice condition." Realized $17.25.

VF-20	EF-40	AU-50	AU-55	MS-60	MS-62	MS-63
$600	$1,250	$2,100	$3,250	$9,000	$15,000	$28,000

1841

Circulation-Strike Mintage: 150–250 (estimated, from the same die pair used to strike Proofs)

Proof Mintage: 25 (estimated by Dannreuther)

"The Little Princess."
Most famous quarter eagle rarity.

In this era, earlier-dated dies that were still serviceable were sometimes used at a later date. Although the scenario is complex, perhaps some circulation strikes dated 1841 were minted in 1842 and included under the mintage figure for the latter year. However, this does not account for the use of a

Proof reverse die for circulation coinage, such die being kept on hand for later Proof coins (such as dated 1846). The situation—far from being settled—is discussed in the sections to follow.

Mention of the 1841 quarter eagle is omitted from the *Annual Report of the Director of the Mint*, which has caused some to believe that only Proofs were made (as Proofs were not listed as part of yearly production figures until decades later). Accordingly, for many years this rare issue has been called a Proof-only date, with the implication that no circulation strikes were minted.[9]

However, as most known pieces show signs of wear and were circulated, it seems likely that a modest coinage of circulation strikes took place, perhaps 150 to 250 as estimated on the previous page. In addition, Proofs were struck, probably for presentation purposes, to the extent of fewer than 15 pieces. There is no reason to believe that the Proof mintage for 1841 was any higher than for other Proofs of the 1840s. Further, there are many other instances in which either circulation-strike coins were omitted from the *Mint Report* (e.g., the 1870-S silver dollar) or the figures given are patently incorrect, at least in regard to the number of coins bearing that particular date. Still further, it was often common practice for the Mint to use polished dies to strike Proofs, then produce circulation strikes afterward (as with virtually the entire series of 1821–1834 quarter eagles).

Estimated Total Population (Mint State). None. All known high-grade coins are Proofs (as discussed in the preceding paragraphs).

Estimated Total Population (Circulated Grades). 12 to 14. Estimates have varied widely over the years, from 5, 6, or 7 to "in the 12–15 range." Probably fewer than 15 different circulation-strike coins exist. It is a matter of opinion as to whether coins were made as circulation strikes (from Proof dies but using regular planchets that had not been specially polished or treated) or many more Proofs were made than normal for the era, perhaps for some long-forgotten ceremony or event, after which the coins were spent (See "Die Data and Notes" under the 1841 Proof entry, page 165). Two are in the Smithsonian Institution, one from the Mint Collection dating from the time of issue and the other acquired in 1967 from the Josiah K. Lilly Collection.

Die Data. *1841 four-digit date logotype:* The top of the second 1 is lower than the tops of the other three numerals. The 8 and 4 are close. The 4 has a thick upright and leans slightly right, (scarcely noticeable) and has a fan-shaped serif at the right end of the crossbar. The 1's have a nearly flat top, with the serif extending to left. The second 1 has a more prominent serif than the first. The top of the second 1 is lower than the tops of 1, 8, and 4. This logotype was used on all dies for all mints.

All 1841 quarter eagles, Proofs as well as circulation strikes, seem to have been struck from the same die pair. The date logotype is high, with the first 1 nearly twice as close to the neck as to the denticles.

All known 1841 quarter eagles have raised die striations within the second S in STATES, indicating that all examples—Proofs as well as circulation strikes—were struck from the same reverse die.

Characteristics of Striking and Die Notes. Well struck.

Selected Auction Records

A large group of listings is given in view of the fame and importance of this date, this at the risk of repeating the same information concerning rarity, the Mitchelson Collection, and so on. In their original context such descriptions were scattered through a period of many years, and each time the details were fresh to many new bidders.

W.H. Strobridge's 1873 catalog of the George Francis Seavey Collection listed an 1841 quarter eagle. However, prior to the sale, collector Lorin G. Parmelee purchased the entire Seavey Collection *en bloc*, and the sale never took place. Parmelee, a Boston baker of beans, was widely considered to have the most important cabinet of federal coins in the 1870s and 1880s—and for the 1870s this may have been true. However, by the mid-1880s Baltimore collector T. Harrison Garrett handily eclipsed him. Parmelee's coins were later dispersed widely, most notably in an auction in 1890, but on other occasions and in other venues as well. This coin finally appeared in the salesroom in June 1890 as lot 1122 in the New York Coin & Stamp Company's sale of the Parmelee Collection: "1841 quarter eagle; Very Good." The catalog was a hasty piece of work, and descriptions were meager except for a few major rarities. This may have sold for $2.90 (scarcely more than face value!), but many of the listed prices represented reserves by Parmelee, who later sold the coins individually. At the time the 1841 was not showcased as a rarity. The market was in a slump period following years of growth in the 1880s.[10]

In Edward Cogan's October 1875 sale of the Col. Mendes I. Cohen Collection, lot 209 said nothing about the elusive nature of the 1841: "1841 But little circulated." Realized $3. In October 1884 W. Elliot Woodward in his 69th sale noted that the coin was elusive; lot 1958: "1841 Good impression; very little circulation, scarce." Realized $3.10.

The situation had changed dramatically by March 1940, as reflected in B. Max Mehl's offering of the Frank A. Baldwin and Charles A. Spencer Collections. Lot 1324:

> 1841 $2.50 gold of the Philadelphia Mint. Strictly Fine; two pinpoint nicks on the upper left reverse edge. Finely milled edge and not the coarse milling as is found on the Charlotte Mint. According to Mint records, no quarter eagles were minted at the Philadelphia Mint in this year. In Mr. Adams' "Official List," published in 1909, he there mentions that only two specimens were then known to exist, one in the Mitchelson Collection of Connecticut, now the property of the State and out of the market for all time; and the other in the U.S. Mint Collection in Philadelphia, also, of course out of the market for all time. Since the publication of that work, four or five specimens have been discovered in that period of more than thirty years. I know of one specimen which sold, about five years ago, for $3,000. Since then, when the other specimens were discovered, I know of another specimen, which sold for $1,100. The coin is undoubtedly one of the rarest of all American gold coins. Considering present market conditions of this class of rarity, it is not worth in the four-figure mark, but certainly should bring well into the three-figure mark. According to the best of my knowledge, this is the first specimen ever to have been offered at auction. I'm sure that the collector who obtains this great rarity will find it a most gratifying source of possession and a profitable investment as well.[11] Realized $605.

Mehl's Dunham sale in June 1941 included a similar commentary. The Dunham coin was described, "This rarity was originally struck as a Proof and still maintains quite a bit of luster around the stars and legend, but has seen some circulation. It can easily be classed as Extremely Fine and only a shade from Uncirculated. I doubt if more than six specimens are known to exist." Realized $525.[12]

Proofs

Estimated Total Population (Proof). 14 to 18 per Dannreuther, assuming all were struck as Proofs.

David W. Akers (1975) writes, "Two or three Proofs are known." Some numismatists believe (incorrectly, in this author's opinion) that all 1841 quarter eagles were struck as Proofs, and certain circulated pieces that one might call, for example, EF-40, have been listed under Proofs as PF-40. As to Proofs with deep mirror finish certified as PF-50 or better, Dannreuther lists four, one of which is in the National Numismatic Collection.

Die Data and Notes. Although the existence of the 1841 quarter eagle was known almost immediately after it was struck, and a Proof was placed in the Mint Cabinet (which had been formed in June 1838), very little was discussed in numismatic circles until these coins were a century old.[13]

In the year after the 1841 quarter eagles were struck, Jacob Reese Eckfeldt and William E. Dubois recorded the existence of an example in the Mint Cabinet in their 1842 book, *A Manual of Gold and Silver Coins of All Nations, Struck Within the Past Century.* The 1841 quarter eagle was illustrated on plate 1 from an engraving taken from a medal-ruling machine, somewhat of an innovation at the time. This device, which may have been invented by Christian Gobrecht but was credited to others, made it possible for a stylus to trace over the surface of a three-dimensional coin or medal and render a two-dimensional engraving of it. The Eckfeldt-Dubois volume was not primarily intended as a numismatic reference, but seems to have been sold mainly to bullion dealers and banks. Thus, no information was given concerning the rarity of the 1841 quarter eagle (if, indeed, it was considered rare at the time), nor was the rarity of other coins highlighted.

In 1860, James Ross Snowden, in *A Description of Ancient and Modern Coins in the Cabinet Collection at the Mint of the United States*, referred to the 1841 issue as a "pattern" coinage. Between pages 128 and 129 is a fold-out "Statement, Exhibiting the Number of Pieces Coined at the Mint of the United States." This statement described the 1841 quarter eagles as "patterns" and notes that "only a few specimens were struck, one of which is now in the Mint Cabinet." Snowden, who became director of the Mint in 1853 and who had a strong interest in numismatics, probably consulted Dubois, who at the time was the Mint historian (and apologist), on the subject of the 1841 quarter eagle. Sometimes the term *pattern* was used interchangeably with *Proof* and referred to limited-production pieces made for cabinet purposes, not necessarily to experimental designs (the definitions are different from what we use today).

Following the 1873 Seavey Collection catalog for the auction that never was (discussed on page 164), the 1841 quarter eagle crossed the auction block several other times in the nineteenth century, but without fanfare. The Seavey coin was offered in the Parmelee sale in 1890 as noted. After this event, nearly two decades elapsed with little notice of the 1841, until Edgar H. Adams issued his *Official Premium List of*

United States, Private, and Territorial Gold Coins in 1909. Adams wrote: "Only two of these coins are known to be in existence. One is owned by a private collector in Connecticut, and the other specimen is in the United States Mint Collection at Philadelphia. The Mint records, however, do not mention the issue of a quarter eagle in this year at the parent mint."[14]

This commentary by Adams was the catalyst for the fame of the 1841, and afterward the coin would be projected into the front rank of American gold rarities. All of a sudden, collectors and dealers sat up and took notice—but there were few coins to be found. Virtually nothing new was mentioned about the 1841 quarter eagle until B. Max Mehl's 1940 offering and the better known 1941 listing (discussed on pages 164–165).

This issue has been nicknamed the *Little Princess* for many years. The first located use of this term seems to have been in the catalog of the Davis-Graves Collection, written by Norman Stack and sold by Stack's in 1954.[15] The text noted: "This 1841 quarter eagle is the only one available today and we like to call it the 'Little Princess' in the coin rarities."

All examples of the 1841 quarter eagle were struck from a single pair of dies.[16] However, it is not known whether, after the Proofs were made, it was the intention of the Mint to produce circulation strikes, or whether any circulation strikes were actually made.

In his *Complete Encyclopedia of U.S. and Colonial Coins*, 1988, Walter Breen noted that these were only struck in Proof. Earlier, in his 1975 auction survey of gold coins, David W. Akers was not convinced that all were struck as Proofs.

Especially significant to the discussion, an offering of an 1841 quarter eagle in the Mid-American sale of May 1985 has a comment originating from John Dannreuther indicating that the 1841 and 1846 Proof quarter eagles in the Eliasberg Collection sale were struck from the same reverse die. This provides additional evidence for those who believe all examples of the Little Princess were intended as Proofs.

In his *Analysis of Auction Records*, 1975, David Akers discussed the Eliasberg coin in detail:

> The 1841 is generally considered to be the most desirable of all Liberty Head quarter eagles. There is no official record of this date having been struck, but obviously a small number were minted. Most numismatists and cataloguers feel that this is a Proof-only date and that all known specimens were originally struck in Proof for inclusion in presentation sets. This seems unlikely to me and I am not convinced that the 1841 is a Proof-only date. First of all, there are far too many specimens known when compared to other Proof quarter eagles (or Proof gold of any other denomination) of the same period. Less than five Proofs are known of every other quarter eagle from 1840 to 1848, and yet I would estimate that at least 12 and possibly as many as 15 1841s are known. Only a few of them are clearly and unequivocally Proofs, such as the coin in the Smithsonian Institution, the piece in Louis Eliasberg's collection, the Davis/Graves coin, and perhaps one or two others. Most of the others are well circulated and, in fact, grade from VG to EF. More importantly, the supposedly "impaired Proofs" just don't look like impaired Proofs. Consider for example the Wolfson specimen, which was subsequently in the Shuford Sale and then in the 1974 NASC Sale conducted by the American Auction Association. Although barely circulated, it has almost no trace of a Proof surface and few of the other characteristics of

> a genuine Proof (such as a square edge), although it does appear to have been struck from the same dies as the Proofs. If indeed the 1841 is a Proof-only date, it would be an interesting research project for someone to determine why such a large number (relatively speaking, of course) were struck. Certainly it was not for presentation sets since such sets would have included a half eagle and eagle as well. Or would they? Could there have been presentation sets that contained the minor coins and just the quarter eagle without the other two gold coins? Was there something special about the year 1841 that justified altering the normal pattern of making gold Proofs? On the other hand, if the 1841 quarter eagle is not a Proof-only date, as I believe, then why were so few struck and why was there no record of the mintage?
>
> Today, some questions have been answered, but others remain. It is now known that there are multiple instances in which dies used to strike Proof gold (and other) coins were, indeed, used to make circulation strikes.
>
> As you can see, this coin poses many interesting questions and, for that reason, it is for me one of the most intriguing and enigmatic of all United States gold coins. All known specimens of the 1841 were apparently struck from the same dies. Since some pieces are obviously Proofs, this would normally indicate that they were all struck as Proofs since I know of no other non-Proof gold coins of any denomination or date that were struck from the same dies as the Proofs of the same year." If all 1841 quarter eagles were struck in Proof format, perhaps the output was partially for collectors and partially for presentation or some other purpose, perhaps for some long-forgotten ceremony. In 1841 the quarter eagle was the smallest gold coin produced by the United States (the gold dollar did not make its debut until 1849). Thus, a civic, political, commercial, or other ceremony requiring gold coins as an honorarium or gift would find the quarter eagle to be convenient. For example, William Henry Harrison was inaugurated in 1841.[17]

To summarize the preceding, all known 1841 quarter eagles are from the same dies, which during part of their career were highly polished and used to strike Proofs. A number of 1841 quarter eagles show signs of circulation and were "spent," which seems logical if some were used for presentation purposes in ceremonies and not sold directly to numismatists. If any coins were made for general circulation, they had Proof surfaces when first issued.

Eliasberg's 1841 "Little Princess": The Story of a Coin

The story of the Eliasberg Collection "Little Princess" is particularly interesting, as this was the final gold coin the well-known Baltimore financier and numismatist needed to complete his set (he already had the unique 1870-S three-dollar gold piece and one of just two 1822 half eagle coins in private hands!).

The saga of this particular quarter eagle goes back to St. Louis dealer Burdette G. Johnson, who purchased a complete 1841 Proof set, including gold, from A.H. Baldwin & Sons, Ltd., of London. Wayte Raymond acquired the set from Johnson for $1,000 and sold one piece from the set, the quarter eagle, to Waldo C. Newcomer for the same amount. Raymond later said that the 1841 Proof $5 and $10 were sold to John Work Garrett of Baltimore, but surviving records of the Garrett Collection, which are very extensive,[18] do not substantiate this, nor was either piece in the Garrett Collection in 1942 when it was gifted to the Johns Hopkins University. Col. E.H.R. Green acquired the 1841 quarter eagle from Newcomer for $1,200. The prized 1841 quarter eagle later found its way to F.C.C. Boyd, a sometime coin dealer who was best known as an executive of the Union News Company, which maintained shops and kiosks in railroad stations and elsewhere to sell magazines, newspapers, tobacco, and sundries.

The background to the gold portion of Boyd's "World's Greatest Collection" and the exciting sale of the 1841 quarter eagle were later recalled by Abe Kosoff in his *Coin World* column:

> Sometime after cataloguing had been started and the date for the auction sale was being considered, Fred Boyd and I were lunching, when he asked if I would be happier if I owned the gold collection rather than just selling it for his account. He realized, he said, that I spent almost all my commission from the silver sale [of the Boyd Collection coins held in 1945] on promotion of that sale.
>
> I acknowledged that he was quite right. We had spent $9,000 out of the $11,000 in commissions on catalogues, advertising, circulars, and so on, and we had sold the silver coins in four sections at four different times. Fred was offering us an opportunity to make up for those efforts by offering us the gold collection.
>
> I readily agreed to the price he set, except that had Boyd promised the four gold $4 Stellas to someone if and when he ever sold the gold coins. "So, we will leave the Stellas out of the deal, and since the set has been valued at $2,000, just take that sum as an allowance. The balance you can pay whenever you feel like it—after the sale, if you wish," Boyd said.
>
> On my return to the office, a check in partial payment was posted—we now owned the collection. No sooner done than the telephone rang. It was J.F. Bell of Chicago.[19] Bell was a frequent caller, several times a week—sometimes several times a day. "Anything new?" he inquired.
>
> I told him about the gold collection. That day he called twice again, and the next morning waiting on the doorstep when we arrived for the start of business was J.F. Bell. He wanted the collection—the price was in six figures. We offered him several options, but we would not break up the collection which is what he really wanted us to do.
>
> Most attractive to him were two of the options: 1. An outright purchase of the entire collection and, 2. A half interest in the collection which would then be sold as per plans which had progressed toward that end.
>
> Finally he decided to purchase the whole collection if we would accept a check for 10% and three promissory notes for the balance, payable in equal installments in 30, 60, and 90 days. His credit was A-1, so the deal was arranged on that basis. The notes were prepared, and as he was signing them and a check, a messenger came in with a package from Charley Ryan, a dealer friend. The package contained a note and a coin, a $50 Kellogg & Co. rarity. I was to call Charley, which I proceeded to do, and the coin was ours—I think for $1,750.
>
> I showed it to Bell, and he bought it for $2,250 or $2,500—I don't recall exactly. He added the $2,500 to the check, and we wound up the transaction, with him taking the coins back to Chicago.

Thirty days later, J.F. Bell called to tell us he was going to have some difficulty meeting the notes. He was okay for the first one, but some business commitments would prevent his paying the next two. We were prepared to extend the period of time for him, but he had other ideas. He now wanted the second option, namely to have a half interest in the collection. He would return the coins, we would catalogue the collection. He would pay the first note plus the difference, an additional 10% of the purchase price, to give him a 50% equity. "When the sale takes place I will be in better shape and will buy what I need," he reflected.

Well, we argued that the second option was only made during our original discussion, and when he decided on an outright purchase, the second option expired. Nevertheless, Bell insisted that he would not be able to carry out the obligations, and I was soon back at work cataloguing the collection.

Finally, the big day came. It was late in January in 1946. Bell had come to the office two or three days earlier. He particularly wanted to buy the 1841 quarter eagle. It was a brilliant Proof coin, undoubtedly the finest of the few known specimens. The coin had not appeared in any sale or list for many years. An unconfirmed report had it that one was sold at private sale in 1930 for $3,000. How much would he have to pay for it?

Obviously, the answer depended on the competition—and the competition was keen and noteworthy. Louis Eliasberg of Baltimore was interested and so was Wayte Raymond. Stack's had examined the coin very carefully. Jerome Kern was coming to New York to attend the sale (it was on this visit that Kern collapsed on the sidewalk on Park Avenue, an attack from which he never recovered—quite likely his stroll was toward the Numismatic Gallery just off Park Avenue).[20] And there were others who also wanted to buy the piece.

For almost three days Bell kept asking how much he would have to pay for the 1841. Finally, an hour before the sale was to begin, he authorized me to bid for him up to $3,500. However, he was to be in the room bidding on other coins. Should the bidding go beyond $3,500 he wanted to take over on his own and I was to look at him—for I was the auctioneer.

Most of those interested in the coin were either present or had representatives there, so the book bids on this lot were just so-so. I think the bidding started at $1,100 and proceeded $50 at a time, then $100 at a time, until it reached $3,000. Morton Stack then represented Louis Eliasberg, and he bid $3,250, to which I countered $3,500, as Bell's final authorized bid.

"$3,750" Morton continued, and I glanced toward Bell's seat—he nodded, it was $4,000, then $4,250—another nod, and now we were at $4,500. Mort went to $4,750, and Bell's nod put it at $5,000. "$5,500" cried Mort, but J.F. seemed determined, and his next nod meant $6,000, and $6,000 it was.

Suddenly things went quiet. The air of expectancy caused a hush of the awed murmurs which had accompanied the bidding. I called the bids, then a second time—and finally gave "fair warning for the third and last time" while Bell sat hopefully—but prepared to continue. After some hesitancy and probing of the mind, Mort shook me off—he was through. "Sold at $6,000 to number 18"—J.F. Bell always wanted number 18.

> Well, after the two sessions of the auction were concluded and all were congratulating us on our successful conduct of the sale, J.F. Bell approached. "You did a marvelous job, but there's one thing I'm not happy about."
>
> "What's that," I asked.
>
> "You should never have let me spend $6,000 for the 1841!" Bell replied.
>
> 'Come on, J.F." I countered, "For three days you nudged [bothered] me with the 1841. Finally, you settled on a price of $3,500. You cautioned me to keep an eye on you—you are over 21. You competed against real competition. However, if you are unhappy, I am sure that Mort Stack will take the coin at his previous bid. He just told me he was bidding for Eliasberg, who was going to be very unhappy about not getting it."
>
> "Chuchim [wise guy]," he responded, "I wouldn't give it up for $10,000!"
>
> Louis Eliasberg was put out—he was mighty unhappy about losing out on this piece. In fact, he telephoned me several days later. "Could I get it say for $7,000?" he asked.
>
> I was due to be in Chicago a week later and would see what I could do, but I did not encourage him because of Bell's previous statement. As it turned out, Bell wouldn't sell. Later, in 1948, we had a rough period economically in the spring, and coin sales dropped sharply as did stock market prices. At this inopportune time, Bell decided to sell. We tried to discourage him, but to no avail. He had his reasons and insisted on going ahead.

On March 1–2, 1948, many of Jake Shapiro's coins were auctioned by Numismatic Gallery under the title "A Memorable Sale of United States and Territorial Gold Coins." The catalog introduction said the event would "appropriately commemorate the opening" of the firm's new office at 8943 Wilshire Boulevard in Beverly Hills, California.[21] The offering was not successful, as just related in Abe Kosoff's recollections. The market was not strong, buyers were scarce, and the material was hardly "fresh" to intending bidders. To Kosoff's partner Abner Kreisberg fell the assignment of "wining and dining" Jake Bell before the auction—anything to get Bell's mind off of the impending sale.[22] The 1841 quarter eagle was given a full page of space and estimated at $10,000, but did not find a buyer.

In February 1949, Kosoff sold Jake Bell's 1841 quarter eagle by private treaty to Louis E. Eliasberg, thus completing his cabinet of U.S. gold coins. The price paid was $4,800.[23]

Following the Baltimore collector's acquisition of the long-sought 1841 quarter eagle, a letter of congratulations was sent by John Zug, who was one of the most important contributors to the development of the Eliasberg Collection over the years and a fine friend as well. Zug wrote that "Everything comes to him who waits." Mr. Eliasberg later related to the author that he appreciated the Zug letter more than any of the accolades he was to receive over the next decade when the absolute completion of his collection became known throughout the numismatic community, and letters poured in from dealers and collectors.

The coin market continued its sluggishness for the next several years, through 1951, when it experienced a reinvigoration, going onward and upward to surpass interest and price levels ever before seen.

VF-20	EF-40	AU-50	AU-55	MS-60	PF-63
$100,000	$125,000	$150,000	$160,000	$225,000	$250,000

1841-C

Circulation-Strike Mintage: 10,281

Incredibly rare in Mint State.

Deliveries of this issue were reported as follows: March 24, 2,070; June 12, 3,980 (these were coined in May); September 25, 3,200; December, 1,027. Total: 10,297. This differs from Mint director R.M. Patterson's cumulative report of a later time, January 23, 1844, of 10,281 (the figure widely used in twentieth-century numismatic publications).

Interestingly, the 1841-C has the largest mintage by far of the three date and mintmark varieties of the 1841 year.

Dr. Montroville W. Dickeson, *American Numismatical Manual:* "1841 [no mention of Charlotte]. The designs the same, with the exception of the letter C on the reverse, which addition, we are advised, referred to California, this emission being a private enterprise designed for that country. There was one type and one variety, but the *Mint Report* does not furnish the number coined."

This listing was one of Dickeson's biggest gaffes, but he can be excused on the grounds that his book was the first comprehensive numismatic guide ever published on American coins, and there was little awareness of or interest in mintmarks.

Estimated Total Population (Mint State). 2 or 3. This issue is exceedingly rare in Mint State, and most of the prominent collections of the past lacked one in this grade. Modern data are inconclusive regarding the difference between high-level About Uncirculated and low-level Mint State coins due to gradeflation.

Estimated Total Population (Circulated Grades). 100 to 150. The 1841-C is very scarce. However, among those that do exist, quite a few are Extremely Fine or About Uncirculated.

Die Data. *1841 four-digit date logotype: See the Philadelphia Mint listing for this year.*

The mintmark C is very small, as also seen on 1840-C, 1842-C, and 1843-C, Small Date, Crosslet 4.

Two reverse die varieties the 1841-C are known: one from a leftover die of 1840 and the other from a die shipped from Philadelphia on February 18, 1841.

The obverse border usually is wide and flat, in effect framing the motifs.

Characteristics of Striking and Die Notes. Examples are nearly always lightly struck on the higher hair curls, although there are rare exceptions. Weakness is seen on the lower part of the eagle. Planchet quality is sometimes rough.

Regardless of the quality of striking, many if not most have a wire rim on the obverse (usually) and/or reverse from loose fitting of the obverse die with relation to the collar in the coining press. The overall appearance of this issue ranges from rustic to poor, with the result that pieces that may have had only light wear can seem well worn. Accordingly, grading is apt to vary widely from one observer to another.

Selected Auction Records

John W. Haseltine, in his 18th sale, December 1875, described lot 1159: "1841-C; Charlotte Mint; Very Fine; rare." In his 69th Sale, June 1883, Haseltine included lot 447: "1841 C Mint. Very Good. Rare." Realized $3.12½. Into the twentieth century, S.H. Chapman described lot 189 in his sale of the S. Wilson Collection: "1841-C Fine." Realized $6.50. In May 1915 in his B.W. Smith Collection, B. Max Mehl offered lot 291: "1841-C. C over and to right of 1 and bar. Very Good. Very rare. Small coinage." Realized $6. This was one of Mehl's earlier catalogs and also an early auction description of the mintmark position. Years later, in his November 1939 sale of the William B. Hale Collection, Mehl included lot 834: "1841-C Small C over fraction. Extremely Fine with some luster. From the Zug Sale in 1909. Rare. Catalogs at $20." Realized $12.50.

Mehl in his May 1950 sale of the Jerome Kern Collection described lot 117: "1841 C. Nearly Uncirculated with considerable mint luster. Record near $40." Realized $30. In November 1956 the New Netherlands sale of the Thomas L. Gaskill Collection included lot 221: "1841-C About Uncirculated. Highly lustrous; complete wire edge upon both sides, which is quite unusual. Just 10,297 struck. Better than the Belden Roach coin at $60, over twelve years ago, for an equal impression." Realized $47.

VF-20	EF-40	AU-50	AU-55	MS-60	MS-62
$1,950	$2,500	$4,500	$6,000	$16,500	$27,500

1841-D

Circulation-Strike Mintage: 4,164

Scarce in any grade. Incredibly rare in Mint State.

During production runs of half eagles in January and February 1841, cracks developed in both of the obverse dies on hand. After this time there were no perfect 1841 half eagle obverse dies on hand, and attention was turned to striking quarter eagles.

The coinage for this year was accomplished by April 30, when 4,164 were delivered. Two melts of bullion were involved, and four coins from the first and three from the second were made for assay (and, as the custom at the time, not included in the annual total). This April figure may have included 500 coins struck by March 27 (see "Die Data" below), or else the March mintage can be added to the above yearly total.

Estimated Total Population (Mint State). 2 or 3 at low Mint State levels. Some of these may have been called About Uncirculated earlier.

Estimated Total Population (Circulated Grades). 50 to 80. Rare at all grade levels, this is the most elusive Dahlonega Mint quarter eagle of the decade. The typical grade encountered for such pieces is Very Fine to Extremely Fine, and at the About Uncirculated level it is, indeed, a rarity.

Die Data. *1841 four-digit date logotype: See the Philadelphia Mint listing for this year.* In his *Gold Coins of the Dahlonega Mint 1838–1861*, Douglas Winter noted three distinct reverse-die varieties for this date.

One 1841-dated obverse die was sent from Philadelphia on December 30, 1840, and arrived in Dahlonega on January 12, 1841.[24] At the time there were no old reverses on hand; thus, coinage could not commence. Two obverse and two reverse dies were sent from Philadelphia on February 3, 1841, and arrived in Dahlonega on February 13, 1841.[25] Three obverse and three reverse dies were sent from Philadelphia on April 12, 1841, and arrived in Dahlonega on April 20, 1840. On January 15, 1842, five obverse and one reverse die were defaced at the Mint. At that time, four old reverses were retained. Notwithstanding all of this preparation, the quantity produced amounted to just 4,164, all in a single delivery, April 30, and from a single die pair.

Dahlonega Mint director Dr. Joseph J. Singleton wrote to the Philadelphia Mint on March 27, 1841, that four quarter eagle dies (apparently a combination of obverses and reverses) had become so cracked that they were unfit for use. Only 500 pieces had been struck (not reflected in the details under "Circulation-Strike Mintage" on the previous page) by coiner David Mason instead of the desired 12,000.[26]

Clair M. Birdsall, author of *The United States Branch Mint at Dahlonega, Georgia,* gives details:

> Because there were no usable half eagle head [obverse] dies, [coiner David] Mason started to strike quarter eagles "from melt No. 4" on March 21st. Although 2 half eagle head dies were received that day, the struggle to coin quarter eagles continued. The first 500 strikes included 2 head and 2 tail varieties—many with die cracks in more than one part of the reverse. The requested quarter eagle dies—1 head and 2 tails—arrived April 20 and the quarter eagle coinage at Dahlonega *for the year* was soon completed. Probably two melts [of bullion on hand], No. 4 and No. 5, were used in the coinage, so that aside from the many varieties, probably six, one has that factor, that may give difference in color.[27]

Characteristics of Striking and Die Notes. Examples are usually lightly struck, although there are exceptions. On some high-grade pieces the surfaces are prooflike.

Selected Auction Records

Thomas L. Elder's March 1911 sale of the William H. Woodin Collection included lot 1092: "1841-D. New head of Liberty. Very Fine. Very rare; coinage very small; seldom offered." Realized $5. In May 1913 the U.S. Coin Co. sale of the Malcolm N. Jackson Collection included lot 249: "1841-D Extremely Fine and very rare." Realized $11.50. B. Max Mehl's May 1915 sale of the B.W. Smith Collection included two examples. Lot 299: "1841-D D over bar. Practically Uncirculated with bright semi Proof surface. An unusually choice specimen and very rare. Record about $15." Realized $12. Lot 300: "1841-D Small D over 1 and bar. About Fine. Very rare." Realized $9.50.

The Stack's sale of the J.F. Bell Collection in December 1944 included lot 208: "1841-D Extremely Fine. Mint mark on reverse. Scarce." Realized $22.50. In October 1947 this coin appeared again in Stack's sale of the H.R. Lee Collection, lot 1112: "1841-D Extremely Fine. This is the Bell Specimen which brought $22.50, but should be worth more today. Scarce." Realized $17.50. In October 1951 the Numismatic Gallery sale of the B.A. Talmadge collection included lot 1214: "1841-D Very Fine. W.G.C." Realized $19. This is the Bell Specimen which brought $22.50, but should be worth more today. Scarce." Realized $17.50. In October 1951 the Numismatic Gallery sale of the B.A. Talmadge collection included lot 1214: "1841-D Very Fine. W.G.C." Realized $19.

VF-20	EF-40	AU-50	AU-55	MS-60	MS-62	MS-63
$3,250	$5,500	$9,000	$12,000	$26,500	$40,000	$55,000

1842

Circulation-Strike Mintage: 2,823

Proof Mintage: 3 (estimated)

Generally unrecognized rarity.
Among rarest Liberty Head $2.50 gold coins.

Estimated Total Population (Mint State). 3 certified in MS-61, 62, and 63. None have been seen by the author.

Estimated Total Population (Circulated Grades). 30 to 50. Very Fine and Extremely Fine are typical grades. A full About Uncirculated specimen is a notable rarity. In nineteenth-century catalogs the 1842 was often showcased as one of the prime rarities of the quarter eagle series, but this distinction has been largely lost in modern times.

Writing in the Pittman II catalog, 1998, David W. Akers noted: "The 1842 quarter eagle is more rare than most of the popular C and D Mint issues, including some of the rarest ones, and it is also more rare, all grades considered, than the ultra-low mintage 1875. In fact, among all Liberty Head quarter eagle issues, only the famous 1841 and 1854-S are indisputably more rare than the 1842."

Die Data. *1842 four-digit date logotype:* The numerals are small, with 8 and 4 closer together than other digits. The 4 has a triangular serif at the right end of the crossbar, and the 2 has a heavy knob and curved base. This logotype was used on all dies for all mints.

Characteristics of Striking and Die Notes. Examples are usually well struck except for the lower left part of the eagle.

Selected Auction Records

The 1842 quarter eagle has one of the strangest market histories of any Liberty Head issue; extra space is devoted to the saga here.

The sale of the estate of engraver James B. Longacre by M. Thomas & Sons took place in January 1870 and included lot 169: "1842 Quarter eagle, good condition." Realized $3.25. There is no way of knowing whether this was a special striking of some kind, or why Longacre selected this date for preservation, for he had only a few federal gold coins, and this particular quarter eagle was struck before he came to the Mint in 1844. The term *good condition* simply means *nice condition*, and is not a reference to the grade later known as *Good.* At the time, the 1842 was considered to be a rarity. The October 1875 sale of the Col. Mendes I. Cohen Collection included Edward Cogan's description of lot 210: "1842 But little circulated." Realized $2.85. Henry Chapman in his June 1908 sale of the Taylor, Windle, and Lincoln Collections stated this for lot 457: "1842 Philadelphia Mint. Fine. One of the greatest rarities in the U.S. series. I know of only one other example and that is in the Collection at the Mint at Philadelphia. Robert C. Davis of this City was the first collector to give his attention to the collection of quarter eagles and though he was a diligent seeker he never succeeding in securing one of this issue. That in the Parmelee Collection was from the New Orleans Mint as I made a memorandum to this effect at the sale though the catalogue failed to state the fact." Realized $155. This was a simply incredible price for the time! S.H. Chapman reoffered the same coin in his October 1918 sale of gold coins from the Granberg Collection, describing lot 89: "1842 Fine. Excessively rare. Bought through Henry Chapman from Mr. Murphy, Quebec, for $170.50. Many of the greatest collections have not contained this coin." Realized $87.50. S.H. Chapman's description suggests that his brother, Henry, collected a 10% buyer's premium at the June 1908 sale.

Thomas L. Elder's March 1911 sale of the William H. Woodin Collection included this description of lot 965: "1842. About Fine. Excessively rare and only offered once in recent years when it sold for $155. The Wilson, Zug, Smith, and other gold sales did not have it." Realized $41. In May 1913 the U.S. Coin Co. sale of the Malcolm N. Jackson Collection included lot 126: "1842 Very Fine and excessively rare. Very few of the large collections contain this coin." Realized $110. In May 1915 B. Max Mehl's catalog of the B.W. Smith Collection included this description of lot 261: "1842. . . . Very Fine, sharp. Excessively rare. Only three or four specimens known, and until a few years ago considered as unique. The first specimen that was ever offered at auction appeared at the Taylor-Windle Sale in 1908 and brought $155.[28] In the past seven years, to the best of my knowledge, only two other specimens were offered, including this specimen, which is from the Griffith Collection at $94.50 and the Jackson Specimen at $110. It is undoubtedly one of the very rarest quarter eagles." Realized $68.

Mehl's May 1922 catalog of the James Ten Eyck Collection included lot 74: "1842. Very Fine. Extremely rare. At one time this coin sold for over $100 but since then a few more specimens were discovered and are not quite as rare, but are still quite valuable, especially in choice condition." Realized $20. The mighty 1842 seems to have fallen from its price perch. The November 1932 sale of the R. Taylor Collection included Mehl's description of lot 126: "1842, Fine. Very rare. At one time this coin brought over $150." Realized $26. Elder's June 1935 sale of the Wendell C. Foster Collection included this description of lot 2789: "1842 A great rarity. Cost $150. Extremely Fine." Realized $78. Mehl's March 1938 sale of the Samuel H. McVitty Collection included this description for lot 2789: "1842 Strictly Fine to Very Fine. Very rare. At one time, back in 1912, it brought $155 at auction.[29] Since then a few other specimens have been discovered, so that today they retail at from $50 to $75." Realized $15. How low can it go?

In his November 1939 sale of the William B. Hale Collection, Mehl described lot 766: "1842 Extremely Fine, just a shade from Uncirculated. Very rare. This coin was purchased by Mr. Hale from the old Chicago dealer, Stevens,[30] in October, 1912, at a time when but very few specimens of this coin were known. At that time Mr. Hale paid $165 as it had an auction record of $155. While a few specimens have been discovered since, but it is still a very rare coin." Realized $57.50. A sharp price uptick. In June 1941 Mehl's sale of the William Forrester Dunham Collection included a market commentary with lot 1933: "1842 Philadelphia Mint. Fine to Very Fine. A light, hardly perceptible scratch on obverse. Very rare. At one time it was hardly known to exist and one of the first to have been offered at auction, nearly thirty years ago, brought $155. It is not worth that amount today, but it does sell for around $50." Realized $42.

Stack's sale of the J.F. Bell Collection in December 1944 included lot 108: "1842 Uncirculated, but not in full brilliancy. A much under-rated coin and seldom offered." Realized $55. In June 1946 Mehl's sale of the William Cutler Atwater Collection included lot 1945: "1842. Extremely Fine with considerable luster. Quite rare. This has a very old record of well over $100, but since then a few specimens have been discovered and its prevailing record is about $50." Realized $18. What a roller-coaster ride the 1842 had by this time! The Will W. Neil Collection sold by Mehl in June 1947 included lot 2421: "Extremely Fine. Rare. Some few years ago there were only a very few specimens of this quarter eagle known and it sold up to $145 [*sic;* what happened to $155?]. A few specimens have been discovered in the past twenty years, but the coin is still very scarce and catalogs at $30. It retails for about $50. This specimen cost $41 in the Roach Sale." Realized $35.

Mehl's sale of the Jerome Kern Collection in May 1950 included lot 31: "1842. Practically Uncirculated with brilliant mint lustre; just the slightest touch of cabinet friction. Very limited number minted. Quite rare, especially so choice. Seldom found better than Fine or Very Fine. Catalogs $30 in Very Fine. This one should be worth watching." Realized $32.50. In November 1956, New Netherlands' sale of the Thomas L. Gaskill Collection included lot 223: "1842 Very Fine. Light, even wear; free of any evidence of maltreatment. One of the most difficult years on the series; only 2,823 coined. Between 1863 and 1915, this date was considered semi-unique, several early records over $100 being made. An example in the Taylor-Windle auction (1908), brought the record price of $155. A few specimens have turned up since, all but one (to our knowledge) about the same as, or nearly equal to this piece.[31] Dunham's was Fine to Very Fine, the obverse scratched. Greatly unappreciated." Realized $35.

PROOFS

Estimated Total Population (Proof). 1.

Documentation is nonexistent, amounting mostly to rumors. The Smithsonian Institution holds one example. Walter Breen (*Proof Encyclopedia*, 1977) stated that Wayte Raymond had seen two examples, perhaps the same as the two impaired coins that Breen had examined in the 1950s.[32]

VF-20	EF-40	AU-50	AU-55	MS-60	MS-62
$2,200	$4,500	$7,000	$12,500	$19,500	$35,000

1842-C

Circulation-Strike Mintage: 6,737

Third-rarest Charlotte $2.50 gold coin. Incredibly rare in Mint State.

Deliveries of this issue were reported as follows:[33] June 7, 3,738; September 3, 2,991; December, 8.[34] Total: 6,737. This figure differs from that reported later by Mint director R.M. Patterson (6,742); elsewhere, the figure of 6,729 was given.

Estimated Total Population (Mint State). 3 to 5. Exceedingly rare in any Mint State level.

Estimated Total Population (Circulated Grades). 60 to 100. Most are Very Fine, this being true of examples in many important collections. Considered to be the third-rarest Charlotte quarter eagle, with only the 1843-C, Small Date, and 1855 being rarer.

Die Data. *1842 four-digit date logotype: See the Philadelphia Mint listing for this year.*

One obverse die for the 1842-C quarter eagle was shipped from the Philadelphia Mint on December 22, 1841, followed by another obverse on March 11, 1842.

The obverse border usually is wide and flat, in effect framing the motifs. The mintmark C is very small, as also seen on 1840-C, 1841-C, and 1843-C, Small Date, Crosslet 4.

Characteristics of Striking and Die Notes. The issue is usually weakly struck in areas, particularly at the stars and the center of the portrait on the obverse and at the lower left of the reverse. The flat border is often wide (reminiscent of the "broad-mill" issues of half eagles of the early 1840s), and sometimes there is a wire rim on part of the border. Douglas Winter has written, "This is one of the most underrated dates in the entire series and, as well, one of the rarest Charlotte quarter eagles. Like its immediate predecessor, this date is found weakly struck . . . any specimen grading Very Fine is quite rare; any piece which grades Extremely Fine or better is very rare."

Selected Auction Records

W. Elliot Woodward's January 1884 sale of the Heman Ely Collection included this lot 909: "1842-C; Very Good." Realized $4.70 to Heath. Thomas L. Elder's March 1911 sale of the William H. Woodin Collection had this description of lot 1119: "1842-C Very Fine. Very rare. Coinage limited." Realized $5. In May 1913 the U.S. Coin Co. sale of the Malcolm N. Jackson Collection included lot 274: "1842-C Extremely Fine, mint luster, Very rare." Realized $4.25. In February 1921 the catalog of B. Max Mehl's sale of the Dr. G.F.E. Wilharm Collection described lot 173: "1842-C Small C over fraction. Practically Uncirculated. Limited coinage. Very scarce." Realized $5. Mehl's February 1944 catalog of the sale of the Belden E. Roach Collection described lot 957: "1842-C About Uncirculated, seldom equaled. Rarest quarter eagle of this mint. Listed at $25 in only Very Fine. This one should be worth double." Realized $21.65.

Stack's sale of the J.F. Bell Collection in December 1944 included lot 191: "1842-C Uncirculated, sharp, scarce." Realized $37.50. Mehl's sale of the William Cutler Atwater Collection included lot 2024: "1842-C. Extremely Fine with traces of mint luster. Bold impression. Rare. Catalogs at $35 in only Very Fine. Recent record of $50 for Uncirculated." Realized $36. In October 1951 the Numismatic Gallery sale of the B.A. Talmadge collection included lot 1197: "1842-C Barely circulated. A rare and desirable coin, worth over . . . $50.00." Realized $42. In June 1957 the New Netherlands sale of Eliasberg duplicates had this for lot 590: "1842-C. Very close to Unc., but a weak strike, and a few mint abrasions. Really rare, only 6,737 minted making this the third rarest Charlotte issue by virtue of the number made, but B.M. Mehl called it the 'rarest quarter-eagle of this Mint.' One of the three finest specimens we have heard of.

We saw the Melish piece, described as 'Extremely Fine. Cost $50.00,' and thought it VF. It brought $52.50. For some idea of true desirability of this lot, read the description of No. 225 in our last sale, where a decidedly inferior one brought all of $50. From the 'Lee' offering, lot 1097, as 'Brilliant Uncirculated.' For the record, Neil's was VF, the Memorable coin VF, Kern's had a loop removed, Menjou's was only Fine, the Graves item VF." Realized $62.50.

VF-20	EF-40	AU-50	AU-55	MS-60	MS-62
$2,000	$3,500	$7,000	$10,000	$23,500	$42,500

1842-D

Circulation-Strike Mintage: 4,643

Rare in any grade.

Coinage was delivered on two days: January 25 (2,469) and November 24 (2,174). The number of additional coins made for the Assay Commission during the year was nine.

Estimated Total Population (Mint State). 4 certified in MS-61 and 62. None have been seen by the author.

Estimated Total Population (Circulated Grades). 60 to 90. Nearly all have disappeared, with the result that the population today is very low, possibly existing only to the extent of several dozen specimens. David W. Akers makes the eye-opening comment that the "1842-D is generally unappreciated for its real rarity; it is every bit as rare as the 1854-D, 1855-D, and 1856-D, and certainly more rare than the latter two in grades better than EF." Walter Breen echoes a similar sentiment, stating, "usually in low grades; prohibitively rare above EF." Most are in the Very Fine range. About Uncirculated examples are very rare, and probably fewer than ten are known.

Die Data. *1842 four-digit date logotype: See the Philadelphia Mint listing for this year.*

One 1842-dated obverse die and one reverse die were sent from Philadelphia on December 20, 1842, and arrived in Dahlonega by January 15, 1842.[35] Four usable old reverse dies remained on hand from 1841. Apparently, a very small coinage was anticipated. Records encountered reveal no back-up for the obverse die, but to have but a single die would have been an unusual situation. Perhaps one or more other dies were sent, but the records are lost today. However, on January 7, 1842, the *single obverse die* and two reverse dies were defaced.

In 1911, Thomas L. Elder, drawing upon the William H. Woodin Collection, described two different die varieties, one with a doubled date (the variety most often seen today), and the other with a perfect date. Woodin in particular was a very careful student of die varieties, and Elder was no amateur either. How this reconciles with the records, apparently incomplete, of but a single obverse die being sent to Dahlonega for the 1842 coinage is not known. Perhaps the perfect-date variety is a later die state with the obverse relapped.

Douglas Winter knew just one die variety, this with a double-punched date. On this die the date logotype was impressed lightly, after which a second impression of the date logotype was made, high and more deeply impressed at the top of the date than at the bottom, indicating that the logotype punch was not driven in a true vertical alignment. As a result, on most specimens the obverse die shows repunching, particularly at the 18. Breen-6164 is the catalog number for early die state coins with noticeable repunching.

The D mintmark on the reverse overlaps the feather, with part of the feather visible at the center of the letter and a tiny part of the feather extending from the left of the upright.

Characteristics of Striking and Die Notes. The obverse and reverse dies were later relapped, removing some lower-relief detail including much of the evidence of the date repunching (perhaps creating the "perfect date" described by Thomas L. Elder in the 1911 Woodin Collection catalog, cited below). Striking quality is about average, with the eagle's leg on the left being slightly weak. In his June 1911 sale of the Summers Collection, Elder noted a specimen from a cracked obverse die, apparently a very rare die state.

Selected Auction Records

John W. Haseltine's description of lot 448 in his sale of the William J. Jenks Collection, June 1883, is an early recognition of rarity: "1842 D Mint. Very Good. Extremely rare." Realized $5. Thomas L. Elder's March 1911 sale of the William H. Woodin Collection included this description of two. Lot 1093: "1842-D. Double cut date. About Fine. Extremely rare." Realized $5.25. Lot 1094: "1842-D. Perfect date. Fine to Very Fine. Extremely rare. No record of both of the varieties being offered together." Realized $10. In May 1913 the U.S. Coin Co. sale of the Malcolm N. Jackson Collection included lot 250: "1842-D Extremely Fine and very rare. Very unusual condition . . . as worn specimens are generally the rule." Realized $22. This would seem to imply that this was *not* a worn coin and may have been Uncirculated. Grading standards were nonexistent at the time. The cataloger of this coin, Wayte Raymond, often erred on the nice side—he was usually quite conservative.

In his November 1939 sale of the William B. Hale Collection, B. Max Mehl described lot 835: "1842-D Small date. Practically Uncirculated, with mint luster. From the famous Woodin Sale. Rare. Listed at $20." Realized $16.75. Which of the two Woodin coins this is was not stated. The Stack's sale of the J.F. Bell Collection in December 1944 included lot 209: "1842-D Extremely Fine, scarce." Realized $25. Likely unsold.

VF-20	EF-40	AU-50	AU-55	MS-60	MS-62
$2,850	$5,500	$8,500	$11,000	$32,500	$60,000

1842-O

Circulation-Strike Mintage: 19,800

Estimated Total Population (Mint State). 2 to 4. Grades range from MS-60 to MS-63. This issue is much rarer than normally realized.

Scarce in any grade.
Very rare in Mint State.

Estimated Total Population (Circulated Grades). 100 to 150. Where did they all go? No one knows. The number surviving is very small, less than 1% of the original mintage. The 1842-O has never had much press—the same is true of most other New Orleans quarter eagles of the era. As a class, the New Orleans coins had a lower survival rate than did those of the Charlotte and Dahlonega Mints.

Die Data. *1842 four-digit date logotype: See the Philadelphia Mint listing for this year.*

All known specimens are from a single pair of dies shipped from Philadelphia on December 23, 1841, to New Orleans.

On the obverse the date logotype is very well centered (as determined by the spacing of the first digit in relation to the bust above and the denticles below). The obverse rim is wide and flat, in effect framing this side of the coin.

On the reverse the mintmark O is very small.

Characteristics of Striking and Die Notes. Examples are usually lightly struck on the portrait and on the eagle's leg at the left side of the reverse. The reverse die later cracked through the base of the letters AMERIC in AMERICA, with the crack continuing to the border at C.

Selected Auction Records

One of the earliest listings mentioning the rarity of a New Orleans gold coin was the description of lot 1556 in W. Elliot Woodward's December 1865 catalog of the Bache, Bertsch, Colburn, Emery, Finotti, Ilsley, Levick, Lilliendahl, Lightbody, McCoy, Semple, and Shurtleff Collections: "1842 From the Orleans [*sic*] Mint; in ordinary condition, rare." In May 1915 B. Max Mehl's catalog of the B.W. Smith Collection included this description of lot 310: "1842-O Small date. Small O over 1 and bar. Extremely Fine, nearly Uncirculated. Rare so choice." Realized $2.80. The Stack's sale of the J.F. Bell Collection in December 1944 included lot 228: "1842-O Brilliant Uncirculated." Realized $15. The 1842-O was a generation away from gaining notable traction in the marketplace.

VF-20	EF-40	AU-50	AU-55	MS-60	MS-62	MS-63
$650	$1,350	$2,000	$4,000	$8,500	$15,000	$25,000

1843, Large Date, Plain 4

Circulation-Strike Mintage: 100,546

Proof Mintage: Fewer than 10 (estimated)

Sometimes simply called "1843." Very rare in Mint State.

Record deposits of gold from mines in the Southeast resulted in record gold coinage figures at all four mints this year.[36]

Estimated Total Population (Mint State). 8 to 12. Most are at lower levels, but as long ago as 1975 David W. Akers commented, "There are a small number of gem Uncirculated pieces known." These have proved to be elusive in the years since then.

Estimated Total Population (Circulated Grades). 300 to 500. Very Fine and Extremely Fine are the grades usually seen. Figuring out how many exist is rather difficult to do with this date, as most lower-grade coins are considered common and achieve little recognition in catalogs or certification-service listings. Hence, the figure given here is less studied than most other estimates presented in this work.

Die Data. *1843 four-digit Large Date logotype:* The 1 and 8 are slightly small, and the 4 and 3 are larger, with the 3 being particularly oversized; *the 4 is plain, without the crosslet at the right end of the crossbar.* The last digit also tilts slightly to the left, and an extension of its top would result in a line intersecting with the adjacent 4 below its peak. The Large Date logotype is rather curious inasmuch as the first two digits are quite small, and the last two much larger! This is true of all Philadelphia Mint quarter eagles of 1843 and all Large Date quarter eagles of 1843-C and 1843-O, which used the same logotype. Interestingly, this same date logotype was also used on dimes of 1843 and 1843-O. The overly large size of the last two date digits is so significant that it really should be mentioned in the standard texts, if only as a footnote.

One might speculate that an amateur was at work preparing date logotypes and punching dies in the Engraving Department of the Philadelphia Mint this year. Die anomalies have been popularly ascribed (especially by Walter Breen) to James B. Longacre, who came to the Mint in 1844 and was considered by Breen to be incompetent. The curious Large Date logotype of 1843 reflects work about as incompetent as can be found anywhere in American numismatics! At the time, Christian Gobrecht was chief engraver, but the work of die preparation was left to others. The identity of the person or persons responsible for the 1843 Large Date may never be known. Breen made immense contributions to numismatics, but a later generation of scholars has found many of his "facts" to be guesswork, often wrong.

As to which came first, the Large Date or the Small Date, the fact that all 1843-D coins are of the Small Date style, from an obverse die shipped to Dahlonega in December 1842, would seem to indicate that the Small Date came first. Why this was later superseded by the ungainly Large Date is not known.

Characteristics of Striking and Die Notes. Examples are usually lightly struck on the eagle's leg on the left side of the reverse.

Selected Auction Records

Thomas L. Elder described lot 1381 in his May 1930 sale of the Sam Guthmann Collection: "1843. Mint bloom. Unc. Rare gem." In his November 1939 sale of the William B. Hale Collection, B. Max Mehl described lot 767: "1843 Uncirculated, with considerable mint luster. Very scarce so choice. From Zug Sale in 1909." Realized $6.80. The Stack's sale of the J.F. Bell Collection in December 1944 included lot 109: "1843 Brilliant Uncirculated." Realized $13. In April 1956 Abe Kosoff's sale of the Melish and Hester Collections included lot 1149: "1843 Uncirculated." Realized $26. Another high-grade coin was offered by Stack's in the February 1957 sale of the J.W. Schmandt Collection, lot 72: "1843 Brilliant Uncirculated. Scarce." Realized $25.

Proofs

Proof Die Data and Notes. On the Proof die the 1 in the date is low and touches a denticle; on circulation strikes the 1 is slightly higher. The date is overly large for the space allotted to it.

Estimated Total Population (Proof). 5. Of the five listed by John Dannreuther, one was stolen and has not been recovered.

Selected Proof Auction Records

Thomas L. Elder's March 1911 sale of the William H. Woodin Collection included this description of lot 966: "1843. Brilliant Proof. As it is unique, it is several times rarer than any 1804 dollar. Numismatists should value it accordingly." Realized $94. The buyer was Virgil Brand (Brand journal item 57049). In January 1947 lot 110 in the "World's Greatest Collection" (F.C.C. Boyd Collection; Numismatic Gallery) was described: "1843 Brilliant Proof. A distinct rarity not listed in any of the great sales of our day. Perhaps only a few Proofs struck. An invaluable addition if acquired for a leading collection. Estimates on this item based only on a feeling acquired through experience with the unusual, and one guess is as good as another." Realized $275. B. Max Mehl's sale of the Jerome Kern Collection in May 1950 included lot 32: "1843. 1843 quarter eagle in Brilliant Proof. Perfect sharp, brilliant Proof gem. Very likely from a Proof set. I doubt very much if more than two or three specimens are known of this quarter eagle in Proof condition. A specimen was offered in 1946 and it brought $27. In fact a coin of this kind is almost priceless." Realized $185.

VF-20	EF-40	AU-50	AU-55	MS-60	MS-62	MS-63	PF-63
$450	$550	$700	$900	$2,500	$4,000	$6,500	$75,000

1843-C, Small Date, Crosslet 4

Circulation-Strike Mintage: 2,988 (estimated, or possibly more than 8,000)

Rarest Charlotte $2.50 gold coin. Especially rare in Mint State.

Deliveries of this issue (all 1843-C regardless of variety) were reported as follows:[37] April, 2,988;[38] June, 5,736; July, 6,570; August, 2,089; October, 3,435. Some pieces were struck in December, but the coiner's records have not been located. There is no relevant total from the coiner in view of missing records. Director R.M. Patterson later stated that 26,096 of the 1843-C quarter eagles were minted. The 2,988 figure is probably from the April 1843 delivery; however, in proportion to the total mintage for the year, this figure seems too small in view of the numbers that exist today. David W. Akers suggests that the figure might be about one-third of the total mintage for 1843-C, or somewhat over 8,000 coins.

Walter Breen writes that the 1843-C Small Date, Crosslet 4, quarter eagles were delivered on April 28, 1843, struck from a pair of dies shipped from Philadelphia on December 23, 1842. The small numerals in the date are consistent with those used from

1840 to 1842. Breen notes that the 1843-C, Large Date, Plain 4, quarter eagles were delivered in five groups between June 30 and December 30, 1843. Using reasoning he employed in many different areas, he apparently made two assumptions: The pair of dies shipped on December 23, 1842, were the Small Date style, as these were sent earlier; and, in general, Small Date coins were made earlier (1840–1842). By default, according to his reasoning, the later coins would have been of the Large Date style.

There are a couple of flaws in this. First, it could have been the case that the Small Date die was sent later or was simply on hand from an earlier time. The Mint did not carefully watch date sizes, and subtleties that are important to numismatists today were not generally recognized back then. Alternatively, the 2,988 pieces delivered in April might have been the Small Date variety, but the die might still have been on hand and used again at a later date (which would account for more than 2,988 being struck, per the Akers estimate). Thus, the 23,076 pieces attributed by Breen as the Large Date might have included some Small Date varieties as well.

If Walter Breen's figures are correct, 2,988 for the 1843-C Small Date and 23,076 for the Large Date, then, all things being equal, Small Date pieces should be about eight times rarer today. However, such does not seem to be the case. Douglas Winter gives an estimate of 45 to 50 pieces known for the Small Date and 75 to 80 known for the Large Date; in other words, the Large Date is not even twice as rare, let alone eight times as rare. In his 1975 study of quarter eagles appearing at auction, David Akers noted that seventeen pieces were described as being Small Dates and fifty-five as Large Dates.

Estimated Total Population (Mint State). 3 to 5, all in lower Mint State levels. The 1843-C, Small Date, is a prime object of desire for the Charlotte Mint specialist.

Estimated Total Population (Circulated Grades). 50 to 75, mostly Very Fine and Extremely Fine, but with enough About Uncirculated pieces in existence that the specialist can find one without too much effort. Conventional wisdom has it that this is the rarest of the Charlotte Mint quarter eagles, and it seems to be true. No doubt part of this reputation is based upon the long-published mintage figure of 2,988. Take away that low number and replace it with, say, 8,000, and the availability of the 1843-C, Small Date, is more logically explained. Still, in comparison to surviving specimens of other Charlotte coins, the 1843-C, Small Date, is less often encountered.

Die Data. *1843 four-digit Small Date logotype:* All digits are small. The digits in 18 and the digits in 43 are close; the 8 and 4 are farther apart. The bases of 1 and 8 are slightly high; the upright of the 4 is heavy and leans slightly right; *Crosslet 4.* This logotype was used for certain dies of 1843-C and 1843-O, and for all of 1843-D.

The mintmark C is very small, as also seen on 1840-C, 1841-C, and 1842-C.

Characteristics of Striking and Die Notes. On nearly all specimens the obverse displays a very prominent die bulge at the point of the bust, extending to the rim; this undoubtedly accounts for its limited use. To the uninitiated the bulge is startling in its appearance (about the only thing that matches or even exceeds it is the curious die state described under 1848-C). The striking is usually light at the centers. Some specimens have partial wire rims. High-grade pieces have virtually full prooflike surfaces, including the areas within the shield stripes on the reverse.

Douglas Winter gives three die states, although there may be intermediate states among these:

I. Perfect obverse die—"This state is very rare."

II. With thin crack from the point of the bust, extending to the rim at 7 o'clock—Some have traces of a bulge.

III. Heavier obverse crack, bulging die—The most commonly seen die state.

Selected Auction Records

Note: Some of the early unattributed (with respect to date size) pieces that are listed under the Large Date heading may be of the Small Date style.

In January 1890 the Robert Coulton Davis Collection, cataloged by H.P. Smith of the New York Coin & Stamp Co., included lot 874: "1843 Charlotte mint: cracked die: Very Fine and sharp; barely touched." No date size was given, but mention of the cracked die suggests the Small Date. Thomas L. Elder's 88th sale, January 1914, included lot 641: "1843-C Small C and date. Excessively rare, possibly only one known." The numismatic community at large was made aware of a new rarity. Milfred H. Bolender's 68th Sale, June 1931, described lot 9: "1843-C Small date. Rare variety with small 'C' mint mark. Die crack connects point of bust and rim. Uncirculated. Cost $12.50." Stack's sale of the J.F. Bell Collection in December 1944 included lot 193: "1843-C Small Date. Brilliant Uncirculated. Very scarce." Realized $15.

VF-20	EF-40	AU-50	AU-55	MS-60	MS-62
$2,750	$5,500	$7,000	$8,500	$22,500	$32,500

1843-C, Large Date, Plain 4

Circulation-Strike Mintage: 23,076 (estimated; the larger part of 26,096 total for 1843-C)

Scarce in any grade. Rare in Mint State.

As described under 1843-C, Small Date, Crosslet 4, the mintage picture for 1843-C in general is complicated by missing coiner's records. Walter Breen may have further complicated things by incorrectly estimating the portion of the mintage composed of Small Date coins. It is likely that about two-thirds of the total mintage are of the Large Date, Plain 4, variety.

Record deposits of gold from mines in the Southeast resulted in record gold coinage figures at all four mints this year.

Estimated Total Population (Mint State). 5 to 8. At least one MS-65 is known.

Estimated Total Population (Circulated Grades). 100 to 200. Very Fine and Extremely Fine are typical grades.

Die Data. *1843 four-digit Large Date logotype: See the 1843, Large Date, Plain 4, listing.*

Some examples exhibit doubling at the date; this fades on later states. The large C mintmark is repunched on some or possibly all. The large C is similar to that used in 1844 and later, and unlike the small C used from 1840 to 1842 and on the 1843-C, Small Date, Crosslet 4. One might think that the Large Date obverse would be combined with a small C on the reverse, as the Large Date seems to be the earlier of the two varieties. The large C was used in later years, 1844 onward.

Characteristics of Striking and Die Notes. Usually seen with fairly decent sharpness, but with some lightness of the highest details at the center. The dies rusted late in their life and were highly polished at the machine shop at the Dahlonega Mint to remove the rust; a few semi-prooflike coins were struck from the dies thereafter.

Selected Auction Records

Note: Some of the early listings that do not mention date size may include some Small Date issues.

J.W. Haseltine's 18th Sale, December 1875, included lot 1163: "1843-C; Charlotte Mint; Very Fine; rare." No date size given. In June 1885, W. Elliot Woodward's sale of the J. Colvin Randall Collection included lot 988: "1843-C; sharp impression, Fine." Realized $2.50 (face value). No date size given. In May 1913 the U.S. Coin Co. sale of the Malcolm N. Jackson Collection included lot 275: "1843-C Large date and mint mark. About Uncirculated, mint luster, rare." Realized $3.50. In May 1915 B. Max Mehl's catalog of the B.W. Smith Collection included this description of lot 292: "1843-C Large C over bar. Extremely Fine, sharp, with considerable mint luster." Realized $3.75. No date size given.

Mehl's February 1944 catalog of the sale of the Belden E. Roach Collection described lot 958: "1843-C Large date. Brilliant Uncirculated. Rare so choice." Realized $16.50. The Stack's sale of the J.F. Bell Collection in December 1944 included lot 192: "1843-C Large Date. Brilliant Uncirculated." Realized $25. In June 1946 Mehl's sale of the William Cutler Atwater Collection included lot 2025: "1843-C. Large Date. Almost Uncirculated with mint luster. Recent record $23.50." Realized $7.50. Mehl's sale of the Jerome Kern Collection in May 1950 included lot 119: "1843 C. Practically Uncirculated with mint luster. Large-date variety. Record over $23." Realized $21.

VF-20	EF-40	AU-50	AU-55	MS-60	MS-62	MS-63
$1,650	$2,300	$3,250	$4,250	$8,000	$12,500	$21,000

1843-D, Small Date, Crosslet 4

Circulation-Strike Mintage: 36,209

Most plentiful Dahlonega $2.50 gold coin. However, a rarity in Mint State.

Record deposits of gold from domestic mines resulted in record gold coinage figures at all four mints this year.

The quarter eagle denomination was exceptionally extensive this year, handily outdistancing every earlier year. Activity was concentrated in January (16,430) and

February (12,993), months during which the half eagle—usually the coin of choice at the Dahlonega Mint—was not coined at all. The explanation for this is simple: Dahlonega had no obverse dies on hand for the $5 gold coin until March. Later in the year, only 3,537 additional quarter eagles were struck, for a delivery of October 7.

Quarter eagles were also delivered on March 6 (3,249) and October 7 (3,537). During the year an additional 72 coins were made for the Assay Commission (they are not included in the yearly total).

Estimated Total Population (Mint State). 8 to 12, mostly in the lower ranges of MS-60 to MS-62.

Estimated Total Population (Circulated Grades). 250 to 400. With the 1843-D, Small Date, Crosslet 4, we encounter the first Liberty Head quarter eagle that can reasonably be described as readily available on the present market, although a comparison of mintage figures will show that it is far more elusive than its Philadelphia or New Orleans counterparts. Among all quarter eagles struck at the Dahlonega Mint, this is the most plentiful.

Die Data.[39] *1843 four-digit Small Date logotype: See the 1843-C, Small Date, Crosslet 4, listing.*

All 1843-D quarter eagles are of the Small Date, Crosslet 4, style; no Large Date, Plain 4, issues were made at Dahlonega.

As of January 9, 1843, three usable reverse dies were on hand from previous times[40]—one 1843-dated obverse and one reverse die sent from Philadelphia on December 22, 1842 (arrival date in Dahlonega not recorded); and one reverse die sent from Philadelphia on July 15, 1842, arriving in Dahlonega on July 30, 1843. This would seem to indicate that the supply of reverses on hand by that time was considered inadequate.

This would also indicate—important in the overall context of 1843 quarter eagle coinage—that the Small Date style was being shipped in December 1842 for use in early 1843; thus, it would seem that the Large Date style (used at other mints) would have come later.

The small D mintmark is the size usually seen for this date. A few 1843-D, Small Date, quarter eagles have a large D mintmark on the reverse, this being the size used later in the series, 1844 through 1859. Presumably, the 1843-D pieces with the large D were the last strikings made in 1843. Over a long span of years the mintmark size on the 1843-D has been overlooked in nearly all catalog listings, the large D variety not being known until comparatively recent times.

Characteristics of Striking and Die Notes. The strike is above average for a Dahlonega quarter eagle, with most details sharp. Weakness is sometimes seen on the eagle's leg on the left. Early die impressions have the date digits close or, in some instances, touching. On coins from relapped dies the digits are separated (sometimes called the "wide date").

On February 21, 1843, Dahlonega Mint superintendent Paul Rossignol wrote to Philadelphia to advise, "Our last tail die is cracked. We will try to coin melt No. 8 with it. . . . If the tail can get through melt No. 8 it will be all it can do." From the preceding, it would seem that as of February 21, all three of the old reverses on hand plus the new reverse had broken. As additional 1842-D quarter eagles were struck in December, it would seem logical that these were from the new reverse die received at the mint on July 20. Thus, five different dies would have been used to consummate the coinage for the year.

Clair M. Birdsall estimates that the five reverses were used in the following order to strike the quantities of 1843-D quarter eagles indicated:[41]

> First new reverse die: Used to strike 12,232 coins; cracked on January 28, 1843.
>
> First old reverse die, left over from 1840: Used to strike 3,198; cracked on January 31, 1843.
>
> Second old reverse die, left over from 1840: Used to strike 3,132; cracked on February 11, 1843.
>
> Third old reverse die, left over from 1840: Used to strike 13,110; cracked on February 21, 1843.
>
> Second new reverse die: Used to strike 3,537; last used, condition unknown, on October 7, 1843.

Such die cracking can be termed excessive and was probably due to improper hardening of the dies. Other variables might include press settings with the dies too close together (in which instances, the coins would be struck with needle-sharp detail, which was not the case) and planchets that were too hard. It is known that in December, for the coinage of half eagles, there was great difficulty in obtaining pure copper as an alloy, and the use of impure copper made it so that the Mint "cannot work the ingots."[42]

Selected Auction Records

Thomas L. Elder's March 1911 sale of the William H. Woodin Collection included several: Lot 1095: "1843-D. Close date, 4 touching 8, the 3 double struck. Small D, just over bar. Fine. Scarce." Realized $3. Lot 1096: "1843-D. Wide date, figures do not touch. Small D on arrow high above bar point. Very Fine; scarce." Realized $3.50. Lot 1097: "1843-D. Wide date, figures do not touch. Small D, high above bar-point. Letters lightly cut, break through first S in 'States.' Very Fine; scarce." Realized $3.75. Lot 1098: "1843-D. Wide date, large D, and heavy cut lettering. Very Fine. Rare." Realized $3.50. In May 1913 the U.S. Coin Co. sale of the Malcolm N. Jackson Collection included three lots. Lot 251: "1843-D Wide date. D over fraction bar. Extremely Fine." Realized $3. Lot 252: "1843-D Similar. Very Fine." Realized $3. Lot 253: "1843-D Similar. D higher. Very Fine." Realized $3.

In his November 1939 sale of the William B. Hale Collection, B. Max Mehl described lot 846: "1943-D The rare small date variety. Nearly Uncirculated. Very rare. Listed at $25 in Very Fine condition. Has been in the Hale Collection for thirty years." Realized $5.40. Mehl's February 1944 catalog of the sale of the Belden E. Roach Collection described lot 984: "1843-D Struck in light yellow gold. Practically Uncirculated brilliant semi-proof surface. Variety with small date. Very scarce so choice." Realized $18.25. The Stack's sale of the J.F. Bell Collection in December 1944 included lot 210: "1843-D Small date. Brilliant Uncirculated." Realized $30. Mehl's sale of the Jerome

Kern Collection in May 1950 included lot 134: "1843-D. Small date. Small mint letter. Just a shade from Uncirculated but with much mint lustre. An Uncirculated specimen has a record of $55." Realized $11.

VF-20	EF-40	AU-50	AU-55	MS-60	MS-62	MS-63
$2,000	$2,500	$3,250	$5,000	$7,500	$15,000	$30,000

1843-O, Small Date, Crosslet 4

Circulation-Strike Mintage: 288,002

Scarce in Mint State.

Record deposits of gold from mines in North Carolina and Georgia resulted in record gold coinage figures at all four mints this year.

Estimated Total Population (Mint State). 20 to 30. This issue is much more readily available in Mint State, and in slightly higher average Mint State grades, than is the Large Date variety from the same Mint.

Estimated Total Population (Circulated Grades). 300 to 500. Most are in Very Fine and Extremely Fine grades, much less often About Uncirculated.

Die Data. *1843 four-digit Small Date logotype: See the 1843-C, Small Date, Crosslet 4, listing.*

For this coinage six obverse and ten reverse dies were sent to New Orleans. It is likely that not all the obverses were employed. Unused reverses, being undated, could be held over for later coinage.

Various logotype and mintmark positions are seen. The O mintmark is large.

Characteristics of Striking and Die Notes. Usually lightly struck at the eagle's leg on the left reverse. With such a large mintage, various die varieties and states exists. Breen-6172, "Tiny Stars," may be from a relapped die. The obverse often has raised areas on the neck from a rusted die.

Selected Auction Records

Note: Certain early listings without date size may represent the rarer Large Date style.

J.W. Haseltine's 18th Sale, December 1875, included lot 1162: "1843-O; New Orleans Mint; Uncirculated; scarce." Date size is not given. The catalog of John W. Haseltine's June 1883 sale of the William J. Jenks Collection described lot 449: "1843-O. Nearly Proof. Extremely rare." Realized $3. Date size is not given. Thomas L. Elder's March 1911 sale of the William H. Woodin Collection included this description of lot 1039: "1843-O. Smallest date, O. away from claw. Very Fine." Realized $2.50 (face value). In May 1913 the U.S. Coin Co. sale of the Malcolm N. Jackson Collection included lot 204: "1843-O Small date. Slight die varieties. Very Fine. [group of] 3 pieces." Realized $2.75 per piece.

In May 1915 B. Max Mehl's catalog of the B.W. Smith Collection included this description of lot 311: "1843-O Small date and large O. Very Fine." Realized $3. In his November 1939 sale of the William B. Hale Collection, Mehl described lot 859: "1843-O Small date. Extremely Fine. From J.W. Scott, the pioneer of the stamp and coin business in this country." Realized $6. Mehl's February 1944 catalog of the sale of the Belden E. Roach Collection described lot 973: "1843-O Small date. Very Fine with considerable mint luster; nearly Uncirculated." Realized $7. The Stack's sale of the J.F. Bell Collection in December 1944 included lot 230: "1843-O Small Date. Brilliant Uncirculated." Realized $15. The Will W. Neil Collection sold by Mehl in June 1947 included lot 2525: "1843-O Small date. Fine to Very Fine." Realized $8.

In March 1956 Abe Kosoff's sale of the Melish and Clinton Collections offered these: Lot 1153: "1843-O. Small date. O is over center of fraction. Very Fine." Realized $12.50. Lot 1154: "1843-O. Small date. O is over left part of fraction and is double-cut. Very Fine." Realized $12.50. Lot 1155: "1843-O. Small date. There is a period in field below right wing opposite E. Uncirculated." Realized $25. Lot 1157: "1843-O. Similar but with an irregular die crack through 2½ D. AC to I [ICA in AMERICA]. Extremely Fine." Realized $20.

VF-20	EF-40	AU-50	AU-55	MS-60	MS-62	MS-63
$500	$600	$650	$750	$1,750	$3,250	$7,000

1843-O, Large Date, Plain 4

Circulation-Strike Mintage: 76,000

Scarce in any grade.
Incredibly rare in Mint State.

The 76,000 figure is a Walter Breen estimate. The total mintage for 1843-O, both date sizes, was 364,002. Considering that the Large Date is about five to seven times rarer than the Small Date, this estimate certainly is in the ballpark.

Estimated Total Population (Mint State). 3 to 5. This issue is exceedingly rare.

Estimated Total Population (Circulated Grades). 50 to 100. Although scarce in comparison to the Small Date, enough of these exist that there is no difficulty in locating one. Most are Very Fine or Extremely Fine.

Die Data. *1843 four-digit Large Date logotype for the quarter eagle: See the 1843, Large Date, Plain 4, listing.*

Various die varieties exist. Some have a wide, flat obverse rim, giving the coin a cameo-like appearance.

Characteristics of Striking and Die Notes. Examples are usually lightly struck on the eagle's leg at the left reverse.

Selected Auction Records

Thomas L. Elder's March 1911 sale of the William H. Woodin Collection included this description of lot 1037: "1843-O. Large date. Fine." Realized $2.50 (face value). In May

1913 the U.S. Coin Co. sale of the Malcolm N. Jackson Collection included lot 205: "1843-O Large date. Extremely Fine, scarce." Realized $3. The Stack's sale of the J.F. Bell Collection in December 1944 included lot 229: "1843-O Large Date. Uncirculated." Realized $37.50. The Will W. Neil Collection sold by B. Max Mehl in June 1947 included lot 2524: "1843-O Large date. Extremely Fine. Very rare; far more so than is generally known. Not in the Atwater Collection. Catalogs $30 in only Very Fine." Realized $23.75.

Mehl's sale of the Jerome Kern Collection in May 1950 included lot 152: "1843 O. Large date. Extremely Fine with some traces of original mint luster. Quite rare. Catalogs $30 in only Very Fine." Realized $9. In October 1951 the Numismatic Gallery sale of the B.A. Talmadge collection included lot 1235: "1843-O Large date. Uncirculated. Very scarce." Realized $47.50. In November 1956 the New Netherlands sale of the Thomas L. Gaskill Collection included lot 233: "1843-O. Large Date. Recut mintmark. About Extremely Fine; traces of rev. tarnish. Clean and choice. A very much underpriced coin; it is at least five times as rare as the Small Date." Realized $29. In June 1957 the New Netherlands sale of Eliasberg duplicates had this for lot 594: "1843-O. Large date. Recut mintmark. Very Fine; lightly struck, clean surfaces. Very much unappreciated; Dunham and Atwater, for instance, had none. At least five times as rare as the small date type." Realized $22.50.

VF-20	EF-40	AU-50	AU-55	MS-60	MS-62	MS-63
$500	$850	$1,750	$2,750	$6,000	$15,000	$25,000

1844

Circulation-Strike Mintage: 6,784
Proof Mintage: 5 or 6 (estimated)

Scarce in any grade.
Incredibly rare in Mint State.

Delivered on August 31.

Estimated Total Population (Mint State). 1 or 2. Exceedingly rare.

Estimated Total Population (Circulated Grades). 60 to 80. The 1844 is very difficult to locate even in circulated grades and is typically seen well worn, with Very Fine being the norm. At the About Uncirculated level the 1844 is a rarity. It has had very little press over the years, especially in comparison to the elusive 1842, which is only slightly rarer.

Die Data. The date is large, deeply impressed into the working die, and somewhat distorted, with the tops of the digits being smaller and more delicate than the bases, the final 4 in particular being bottom heavy. To accommodate the logotype, the denticles were modified, with the curious result that they are indented under the first and last digits. The die also shows some unusual finish lines between the first digit and the first star, extending clockwise past star 2. On the reverse the left-most raised line in the two-part stripes, as well as the right-most line, extend upward through the horizontal shield stripes.

Only one die pair has been recognized for this issue.

Characteristics of Striking and Die Notes. Examples are usually fairly well struck.

Selected Auction Records

The October 1875 sale of the Col. Mendes I. Cohen Collection included Edward Cogan's description of lot 212: "1844 Very Fine." Realized $2.80. Thomas L. Elder's March 1911 sale of the William H. Woodin Collection included this description of lot 967: "1844. Uncirculated with luster; scarce so fine." Realized $16. May 1913 the U.S. Coin Co. sale of the Malcolm N. Jackson Collection included lot 128: "1844 Extremely Fine, only slight trace of circulation. Very rare." Realized $27.

In his November 1939 sale of the William B. Hale Collection, B. Max Mehl described lot 768: "1844 Practically Uncirculated. Rare. From the famous Woodin Sale in 1911. (Cost then $16.)" Realized $10.25. The Stack's sale of the J.F. Bell Collection in December 1944 included lot 110: "1844 Brilliant Uncirculated." Realized $30. Mehl's sale of the Jerome Kern Collection in May 1950 included lot 33: "1844 Nearly Uncirculated; just the slightest touch of cabinet friction. Considerable mint luster. Scarce date. Catalogs $20 in Very Fine." Realized $22.50. In April 1956 Abe Kosoff's sale of the Melish and Hester Collections included lot 1160: "1844 About Uncirculated." Realized $21.

Proofs

Estimated Total Population (Proof). 3. The National Numismatic Collection has an example. Another was in the Pittman Collection, part I (David W. Akers, 1997), part of an 1844 Proof set; this was called "the lone specimen in private hands" and was later certified by PCGS as PF-61.

Selected Proof Auction Record

In January 1946 lot 111 in the Numismatic Gallery sale of the "World's Greatest Collection" was described: "1844 Brilliant Proof." Realized $275.

VF-20	EF-40	AU-50	AU-55	MS-60	MS-62	MS-63
$850	$1,100	$2,250	$3,250	$8,500	$18,000	$22,500

1844-C

Circulation-Strike Mintage: 15,821

Incredibly rare in Mint State.

Deliveries of this issue were reported as follows:[43] February, 2,120; March, 2,079; April 30, 3,975; May, 3,522; July 18, 4,125. Total: 15,821. This includes 8 coins for assay. Breen gives the disparate figure of 11,622.

On July 27, 1844, the Charlotte Mint was burgled. The miscreant responsible for the act also set the Mint afire, preventing coinage in 1845.

Estimated Total Population (Mint State). 2 or 3. The 1844-C is exceedingly rare in Mint State.

In 1975 David W. Akers commented: "I have not seen a fully Mint State piece, although I have seen several choice AU ones." In his 1986 study *The Quarter Eagles,*

Paul F. Taglione wrote: "Over the past decade or so a few 1844-C's were catalogued as Mint State, and of the examples which I witnessed (all but one), none were, in my opinion, Uncirculated." In one instance, a piece called a "Gem" was graded by Taglione as AU-50. The numismatic equivalent of Charles Dana Gibson's famous "The Eternal Question" is this: What is the difference between a high-level About Uncirculated and a Mint State coin?

Estimated Total Population (Circulated Grades). 150 to 200. Most are well worn, with Very Fine being the norm. At the About Uncirculated level the 1844-C is sufficiently elusive that examples are usually seen only when specialized collections are dispersed.

Die Data. Apparently an extensive mintage was contemplated, as in December 1843 three obverse and five reverse dies were sent from Philadelphia. However, it seems that but a single pair was used.

The mintmark is large and high, embedded in the arrow feather, with a small part of the feather visible within the upper curve. The large C mintmark was continued through the end of the series on various reverse dies.

Characteristics of Striking and Die Notes. Typically, specimens are lightly struck at the obverse and reverse centers. Douglas Winter writes: "The 1844-C is one of the worst struck quarter eagles from the Charlotte Mint."

Selected Auction Records

The catalog of John W. Haseltine's June 1883 sale of the William J. Jenks Collection described lot 450: "1844 C Mint. Good." Realized $3. "Good" probably meant "very nice." In June 1885, W. Elliot Woodward's sale of the J. Colvin Randall Collection included lot 990: "1844-C Fine." Realized $2.90. Thomas L. Elder's March 1911 sale of the William H. Woodin Collection included this description of lot 1121: "1844-C. Fine. Rare. Cost $8." Realized $5. Woodin profited so immensely from this sale that he was moved to write an article on the benefits of rare coin investment for *The Numismatist*. However, the financial result for this particular coin was an exception. In May 1913 the U.S. Coin Co. sale of the Malcolm N. Jackson Collection included lot 276: "1844-C Very Fine and very rare." Realized $3.50. In retrospect the Woodin coin performed well. In May 1915 B. Max Mehl's catalog of the B.W. Smith Collection included this description of lot 293: "1844-C. C directly over bar. Very Fine." Realized $2.75. The market for mintmarked gold did not catch on in a large way until the 1930s.

Thomas L. Elder's June 1935 sale of the Wendell C. Foster Collection included this description of lot 2792: "1844-C Extremely Fine. Very rare. Any 1844 quarter eagle is very rare. One of the best, about Uncirculated and bold example." Realized $19. Mehl's February 1944 catalog of the sale of the Belden E. Roach Collection described lot 959: "1844-C Uncirculated with brilliant mint luster. Just the very slightest touch of cabinet friction. Very scarce so choice. Listed at $15 in only Very Fine." Realized $16.25. The Stack's sale of the J.F. Bell Collection in December 1944 included lot 194: "1844-C Extremely Fine. Choice." Realized $37.50.

In June 1946 Mehl's sale of the William Cutler Atwater Collection included lot 2026: "1844-C Nearly Uncirculated with considerable luster. Record over $35." Realized $7.50. Oops! Wonder what happened? Mehl's sale of the Jerome Kern Collection in May 1950 included lot 120: "1844 C. Practically Uncirculated with mint luster. I doubt if this coin was ever in circulation. Not rare, but very scarce so choice. Has an auction record of over $22." Realized $20.50.

VF-20	EF-40	AU-50	AU-55	MS-60	MS-62	MS-63
$1,700	$2,850	$5,000	$6,500	$15,000	$22,500	$40,000

1844-D

Circulation-Strike Mintage: 17,332
Proof Mintage: 4 (Dannreuther)

Scarce in any grade.

Quarter eagle coinage for the year was spread across the calendar. Delivery dates included February 5 (2,575 + 6 for assay), April 12 (3,837 + 9), May 17 (4,551 + 10), September 14 (3,234 + 7), and December 16 (3,135 + 7). Assay coins are not included in the annual total.

Estimated Total Population (Mint State). 20 to 35. In the context of early Dahlonega quarter eagles, Mint State coins are more readily available than usual—but when it comes to finding one quickly, all of a sudden the 1844-D is apt to be quite rare! As is the case with any Mint State quarter eagle in the early reach of the Liberty Head series, such examples are where you find them, and this often means waiting until a specialized cabinet comes to market.

In *The Quarter Eagles* (1986), Paul F. Taglione writes, "Some years ago M.B. Simons related to me that he had seen a small cache of Uncirculated 1844-Ds, and I find this tale quite plausible given the fact that at least 14 or 15 Mint State examples of this issue are known to me. 'Britt' (as friends knew him) allowed me to view 3 coins from this group (of 10 or so) and one of these was an absolutely gorgeous MS-65 with an exceptional strike."[44]

Estimated Total Population (Circulated Grades). 150 to 200. Grades vary, with Very Fine and Extremely Fine being the norm, although enough About Uncirculated specimens exist that one will have no difficulty in finding them.

Die Data.[45] One 1844-dated obverse die and one reverse die were sent from Philadelphia on December 21, 1843; they arrived in Dahlonega on January 6, 1844. One obverse die and one reverse were sent from Philadelphia on January 8, 1844, and another pair was sent on January 10; all arrived in Dahlonega on January 22, 1844.

On January 2, 1845, four obverse dies and four reverse dies were defaced at the Mint. If these data are correct, this would indicate that one or more of the destroyed obverses was dated prior to 1844—that is, in 1844 one or more earlier-dated obverse dies was still being used for coinage.[46]

Characteristics of Striking and Die Notes. Examples are generally lightly struck at the centers, but are sharper than most Dahlonega Mint quarter eagles of other dates. There are exceptions, and some are well struck, these probably from a different coining batch (as lightness of striking indicates that the dies were set too far apart on the press, and sharpness indicates they were set just right). Some examples are highly prooflike.

Selected Auction Records

W. Elliot Woodward's 69th sale, October 1884, included lot 1961: "1844-D Very Good, rare." Realized $3.10. In his 1907 fixed-price list Elmer S. Sears offered lot 208: "1844 Dahlonega Mint. Beautiful specimen of bright yellow gold. Uncirculated, with mint lustre. Rare coin in a very high state of preservation. $20." Thomas L. Elder's March 1911 sale of the William H. Woodin Collection included this description of lot 1099: "1844-D. Figure 1 touches bust and rim. Large D over bar point. Very Fine." Realized $4.25. In May 1913 the U.S. Coin Co. sale of the Malcolm N. Jackson Collection included two: Lot 254: "1844-D D high over fraction bar. Extremely Fine, rare." Realized $3.50. Lot 255: "1844-D. D touches fraction bar. Very Fine, rare." Realized $3.50. An early offering of two different die varieties of this issue. In May 1915 B. Max Mehl's catalog of the B.W. Smith Collection included this description of lot 301: "1844-D D over bar. Practically Uncirculated, but a dent on reverse. Scarce." Realized $4.

In his November 1939 sale of the William B. Hale Collection, Mehl described lot 847: "1844-D Uncirculated, with full mint luster; the highest portions show only the slightest cabinet friction. Very rare so choice." Realized $11.60. Mehl's February 1944 catalog of the sale of the Belden E. Roach Collection described two: Lot 985: "1844-D Variety with mint letter D over fraction. Fine to Very Fine. Scarce." Realized $7. Lot 986: "1844-D Variety with mint letter over fraction line. Strictly Fine." Realized $7. The Stack's sale of the J.F. Bell Collection in December 1944 included lot 211: "1844-D Brilliant Uncirculated." Realized $17.50. The Will W. Neil Collection sold by Mehl in June 1947 included a pair: Lot 2513: "1844-D The mint letter touches fraction bar and almost touches 1 of fraction. Fine." Realized $10.75. Lot 2514: "1844-D Mint letter touches fraction bar and 1 of fraction and feather. Nearly Uncirculated. Scarce so choice." Realized $16.75.

Mehl's sale of the Jerome Kern Collection in May 1950 included lot 135: "1844 D. Mint letter D directly over fraction. Practically Uncirculated with mint luster. Record of $35.00 for an Uncirculated specimen." Realized $19. October 1951 the Numismatic Gallery sale of the B.A. Talmadge collection included lot 1217: "1844-D About Uncirculated." Realized $19. Abe Kosoff's November 1956 sale of the William P. Donlon Collection offered some philosophy in the description of lot 1189: "1844-D Very Fine. Scarce. There are indications that the general trend of coin prices is finally catching up to these intriguing quarter eagles [referring to this and other $2.50 in the sale]. Wise buyers will acquire these coins today while prices for quarter eagles are comparatively modest."

Proofs

Estimated Total Population (Proof). 2.

Selected Proof Auction Record

In January 1946 Lot 111 in the Numismatic Gallery auction of the "World's Greatest Collection" (F.C.C. Boyd Collection) was described by Abe Kosoff: "1844 Brilliant Proof." Realized $275.

VF-20	EF-40	AU-50	AU-55	MS-60	MS-62	MS-63
$1,850	$2,500	$3,500	$4,750	$8,000	$12,500	$25,000

1845

Circulation-Strike Mintage: 91,051
Proof Mintage: 5 or 6 (estimated)

Scarce in Mint State.

Estimated Total Population (Mint State). 30 to 60, mostly in lower Mint State levels. Although plentiful in the context of quarter eagles of the 1840s, Mint State 1845 coins are certainly rare compared to coins of the same design minted 60 years later, in the first decade of the twentieth century.

Estimated Total Population (Circulated Grades). 300 to 500. In circulated condition the 1845 is a very plentiful issue among early Liberty Head quarter eagles, although an estimate is difficult to make, as relatively few circulated coins have been submitted to certification services or featured in auctions. Such published data overlook countless coins that are routinely bought, sold, and traded in private transactions.

Die Data. *1845 four-digit date logotype:* This was rather carelessly made, with the bases of 1 and 8 higher than the bases of 4 and 5. The 1 and 8 are farther apart than are other digits; 4 and 5 lean slightly to the right. This logotype was used on quarter eagles of all mints as well as for dimes of the various mints.

Characteristics of Striking and Die Notes. Usually sharply struck except for the eagle's leg at the lower left of the reverse. High-grade specimens often display prooflike surfaces. Most have die cracks on the reverse, as reflected in the multiple citations that follow.

Selected Auction Records

The October 1875 sale of the Col. Mendes I. Cohen Collection included Edward Cogan's description of lot 213: "1845 Very Fine." Realized $2.80. In his 1907 fixed-price list Elmer S. Sears offered lot 210: "1845 Uncirculated. Mint bloom. Handsome and choice. Rare in this unusual condition. $7.50." Thomas L. Elder's March 1911 sale of the William H. Woodin Collection included three coins that each realized its face value of $2.50: Lot 968: "1845. Perfect die. Nearly Fine." Lot 969: "1845. Die crack through center of 2 on reverse. Very Fine, sharp. Scarce." Lot 970: "1845. Die crack along left side of 2 on reverse. Fine." In May 1913 the U.S. Coin Co. sale of the Malcolm N. Jackson Collection included lot 129: "1845 Reverse die cracked. Uncirculated." Realized $3.25.

In his November 1939 sale of the William B. Hale Collection, B. Max Mehl described lot 769: "1845 Nearly Uncirculated with considerable mint luster. Scarce date in very scarce condition." Realized $7.35. The Stack's sale of the J.F. Bell Collection in December 1944 included lot 111: "1845 Brilliant Uncirculated." Realized $15. In June 1946 Mehl's sale of the William Cutler Atwater Collection included lot 1948: "1845 Practically Uncirculated with mint luster. Catalog at $12.50 in Very Fine. Recent record of $26 for an Uncirculated specimen." Realized $8.25. The Will W. Neil Collection sold by Mehl in June 1947 included lot 2424: "1845 Light die breaks.

Uncirculated with mint luster. The reverse is a semi-proof. Record over $20." Realized $17.50. Mehl's sale of the Jerome Kern Collection in May 1950 included lot 34: "1845 Nearly Uncirculated with semi-Proof surface. Scarce so choice." Realized $10.55. The June 1957 New Netherlands sale of Eliasberg duplicates had this for lot 596: "1845. Reverse die cracked. Almost Very Fine, somewhat mishandled. Ex Mehl at $12.50, years ago." Realized $11.50.

PROOFS

Estimated Total Population (Proof). 3 (Dannreuther).

VF-20	EF-40	AU-50	AU-55	MS-60	MS-62	MS-63	PF-63
$500	$525	$550	$600	$1,250	$2,500	$5,000	$55,000

1845-D

Circulation-Strike Mintage: 19,460

Scarce in any grade. Incredibly rare in Mint State.

Quarter eagle mintage extended throughout the year. Delivery dates included January 15 (2,363 + 5 for assay), April 5 (2,540 + 6), May 7 (2,461 + 5), May 31 (2,752 + 6), July 3 (2,295 + 5), August 19 (1,959 + 4), September 15 (2,338 + 5), and November 22 (2,752 + 6). Assay coins are not included in the annual total.

In November 1845 there was some small excitement at Dahlonega when a 6.8 grain (2.2 carat) diamond was found in a gold placer. It was thought for a time that a diamond field would be discovered, bringing more wealth to the area, but few additional diamonds were located.[47]

Estimated Total Population (Mint State). 2 to 4. The 1845-D is an extreme rarity in Mint State.

Estimated Total Population (Circulated Grades). 110 to 150. Most are in Very Fine and Extremely Fine grades, although several dozen About Uncirculated pieces exist. Most circulated specimens are very attractive. Thus, the collector seeking just one Dahlonega Mint quarter eagle for a type set or an object of fascination would do well to consider the 1845-D.

Die Data. *1845 four-digit date logotype: See the Philadelphia Mint listing for this year.*

Two 1845-dated obverse dies were sent from Philadelphia December 9, 1844, and two reverse dies were sent the next day; all arrived in Dahlonega on December 21, 1844, packed with half eagle dies in four boxes.[48]

It is believed that just one obverse die was used. Its date logotype was placed extremely close to the neck truncation, notably separated from the denticle below, but still close.[49] The logotype was also punched more deeply into the die at the first part of the date than toward the end.

Among the reverse varieties known is the 1845-D, Large D, on which a large Denver mintmark just touches the arrow feather, with no traces of the feather appearing within the opening. The lower left serif of the mintmark touches the 1 in the numerator of the denomination. This reverse had been used earlier in 1844.

Clair M. Birdsall described a die pair: "One variety has the axis of the 5 canting to the right away from the plain 4. 10 or 11 beads are discernible in the vertical section of the hair binding. The mintmark touches the arrow feather and the 1 and bar in the fraction."[50]

A Large D Over Small D was described by David W. Akers in the Pittman Collection II sale, May 1998, lot 1750. This was, apparently, an early die state of the normal Large D variety, not otherwise reported and not noticed by Douglas Winter.

In his October 1921 sale Thomas L. Elder described a Small D variety different from any of the others he had handled earlier. He described lot 1625 as follows: "1845-D Small D. Only one known. Ex. rare. Fine. First offered." The Small D variety is not known today, and may have incorporated a reverse of 1843 (which had a small mintmark). Elder had studied other 1845-D quarter eagles and had offered them in earlier sales (see the selected auction records). Thus, this must have been a new variety.

Characteristics of Striking and Die Notes. Examples are usually well struck on the peripheries but somewhat lightly at the center.

Selected Auction Records

In June 1885, W. Elliot Woodward's sale of the J. Colvin Randall Collection included lot 991: "1845-D Very Good." Realized $2.85. In his 1907 fixed-price list Elmer S. Sears offered lot 212: "1845 Dahlonega Mint. Practically Uncirculated, with mint lustre. Rare in such a perfect state. $12." Thomas L. Elder's March 1911 sale of the William H. Woodin Collection included this description of lot 1100: "1845-D. D just over point of fraction bar. Very Fine. Very rare." Realized $4. In May 1913 the U.S. Coin Co. sale of the Malcolm N. Jackson Collection included lot 256: "1845-D D over fraction bar. Extremely Fine, scarce." Realized $5.25. The Will W. Neil Collection sold by B. Max Mehl in June 1947 included lot 2515: "1845-D D directly over fraction. Extremely Fine. Catalogs $15." Realized $13.50. Mehl's sale of the Jerome Kern Collection in May 1950 included lot 136: "1845 D. Struck in light yellow gold. Just About Uncirculated with mint luster. Scarce so choice." Realized $13.

VF-20	EF-40	AU-50	AU-55	MS-60	MS-62	MS-63
$1,800	$2,450	$3,250	$4,250	$10,000	$25,000	$40,000

1845-O

Circulation-Strike Mintage: 4,000

Incredibly rare in Mint State.
Fascinating "story coin."

All 1845-O quarter eagles were delivered on January 22, 1846, which was two days before the 1846-O dies arrived. Logically, these pieces were included in the 1846-O mintage figure,[51] and the production for the 1845-O was omitted from early *Mint Reports.* The discovery of the mintage and the first publication of it in the 1890s came as a surprise. For a long time it was considered to be incredibly rare, then quite rare, then "only" rare—with a few dozen pieces known. In later years the story has been pieced together, as follows.

The Numismatist, December 1894, contained this note: "Quarter eagle pieces of 1845, New Orleans Mint, have lately been found, although no coinage that year appears in the Mint Report." Then, in June 1903, the same journal printed the news that Elmer S. Sears, of Fall River, Massachusetts, "found in Fine grade a rare 1845-O quarter eagle. The Mint report shows no coinage, and Heaton in his *Mint Marks* did not know of it." *The Numismatist*'s editor (George F. Heath, M.D.) had forgotten that he himself had reported the discovery of a similar piece nearly a decade earlier. This coin was soon sold to enthusiastic Washington, D.C., numismatist John M. Clapp, in whose cabinet it remained for a long time. It eventually became part of the Louis E. Eliasberg Sr. Collection.

Estimated Total Population (Mint State). 3 to 5. Typical grades are MS-60 or thereabouts. The issue is exceedingly rare at this level.

Estimated Total Population (Circulated Grades). 100 to 150, making the issue very elusive. It is a wonder that multiple dozens exist today when in the last century the 1845-O was considered to be a major rarity, as described above.

Die Data. *1845 four-digit date logotype: See the Philadelphia Mint listing for this year.*

Four pairs of dies were shipped from the Philadelphia Mint for this coinage, but only one pair of dies is known to have been used.

The 1 and 8 in the date are repunched, later fading so that just the 1 has notable repunching.

Characteristics of Striking and Die Notes. Examples are usually sharply struck except for some truly minor weakness at the centers.

Selected Auction Records

Note: Among quarter eagle sale records of the early twentieth century, the 1845-O was unique for its "breakout" market price. Various accounts were given as to the discovery of this variety.

In his 1907 fixed-price list Elmer S. Sears offered lot 214: "1845 New Orleans Mint. I know of but five specimens of this extremely rare coin. There is no record of any coinage of quarter eagles at the New Orleans Mint for this year, but this is but one of the many instances where the mint records are at fault. Extremely Fine specimen of a very rare coin, and I think this is the finest of the 5 known specimens and I have handled four of them. This specimen still retains much of the original lustre, and is practically Uncirculated. $300." Thomas L. Elder's March 1911 sale of the William H. Woodin Collection included this description of lot 1040: "1845-O. No record of coinage for this date! This sold for $161.50 in the Raymond Sale, 1910. Very few are known. About Fine." Realized $76. The bloom was off of the rose, price-wise. In May 1913 the U.S. Coin Co. sale of the Malcolm N. Jackson Collection included lot 206: "1845-O Extremely Fine, mint luster, excessively rare, probably not over 10 specimens known." Realized $42.50. In May 1915 B. Max Mehl's catalog of the B.W. Smith Collection included this description of lot 312: "1845-O O over bar. Strictly Fine.

Excessively rare. The Mint gives no record of the coinage of quarter eagles at this mint for this year. Record over $100." Realized $65.

In February 1921 the catalog of Mehl's sale of the Dr. G.F.E. Wilharm Collection described lot 189: "1845-O. O over fraction. Fine. Excessively rare. The Mint records do not mention this variety. When first discovered, several years ago, it sold for $300." Realized $38.50. The November 1932 sale of the R. Taylor Collection included Mehl's description of lot 174, obviously copied from this earlier offering: "1845-O, Fine. Rare. The *Mint Report* states that no quarter eagles were coined at New Orleans Mint in 1845. At one time, this coin sold up to $300. It is still quite rare." Realized $41.50. Somewhat similarly, we have this for lot 267 in Mehl's sale in March 1938 of the Samuel H. McVitty Collection: "1845-O No record of any mintage of this year and mint. Fine. Rare. At one time it brought over $300, but since then several have been discovered and they now retail at $50." Retailed $25. How the mighty had fallen! Mehl's February 1944 catalog of the sale of the Belden E. Roach Collection described lot 974: "1845-O Very Fine with considerable luster. Very rare. According to the mint report none were minted this year at the New Orleans Mint. I discovered the first specimen some thirty-five years ago at which time it sold for over $300. Since then several specimens have been discovered, but the coin is still a rarity." Realized $42. Mehl states that he was the discoverer of the first 1845-O (but see below).

Stack's sale of the J.F. Bell Collection in December 1944 included lot 231: "1845-O Extremely Fine, with high auction records. One of the finest ever seen." Realized $87.50. June 1946 Mehl's sale of the William Cutler Atwater Collection included lot 2063: "1845-O. (None coined in 1844.) Extremely Fine with some luster. There is no record in the Mint report of any quarter eagle of 1845 having been minted at the New Orleans Mint. Until about twenty-five years ago not a single specimen was known to exist. Since then a few have been discovered. At one time the coin sold for well into the three-figure mark. It now has an auction record of $87.50." Realized $28. Mehl now places the discovery to about 1920! It is interesting across the board to compare what various of the same catalogers said over the years.

In October 1951 the Numismatic Gallery sale of the B.A. Talmadge collection included lot 1237: "1845-O None minted in 1844. Only About Fine but rare. Seldom offered." Realized $21." In November 1956 the New Netherlands sale of the Thomas L. Gaskill Collection included lot 241: "1845-O. 18 plainly double cut, as on all seen. Fully Very Fine, the obv. tarnished. A nice, highly desirable piece, in spite of a nick-like flaw on the obverse border above the 7th star, and an (old) shallow scratch from Liberty's neck to the 13th star. A well-known rarity (ignored in the Mint Report); only 4,000 coined in January, 1846. When first unearthed by friend B. Max Mehl, circa 1909,[52] this mintmark readily sold for over $300. Since that time several specimens have been discovered, but it is still a real rarity, even though now somewhat neglected. Waldo Newcomer never had one; the comparable[53] Bell example commanded $87.50 in 1944." Realized $43.

VF-20	EF-40	AU-50	AU-55	MS-60	MS-62	MS-63
$1,850	$3,500	$7,000	$9,500	$26,500	$45,000	$115,000

1846

Circulation-Strike Mintage: 21,598
Proof Mintage: 7 to 9 (estimated)

Notably rare in Mint State.

Estimated Total Population (Mint State). 6 to 10, mostly at or close to MS-60. In Mint State the 1846 is exceedingly rare.

Estimated Total Population (Circulated Grades). 200 to 300, mostly Very Fine and Extremely Fine. The 1846 is truly scarce, much more so than its generous mintage figure suggests.

Die Data. *1846 four-digit date logotype:* The logotype punch was crudely made, with the last two figures (46) leaning right. The first three digits are spaced evenly; the 6 is distant. The 6 is also heavier (i.e., fatter at the bottom) than the other figures and appears repunched (this was in the logotype and is common to all dies and mints; the intensity of the repunching varies with the depth to which the logotype was punched into a given working die). The crossbar of the 4 is oriented slightly upward to the right. In this year it was perpetual amateur night in the date-logotype preparation department, and punches vary across the different denominations, sometimes being short and squat with irregular numerals, other times tall with thin numerals. There seem to be no rhyme, reason, or consistency to it. This date logotype was used on all quarter eagle dies for all mints, and was also used on dime dies.

Due to the peculiarities of the date logotype, many catalogers have given widely varying descriptions of its characteristics. In New Netherlands' offering of an 1846-O in their 48th sale, November 1956, this comment appeared with lot 245: "The 'overdate' appearance of the various quarter eagles of 1846 results from use of the same imperfect punches on these as on the dime."[54]

Characteristics of Striking and Die Notes. Examples are usually sharply struck except on the eagle's leg at the lower left of the reverse. High-grade pieces show diagonal die striae.

Selected Auction Records

The October 1875 sale of the Col. Mendes I. Cohen Collection included Edward Cogan's description of lot 214: "1846 Very Fine." Realized $2.80. In his 1907 fixed-price list Elmer S. Sears offered lot 215: "1846 Uncirculated, with mint lustre. Scarce. $10."

S.H. Chapman described lot 199 in the March 1907 sale of the David S. Wilson Collection: "1846 Uncirculated. Mint luster." Realized $8. In May 1913 the U.S. Coin Co. sale of the Malcolm N. Jackson Collection included two: Lot 130: "1846 Recut date. Extremely Fine." Realized $3.25. Lot 131: "1846 Same variety. Extremely Fine." Realized $3.25. In his November 1939 sale of the William B. Hale Collection, B. Max Mehl described lot 770: "1846 Extremely Fine; just a shade from Uncirculated. Listed at $10." Realized $8.60.

Stack's sale of the J.F. Bell Collection in December 1944 included lot 112: "1846 Brilliant Uncirculated, with proof-like surface, Choice." Realized $17.50. The Will W. Neil Collection sold by Mehl in June 1947 included lot 2425: "1846 The 4 of date re-cut. Very Fine. Scarce. Record over $20." Realized $14. Mehl's sale of the Jerome Kern Collection in May 1950 included lot 35: "1846 Uncirculated with frosty mint surface; just the barest touch of cabinet friction. Scarce so choice." Realized $10. In October 1951 the Numismatic Gallery sale of the B.A. Talmadge collection included lot 1103: "1846 Barely circulated, scarce." Realized $10.50.

Proofs

Estimated Total Population (Proof). 4 (Dannreuther).

Proof Die Data and Notes. The standard four-digit logotype with anomalies used to make circulation-strike dies appears to have been employed for Proofs as well. In his 1977 *Proof Encyclopedia* Walter Breen commented that the Wetmore specimen (cited below) was from this die, but that the American Numismatic Society specimen has a "normal date."

Selected Proof Auction Records

Lot 107 in the June 1906 sale of the Major W.B. Wetmore by the Chapman brothers was described as: "1846 . . . The 4 and 6 are more or less filled up and may be an over date, but which previous date it is impossible to determine. Brilliant Proof. Extremely rare in this preservation." Realized $26. An early "may be an overdate" type of description, of which many have appeared in listings over the years. The same coin reappeared in the December 1921 sale of the John Story Jenks Collection by Henry Chapman, lot L 5810: "1846. Brilliant Proof. The 46 of date is either over a date or a recut. A wonderful example of the greatest rarity. From Wetmore sale, 1906." Realized $90. In his 1977 *Proof Encyclopedia* Walter Breen commented that this coin had been "seen by Wayte Raymond, not now located," and had an "oddly recut date, like an overdate."

An "1846 Proof" from the ANS Collection was recorded in the 1914 American Numismatic Society Exhibition catalog.

VF-20	EF-40	AU-50	AU-55	MS-60	MS-62	MS-63	PF-63
$500	$550	$900	$1,000	$5,000	$13,500	$20,000	$55,000

1846-C

Circulation-Strike Mintage: 4,808

Exceedingly rare in Mint State.

The entire mintage of the year—4,808—was delivered in December.[55] (Eight assay coins were also included.) This is far and away the smallest production of quarter eagles of the four mints this year. Moreover, it is the second-lowest mintage of any date of the Charlotte quarter eagle.

During this era the denomination of choice for those depositing gold bullion at the Charlotte Mint was the half eagle, as it would continue to be through the following decade. A given amount of gold dust and nuggets could be converted to gold coin more efficiently by using the $5 denomination, which required only about half the work needed to strike two quarter eagles. Thus, quarter eagle mintages tended to be low.

Estimated Total Population (Mint State). 4 to 6. The data are inconclusive relating to Mint State examples. The finest seen by David Akers (1975) was a saltwater-etched Uncirculated. How many *true* Mint State coins exist is a matter of debate.

Estimated Total Population (Circulated Grades). 100 to 140. These are usually seen in Very Fine or Extremely Fine, and are very rare in About Uncirculated.

Die Data. *1846 four-digit date logotype: See the Philadelphia Mint listing for this year.*

Two pairs of dies were sent to Charlotte from Philadelphia, but it seems that just one pair was used, apparently over a period of time during the year.

Characteristics of Striking and Die Notes. Examples usually show light striking on the eagle's leg at the left reverse. Also frequently seen is evidence of rusted dies, sometimes very prominent, in the form of raised lumps—especially on the reverse. Planchet quality usually ranges from subpar to poor.

Collars with wide reeding were used to strike 1838-C to 1844-C quarter eagles (and all quarter eagles at Dahlonega from 1839-D to 1859-D); in contrast, narrow reeding was used on Philadelphia and New Orleans quarter eagles. The Charlotte Mint was destroyed by fire during the summer of 1844. When Charlotte quarter eagles were again struck in 1846 a narrow reeding was used. All Charlotte quarter eagles from the 1846-C to the 1860-C have the narrow reeding.[56]

Selected Auction Records

In January 1890 the Robert Coulton Davis Collection sold by the New York Coin & Stamp Co. included lot 878: "1846 Charlotte mint: struck from rusty die: sharp; barely touched by circulation." In his 1907 fixed-price list Elmer S. Sears offered lot 217: "1846 Charlotte Mint. Practically Uncirculated, with mint lustre. Extremely rare. $20." In May 1913 the U.S. Coin Co. sale of the Malcolm N. Jackson Collection included lot 277: "1846-C Very Fine and very rare." Realized $3.50.

Stack's sale of the J.F. Bell Collection in December 1944 included lot 195: "1846-C Uncirculated. Very scarce." Realized $37.50. B. Max Mehl's sale of the Jerome Kern Collection in May 1950 included lot 121: "1846 C. (None minted in 1845) Uncirculated with semi-Proof surface. Very scarce and quite rare so choice. Record $30." Realized $47.50.

VF-20	EF-40	AU-50	AU-55	MS-60	MS-62	MS-63
$1,750	$3,250	$5,750	$9,000	$16,000	$27,500	$42,500

1846-D

Circulation-Strike Mintage: 19,303

Incredibly rare in Mint State.

Coinage delivery dates and amounts were recorded as follows: January 22, (2,360 + 5 for assay); March 23, 1,822 + 4; April 30, 1,511 + 4; May 27, 2,698 + 6; July 8, 1,675 + 4; August 21, 1,863 + 4; September 2, 2,198 + 5; September 25, 1,400 + 3; November, 2,256 + 5; December 31, 1,520 + 4. Assay coins are not included in the annual total.

Estimated Total Population (Mint State). 3 to 5. In Mint State the 1846-D is exceedingly rare. One is in the National Coin Collection in the Smithsonian Institution.

Estimated Total Population (Circulated Grades). 175 to 250. Most are in grades of Very Fine to Extremely Fine, but enough About Uncirculated coins exist that the specialist will have no difficulty obtaining one.

Die Data.[57] *1846 four-digit date logotype: See Philadelphia listing for this year.*

One obverse and one reverse die were sent from Philadelphia on January 2, 1846, and arrived in Dahlonega on January 11, 1846. Another obverse and reverse were sent from Philadelphia on March 4, 1846, and arrived in Dahlonega on March 11, 1846. On January 4, 1847, four obverse dies and six reverse dies were defaced at the Mint. If these data are correct, then at least two dies dated prior to 1846 were destroyed at that time. This may be an indication that in 1846, two or more earlier-dated obverse dies were still being used for coinage. As of January 4, 1847, the reserve of old obverses seems to have been cleared, and no older ones were on hand; two usable reverse dies were still on hand.

Varieties include the Normal D and the curious Doubled D. The latter was discovered by Harry W. Bass Jr. in the 1970s, after which the other available pieces were studied by their owners—with the result that today this is the most widely available variety! In the die shop at the Philadelphia Mint, the mintmark punch had first been entered far to the left, above the numerator in the fraction, then entered a letter's width away to the right. The final mintmark is to the right and leans about 20° left, itself an interesting feature. Under even low magnification the appearance is startling. Later the reverse die was relapped, removing much of the first D, although under magnification enough remains on the typical specimen to permit identification. Douglas Winter calls the Doubled D varicty "the D near D variety" and comments that this applies only to early die states, "however, early or late, the same die was used to create the variety, it is just that later die states were relapped and show only a portion of the doubled D." Walter Breen (*Encyclopedia*, 1988) states his opinion that specimens were coined on January 22, 1846, from the first pair of dies received from the Philadelphia Mint (which had arrived on January 11).

Characteristics of Striking and Die Notes. Examples are usually fairly well struck. Indeed, among all Dahlonega quarter eagles, this year stands out for its sharpness.

Selected Auction Records

The catalog of John W. Haseltine's June 1883 sale of the William J. Jenks Collection described lot 452: "1846 D Mint. Fine. Scarce." Realized $3.35. In his 1907 fixed-price list Elmer S. Sears offered two examples: Lot 218: "1846 Dahlonega Mint. Mint mark 'D' placed over 2 and D of 1/2D. Uncirculated, with bright yellow lustre. A gem. Very rare. $20." Lot 219: "1846 Another. But with mint mark placed over dividing line of fraction. Extremely Fine with bloom. $20." Thomas L. Elder's March 1911 sale of the William H. Woodin Collection included two examples: Lot 1101: "1846-D. D over fraction bar. Nearly Fine. Very scarce." Realized $4. Lot 1102: "1846-D. The D between 2 and D. Extremely Fine; rare." Realized $6.50. In May 1913 the U.S. Coin Co. sale of the Malcolm N. Jackson Collection included a pair: Lot 257: "1846-D D over fraction bar. Fine, scarce." Realized $3.75. Lot 258: "1846-D. D over 2 and D. Very Fine, scarce." Realized $3.35.

In May 1915 B. Max Mehl's catalog of the B.W. Smith Collection included this description of lot 302: "1846-D D over bar. Fine. Rare. Record about $10." Realized $2.75. Mehl's February 1944 catalog of the sale of the Belden E. Roach Collection described lot 988: "1846-D Uncirculated; brilliant, with semi-proof surface. Raised borders. Very scarce date in rare condition." Realized $9.45. The Will W. Neil Collection sold by Mehl in June 1947 included lot 2516: "1846-D D over 2 of fraction. Extremely Fine, sharp. Scarce." Realized $12.75. Mehl's sale of the Jerome Kern Collection in May 1950 included lot 137: "1846 D. Extremely Fine, nearly Uncirculated; strong impression. One of the scarcest dates of this mint. Catalogs $12.50 in Very Fine." Realized $17.75. In October 1951 the Numismatic Gallery sale of the B.A. Talmadge collection included lot 1219: "1846-D Uncirculated, choice. W.G.C." Realized $25. In April 1956 Abe Kosoff's sale of the Melish and Hester Collections included lot 1172: "1846-D Reverse die lines. About Uncirculated." Realized $30.

VF-20	EF-40	AU-50	AU-55	MS-60	MS-62	MS-63
$1,850	$2,750	$3,250	$4,000	$9,500	$13,500	$30,000

1846-O

Very rare in Mint State.

Circulation-Strike Mintage: 62,000

Estimated Total Population (Mint State). 6 to 10, concentrated in the MS-60 to MS-63 range. The 1846-O is very rare in uncirculated grades. Historically, very few Mint State coins have appeared in even the most important collections. One cannot help but contemplate that some coins called Mint State today may have been graded as About Uncirculated years ago.

Estimated Total Population (Circulated Grades). 150 to 225, perhaps more. Most are in the Very Fine range, although Extremely Fine pieces are occasionally seen. About Uncirculated coins are exceedingly scarce. In general, New Orleans gold coins of this era saw extensive circulation. As well-worn pieces have not attracted much attention, there may be more pieces in existence than the written record indicates.

Die Data. *1846 four-digit date logotype: See the Philadelphia listing for this year.*

Four obverse and two reverse dies were sent to New Orleans for this coinage, but not all dies are known to have been used.

The 1846-O is Breen-6186, imaginatively described as "Repunched 4, microscopic traces of 4 within 6." There is a small line in the top of the 6 that might lead someone to think it is a diagonal from a 4, but within the base of the 6 the repunchings are all curved or circular in appearance, indicating a repunching of a 6, certainly not a 4. Regarding this characteristic, Douglas Winter, in *New Orleans Mint Gold Coins: 1839–1909*, comments: "It has long been claimed that an 1846/44-O overdate exists. In my opinion, such pieces are not overdates."

Characteristics of Striking and Die Notes. Examples are usually lightly struck, including on the eagle's leg at the lower left of the reverse. Some have raised die-finish lines. Many if not most have rotated reverses at varying orientations from the normal 180° opposition to the obverse.

Selected Auction Records

In October 1844, W. Elliot Woodward's Collection of Coins, Medals, Etc. offered lot 1963: "1846 Orleans mint; Very Good, rare." Realized $2.50 (face value). In his 1907 fixed-price list Elmer S. Sears offered lot 220: "1846 New Orleans Mint. Mint mark 'O' placed over dividing line of fraction. $10." In the same list, he also offered a "peach" in lot 221: "1846 Another with mint mark 'O' placed over figure 1 of fraction. Uncirculated specimen of bright yellow gold, with original lustre. A peach. $15." Thomas L. Elder's March 1911 sale of the William H. Woodin Collection included these: Lot 1041: "1846-O, the O between 1 and dividing line. Fine." Realized $2.50 (face value). Lot 1042: "1846-O. The O directly over top of dividing line. Fine." Realized $2.50 (face value). In May 1913 the U.S. Coin Co. sale of the Malcolm N. Jackson Collection included lot 207: "1846-O Mint mark between 1 and fraction bar. Extremely Fine." Realized $3.25. The November 1932 sale of the R. Taylor Collection included B. Max Mehl's description of lot 175: "1846-O, O over 2 of fraction. Very Fine. Rare." Realized $5.25.

In June 1941 Mehl's sale of the William Forrester Dunham Collection included lot 1939: "1846-O Nearly Uncirculated with bright mint luster. Very scarce in any condition, but quite scarce so choice. Listed at $12.50 in Very Fine." Realized $7.25. Mehl's February 1944 catalog of the sale of the Belden E. Roach Collection described lot 975: "1846-O Extremely Fine with considerable luster. Very scarce, especially so choice." Realized $7. The Stack's sale of the J.F. Bell Collection in December 1944 included lot 232: "1846-O Brilliant Uncirculated." Realized $35. The Will W. Neil Collection sold by Mehl in June 1947 included lot 2526: "1846-O 4 of date re-cut. Very Fine. Catalogs $10." Realized $9.50. Mehl's sale of the Jerome Kern Collection in May 1950 included lot 153: "1846 O. Practically Uncirculated with frosty mint surface. Scarce so choice. Record over $25." Realized $21. In November 1956 the New Netherlands sale of the Thomas L. Gaskill Collection included lot 245: "1846-O. Last two numerals in date crudely cut. Very Fine; a flat strike. The 'overdate' appearance of the various quarter eagles of 1846 results from use of the same imperfect punches on these as on the dime."[58] Realized $13.50. In June 1957 the New Netherlands sale of Eliasberg duplicates had this for lot 598: "1846-O. Last two numerals in date crudely cut. Very Fine, bright but a flat strike, like the Gaskill lot. Minute reverse rim nick. Seldom found as choice, much less better." Realized $13.

VF-20	EF-40	AU-50	AU-55	MS-60	MS-62	MS-63
$525	$650	$1,100	$1,900	$5,500	$10,000	$18,500

1847

Circulation-Strike Mintage: 29,814
Proof Mintage: 2 or 3 (estimated)

Rare in Mint State.

Estimated Total Population (Mint State). 15 to 22, mostly ranging from MS-60 to MS-63. In *true* Mint State the 1847 is quite rare, and most of the finer specialized cabinets auctioned in the past have lacked an example. Accordingly, it seems reasonable that some of the pieces accepted as Mint State today were probably called high-level About Uncirculated coins earlier. In his 1986 book, *The Quarter Eagles*, Paul F. Taglione estimated that seven or eight different Mint State coins were known.

Estimated Total Population (Circulated Grades). 200 to 300. Most are in the Very Fine to Extremely Fine range. As this has been considered a common date, little attention has been paid to it. Thus, an estimate of the population is difficult to formulate.

Die Data. *1847 four-digit date logotype:* The 1, 8, and 4 are about evenly spaced at a medium distance. The bases of 4 and 7 are closer, with the base of 7 low. The top and bottom interior of 8 are each about the same size; the 4 has a crosslet with a square top and a triangular or pointed bottom. The base of the 7 is squared off. The logotype was casually made overall, and the 8 and 4 lean slightly right—the type of workmanship that Walter Breen was fond of attributing to James B. Longacre, but was probably done by some assistant. The logotype this year was too high and wide to comfortably fit on the quarter eagle, and thus on all specimens its position appears crowded, sometimes overlapping the denticles or bust. This logotype was used on all dies of all mints.

Varieties exist with normal numerals and repunched 18 in the date, from two impressions of the date logotype into the working die.

Characteristics of Striking and Die Notes. Examples are usually lightly struck at the eagle's leg on the left. Early impressions have die striations. High-grade pieces are usually prooflike.

Selected Auction Records

In his January 1884 sale of the Ely Collection, W. Elliot Woodward described lot 914: "1847 Fine." Realized $3.10 to Heath. In his 1907 fixed-price list Elmer S. Sears offered lot 222: "1847 Uncirculated, with mint lustre. Rare. A gem. $10." Thomas L. Elder's March 1911 sale of the William H. Woodin Collection included this description of lot 972: "1847. Figure 1 in date double-struck. Die broken on reverse through eagle down to rim." Realized $2.70. In May 1913 the U.S. Coin Co. sale of the Malcolm N. Jackson Collection included lot 132: "1847 Reverse die cracked. Extremely Fine." Realized $4.25. In May 1915 B. Max Mehl's catalog of the B.W. Smith Collection included this description of lot 263: "1847 1 of date and point of & touch bust. Extremely Fine, some mint luster. Very scarce." Realized $3.

In his November 1939 sale of the William B. Hale Collection, Mehl described lot 771: "1847 Very Fine. Very scarce. From the Zug Sale in 1909." Realized $5.15. The Stack's sale of the J.F. Bell Collection in December 1944 included lot 113: "1847 Brilliant Uncirculated." Realized $18.50. Mehl's sale of the Jerome Kern Collection in May 1950 included lot 36: "1847 Practically Uncirculated with considerable luster." Realized $17.25. April 1956 Abe Kosoff's sale of the Melish and Hester Collections included lot 1175: "1847 Uncirculated, mint bloom." Realized $40. In June 1957 the New Netherlands sale of Eliasberg duplicates had this for lot 599: "1847. In date, 1 and 7 touch above; the reverse die cracked down to O in OF. Strictly Very Fine, obtained as EF. A hard year to locate; the EF one in our last sale was bid up to $35." Realized $17.

Proofs

Estimated Total Population (Proof). 2 or 3 estimated by David W. Akers (1975). Walter Breen (*Proof Encyclopedia*, 1977) knew only of the Mint Collection Proof.

VF-20	EF-40	AU-50	AU-55	MS-60	MS-62	MS-63
$500	$650	$800	$1,050	$3,000	$5,000	$12,000

1847-C

Circulation-Strike Mintage: 23,226

Most plentiful Charlotte Mint $2.50 gold coin. Scarce on an absolute basis.

Deliveries of this issue were reported as follows:[59] March; 4,103; April; 4,624; September, two deliveries, 4,564 and 5,014; October, 4,921. Total: 23,226.

Estimated Total Population (Mint State). 30 to 45. Mint State examples are plentiful in the context of Charlotte Mint quarter eagles, but on an absolute basis an issue with only a few dozen known Mint State specimens cannot be called common. For a reality check, consider that about 100 to 200 Mint State specimens are known of the most highly prized mintmark variety in the Morgan silver dollar series, the 1893-S, and that when even an MS-60 examples of an 1893-S dollar is featured at auction, it is given a very extensive spread.

Estimated Total Population (Circulated Grades). 200 to 300. This is the most widely available Charlotte Mint quarter eagle.

Die Data. *1847 four-digit date logotype. See the Philadelphia listing for this date.*

Three die pairs were shipped from Philadelphia, but no accounting has been made of what slight variations may have been struck.

Characteristics of Striking and Die Notes. Examples are usually lightly struck in areas, particularly on the eagle's leg on the left reverse, although well-struck pieces are sometimes encountered, sometimes of remarkable sharpness (in the context of Charlotte Mint quarter eagles). The rims are often wide. Luster tends to be satiny rather than deeply frosty.

Selected Auction Records

The catalog of John W. Haseltine's June 1883 sale of the William J. Jenks Collection described lot 453: "1847 C Mint. Fine. Scarce." Realized $3.35. In his 1907 fixed-price list Elmer S. Sears offered lot 224: "1847 Charlotte Mint. Uncirculated. Mint lustre. Rare. $12." Thomas L. Elder's March 1911 sale of the William H. Woodin Collection included this description of lot 1123: "1847-C Very Fine. Scarce." Realized $4.25. May 1913 the U.S. Coin Co. sale of the Malcolm N. Jackson Collection included lot 278: "1847-C Extremely Fine, scarce." Realized $3.78. In May 1915 B. Max Mehl's catalog of the B.W. Smith Collection included this description of lot 294: "1847-C. C over 2 of fraction. Light yellow gold. Very Fine. Very scarce." Realized $2.75.

Mehl's February 1944 catalog of the sale of the Belden E. Roach Collection described lot 960: "1847-C Practically Uncirculated with mint luster." Realized $7.50. The Stack's sale of the J.F. Bell Collection in December 1944 included lot 196: "1847-C About Uncirculated. Sharp." Realized $17.50. Mehl's sale of the Jerome Kern Collection in May 1950 included lot 122: "1847 C. Very Fine, strictly so. Mint letter C over 2 of fraction." Realized $15.75. In October 1951 the Numismatic Gallery sale of the B.A. Talmadge collection included lot 1201: "1847-C Uncirculated." Realized $18.

VF-20	EF-40	AU-50	AU-55	MS-60	MS-62	MS-63
$1,650	$2,250	$3,000	$3,500	$5,750	$7,500	$15,000

1847-D

Circulation-Strike Mintage: 15,784

Scarce in any grade.

Coinage delivery dates and amounts: February 27, 1,816 + 4 for assay; April 28, 2,856 + 6; June 24, 1,455 + 3; August 6, 1,981 + 4; September 23, 3,220 + 7; November 4, 2,422 + 5; and December 30, 2,034 + 5). Assay coins are not included in the annual total.

Estimated Total Population (Mint State). 20 to 30, mostly in lower levels. Some of these must have been called About Uncirculated years ago. Any 1847-D that is *really* MS-63 or finer is a first-class rarity.

Estimated Total Population (Circulated Grades). 175 to 250. This is one of the three or four most commonly available D-Mint quarter eagles; however, most of the available specimens are only Very Fine or Extremely Fine, and About Uncirculated examples are very scarce, if not rare.

Die Data. *1847 four-digit date logotype: See the Philadelphia listing for this year.*

One 1847-dated obverse and one reverse die were sent from Philadelphia on November 19, 1846; another pair was sent on November 20 and a further pair on November 21; all six dies arrived in Dahlonega on December 2, 1846.[60] On March 1, 1848, three old obverse and three old reverse dies were defaced at the mint. After this time there were two usable reverse dies carried over.

So-called "1847/6-D": Apparently, all known 1847-D quarter eagles are from the same die pair, often in different states. Breen-6191 was designated by that author as an "overdate" with "strong repunching at bases of 47, not matching curves of 7"; this variety has not been widely accepted. It seems that to be a true overdate, the 1847 logotype, which is in large numerals, would have been punched over a full 1846 date, which is in smaller numerals.

Characteristics of Striking and Die Notes. Most examples are better struck than usually seen for a Dahlonega quarter eagle, but some lightness is typical at the highest area of the portrait and on the lower left of the eagle. The fields are sometimes prooflike.

One specimen examined was from rusted dies that had been relapped in the fields, but which still retained rust on the higher areas.

Selected Auction Records

In October 1884 W. Elliot Woodward's Collection of Coins, Medals, Etc. described lot 1964: "1847 Dahlonega mint; Very Good, rare." Realized $3.55." In his 1907 fixed-price list Elmer S. Sears offered lot 227: "1847 Dahlonega Mint. Almost Uncirculated, with mint lustre. Rare. $12." Thomas L. Elder's March 1911 sale of the William H. Woodin Collection included this description of lot 1103: "1847-D. Figures 1 and 7 touch bust. D directly above fraction bar. Extremely Fine. Very rare. Coinage small." Realized $4.50. In February 1921 the catalog of B. Max Mehl's sale of the Dr. G.F.E. Wilharm Collection described lot 161: "1847-D Beautiful Uncirculated specimen. Sharp with bright Mint luster. A little gem and as such very rare." Realized $7.35. In June Mehl's sale of the William Cutler Atwater Collection included lot 2047: "1847-D Nearly Uncirculated with considerable luster. Record nearly $30." Realized $12.50. The Will W. Neil Collection sold by Mehl in June 1947 included lot 2517: "1847-D Nearly Uncirculated with considerable luster. Record near $30." Realized $15.75. Mehl's sale of the Jerome Kern Collection in May 1950 included lot 138: "1847 D. Extremely Fine; just a shade from Uncirculated. Record near $30." Realized $12.

VF-20	EF-40	AU-50	AU-55	MS-60	MS-62	MS-63
$1,650	$2,500	$3,250	$4,500	$8,750	$13,500	$25,000

1847-O

Major rarity in Mint State.

Circulation-Strike Mintage: 124,000

Estimated Total Population (Mint State). 8 to 12, mostly at lower levels. A major rarity at the MS-63 or any higher level.

In 1986 in *The Quarter Eagles*, Paul F. Taglione commented: "Until early 1985, the Mint State 1847-O was exceedingly rare with no more than 3 or 4 example known, but a small group was discovered in the Southwest in the early months of that year. This group, numbering 6 or 7 pieces, was lightly cleaned at some point and none of the coins graded better than Mint State-60 although the cleaning was not particularly harsh or detracting."

Estimated Total Population (Circulated Grades). 200 to 400, with Very Fine being a typical grade. At the About Uncirculated level the 1847-O is very scarce. The estimate covers a wide range, but as little attention is paid to Very Fine coins, these being considered common, specimens of 1847-O have not been extensively publicized, a situation quite unlike that for Charlotte and Dahlonega coins.

Die Data. *1847 four-digit date logotype: See the Philadelphia Mint listing for this year.*

Three obverse and five reverse dies were sent to New Orleans in December 1846 in anticipation of the 1847-O coinage. Multiple dies were used, with the result that many variations and states exist.

Doubled Date: Breen-6194.[61] The distinct remnants of a previously punched 1 and 8, in a slightly higher position, are visible at the respective numerals in the date. The repunched numerals were punched lower in the die than the first pair, with the result that the 1 in the date is now *embedded* in the denticles below that numeral. There is no sign of repunching at the 4 or 7 in the date. At the upper right, the 7 touches the neck truncation, while the bottom of the 7 does not touch a denticle, simply because the denticles have been shortened at this point.

Characteristics of Striking and Die Notes. Usually lightly struck at the centers and on the obverse stars. Clash marks are often seen. Some have light die cracks.

Selected Auction Records

In his 1907 fixed-price list Elmer S. Sears offered lot 230: "1847 Another with mint mark placed over figure 1 of fraction, but not touching it. Very Fine. Rare. $8." Thomas L. Elder's March 1911 sale of the William H. Woodin Collection included these: Lot 1044: "1847-O. The O directly over top of dividing line. Fine." Realized $2.60. Lot 1045: "1847-O. The O between 1 and dividing line, and touching 1. Fine." Realized $2.50 (face value). Lot 1046: "1847-O. The bottom of 1 barely touches rim. The O rests between 1 and dividing line, touching both. Fine." Realized $2.60. Lot 1047: "1847-O. The 1 does not touch rim. The O between 2 and dividing line but does not touch. Fine." Realized $2.50 (face value). In May 1913 the U.S. Coin Co. sale of the Malcolm N. Jackson Collection included a trio: Lot 208: "1847-O 1 in date touches border. 0 over fraction bar. Very Fine." Realized $3. Lot 209: "1847-O 1 touches border. 0 between I and fraction bar. Fine." Realized $2.75 Lot 210: "1847-O 1 does not touch border. 0 high between I and fraction bar. Very Fine." Realized $2.75.

In May 1915 B. Max Mehl's catalog of the B.W. Smith Collection included this description of lot 314: "1847-O O over 1 and bar. Very Fine." Realized $3.25. In his November 1939 sale of the William B. Hale Collection, Mehl described lot 861: "1847-O Nearly Uncirculated. Rare variety with die break connecting bottom of AMERICA and D. About Uncirculated. I believe this is the first specimen of this variety I have ever seen." Realized $7.60. The Stack's sale of the J.F. Bell Collection in December 1944 included lot 233: "1847-O Brilliant Uncirculated." Realized $20. The Will W. Neil Collection sold by Mehl in June 1947 included lot 2527: "1847-O O over fraction. Nearly Uncirculated with mint luster. Catalogs $10 in only Very Fine." Realized $9. In November 1956 the New Netherlands sale of the Thomas L. Gaskill Collection included lot 249: "1847-O. 18 plainly recut, particularly the 1. Actually, a hair's breadth from Uncirculated, but bag-marked, and a very weak strike. Coins like this make grading an art, and one often paradoxical in results. Very scarce choice." Realized $21.

VF-20	EF-40	AU-50	AU-55	MS-60	MS-62	MS-63
$500	$650	$1,000	$1,350	$4,500	$10,000	$16,000

1848

Circulation-Strike Mintage: 7,497

Proof Mintage: 5 to 7 (estimated)

Notably rare in Mint State.

Estimated Total Population (Mint State). 12 to 20, mostly at lower Mint State levels. It is very rare in Mint State. No doubt some that were earlier offered as

About Uncirculated are now called MS-60 or MS-61. In Mint State the 1848 is notably rarer than the more famous 1848 CAL.

Estimated Total Population (Circulated Grades). 150 to 225. Very scarce in all grades. Most are Very Fine or Extremely Fine. With a mintage of 7,497, the 1848 quarter eagle has long been recognized as scarce. Walter Breen described the elusive quality of the issue as follows: "Touted as a rarity since about 1958, when J.F. Bell circulated want lists including this date; dealers found none in stock, and the hunt was on. Survivors were usually VF to EF, extremely rare AU."[62]

"Touted" or otherwise, the 1848 is indeed rare and, as is true of so many quarter eagles of this era, its elusive quality is mainly known to dealers and specialists. The 1848 CAL. counterstamp has garnered nearly all of the limelight for this date, and whenever an example crosses the block, it creates a lot of attention. However, at the Mint State level the 1848 "regular" quarter eagle is much more elusive than the famous lower-mintage 1848 CAL. The reason is that the pieces with the CAL. counterstamp were deliberately saved, whereas the regular issues slipped unnoticed into circulation.

Die Data. *1848 four-digit date logotype:* Numerals are slightly smaller than the preceding year, and thus they fit more comfortably in the dies, 48 being closer than the others. The upper and lower interior of the first 8 are about the same size, and 8 leans slightly right. The 4 has a crosslet, with the top and bottom of the crosslet each with a flat top and bottom end and normal (in comparison to the 1847). The second 8 is upright (does not lean right). This logotype was used on all dies of all mints.

Characteristics of Striking and Die Notes. Examples are usually lightly struck on the eagle at the left side of the reverse.

Selected Auction Records

In June 1885 W. Elliot Woodward's sale of the J. Colvin Randall Collection included lot 993: "1848 Sharp impression, nearly Proof." Realized $2.85. In May 1913 the U.S. Coin Co. sale of the Malcolm N. Jackson Collection included lot 133: "1848 Uncirculated. Small edge nick on reverse. Very rare." Realized $6.75. An early notation regarding the great rarity of this issue. In May 1915 B. Max Mehl's catalog of the B.W. Smith Collection included this description of lot 264: "1848 Practically Uncirculated, unusually sharp and well struck specimen. Very rare. Record over $10." Realized $6.75. The Stack's sale of the J.F. Bell Collection in December 1944 included lot 114: "1848 Brilliant Uncirculated." Realized $27.50. In June 1946 Mehl's sale of the William Cutler Atwater Collection included lot 1951: "1848 About Uncirculated with mint luster. Scarce date. Catalogs at $25 in Very Fine. This, of course, is much better." Realized $12.50. Mehl's sale of the Jerome Kern Collection in May 1950 included lot 38: "1848 Regular issue. Uncirculated with semi-Proof surface. Just the slightest evidence of cabinet friction. Mention is made of this only for the sake of accuracy. The coin is a beautiful specimen and as such, very scarce. Catalogs $20 in only Very Fine." Realized $27.

Proofs

Estimated Total Population (Proof). 3 confirmed. One is in the Mint Collection, and the two others are the Woodin and Melish coins.

Proof Die Data and Notes. On the Proof die, the date logotype is lower in the field than it is on the regular issues, and there is also a prominent die chip on the neck. On the reverse, the lowest arrowhead is detached from CA in AMERICA, while on the regular issue it barely touches. The right leg of the eagle is weakly struck on the Proofs as it is on the Proofs of other years in the 1840s (cf. Akers, 1975).

Selected Proof Auction Records

In January 1884 for the Heman Ely Collection, W. Elliot Woodward described lot 915: "1848 Proof, scarce." Realized $4.40 to Akers. In December 1898, Lyman H. Low offered the James T. Callender Collection with lot 378a: "1848 Brilliant Proof, a few slight blemishes, scarcely noticeable to the naked eye, extremely rare and valuable." Realized $16.

VF-20	EF-40	AU-50	AU-55	MS-60	MS-62	MS-63	PF-60	PF-63
$750	$1,200	$2,250	$3,850	$5,500	$8,500	$15,000	$40,000	$55,000

1848, CAL.

Circulation-Strike Mintage: 1,389

First United States commemorative coin. Struck from California gold.

Gold was discovered in quantity in California starting on January 24, 1848, when James Marshall, an employee of John Sutter, spotted gold flecks in the race of a sawmill he was helping to construct at Coloma on the American River. Soon, additional deposits were discovered up and down the river, and the area attracted dozens, then hundreds of miners. Word soon spread further, and by autumn 1848 newspapers in the East contained many articles on the alluring prospect of becoming rich overnight. In November 1848 several ships left the East to go to San Francisco. By December a veritable stampede was in progress. Old schooners, transport steamers, and virtually any other vessels considered remotely seaworthy were pressed into service. Between December 14, 1848, and February 1, 1849, 61 ships with an average of 50 passengers each left Boston, Salem, New York, Philadelphia, Baltimore, and Norfolk. Additional vessels left from Charleston, New Orleans, and other ports.

We can trace the advent of coins specifically linked to California, and easily identifiable as such, to the purchase of 228 ounces of gold, averaging .894 fine, by Assistant Quartermaster Joseph L. Folsom in California, who had obtained the metal for the bargain rate of $10 per ounce at a time when the metal was common and Spanish-American and other coins in exchange were scarce. The money came from a civil fund. Col. R.B. Mason Jr., acting governor, shipped the metal, with a letter dated August 17, to the East via Lieutenant Lucien Loeser, who carried it in a small oyster can or, more elegantly, a tea caddy.[63] When Loeser subsequently arrived in the capital on December 9, *The Washington Union* informed readers of the following:

> We readily admit that the account so nearly approached the miraculous that we were relieved by the evidence of our own senses on the subject. The specimens have

> all the appearance of the native gold we had seen from the mines of North Carolina and Virginia; and we are informed that the Secretary will send the small chest of gold to the Mint, to be melted into coin and bars, and most of it to be subsequently fashioned into medals commemorative of the heroism and valor of our officers.
>
> Several of the other specimens he will retain for the present in the War Office as found in California in the form of lumps, scales, and sand; the last named being of different hues, from bright yellow to black, without much appearance of gold. However skeptical any man may have been, we defy him to doubt that if the quantity of such specimens as these be as great as has been represented, the value of gold in California must be greater than has been hitherto discovered in the old or new continent; and great as may be the immigration to this new El Dorado, the frugal and industrious will be amply repaid for their enterprise and toil.

Secretary of War W.L. Marcy wrote the following to Mint Director Patterson on December 8, 1848, concerning the first official government deposit of 228 ounces, which subsequently arrived via Lt. Loeser: "If the metal is found to be pure gold, as I doubt not that it will be, I request you to reserve enough of it for two medals ordered by Congress and not yet completed, and the remainder, with the exception of one or two small bars, I wish to have coined and sent with the bars to this department. As many may wish to procure specimens made with California gold, by exchanging other coin for it, I would suggest that it be made into quarter eagles with a distinguishing mark on each, if any variation from the ordinary issues from the Mint would be proper and could be conveniently made."

Nothing was heard from the Mint, and Marcy inquired concerning the progress of the coinage. On January 5, 1849, Mint Director Patterson replied: "The amount of your deposit of gold, made on the 15th ult., is now ready for delivery in California gold. It is our practice to pay for deposits as soon as their value is ascertained; but this could not be done in the present case because payment was required in coins made of the bullion deposited. Before the Cal. gold could be used it had to undergo the process of *parting* in order to separate it from the excess of silver which it contains. This was one source of delay. Another occurred by the time required for stamping the letters CAL. on the quarter-eagles as you desired. Your payment of $3,910.10 will be made up of $3,474.64 in coins and $435.46 in two bars of gold as melted from the grains. The California gold reserved for the medals is from another deposit. . . ."

At the time the smallest United States gold coin was the $2.50 piece. Accordingly, it was selected as being ideal for wide distribution. The estimated 1,389 quarter eagles from the first government deposit bore the notation CAL. on the reverse, thus making them the first commemorative coins ever issued by a United States mint. The fact that these are true commemoratives is without a doubt, as the above government correspondence indicates that the pieces were to have been made to satisfy those seeking a souvenir coin specifically made from California gold.

Apparently, 1848 CAL. quarter eagles were available at face value to anyone desiring them. Although 1,389 pieces were minted, probably fewer than two or three dozen numismatists—if, indeed, even that many—learned of them at or near the time of issue and added the coins to their cabinets. Among those acquiring such pieces was Chief Engraver James B. Longacre, who preserved at least three prooflike specimens in his personal collection. Most were probably distributed to the general public, for interest in the California Gold Rush was extremely intense at that time and news of treasure in the West dominated the newspapers. Any unsold coins were undoubtedly put into circulation at face value, as evidenced by the fact that the majority of the examples known today show evidence of wear. The writer has never seen any publicity or outside notices, apart from government correspondence, pertaining to this early issue. The history of the 1848, CAL., quarter eagle is laid out in *1849: The Philadelphia Mint Strikes Gold*, by Michael F. Moran and Jeff Garrett.

Estimated Total Population (Mint State). 25 to 40, mostly toward the MS-60 end of the spectrum. Grading interpretations differ, often widely. Mint State specimens are usually highly prooflike, and some have been called "Proof" for this reason.[64] A few beautiful gems exist.

Estimated Total Population (Circulated Grades). 125 to 175. These exist in grades from Very Good to Fine (unusual) through Very Fine and Extremely Fine (the grades typically encountered), to About Uncirculated, the last often displaying prooflike surface.

The reverse has the CAL. counterstamp, with a square period after the L, punched into the coin; the letters are thus *recessed* in the die surface.

Characteristics of Striking and Die Notes. Most show obverse die striae from the preparation process and file marks from the border (below the left side of the date). When first struck, specimens had prooflike surfaces rather than lustrous mint frost. The prooflike surface on the reverse extends to within the shield stripes, indicating that the die was intentionally polished. However, the die polishing was not of the caliber used on contemporary Proof gold coins. All specimens have slight weakness on the obverse, in the curl of the hair under the ear.

Selected Auction Records

Note: These listings emphasize early auction appearances in combination with later issues, the later ones selected to reflect Mint State coins or listings with expanded information. Several of the later descriptions included lengthy historical information not quoted here (to avoid repetition).

The 1848 CAL. quarter eagle has attracted a numismatic following virtually from day one. The earliest auction appearance located is a specimen appearing in the February 20, 1851, sale of the Dr. Lewis Roper Collection held in Philadelphia by M. Thomas & Sons, Lot 22, No. 13,[65] "Quarter eagle (struck from California gold) 1848." The coin, which sold for face value(!) to the auction house itself, was probably obtained by Roper at the time it was issued by the nearby Mint.[66] Lot 812, in W. Elliot Woodward's March 1865 auction of the Bache, Bertsch, Lightbody, Lilliendahl, Vinton, and Watson Collections was described as: "1848 Brilliant Proof, having on the reverse Cal., to indicate that it was coined from the first gold of California received that year, *excessively rare.*" Realized $4.25 to J. Osborn Emery. In his 1907 fixed-price list Elmer S. Sears offered two: Lot 233: "1848 Another with (CAL.) stamped on reverse. It is said that this was done at the Mint to show that the gold used in the coinage was mined in California. Almost Uncirculated specimen with semi-Proof surface. Very rare. $40." Lot 234: "1848 Another as the lot preceding. Almost its equal. $35." Thomas L. Elder's March 1911 sale of the William H. Woodin Collection included this description of lot 974: "1848. Different die, with heavier arrows, one barely touching left part of A. Incuse over the eagle's head the letters, 'Cal.' Made from gold from the California placer mines. Very rare. Records of $85 and $75.50 have been made for this interesting piece. About Uncirculated, with some Proof surface." Realized $54. In February 1921 the catalog of B. Max Mehl's sale of the Dr. G.F.E. Wilharm Collection described lot 347: "1848 Head of Liberty to left, coronet inscribed Liberty 13 stars, date below. Rev. eagle with U. S. shield. Around, United States Of America 2 ½ D. In the field, over the head of eagle, are the letters Cal. stamped in. This was done while the coin was yet in the die. Struck at the United States Mint at Philadelphia, from the first gold received from California. Proof. Finest known specimen. Cost $75, and in this condition certainly worth it." Realized $77.50.

The Stack's sale of the J.F. Bell Collection in December 1944 included lot 115: "1848 Head of Liberty left, 13 stars 1848 Reverse: Eagle with U.S. shield on breast, U.S.A. over the head of eagle are the letters "CAL" (California) punched in while the coin was in the die. Struck at the Philadelphia Mint from the first gold received from California. Uncirculated semi-Proof, very rare, with private sales records as high as $250." Realized $250. June 1946 Mehl's sale of the William Cutler Atwater Collection included lot 1952: "1848 With CAL on Reverse. Type of regular issue, but with CAL. counterstamped on reverse directly above eagle. The CAL stands for California. This was stamped in at the Mint while the coin was still in the die. It is to signify that it was struck from the first mined gold received at the Philadelphia Mint from California. Only a limited number were struck. Beautiful semi-Proof; the left field on obverse is very slightly rubbed. But it is a magnificent specimen. Very rare and of historical interest. Auction record up to $250." Realized $120. Mehl's sale of the Jerome Kern Collection in May 1950 included lot 37: "1848. Gem specimen of the 1848 $2.50 gold with CAL on Reverse. Type of regular issue. CAL (for California) counterstamped on reverse directly above eagle. This was stamped at the Mint while the coin was still in the die. It is to signify that it was minted from the first mined gold received at the Philadelphia Mint from California. We do not have a record of the exact number struck, but apparently the number was small. This is as beautiful a specimen of this rarity as I have ever seen. It was purchased by Mr. Kern as a brilliant Proof. The coin measures up to that description. As such, it is very rare indeed and valuable. Cost $250. Certainly worth it and even more in this beautiful condition." Realized $262.50.

In November 1956 the New Netherlands sale of the Thomas L. Gaskill Collection included lot 252: "1848 CAL. incused in field about eagle on reverse. Made to signify that this coin was composed of the first mined gold received at the Philadelphia Mint from California. Paler, slightly greenish metal, typical of California pieces and unlike the Carolina, Georgia, and African gold which made up the Mint's principal pre-1848 supply. A splendid first-strike; displays considerable proof-like lustre, a partial wire edge. Slight evidence of handling in the upper reverse field. Only 1,389 made. Several months ago, a top-flight example realized $600. Most of the specimens offered recently have been VF or thereabouts. We have seen possibly three that would match this coin, and only one (Eliasberg's) that would exceed it even slightly. Ex Henry Chapman, 1935."[67] Realized $575.

VF-20	EF-40	AU-50	AU-55	MS-60	MS-62	MS-63
$40,000	$50,000	$60,000	$70,000	$85,000	$115,000	$150,000

1848-C

Circulation-Strike Mintage: 16,788

Incredibly rare in Mint State.

Estimated Total Population (Mint State). 2 to 5. The data are inconsistent, and in-person examination of several pieces called "Uncirculated" has revealed that some would be better called About Uncirculated. As always, grading is a matter of opinion, but it seems to be especially liberal for the gold coins of Charlotte and Dahlonega. Although modern certification services list multiple examples in low ranges of Mint State, perhaps David W. Akers' 1975 comment is reflective of the rarity of *true* Mint State coins: "I have never seen a full Mint State 1848-C, although I have seen three or four very nice AUs." In his reference on the series, Douglas Winter listed only two pieces that he considered to be Mint State, with the notation that both listings might have referred to the same coin!

The rarity of the 1848-C in high grades is explained by the manner of distribution, unknown but apparently involving placing nearly all coins into circulation at the time of mintage. On the other hand, several dozen Mint State examples are known of the 1847-C of the previous year, of only slightly higher mintage (23,226 for 1847-C, as compared to 16,788 for 1848-C). Perhaps a small cache, today unrecorded, was saved of Mint State 1847-C quarter eagles.

Estimated Total Population (Circulated Grades). 125 to 175. Most are Very Fine or Extremely Fine. The About Uncirculated level represents the highest grade reasonably available, and these are few and far between.

Die Data. *1848 four-digit date logotype: See the Philadelphia Mint listing for this year.*

Four 1848 obverse dies were sent from Philadelphia to Charlotte, but no reverses, indicating that a supply of reverses was on hand from earlier years. Apparently a fairly extensive mintage was anticipated.

Characteristics of Striking and Die Notes. The 1848-C is nearly always weakly struck, this being most obvious on the stars and on the highest hair strands. Some are lightly struck at the obverse and reverse centers. However, there are a few dozen well-struck pieces, although these are largely unnoticed, for in today's world of certification, one numerical designation is all that is needed for many buyers—and such numbers do not indicate striking quality. Die striae are common on higher grade pieces. One variety has the obverse die dramatically buckled.

Selected Auction Records

In June 1885 W. Elliot Woodward's sale of the J. Colvin Randall Collection included lot 994: "1848-C Fine." Realized $2.60. Thomas L. Elder's March 1911 sale of the William H. Woodin Collection included this description of lot 1124: "1848-C. Fine. Very scarce." Realized $3.75. In May 1913 the U.S. Coin Co. sale of the Malcolm N. Jackson Collection included three: Lot 279: "1848-C Date close to bust. Very Fine, scarce." Realized $3.25. Lot 280: "1848-C Similar. Fine." Realized $3. Lot 281: "1848-C Part of date slightly lower. Very Fine, scarce." Realized $3.25.

In June 1941 B. Max Mehl's sale of the William Forrester Dunham Collection included lot 1943: "1848-C Extremely Fine, with considerable mint luster; just a shade from Uncirculated. Very scarce." Realized $6.50. Mehl's February 1944 catalog of the sale of the Belden E. Roach Collection described lot 961: "1848-C About Uncirculated. Very scarce, especially so choice." Realized $15.75. The Stack's sale of the J.F. Bell Collection in December 1944 included lot 197: "1848-C Brilliant Uncirculated." Realized $32.50. Mehl's sale of the Jerome Kern Collection in May 1950 included lot 123: "1848 C. Practically Uncirculated with mint luster. Very scarce so choice. Record of $30." Realized $25.75.

VF-20	EF-40	AU-50	AU-55	MS-60	MS-62	MS-63
$1,500	$2,850	$3,500	$4,500	$11,000	$20,000	$32,500

1848-D

Circulation-Strike Mintage: 13,771

Rare in Mint State.

Delivery dates and amounts: February 21 (2,960+6 for assay), April 3 (1,713+6), May 30 (2,765+6), August 11 (3,036+6), month of October (2,368+5), December 30 (929+2). Assay coins are not included in the annual total.

Estimated Total Population (Mint State). 10 to 18, mostly at lower levels.

Estimated Total Population (Circulated Grades). 200 to 300. Quite a few exist in higher grades such as Extremely Fine and About Uncirculated, these being the typical levels of pieces offered as part of collections in recent decades. Why the higher mintage 1848-C should be so rare in high grades, while the 1848-D is more or less available, is one of the little mysteries that make collecting *C* and D mint gold coins so interesting.

Die Data. *1848 four-digit date logotype: See the Philadelphia Mint listing for this year.*

Three obverse and three reverse dies were sent from Philadelphia on January 11, 1848, and arrived in Dahlonega by February 3, 1848.[68] On January 3, 1849, three obverse and two reverse dies were defaced at the mint, leaving three old but usable reverses on hand.

At least two die varieties are known, these being Douglas Winter's 10-L and 10-M, both from the same obverse.

Characteristics of Striking and Die Notes. Sometimes seen lightly struck at the center of the obverse, but usually quite sharp overall, sometimes remarkably so.

Selected Auction Records

In his 1907 fixed-price list Elmer S. Sears offered lot 237: "1848 Dahlonega Mint. Uncirculated, with mint lustre. Superb example of a rare quarter eagle. $15." Thomas L. Elder's March 1911 sale of the William H. Woodin Collection included two: Lot 1104: "1848-D. The D high above 1/2. Very Fine. Very rare and seldom offered." Realized $6. Lot 1105: "1848-D. The D low and close to 1. Good. Very rare." Realized $3.75. In May

1913 the U.S. Coin Co. sale of the Malcolm N. Jackson Collection included lot 260: "1848-D D high over fraction bar. Extremely Fine, mint luster." Realized $4.25. In May 1915 B. Max Mehl's catalog of the B.W. Smith Collection included this description of lot 303: "1848-D D over bar. Extremely Fine, mint luster. Rare." Realized $3.

In June 1941 Mehl's sale of the William Forrester Dunham Collection included lot 1944: "1848-D Bold impression. Extremely Fine, with some luster. Very scarce." Realized $7.50. Mehl's February 1944 catalog of the sale of the Belden E. Roach Collection described lot 990: "1848-D Brilliant Uncirculated with Proof surface. A real rarity in this beautiful condition." Realized $11.50. The Stack's sale of the J.F. Bell Collection in December 1944 included lot 215: "1848-D Brilliant Uncirculated. Scarce." Realized $15. In April 1956 Abe Kosoff's sale of the Melish and Hester Collections included lot 1185: "1848-D Uncirculated, choice." Realized $38.

VF-20	EF-40	AU-50	AU-55	MS-60	MS-62	MS-63
$1,700	$2,650	$3,750	$4,250	$8,000	$12,500	$28,000

1849

Circulation-Strike Mintage: 23,294

Proof Mintage: None known

Remarkably rare in Mint State.

Estimated Total Population (Mint State). 5 to 10. Extremely rare in Mint State. Of those that do exist, most are in lower grade ranges. As is the case with virtually every early quarter eagle, certification service submission totals are significantly higher than our estimate. As years go by and *re*submissions increase, the totals will continue to climb, without necessarily any real increase in the number of specimens known.

Estimated Total Population (Circulated Grades). 300 to 450. Extremely Fine is about par for historical listings, although many About Uncirculated examples have surfaced in "name" collections. As the 1849 is a so-called "common date," it is under-represented in certification service listings.

Die Data. *1849 four-digit date logotype:* The numerals are small (permitting easy placement between the denticles and bust, in contrast with the large logotypes of 1847–1848) and very close together. The numerals often seem to touch, but on light impressions they are separated. The top and bottom interior of 8 are about the same size; the 8 leans slightly right. The 4 leans slightly right, and the serif is normal. The 9 leans right, is somewhat "lumpy" at the bottom, and seems to have the ball added as an afterthought, the ball being close to the upright. Extra material is seen at the 4 and the 9, a feature of the logotype, as this is common to dies from all mints. On light strikings the material is less evident and, as noted, the numerals seem to be slightly wider apart. On deep strikes this material can give the 1849 the appearance of an overdate. This logotype was used on all dies of all mints.

There are various logotype position varieties, including doubled dates.

Characteristics of Striking and Die Notes. Striking varies but is often lightly defined on the eagle's leg to the left. Examples are sometimes seen with prooflike surfaces.

Selected Auction Records

The catalog of John W. Haseltine's June 1883 sale of the William J. Jenks Collection described lot 454: "1849 Uncirculated." Realized $3.90. In May 1913 the U.S. Coin Co. sale of the Malcolm N. Jackson Collection included lot 135: "1849 Extremely Fine." Realized $3. The Stack's sale of the J.F. Bell Collection in December 1944 included lot 116: "1849 About Uncirculated, yet choice." Realized $11. B. Max Mehl's sale of the Jerome Kern Collection in May 1950 included lot 39: "1849 Uncirculated with mint luster; slight evidence of having been handled. Brilliant. Very scarce so choice." Realized $12. In June 1957 the New Netherlands sale of Eliasberg duplicates had this for lot 602: '1849. Crudely cut 49 in date. Uncirculated. Brilliant; some evidence of handling, particularly upon the reverse rim. The Melish lot, called Unc., didn't quite make that grade, and brought $35. None in Dunham; most other sales had only Fine to VF examples." Realized $23.

VF-20	EF-40	AU-50	AU-55	MS-60	MS-62	MS-63
$550	$750	$950	$1,250	$2,750	$4,000	$7,500

1849-C

Circulation-Strike Mintage: 10,220

Incredibly rare in Mint State.

Estimated Total Population (Mint State). 1 or 2. Exceedingly rare. The Bass II coin may be the finest known. In *The Quarter Eagles*, 1986, Paul F. Taglione noted that in his studies he had encountered just one Mint State specimen.

Estimated Total Population (Circulated Grades). 90 to 125. Very Fine and Extremely Fine grades are typical. At the About Uncirculated level the 1849-C is very rare.

Die Data. *1849 four-digit date logotype: See the Philadelphia Mint listing for this year.*

Three pairs of dies were sent from Philadelphia.

At least two obverse dies were used, one showing light repunching on the last two date digits. Sometimes the repunched variety is called "1849/8-C," but it is not an overdate; the same situation occurs with 1849-D.

Characteristics of Striking and Die Notes. It is usually well struck, save for the eagle's leg at the lower left of the reverse. Early impressions are apt to show prominent die striations.

"[A certain reverse die] was used for three years to strike 1849-C, 1850-C and 1851-C quarter eagles. This C mintmark is located far to the left over the 1 in the fraction. This reverse becomes badly clashed during the striking of 1850-C coins and the clash marks are still visible on 1851-C coins."[69]

Selected Auction Records

In his 1907 fixed-price list Elmer S. Sears offered lot 240: "1849 Charlotte Mint. Uncirculated. Superb specimen with semi-Proof surface. Exceedingly rare. $25." Thomas L. Elder's March 1911 sale of the William H. Woodin Collection included this description of lot 1125: "1849-C. Fine to V.F. Very rare and coinage small. Recent records of $9.50 and $10 for this." Realized $7. In May 1913 the U.S. Coin Co. sale of the Malcolm N. Jackson Collection included lot 282: "1849-C Extremely Fine and very rare." Realized $5.25. In February 1921 the catalog of B. Max Mehl's sale of the Dr. G.F.E. Wilharm Collection described lot 177: "1849-C Brilliant semi-Proof, nearly equal to a perfect Proof. Very rare so choice. Old records of $10 and this one is certainly worthy of new high record." Realized $8.40.

Elder's June 1935 sale of the Wendell C. Foster Collection included this description of lot 2793: "1849-C over '48? Ex. Fine and very rare." Realized $9. In his November 1939 sale of the William B. Hale Collection, Mehl described lot 838: "1849-C Very Fine. Very scarce; in fact all of the quarter eagles of the Charlotte Mint are very scarce and most of them are rare. none of them are listed at less than $15." Realized $12.60. During this decade a widespread interest in collecting branch mint gold coins developed. Prices increased, but did not soar. In June 1941 Mehl's sale of the William Forrester Dunham Collection included lot 1945: "1849-C C very high. Nearly Uncirculated. Very scarce." Realized $7.20. Mehl's sale of the Jerome Kern Collection in May 1950 included lot 124: "1849 C. Just About Uncirculated with mint luster. Record over $30." Realized $26. In Abe Kosoff's sale of the Melish and Hester Collections, April 1956, this was the description of lot 1189: "1849-C. Planchet break over M and other cracks, evidence of crumbling die. Extremely Fine." Realized $32.50.

VF-20	EF-40	AU-50	AU-55	MS-60	MS-62
$1,650	$3,000	$5,000	$6,500	$13,500	$20,000

1849-D

Circulation-Strike Mintage: 10,945

Coinage delivery dates and amounts: March (2,125 + 5 for assay), May (2,847 + 6), August (2,720 + 6), October (1,577 + unknown number of assay coins, probably 4), December 17 (1,696 + 4). Assay coins are not included in the annual total.

Incredibly rare in Mint State.

Estimated Total Population (Mint State). 2 or 3. This issue is exceedingly rare. Douglas Winter knew of only a single example, and to this can be added the Bass II coin. Historical offerings include the Renz-Bareford and Fairfield (later Bass) coins.

Estimated Total Population (Circulated Grades). 175 to 275, mostly Very Fine and Extremely Fine.

Die Data. *1849 four-digit date logotype: See the Philadelphia Mint listing for this year.*

Three 1849-dated obverse and three reverse dies were sent from Philadelphia on September 20, 1848, a very early date for the succeeding year's coinage.[70] The dies arrived in Dahlonega on October 3, 1848, carried with other items from Philadelphia, with a stop in Washington, by Valentine Hodgson.[71] At the time Hodgson, a Georgian who had worked at the Dahlonega Mint and also had received training in Philadelphia, was visiting the north to seek appointment as coiner at the Dahlonega Mint. However, John D. Field Jr. was chosen instead.

On January 3, 1850, three obverse dies were defaced; thus, it can be concluded that the mintage figure for 1849 is correct. Six reverse dies were carried forward for further use.

Sometimes a variety with repunched numerals 49 is called "1849/8-D," but it is not an overdate; the same situation occurs with 1849-C. Another is repunched at the first digit.

On the reverse die used on all Dahlonega quarter eagles from 1849 to 1859, the center of the D mintmark is about 40% occupied by a part of the arrow feather. Some raised die marks are seen at the tip of the lowest arrow. John W. McCloskey: "All . . . were struck from the same reverse die. This can be verified by a series of die scratches running through the reverse shield. And then there is the die crack that connects the base of the OF for all the rare dates from the 1854-D to the 1859-D. . . . Many of the Dahlonega quarter eagles have weaknesses in the dentils from the 1849-D through to the 1859-D. But this weakness in the dentils was not caused by any permanent damage to the coinage dies. I can only assume that the dies were clogged by some substance that was cleaned out for further use of the dies. The die was used for many years and in some years shows strong dentils after very weak dentils from the year before."[72]

Characteristics of Striking and Die Notes. Examples are often lightly struck in areas including at the eagle's neck feathers and on the denticles.

Selected Auction Records

In June 1885 W. Elliot Woodward's sale of the J. Colvin Randall Collection included lot 995: "1849-D Fine." Realized $2.65. In his 1907 fixed-price list Elmer S. Sears offered lot 242: "1849 Dahlonega Mint. Extremely Fine. Bright yellow lustre. Choice and very rare. $20." Thomas L. Elder's March 1911 sale of the William H. Woodin Collection included this description of lot 1106: "1849-D. The D directly above fraction bar. Very Fine. Very rare." Realized $6.50. In May 1913 the U.S. Coin Co. sale of the Malcolm N. Jackson Collection included lot 261: "1849-D D over fraction bar. Extremely Fine. Mint lustre." Realized $5.10. In May 1915 B. Max Mehl's catalog of the B.W. Smith Collection included this description of lot 304: "1849-D D over bar. A pin-point nick on reverse edge. Extremely Fine, mint luster. Rare." Realized $2.75. The Stack's sale of the J.F. Bell Collection in December 1944 included lot 216: "1849-D About Uncirculated." Realized $12.50. Mehl's sale of the Jerome Kern Collection in May 1950 included lot 140: "1849 D. Extremely Fine. Catalogs $12.50 in Very Fine." Realized $15.75.

VF-20	EF-40	AU-50	AU-55	MS-60	MS-62	MS-63
$2,000	$2,750	$3,750	$5,500	$14,000	$25,000	—

1850

Circulation-Strike Mintage: 252,923

Proof Mintage: 2 or 3 (estimated)

Estimated Total Population (Mint State). 50 to 100. While most are in lower Mint State ranges, a few choice and gem pieces exist. One of the more plentiful Mint State varieties among early quarter eagles.

Among the more plentiful $2.50 gold coins of the era.

Estimated Total Population (Circulated Grades). 1,000 to 2,000. Common. Usually seen in Very Fine or Extremely Fine grade, less often About Uncirculated. This is a very common coin in worn grades.

Die Data. *1850 four-digit date logotype:* The date is in larger numerals than the preceding year, but is still small enough to permit easy placement between the denticles and bust. The date is fairly widely spaced: 18 is closest, 85 is slightly wider, and 50 is wider yet. The digit 1 is thin with wide serifs. The 8 is wide with unusually large interior spaces, the top interior space being as large as the bottom. The 5 is of the italic style with the top flag distant from the bottom curve, the ball separated from the upright (except on deep impressions), and with the ball extending slightly to the left of the upright. The 5 is very slightly low and the 0 is lower yet and leaning right, with a large interior space, nicely rounded at the top, and somewhat irregularly rounded at the bottom interior. This logotype was used on all dies of all mints.

Many dies were used, and thus multiple varieties exist, most notable in the position of the date logotype.

Characteristics of Striking and Die Notes. Generally well struck, although there are minor exceptions. Most pieces are from normally basined dies; the Bass II coin, Lot 425, had flat fields.

The "Thin Numerals" variety (Breen-6205) is simply from a relapped die, not from a different logotype. Thin numerals can be created in one of two ways: By lightly punching the four-digit date logotype into the working die, or by relapping or grinding away the surface of the working die, thus reducing the mass of the numerals.

Selected Auction Records

The catalog of John W. Haseltine's June 1883 sale of the William J. Jenks Collection described lot 455: "1850 Uncirculated. Scarce." Realized $3. In his 1907 fixed-price list Elmer S. Sears offered lot 243: "1850 Uncirculated, handsome little coin in almost full mint bloom. $7." In his November 1939 sale of the William B. Hale Collection, B. Max Mehl described lot 775: "1850 Variety with die break on reverse at R in AMERICA. Extremely Fine. Rare." Realized $6.30. In April 1956 Abe Kosoff's sale of the Melish and Hester Collections included lot 1191: "1850 Uncirculated." Realized $18.50.

Proofs

A Proof *may have been* included in a set produced for the Congressional Committee on the Library (cf. a letter by Mint Director Robert Maskell Patterson, September 26, 1850, which mentions coins were sent; Walter Breen has assumed these were Proofs). This piece is not traced today. No example was retained for the Mint Cabinet.

Estimated Total Population (Proof). 1 verified. The only one known to the writer is the specimen believed to have been found in Europe by Marc Emory in 1980 or 1981.

Selected Proof Auction Record

In June 1885 W. Elliot Woodward's sale of the J. Colvin Randall Collection included lot 996: "1850 Brilliant Proof; scarce." Realized $4.25. The present status of the Randall coin is not known.

VF-20	EF-40	AU-50	AU-55	MS-60	MS-62	MS-63
$500	$525	$550	$575	$1,000	$2,500	$3,750

1850-C

Circulation-Strike Mintage: 9,148

Scarce in any grade.
Incredibly rare in Mint State.

Estimated Total Population (Mint State). 2 to 4. These few are at lower levels.

Estimated Total Population (Circulated Grades). 100 to 150. Most are in the Very Fine or Extremely Fine categories.

Die Data. *1850 four-digit date logotype: See the Philadelphia Mint listing for this year.*

Three pairs of dies were sent to Charlotte for this coinage, but it seems that not all were used.

Characteristics of Striking and Die Notes. Usually lightly struck at the center of the reverse, especially at the eagle's leg at the left. Planchet quality is usually low.

Dr. John McCloskey: "[A certain reverse die] was used for three years to strike 1849-C, 1850-C and 1851-C quarter eagles. This C mintmark is located far to the left over the 1 in the fraction. This reverse becomes badly clashed during the striking of 1850-C coins and the clash marks are still visible on 1851-C coins."[73] However, there are exceptions with 1851-C, and an example in the Bowers and Merena Galleries Rarities Sale (July 2002) had such marks that were, if present, barely discernible at best.

Selected Auction Records

In his 1907 fixed-price list Elmer S. Sears offered lot 245: "1850 Charlotte mint, with mint mark placed over figure 1 of fraction. Very choice. Nearly Uncirculated, with bloom. Rare. $17." Lot 247: "1850 Another, but mint mark placed over dividing line of fraction. Absolutely Uncirculated example of bright yellow gold, with semi-Proof surface and the only specimen of the variety that I have ever seen. Must be seen to be appreciated. $50." In May 1913 the U.S. Coin Co. sale of the Malcolm N. Jackson Collection included lot 283: "1850-C Extremely Fine and very rare." Realized $3.25. In May 1915 B. Max Mehl's catalog of the B.W. Smith Collection included this description of lot 295: "1850-C C over 1 of fraction. Fine. Very scarce." Realized $2.80.

In June 1946 Mehl's sale of the William Cutler Atwater Collection included lot 2031: "1850-C Nearly Uncirculated with considerable semi-Proof surface. Record $25." Realized $21. Mehl's sale of the Jerome Kern Collection in May 1950 included lot 125: "1850 C. Mint letter C over 1 of fraction. Uncirculated, frosty mint surface. Catalogs $25.00." Realized $27.50. In Abe Kosoff's sale of the Melish and Hester Collections, April 1956, this was the description of lot 1192: "1850-C. C is over 1 in fraction. Extremely Fine." Realized $22.

VF-20	EF-40	AU-50	AU-55	MS-60	MS-62	MS-63
$1,500	$2,500	$3,500	$5,000	$12,500	$25,000	$35,000

1850-D

Circulation-Strike Mintage: 12,148

Incredibly rare in Mint State.

Deliveries were as follows: January, 1,610; February, 1,877; April, 1,557; August, 1,806; September, 2,325; November, 1,682; and December, 1,291. Assay coins were not recorded.

Estimated Total Population (Mint State). 2 to 4. These are at lower levels.

Estimated Total Population (Circulated Grades). 200 to 300. Very Fine and Extremely Fine are typical grades, although quite a few About Uncirculated coins are listed in catalogs of major collections.

Die Data. *1850 four-digit date logotype: See the Philadelphia Mint listing for this year.*

Three obverse and three reverse dies were sent from Philadelphia at an unknown time and arrived in Dahlonega by January 3, 1850.[74] On January 13, 1851, three obverse dies were defaced at the mint. Nine reverse dies remained on hand for further use.

Only one die pair has been identified: The obverse has the date far too high and left, piercing the neck of Miss Liberty and distant from the denticles.

Reverse die used on all Dahlonega quarter eagles from 1849 to 1859: See description under 1849-D on pages 220–221.

Characteristics of Striking and Die Notes. Examples are lightly struck at the center of the reverse and usually have weak denticles and borders, although variations exist, no doubt from the different production runs. Planchet quality is usually low.

Late in its life the obverse die was relapped.

Selected Auction Records

In his 1907 fixed-price list Elmer S. Sears offered lot 248: "1850 Dahlonega Mint. Uncirculated, handsome specimen with mint bloom. Exceedingly rare. $20." Thomas L. Elder's March 1911 sale of the William H. Woodin Collection included this description of lot 1107: "1850-D. The D high above bar point. Fine. Very rare." Realized $4. In May 1915 B. Max Mehl's catalog of the B.W. Smith Collection included this description of lot 305: "1850-D D over bar. Extremely Fine, sharp, with considerable mint luster." Realized $2.75. The Stack's sale of the J.F. Bell Collection in December 1944 included lot 217: "1850-D Brilliant Uncirculated." Realized $27.50. In June 1946 Mehl's sale of the William Cutler Atwater Collection included lot 2050: "1850-D Practically Uncirculated with full mint luster; bold impression. Quite rare so choice." Realized $8.

VF-20	EF-40	AU-50	AU-55	MS-60	MS-62	MS-63
$1,600	$2,750	$3,750	$5,500	$12,500	$22,500	$40,000

1850-O

Circulation-Strike Mintage: 84,000

Notably rare in Mint State.

Gold was aplenty in New Orleans, a secondary minting destination for metal brought from California, thus reactivating the quarter eagle denomination—which had not been coined in New Orleans since 1847.

As a general rule, *any* New Orleans quarter eagle at the MS-63 or higher level is a fantastic rarity.

Estimated Total Population (Mint State). 20 to 30.

Estimated Total Population (Circulated Grades). 250 to 400, possibly more. The mintage is quite large, and yet the supply of available specimens is unusually small. Most are in the Very Fine level, indicating that this issue circulated extensively. However, a fair number of About Uncirculated pieces have appeared in auctions during the past several decades.

Die Data. *1850 four-digit date logotype: See the Philadelphia Mint listing for this year.*

Four obverse dies were prepared for the 1850-O coinage. Eighteen reverses from earlier years remained on hand.

Characteristics of Striking and Die Notes. Lightly struck at the centers, although there are some exceptions.

Selected Auction Records

In his 1907 fixed-price list Elmer S. Sears offered these: Lot 249: "1850 New Orleans mint, with mint mark placed over 1 of fraction. Very Fine. Scarce. $6." Lot 250: "1850 Another, with mint mark placed over 2 of fraction. Very Fine and very rare variety. $10." Thomas L. Elder's March 1911 sale of the William H. Woodin Collection included these: Lot 1048: "1850-O. Date close to bust, figure 1 touching it; O between 2 and dividing fraction, and not close. Fine." Realized $2.50 (face value). Lot 1049: "1850-O. Date away from bust; the O between second 2 and D. Fine." Realized $2.50 (face value). Lot 1050: "1850-O. Date close to bust. O touches claw. Fine." Realized $2.60. In May 1913 the U.S. Coin Co. sale of the Malcolm N. Jackson Collection included lot 212: "1850-O Date higher. O over 2 in fraction. Extremely Fine." Realized $3.

In May 1915 B. Max Mehl's catalog of the B.W. Smith Collection included this description of lot 315: "1850-O O over 2 of fraction. Extremely Fine." Realized $3. The Stack's sale of the J.F. Bell Collection in December 1944 included lot 234: "1850-O Brilliant Uncirculated." Realized $22.50. In June 1946 Mehl's sale of the William Cutler Atwater Collection included lot 2066: "1850-O Uncirculated. Scarce so choice." Realized $13.50. In Abe Kosoff's sale of the Melish and Hester Collections, April 1956, these were included: Lot 1195: "1850-O. O is over 1 and fraction bar. Very Fine." Realized $13." Lot 1196: "1850-O. O is over 2 infraction. Very Fine." Realized $12. Realized $13. Lot 1197: "1850-O. O is over 2 but date closer to bust. Very Fine." Realized $11.50.

VF-20	EF-40	AU-50	AU-55	MS-60	MS-62	MS-63
$500	$550	$1,000	$1,500	$4,000	$8,500	$20,000

1851

Circulation-Strike Mintage: 1,372,748

Proof Mintage: None known

Plentiful in the context of this era.

In the entire quarter eagle series of 1796 to 1929, only four issues had a mintage of over 1,000,000 coins: 1851, 1852, 1853, and 1861. The three earlier dates were produced when California gold was available in quantity, while the 1861 quarter eagles were struck from melted-down coins of earlier times, including Type I (Coronet or Liberty Head) gold dollars.

Estimated Total Population (Mint State). 100 to 200. Most Mint State 1851 quarter eagles are in lower grade levels. Any coin of choice or gem quality is a prize, with gems being exceedingly rare.

Estimated Total Population (Circulated Grades). 2,000 to 4,000. This is considered a common date, though relatively few 1851 quarter eagles have been certified.

Die Data. *1851 four-digit date logotype:* The numerals are fairly large and widely separated, the most widely separated of any recent quarter eagle date. The 18 is closest, 85 is slightly wider, and 51 is slightly wider yet, but the differences are slight. The top and bottom interiors of 8 are open, and the numeral is wide and leans slightly right. The 5 is italic style as in 1850, a very "open" and eye-pleasing arrangement. The logotype was sufficiently large that some care was needed to place it on the working die, sometimes resulting in the first and last digits touching an element above or below. This logotype was used on all dies of all mints.

This item in the personal diary of James B. Longacre indicates that, presumably, five different sizes of date logotypes for the 1851 coinage were prepared by an outside engraver, W. Dougherty, who had done other work for the Mint:[75] "*Saturday, August 31, 1850:* Certified W. Dougherty's bill to mint U.S. for 5 date punches for 1851, $4 each, $20."

Ten obverse and nine reverse dies were made available for use this year, and many were actually employed. Thus, they probably never will all be identified or cataloged.

Characteristics of Striking and Die Notes. Multiple dies were used, and thus sharpness varies from one die and press run to another. Examples are sometimes seen with weak definition at the left side of the reverse.

Selected Auction Records

The catalog of John W. Haseltine's June 1883 sale of the William J. Jenks Collection described lot 456: "1851 Uncirculated. Scarce." Realized $3. In his September 1885 sale of the J. Colvin Randall Collection, W. Elliot Woodward offered lot 1087: "1851 Nearly Proof, doubtless false, but bought for genuine in the Fowle Sale." Realized 40¢. An interesting description; apparently it was not a false *Proof,* but an overall counterfeit—or else it would have realized at least face value. In his 1907 fixed-price list Elmer S. Sears offered lot 251: "1851 Uncirculated example, with handsome mint lustre. Nice. $7.50." Thomas

L. Elder's March 1911 sale of the William H. Woodin Collection included these: Lot 981: "1851. Yellow gold, first 1 touching bust, last 1 away from rim. Break from last 1. Mint bloom." Realized $5.70. Three other coins in circulated grades each sold for face value.

In his 1907 fixed-price list Elmer S. Sears offered lot 251: "1851 Uncirculated example, with handsome mint lustre. Nice. $7.50." In May 1913 the U.S. Coin Co. sale of the Malcolm N. Jackson Collection included lot 137: "1851 Uncirculated." Realized $2.75. In June 1941 B. Max Mehl's sale of the William Forrester Dunham Collection included lot 1948: "1851 Uncirculated; yellow gold. Full mint luster. Not a rare date but quite rare so choice." Realized $5. The Stack's sale of the J.F. Bell Collection in December 1944 included lot 118: "1851 Brilliant Uncirculated." Realized $9. In Abe Kosoff's sale of the Melish and Hester Collections, April 1956, these were offered: Lot 1198: "1851. Date high, first 1 touches bust; crack connects 1851. Very Fine." Realized $12.50. Lot 1199: "1851. Date lower, 1 does not touch bust but touches a denticles. About Extremely Fine." Realized $14.

VF-20	EF-40	AU-50	AU-55	MS-60	MS-62	MS-63
$500	$515	$525	$535	$550	$750	$1,100

1851-C

Circulation-Strike Mintage: 14,923

Scarce in any grade.
Incredibly rare in Mint State.

Of the total mintage, 12 coins were reserved to send to the Assay Commission.

Estimated Total Population (Mint State). 2 to 4. This is a major rarity by any standard. All are in lower grade ranges. The go-around whereby the same coins are often sent again and again to the grading services, with the result that a single specimen can "expand" and occupy multiple listings, does not make it easy to estimate the population. This, of course, is a problem in just about every other area of numismatics where high grade and high value are coincident.

Estimated Total Population (Circulated Grades). 75 to 125. The 1851-C is quite scarce in worn grades, but enough exist that every specialist can find a nice one, such as Extremely Fine or the occasional About Uncirculated. The typically encountered 1851-C is Very Fine. Such pieces saw extensive use in commerce in the region in which they were minted.

Die Data. *1851 four-digit date logotype: See the Philadelphia Mint listing for this year.*

Three pairs of dies were sent to Charlotte for this coinage.

It is believed that just one pair of dies was used. The date logotype is lightly impressed into the die. It is centered quite far left, with the tip of 1 embedded into the neck truncation. The lower left serif of 1 is barely separated from the denticle, but seemingly connected to it with a very light die line. The reverse has the C mintmark placed high and into the claw. The tip of the arrow feather touches the lower right of C, below the opening, indicating a particularly high position; this die also used in 1849 and 1850.

Characteristics of Striking and Die Notes. "[A certain reverse die] was used for three years to strike 1849-C, 1850-C and 1851-C quarter eagles. This C mintmark is located far to the left over the 1 in the fraction. This reverse becomes badly clashed during the striking of 1850-C coins and the clash marks are still visible on 1851-C coins."[76]

The usual coin has some lightness of striking at the highest area of Miss Liberty's hair. The reverse die nearly always shows evidence of rust, but there are exceptions.

Selected Auction Records

Thomas L. Elder's March 1911 sale of the William H. Woodin Collection included this description of lot 1127: "1851-C Very Fine. Very rare." Realized $5.75. B. Max Mehl's February 1944 catalog of the sale of the Belden E. Roach Collection described lot 964: "1851-C Uncirculated. Very scarce." Realized $21. The Stack's sale of the J.F. Bell Collection in December 1944 included lot 200: "1851-C About Uncirculated." Realized $20. The Will W. Neil Collection sold by Mehl in June 1947 included lot 2504: "1851-C Nearly Uncirculated with considerable mint luster. Rare so choice." Realized $11.25. Mehl's sale of the Jerome Kern Collection in May 1950 included lot 126: "1851 C. Nearly Uncirculated with frosty mint surface." Realized $21.

VF-20	EF-40	AU-50	AU-55	MS-60	MS-62	MS-63
$1,500	$2,450	$3,750	$4,500	$8,500	$15,000	$35,000

1851-D

Circulation-Strike Mintage: 11,264

Scarce in any grade.
Exceedingly rare in Mint State.

Deliveries were reported as follows: February, 1,731; March, 1,952; May, 787; June, 2,626; July, 1,912; and August, 2,256. Assay coins were not recorded.

Estimated Total Population (Mint State). 3 to 5. These are mostly lower range specimens. In 1975 David W. Akers wrote that as of that time he had never seen a Mint State coin (this being before the Eliasberg coin came on the market in 1982). It is probably the case that some called "Mint State" today were called About Uncirculated years ago.

Estimated Total Population (Circulated Grades). 90 to 130. Very scarce in all grades. Very Fine and Extremely Fine grades are usually seen, although About Uncirculated specimens occasionally come on the market.

Die Data. *1851 four-digit date logotype: See the Philadelphia Mint listing for this year.*

Three obverse dies were sent from Philadelphia as part of shipments from December 9 to 13, 1850, and arrived in Dahlonega in the period from December 18, 1850, to January 4, 1851.[77] On January 3, 1852, the three 1851 obverse dies were defaced at the mint. On hand for further use were nine reverse dies. However, only one reverse die was used.

Reverse die used on all Dahlonega quarter eagles from 1849 to 1859: See description under 1849-D on pages 220–221.

Characteristics of Striking and Die Notes. Examples are usually lightly struck on the denticles and to the left on the eagle on the reverse, although there are exceptions, and a few are sharply struck.

Selected Auction Records

In his 1907 fixed-price list Elmer S. Sears offered lot 254: "1851 Dahlonega Mint. Almost if not quite Uncirculated, with mint bloom. A very choice example of one of the rare mint marked quarter eagles. $20." Thomas L. Elder's March 1911 sale of the William H. Woodin Collection included this description of lot 1108: "1851-D. The D above bar point. Fine. Rare." Realized $4.25. In May 1913 the U.S. Coin Co. sale of the Malcolm N. Jackson Collection included lot 263: "1851-D Extremely Fine, mint luster, rare." Realized $4.75. B. Max Mehl's February 1944 catalog of the sale of the Belden E. Roach Collection described lot 993: "1851-D Extremely Fine; sharp." Realized $13.25. The Stack's sale of the J.F. Bell Collection in December 1944 included lot 218: "1851-D Brilliant Uncirculated." Realized $20. The Will W. Neil Collection sold by Mehl in June 1947 included lot 2520: "1851-D About Uncirculated with mint luster. Scarce." Realized $10.50.

VF-20	EF-40	AU-50	AU-55	MS-60	MS-62	MS-63
$1,650	$2,600	$4,000	$5,500	$11,500	$20,000	$32,500

1851-O

Circulation-Strike Mintage: 148,000

Incredibly rare in Mint State.

Gold was aplenty in New Orleans, a secondary minting destination for metal brought from California.

Estimated Total Population (Mint State). 4 to 6, mostly in lower grades. This issue is extremely rare in Mint State, but largely unrecognized as such, as, unlike the situation for Charlotte and Dahlonega coins, relatively few specialists concentrate upon New Orleans issues. This is a good situation for those who do, for high grade O-Mint quarter eagles can hold their own with any others of their era, including the generally lower mintage C and D coins.

Estimated Total Population (Circulated Grades). 200 to 400. The 1851-O is under-represented in grading service data. It is fairly scarce in all grades, this being true of nearly all New Orleans Mint quarter eagles. Very Fine is the usually seen grade, this also being true of most quarter eagles from this mint.

Die Data. *1851 four-digit date logotype: See the Philadelphia Mint listing for this year.*

Eight obverse and four reverse dies were sent to New Orleans for this coinage, in anticipation of a generous production.

Multiple dies were used. One often-seen variety has a repunched date, with the earlier date being slightly low and slightly left of the final date figures. Actually, two different variations on the repunched date have been described.[78] An example in the Bowers and Merena Galleries sale of March 2003 showed especially prominent traces of the earlier-punched final 1 and clear vestiges of the 8 and 5, but no doubling on the first 1. The original date slanted down to the right and was repunched to make it more level.

Characteristics of Striking and Die Notes. Examples are usually well struck on the obverse, and on the reverse lightly struck on portions of the eagle.

Selected Auction Records

In his 1907 fixed-price list Elmer S. Sears offered lot 255: "1851 New Orleans Mint. About Uncirculated. $6." S.H. Chapman's June 1909 sale of the Henry L. Jewett Collection included lot 897: "1851 New Orleans mint. Very Fine." Realized $2.70. Thomas L. Elder's March 1911 sale of the William H. Woodin Collection included this description of lot 1051: "1851-O. Extremely Fine." Realized $2.50 (face value). In May 1915 B. Max Mehl's catalog of the B.W. Smith Collection included this description of lot 316: "1851-O O over bar. Very Fine." Realized $3. Mehl's February 1944 catalog of the sale of the Belden E. Roach Collection described lot 978: "1851-O Nearly Uncirculated with brilliant luster. A very slight die depression on reverse to right of eagle." Realized $11.50.

The Stack's sale of the J.F. Bell Collection in December 1944 included lot 235: "1851-O Brilliant Uncirculated." Realized $12.50. In June 1946 Mehl's sale of the William Cutler Atwater Collection included lot 2067: "1851-O Just About Uncirculated with considerable mint luster. Recent record for an only Very Fine one, $15." Realized $7.50. The Will W. Neil Collection sold by Mehl in June 1947 included lot 2529: "1851-O O directly over fraction. Extremely Fine." Realized $8. Abe Kosoff's sale of the Melish and Hester Collections, April 1956, offered two: Lot 1202: "1851-O. O is over center of fraction. About Extremely Fine." Realized $14. Lot 1203: "1851-O. O is a bit left over fraction. Very Fine." Realized $13. In June 1957 the New Netherlands sale of Eliasberg duplicates had this for lot 607: "1851-O. 'Double date'-traces of a second date below the first, slanting down to right, mostly effaced. First published in our last sale. Very Fine and lustrous, a single pinpoint nick in the right obv. field." Realized $16.

VF-20	EF-40	AU-50	AU-55	MS-60	MS-62	MS-63
$500	$575	$800	$1,350	$4,000	$7,000	$11,500

1852

Plentiful in most grades.

Circulation-Strike Mintage: 1,159,681
Proof Mintage: None known

In the entire quarter eagle series from 1796 to 1929, only four issues had a mintage of over 1,000,000 coins: 1851, 1852, 1853, and 1861. The three earlier dates were produced when California gold was available in quantity, while the 1861 quarter eagles were struck from melted-down coins of earlier times, including Type I (Coronet or Liberty Head) gold dollars.

Estimated Total Population (Mint State). 200 to 400. Examples are easily available, although most are in lower grade ranges. However, enough choice and gem pieces exist that there will be no trouble in finding one. The typical Mint State 1852 is very lustrous and frosty, a thoroughly attractive quarter eagle.

Estimated Total Population (Circulated Grades). 3,000 to 5,000. Very Fine and Extremely Fine are the usual grades, but hundreds of About Uncirculated coins exist. This common date is grossly under-represented in the grading service data.

Die Data. *1852 four-digit date logotype:* The numerals are fairly widely spaced and nicely arranged. The 18 and 52 are about the same distance apart, and 85 is ever so slightly closer; the base of 2 is low. The top interior of 8 is slightly smaller than its bottom interior. The 5 is of the italic style, from a different numeral punch than used in the preceding year, with the flag far above the curve below, and the ball distant from the upright; the left side of the upright, if extended below, would graze the left side of the ball. The 2 is heavy at the right and bottom, with a rather small knob close to the diagonal and a curved base. This logotype was used on all dies of all mints.

Eleven obverse and ten reverse dies were prepared for this coinage, and multiple pairs were actually used. Several logotype position varieties have been seen.

Characteristics of Striking and Die Notes. The strike varies depending upon the die combination and production run. Often, there is some light striking at the reverse on the eagle's leg beyond the lower left of the shield—this being the point in the die opposite the highest relief portion of the obverse, creating a demand for metal flow in both directions.

Selected Auction Records

Note: There are so many Mint State listings that only a few can be given here.

The catalog of John W. Haseltine's June 1883 sale of the William J. Jenks Collection described lot 457: "1852 Uncirculated. Scarce." Realized $3. In his 1907 fixed-price list Elmer S. Sears offered lot 256: "1852 Uncirculated (copper alloy). Brilliant mint bloom. $6." Thomas L. Elder's March 1911 sale of the William H. Woodin Collection included these: Lot 986: "1852. Silver alloy, 1 off bust.[79] Mint State." Realized $2.60. Lot 987: "1852. Figure 1 very close to bust. Extremely Fine." Realized $2.60. Lot 988: "1852. Yellow gold, figure 1 away from bust. Extremely Fine." Realized $2.60. In his November 1939 sale of the William B. Hale Collection, B. Max Mehl described lot 778: "1852 Uncirculated, frosty mint luster." Realized $4.25.

In June 1946 Mehl's sale of the William Cutler Atwater Collection included lot 1956: "1852 Uncirculated with frosty mint surface. Catalogs and sells at $10." Realized $10.50. Mehl's sale of the Jerome Kern Collection in May 1950 included lot 42: "1852 Uncirculated." Realized $10. In October 1951 the Numismatic Gallery sale of the B.A. Talmadge collection included lot 1110: "1852 Uncirculated. Choice." Realized $10.

VF-20	EF-40	AU-50	AU-55	MS-60	MS-62	MS-63
$500	$515	$525	$535	$550	$800	$1,100

1852-C

Circulation-Strike Mintage: 9,772

Scarce in any grade.
Incredibly rare in Mint State.

Estimated Total Population (Mint State). 2 to 5. The data are inconsistent. A few Mint State specimens are said to have been found in a Southern hoard that came to light in May 1986, but the writer has no specific information.[80] Apart from this group, the population is probably 2 or 3.

Estimated Total Population (Circulated Grades). 70 to 110. Very Fine is the typical grade seen, although Extremely Fine and, occasionally, About Uncirculated pieces are seen. A key issue by any standard.

Die Data. *1852 four-digit date logotype: See the Philadelphia Mint listing for this year.*

Three pairs of dies were sent to Charlotte in anticipation of this coinage.

On the 1852-C the date logotype is placed somewhat left and slightly closer to the neck truncation than to a denticle. The first two digits are repunched at the bottom, the third digit less so.

The same reverse die was used to strike 1852-C, 1854-C, and 1855-C quarter eagles, to the exclusion of any other die(s). The C is very close to the numerator 1 in the fraction and touches the fraction bar. The tip of the arrow feather pierces the upper curve of the C and is seen within it.[81]

Characteristics of Striking and Die Notes. Examples are usually lightly struck on the highest part of the hair on the obverse and on portions of the eagle.

David W. Akers commented (1975): "Many specimens show a distinct wire rim. Whereas on many coins, a wire rim denotes a sharp strike, the wire rim that is seen on many C Mint coins is not the result of a strong strike but rather the result of improperly matched dies and collars."

Selected Auction Records

Thomas L. Elder's March 1911 sale of the William H. Woodin Collection included this description of lot 1128: "1852-C. Fine. Very scarce, and coinage small." Realized $3.50. In May 1915 B. Max Mehl's catalog of the B.W. Smith Collection included this description of lot 296: "1852-C C over 1 and bar. Fine. Scarce." Realized $2.80. Mehl's sale of the Jerome Kern Collection in May 1950 included lot 127: "1852 C. Extremely Fine with some luster. Not rare, but scarce so choice." Realized $21.50.

VF-20	EF-40	AU-50	AU-55	MS-60	MS-62	MS-63
$1,500	$2,500	$4,000	$5,500	$10,000	$21,000	$35,000

1852-D

Circulation-Strike Mintage: 4,078

Elusive in any grade.
Exceedingly rare in Mint State.

Deliveries were reported as follows: January, 2,061; and April, 2,017. Assay coins not recorded. Although half eagles were coined each month, gold dollars and quarter eagles were coined only in January and April.

In contrast to the trend evidenced in immediately preceding years, the mintage of the 1852-D dips to a low level, just 4,078. From this point to the end of the Dahlonega series, quarter eagle mintages are very small.

Estimated Total Population (Mint State). 4 to 6. A major rarity in any Mint State grade, and "any" means MS-60 to MS-62. No gems are known. For this and other low-population Dahlonega (and Charlotte) rarities the data are inconsistent, as in response to the demand for Mint State issues, it seems that some erstwhile About Uncirculated coins are now "Mint State." In collecting such pieces, a degree of connoisseurship is useful, as it is better to buy the coin than the holder, although the writer fully recognizes that there are many buyers who would rather have an ugly coin certified as MS-60 than a sharp, attractive coin certified as AU-58.

Estimated Total Population (Circulated Grades). 80 to 120. This issue is very scarce. Very Fine and Extremely Fine coins are the norm, although a few exist above and below this range.

Die Data. *1852 four-digit date logotype: See the Philadelphia Mint listing for this year.*

One obverse and one reverse die were sent from Philadelphia on December 8, 1851; another pair was sent on December 12; and another pair on an unrecorded day the same month.[82] The three obverse and three reverse dies arrived in Dahlonega by January 1, 1852. On January 17, 1853, the three 1852-dated obverse dies were defaced at the mint. Twelve usable reverses remained on hand, all but one of which were redundant.

On the obverse the date is very high and about three times closer to the neck truncation than to the denticles. There is a raised die line from the border through star 3.

Reverse die used on all Dahlonega quarter eagles from 1849 to 1859: See description under 1849-D on pages 220–221.

Characteristics of Striking and Die Notes. Examples are usually lightly struck on the highest hair areas and on the eagle, although exceptions exist.

Selected Auction Records

In his 1907 fixed-price list Elmer S. Sears offered lot 259: "1852 Dahlonega Mint. Uncirculated specimen of bright yellow gold and among the rarest of the series. Handsome. $35." Thomas L. Elder's March 1911 sale of the William H. Woodin Collection included this description of lot 1109: "1852-D. Large D, over arrow, above bar. About Uncirculated. Excessively rare. Not in any recent sale." Realized $16. In May 1913 the U.S. Coin Co. sale of the Malcolm N. Jackson Collection included lot 264: "1852-D Very Fine and extremely rare." Realized $42. The elusive nature of the

1852-D was widely recognized in the early twentieth century, in contrast to most other branch mint issues. In May 1915 B. Max Mehl's catalog of the B.W. Smith Collection included this description of lot 306: "1852-D Only Very Good but extremely rare. One of our rarest mint mark quarter eagles. Record over $50." Realized $32.

In his November 1939 sale of the William B. Hale Collection, Mehl described lot 853: "1852-D Beautiful Uncirculated specimen, with full mint luster. Rare in any condition, but excessively rare so choice. From the famous Woodin Sale." Realized $20. Elder called this coin "About Uncirculated" in the Woodin catalog. It seems that gradeflation is not a new situation. Mehl's February 1944 catalog of the sale of the Belden E. Roach Collection described lot 994: "1852-D Very Fine; in fact extremely so, but there seems to have been something removed from the center obverse, probably some solder. But it is hardly noticeable. It is a most acceptable specimen of this rarity."[83] Realized $18.75. The Stack's sale of the J.F. Bell Collection in December 1944 included lot 219: "1852-D Brilliant Uncirculated. Scarce." Realized $45. In June 1946 Mehl's sale of the William Cutler Atwater Collection included lot 2052: "1852-D Just a shade from Uncirculated with considerable mint luster. Tiny die depression on upper reverse left border. Record of $50." Realized $47.50. Mehl's sale of the Jerome Kern Collection in May 1950 included lot 143: "1852 D. Uncirculated. Not a particularly rare date, but in this beautiful condition I consider it very rare. Full mint luster. Catalogs at $50. Has a record for that amount and certainly worth it." Realized $50.

VF-20	EF-40	AU-50	AU-55	MS-60	MS-62	MS-63
$1,850	$3,250	$6,250	$8,000	$17,000	$30,000	$45,000

1852-O

Circulation-Strike Mintage: 140,000

Incredibly rare in Mint State.

Gold continued to be plentiful in New Orleans, a secondary minting destination for metal brought from California.

Estimated Total Population (Mint State). 2 to 4. The 1852-O is extremely rare in Mint State. When seen, which is not very often, the typical specimen is apt to be around MS-60 and might be called "AU" by the next observer. In his collecting career of 30+ years, Harry W. Bass Jr. was never able to buy a specimen that he considered to be Mint State!

Estimated Total Population (Circulated Grades). 300 to 400. It is considered by some to be a "common date" and thus fairly well ignored. As is par for New Orleans quarter eagles of this era, the usually seen grade is Very Fine. Only occasionally do Extremely Fine coins appear, and only infrequently are About Uncirculated specimens available.

Die Data. *1852 four-digit date logotype: See the Philadelphia Mint listing for this year.*

Six obverse dies were sent to New Orleans for this coinage, but it is not known if all were used. Adequate reverses were on hand from earlier times.

One reverse die has the O mintmark heavy and irregular; perhaps it was added by hand in New Orleans to a die that arrived with the mintmark omitted in error.

Characteristics of Striking and Die Notes. Examples are usually fairly well struck.

Selected Auction Records

In his 1907 fixed-price list Elmer S. Sears offered lot 260: "1852 New Orleans Mint. Mint mark over dividing line of fraction. Very Fine, with semi-Proof surface. $5." His list also offered lot 261: "1852 Another with mint mark placed over figure 1 of fraction. A superb, Uncirculated example with Proof surface. A beauty. Rare. $10."

Thomas L. Elder's March 1911 sale of the William H. Woodin Collection included this trio: Lot 1052: "1852-O Figure 1 just touches bust; the O directly above second 2. Very Fine." Realized $2.60. Lot 1053: "1852-O. The 1 farther away from bust. Top leaf very close to "I", O between 1 and dividing bar. Silver alloy. About. fine." Realized $2.50 (face value). Lot 1054: "1852-O. Fig. 1 away from bust, top leaf farther away from I, O close to, but does not touch, claw. Fine." Realized $2.50 (face value). In May 1913 the U.S. Coin Co. sale of the Malcolm N. Jackson Collection included these: Lot 214: "1852-O O between I and fraction bar. Very Fine." Realized $3. Lot 215: "1852-O Similar. Very Fine." Realized $2.75.

In May 1915 B. Max Mehl's catalog of the B.W. Smith Collection included these: Lot 317: "1852-O O over 1 and bar. Semi Proof. Rare so choice." Realized $4. Lot 318: "1852-O O directly over bar. Fine." Realized $3. The Stack's sale of the J.F. Bell Collection in December 1944 included lot 236: "1852-O Brilliant Uncirculated." Realized $12.50. In June 1946 Mehl's sale of the William Cutler Atwater Collection included lot 2068: "1852-O. A difficult coin to describe its condition. It is almost a semi-proof, but the field shows cabinet friction. I consider it quite rare in this choice condition." Realized $7.50. In Abe Kosoff's sale of the Melish and Hester Collections, April 1956, these were offered: Lot 1207: "1852-O. The O is over the center of the fraction. Very Fine." Realized $13. Lot 1208: "1852-O. Similar but with reverse die breaks. Very Fine." Realized $12.50. Lot 1209: "1852-O. The O is left over the fraction. Fine." Realized $12.

VF-20	EF-40	AU-50	AU-55	MS-60	MS-62	MS-63
$500	$575	$850	$1,000	$4,500	$7,000	$11,000

1853

Circulation-Strike Mintage: 1,404,668
Proof Mintage: None known

Highest mintage of all quarter eagles 1796–1929. Plentiful in all grades.

In the entire quarter eagle series of 1796 to 1929, only four issues had a mintage of over 1,000,000 coins: 1851, 1852, 1853, and 1861. The three earlier dates were produced when California gold was available in quantity, while the 1861 quarter eagles were struck from melted-down coins of earlier times, including Type I (Coronet or Liberty Head) gold dollars. Of these dates, the 1853 had the highest mintage of all.

Estimated Total Population (Mint State). 500 to 800. The 1853 is common in the context of quarter eagles in this era. Available specimens run all the way from MS-60 up to gem.

Paul F. Taglione (*The Quarter Eagles*, 1986): "In 1985, at least 125 Mint State examples were discovered although quite a few were dull, likely from burial. From that group only a small percentage exceeded MS-60." Similarly, Walter Breen (*Encyclopedia*, 1988): "Common Uncirculated, from a hoard said to number at least 500."

Estimated Total Population (Circulated Grades). 5,000 to 8,000. Very Fine and, more often, Extremely Fine are the grades typically seen. Not much attention has ever been paid to these, as they are very plentiful. In fact, just about any unsorted group of pre-Civil War quarter eagles is apt to have multiple examples.

Die Data. *1853 four-digit date logotype:* The numerals are slightly smaller this year. The 18 is closely spaced, the 85 and 53 are wider and each about the same distance apart. The 5 is italic, and the ball is close to the upright and will touch on deep impressions. The 3 is rather irregularly made at the bottom, and somewhat awkward in appearance; the lower ball is slightly flattened and small; the 3 leans slightly right. This logotype was used on all dies of both mints.

Multiple die pairs were used.

Breen-6221 was called an "overdate" by that author: "upper and lower edges of base stroke of 2 plain between 53; ex New Netherlands 54th Sale, Lot 873." Paul F. Taglione:[84] "A tiny number (six which the present author has seen) evidence a hint of a 2 under the 3 in the date and this is sometimes claimed to be an overdate but is not sure."

Characteristics of Striking and Die Notes. Striking varies, but most are fairly sharp.

Selected Auction Records

The catalog of John W. Haseltine's June 1883 sale of the William J. Jenks Collection described lot 458: "1853 Uncirculated. Scarce." Realized $3. In his 1907 fixed-price list Elmer S. Sears offered lot 262: "1853 Magnificent, Uncirculated specimen, with full mint lustre untouched. $8." Thomas L. Elder's March 1911 sale of the William H. Woodin Collection included these coins: Lot 989: "1853. Figure 1 very close to bust, and 3 close to rim. Mint bloom." Realized $2.60. Lot 990: "1853. Figure 1 imperfect and close to bust, figure 3 more distant from rim than last. Uncirculated; rare." Realized $2.50 (face value). Lot 991: "1853. Entire date far below bust but not touching rim, differing from preceding lots. Very Fine." Realized $2.50 (face value).

In June 1941 B. Max Mehl's sale of the William Forrester Dunham Collection included lot 1951: "1853 Bright Uncirculated, with full mint luster." Realized $6. The Stack's sale of the J.F. Bell Collection in December 1944 included lot 120: "1853 Brilliant Uncirculated." Realized $9. In October 1951 the Numismatic Gallery sale of the B.A. Talmadge collection included lot 1111: "1853 Uncirculated. Choice." Realized $11. Abe Kosoff's sale of the Melish and Hester Collections, April 1956, included these circulated coins: Lot 1210: "1853. Low date. Very Fine." Realized $12.50. Lot 1211: "1853. High date, close to bust. Very Fine." Realized $12. Lot 1212: "1853. One touches bust. About Extremely Fine." Realized $14.50.

VF-20	EF-40	AU-50	AU-55	MS-60	MS-62	MS-63
$500	$515	$525	$535	$550	$600	$1,000

1853-D

Circulation-Strike Mintage: 3,178

Scarce in any grade.
Exceedingly rare in Mint State.

Deliveries were as follows: February, 642; July, 1,814; and October, 722. Assay coins were not recorded. Two of the production runs were small. Yearly production was the smallest mintage up to this time in the Dahlonega Mint's history of the denomination.

With the 1853-D, mintage quantities changed dramatically. Production fell to just over 3,000 pieces, beginning a series of low mintages that would last to the end of the Dahlonega quarter eagle series. This was directly the result of depositors not requesting coins of this denomination.

Although California gold bullion had been shipped to Dahlonega for coinage since 1850, in 1853 the high mark was achieved when 79.4% of the metal used for coinage at Dahlonega came from California.

Estimated Total Population (Mint State). 4 to 6. This issue is very rare in Mint State. When seen, such pieces are usually at the low end of the Mint State scale.

Estimated Total Population (Circulated Grades). 70 to 100. Very Fine is the grade usually seen. It is highly prized in *any* grade. The elusive quality of the 1853-D was recognized at an early date, and pieces appearing at auction in the early twentieth century met with an enthusiastic bidder reception.

Die Data. *1853 four-digit date logotype: See the Philadelphia Mint listing for this year.*

Three 1853-dated obverse dies were sent from Philadelphia on December 14, 1852, and arrived in Dahlonega by December 24, 1852.[85] No meaningful records exist to reveal the number of dies defaced and/or carried over for further use at Dahlonega for the coinages of 1853 and later years. However, with regard to the reverse, the point seems moot.

On several specimens observed, on the obverse there are several raised die lines, oriented at an angle, including one from the rim at the left of star 8, continuing to the head, and others from the border at the right, to the hair at the back of the head. On this die the date is far to the left, being squeezed between the neck truncation and the denticles, but with much open space on the right side of the logotype and above and below the right side.

Reverse die used on all Dahlonega quarter eagles from 1849 to 1859: See description under 1849-D on pages 220–221.

Characteristics of Striking and Die Notes. Always with light striking, usually on the higher areas of the obverse and on the denticles.

Selected Auction Records

In his 1907 fixed-price list Elmer S. Sears offered lot 263: "1853 Dahlonega Mint. Excessively rare and one of the scarcest mint marks in the entire collection. Very Fine. $35." In May 1913 the U.S. Coin Co. sale of the Malcolm N. Jackson Collection included lot 265: "1853-D About Uncirculated, brilliant mint luster, extremely rare."

Realized $45. In his November 1939 sale of the William B. Hale Collection, B. Max Mehl described lot 854: "1853-D Uncirculated, with bright mint luster. Very rare in any condition. Listed at $50 in Very Fine. This is one of the finest specimens I have ever seen or handled; it has full raised borders; well centered and boldly stuck. It has full mint luster. Purchased by Mr. Hale in 1910, over a quarter of a century ago, from that old famous dealer and prince of good fellows, the late Elmer S. Sears.[86] In original box as are most of the scarcer items in the collection." Realized $47.50.

Stack's sale of the J.F. Bell Collection in December 1944 included lot 220: "1853-D Brilliant Uncirculated, seldom offered in this condition. Rare." Realized $110. In June 1946 Mehl's sale of the William Cutler Atwater Collection included lot 2053: "1853-D. Uncirculated. Struck in light yellow gold. Rare in any condition, especially so choice. Catalogs at $75 in Very Fine. Recent record $125." Realized $105. Mehl's sale of the Jerome Kern Collection in May 1950 included lot 144: "1853 D. Extremely Fine; nicely struck and well centered. Rare and valuable. A somewhat better specimen in my Atwater Sale brought $105." Realized $115.

VF-20	EF-40	AU-50	AU-55	MS-60	MS-62	MS-63
$2,000	$3,500	$6,000	$7,000	$15,000	$35,000	$50,000

1854

Circulation-Strike Mintage: 596,258
Proof Mintage: 1 to 3 (estimated)

Plentiful for the era.

Estimated Total Population (Mint State). 100 to 175. One of the more available quarter eagles of this era. Examples are mostly in lower ranges, but a number of choice and gem specimens exist.

Estimated Total Population (Circulated Grades). 1,000 to 1,500. Most specimens are in the Very Fine or Extremely Fine range, but About Uncirculated examples are easy to find. As is the case with most high-mintage Philadelphia Mint quarter eagles, the 1854 in worn grades is grossly under-represented in certification data.

Die Data. *1854 four-digit date logotype:* The digits are large and fairly closely spaced, the 54 is nearly touching (and may touch on deep impressions), the 18 is slightly wider, and the 85 is wider yet, but the difference is not particularly noticeable. The top interior of the 8 is the same size as the bottom interior; the 8 leans slightly right. The 5 is of the italic style, with the ball very close to the upright and touching on many logotype impressions. The 4 leans slightly right, the crossbar is flat at the top and pointed at the top and bottom. This logotype was used on all dies of all mints. Multiple die pairs were used, and thus positional varieties exist. One has the tip of the 1 (1854) embedded in the neck truncation.

Characteristics of Striking and Die Notes. Examples are usually sharp, but there are exceptions. One reverse has a massive rim cud on the rim from 8 to 9 o'clock; several examples have been seen.

Selected Auction Records

The catalog of John W. Haseltine's June 1883 sale of the William J. Jenks Collection described lot 459: "1854 Uncirculated. Scarce." Realized $3. In his 1907 fixed-price list Elmer S. Sears offered lot 264: "1854 Uncirculated, or nearly so, with mint lustre. $6." Thomas L. Elder's March 1911 sale of the William H. Woodin Collection had two: Lot 992: "1854. Figures lightly cut, 1 touching bust. Fine." Realized $2.50 (face value). Lot 993: "1854. Heavier cut date figures, 1 touching bust, and date narrower. Very Fine." Realized $2.50 (face value). Lot 994: "1854. Still thicker date figures, the figure 1 barely touching bust. Fine." Realized $2.50 (face value).

In his November 1939 sale of the William B. Hale Collection, B. Max Mehl described lot 780: "1854 Uncirculated, with full mint luster." Realized $4.40. In Abe Kosoff's sale of the Melish and Hester Collections, April 1956, two were described: Lot 1215: "1854. Reverse die breaks connect ITED, etc. About Uncirculated." Realized $14. Lot 1216: 1216: "1854 Incused head of Liberty outlined on reverse. Very Fine." Realized $13. Seemingly from clashed dies.

Proofs

Estimated Total Population (Proof). 1 confirmed (Harry W. Bass Jr. Collection).

Proof Die Data and Notes. A specimen in the Bass Foundation holdings (ex the Stack's 1976 ANA sale) has the date logotype high with the 1 (1854) close to but not quite touching the neck. On the reverse there is mounding in the field near the arrowheads.

VF-20	EF-40	AU-50	AU-55	MS-60	MS-62	MS-63
$500	$515	$525	$535	$575	$700	$1,250

1854-C

Circulation-Strike Mintage: 7,295

Scarce in any grade.
Incredibly rare in Mint State.

Estimated Total Population (Mint State). 2 to 4. This issue is exceedingly rare.

Estimated Total Population (Circulated Grades). 70 to 100. The 1854-C is typically encountered in Very Fine grade. Higher level specimens are very elusive.

Die Data. 1854 *four-digit date logotype: See the Philadelphia Mint listing for this year.*

Three obverse dies were sent from Philadelphia, but apparently only one die was used. Enough reverses were on hand from earlier times that no new ones were needed. All known 1854-C quarter eagles are from a single die pair and were struck to the extent of 7,295 examples. The date logotype is high, with the peak of the 1 piercing the neck truncation.

The same reverse die was used to strike 1852-C, 1854-C, and 1855-C quarter eagles, to the exclusion of any other die(s). The C is very close to the numerator 1 in the fraction and touches the fraction bar. The tip of the arrow feather pierces the upper curve of the C and is seen within it.[87]

Characteristics of Striking and Die Notes. Obverse striking varies from strong to weak, indicating different press runs. Most have some areas of light striking, particularly on the eagle. The reverse is usually weak at the centers. The dies clash, and later strikings show evidence of this. Some have wire rims from mismatching of the dies and collar (also see the comment under 1852-C, page 232).

Selected Auction Records

In his 1907 fixed-price list Elmer S. Sears offered lot 266: "1854 Charlotte Mint. Uncirculated specimen of one of the rarities. Very choice and exceedingly difficult to obtain at any price. $25." Thomas L. Elder's March 1911 sale of the William H. Woodin Collection included this description of lot 1129: "1854-C. As the number coined was only 7,000, the piece is rare. About Fine." Realized $3. In February 1921 the catalog of B. Max Mehl's sale of the Dr. G.F.E. Wilharm Collection described lot 181: "1854-C Uncirculated, considerable bright Mint luster. Very rare." Realized $6. The November 1932 sale of the R. Taylor Collection included Mehl's description of lot 168: "1854-C, Slanting C. Very Fine. Very scarce. Cost several years ago, $16." Realized $5.50.

In his November 1939 sale of the William B. Hale Collection, Mehl described lot 842: "1854-C Very Fine, sharp, with proof-like surface. From the Zug Sale in 1909." Realized $7.40. Mehl's February 1944 catalog of the sale of the Belden E. Roach Collection described lot 966: "1854-C About Uncirculated with considerable mint luster." Realized $13.75. The Stack's sale of the J.F. Bell Collection in December 1944 included lot 202: "1854-C Brilliant Uncirculated." Realized $22.50. Mehl's sale of the Jerome Kern Collection in May 1950 included lot 128: "1854 C. Not very far from Uncirculated. Catalogs $15 in only Very Fine." Realized $17.50.

VF-20	EF-40	AU-50	AU-55	MS-60	MS-62	MS-63
$2,000	$3,000	$4,250	$6,000	$10,000	$20,000	$37,500

1854-D

Circulation-Strike Mintage: 1,760

Rare in any grade.
Incredibly rare in Mint State.

Deliveries were reported as follows: January, 1,720; and November, 490. Assay coins were not recorded. Coinage hit another new low for Dahlonega.

Estimated Total Population (Mint State). 3 to 5. This issue is exceedingly rare.

Estimated Total Population (Circulated Grades). 40 to 60. It is very elusive in all circulated grades. Most are well worn, with Fine to Very Fine being typical. Extremely Fine coins are rare and About Uncirculated pieces are especially so. From the viewpoint of rarity, the famous 1854-D is about tied with the relatively unappreciated 1840-D.

Die Data. *1854 four-digit date logotype: See the Philadelphia Mint listing for this year.*

Three obverse dies were sent from Philadelphia on December 20, 1853, and arrived in Dahlonega on December 29, 1853.[88]

Reverse die used on all Dahlonega quarter eagles from 1849 to 1859: See description under 1849-D on pages 220–221.

Characteristics of Striking and Die Notes. Examples are always seen with some lightness of striking at the eagle's leg to the left. Denticles are usually weak or incomplete, although the literature discloses a few exceptions.

Selected Auction Records

Thomas L. Elder's March 1911 sale of the William H. Woodin Collection included this description of lot 1111: "1854-D. Large D, high over bar point. Good. Excessively rare. Only one record of public sale, and that $130." Realized $39. In May 1913 the U.S. Coin Co. sale of the Malcolm N. Jackson Collection included lot 266: "1854-D Very Fine and excessively rare." Realized $70. The November 1932 sale of the R. Taylor Collection included B. Max Mehl's description of lot 164: "1854-D, D over fraction. Very Good. Very rare. At one time sold up to $50." Realized $27. Mehl's February 1944 catalog of the sale of the Belden E. Roach Collection described lot 996: "1854-D Extremely Fine; just a shade from Uncirculated with frosty mint surface. Bold impression with usual raised borders which is characteristic of the gold coins struck at this mint. Extremely rare. Listed at $150 in only Very Fine." Realized $147.

Stack's sale of the J.F. Bell Collection in December 1944 included lot 221: "1854-D Brilliant Uncirculated. Very rare in this state of preservation, one of the finest known." Realized $230. In April 1956 Abe Kosoff's sale of the Melish and Hester Collections included lot 1218: "1854-D Very Fine, Rare. A top-grade coin, seldom offered." Realized $200. In June 1957 the New Netherlands sale of Eliasberg duplicates had this for lot 613: "1854-D. Better than the conventional Very Fine, nearly EF for coin. A beautiful, highly attractive impression, struck rather weakly as always from defective dies. We have seen just six examples and heard of four others, out of a total coinage of only 1,760. Most of them are decidedly inferior to this one, and the high records have been racked up by coins that were not fully VF: W.G.C. at $187.50, Graves at $250., Melish at $200. (cost $265.), Gaskill at $175. Atwater only had a Fine one, the Dr. Green and Menjou lots were called Fine to VF. Ex 'Lee,' Lot 1125. A top-flight specimen of a very important rarity." Realized $210.

VF-20	EF-40	AU-50	AU-55	MS-60	MS-62	MS-63
$3,500	$7,500	$10,000	$15,000	$28,500	$40,000	$65,000

1854-O

Circulation-Strike Mintage: 153,000

An unrecognized rarity in Mint State.

Gold remained in New Orleans, a secondary minting destination for metal brought from California. However, no quarter eagles had been coined since 1852.

Estimated Total Population (Mint State). 8 to 12. These are clustered in the lower Mint State ranges. The rarity of the 1854-O in Mint State is neither widely known nor appreciated.

Estimated Total Population (Circulated Grades). 300 to 600. Examples are usually seen in Very Fine or Extremely Fine grade. It is quite scarce in About Uncirculated. This issue is under-represented in certification service listings.

Die Data. *1854 four-digit date logotype: See the Philadelphia Mint listing for this year.*

Die characteristics for 1854-O quarter eagles in the Bowers and Merena March 2003 auction:

> 1. The four-digit date logotype was "rocked" when it was entered into the die, making the top and bottoms of the numerals bolder than the centers, although the centers themselves are very well defined. The logotype is too low and too far to the left, with the lower left serif of the 1 intruding upon two denticles. The obverse displays what either is a complete or perhaps incipient vertical bisecting break from the top border through the right side of star 7, to the hair, then disappearing and re-emerging at the truncation and touching the upper right of the 5, then within the 5 exiting from the knob to the lower left. Reverse with O mintmark high, and with but the barest hint of a feather element at the upper inside right. Vertical shield stripes somewhat irregular, with the leftmost pair of vertical shield stripes having an overly heavy element to the left, and on the second pair the right hand element being about two-thirds missing.
>
> 2. Date logotype about equally spaced from the denticles and the neck truncation (as determined by the digit 1). Date punched deeply and evenly into the die. Reverse different from the preceding with the arrow feather occupying the upper left of the interior of the O; vertical shield stripes different, but with part of the right element of the second leftmost pair missing, and with other peculiarities.

Characteristics of Striking and Die Notes. Examples are often seen with prominent die clash marks. High grade coins are often prooflike.

Selected Auction Records

In his 1907 fixed-price list Elmer S. Sears offered lot 268: "1854 New Orleans Mint. Mint mark placed far from fraction. Very Fine. $6." Thomas L. Elder's March 1911 sale of the William H. Woodin Collection included these: Lot 1055: "1854-O. Date midway between bust and rim; the O between 1 and dividing bar, touching arrow. Fine." Realized $2.50 (face value). Lot 1056: "1854-O. The figure 1 closer to bust, the O higher." Realized $2.50 (face value). Lot 1057: "1854-O. Figure 1 touching both bust and rim, the O between 2 and D. Fine." Realized $2.50 (face value). In May 1913 the U.S. Coin Co. sale of the Malcolm N. Jackson Collection included multiples: Lot 216: "1854-O Date very low. O between 1 and fraction bar. Extremely Fine." Realized $2.75. Lot 217: "1854-O Date higher. 1 touches bust. Very Fine." Realized $2.75. Lot 218: "1854-O 1 does not quite touch bust. Extremely Fine." Realized $2.75. Lot 219: "1854-O 1 touches bust. O over 2 in fraction and D. Very Fine." Realized $2.75.

In May 1915 B. Max Mehl's catalog of the B.W. Smith Collection included this description of lot 319: "1854-O O between 1 and bar. Extremely Fine, some mint luster." Realized $3.25. Mehl's February 1944 catalog of the sale of the Belden E. Roach Collection described lot 980: "1854-O About Uncirculated with semi-proof surface."

Realized $7. In June 1946 Mehl's sale of the William Cutler Atwater Collection included lot 2069: "1854-O Practically Uncirculated. Scarce so choice. (None coined in 1853)." Realized $9.25. Abe Kosoff's sale of the Melish and Hester Collections, April 1956, offered these: 1219: "1854-O. O is over center of fraction. About Extremely Fine." Realized $16. Lot 1220: "1854-O. O is a bit left. Obverse die is buckling; a crack from chin to rim. Very Fine." Realized $12.50. Lot 1221: "1854-O. Similar. A series of cracks emanates from lips, neck and hair. Very Fine." Realized $12.

VF-20	EF-40	AU-50	AU-55	MS-60	MS-62	MS-63
$500	$550	$625	$700	$1,500	$4,500	$9,000

1854-S

Circulation-Strike Mintage: 246

The rarest quarter eagle date and mint. Landmark classic rarity.

This is the lowest mintage figure for any circulation strike quarter eagle. At the time, denominations were coined to the order of bullion depositors, and quarter eagles were not desired.

The 1854-S, produced during the first year of operation of the San Francisco Mint, has the lowest recorded mintage (only 246 were struck) of all quarter eagles issued as circulation strikes from 1796 to 1929. Only about a dozen examples survive today, and all of these are in worn grades.

In Edgar H. Adams' *Official Premium List of United States, Private, and Territorial Gold Coins*, published in 1909, he found "no record of public sale" for the 1854-S. However, that was soon to change. The following commentary by Adams appeared in the May 1911 issue of the periodical mentioned:

> *The Numismatist* is in a position to state for the benefit especially of the quarter eagle collectors that the long-sought-for 1854 $2.50 gold piece of the San Francisco Mint has come to light, and is now in the collection of Mr. H.O. Granberg of Oshkosh, Wisconsin. This rare mintmark recently came to Mr. Granberg's notice, and of course was carefully examined by him. It was found to be authentic beyond a doubt. Mr. Hudson Chapman has also examined the coin, and has stated that it was the only specimen of the variety that had ever been located. The coin is in a good state of preservation, but has seen considerable circulation. According to the mint report of 1854 exactly 246 quarter eagles were struck at San Francisco, but all seem to have disappeared until this specimen came to notice. This was the first year of the operation of the San Francisco Mint, which produced very few coins for the reason that there was a great scarcity of acids used for refining the gold and also of silver used to alloy the gold to bring it up to the United States coin standard. It was this scarcity of acids and silver that often compelled the branch mint to suspend coinage in the early fifties, and accounts for the tremendous productions of the private coining establishments of Wass, Molitor & Co. and Kellogg & Co.

The theory that there was a "great scarcity of acids" has no relevance, for large quantities were struck of the higher denominations such as $10 and, in particular, $20.

Coins were struck to the order of depositors who requested certain values, and the small-denomination $2.50 and $5 pieces were not wanted in quantity.

In a biography of Texas dealer B. Max Mehl in the *Numismatic Scrapbook*, March 1939, this was included: "The Fort Worth dealer has discovered rarities by the score. . . . He found six of the five known [*sic!*] 1854-S quarter eagles, one of the two known 1854-S half eagles."

In his sale of the Belden Roach specimen sold by B. Max Mehl in February 1944, Mehl noted at the time: "Until 1910 not a single specimen of this coin was known to exist in any collection. I discovered one specimen through my extensive advertising. It was sold to Mr. John Clapp of Washington at over $500."

Mehl has been known to exaggerate on occasion and sometimes confuse facts, not a surprising situation in view of the literally millions of transactions he conducted over the years. However, the story of the sale to Clapp is divergent from the 1911 commentary by Edgar H. Adams quoted on the previous page.

Possibly, Mehl sold the 1854-S to Granberg, who may have disposed of it later. It was not part of the 1913 Granberg Collection sold at auction by Mehl, but Granberg is known to have sold pieces on other occasions as well. The Clapp notebooks revealed that an 1854-S quarter eagle was purchased from Elmer S. Sears for $395 in August 1915. This coin subsequently went to Louis E. Eliasberg Sr. in 1942 and was sold by Bowers and Ruddy Galleries in October 1982 as part of the Eliasberg Collection.

Fast forward to 1988 and *Walter Breen's Complete Encyclopedia of U.S. and Colonial Coins*. In that publication he offered the following commentary and registry:

1. Davis-Graves: 825, Harry Bass? VF+, horizontal abrasion above eagle.
2. Atwater, Grant Pierce, Miles, 1973 ANA: 826, $9,000, 1974 MANA: 1547, $24,000, Arthur Lamborn, "Fairfield": 1544, $10,000 (1977), Scott-Kinnear: 13, $9,900. VF, nick above 13th star, rough on upper left obverse, lower left reverse.
3. F.C.C. Boyd, WGC, "Bell," "Memorable," Clinton Hester or C.M. Williams, Menjou: 1326, NN 51:837, private collections, "Rio Rancho": 89, VF+, scratch from arrow to M. [This is the Bass coin]
4. Waldo Newcomer, Col. E.H.R. Green, "Bell," Farouk: 278, Gilhousen: 184, "Rio Rancho": 90, $13,000, Dr. Altany, Windsor: 307, F to VF.
5. Roach, Wolfson, S. Hallock to duPont: 85, 1983 Grand Central: 2762, F, scratch above eagle's head, another (parallel upper wing) to rim close to F.
6. Kreisberg/Schulman 2/60: 2592, 1979 ANA: 82, $8,750. Auction 81: 1405. VG-F, $9,200.
7. 'Western bank,' B. Max Mehl, 1910, H.O. Granberg, Mehl, Elmer Sears, John H. Clapp, Eliasberg: 170, $7,150. VG/G.
8. Texas private collection. Loop removed, traces of solder.
9. Texas private collection. Obverse VF, scratched; reverse shank removed, affecting NITE and MERI.

There are probably at least two others around.

No. 3 in the above list (but not identified by Breen as such), was cataloged by Walter Breen and finessed by John J. Ford Jr.—the procedure in effect at New Netherlands coin company at the time—as follows in their 51st catalog of June 19–20, 1958, as Lot 837:

> 1854-S. In date, 1 embedded in bust; upper right corner of mintmark joins tip of arrow shaft, but the S is elsewhere clear. Strictly Very Fine; bold, the obverse more so than the reverse (as on all others known). Although this piece has minor handling marks, the most obvious of which is a faint reverse scratch from the top arrow to M, it still retains traces of original lustre on the reverse, confirming our contention that the flatness on the eagle's head and upper parts of wings is a result of the way the coin was struck. Beyond doubt, this is *one of the two finest of only five so far traced (a sixth is reported, but still unverified). Other than two half eagles, the 1841-O and 1875, this coin has the lowest mintage of any gold piece struck for circulation and so used.* Also, likewise an unappreciated fact, the 1854-S quarter eagle is an initial type coin, being the first San Francisco Mint issue of that denomination.
>
> Of the 246 pieces made 104 years ago, this coin was the second specimen to be discovered and the first choice one. It was Lot 242 of the 1946 'World's Greatest Collection;' Lot 222 of the 1948 Memorable Sale; Lot 1326 of the 1950 Menjou offering. The other four examples known to us are as follows: (1) Davis-Graves, 1954, Lot 825, VF plus; (2) Bell, 1944, Lot 240, Farouk, 1954, part of Lot 278, VF; (3) Atwater, 1946, Lot 2072, Fine, obverse field dig; (4) Eliasberg Collection, discovered circa 1910 in a western bank, sold by B.M. Mehl to J.H. Clapp for a reported $850, to Eliasberg with the Clapp Collection, 1942. VG.
>
> Clearly, one of the most underrated United States coins in any metal manufactured to be used as a circulating medium, and completely free of the stigma of Mint experimentation or chicanery. In comparison with commoner, but more touted coins such as the 1815 half eagle (and many others we could name), this mintmark has a tremendous potential, perhaps in the $4,000 to $5,000 class. A true American classic!

The "New Netherlands style" was quite advanced for its era, and had its genesis in 1952 when John J. Ford Jr. compiled a section of the ANA convention catalog. The philosophy at the time was to say as much as possible about the coin—the specimen itself as well as its history, background, and, if merited, other known pieces. Descriptions were interesting reading at the time, but many "facts" expressed by writer Breen proved to be imaginary.

In 1893 Augustus G. Heaton, in *Mint Marks*, commented: "The San Francisco issues are from 1854 to '79, except '55, '64, and '74. The great prize of the series is 1858. . . ."[89] In 1909 Edgar H. Adams, in *Adams' Official Premium List of United States, Private, and Territorial Gold Coins*, studied the availability of such coins in recent auctions. For San Francisco Mint issues he noted these grades: 1854-S ("no record of public sale"); 1856-S (Uncirculated, W.S. Appleton sale, 1907); 1857-S (Uncirculated, W.S. Appleton sale, 1907); 1858-S ("no record of public sale"—Adams was not aware that *none were minted*); 1859-S ("no record of public sale"); and 1860-S (Fine, Appleton sale, 1907). In contrast, most Philadelphia Mint coins in the survey were Uncirculated.

Estimated Total Population (Circulated Grades). 12 to 14. The 1854-S is exceedingly rare, on a par with or rarer than the 1841 and 1863.

Die Data. *1854 four-digit date logotype: See the Philadelphia Mint listing for this year.*

Five pairs of dies were shipped to San Francisco for the 1854-S $2.50 coinage, but only one pair was used.

On the obverse the 1 of the date is embedded in the neck. The undated reverses were held over as they could be used later.

Characteristics of Striking and Die Notes. Some minor lightness of details is usual at the center reverse.

Selected Auction Records

Note: Extensive information is given in view of the rarity and importance of the 1854-S, including the following listings.

B. Max Mehl's February 1944 catalog of the sale of the Belden E. Roach Collection described lot 1001:

> 1854-S $2.50 Gold, S Mint. First year of issue of this Mint. The first specimen of this great rarity ever to be offered at auction.[90] Only 246 specimens minted. Until 1910 not a single specimen of this coin was known to exist in any collection. I discovered one specimen in About Good condition, through my extensive advertising. It was sold to John Clapp of Washington at over $500. About ten years later a second specimen was also discovered by me and sold at a much higher price. Since then I believe that one or two other specimens were discovered. In all, I am sure that not more than five specimens are known to exist. Including the one here offered. This specimen is in fine condition, strictly so. I know of one specimen which was offered some time ago for $650. considering the number of specimens minted, and the number now known to exist, I consider it the rarest of all quarter eagles. A coin that is really worth up to the four-figure mark.

Realized $615.

The Stack's sale of the J.F. Bell Collection in December 1944 included lot 240: "1854-S Strictly Very Fine, this coin is considered one of the finest known with records in fine condition, as high as $850." Realized $950. In June 1946 Mehl's sale of the William Cutler Atwater Collection included lot 2072:

> 1854-S. The coin is fine but shows, of course, evidence of circulation. On the upper left obverse field there is a slight indentation or probably a tiny nick. The coin is evenly struck and evidence of circulation evenly distributed. While I catalog this rarity as fine, I believe it is as fine as exists. The coin is excessively rare. A total of only 246 specimens were struck in all. And until 1910 not a single specimen was known to exist. During that year, through my extensive advertising, I secured from a Western bank the first specimen discovered. It is in good condition only and shows considerable wear. I sold it to the late John Clapp of Washington, D.C. It is now in the great Collection owned by Mr. Louis Eliasberg of Baltimore. I doubt very much if more than six or seven specimens are known today. Until 1944 not a single specimen was ever offered at auction. In a recent sale a specimen brought $1,000. I consider it one of the very rarest of all branch mint gold coins.

Realized $715.

VF-20	EF-40	AU-50
$250,000	$300,000	$450,000

1855

Circulation-Strike Mintage: 225,480
Proof Mintage: Unknown, very small

Plentiful for the era.

Estimated Total Population (Mint State). 50 to 100. Most are in lower Mint State ranges, although choice and gem pieces are seen on occasion. Mint State coins have appeared at auction over a long range of years, most probably pieces saved by chance. No hoards have ever been reported.

Estimated Total Population (Circulated Grades). 600 to 1,000. This issue is underreported as 1855 is considered to be a common date. Extremely Fine and About Uncirculated are typical grades.

Die Data. *1855 four-digit date logotype:* The date numerals are slightly smaller than for the preceding year. The logotype is open. The 18 is closely spaced, and 85 and 55 are about twice as far apart and each the same. The 1 has prominent lower serifs. The top and bottom interior space of the 8 are about the same size, and 8 leans right. The 5's are italic with the upright, if extended below, intersecting the ball near its left edge. On the first 5 the flag is more distant from the curve below than it is on the second 5; the ball is closer to the upright on the second 5, this due to the logotype preparation process, in which the final digit was punched more deeply into the logotype *matrix*. This logotype was used on all dies of all mints.

Characteristics of Striking and Die Notes. Examples are usually fairly well struck.

Selected Auction Records

The October 1875 sale of the Col. Mendes I. Cohen Collection included Edward Cogan's description of lot 223: "1855 Uncirculated." Realized $2.85. The catalog of John W. Haseltine's June 1883 sale of the William J. Jenks Collection described lot 460: "1855 Uncirculated. Scarce." Realized $3. Thomas L. Elder's March 1911 sale of the William H. Woodin Collection included these examples: Lot 995: "1855. Yellow gold. Figure 1 barely touches bust and rim, 55 distant from bust. Extremely Fine, sharp." Realized $2.50 (face value). Lot 996: "1855. Silver alloy, figures close to bust but do not touch. Extremely Fine." Realized $2.50 (face value). In May 1913 the U.S. Coin Co. sale of the Malcolm N. Jackson Collection included lot 141: "1855 Uncirculated." Realized $3.

In February 1921 the catalog of B. Max Mehl's sale of the Dr. G.F.E. Wilharm Collection described lot 91: "1855 Bright Uncirculated." Realized $3.40. In his November 1939 sale of the William B. Hale Collection, Mehl described lot 781: "1855 Uncirculated." Realized $4.40. The Will W. Neil Collection sold by Mehl in June 1947 included lot 2433: "1855 Uncirculated, mint luster. Catalogs $12.50." Realized $8.25. In November 1956 the New Netherlands sale of the Thomas L. Gaskill Collection included lot 279: "1855 Brilliant Uncirculated. With full, frosty mint surfaces. Not often found so!" Realized $18.

Proofs

Estimated Total Population (Proof). 1 or 2?

These coins are not traced today. One was reported to have been in the Yale University Collection, stolen and not recovered. An impaired Proof was reported by Breen, but not presently confirmed.

VF-20	EF-40	AU-50	AU-55	MS-60	MS-62	MS-63
$500	$515	$535	$550	$575	$1,100	$1,650

1855-C

Circulation-Strike Mintage: 3,677

These were made in a single production run.

The second rarest Charlotte $2.50 gold coin. Especially rare in Mint State.

Estimated Total Population (Mint State). 2 to 4. The finest seems to be the MS-64 coin in the Bass Part II sale, 1999.

Estimated Total Population (Circulated Grades). 60 to 80. This is considered to be the second rarest Charlotte Mint quarter eagle (the 1843-C Small Date is considered to be the rarest, but it is a variety rather than a stand-alone date and mintmark). Extremely Fine and About Uncirculated are the typical grades. Most probably, these and other C and D mint quarter eagles only circulated up to the Civil War, 1861, after which they were hoarded.

Die Data. *1855 four-digit date logotype: See the Philadelphia Mint listing for this year.*

The same reverse die was used to strike 1852-C, 1854-C, and 1855-C quarter eagles, to the exclusion of any other die(s). The C is very close to the numerator 1 in the fraction and touches the fraction bar. The tip of the arrow feather pierces the upper curve of the C and is seen within it."[91]

Characteristics of Striking and Die Notes. Examples are lightly struck at the centers and obverse stars. This was due to the overly wide spacing of the dies on the coining press. It is usually seen with a small rim cud on the bottom of the reverse.

Selected Auction Records

In his 1907 fixed-price list Elmer S. Sears offered lot 271: "1855 Charlotte Mint. The rarest issue of this mint. Almost Uncirculated and excessively rare. $40." Thomas L. Elder's March 1911 sale of the William H. Woodin Collection included this description of lot 1130: "1855-C. Extremely Fine. Excessively rare. Has a recent record of $22.50. Only 3,667 coined." Realized $16. In May 1913 the U.S. Coin Co. sale of the Malcolm N. Jackson Collection included two: Lot 287: "1855-C Very Fine and extremely rare." Realized $4. Lot 288: "1855-C Similar. Very Fine and extremely rare." Realized $4.50. Cataloged by Wayte Raymond.

B. Max Mehl's February 1944 catalog of the sale of the Belden E. Roach Collection described lot 967: "1855-C Nearly Uncirculated. Very rare, especially so choice."

Realized $15.75. The Stack's sale of the J.F. Bell Collection in December 1944 included lot 203: "1855-C Brilliant Uncirculated." Realized $42.50. June 1946 Mehl's sale of the William Cutler Atwater Collection included lot 2035: "1855-C Very Fine, sharp; light nick on obverse. Very scarce. Record for an Extremely Fine specimen, $35." Realized $8.50. In October 1951 the Numismatic Gallery sale of the B.A. Talmadge collection included lot 1208: "1855-C About Uncirculated; very scarce." Realized $21.

VF-20	EF-40	AU-50	AU-55	MS-60	MS-62	MS-63
$2,250	$4,250	$6,000	$7,500	$20,000	$27,500	$42,500

1855-D

Circulation-Strike Mintage: 1,123

Rarest gold coin from the Dahlonega Mint.

Coinage took place only in January, and to the extent of just 1,123 pieces. Assay coins were not recorded. The production hit still another new low for Dahlonega Mint quarter eagles.

Estimated Total Population (Mint State). None seen. The writer has never seen a Mint State 1855-D, nor have David W. Akers or Douglas Winter. One piece has been certified as MS-60.

Estimated Total Population (Circulated Grades). 30 to 50. The 1855-D seems to edge out the 1856-D by a small margin for the title of the rarest Dahlonega Mint quarter eagle.

Die Data.[92] *1855 four-digit date logotype: See the Philadelphia Mint listing for this year.*

Three 1855-dated obverse and three reverse dies were sent from Philadelphia on November 24, 1854. The shipment, comprising three pairs of each of the gold $1, $2.50, and $5 denominations, was sent in one box and forwarded by Adams' Express from Philadelphia but was lost for a time in Savannah, Georgia; after it was found, it was forwarded to Dahlonega and arrived there on December 27, 1854. As is seen from the mintage figures, more dies were sent than were needed for quarter eagles.

Reverse die used on all Dahlonega quarter eagles from 1849 to 1859: See description under 1849-D on pages 220–221.

Characteristics of Striking and Die Notes. Lightly struck at the centers of both sides and on the denticles of the obverse.

Selected Auction Records

B. Max Mehl's February 1944 catalog of the sale of the Belden E. Roach Collection described lot 997: "1855-D Strictly Fine to Very Fine. Only 1,123 minted. High auction record. Catalogs at $150 and worth it. I know of specimens which have sold for more." Realized $140. This coin was later offered by Stack's in the October 1947 sale of the H.R. Lee Collection, lot 1126: "1855-D Strictly Very Fine. From the Mehl

Sale, $140 was paid for same. Very rare." Realized $125. The Stack's sale of the J.F. Bell Collection in December 1944 included lot 222: "1855-D Brilliant Uncirculated condition." Realized $190.

VF-20	EF-40	AU-50	AU-55	MS-60	MS-63
$4,500	$8,000	$15,000	$20,000	$50,000	$100,000

1856

Circulation-Strike Mintage: 384,240
Proof Mintage: 6 or 7 (estimated)

Plentiful for the era.

Estimated Total Population (Mint State). 100 to 150, including dozens that grade choice or finer. This estimate may be conservative, for in 1986 Paul F. Taglione commented, "Scarce MS-63 or finer with no more than 160 existing in MS-63 to MS-65."

Estimated Total Population (Circulated Grades). 1,000 to 1,500. One of the more plentiful pre-Civil War quarter eagle varieties. It is available in just about any grade desired, with Extremely Fine and About Uncirculated being about the norm.

Die Data. *1856 four-digit date logotype:* The date is in very small numerals, reminiscent of 1849, but in the present instance widely spaced and of good proportions. The 18 and 56 are about the same distance apart, and the 85 is ever so slightly closer. The top interior space of the 8 is about the same or slightly smaller than the bottom interior space, and the digit leans very slightly right. The 5 is of the italic style, with a prominent ball close to or touching the upright above, and the flag fairly close to the curve below. The 6 leans right and has a large top ball that virtually touches the curve below, the digit being thick at the left and right; the base of 6 is slightly lower than the bases of other figures. This logotype was used on all dies of all mints and also used on the 1856 Small Date *dime.*

Fifteen pairs of dies were produced for the 1856 quarter eagle coinage, and probably the use of all of them will never be recorded, as differences in placement may be small.

Large Date reported: Two examples in the Gray and Dickie Collection (Elder, March 1938) were called "Small date" (mentioned here for contrast), while a specimen in the Hall Collection (Stack's, May 1945, see the following page) was called "Large date." If the Hall coin is with large numerals, the variety has not been seen in recent times and would represent a major find if discovered.

Characteristics of Striking and Die Notes. Examples are usually well struck.

Selected Auction Records

The October 1875 sale of the Col. Mendes I. Cohen Collection included Edward Cogan's description of lot 224: "1856 Uncirculated." Realized $2.85. The catalog of John W. Haseltine's June 1883 sale of the William J. Jenks Collection described lot 461: "1856 Uncirculated. Scarce." Realized $3. In his 1907 fixed-price list Elmer S. Sears offered lot 272: "1856 Uncirculated. Mint lustre. $8." Thomas L. Elder's March

1911 sale of the William H. Woodin Collection included this description of lot 998: "1856. Uncirculated." Realized $2.60. In May 1913 the U.S. Coin Co. sale of the Malcolm N. Jackson Collection included lot 142: "1856 Uncirculated." Realized $2.75. In May 1915 B. Max Mehl's catalog of the B.W. Smith Collection included this description of lot 270: "1856 Uncirculated, mint luster." Realized $3.

In his November 1939 sale of the William B. Hale Collection, Mehl described lot 782: "1856 Uncirculated." Realized $4.50. The Stack's sale of the J.F. Bell Collection in December 1944 included lot 123: "1856 Brilliant Uncirculated." Realized $15.50. A mystery was introduced by Stack's description of lot 1757 in the May 1845 sale of the George H. Hall Collection: "1856 Large date, Uncirculated." Realized $11. The "Large date" notation may signify a different variety from the usually seen 1856, which has small numerals. It is untraced today. In June 1957 the New Netherlands sale of Eliasberg duplicates had this for lot 616: "1856. Small date, as usual. Extremely Fine. Presumably 'Lee' 1028. We have never seen the large date variety reported in Stack's G.H. Hall auction, and seriously doubts if it exists." Realized $12.

Proofs

Estimated Total Population (Proof). 3 or 4 (Dannreuther).

VF-20	EF-40	AU-50	AU-55	MS-60	MS-62	MS-63	PF-60	PF-63
$500	$515	$525	$550	$575	$850	$1,250	$35,000	$55,000

1856-C

Circulation-Strike Mintage: 7,913

Scarce in any grade.
Incredibly rare in Mint State.

Estimated Total Population (Mint State). 2 to 4. Pieces that have been graded as Mint State are at the lower end of the spectrum. In 1975 David W. Akers stated that he had never seen a true Mint State coin. Any Mint State coin with attractive appearance and unequivocal credentials would be a numismatic showpiece.

Estimated Total Population (Circulated Grades). 75 to 125. Very Fine is about the norm. Any coin with legitimate claim to About Uncirculated is a prize, as only a few such pieces have been represented in the major collections over the years.

Die Data. *1856 four-digit date logotype: See the Philadelphia Mint listing for this year.*

Examples often have rough or irregular fields, including a depression on the reverse.

Selected Auction Records

In his 1907 fixed-price list Elmer S. Sears offered lot 273: "1856 Charlotte Mint. Extremely Fine and rare. $20." Thomas L. Elder's March 1911 sale of the William H. Woodin Collection included this description of lot 1131: "1856-C. About Fine. Rare. Recent record of $6.50." Realized $4.25. In his November 1939 sale of the William B. Hale Collection, B. Max Mehl described lot 843: "1856-C Just a shade from Uncirculated. Light planchet dent on reverse field. Rare in choice condition." Realized $9.60. Mehl's February 1944 catalog of the sale of the Belden E. Roach Collection described lot 968: "1856-C Light die depression on obverse. Very Fine. Very scarce." Realized $7.

The Stack's sale of the J.F. Bell Collection in December 1944 included lot 204: "1856-C Extremely Fine." Realized $14. In June 1946 Mehl's sale of the William Cutler Atwater Collection included lot 2036: "1856-C. Extremely Fine, nearly Uncirculated. Slight die depression on reverse. Characteristic of this date and mint. Record of $22.50 for a Very Fine specimen." Realized $27.50. In November 1956 the New Netherlands sale of the Thomas L. Gaskill Collection included lot 283: "1856-C. Fully Extremely Fine. Granular chips out of the flan before striking, mainly upon the reverse. Rare, some 7,913 struck. Very much underrated, particularly so fine. This date was not in the Dunham, Memorable, Dr. Green and H.P. Graves collections; the Roach, WGC coins were VF, the Menjou, Melish ones but F/VF. A 'sleeper,' worth a good price." Realized $40.

VF-20	EF-40	AU-50	AU-55	MS-60	MS-62	MS-63
$1,650	$2,750	$4,000	$6,000	$11,500	$20,000	$25,000

1856-D

Circulation-Strike Mintage: 874

Lowest mintage Dahlonega $2.50 gold coin. Rare in all grades. Landmark rarity in Mint State.

There was but one mintage, in February, with 874 coins for circulation plus 2 for assay. Again, the quarter eagle hit a new low at the Dahlonega Mint, dipping below the 1,000 mark. This would stand as a record.

At the annual Assay Commission meeting in 1857, to test the silver and gold coins struck at various mints in 1856, it was found that several Dahlonega Mint gold coins were below the legal limit in weight. This was startling news to Dahlonega Mint Superintendent Julius M. Patton, who informed Mint Director James Ross Snowden that the person adjusting the planchet weights in 1856 was the same employee who had been doing this since the first gold coinage in 1838. Moreover, although a few stray single pieces may have been of low weight, the deviation of Dahlonega Mint gold coins when weighed in quantity and averaged was within statutory limits. Apparently, more care was given to planchet adjusting at Dahlonega after that time, for the subject did not arise again.[93]

Estimated Total Population (Mint State). 2 to 4. The 1856-D is exceedingly rare. In 1986 in *The Quarter Eagles*, Paul F. Taglione stated that he knew of three Mint State coins.

Estimated Total Population (Circulated Grades). 40 to 55. A major rarity in the series.

Die Data.[94] *1856 four-digit date logotype: See the Philadelphia Mint listing for this year.*

Three 1856-dated obverse and three reverse dies were sent from Philadelphia on December 13, 1855, as part of a shipment containing three pairs each of quarter eagle and half eagle dies. Dahlonega Mint Director Julius M. Patton became concerned that they did not arrive on a timely basis, and on January 5, 1856, wrote to Philadelphia to ask about them. The shipment arrived in Dahlonega at an unknown later date (it is to be recalled that the year before, a shipment of 1855-dated dies had been lost by Adams' Express and later found in Savannah).

Reverse die used on all Dahlonega quarter eagles from 1849 to 1859: See description under 1849-D on pages 220–221.

Characteristics of Striking and Die Notes. Examples are lightly struck at the centers. Die rust is on the lower part of the portrait.

Selected Auction Records

Thomas L. Elder's March 1911 sale of the William H. Woodin Collection included this description of lot 1112: "1856-D. The D high above bar point. Very Fine. Excessively rare. 'No record of public sale.' The Mint record gives the number struck as 874 pieces, making this the rarest quarter eagle struck at the D. Mint." Realized $66. In his November 1939 sale of the William B. Hale Collection, B. Max Mehl described lot 855: "1856-D The rarest quarter eagle of this Mint, and one of the rarest of the entire series. Only 874 coined. Extremely Fine, with considerable luster. According to Mr. Hale's memorandum, it was purchased as Uncirculated in 1911, and at that time, nearly thirty years ago he paid $90 for it." Realized $210. Mehl's February 1944 catalog of the sale of the Belden E. Roach Collection described lot 998: "1856-D $2.50. D. Mint. Uncirculated with full mint luster. Broad raised borders. I do not recall ever having seen an equal specimen of this, the rarest quarter eagle of this Mint and one of the rarest of the entire issue of quarter eagles. Extremely rare in any condition, but in this choice condition it is almost priceless. Listed at $200 in only Very Fine. This beautiful specimen is certainly worthy of a high new record." Realized $236. The Stack's sale of the J.F. Bell Collection in December 1944 included lot 223: "1856-D Brilliant Uncirculated. One of the finest strikes ever seen, also one of the rarest mintmarks. Seldom offered for Sale either privately or by auction." Realized $237.50.

In November 1956 the New Netherlands sale of the Thomas L. Gaskill Collection included lot 284: "186-D. Though weakly and flatly struck, as usual on coins of this mint, we can call this rarity Very Fine. Hardly visible obverse planchet defect; scratch-like, one end at bottom of bust (between curls), other diagonally below on border. Only 874 coined; the rarest-D Mint quarter eagle, one of the rarest coins in the entire series. This piece is the twin brother of the WGC coin which was sold for $225 in 1946, and apparently equal to the 'About Extremely Fine' Melish example. None in any of the big Chapman sales; less than half-a-dozen auction records known to us.[95] A 'good buy' at $400 (or anything near it), considering the steady advance of the market. The collector fortunate enough to get this one, will have little cause to worry about 'finds' being made in Treasury or bank vaults." Realized $300. The sale was negated, and in 1957 the New Netherlands sale of Eliasberg duplicates had this for lot 617: "1856-D. Strictly Very Fine. . . . Equal to, or a shade better than, the Melish piece, estimated at $400, but which realized $285. This example from the Gaskill coll., sold in our Forty-Eighth sale for $300, is herewith re-offered on behalf of a delinquent account." Realized $260.

In *The Numismatist* of September 1967, H.D. Holt, of Dunedin, Florida, advertised an 1856-D quarter eagle, noting: "One of the real rarities as only 874 were struck.

This one is a sharp strict AU. I have bought hundreds of Dahlonegas and in most series this would be graded a struck brilliant Uncirculated. This little sweetheart is worth much more than my asking price of $1,995."

VF-20	EF-40	AU-50	AU-55	MS-60
$12,500	$22,000	$30,000	$37,500	$75,000

1856-O

Circulation-Strike Mintage: 21,100

Elusive in any grade.
Incredibly rare in Mint State.

The first New Orleans quarter eagle coinage since 1854-O. The mintage figure was lower than in the earlier era, for after the San Francisco Mint opened for business (in 1854), the New Orleans facilities were not as essential.

Estimated Total Population (Mint State). 1 or 2. This issue is exceedingly rare in actuality, although a handful of pieces can be found in the literature. Mint State coins tend to be toward the lower end of the range.

Estimated Total Population (Circulated Grades). 150 to 250. It is very elusive in circulated grades. The norm is Very Fine, and any coin significantly higher, such as About Uncirculated, is a notable specimen.

Die Data. *1856 four-digit date logotype: See the Philadelphia Mint listing for this year.*

Mintmark positional varieties exist, including O overlapping the arrow feather and O clear of the feather.

Characteristics of Striking and Die Notes. Examples are about average in sharpness. Sometimes the strike is weak on the eagle's leg on the left side of the reverse.

Selected Auction Records

Thomas L. Elder's March 1911 sale of the William H. Woodin Collection included this description of lot 1059: "1856-O, the O between 2 and D. Very Fine. Rare." Realized $9. In May 1913 the U.S. Coin Co. sale of the Malcolm N. Jackson Collection included lot 220: "1856-O Extremely Fine." Realized $3.25. In May 1915 B. Max Mehl's catalog of the B.W. Smith Collection included this description of lot 320: "1856-O O over 2 of fraction. Fine. Scarce." Realized $2.75. In his November 1939 sale of the William B. Hale Collection, B. Mehl described lot 866: "1856-O Nearly Uncirculated. Very scarce. Listed at $10." Realized $9.45. The Stack's sale of the J.F. Bell Collection in December 1944 included lot 238: "1856-O About Uncirculated." Realized $15.

In June 1946 Mehl's sale of the William Cutler Atwater Collection included lot 2070: "1856-O. Uncirculated with semi-proof surface. Just the slightest touch of cabinet friction. Very scarce so choice. (None coined in 1855.)" Realized $19. In October 1951 the Numismatic Gallery sale of the B.A. Talmadge collection included lot 1244: "1856-O None minted [at New Orleans] in 1855. Extremely Fine." Realized $12.75.

In November 1956 the New Netherlands sale of the Thomas L. Gaskill Collection included lot 285: "1856-O. Mintmark partly hidden by feather. About Uncirculated, almost full mint lustre. Unimportant bag scratch in reverse field near eagle's head. Uncommon date, only 21,100 made. More or less of a 'sleeper.' The WGC example, only Very Fine, estimated at $14., brought $18. ten years ago." Realized $18.

VF-20	EF-40	AU-50	AU-55	MS-60	MS-62
$500	$800	$1,750	$2,500	$8,250	$40,000

1856-S

Circulation-Strike Mintage: 71,120

Very rare in Mint State.

Estimated Total Population (Mint State). 6 to 10. The 1856-S is a prime rarity in Mint State, and probably no more than 6 to 10 specimens are presently known in collections. Most such pieces are in lower Mint State numerical ranges. As is the case with virtually all San Francisco Mint quarter eagles (possible SS *Central America* finds excepted, and these would apply only to 1857-S and earlier), this is a *condition rarity.*

Estimated Total Population (Circulated Grades). 140 to 225. Repeating a familiar scenario, the 1856-S $2.50 is readily available but hardly common in worn grades such as Very Fine, which is about par, or the occasional Extremely Fine or About Uncirculated.[96]

Die Data. *1856 four-digit date logotype: See the Philadelphia Mint listing for this year.*

Ten 1856-dated obverses and six reverses were sent from the die shop at the Philadelphia Mint to San Francisco from November 1855 to March 1856.

Characteristics of Striking and Die Notes. Usually lightly struck at the leg of the eagle on the left.

Selected Auction Records

In his 1907 fixed-price list Elmer S. Sears offered two: Lot 275: "1856 San Francisco Mint. First year of quarter eagles at this mint. Mintmark placed over figure 1 of fraction. Very Fine and very rare variety. $10." 276: "1856 Another, but mint mark is placed over figure 2 of fraction. Uncirculated, with beautiful mint bloom. $10." In May 1913 the U.S. Coin Co. sale of the Malcolm N. Jackson Collection included lot 222: "1856-S, S over 1 in fraction. Extremely Fine, mint luster, scarce." Realized $3. May 1915 B. Max Mehl's catalog of the B.W. Smith Collection included this description of lot 322: "1856-S S between bar and D. Very Fine. Scarce." Realized $3.50.

Mehl's sale of the William Cutler Atwater Collection included lot 2073: "1856-S Practically Uncirculated with considerable frosty mint luster (None were minted in 1855) Recent record $27.50 for a specimen which was cataloged as Uncirculated." Realized $8. The Will W. Neil Collection sold by Mehl in June 1947 included lot 2533: "1856-S About Uncirculated with frosty mint surface. Scarce, especially so choice." Realized $8. Mehl's sale of the Jerome Kern Collection in May 1950 included lot 161: "1856-S. Originally purchased as brilliant Uncirculated. I classify it as practically Uncirculated with mint lustre. Cost $20. I hardly think it is worth that much. It catalogs at $17.50." Realized $14.75. In April 1956 Abe Kosoff's sale of the Melish and Hester Collections included lot 1235: "1856-S Extremely Fine." Realized $22. In November 1956 the New Netherlands sale of the Thomas L. Gaskill Collection included two: Lot 286: "1856-S. Letter S held between claw and feather. Extremely Fine. Highly lustrous, faintly sack marked. Decidedly uncommon; the first San Francisco Mint quarter eagle except for the impossible 1854." Realized $19. Lot 287: "1856-S. Similar. S grazing feather, D, and fraction bar. Very Fine, the obverse especially sharp. Few microscopic obv. rim nicks. Much rarer than preceding." Realized $15.

VF-20	EF-40	AU-50	AU-55	MS-60	MS-62	MS-63
$500	$515	$850	$1,250	$5,000	$8,000	$12,000

1857

Circulation-Strike Mintage: 214,130
Proof Mintage: 5 to 7 (estimated)

Plentiful for the era.

Estimated Total Population (Mint State). 75 to 125. Choice and finer examples are sometimes seen.

Estimated Total Population (Circulated Grades). 500 to 800. The 1857 is plentiful in all grades including Extremely Fine and About Uncirculated.

Die Data. *1857 four-digit date logotype:* The digits are small and quite widely spaced. The 18 is closest, 85 is significantly wider, and 57 is wider yet. The top interior of 8 is slightly smaller than the bottom interior; the 8 leans right. The 5 leans slightly right, with a heavy flag and thick right side, and the bottom is rather irregular; the 5 appears somewhat lighter than the other figures (from not having been punched in as deeply on the matrix used to make the logotype). The lower right outside curve of the 8 has a *nick* or recess—a very distinctive feature. This logotype was used on all dies of all mints.

Multiple die pairs were used. Thus, there are different date logotype positions.

One reverse shows a "ring" at the top of the second vertical shield stripe, a characteristic seen on several varieties of $10 gold coins in the era but generally unreported in the quarter eagle denomination.

Characteristics of Striking and Die Notes. Striking varies depending upon the die pair and the press set up. Most have some lightness on the leg of the eagle at the left.

Selected Auction Records

The catalog of John W. Haseltine's June 1883 sale of the William J. Jenks Collection described lot 462: "1857 Uncirculated. Scarce." Realized $3. In his 1907 fixed-price list Elmer S. Sears offered lot 278: "1857 Uncirculated. Mint lustre. $6.50." In May 1913 the U.S. Coin Co. sale of the Malcolm N. Jackson Collection included lot 143: "1857 Uncirculated." Realized $3. In his November 1939 sale of the William B. Hale Collection, B. Max Mehl described lot 783: "1857 Uncirculated." Realized $7.35.

Mehl's sale of the William Forrester Dunham Collection included lot 1956: "1857 About Uncirculated, with mint luster. Very scarce, especially so choice." Realized $7. The Stack's sale of the J.F. Bell Collection in December 1944 included lot 124: "1857 Brilliant Uncirculated." Realized $9. In April 1956 Abe Kosoff's sale of the Melish and Hester Collections included lot 1236: "1857 Uncirculated, choice." Realized $21.

Proofs

Estimated Total Population (Proof). 2 or 3 (Dannreuther).

Selected Proof Auction Records

Charles Steigerwalt's June 1891 sale of the George Morris Collection included lot 84: "1857 Brilliant Proof." Realized $2.90. Lot 841 of Henry Chapman's July 1922 sale of the A. Reimers, J.P. Hale Jenkins, Mrs. Marvin Preston, and Dr. Wallace Bardeen Collections included lot 841: "1857 Brilliant Proof. Excessively rare."

VF-20	EF-40	AU-50	AU-55	MS-60	MS-62	MS-63	PF-60	PF-63
$500	$515	$525	$535	$575	$850	$1,250	$35,000	$57,500

1857-D

Circulation-Strike Mintage: 2,364

Scarce in any grade.
Notably rare in Mint State.

Deliveries were reported as follows: June, 1,464; and December, 900. Assay coins were not recorded. After several years of trending downward, the annual mintage had an uptick.

Estimated Total Population (Mint State). 5 to 8. This issue is rare in any degree of Mint State. Known examples are at the lower end of the range.

Estimated Total Population (Circulated Grades). 80 to 110. About Uncirculated is a typical grade. Seemingly, a number of these were hoarded on the eve of the Civil War, this also being true of other C and D issues of the late 1950s.

Die Data. *1857 four-digit date logotype: See the Philadelphia Mint listing for this year.*

Two 1857-dated obverse and two reverse dies were sent from Philadelphia on November 26, 1856, and arrived in Dahlonega over a month later, on January 4, 1857 (the dies had been sent by Adams' Express; the delayed shipment was a repeat of the scenarios of the preceding two years).[97] *For an anticipated 1858-D coinage that never materialized*, two obverse and two reverse dies were sent from Philadelphia on November 14 or 16, 1857, by Adams' Express, and arrived in Dahlonega on January 6, 1858. The new reverse dies were never used.

Reverse die used on all Dahlonega quarter eagles from 1849 to 1859: See description under 1849-D on pages 220–221.

Characteristics of Striking and Die Notes. Examples are usually fairly well struck.

Selected Auction Records

Thomas L. Elder's March 1911 sale of the William H. Woodin Collection included this description of lot 1113: "1857-D. Uncirculated, partly bright. Possibly but one record of public sale. One of the rarest of this denomination. Value $150." Realized $75. In his November 1939 sale of the William B. Hale Collection, B. Max Mehl described the same coin as lot 856: "1857-D Uncirculated, with semi-proof surface; the highest portions show just the slightest cabinet friction. From the great Wm. H. Woodin Collection, at $60, in 1911." Realized $25. In February 1921 the catalog of Mehl's sale of the Dr. G.F.E. Wilharm Collection described lot 168: "1857-D Practically Uncirculated, sharp, with some Mint luster. Extremely rare, more so than the 1852 and 1853." Realized $15.25. Mehl's February 1944 catalog of the sale of the Belden E. Roach Collection described lot 999: "1857-D Practically Uncirculated with mint luster. Rare in any condition, but extremely so in Uncirculated." Realized $45.

Stack's sale of the J.F. Bell Collection in December 1944 included lot 224: "1857-D Brilliant Uncirculated, very scarce." Realized $55. Mehl's sale of the William Cutler Atwater Collection included lot 2057: "1857-D. Just about Uncirculated with full frosty mint surface. Rare so choice. Catalogs at $45 in only Very Fine. Recent record $55." Realized $47.50. In October 1951 the Numismatic Gallery sale of the B.A. Talmadge collection included lot 1230: "1857-D Uncirculated, scarce." Realized $45. In November 1956 the New Netherlands sale of the Thomas L. Gaskill Collection included lot 289: "1857-D. Dull, lustrous Uncirculated. An exceptionally sharp strike, almost entirely free of handling or bag marks. Obverse die lightly cracked; reverse with planchet defect at border below fraction. A truly lovely coin, and a rare one; only 2,364 coined. As fine as any known to us. Supposedly cost $100. years ago." Realized $102.50.

VF-20	EF-40	AU-50	AU-55	MS-60	MS-62	MS-63
$1,750	$2,800	$4,500	$7,000	$12,000	$22,000	$35,000

1857-O

Circulation-Strike Mintage: 34,000

Very rare in Mint State.

The final New Orleans Mint coin of this denomination.

Estimated Total Population (Mint State). 7 to 11. The 1857-O is very rare. Most are in lower ranges, nearer to MS-60 than to MS-63. Although 34,000 1857-O quarter eagles were minted, there was no numismatic interest in them at the time, and virtually all circulated extensively. The appearance of pieces in Mint State today is due to remote chance. Often a period of *years* will elapse between offerings of such coins.

Estimated Total Population (Circulated Grades). 300 to 400. Very Fine and Extremely Fine are about par. When the Civil War began in 1861, vast quantities of southern mint coins were hoarded. Thus, such pieces saw circulation from the time of mintage, in the present case 1857, up to 1861. Because of this, extant southern mint

(Charlotte, Dahlonega, and New Orleans) coins tend to have higher average grades as the years of the decade elapse.

Die Data. *1857 four-digit date logotype: See the Philadelphia Mint listing for this year.*

Characteristics of Striking and Die Notes. Examples are usually lightly struck in the centers. Higher grades are usually prooflike.

Selected Auction Records

In his 1907 fixed-price list Elmer S. Sears offered lot 280: "1857 New Orleans Mint. Uncirculated. Mint lustre. Scarce in this condition. $6.50." Thomas L. Elder's March 1911 sale of the William H. Woodin Collection included this description of lot 1060: "1857-O, the O between 2 and D. Extremely Fine. Rare." Realized $2.50 (face value). In May 1915 B. Max Mehl's catalog of the B.W. Smith Collection included this description of lot 321: "1857-O O over 2 of fraction. Uncirculated, bright mint luster. Rare. The last date of the quarter eagle of this mint." Realized $4. Mehl's May 1922 catalog of the James Ten Eyck Collection included lot 90: "1857-O. O over 2 of fraction. Brilliant Uncirculated. Very rare so choice." Realized $5.25. In his November 1939 sale of the William B. Hale Collection, Mehl described lot 867: "1857-O Last year of issue. Brilliant Uncirculated, with full mint luster; almost equal to a Proof. Scarce in any condition, but very rare so choice." Realized $5.40.

Mehl's February 1944 catalog of the sale of the Belden E. Roach Collection described lot 981: "1857-O Uncirculated with semi-proof surface; brilliant. Very scarce, especially so choice." Realized $7.50. The Stack's sale of the J.F. Bell Collection in Mehl's sale of the William Cutler Atwater Collection included lot 2071: "1857-O. Last year of issue. Uncirculated, slight cabinet friction. Very scarce so choice. Recent record $27." Realized $8.50.

VF-20	EF-40	AU-50	AU-55	MS-60	MS-62	MS-63
$500	$600	$1,250	$1,700	$4,250	$8,000	$14,500

1857-S

Circulation-Strike Mintage: 69,200

Traditionally a rarity in Mint State.

The mintage figure includes 1,200 coins struck on January 19, *1858*. There is no known way of distinguishing the 1857-S quarter eagles actually struck in 1858. There is no such thing as an 1858-dated San Francisco Mint quarter eagle (although ten obverse dies were on hand at the Mint), thus effectively revealing these to be 1857-S (unless at some future date an authentic 1858-S is discovered, and what a fantastic find that would be!).

No quarter eagles were made at the San Francisco Mint in the following year, 1858. Writing in the August 1903 issue of *The Numismatist*, Augustus G. Heaton, in "Eccentricities of Coin Valuation," commented (excerpt): "As gold collecting is generally the interest of the more experienced class, its branch as well as Philadelphia rarities are fully appreciated, and such pieces as the Philadelphia Mint double eagle of 1883, the eagle of 1875, the half eagle of 1887, the $3 or $1 of 1875, and the S mint quarter eagle of 1858, the S mint dollar of 1870, the D mint dollars of 1855, 1856, and 1861, would raise the numismatic temperature of an auction room to fever heat." Heaton, whose 1893 monograph, *Mint Marks*, had caused much attention a few years earlier, was not aware that there was no such coin as an 1858-S quarter eagle.

Estimated Total Population (Mint State). 2 to 4, this per the numismatic record. This issue is very rare.

This estimate does not include any specimens that may have been retrieved from the wreck of the SS *Central America* (sunk on September 12, 1857, with many gold coins aboard, mostly but not entirely $20 double eagles). *The Numismatist*, July 1990, "The S.S. Central America: Tragedy and Treasure," by Walter Breen: "There are far smaller numbers of gem 1857-S eagles, half eagles and quarter eagles. Eagles shown me are the 'low date' variety (*Encyclopedia* 6927); half eagles include three varieties of *Encyclopedia* 6632 (large S, 7 free or touching truncation, one of latter with 57 repunched at bases) and 6633 (small S). Few coins retain traces of reddish iron oxide coating; most are pristine. I saw one 1856-S medium-S Uncirculated eagle and one 1856-S $3, small S (*Encyclopedia* 6922 and 6356)."

Estimated Total Population (Circulated Grades). 150 to 250. This issue is most often seen in Very Fine and Extremely Fine grades, but a fair number of About Uncirculated coins have been included in major collections that have come to market in recent decades.

Die Data. *1857 four-digit date logotype: See the Philadelphia Mint listing for this year.*

Minor variations exist in date and mintmark placement.

Characteristics of Striking and Die Notes. Most specimens are somewhat flatly struck, this being most evident on the eagle's leg at the left side of the reverse. This general rule fits most other San Francisco quarter eagles of the era.

Selected Auction Records

In his 1907 fixed-price list Elmer S. Sears offered these: Lot 282: "1857 San Francisco Mint. Mint mark placed over figure 1 of fraction. Uncirculated. Mint lustre. Scarce. $6." Lot 284: "1857 Another, with mint mark placed over dividing line of fraction. Very Fine. $6." Thomas L. Elder's March 1911 sale of the William H. Woodin Collection included this description of lot 1063: "1857-S. The S over 1. Very Good. Scarce." Realized $2.60. In May 1913 the U.S. Coin Co. sale of the Malcolm N. Jackson Collection included two examples: Lot 223: "1857-S, S over 1 in fraction. Very Fine." Realized $3.25. Lot 224: "1857-S 5 between 1 and fraction bar. Extremely Fine and rare." Realized $3.50. In May 1915 B. Max Mehl's catalog of the B.W. Smith Collection included this description of lot 323: "1857-S S between 1 and bar. A pin-point nick on obverse edge. Fine." Realized $3.25.

In his November 1939 sale of the William B. Hale Collection, Mehl described lot 869: "1857-S Bright Uncirculated, with full mint luster. Highest portions show slight cabinet friction. Very scarce." Realized $6.30. The Stack's sale of the J.F. Bell Collection in December 1944 included lot 242: "1857-S Brilliant Uncirculated." Realized

$16. The Will W. Neil Collection sold by Mehl in June 1947 included lot 2534: "1857-S, S over 1 of fraction. About Uncirculated with mint luster. Scarce so choice. Record over $20." Realized $10. Abe Kosoff's sale of the Melish and Hester Collections, April 1956, included two: Lot 1239: "1857-S. The S is over the 1 in fraction. About Uncirculated." Realized $21. Lot 1240: "1857-S. The S is centered over the fraction. Uncirculated." Realized $27.50.

VF-20	EF-40	AU-50	AU-55	MS-60	MS-62	MS-63
$525	$650	$1,200	$1,650	$5,500	$7,500	$13,500

1858

Circulation-Strike Mintage: 47,377
Proof Mintage: 8 to 10 (estimated)

Rare in Mint State.

Estimated Total Population (Mint State). 15 to 30. This issue is very rare in Mint State. Most are at lower ranges, closer to MS-60 than to MS-63—an unappreciated rarity.

Estimated Total Population (Circulated Grades). 250 to 400. Very Fine and Extremely Fine are the typical grades.

Die Data. *1858 four-digit date logotype:* The numerals are more evenly spaced than for the preceding year; quite well done, except that the vertical axes of the 8's are not parallel, and the last 8 seems to lean ever so slightly right. This logotype was used on all dies for both mints.

Characteristics of Striking and Die Notes. Examples are usually lightly struck on the eagle's leg to the left, the typical area of lightness on this design because this spot is opposite in the dies to the highest area of the obverse.

Selected Auction Records

The October 1875 sale of the Col. Mendes I. Cohen Collection included Edward Cogan's description of lot 226: "1858 Uncirculated." Realized $2.85. In June 1941 B. Max Mehl's sale of the William Forrester Dunham Collection included lot 1957: "1858 Just a shade from Uncirculated, but with considerable original mint luster. Scarce so choice." Realized $4.75. In October 1951 the Numismatic Gallery sale of the B.A. Talmadge collection included lot 1116: "1858 Uncirculated. Scarce." Realized $20. In Abe Kosoff's sale of the Melish and Hester Collections, April 1956, this was the description of lot 1241: "1858. Uncirculated, choice." Realized $26.

Proofs

Estimated Total Population (Proof). 6 to 8. A very rare coin, but in absolute terms the second most available Proof gold coin of this year (the gold dollar being the most available).

Proof Die Data and Notes. The small date numerals are evenly spaced. There are die lines around stars 11 and 12. This die was only used for Proofs.

Selected Proof Auction Records

Thomas L. Elder's March 1911 sale of the William H. Woodin Collection included this description of lot 1000: "1858. Brilliant Proof. Excessively rare. This may be the first offered in such preservation. Parmelee Collection." Realized $29. B. Max Mehl's May 1922 catalog of the James Ten Eyck Collection included lot 91: "1858. Brilliant Proof. Extreme edge on reverse slightly stained. Excessively rare in Proof condition." Realized $8.75. In November 1956 the New Netherlands sale of the Thomas L. Gaskill Collection included lot 294: "1858 Choice, brilliant Proof. Wire edge; a glittering "gem." The first year of publicly sold Proofs. Chapman once estimated that not over five of these were around. It is remarkable that we cannot locate a Proof '58 in any modern sale, including the Dunham, Roach, Flanagan, Bell, WGC, Atwater, H.R. Lee (1947), Memorable, Dr. Green, Menjou, Davis-Graves or Melish offerings. From the celebrated Virgil Brand Collection, ex Ira Reed." Realized $320.

VF-20	EF-40	AU-50	AU-55	MS-60	MS-62	MS-63	PF-60	PF-63
$500	$515	$525	$535	$1,100	$1,850	$3,000	$25,000	$45,000

1858-C

Circulation-Strike Mintage: 9,056

Scarce in any grade.
Rare in Mint State.

Estimated Total Population (Mint State). 12 to 18. This issue is very rare. Most are in lower ranges, and no doubt some would be better designated as About Uncirculated.

Estimated Total Population (Circulated Grades). 125 to 175; very scarce. Extremely Fine is about par for the typical specimen seen, although there are quite a few Extremely Fine coins. At the About Uncirculated level, the 1858-C is rare.

Die Data. *1858 four-digit date logotype: See the Philadelphia Mint listing for this year.*

The die characteristics for the 1858-C quarter eagle listed in the Bowers and Merena March 2003 auction are as follows: The four-digit 1858 logotype is deeply punched into the die and slightly closer to the denticles than to the neck truncation, but clear of both. On the obverse a tiny, raised ridge extends from the earlobe to the lower left to near the front of the neck. On the reverse the C mintmark overlaps the tip of the arrow feather.

Characteristics of Striking and Die Notes. Usually with slight lightness of strike at the centers, but not necessarily much different from the typical quarter eagle struck at other mints of the era. Planchet quality is usually poor.

Selected Auction Records

In his 1907 fixed-price list Elmer S. Sears offered lot 287: "1858 Charlotte Mint. Uncirculated, with some lustre. Very rare. $15." Thomas L. Elder's March 1911 sale of the William H. Woodin Collection included this description of lot 1132: "1858-C. Fine. Very rare." Realized $4. In May 1913 the U.S. Coin Co. sale of the Malcolm N.

Jackson Collection included lot 290: "1858-C About Uncirculated, mint luster, rare." Realized $3.25. In May 1915 B. Max Mehl's catalog of the B.W. Smith Collection included this description of lot 297: "1858-C C over 1 and bar. Very Fine. Scarce." Realized $3.10. In February 1921 the catalog of Mehl's sale of the Dr. G.F.E. Wilharm Collection described lot 182: "1858-C Uncirculated, Mint luster. Rare." Realized $3.75. In his November 1939 sale of the William B. Hale Collection Mehl described lot 844: "1858-C About Uncirculated, with mint luster." Realized $5.60. Stack's sale of the J.F. Bell Collection in December 1944 included lot 205: "1858-C Brilliant Uncirculated." Realized $28.50. In June 1946 Mehl's sale of the William Cutler Atwater Collection included lot 2037: "1858-C. Extremely Fine; considerable luster. A very light die depression on upper reverse and light hardly noticeable die file mark. Very scarce. (None minted in 1857.)" Realized $8.75. Mehl's sale of the Jerome Kern Collection in May 1950 included lot 129: "1858 C. Uncirculated; just the slightest touch of cabinet friction; mint luster. Cost $23." Realized $23.50.

VF-20	EF-40	AU-50	AU-55	MS-60	MS-62	MS-63
$1,700	$2,500	$3,500	$4,250	$8,000	$13,500	$25,000

1859

Circulation-Strike Mintage: 39,364
Proof Mintage: 80

This represents the smallest quantity for any Philadelphia Mint quarter eagle of the 1850s.

Elusive in Mint State.

Estimated Total Population (Mint State). 30 to 45. It is fairly scarce in Mint State. Among those that do exist, there are a few choice and gem examples, although most are MS-60 to MS-62.

Estimated Total Population (Circulated Grades). 200 to 350. The 1859 is mostly seen in Extremely Fine and About Uncirculated grades, as the issue circulated but briefly before gold coins were hoarded in the East (beginning in December 1861).

Die Data. *1859 four-digit date logotype:* The 18 is close, 85 is farther apart, and 59 is farthest. The digits are of a different style than used earlier or later, sometimes attributed to Paquet. The 1 has a thick upright and very thin upper left serif; the left serif is longer than the right serif. The top part of the 8 is smaller than the bottom part, and the 8 leans slightly left. The 5 is large, thin, and "open," slanting slightly, with the flag extending nearly to the width of the curve below, and the ball is small and close to the upright. The 9 leans right; the bottom of the 9 is thin and has the ball touching or nearly touching the curve above it. This logotype was used on all dies of all mints.

In 1859 a new hub or master reverse die was employed, creating the New Reverse variety, which Walter Breen designated Type II. The Old Reverse (which Breen called Type I; in use since 1840) and New Reverse are differentiated as follows:

Old Reverse: The lower arrowhead almost touches CA (AMERICA). *The top two arrowheads touch each other.* The eagle's claws are closed.

New Reverse: The smaller arrowheads are distant from CA. The eagle's claws are open. *The top two arrowheads are distinctly separated.* Most 1859 circulation strikes seem to be of this type, perhaps 80% or more of the population.

Characteristics of Striking and Die Notes. The 1859 is typically weakly struck on the eagle's leg at the left reverse. High-grade pieces usually show prooflike surfaces.

Selected Auction Records

Thomas L. Elder's March 1911 sale of the William H. Woodin Collection included this description of lot 1001: "1859. Uncirculated." Realized $4. B. Max Mehl's sale of the Jerome Kern Collection in May 1950 included lot 49: "1859 Uncirculated with Proof surface. It appears as having been polished." Realized $8.50. In October 1951 the Numismatic Gallery sale of the B.A. Talmadge collection included lot 1117: "1859 Uncirculated, very scarce." Realized $26. In April 1956 Abe Kosoff's sale of the Melish and Hester Collections included lot 1243: "1859 Uncirculated, choice." Realized $45. In November 1956 the New Netherlands sale of the Thomas L. Gaskill Collection included lot 296: "1859 'gem' first-strike or 'Semi-proof.' Partial wire edge (on either side). Obtained as a "Brilliant Proof" from the late Ira Reed. A highly deceptive coin, actually rarer than a Proof in this preservation. Should bring about $50." Realized $35.

Proofs

Based on the number of known examples, this mintage figure is either inaccurate or reflects a large number of Proofs minted, but never sold and later remelted.

Estimated Total Population (Proof). 15 to 20. John Dannreuther traces ten of the Old Reverse (heavy arrows) with others reported, and three of the New Reverse.

Proof Die Data and Notes. The 1 in 1859 is about centered between the denticles and bust, somewhat to the left; the ball of the 5 logotype is upright; the ball of the 9 is touching the curve above it. There is a tiny brilliant patch of Proof surface deep within Miss Liberty's ear. The reverse has the bottom parts of the second and third vertical stripe pairs polished and showing Proof surface within the line elements. The date logotype is ever so slightly closer to the denticles than to the neck truncation, but the difference is hardly noticeable.

Nearly all Proofs were struck from an Old Reverse die, although an example with the New Reverse is reported from the Byron Reed Collection.

Selected Proof Auction Records

The October 1875 sale of the Col. Mendes I. Cohen Collection included Edward Cogan's description of lot 227: "1859 Fine Proof." Realized $2.85. In February 1921 the catalog of B. Max Mehl's sale of the Dr. G.F.E. Wilharm Collection described lot 95: "1859 Perfect brilliant Proof. Gem. Very rare so choice. Valued at $20." Realized $15.75. The Stack's sale of the J.F. Bell Collection in December 1944 included lot 126: "1859 Brilliant Proof gem." Realized $65. In June 1946 Mehl's sale of the William Cutler Atwater Collection included lot 1963: "1859 Perfect brilliant Proof. Extremely rare in Proof. Recent record $75, but in my humble opinion these beautiful gold coins in brilliant Proof condition are almost priceless and worth much more than their present market." Realized $70.

	VF-20	EF-40	AU-50	MS-60	MS-63	PF-60	PF-63
Old Reverse	$500	$550	$850	$2,000	$6,000	$15,000	$30,000
New Reverse	$500	$515	$525	$1,200	$3,000		—

1859-D

Final Dahlonega Mint quarter eagle. Scarce in any grade. Very rare in Mint State.

Circulation-Strike Mintage: 2,244

Deliveries of this issue were reported as follows: First quarter, 642; third quarter, 730; fourth quarter, 872. Assay coins were not recorded.

Estimated Total Population (Mint State). 7 to 10. This issue is very rare. Virtually all Mint State examples are in lower levels, in the MS-60 and MS-61 range.

Estimated Total Population (Circulated Grades). 90 to 130. The 1859-D is very elusive, and most are in higher grades such as Extremely Fine and About Uncirculated.

Die Data. *1859 four-digit date logotype: See the Philadelphia Mint listing for this year.*

Two 1859-dated obverse dies were sent from Philadelphia sometime on or after September 15, 1858 (this being the date of a note by Chief Engraver J.B. Longacre stating that the request for dies had been complied with), and arrived in Dahlonega in early January 1859.[98] Dies were sent from Philadelphia to Dahlonega for anticipated 1860-D and 1861-D quarter eagle coinages that never materialized. The 1860-D dies were in response to a request sent by Dahlonega Mint Director Patton to Philadelphia, asking for two pairs each of the $1, $2.50, and $5 dies.

Reverse die used on all Dahlonega quarter eagles from 1849 to 1859: See description under 1849-D on pages 220–221.

Characteristics of Striking and Die Notes. Usually fairly well struck on the obverse, but with areas of lightness on the reverse.

Selected Auction Records

Thomas L. Elder's March 1911 sale of the William H. Woodin Collection included this description of lot 1114: "1859-D. Fine. Excessively rare. 'No record of public sale.' It should be valued highly." Realized $30. In May 1913 the U.S. Coin Co. sale of the Malcolm N. Jackson Collection included lot 268: "1859-D Very Fine and extremely rare. The preceding collection of the Dahlonega Mint [in the Jackson catalog] is the most remarkable in regard to condition ever offered for public sale." Realized $31. In May 1915 B. Max Mehl's catalog of the B.W. Smith Collection included this description of lot 307: "1859-D Last date of the quarter eagle of this mint. Extremely Fine, practically Uncirculated, with mint luster. Latest record for only a Very Fine specimen $31. Extremely rare." Realized $18.60. The same coin reappeared as lot 297 in November 1956 in New Netherlands' sale of the Thomas L. Gaskill Collection: "1859-D. The last year of issue from Dahlonega. Very Fine or better, the usual rather flat strike. Cleaner than most; a tiny planchet defect in field behind Liberty's head. An underrated item; only 2,244 minted. The almost identical WGC coin obtained $42.50 in 1946, when a great many items were a lot cheaper than they are today. Ex B.W. Smith Collection, lot 307 (Mehl, 1915)." Realized $54.

Mehl's February 1944 catalog of the sale of the Belden E. Roach Collection described lot 1000: "1859-D Last year of issue. Nearly Uncirculated with considerable luster. Bold impression. A beautiful specimen of this rarity." Realized $26.65. The Stack's sale of the J.F. Bell Collection in December 1944 included lot 225: "1859-D Last year of issue. Uncirculated, very scarce." Realized $40. In June 1946 Mehl's sale of the William Cutler Atwater Collection included lot 2058: "1859-D. Uncirculated with brilliant mint luster. Rare and valuable. Last year of issue. (None minted in 1858.) Record of $42.50 for a much inferior specimen."[99] Realized $41. In Abe Kosoff's sale of the Melish and Hester Collections, April 1956, this was the description of lot 1244: "1859-D. Last year of the Dahlonega Mint quarter eagles. About Uncirculated, mint luster. A lovely coin." Realized $52.50.

VF-20	EF-40	AU-50	MS-60
$2,200	$3,250	$4,500	$17,500

1859-S

Circulation-Strike Mintage: 15,200

Scarce in any grade.
Very rare in Mint State.

Estimated Total Population (Mint State). 4 to 6. This is a major rarity by any evaluation. No hoard coins are known to exist. Examples are encountered one at a time on the market, and not often.

Estimated Total Population (Circulated Grades). 70 to 90. The 1859-S quarter eagle is scarce in all worn grades due to its low mintage. Extremely Fine is about the median grade for specimens appearing at auction over the years. When David W. Akers was preparing the manuscript for his 1975 book, he noted that in the preceding seven years, only one coin better than Extremely Fine had appeared at auction.

As is the case with just about any gold coin of this era, estimates are apt to vary. In 1986 in *The Quarter Eagles*, Paul F. Taglione suggested that "about 125 exist; about 4 are Uncirculated."

Die Data. *1859 four-digit date logotype: See the Philadelphia Mint listing for this year.*

The Old Reverse hub is used.

Six 1859-dated obverse dies were shipped to the San Francisco Mint in November 1858. For reverses, dies already on hand were used.

The mintmark S is small on the specimens seen, including one S that is very thin, having been weakly punched into the die (from the same small S punch used on other dies). In his 1964 monograph, Walter Breen described three different mintmark variations, later finding a fourth (mentioned in his 1968 *New Varieties* monograph update).

Characteristics of Striking and Die Notes. The 1859-S is often seen weakly struck.

Selected Auction Records

In his 1907 fixed-price list Elmer S. Sears offered two: Lot 291: "1859 San Francisco Mint. Almost Uncirculated. Scarce. $7." Lot 292: "1859 Another with solid ('s'). Uncirculated. Mint lustre. Very rare. $12." Thomas L. Elder's March 1911 sale of the William H. Woodin Collection included this description of lot 1064: "1859-S. The S between 1 and bar. Extremely Fine. Very rare, and seldom offered." Realized $9.50. This coin came on the market again as lot 870 in the November 1939 sale by B. Max Mehl of the William B. Hale Collection: "1859-S Extremely Fine, with some luster. Very rare. From the Wm. H. Woodin Collection. Not even priced in the Standard Catalogue." Realized $42. In May 1913 the U.S. Coin Co. sale of the Malcolm N. Jackson Collection included lot 225: "1859-S. S between 1 and fraction bar. Good, extremely rare." Realized $3.50. In June 1941 Mehl's sale of the William Forrester Dunham Collection included lot 1958: "1859-S Practically Uncirculated, with considerable mint luster. Rare in any condition, especially so choice. Listed at $20 in Very Fine." Realized $21.

Mehl's February 1944 catalog of the sale of the Belden E. Roach Collection described lot 1003: "1859-S Extremely Fine. Rare. Listed at $20 in only Very Fine. (Although the mint records show that 1,200 specimens were struck in 1858, not a single specimen is known to exist as far as I know.)" Realized $26. The Stack's sale of the J.F. Bell Collection in December 1944 included lot 243: "1859-S Brilliant Uncirculated." Realized $37.50. In June Mehl's sale of the William Cutler Atwater Collection included lot 2075: "1859-S. About Uncirculated with mint luster. Limited coinage. Quite rare. Recent record $37.50." Realized $16. In November 1956 the New Netherlands sale of the Thomas L. Gaskill Collection included lot 298: "1859-S. A curiosity; lower half of mintmark filled up by a die defect. Strictly Very Fine. Highly attractive desirable. Limited coinage of 15,200 pieces. A 'sleeper.' The 'World's Greatest' specimen (also VF) realized $37.50 against a $30 estimate; the EF plus Peake example, in our 46th sale over a year ago, sold for $45. The 1859 Philadelphia Mint quarter eagle above has small slender arrows and letters upon the reverse, as on 1860 and later coins. In contrast, the-D and-S mintmarks have heavy arrows and letters, as in preceding years." Realized $29.

VF-20	EF-40	AU-50	MS-60	MS-63
$525	$1,000	$2,000	$5,500	$17,500

1860

Circulation-Strike Mintage: 22,563
Proof Mintage: 112

Scarce in Mint State.

Estimated Total Population (Mint State). 30 to 50. This issue is scarce in Mint State and usually seen in lower ranges, but a few choice and gem specimens exist. The certification data are inconclusive.

Estimated Total Population (Circulated Grades). 175 to 350. Extremely Fine and About Uncirculated are the typical grades.

Die Data. *1860 four-digit date logotype:* The numerals are small and fairly evenly spaced. The upright of the 1 is thick; the top interior of the 8 is smaller than the bottom interior, and the 8 leans ever so slightly right. The 6 leans slightly right, and its ball is not completely circular, separated from the curve below on most impressions. The left and right side of the 6 are thick, and the bottom interior of 6 has more or less straight sides. The 0 leans right, and its interior is long and narrow with straight sides and a rounded top; the base of 0 is lower than the base of the adjacent 6. This logotype was used on all dies of all mints.

Old Reverse: The lower arrowhead almost touches CA (AMERICA). *The top two arrowheads touch each other.* The eagle's claws are closed. Relatively few coins of this year are of the Old Reverse type. The rarity was noted by Walter Breen in his *Encyclopedia*, 1988, when he observed that these "possibly exist," but had not seen one. The Bowers and Merena sale of November 2002 included a Mint State example.

New Reverse: The smaller arrowheads are distant from CA. The eagle's claws are open. *The top two arrowheads are distinctly separated.* Most 1859 circulation strikes seem to be of this type, perhaps 80% or more of the population.

Characteristics of Striking and Die Notes. The 1860 is usually well struck.

Selected Auction Records

The catalog of John W. Haseltine's June 1883 sale of the William J. Jenks Collection described lot 465: "1860 Uncirculated. Scarce." Realized $3. In May 1913 the U.S. Coin Co. sale of the Malcolm N. Jackson Collection included lot 146: "1860 Uncirculated." Realized $3. B. Max Mehl's sale of the Jerome Kern Collection in May 1950 included lot 50: "1860 Uncirculated with semi-Proof surface. Slight cabinet friction on obverse, but a beautiful coin. Not a rarity, but very scarce so choice. Catalogs $25. This coin was originally purchased by Mr. Kern as a Proof at $35." Realized $11.

Proofs

It is likely that fewer than 30 to 40 pieces at most were sold from this mintage; the rest were spent or melted.

Estimated Total Population (Proof). 14 to 18.

Proof Die Data and Notes. The date logotype is lightly impressed into the die and is placed high, significantly closer to the bust than to the denticles. The bottom of the interior ear has a polished Proof surface. The reverse is from the new die with arrowheads separated, etc. There are polished areas between the elements of the third and fourth vertical shield stripes. On the reverse there is a small projection from the left side of the numerator 1 in the fraction, which serves to hallmark this die (which was also used throughout the 1860s).

The New Reverse was used on all Proofs from this year forward.

Selected Auction Records

Note: Proof listings are very extensive, representing a much smaller number of different coins coming on the market multiple times. Cited here are representative listings. The Proof 1860 has been given a lot of "press" for its rarity, more so than a number of the other Proof dates of the 1860s and 1870s that are equally or more elusive.

In June 1946 B. Max Mehl's sale of the William Cutler Atwater Collection included lot 1964: "1860 Brilliant Proof. Just a tiny pin-point nick on left obverse field. This is hardly noticeable. Recent record $75." Realized $55. In April 1956 Abe Kosoff's sale of the Melish and Hester Collections included lot 1247: "1860 Superb brilliant Proof." Realized $140. In November 1956 the New Netherlands sale of the Thomas L. Gaskill Collection included lot 299: "1860 Brilliant Proof. Unsullied; traces of tarnish, easily removable by ammonia. Extremely rare, should bring $150. Ex V. Brand, Ira Reed." Realized $175.

	VF-20	EF-40	AU-50	MS-60	MS-63	PF-60	PF-63
Old Reverse	$1,250	$2,000	$2,750	$5,000	$10,000		
New Reverse	$500	$515	$525	$1,100	$3,000	$14,000	$22,500

1860-C

Circulation-Strike Mintage: 7,469

Last Charlotte Mint quarter eagle. Scarce in any grade. Incredibly rare in Mint State.

Estimated Total Population (Mint State). 3 or 4. These are in lower levels, MS-60 or thereabouts, with none attaining MS-64 or finer level. As of 1975, David W. Akers had seen only one Mint State coin.

Estimated Total Population (Circulated Grades). 80 to 110. Very Fine is about the norm, representing pieces that *appear* to be Very Fine but in reality have sustained relatively little wear (see "Characteristics" below). Population estimates are difficult to determine for Charlotte (and Dahlonega) coins because of so much churning of them in and out of the grading services—their generally high market value makes this activity worthwhile to the owners of the coins and, of course, to the grading services.

Die Data. *1860 four-digit date logotype: See the Philadelphia Mint listing for this year.*

Characteristics of Striking and Die Notes. These are nearly always weakly struck on the reverse at the lower left, although the occasional exception is encountered. Struck from roughly finished dies on imperfect planchets. This makes them very difficult to grade.

Selected Auction Records

In his 1907 fixed-price list Elmer S. Sears offered lot 294: "1860 Charlotte Mint. Practically Uncirculated and an extremely rare mint mark. $25." Thomas L. Elder's March 1911 sale of the William H. Woodin Collection included this description of lot 1133: "1860-C. Fine. Very scarce, coinage small." Realized $4. In May 1913 the U.S. Coin Co. sale of the Malcolm N. Jackson Collection included lot 291: "1860-C Extremely Fine, mint luster, rare." Realized $3.25. In May 1915 B. Max Mehl's catalog of the B.W. Smith Collection included this description of lot 298: "1860-C Last year of issue. Very Fine, sharp. Rare. Record $12.50." Realized $3.10. The record was not challenged! In February 1921 the catalog of Mehl's sale of the Dr. G.F.E. Wilharm

Collection described lot 183: "1860-C Last year of issue at this Mint. About Uncirculated. Rare. Old records of $12." Realized $6.10. The Stack's sale of the J.F. Bell Collection in December 1944 included lot 206: "1860-C Last year of issue. Extremely Fine." Realized $17.50. The Will W. Neil Collection sold by Mehl in June 1947 included lot 2506: "1860-C Last year of issue. Extremely Fine with some luster. Very scarce with record over $20." Realized $10. In November 1956 the New Netherlands sale of the Thomas L. Gaskill Collection included lot 300: "1860-C. Last year. Extremely Fine for this poorly struck coin, some of the appearance of weakness from die wear. A rare date; only 7,469 struck, putting this in a class with the 1866 gold dollar. Records to $37, for comparable pieces." Realized $33.

VF-20	EF-40	AU-50	MS-60	MS-63
$1,850	$2,500	$3,250	$13,000	$30,000

1860-S

Circulation-Strike Mintage: 35,600

Scarce in any grade.
Especially rare in Mint State.

Estimated Total Population (Mint State). 4 to 7. The 1860-S is a first-class rarity in Mint State, and only a handful exist. Nearly all are in lower ranges of the category.

Estimated Total Population (Circulated Grades). 80 to 100. Typical grades are Very Fine and Extremely Fine, the average being slightly finer than quarter eagles of the preceding decade.

In perusing the availability of quarter eagles from this era, one cannot help but contemplate that if the collecting of San Francisco issues ever became as popular as the pursuit of Charlotte and Dahlonega pieces, prices would multiply many times—as, in general, the supply of high-grade S-Mint pieces of the 1850s is much smaller.

Die Data. *1860 four-digit date logotype: See the Philadelphia Mint listing for this year.*

Four obverse dies were shipped to San Francisco for the coinage, but it is probable that not all were used. Old reverse dies were still on hand, these being of the hub style used through 1876.

One obverse die has a repunched date (Breen-6255), this being most evident at 860. This variety is not particularly rare.

Characteristics of Striking and Die Notes. These are usually seen with some lightness at the centers.

Selected Auction Records

In his 1907 fixed-price list Elmer S. Sears offered lot 295: "1860 San Francisco Mint. Nearly Uncirculated, with mint lustre. $7." Thomas L. Elder's March 1911 sale of the William H. Woodin Collection included this description of lot 1065: "1860-S. The S just touching 1. About Fine; rare." Realized $2.85. In February 1921 the catalog of B.

Max Mehl's sale of the Dr. G.F.E. Wilharm Collection described lot 201: "1860-S Variety as last. Nearly Uncirculated. Very scarce." Realized $3.75. In his sale of the Morris Collection, April 1931, Mehl described lot 599: "1860-S Slanting S over 1 of fraction. Fine. Rare." Realized $6. The Stack's sale of the J.F. Bell Collection in December 1944 included lot 244: "1860-S Extremely Fine." Realized $13.50. The sale of the Philpott and Zander Collections by Mehl in November 1945 included lot 1214: "1860-S Uncirculated. Very scarce so choice." Realized $15.50. In the Numismatic Gallery sale of the "World's Greatest Collection" (F.C.C. Boyd Collection, January 1946) Abe Kosoff described lot 246: "1860-S Very Fine." Realized $20. In October 1951 the Numismatic Gallery sale of the B.A. Talmadge collection included lot 1249: "1860-S Very Fine. W.G.C." Realized $9.25. This coin was bought at the height of the coin market in 1946 and sold near the low in 1951.

VF-20	EF-40	AU-50	MS-60	MS-63
$550	$675	$1,250	$3,750	$20,000

1861

Circulation-Strike Mintage: 1,283,788
Proof Mintage: 90

Readily available in most grades.

In the entire quarter eagle series from 1796 to 1929 only four issues had a mintage of over 1,000,000 coins: 1851, 1852, 1853, and 1861. The three earlier dates were produced when California gold was available in quantity, while the 1861 quarter eagles were struck from melted-down coins of earlier times including Type I gold dollars.

Estimated Total Population (Mint State). 700 to 1,000. Mint State specimens are widely available, and no trouble will be experienced in acquiring an example in the choice or gem category, although the vast majority are closer to MS-60. Most 1861 quarter eagles are of very pleasing appearance, yielding a coin that is at once affordable and a pleasure to own. It is likely that many of these were hoarded toward the end of the year and kept secure for years afterward during the uncertainties of the Civil War.

Estimated Total Population (Circulated Grades). 5,000 to 7,000. These are very plentiful, as the high mintage suggests. Typical grades are Extremely Fine and About Uncirculated, as such coins were hoarded during and after the Civil War and were not seen again in circulation until December 1878, after which time they did not circulate extensively. The same comment can be made for all other Philadelphia Mint quarter eagles of the era.

Die Data. *1861 four-digit date logotype:* The 18 are closely spaced, the 86 are slightly farther apart, and the 61 are still slightly farther apart, but the entire ensemble is spaced so as to be attractive to the eye. Both 1's are slightly bulged on the left side of the upright. The 8 leans slightly right, and its lower interior is slightly larger than the upper interior. The 6 leans right, the knob of the 6 is small and distant from the curve below, and the left side of the 6 is thick. The base of the final 1 is slightly low; there is a slight bulge to each digit 1 on the left side of the upright. This logotype was used on all dies of both mints.

Multiple die pairs were used—from 21 obverse and 24 reverse dies prepared. Thus, the date logotype positions vary. These have not been widely studied and can only be appreciated when several different coins are compared side by side.

The reverse is seen with old (rare) and new hub styles.[100]

Although Old Reverse coins are very rare, serious numismatists seeking them are rarer yet, and little notice has been taken of them by dealers or certification services. Thus, the 1860 with the Old Reverse is a candidate for cherrypicking.

Characteristics of Striking and Die Notes. Dies of this and other circulation-strike quarter eagles of the next several years were hastily finished. Thus, early strikings nearly always show parallel die striae. As the dies wore, the striae wore away, and later strikings show them less prominently.

Selected Auction Records

The catalog of John W. Haseltine's June 1883 sale of the William J. Jenks Collection described lot 466: "1861 Uncirculated. Scarce." Realized $3. Thomas L. Elder's March 1911 sale of the William H. Woodin Collection included this description of lot 1004: "1861. Date farther away from bust. Very Fine." Realized $2.50 (face value). In June 1941 B. Max Mehl's sale of the William Forrester Dunham Collection included lot 1960: "1861 Uncirculated, with full mint luster." Realized $4.80. In October 1951 the Numismatic Gallery sale of the B.A. Talmadge collection included lot 1119: "1861 Uncirculated." Realized $14. In Abe Kosoff's sale of the Melish and Hester Collections, April 1956, there were two: Lot 1251: "1861. 1 close to bust; outlines below 18. Very Fine." Realized $12. Lot 1252: "1861. 1 distant from bust. Very Fine." Realized $12.

PROOFS

It is likely that no more than 20 to 25 were distributed, as today the 1861 Proof is rarer, for example, than the 1863 (30 mintage).

Estimated Total Population (Proof). 12 to 15.

Proof Die Data and Notes. The obverse has its date logotype high, at least twice as close to the neck as to the denticles. Some area of semi-Proof finish, visible when coins are held at an angle, is seen at the intersection of the chest and neck of Miss Liberty as well as below her ear; the inner ear has Proof polish. The reverse is seen with a distinctive die with little projection from the left side of the vertical element of the numerator in the fraction, the interiors of shield stripes 4 and 5 highly polished, and with stripes each side being slightly more polished than in 1860.

Selected Auction Records

Note: Proof listings are very extensive, representing a much smaller number of different coins coming on the market multiple times.

Thomas L. Elder's March 1911 sale of the William H. Woodin Collection included this description of lot 1003: "1861 Date near to bust. Brilliant Proof. Very rare." Realized

$14.50. The Stack's sale of the J.F. Bell Collection in December 1944 included lot 128: "1861 Brilliant Proof gem." Realized $46. In the Numismatic Gallery sale of the "World's Greatest Collection" (F.C.C. Boyd Collection, January 1946) Abe Kosoff described lot 129: "1861 Brilliant Proof." Realized $50. In June 1946 Mehl's sale of the William Cutler Atwater Collection included lot 1965: "1861 Perfect brilliant Proof. record $50." Realized $50. In November 1956 the New Netherlands sale of the Thomas L. Gaskill Collection included lot 302: "1861 Small, light arrows and letters, as on all Philadelphia coins to follow. Brilliant Proof; a few light stains easily removable. At least as rare as the famous 1863, but not valued so highly since this date is available in grades other than Proof. The recently sold Davis-Graves and Melish coins were only circulated examples." Realized $175.

	VF-20	EF-40	AU-50	MS-60	MS-63	PF-60	PF-63
Old Reverse	$550	$1,000	$1,500	$3,750	$7,500		
New Reverse	$500	$515	$525	$700	$1,750	$12,000	$20,000

1861-S

Circulation-Strike Mintage: 24,000

Scarce in any grade.
Incredibly rare in Mint State.

Estimated Total Population (Mint State). 2 or 3. These are exceedingly rare, lacking in just about every major cabinet ever formed. As of 1975 David W. Akers had never seen a Mint State coin, nor had Paul F. Taglione (1986) or Breen (1988). For the classic gold collections of yesteryear, Extremely Fine and About Uncirculated were the order of the day.

Estimated Total Population (Circulated Grades). 80 to 100. These are somewhat scarce, but examples appear on the market regularly. Most are Very Fine or, less often, Extremely Fine coins are seen, and still less often, About Uncirculated examples are encountered.

Die Data. *1861 four-digit date logotype: See the Philadelphia Mint listing for this year.*

The Old Reverse hub is used. One 1861-dated obverse was shipped to the San Francisco Mint in November 1860 and another obverse was sent in June 1861. It seems that only a modest coinage was anticipated. Coinage was performed at the request of depositors, most of whom preferred larger denominations.

Variations exist in mintmark positions.

Characteristics of Striking and Die Notes. These are usually lightly struck on the hair details below the coronet and, on the reverse, on the eagle.

Selected Auction Records

In his 1907 fixed-price list Elmer S. Sears offered two: Lot 298: "1861 San Francisco Mint. Mint mark placed over figure 2 of fraction. Very Fine. Scarce. $6." Lot 299: "1861 Another with mint mark placed over figure 1 of fraction. Uncirculated, with full mint lustre. $9." Thomas L. Elder's March 1911 sale of the William H. Woodin Collection included this description of lot 1066: "1861-S. S between 2 and D. Fine; rare." Realized $2.80. Early mention of mintmark position. In May 1913 the U.S. Coin Co. sale of the Malcolm N. Jackson Collection included two: Lot 227: "1861-S. S over 2 and D. Very Fine, scarce." Realized $4. Lot 228: "1861-S, S between 1 and fraction bar. Fine." Realized $3. Relatively few numismatists collected mintmark positional varieties at this time, and Jackson did not have many. However, of those that he had, most were in the quarter eagle series. In his sale of the Morris Collection, April 1931, Mehl described lot 600: "1861-S, S over 2 of fraction. Very Fine. Rare." Realized $3.60.

Stack's sale of the J.F. Bell Collection in December 1944 included lot 245: "1861-S Brilliant Uncirculated." Realized $27.50. In the Numismatic Gallery sale of the "World's Greatest Collection" (F.C.C. Boyd Collection, January 1946) Abe Kosoff described lot 247: "1861-S Very Fine." Realized $20. In October 1951 the Numismatic Gallery sale of the B.A. Talmadge collection included lot 1250: "1861-S Very Fine. W.G.C." Realized $9.25. Another "buy high, sell low" case of bad market timing. Abe Kosoff's sale of the Melish and Hester Collections, April 1956, had two: Lot 1253: "1861-S. S is over center of fraction. About Extremely Fine." Realized $16. Lot 1254: "1861-S. S is over right side of fraction. Very Fine." Realized $14. In November 1956 the New Netherlands sale of the Thomas L. Gaskill Collection included lot 303: "1861-S. Rev of 1859, as always. Abt. Extremely Fine. Bright and lustrous. Limited coinage." Realized $17.

VF-20	EF-40	AU-50	MS-60
$650	$1,100	$3,500	$13,500

1862, 2 Over 1

Circulation-Strike Mintage: Small part of total mintage of 98,543 for 1862

So-called overdate (but may be over inverted date). Not published until 1963.

Estimated Total Population (Mint State). 2 to 4. These are very rare. The known pieces are at lower Mint State levels.

Estimated Total Population (Circulated Grades). 30 to 50. The typical grades are Extremely Fine and About Uncirculated, as such coins did not circulate extensively. Most probably, the 1862, 2 Over 1, die accounted for a sizable fraction of the year's mintage, say a quarter of it. Many 1862 quarter eagles have not been checked for the overdate feature. As time goes on, more will be identified. Meanwhile, specimens that are run through the certification services will be attributed correctly.

Die Data. *1862 four-digit date logotype: See the listing for 1862 (normal date).*

Eight pairs of dies were prepared for the 1862 quarter eagle coinage, of which one was of the 1862, 2 Over 1, as discussed here.

On this particular obverse die, traces of roughness resembling part of the *upright* of a 1 are seen under the 2 of the date. However, there is no trace of a serif at the upper left of the digit, nor does the upright seem to be slightly bulged at its left (it should be slightly bulged if it is over 1861). The die may have been first punched with the *1862* date *inverted* (this would account for the lack of a bulge on the left side of the undertype), nearly completely erased from the die, then overpunched with an 1862 in the right position. From evidence on hand at this point, the writer sees no reason to call this an 1862, 2 Over 1, overdate. It may be 1862 over inverted date, or the final under-digit may be a stray mark.

All 1862 and later Philadelphia Mint quarter eagles have the New Reverse.

Selected Auction Records

The Stack's Public Auction Sale of U.S. Gold, Silver & Copper Coins, and U.S. and World Paper Money (June 2005) included a Brilliant Uncirculated example of this overdate, with "intensely flashing red-gold lustre" and superficial bagmarks. Realized $13,800. At the August 2010 Boston Rarities auction, Stack's offered an AU-53 coin, described as "minimally worn, predominantly lustrous AU. Generally bold in detail, with pretty rose-gold color and only the expected number of mostly small-size abrasions for a lightly circulated gold coin from the Civil War era." Realized $2,645. An AU-58 coin was offered at the Stack's June 2012 Baltimore Auction: "Bright and lustrous with appealing quality overall. A shallow dig above Liberty's head in the field will serve to identify." Realized $4,700. Other modern auction listings can be found online.

VF-20	EF-40	AU-50	MS-60	MS-63
$1,000	$1,850	$3,000	$8,500	$32,500

1862

Circulation-Strike Mintage: Majority of the total of 98,543 for 1862

Proof Mintage: 35

Scarce in any grade.
Of unexplained rarity in Mint State.

No quarter eagles or other gold coins minted at Philadelphia from 1862 through autumn 1878 were paid out at par; such pieces were stored by the Treasury and were available only by paying a premium.

Estimated Total Population (Mint State). 12 to 18. Mint State coins are very rare. Where did they all go? In 1975 David W. Akers was able to track the appearance of more Proofs than of Mint State coins!

Estimated Total Population (Circulated Grades). 90 to 120. Extremely Fine and About Uncirculated are the typical grades, for these coins did not circulate to any significant extent. There was a flurry of activity among the populace with regard to hoarding "hard" money, and although the Treasury Department did not pay out gold coins after late December 1861, it seems that many of the 1862 gold dollars and quarter eagles were distributed, no doubt to those caring to pay a small premium for them. In any event, high-grade circulation strikes of 1862 are seen with some frequency today, but not in Mint State.

Die Data. *1862 four-digit date logotype:* The 18 are close, but still with generous separation; 86 are slightly wider, and 62 are wider yet, giving the entire logotype a wide or spread-out appearance. The 1 leans slightly right; there is a slight bulge on the left side of the upright (similar to the 1 used in 1861). The top interior of 8 and the bottom interior are about the same size, or perhaps the bottom is very slightly larger, and the 8 leans slightly right. The 6 has an irregularly shaped ball close to but not touching the curve below (except on deep impressions), and the numeral leans slightly right. The 2 has a hook rather than a ball at the top, its upright and base are thick, and the base is curved. The base of 2 is slightly lower than other figures. This logotype was used on all dies of both mints.

Eight pairs of dies were prepared for the 1862 quarter eagle coinage, of which one was of the "1862, 2 Over 1," as discussed earlier. It is not known if all eight pairs were actually used, and it is not likely that they all were.

All 1862 and later Philadelphia Mint quarter eagles have the New Reverse.

Characteristics of Striking and Die Notes. Most have die striae, and many show evidence of clashed dies. The striking is usually sharp. Surfaces are usually frosty and satiny, rather than prooflike.

Selected Auction Records

The catalog of John W. Haseltine's June 883 sale of the William J. Jenks Collection described lot 467: "1862 Uncirculated. Scarce." Realized $3.10. In his 1907 fixed-price list Elmer S. Sears offered lot 301: "1862 Uncirculated. Mint lustre. $4." In May 1913 the U.S. Coin Co. sale of the Malcolm N. Jackson Collection included lot 148: "1862 Uncirculated." Realized $3. In October 1951 the Numismatic Gallery sale of the B.A. Talmadge collection included lot 1121: "1862 Uncirculated, choice." Realized $18.

Proofs

Estimated Total Population (Proof). 14 to 18.

Proof Die Data and Notes. Proofs have the date logotype punched deep into the die. The final digit is particularly deep (Breen's "partly filled 2, effaced overdate?").

Notes on a Proof in the Bass III sale: On the obverse there are small areas of extra polish beneath earlobe and below E (LIBERTY) that can be noticed upon very close inspection. On the reverse the upper interior of 2 is not completely polished, and the area above the curved base of 2 is not completely polished in the die. The date logotype is significantly lower to the denticles than to the bust. The reverse die is as used on other Proofs of the 1860s.

Selected Auction Records

Note: Certain of these "Proofs" may have been prooflike circulation strikes, although for 1862 most circulation issues are frosty.

In June 1885 W. Elliot Woodward's sale of the J. Colvin Randall Collection included these: Lot 998: "1862 Splendid Proof; very rare as Proof." Realized $2.50 (face value). Lot 999: "1862 Scarce; and, as Proof, very rare." Realized $2.50 (face value). Such price realizations are poignant reminders of why so many nineteenth-century Proof gold coins were simply spent. There was little resale market for them until years later. In his 1907 fixed-price list Elmer S. Sears offered lot 300: "1862 Brilliant Proof. Exceedingly rare in this condition. $15." Thomas L. Elder's March 1911 sale of the William H. Woodin Collection included this description of lot 1005: "1862. Brilliant Proof. Very rare." Realized $11.25.

In February 1921 the catalog of B. Max Mehl's sale of the Dr. G.F.E. Wilharm Collection described lot 99: "1862 Brilliant Proof. Very rare in Proof condition. Cost $18." Realized $8.50. The Stack's sale of the J.F. Bell Collection in December 1944 included lot 129: "1862 Brilliant Proof gem." Realized $50. In the Numismatic Gallery sale of the "World's Greatest Collection" (F.C.C. Boyd Collection, January 1946) Abe Kosoff described lot 130: "1862 Brilliant Proof." Realized $60.

In the 93rd Catalogue Sale (Barney Bluestone) there was Lot 1155: "1862 Brilliant, glittering Proof, Superb in every respect. Very rare." In June 1946 Mehl's sale of the William Cutler Atwater Collection included lot 1966: "1862 Struck in yellow gold. Perfect brilliant Proof with raised borders. Truly a gem. Record $60 and worth more." Realized $57.50. In November 1956 the New Netherlands sale of the Thomas L. Gaskill Collection included lot 304: "1862 Mostly brilliant Proof. About as rare as the 1861 and 1863; it is doubtful if even fifteen specimens are in collectors' hands. Catalog valuations are still too low." Realized $125.

VF-20	EF-40	AU-50	MS-60	MS-63	PF-60	PF-63
$500	$600	$1,450	$4,750	$11,000	$12,000	$20,000

1862-S

Circulation-Strike Mintage: 8,000

Scarce in any grade.
Incredibly rare in Mint State.

These circulated at par in the West at a time when quarter eagles were not seen in circulation in the East or Midwest.

Estimated Total Population (Mint State). 2 or 3. The Mint State coins believed to exist are around MS-60 or MS-61. San Francisco Mint quarter eagles of this era are rare enough in such grades as About Uncirculated or even MS-60, but at the MS-62 level they are so elusive that a span of *years* may elapse between offerings of them. Such pieces were not used in large bullion shipments, as $20 pieces were easier to count. Rather, these saw extensive service in everyday commerce.

In 1862, while the Treasury Department was no longer paying out Philadelphia Mint quarter eagles at par, on the West Coast, in San Francisco, freshly minted coins were placed directly into commerce. The West Coast operated on an entirely different monetary system during the Civil War—with scarcely a Legal Tender note in circulation in San Francisco, but many gold coins in evidence. On the East Coast just the opposite was true: paper money abounded, and silver and gold coins were nowhere to be seen.

Estimated Total Population (Circulated Grades). 50 to 70. Very Fine is about average, although a few Extremely Fine and About Uncirculated coins have appeared in sales.

In his supplemental monograph, *New Varieties of $1, $2.50 and $5.00 United States Gold*, 1968, Walter Breen paid this tribute to the 1862-S: "One of the most undervalued of all S Mint quarter eagles; fewer are around than of 1875-S or '76-S. Two EFs are known, but the only grade available is VG to Fine."

Die Data. *1862 four-digit date logotype: See the Philadelphia Mint listing for this year.*

The Old Reverse hub is used. Two 1862-dated obverse dies were shipped to the San Francisco Mint in November 1861.

Characteristics of Striking and Die Notes. These usually have some lightness of striking, particularly on the eagle, but there are exceptions.

Selected Auction Records

Thomas L. Elder's March 1911 sale of the William H. Woodin Collection included this description of lot 1067: "1862-S. S between 2 and D. Extremely Fine. Very small coinage: Very rare." Realized $10. In May 1913 the U.S. Coin Co. sale of the Malcolm N. Jackson Collection included lot 229: "1862-S Extremely Fine and very rare." Realized $5.50. The Stack's sale of the J.F. Bell Collection in December 1944 included lot 246: "1862-S Brilliant Uncirculated." Realized $37.50. S Just About Uncirculated with full mint luster. Very scarce. Recent record of $23 for an only Very Fine specimen." Realized $25. The Will W. Neil Collection sold by B. Max Mehl in June 1947 included lot 2537: "1862-S Strictly Very Fine; strong impression. Very scarce. A slightly better specimen in my Atwater Sale brought $25." Realized $16.75. In October 1951 the Numismatic Gallery sale of the B.A. Talmadge collection included lot 1251: "1862-S Fine—Very Fine. Scarce." Realized $14.50. In November 1956 the New Netherlands sale of the Thomas L. Gaskill Collection included lot 305: "1862-S. Rev. of 1859, as always. (There was a surplus of reverse dies in 1859, and for the next few years, only obverses were sent out from Philadelphia.) Strictly Very Fine; usual light handling marks, mainly upon the rev. border. Rare date only 8,000 made. Lacking in the Memorable, Melish offerings." Realized $32.

VF-20	EF-40	AU-50	MS-60	MS-63
$1,850	$2,650	$4,250	$16,000	$45,000

1863

Circulation-Strike Mintage: None

Proof Mintage: 30

Proof-only issue.
Landmark quarter eagle rarity.

PROOFS

Thirty $2.50 Proofs were struck this year, the same number as for $5 Proofs and about the same as for $3 Proofs (of which 39 are believed to have been struck).[101]

On September 13, 1883, Harold P. Newlin informed T. Harrison Garrett that he had recently "secured two pieces which were obtained at the Mint in the year they were struck, by the gentleman from whom I got them. They are the gold dollar and quarter eagle of 1863. They are in beautiful brilliant Proof condition. The former is rare, and the latter in my estimation is the rarest of the series of quarter eagles.

"In my former gold collection (originally the Adams Collection) I had an 1863 $5 gold piece but never could obtain the quarter eagle. There were I believe but thirty struck in this year, and certainly not a half dozen of these are now known to collectors. I do not know if you have the piece, but if you care for it I am willing to dispose of it as long as I have broken up my set. The price is $30, and $5 for the 1863 dollar. Will you kindly let me know what you lack in gold as I have one or two fine pieces left."[102]

The foregoing demonstrates vividly that in 1883, just 20 years after the coinage, the 1863 quarter eagle was a great rarity. Newlin, who was a careful correspondent and scholar (he wrote the first technical work on half dimes, for example), was quite aware of the rarity of various issues but knew of not as many as a half dozen 1863 Proof quarter eagles still in existence. There were more in the hands of collectors, but in any event the issue was recognized as a major rarity.

Caveat: Any worn "1863" should be authenticated, to be sure it is not an 1863-S with the mintmark removed.

Estimated Total Population (Proof). 18 to 22.

Proof Die Data and Notes. *1863 four-digit date logotype: The* 18 are close, 86 are wider, and 63 are wider yet. The 1 leans very slightly right. the 8 leans slightly right, and the top interior of the 8 is smaller than the bottom interior. The 6 leans slightly right, the ball is small and slightly truncated, and distant from curve below. The 3 is quite "open" with the top ball only half visible, cut off in a line, and the bottom ball is small and irregular. This logotype was used on all dies of both mints.

The date logotype is low; the 1 (1863) is twice as close to the denticles as to the neck. The left tip of the lowest hair curl is barely to the right of the 6; the 1 and 3 are each about over the space between two denticles (such space, if extended upward, would be at about the center of each digit). There are some patches of Proof brilliance below the earlobe and below BER.

Selected Proof Auction Records

The following is a generous selection from *many* Proof citations over the years:

J.W. Haseltine's 18th Sale, December 1875, included lot 1181: "1863; brilliant Proof; scarce. Fine and excessively rare. Only 30 specimens struck. This coin is as rare as any in the series and should bring a very high price, fully as much as the 1875 three dollar piece." Realized $171. Well into the twentieth century, B. Max Mehl's February 1944 sale of the Belden E. Roach Collection described lot 898: "1863 Perfect brilliant Proof gem. Perfectly centered with raised borders and partly wire edge. Struck in yellow gold. A total of only 30 specimens were struck in all. Probably all were struck on order from collectors. This gives us an idea how rare the early Proof gold coins are today. I doubt if more than ten or twelve specimens are known to exist of this coin now. I consider it as rare as any quarter eagle. It is listed now at $1,000, and I know of a specimen that has sold for more. Only available when great collections come on the market. This specimen is truly a gem and worthy of its highest record. Its acquisition will prove not only a most gratifying source of possession but a good investment as well." Realized $950. The Stack's sale of the J.F. Bell Collection in December 1944 included lot 130: "1863 Brilliant Proof, a flawless gem. One of the finest we have ever handled and also one of the most difficult to obtain. Many of the large collections lack this coin, only 30 said to have been struck, but only a few have ever come up either in private or public auction. This coin should break all records." Realized $1,150.

In June 1946 Mehl's sale of the William Cutler Atwater Collection included lot 1967: "1863. As perfect a brilliant Proof gem as exists. Just as perfect as the moment it dropped from the die. Truly a gem coin! According to the U.S. Mint records only 30 specimens were minted in all of this coin. This can easily be understood, as it was during the War Between the States, when gold was at a high premium. Apparently these coins were struck only on orders from collectors. I doubt very much if one-half of the number of specimens reported struck now exist, as they are available only when such great collections as this come on the market. In 1944, when I sold the Roach Collection, a specimen in that sale brought $950. Another specimen offered at auction just a few months later in the same year brought $1,150. This is one rarity which I believe is destined to advance greatly in value. It would not surprise me to see this coin reach the $2,000 figure in the not distant future." Realized $1,225. Mehl's sale of the Jerome Kern Collection in May 1950 included lot 53: "1863. The Exceedingly Rare 1863 quarter eagle. Perfect brilliant Proof gem. Exceedingly rare, as only 30 specimens were minted in all. The coins were undoubtedly struck only on orders from collectors. Of the number minted, probably not more than one half exist today. While it is true that several specimens have been offered in the last ten years, but it is also true that practically all of them were duplicates or the same coin being re-offered. Catalogs $1,250 and has an auction record for that amount. This specimen is from the great Colonel Green Collection. It is as glittering a Proof as exists." Realized $1,025.

In June 1957 the New Netherlands sale of Eliasberg duplicates had this for lot 627: "1863. Brilliant, just about 'gem' Proof. Only a glass reveals three or four places where lint remained in the dies prior to striking. Just 30 impressions were taken of this date, all Proofs. In addition to this coin, we have located records of eight other sales (representing not over seven different coins, and probably less), since 1946. This agrees well with the usual story that about a dozen examples are now known in all, including those impounded in the Mint, the Eliasberg and a famous Midwestern collection, one or two other institutions and at least one estate. This date has a private sale records to $1,650. (Davis-Graves catalog, p. 39), and dealer Kosoff states that he has sold one for $1,500 at private sale (Melish catalog, p. 57). Ex J.F. Bell auction, December, 1944, at $1,150.00. The 1863 was one of but four quarter eagles lacking in our sale of the Judge Gaskill collection, last November 24th. It was also lacking in such famous offerings as the Dunham, Flanagan, Geiss and Neil auctions, among others." Realized $915. In Abe Kosoff's sale of the Melish and Hester Collections, April 1956, this was the description of lot 1256: "1863. Brilliant Proof; very rare, only 30 pieces having been struck. I have sold an 1863 for $1,500, and this gem should certainly bring no less." Realized $1,250.

PF-60	PF-63	PF-65
$50,000	$75,000	$125,000

1863-S

Circulation-Strike Mintage: 10,800

Very elusive in any grade. Incredibly rare in Mint State.

These circulated at par in the West at a time when quarter eagles were not seen in circulation in the East or Midwest.

Estimated Total Population (Mint State). 2 or 3. The finest may be the amazing coin from the Eliasberg Collection. However, in 1986 Paul F. Taglione (*The Quarter Eagles*) stated that he knew of four Mint State coins.

Estimated Total Population (Circulated Grades). 55 to 80. The 1863-S quarter eagle is scarce in any grade and, in fact, is one of the rarities of the quarter eagle series, almost in a class with the 1862-S. Very Fine is the norm for auction appearances, although occasional Extremely Fine and About Uncirculated pieces enter the record books.

Die Data. *1863 four-digit date logotype: See the Philadelphia Mint listing for this year.*

Eliasberg specimen: The date logotype is low; the 1 (1863) is twice as close to the denticles as to the neck. The left tip of the lowest hair curl is barely to the right of the 6; the 1 and 3 are each *over a denticle* (such denticle, if extended upward, would be at about the center of each digit). Another obverse die has the date logotype higher.

The Old Reverse hub is used.

The S mintmark is tilted right.

Characteristics of Striking and Die Notes. These are lightly struck on the reverse.

Selected Auction Records

In his 1907 fixed-price list Elmer S. Sears offered lot 303: "1863 San Francisco Mint. Uncirculated. Full mint lustre. Beauty. $10." Thomas L. Elder's March 1911 sale of the William H. Woodin Collection included this description of lot 1068: "1863-S Very crooked S leaning to right, between 2 and D. Fine. Rare; coinage small." Realized $3.75. In May 1913 the U.S. Coin Co. sale of the Malcolm N. Jackson Collection included lot 230: "1863-S Extremely Fine and very rare." Realized $3.75. In June 1941 B. Max Mehl's sale of the William Forrester Dunham Collection included lot 1962: "1863-S About Uncirculated, with considerable original mint luster. Rare, especially so choice." Realized $11.25. The Stack's sale of the J.F. Bell Collection in December 1944 included lot 247: "1863-S About Uncirculated." Realized $15. In November 1956 the New Netherlands sale of the Thomas L. Gaskill Collection included lot 306: "1863-S. About Extremely Fine. Minute obv. rim nick; few faint rev. rim abrasions. Just 10,800 coined. Very difficult to locate choice; the Uncirculated Graves example brought $80, two years ago, in spite of a $37.50 *Red Book* listing." Realized $22.

VF-20	EF-40	AU-50	MS-60	MS-64
$1,350	$2,500	$4,500	$15,000	$75,000

1864

Circulation-Strike Mintage: 2,824

Proof Mintage: 50

A fantastic "sleeper" rarity.

Deliveries of this issue were reported as follows: February 25, 424; December 6, 2,400.

No quarter eagles or other gold coins minted at Philadelphia from 1862 through autumn 1878 were paid out at par; such pieces were stored by the Treasury and were available only by paying a premium. The December delivery may indicate that there was a demand for quarter eagles as holiday gifts.

In this year there was no San Francisco quarter eagle coinage.

Estimated Total Population (Mint State). 2 certified. None have been seen by the author.

Estimated Total Population (Circulated Grades). 10 to 15. While the 1864 is not a Proof-only date, only 2,824 circulation strikes were minted, and few of those exist today. The date is incredibly rare. Most of the "name" collections of the past have had Proofs. As a circulation strike, the 1864 is a fantastic "sleeper," one of the very rarest of all American gold coins, but not generally recognized as such.

The demand for the 1864 is increased by the need for *date* collectors to acquire one of the Philadelphia issues, for there was no San Francisco coinage this year.

Die Data. *1864 four-digit date logotype:* The 18 are close, the 86 are closer, and 64 are closer yet, nearly touching. The top of the 8 is smaller than the bottom of the 8; the digit leans right. The ball of the 6 is close to the upright and may touch on uncertain impressions; the 6 leans slightly right. The 4 leans slightly right, with a large upright, a slightly low base, and no crosslet; the end of the bar is about the same length as the serif below it; the 4 is deeply punched into the logotype matrix, making it appear a bit larger than the other numerals. This logotype was used on all dies.

So far as is known, all circulation strikes are from a single pair of dies. The date logotype is about centered. The obverse shows the first two digits of the date, 18, recut, with the upper serif of an earlier 1 appearing significantly below the final figure. The obverse die has "brush marks," actually *raised* die lines, indicating that the die was not completely finished but was pressed into service without having the grinding marks removed (this is common to all genuine circulation strikes of this date and is a general characteristic of other gold coins of the Civil War years).

Characteristics of Striking and Die Notes. Sharp striking is the rule.

Selected Auction Records

In May 1913 the U.S. Coin Co. sale of the Malcolm N. Jackson Collection included lot 150: "1864 Extremely Fine and very rare." Realized $22. In his November 1939 sale of the William B. Hale Collection, B. Max Mehl described lot 789: "1864 Extremely Fine, just a shade from Uncirculated, but with considerable mint luster. Very rare." Realized $82.50. The same coin was featured by M.H. Bolender in his March 1951 sale of the

Marmaduke Fox Collection: Lot 1142: "1864 Phila. mint. Extremely Fine. Very rare. From Hale coll'n." Realized $76. In Abe Kosoff's sale of the Melish and Hester Collections, April 1956, this was the description of lot 1258: "1864. Very Fine, plus (acquired as practically Uncirculated). A nice coin and a scarce one." Realized $87.50.

Proofs

It is likely that not all were distributed.

Estimated Total Population (Proof). 15 to 18.

Proof Die Data and Notes. The date logotype is positioned slightly higher than on circulation strikes and seems to slant ever so slightly down to the right. However, this is an optical illusion as the base of the 1 and the base of the 4 are each about the same distance from the denticles. The date is placed too far to the left, giving a large amount of space between the top of the 4 and the neck.

Selected Proof Auction Records

Note: Certain of these "Proofs" may have been prooflike circulation strikes (if so, they would have been far rarer than Proofs).

Thomas L. Elder's March 1911 sale of the William H. Woodin Collection included this description of lot 1007: "1864 Brilliant perfect Proof. Another precious date with very small number of pieces coined. The Stickney, Smith, Wilson, Zug, and other gold sales did not have it outside of one or two Proof sets." Realized $41. In February 1921 the catalog of B. Max Mehl's sale of the Dr. G.F.E. Wilharm Collection described lot 100: "1864 Perfect brilliant Proof. Excessively rare. I doubt if more than a dozen Proof exist. Record near $100. This specimen cost $75 six years ago." Realized $45. In June Mehl's sale of the William Forrester Dunham Collection included lot 1963: "1864 Originally struck as a Proof, but can only classed as About Uncirculated now, as it has been slightly handled but still maintains considerable original mint luster. Extremely rare. Listed up to $125. An Extremely Fine specimen in the Hale Sale brought $82.50." Realized $62.50. The Stack's sale of the J.F. Bell Collection in December 1944 included lot 131: "1864 Brilliant Proof, struck in deep yellow gold flawless in every respect." Realized $210.

Mehl's sale of the Jerome Kern Collection in May 1950 included lot 54: "1864 Perfect brilliant Proof gem. Probably not more than 25 proofs struck; even a fewer number known to exist today. Extremely rare. Record over $200." Realized $185. In November 1956 the New Netherlands sale of the Thomas L. Gaskill Collection included lot 307: "1864 Superb, brilliant Proof. A real "gem," even though examination with a glass reveals two truly microscopic nicks (from their appearance, inflicted during manufacture), upon the obverse between the 10th and 11th stars. Extremely rare, but 2,874 coined in all, probably only 24 Proofs. Seldom offered in Proof; fairly valued at $250. today, the WGC specimen having brought $190 a decade ago. Melish only had a Very Fine plus one, which commanded $87.50." Realized $265.

VF-20	EF-40	AU-50	MS-60	PF-60	PF-63
$20,000	$37,500	$55,000	$100,000	$12,000	$25,000

1865

Circulation-Strike Mintage: 1,520
Proof Mintage: 25

A great unrecognized rarity.

The coinage was delivered to the Mint on January 27. No quarter eagles or other gold coins minted at Philadelphia from 1862 through autumn 1878 were paid out at par; such pieces were stored by the Treasury and were available only by paying a premium.

Estimated Total Population (Mint State). 1 or 2. A fantastic rarity.

Estimated Total Population (Circulated Grades). 12 to 18. A major rarity in circulation-strike form, a coin that over the years has appeared at auction less often than Proofs (cf. Akers, 1975). Another great "sleeper," a rarity that is by and large unrecognized.

Die Data. *1865 four-digit date logotype:* The 18 are close, the 68 are slightly wider, and the 65 are ever so slightly wider yet. The 1 is very solid, with especially thick serifs to the left and right, the right serif being defective in having a point at its upper right. The 8 has top and bottom interior spaces that are about the same size, with the top perhaps slightly larger, and the digit leans right. The 6 has an interior space with nearly straight sides; the ball is separated from the curve below, with the top of the 6 extending about as far to the right as the right side of the lower curve. The 5 is broad and with a prominent flag, somewhat reminiscent of the 5 in the 1859 "Paquet" quarter eagle logotype; the ball is very close or on some impressions touching the upright above it; the lower right of the 5 is very heavy. The 5 leans slightly right. This logotype was used on all dies of both mints.

Date logotype high and deeply punched into the die. Walter Breen (*Encyclopedia*, 1988) states that one obverse die and two reverse dies were made for circulation strikes.

Characteristics of Striking and Die Notes. These are fairly sharply struck. High-grade pieces show prooflike surfaces.

Selected Auction Records

In October 1884 W. Elliot Woodward's 69th sale included lot 1982: "1865 Fair, scarce." Realized $3. In June 1941 B. Max Mehl's sale of the William Forrester Dunham Collection included lot 1964: "1865 Brilliant Uncirculated, with Proof surface. Extremely rare and valuable. Edge is like a Proof. Listed at $125 in Proof condition." Realized $42.50. Particularly notable was lot 1036 in Stack's October 1947 sale of the H.R. Lee Collection: "1865 Brilliant Uncirculated with prooflike surface. Really choice. Far above average. Scarce." Realized $71. In October 1951 the Numismatic Gallery sale of the B.A. Talmadge collection included lot 1123: "1865 Very Fine, very rare." Realized $55.

PROOFS

Estimated Total Population (Proof). 15 to 18.

Proof Die Data and Notes. The date logotype is high. There are raised arc-like ridges at the date and in the lower field.

Selected Proof Auction Records

Note: Certain of these "Proofs" may have been prooflike circulation strikes (if so, they would have been far rarer than Proofs).

In his 1907 fixed-price list Elmer S. Sears offered lot 304: "1865 Brilliant Proof. Very rare in any condition and proofs are extremely so. $35." L. Elder's March 1911 sale of the William H. Woodin Collection included this description of lot 1008: "1865. Brilliant Proof. Another very rare piece, which most of the sales, big or little, did not have." Realized $25. In May 1913 the U.S. Coin Co. sale of the Malcolm N. Jackson Collection included lot 151: "1865 Brilliant Proof, excessively rare." Realized $53. B. Max Mehl's May 1922 catalog of the James Ten Eyck Collection included lot 97: "1865. Perfect brilliant Proof. Extremely rare and valuable." Realized $42.

Stack's sale of the J.F. Bell Collection in December 1944 included lot 132: "1865 Brilliant Proof gem." Realized $150. In June 1946 Mehl's sale of the William Cutler Atwater Collection included lot 1969: "1865 Perfect brilliant Proof, sharp wire edge. Recent record of $150." Realized $125. In November 1956 the New Netherlands sale of the Thomas L. Gaskill Collection included lot 308: "1865 Magnificent, brilliant Proof. Nearly complete wire edge. Likewise RRR, only 1,520 business strikes and 25 Proofs struck. Despite the contrary *Red Book* listing, should bring appreciably more than last. Rarer than either the one or three dollar gold pieces of this date." Realized $270.

VF-20	EF-40	AU-50	MS-63	PF-60	PF-63
$4,750	$10,000	$20,000	$100,000	$13,500	$20,000

1865-S

Circulation-Strike Mintage: 23,376

These circulated at par in the West at a time when quarter eagles were not seen in circulation in the East or Midwest.

Scarce in any grade.
Incredibly rare in Mint State.

Estimated Total Population (Mint State). 3 to 5. Exceedingly scarce. When seen, the grade is apt to be closer to MS-60 than to the choice level. Paul F. Taglione (*The Quarter Eagles*, 1986) stated that in 1979 an MS-60 and an MS-63 "turned up in the Far East."

Estimated Total Population (Circulated Grades). 75 to 95. The 1865-S quarter eagle is hardly common, but enough exist that an example is usually obtainable with only a moderate amount of searching, not because there are many around—for there are not—but because there are enough to satisfy the needs of those few numismatists forming systematic collections of Liberty Head quarter eagles. Fine and Very Fine seem to be about par for the grades seen, with Extremely Fine and About Uncirculated coins being in the distinct minority.

Die Data. *1865 four-digit date logotype: See the Philadelphia Mint listing for this year.*

Three 1865-dated obverse dies were shipped to San Francisco in November 1864, and at least two of these were used (one showing repunching).

The Old Reverse hub is used. At least two reverse dies were used, one with the S mintmark at an angle.

Characteristics of Striking and Die Notes. These are usually lightly struck at the centers, particularly on the higher points of the hair on the obverse and on the left side of the reverse.

Selected Auction Records

The catalog of John W. Haseltine's June 1883 sale of the William J. Jenks Collection described lot 468: "1865-S Good. Rare." Realized $4. In May 1913 the U.S. Coin Co. sale of the Malcolm N. Jackson Collection included lot 231: "1865-S Very Good. scarce." Realized $3. In May 1915 B. Max Mehl's catalog of the B.W. Smith Collection included this description of lot 324: "1865-S Slanting S over 2 of fraction. Very Good. Very scarce." Realized $4. February 1921 the catalog Mehl's sale of the Dr. G.F.E. Wilharm Collection described lot 204: "1865-S Variety as last. Nearly Uncirculated. Very scarce." Realized $3.60.

Mehl's February 1944 catalog of the sale of the Belden E. Roach Collection described lot 1006: "1865-S Extremely Fine with brilliant luster." Realized $11.25. The Stack's sale of the J.F. Bell Collection in December 1944 included lot 248: "1865-S Brilliant Uncirculated." Realized $17.50. This was an incredible rarity in an era in which high grades did not bring a premium of many multiples over circulated coins. In November 1956 the New Netherlands sale of the Thomas L. Gaskill Collection included lot 309: "1865-S. Apparently from the badly worn reverse die of 1863. Very Fine plus; lightly impaired about the obverse rim. Some mint lustre; acceptable. Marked $23." Realized $18. In June 1957 the New Netherlands sale of Eliasberg duplicates had this for lot 629: "1865-S. Date faintly re-engraved; the same reverse die as last, not showing evidence of extensive use. Fully Very Fine. The obverse border with a small defect between the first and second stars; minor signs of handling upon the obverse rim. Really scarce choice." Realized $13.

VF-20	EF-40	AU-50	MS-60	MS-63
$800	$1,300	$2,150	$4,500	$17,500

1866

Circulation-Strike Mintage: 3,080

Proof Mintage: 30

A rarity in any grade.

No quarter eagles or other gold coins minted at Philadelphia from 1862 through autumn 1878 were paid out at par; such pieces were stored by the Treasury and were available only by paying a premium.

Estimated Total Population (Mint State). 3 to 5. A tremendous rarity in Mint State, so rare that most advanced collectors and dealers have never *seen* one.

Estimated Total Population (Circulated Grades). 25 to 40. These are very elusive, a major rarity. Very Fine and Extremely Fine are the typical grades.

Die Data. *1866 four-digit date logotype:* The numerals are about evenly spaced. The 1 is prominent, taller than the other numerals, which is particularly noticeable at the top. The 8 has a slightly smaller top interior space than the bottom interior space; the 8 leans slightly right. The first 6 leans right, the ball is distinctly separated from the curve below. The second 6 also leans right, from same digit punch (in the logotype matrix), but driven deeper into the matrix, with the result that the ball is slightly closer to the curve below and the center opening is slightly smaller. On the Proof die, the date logotype is about twice as close to the neck as to the denticles and is somewhat left. This logotype was used on all dies of both mints.

There is minor repunching on the 1 in the date. The date logotype is deeply punched into the die, slightly more heavily on the right, making the final digit appear slightly larger than the third digit.

Characteristics of Striking and Die Notes. These are usually well struck except for some lightness on the eagle's leg at the lower left reverse. These sometimes have a wire rim around part of the reverse, from slight mismatching of the reverse die and collar diameters.

Selected Auction Records

In December 1884 the catalog of Dr. George W. Massamore's twenty-fifth sale described lot 947: "1866 Uncirculated." Realized $2.55. In May 1913 the U.S. Coin Co. sale of the Malcolm N. Jackson Collection included lot 152: "1866 Extremely Fine, very rare." Realized $11. The Stack's sale of the J.F. Bell Collection in December 1944 included lot 133: "1866 Brilliant Uncirculated." Realized $32.50. A remarkable coin.

Stack's April 1959 catalog of the Robert H. Pelletreau Collection described 323: "1866 Extremely Fine. Rare. 3780 struck." Realized $82.

Proofs

Estimated Total Population (Proof). 15 to 18.

Proof Die Data and Notes. On the Proof die, the date logotype is about twice as close to the neck as to the denticles and is somewhat left. The reverse die continues to be the same as used on earlier Proof quarter eagles of the decade (with a tiny bulge at the left side of the upright of the 1 in the fraction numerator).

Selected Proof Auction Records

Note: Certain of these "Proofs" may have been prooflike circulation strikes (such being rarer than Proofs).

In June 1885 W. Elliot Woodward's sale of the J. Colvin Randall Collection included lot 1000: "1866 Splendid Proof; very scarce." Realized $3. Thomas L. Elder's March 1911 sale of the William H. Woodin Collection included this description of lot 1009: "1866. Magnificent, brilliant Proof. Of extreme rarity, as attested by Adams' book, which does not list it. Very limited coinage." Realized $20. In June 1946 B. Max Mehl's sale of the William Cutler Atwater Collection included lot 1970: "1866 Perfect brilliant Proof with wire edge. Seldom offered. Recent record $130." Realized $132.50. In November 1956 the New Netherlands sale of the Thomas L. Gaskill Collection included lot 310: "1866 "Gem," brilliant, Proof. Comparable to the 1864, only 3,080 regulars and 30 Proofs made. A 'sleeper,' the Roach, Bell, Menjou and Davis-Graves coins only Fine to Uncirculated; this date completely lacking in the Dunham, Dr. Green, Melish offerings. Ex V. Brand, Ira Reed." Realized $255.

VF-20	EF-40	AU-50	MS-60	MS-63	PF-60	PF-63
$1,150	$3,500	$5,250	$12,500	$27,500	$10,000	$17,500

1866-S

Circulation-Strike Mintage: 38,960

Scarce in any grade.
Extremely rare in Mint State.

These circulated at par in the West at a time when quarter eagles were not seen in circulation in the East or Midwest.

Estimated Total Population (Mint State). 2 or 3. One specimen was in the Bass Collection II offering, and another has been reported at the MS-63 level but not seen by the writer. Scattered others, not necessarily representing different coins and not necessarily representing pieces that would be graded Mint State today, were reported in catalogs years ago.

Estimated Total Population (Circulated Grades). 110 to 140. Fine and Very Fine are typical grades. Scarce.

Die Data. *1866 four-digit date logotype: See the Philadelphia Mint listing for this year.*

The Old Reverse hub is standard.

Reports of a New Reverse have surfaced. Regarding this, David W. Akers wrote (1975): "Walter Breen's monograph indicates that the reverse of the 1866-S is from the 1859 hub, but as one can tell from the photograph above, the old hub of 1840 to 1858 was used. (Perhaps the new hub was also used for the reverse of the 1866-S, but I have never seen such a specimen. Furthermore, the old reverse is used on all subsequent S Mint quarter eagles until 1877.)" Paul F. Taglione (1986) reported seeing two specimens with the New Reverse hub, each MS-63 in grade, in a Detroit-area collection in 1984; he was not allowed to borrow them for further study.

Obverses are known with high and centered logotypes. The reverse is seen with a perfect or repunched S mintmark.[103] In 1911 Elder (Woodin sale, see below) described three different reverse dies.

Characteristics of Striking and Die Notes. These are usually well struck.

Selected Auction Records

The catalog of John W. Haseltine's June 1883 sale of the William J. Jenks Collection described lot 469: "1866-S Fine. Rare." Realized $3.70. In his 1907 fixed-price list Elmer S. Sears offered lot 307: "1866 San Francisco Mint. Mint mark placed over figure 1 of fraction. Very Fine. $6." Thomas L. Elder's March 1911 sale of the William H. Woodin Collection included three: Lot 1070: "1866-S. The S directly over 1, and open. Nearly

Fine." Realized 2.60. Lot 1071: "1866-S. The S. between 2 and D and closed. Fine." Realized $2.75. Lot 1072: "1866-S. The S wide open and between 2 and D. About. Fine." Realized $2.50 (face value). The November 1932 sale of the R. Taylor Collection included B. Max Mehl's descriptions of two: Lot 185: "1866-S, S over 1 of fraction. Fine." Realized $4.75. Lot 186: "1866-S, S over 2 of fraction. About Fine." Realized $3.25. In June 1941 Mehl's sale of the William Forrester Dunham Collection included lot 1965: "1866-S Just a shade away from Uncirculated, but with brilliant luster." Realized $7.35. Mehl's February 1944 catalog of the sale of the Belden E. Roach Collection described two examples: Lot 1007: "1866-S Variety with mint letter S directly over 2 of fraction and touching fraction bar. Fine." Realized $7. Lot 1008: "1866-S Variety with S over 2 of fraction and over D and does not touch fraction bar. Fine." Realized $7.

The Stack's sale of the J.F. Bell Collection in December 1944 included lot 249: "1866-S Brilliant Uncirculated." Realized $14. This was an amazing coin. In June 1946 Mehl's sale of the William Cutler Atwater Collection included lot 2081: "1866-S Extremely Fine. Record of $27.50 for an Uncirculated coin." Realized $8.50. The Will W. Neil Collection sold by Mehl in June 1947 included lot 2540: "1866-S Extremely Fine with mint surface. Catalogs $12.50 in Very Fine." Realized $9. Mehl's sale of the Jerome Kern Collection in May 1950 included lot 169: "1866 S. Extremely Fine, nearly Uncirculated. Originally purchased as Uncirculated. Record for an Uncirculated specimen over $27." Realized $10.50. In Abe Kosoff's sale of the Melish and Hester Collections, April 1956, two were offered: Lot 1261: "1866-S. Date is high. Very Fine." Realized $16. Lot 1262: "1866-S. Low date, Fine." Realized $11.50. In November 1956 the New Netherlands sale of the Thomas L. Gaskill Collection included lot 311: "1866-S. Evidently from the new small letters hub, but a heavy strike from rather worn dies. Abt. Very Fine. Indications of handling, mainly about the reverse rim. Menjou only had a Very Good one." Realized $13.

VF-20	EF-40	AU-50	MS-60	MS-63
$525	$750	$1,250	$6,500	$22,500

1867

Circulation-Strike Mintage: 3,200

Proof Mintage: 50

Rare in any grade.
Exceedingly rare in Mint State.

These coins were delivered to the Mint on January 22. No quarter eagles or other gold coins minted at Philadelphia from 1862 through autumn 1878 were paid out at par; such pieces were stored by the Treasury and were available only by paying a premium.

Estimated Total Population (Mint State). 4 to 6. This is a formidable rarity, extending to the choice and gem range, the latter being very notable specimens. As is the case with most other quarter eagles of this era, contemporary numismatists ignored them at the time of issue and purchased Proofs instead. Thus, even for a variety with a mintage in the thousands of coins, the survival of a Mint State coin was a matter of rare change.

Estimated Total Population (Circulated Grades). 25 to 40. Extremely Fine and About Uncirculated are the typical grades.

Die Data. *1867 four-digit date logotype:* The 18 are close, and the 86 and 67 are wider and each about the same distance apart. The lower left serif of the 1 is heavier than the lower right serif; the 8 leans noticeably to the right. The 6 leans slightly right, with the ball to the 6 close to the upright but not touching. The base of the 7 is slightly lower than the bases of the other figures. This logotype was used on all dies of both mints.

Apparently, only one die pair was used to make circulation strikes.

Characteristics of Striking and Die Notes. These are usually very well struck. Prooflike surfaces are seen on higher grade pieces.

Selected Auction Records

In his 1907 fixed-price list Elmer S. Sears offered lot 309: "1867 Uncirculated, or nearly so, with some prooflike lustre. Very rare. $15." In May 1913 the U.S. Coin Co. sale of the Malcolm N. Jackson Collection included lot 153: "1867 Extremely Fine, very rare." Realized $10. In his November 1939 sale of the William B. Hale Collection, B. Max Mehl described lot 791: "1867 Uncirculated, with brilliant semi-proof surface, especially on obverse. Rare. Especially so choice." Realized $16. In June 1941 B. Mehl's sale of the William Forrester Dunham Collection included lot 1966: "1867 Brilliant Uncirculated, with almost full bright mint luster, but shows slight cabinet friction or handling. Very rare. Listed at $20 to $50." Realized $15. Mehl's sale of the Jerome Kern Collection in May 1950 included lot 56: "1867 Uncirculated with semi-Proof surface. Just the slightest evidence of having been handled with other coins. Rare. Catalogs $35." Realized $27.50. In October 1951 the Numismatic Gallery sale of the B.A. Talmadge collection included lot 1125: "1867 About Extremely Fine, scarce." Realized $22.

Proofs

Probably not all were distributed.

Estimated Total Population (Proof). 15 to 18.

Proof Die Data and Notes. The date logotype is high; the 1 is close to the bust, and the 7 nearly touches.

Selected Proof Auction Records

Note: Certain of these "Proofs" may have been prooflike circulation strikes (rarer than Proofs).

In June 1885 W. Elliot Woodward's sale of the J. Colvin Randall Collection included lot 1001: "1867 Splendid Proof." Realized $2.50 (face value). A concise explanation of why so many nineteenth-century Proof gold coins were spent by their owners. Thomas L. Elder's March 1911 sale of the William H. Woodin Collection included this description of lot 1010: "1867. Brilliant Proof. Excessively rare in this condition." Realized $15.

VF-20	EF-40	AU-50	MS-60	MS-63	PF-60	PF-63
$600	$1,000	$1,500	$8,000	$23,000	$10,000	$16,000

1867-S

Scarce in any grade. Exceedingly rare in Mint State.

Circulation-Strike Mintage: 28,000

These circulated at par in the West at a time when quarter eagles were not seen in circulation in the East or Midwest.

Estimated Total Population (Mint State). 3 to 5. Most are at or near MS-60. This is a rarity at the Mint State level.

Estimated Total Population (Circulated Grades). 95 to 135.

Die Data. *1867 four-digit date logotype: See the Philadelphia Mint listing for this year.*

The Old Reverse hub is used. One reverse has slight doubling on the letters (Breen-6272).

Characteristics of Striking and Die Notes. These are typically lightly struck on the eagle's leg on the left side of the reverse, this being opposite the deepest recess in the obverse die, causing metal flow problems.

Selected Auction Records

In June 1883 John W. Haseltine's sale of the William J. Jenks Collection had lot 470: "1867-S Fine. Rare." Realized $3. Thomas L. Elder's March 1911 sale of the William H. Woodin collection included lot 1073: "1867-S. The S between 2 and D. About Fine; rare." Realized $2.60. B. Max Mehl in his February 1921 sale of the Dr. G.F.E. Wilharm Collection described lot 206: "1867-S Upright S over 2 of fraction. Uncirculated. Very scarce." Realized $3.35. In his sale of the Morris Collection, April 1931, Mehl described lot 603: "1867-S Upright S over and to right of fraction. Very Good." Realized $3.40. In the Numismatic Gallery sale of the "World's Greatest Collection" (F.C.C. Boyd Collection, January 1946) Abe Kosoff described lot 252: "1867-S Very Fine." Realized $19. Mehl's Will W. Neil Collection, June 1947, included lot 2541: "1867-S Extremely Fine, frosty mint surface. Very scarce. A similar specimen in my Atwater Sale brought $21." Realized $11.50. The catalog of the New Netherlands November 1956 sale of the Thomas L. Gaskill Collection described lot 313: "1867-S. Mostly brilliant Uncirculated. Choice, though not too boldly struck. We have never seen a comparable specimen! Unappreciated so, like most of these." Realized $66.

VF-20	EF-40	AU-50	MS-60	MS-63
$500	$650	$1,250	$4,000	$15,000

1868

Scarce in any grade. Exceedingly rare in Mint State.

Circulation-Strike Mintage: 3,600

Proof Mintage: 25

Circulation strikes were delivered on January 20, 1868, early in the year. Apparently, there was no later call for additional coins. No quarter eagles or other gold coins minted at Philadelphia from 1862 through autumn 1878 were paid out at par; such pieces were stored by the Treasury and were available only by paying a premium.

Estimated Total Population (Mint State). 6 to 10. Nearly all are in lower Mint State levels, but at least one or two gems exist.

Estimated Total Population (Circulated Grades). 90 to 120. Extremely Fine and About Uncirculated are the grades typically encountered.

Die Data. *1868 four-digit date logotype:* The 18 are close, the 86 are wider, and the 68 are wider yet. The top interior of the 8 is slightly smaller than the bottom. The 6 has a large ball separated from the curve below; the digit leans slightly right. The second 8 leans slightly right (the second 8 leans almost perceptibly right, while the leaning of the first 8 is quite noticeable). This logotype was used on all dies of both mints.

Production was from a single pair of dies. The date logotype is deeply punched in the die, positioned left, and very close to but not touching the truncation. All known circulation strikes have raised rust marks on the neck of Miss Liberty.

Characteristics of Striking and Die Notes. Usually sharply struck. High-grade pieces usually have prooflike surfaces.

Selected Auction Records

In June 1883 John W. Haseltine's sale of the William J. Jenks Collection had lot 471: "1868 Nearly Proof." Realized $3.50. Dr. George W. Massamore's sale of the Washington Collection in December 1884 included lot 948: "1868 Uncirculated." Realized $2.55. The William B. Hale Collection sold by B. Max Mehl in November 1939 included lot 792: "1868 Uncirculated; highest portions show slight cabinet friction, but almost full bright mint luster. Another rarity." Realized $7.40. In the J.F. Bell Collection in December 1944 Stack's described lot 135: "1868 Brilliant Uncirculated." Realized $18.

The catalog of the New Netherlands November 1956 sale of the Thomas L. Gaskill Collection described lot 314: "1868 Extremely Fine. Cleaned with metal polish or the like; unnatural brilliance. Sold to the former owner of this collection as a 'Proof' by a well-known firm.[104] Nevertheless a rarity; only 3,600 pieces regularly struck." Realized $19. The New Netherlands June 1957 sale of Eliasberg duplicates included lot 632: "1868. Extremely Fine, cleaner than most. Only 3,600 business strikes made. Menjou's was looped, Gaskell's buffed; Mason Williams, Memorable and Donlon had none. Really rare, and seldom offered." Realized $26. April 1959 the Robert H. Pelletreau Collection sold by Stack's included lot 324: "1868 About Uncirculated! Rare. 3600 struck." Realized $66.

Proofs

Proof Die Data and Notes. The portrait does not have rust pits on the neck.

Estimated Total Population (Proof). 10 to 12. In Proof format this is one of the *great rarities* in the quarter eagle series after 1860.

Selected Proof Auction Records

Note: Certain of these "Proofs" may have been prooflike circulation strikes (which are rarer than Proofs).

Thomas L. Elder's March 1911 sale of the William H. Woodin collection included lot 1011: "1868. Proof. Very rare state, and coinage limited. Parmelee Collection. Most large sales did not include it." Realized $29. The June 1941 William Forrester Dunham Collection sold by B. Max Mehl included lot 1967: "1868 Brilliant Proof. Very rare." Realized $41. In June 1946 in his sale of the William Cutler Atwater Collection. Mehl offered lot 1972: "1868 Perfect brilliant Proof. Unusually bold impression. A gem in every respect. a scarce date, but extremely rare so perfect. This and practically all other Proof gold coins in this collection are from complete Proof sets." Realized $55.

VF-20	EF-40	AU-50	MS-60	MS-63	PF-60	PF-63
$500	$515	$725	$2,250	$8,000	$9,500	$16,500

1868-S

Circulation-Strike Mintage: 34,000

Elusive in any grade.
Exceedingly rare in Mint State.

These circulated at par in the West at a time when quarter eagles were not seen in circulation in the East or Midwest.

Estimated Total Population (Mint State). 8 to 12. Most are at or near MS-60. These are very rare in Mint State.

Estimated Total Population (Circulated Grades). 125 to 200. As is to be expected with San Francisco Mint quarter eagles, which circulated extensively, the typical grade is Very Fine.

Die Data. *1868 four-digit date logotype: See the Philadelphia Mint listing for this year.*
Two obverse dies were sent to San Francisco in February 1868 for this coinage.[105] The Old Reverse hub is used.

Characteristics of Striking and Die Notes. These are typically lightly struck on the eagle's leg at left side of reverse.

Selected Auction Records

Elmer S. Sears in his 1907 fixed-price list offered lot 312: "1868 San Francisco Mint. Uncirculated. Mint lustre. Choice. $6." Thomas L. Elder's March 1911 sale of the William H. Woodin collection included lot 1074: "1868-S. S between 2 and D. About Fine." Realized $3.10. The Malcolm N. Jackson Collection, sold in May 1913 by the U.S. Coin Co., included lot 234: "1868-S Extremely Fine, rare." Realized $3.25. In his sale of the Morris Collection, April 1931, B. Max Mehl described lot 604: "1868-S, S over 2 of fraction. Very Good." Realized $4. The William B. Hale Collection sold Mehl in November 1939 included lot 875: "1868-S About Uncirculated, with mint luster." Realized $8.40.

In the J.F. Bell Collection in December 1944, Stack's described lot 251: "1868-S Brilliant Uncirculated." Realized $15. In the Numismatic Gallery sale of the "World's Greatest Collection" (F.C.C. Boyd Collection, January 1946) Abe Kosoff described lot 253: "1868-S Extremely Fine." Realized $21. In June 1946 in his sale of the William

Cutler Atwater Collection. Mehl offered lot 2083: "1868-S Extremely Fine, nearly Uncirculated, but light nick on edge. Record $21." Realized $8. The Will W. Neil Collection, June 1947, included lot 2542: "1868-S Practically Uncirculated with frosty mint surface. Scarce so choice. Record over $20." Realized $10.

VF-20	EF-40	AU-50	MS-60	MS-63
$500	$525	$700	$3,000	$8,500

1869

Circulation-Strike Mintage: 4,320

Proof Mintage: 25

Scarce in any grade.
Exceedingly rare in Mint State.

These were delivered on February 5.

Estimated Total Population (Mint State). 5 to 8. The grades are mostly toward the MS-60 end of the scale. These are very rare in Mint State. No quarter eagles or other gold coins minted at Philadelphia from 1862 through autumn 1878 were paid out at par; such pieces were stored by the Treasury and were available only by paying a premium. Others have suggested that the 1869 is more plentiful than this,[106] but the writer believes the true number is quite small.

Estimated Total Population (Circulated Grades). 90 to 120. Another Philadelphia Mint rarity. Extremely Fine and About Uncirculated are typical grades encountered.

Die Data. *1869 four-digit date logotype:* The 18 are very close, the 86 are wider, and the 69 are wider yet. The 1 is rather ungainly, with a large top flag, and with the lower left serif larger than the lower right serif. The top interior of the 8 is smaller than the bottom interior; the 8 leans slightly right. The ball of the 6 is large, slightly flattened at the bottom, and close but not touching the curve below; the 6 leans slightly left. The 9 leans slightly right and has a top interior space smaller than the bottom interior space of the adjacent 6; the two *tête-bêche* digits are slightly different in style, and if they are from the same punch in the matrix, they were differently impressed. This logotype was used on all dies of both mints.

The logotype is high and farther right than on the Proof die; the 1 is farther above the denticles than on the Proof die.

Characteristics of Striking and Die Notes. These are usually sharply struck. All high-grade examples seen have prooflike surfaces, including within the shield stripes on the reverse. These are sometimes seen with a minor area of light striking at the center obverse.

Selected Auction Records

In June 1883 John W. Haseltine's sale of the William J. Jenks Collection had lot 472: "1869 Uncirculated." Realized $3.60. B. Max Mehl in his February 1921 sale of the Dr. G.F.E. Wilharm Collection described lot 103: "1869 Uncirculated, Mint luster. Rare. Small coinage." Realized $4.10. In March 1934, Sale 331 of J.C. Morgenthau & Co. included 364: "1869 Uncirculated." Realized $7.50. The sale of the Philpott and

Zander Collections by Mehl in November 1945 included lot 1119: "1869 Just a shade from Uncirculated; tiny nick on obverse. Rare date." Realized $5.50.

Proofs

Estimated Total Population (Proof). 12 to 16.

Proof Die Data and Notes. The date logotype is to the left with the 1 (1869) close to both the neck and the denticles.

Selected Proof Auction Records

Note: Certain of these "Proofs" may have been prooflike circulation strikes (which are rarer than Proofs).

Thomas L. Elder's March 1911 sale of the William H. Woodin collection included lot 1012: "1869. Brilliant Proof. Extremely rare. The largest sales did not have it. . . . Parmelee Collection." Realized $20. The June 1941 William Forrester Dunham Collection sold by B. Max Mehl included lot 1968: "1869 Bright Uncirculated, but shows slight evidence of handling, but with semi-Proof surface. Rare. Listed at $50 in Proof." Realized $20. In the Numismatic Gallery sale of the "World's Greatest Collection" (F.C.C. Boyd Collection, January 1946) Abe Kosoff described lot 137: "1869 Brilliant Proof." Realized $80. In June 1946 in his sale of the William Cutler Atwater Collection, Mehl offered lot 1973: "1869 Perfect brilliant Proof. Catalogs at $75, but a specimen recently brought $80 at auction." Realized $72.50.

VF-20	EF-40	AU-50	MS-60	MS-63	PF-60	PF-63
$500	$525	$800	$3,000	$10,000	$8,500	$15,000

1869-S

Circulation-Strike Mintage: 29,500

Somewhat scarce in any grade. Very rare in Mint State.

These circulated at par in the West at a time when quarter eagles were not seen in circulation in the East or Midwest.

Estimated Total Population (Mint State). 7 to 10. Several choice and gem pieces are among these and are extremely rare.

Estimated Total Population (Circulated Grades). 125 to 200. These are usually seen in Very Fine grades, occasionally Extremely Fine, and rarely About Uncirculated, although a number of About Uncirculated coins have appeared in major collections over the years.

Die Data. *1869 four-digit date logotype: See the Philadelphia Mint listing for this year.*

Six obverse dies were shipped from Philadelphia in October 1868 in anticipation of the 1869-S coinage, but most remained unused. Serviceable dies of the Old Reverse hub style remained on hand from years earlier.

Characteristics of Striking and Die Notes. These are usually somewhat lightly struck on the hair below the coronet on the obverse and on the left side of the reverse.

Selected Auction Records

Elmer S. Sears in his 1907 fixed-price list offered lot 314: "1869 San Francisco Mint. Uncirculated. Mint lustre. $7." Thomas L. Elder's March 1911 sale of the William H. Woodin collection included lot 1075: "1869-S. Fine. Scarce." Realized $2.50 (face value). The Malcolm N. Jackson Collection sold in May 1913 by the U.S. Coin Co. included lot 235: "1869-S Extremely Fine, mint luster, rare." Realized $3.50. In the J.F. Bell Collection in December 1944, Stack's described lot 252: "1869-S Brilliant Uncirculated." Realized $15.

In the Numismatic Gallery sale of the "World's Greatest Collection" (F.C.C. Boyd Collection, January 1946) Abe Kosoff described lot 254: "1869-S Uncirculated. With frosty mint surface. Choice." Realized $21. Max Mehl's Will W. Neil Collection, June 1947, included lot 2543: "1869-S Extremely Fine. Catalogs $12.50." Realized $11.50. The New Netherlands June 1957 sale of Eliasberg duplicates included lot 635: "1869-S. Extremely Fine plus, lustrous. Unusually clean and desirable. With two exceptions (one an impaired Unc. coin), all examples offered of this mintmark, within recent years, have been inferior. Unappreciated, as are 11 of these." Realized $15.

VF-20	EF-40	AU-50	MS-60	MS-63
$500	$525	$700	$3,500	$9,250

1870

Circulation-Strike Mintage: 4,520
Proof Mintage: 35

Scarce in any grade.
Very rare in Mint State.

These were delivered from the coiner on January 17, 1870. No quarter eagles or other gold coins minted at Philadelphia from 1862 through autumn 1878 were paid out at par; such pieces were stored by the Treasury and were available only by paying a premium.

Estimated Total Population (Mint State). 6 to 10. A major rarity. These are mostly in lower Mint State levels.

Estimated Total Population (Circulated Grades). 90 to 120. These are very scarce. Extremely Fine is about par, although About Uncirculated coins come on the market now and then.

Die Data. *1870 four-digit date logotype:* The 18 are very close, 87 are widest, and the 70 has intermediate spacing. The lower left serif of the 1 is more prominent than the lower right serif. The top interior space of the 8 is slightly smaller than the bottom interior; the 8 leans slightly right. The 0 leans slightly right (best seen by the orientation of the space within). This logotype was used on all dies for both mints.

The date is very high and close to the neck truncation, but not quite touching.[107] The first and last digits are about equidistant from the denticles, conflicting with Walter Breen's comment, "Circulation strikes . . . have dates slanting down to the right." Actually, the date position tends to fool the eye, and if the neck truncation of Miss Liberty is used as the only focal point, the date does *seem* to slant down to the right—even though it does not. The portrait of Miss Liberty bears some raised finish lines at the neck, before and after the curls, some of which are in an arc, sufficient enough that these can be called *circular lathe marks.*"

Characteristics of Striking and Die Notes. These are usually well struck. Higher-grade pieces display prooflike surfaces.

Selected Auction Records

In June 1883 John W. Haseltine's sale of the William J. Jenks Collection had lot 473: "1870 Uncirculated." Realized $3.50. Dr. George W. Massamore's sale of the Washington Collection in December 1884 included lot 949: "1870 Very Fine." Realized $2.80. The June 1941 William Forrester Dunham Collection sold by B. Max Mehl included lot 1969: "1870 Brilliant Uncirculated; slightest marks of cabinet friction, but with full mint luster. Quite rare." Realized $7.50.

Proofs

Estimated Total Population (Proof). 12 to 15. This is for Proofs grading PF-60 or finer. Considerably rarer than the 1869 Proof (mintage 25), creating a little mystery as to why.[108] More than a few are impaired (not cited here), indicating that this issue must have had a high "spending rate."

Proof Die Data and Notes. The reverse is from a different die than that used in the 1860s, without a little raised area projecting from the left side of the numerator of the fraction.

Selected Proof Auction Records

Note: Certain of these "Proofs" may have been prooflike circulation strikes (which are rarer than Proofs).

Thomas L. Elder in his sale of the Robert J. Bouvier Collection, September 1939, described lot 1085: "1870 Brilliant Proof. A very rare date of quarter eagle. Any quarter eagle of this date is Rare." Realized $9.25. In the J.F. Bell Collection in December 1944, Stack's described lot 137: "1870 Brilliant Proof gem." Realized $50.

VF-20	EF-40	AU-50	MS-60	MS-63	PF-60	PF-63
$500	$550	$850	$3,250	$8,000	$8,500	$15,000

1870-S

Circulation-Strike Mintage: 16,000

Scarce in any grade.
Very rare in Mint State.

These circulated at par in the West at a time when quarter eagles were not seen in circulation in the East or Midwest.

Estimated Total Population (Mint State). 6 to 10. It is amazing that from a mintage of 16,000 coins, fewer than a dozen Mint State coins survive. Most are in lower Mint State ranges.

Estimated Total Population (Circulated Grades). 75 to 100. These are usually seen in Extremely Fine grade, although a number of higher grade pieces exist. As is typical of small denomination San Francisco gold coins of the era, these pieces circulated extensively. In the 1874 *Annual Report of the Director of the Mint* the recommendation was made that worn coins in commerce on the West Coast be called in by the Treasury Department for recoinage.

Die Data. *1870 four-digit date logotype: See the Philadelphia Mint listing for this year.*

The date logotype is high. The Old Reverse hub is used.

Characteristics of Striking and Die Notes. These are lightly struck at the centers, although a very few are sharp.

Selected Auction Records

Elmer S. Sears in his 1907 fixed-price list offered lot 317: "1870 San Francisco Mint. Extremely Fine, with mint lustre. $6." Thomas L. Elder's March 1911 sale of the William H. Woodin collection included lot 1076: "1870-S. The S between 1 and dividing bar. Fine; scarce." Realized $3. In the J.F. Bell Collection in December 1944, Stack's described lot 253: "1870-S Brilliant Uncirculated." Realized $20. In the Numismatic Gallery sale of the "World's Greatest Collection" (F.C.C. Boyd Collection, January 1946) Abe Kosoff described lot 255: "1870-S Uncirculated." Realized $25.

VF-20	EF-40	AU-50	MS-60	MS-63
$500	$550	$900	$4,000	$12,500

1871

Circulation-Strike Mintage: 5,320

Proof Mintage: 30

Scarce in any grade.

Delivered on February 9.

No quarter eagles or other gold coins minted at Philadelphia from 1862 through autumn 1878 were paid out at par; such pieces were stored by the Treasury and were available only by paying a premium.

Estimated Total Population (Mint State). 25 to 40. Most are in lower Mint State levels.

Estimated Total Population (Circulated Grades). 90 to 140. Most are Extremely Fine or About Uncirculated.

Die Data. *1871 four-digit date logotype:* Date numerals large, 18 close, 87 wider than any others, 71 extremely close and almost touch. Both 1's have very large bottom serifs, giving each numeral a somewhat unusual appearance. The top interior of the 8 narrower and smaller than bottom interior. This logotype was used on all dies of both mints.

Date logotype high; 1 (1871) closer to neck that on the Proof die.

Characteristics of Striking and Die Notes. Neck details indistinct due to insufficient depth of impression by the master die (alternatively, relapping; not probable on such a short production run).

Selected Auction Records

In June 1883 John W. Haseltine's sale of the William J. Jenks Collection had lot 474: "1871 Uncirculated." Realized $3.50. Lot 1779 in Stack's May 1945 sale of the George H. Hall Collection was described as "1871 Uncirculated, scarce." Realized $18. The catalog of the New Netherlands November 1956 sale of the Thomas L. Gaskill Collection described lot 320: "1871 A brilliant, glittering "first-strike" or quasi-Proof. Signs of contact with other coins. Like the 1859 and '68, sold as a proof—the common fate of coins with any trace of a reflective surface. Rare, but 5,320 (and 30 Proofs) manufactured." Realized $55.

Proofs

Estimated Total Population (Proof). 12 to 15. An incredible rarity with a low survival rate vis-à-vis the Proof mintage. The explanation is unknown.

Proof Die Data and Notes. Date logotype high. Raised spot on neck from rust on die.

Selected Proof Auction Records

Thomas L. Elder's March 1911 sale of the William H. Woodin collection included lot 1014: "1871. Proof. Very rare and seldom offered." Realized $8.75. The June 1941 William Forrester Dunham Collection sold by B. Max Mehl included lot 1970: "1871 Brilliant Proof, with wire edge. The field on reverse shows slightest cabinet friction. These gold coins in Proof condition are far more rare than we realize. Only a limited number were struck and of that number probably not half are in existence today." Realized $31. This is an early expanded comment about rarity. In the J.F. Bell Collection in December 1944, Stack's described lot 138: "1871 Brilliant Proof." Realized $46. In the Numismatic Gallery sale of the "World's Greatest Collection" (F.C.C. Boyd Collection, January 1946) Abe Kosoff described lot 139: "1871 Proof, though not in full brilliance." Realized $37. In June 1946 in his sale of the William Cutler Atwater Collection, Mehl offered lot 1975: "1871 Perfect brilliant Proof with wire edge. Just as rare and valuable as last." Realized $50. Mehl's sale of the Jerome Kern Collection, May 1950, included lot 60: "1871 Perfect brilliant Proof. From the Roach Collection. Catalogs $50." Realized $42.

VF-20	EF-40	AU-50	MS-60	MS-63	PF-60	PF-63
$500	$600	$750	$2,000	$4,500	$8,500	$15,000

1871-S

Circulation-Strike Mintage: 22,000

Scarce in any grade. Rare in Mint State.

These circulated at par in the West at a time when quarter eagles were not seen in circulation in the East or Midwest.

Estimated Total Population (Mint State). 12 to 15. The grades vary, but include a handful of choice, lustrous pieces—great attractions whenever offered. This is the earliest-dated San Francisco Mint quarter eagle for which Mint State coins have been seen in several old-time collections.

Estimated Total Population (Circulated Grades). 85 to 130. Very Fine and Extremely Fine grades are normal, although enough About Uncirculated pieces exist that the specialist should have no difficulty in acquiring one.

Die Data. *1871 four-digit date logotype: See the Philadelphia Mint listing for this year.* The Old Reverse hub is used.

Characteristics of Striking and Die Notes. These are usually lightly struck at the centers, most noticeably on the eagle's leg at the left.

Selected Auction Records

Elmer S. Sears in his 1907 fixed-price list offered lot 321: "1871 San Francisco Mint. Nearly Uncirculated, with lustre. $5." The Malcolm N. Jackson Collection sold in May 1913 by the U.S. Coin Co. included lot 237: "1871-S Extremely Fine, rare." Realized $3.25. In his sale of the Morris Collection, April 1931, B. Max Mehl described lot 607: "1871-S Slanting S over 1 of fraction. Strictly Fine." Realized $4.50. In the J.F. Bell Collection in December 1944, Stack's described lot 254: "1871-S Brilliant Uncirculated." Realized $13. In the Numismatic Gallery sale of the "World's Greatest Collection" (F.C.C. Boyd Collection, January 1946) Abe Kosoff described lot 256: "1871-S Uncirculated." Realized $27.50. In June 1946 in his sale of the William Cutler Atwater Collection, Mehl offered lot 2086: "1871-S About Uncirculated with full mint luster. Recent record $27.50." Realized $8.50. The sale of the Melish and Hester Collections by Abe Kosoff in April 1956 included lot 1273: "1871-S Uncirculated." Realized $27. The catalog of the New Netherlands November 1956 sale of the Thomas L. Gaskill Collection described lot 321: "1871-S. Bright, lustrous Uncirculated. Somewhat weakly struck, but with full mint frost. Mintmarked gold in this preservation is almost impossible to locate, and catalog prices should be adjusted accordingly, particularly when a limited coinage is involved." Realized $41.

VF-20	EF-40	AU-50	MS-60	MS-63
$500	$550	$650	$2,000	$4,350

1872

Circulation-Strike Mintage: 3,000
Proof Mintage: 30

Scarce in any grade. Incredibly rare in Mint State.

These were made early in the year, and the entire batch was delivered on January 22, 1872. No quarter eagles or other gold coins minted at Philadelphia from 1862 through autumn 1878 were paid out at par; such pieces were stored by the Treasury and were available only by paying a premium.

Estimated Total Population (Mint State). 2 or 3—an amazing situation. Apparently, no attention at all was paid to Mint State coins upon their issuance, collectors acquiring Proofs instead. This is one of the great "condition rarities" among late-nineteenth-century quarter eagles.

Estimated Total Population (Circulated Grades). 50 to 70. Extremely Fine to About Uncirculated is the usual range seen. These are very elusive in all grades.

Die Data. *1872 four-digit date logotype:* The bases of 72 in the date are very low; 18 are very close, 87 are slightly wider, and 72 are very close. This logotype was used on all dies for both mints.

Characteristics of Striking and Die Notes. These are usually lightly struck on the eagle's leg on the left reverse.

Selected Auction Records

In June 1883 John W. Haseltine's sale of the William J. Jenks Collection had lot 475: "1872 Uncirculated." Realized $3.60. Dr. George W. Massamore's sale of the Washington Collection in December 1884 included lot 950: "1872 Uncirculated." Realized $2.60. Elmer S. Sears in his 1907 fixed-price list offered lot 323: "1872 Uncirculated. Mint lustre. Very rare. $8."

Proofs

These coins were delivered to the Mint on February 3.

Estimated Total Population (Proof). 12 to 16. These are very rare.

Proof Die Data and Notes. The date logotype is high.

Selected Proof Auction Records

Note: Certain of these "Proofs" may have been prooflike circulation strikes (which are rarer than Proofs).

Thomas L. Elder's March 1911 sale of the William H. Woodin collection included lot 1015: "1872. Proof. Very rare, not in any recent large sale in this condition." Realized $15.50. The June 1941 William Forrester Dunham Collection sold by B. Max Mehl included lot 1971: "1872 Perfect brilliant Proof, with bold impression, raised borders and wire edge. A gem. Just as perfect as the day it was struck. Catalogs at $35 and certainly worth it." Realized $36. In the J.F. Bell Collection in December 1944, Stack's described lot 139: "1872 Brilliant Proof." Realized $48. Mehl's sale of the Jerome Kern Collection, May 1950, included lot 61: "1872 Perfect brilliant Proof. Very scarce. Catalogs $55. From the Colonel Green Collection." Realized $45. The catalog of the New Netherlands November 1956 sale of the Thomas L. Gaskill Collection described lot 322: "1872 Sparkling, brilliant Proof. between the 1864 and the 1866 in rarity; only 3,000 business strikes, 30 Proofs. Recent public sale record of $170." Realized $230.

VF-20	EF-40	AU-50	MS-60	MS-63	PF-60	PF-63
$500	$850	$1,650	$4,350	$15,000	$8,500	$15,000

1872-S

Circulation-Strike Mintage: 18,000

Scarce in any grade.
Very rare in Mint State.

These circulated at par in the West at a time when quarter eagles were not seen in circulation in the East or Midwest.

Estimated Total Population (Mint State). 5 to 7. These are very rare in Mint State and are known levels from MS-60 to about MS-63.

Estimated Total Population (Circulated Grades). 100 to 150. Very Fine is the grade typically found.

Die Data. *1872 four-digit date logotype: See the Philadelphia Mint listing for this year.* The Old Reverse hub is used.

Characteristics of Striking and Die Notes. These are sometimes lightly struck and the centers, but usually a decent strike.

Selected Auction Records

Elmer S. Sears in his 1907 fixed-price list offered lot 324: "1872 San Francisco Mint. Uncirculated. Mint lustre. $6." In his sale of the Morris Collection, April 1931, B. Max Mehl described lot 608: "1872-S S directly over fraction. Fine; sharp. Rare." Realized $7. Thomas L. Elder in his sale of the Robert J. Bouvier Collection, September 1939, described lot 1476: "1872-S Extremely Fine. Very rare." Realized $5. The William B. Hale Collection sold by Mehl in November 1939 included lot 878: "1872-S Extremely Fine, with mint luster. Very scarce." Realized $9.40. In the J.F. Bell Collection in December 1944, Stack's described lot 255: "1872-S Brilliant Uncirculated." Realized $16. The sale of the Philpott and Zander Collections by Mehl in November 1945 included lot 1223: "1872-S Practically Uncirculated with mint luster." Realized $11. In the Numismatic Gallery sale of the "World's Greatest Collection" (F.C.C. Boyd Collection, January 1946) Abe Kosoff described lot 257: "1872-S About Uncirculated." Realized $24. Mehl's sale of the Jerome Kern Collection, May 1950, included lot 174: "1872-S. Uncirculated, mint lustre. Catalogs $20." Realized $16.50. At the time the market did not place a high premium on Mint State coins vis-à-vis Extremely Fine and About Uncirculated.

VF-20	EF-40	AU-50	MS-60	MS-63
$500	$550	$950	$4,000	$10,500

1873, Close 3

Circulation-Strike Mintage: 55,200 (estimated)

Proof Mintage: 25

Scarce in any grade.

The mintage distribution of Close 3 vis-à-vis Open 3 quarter eagles is an estimate by Walter Breen.

No quarter eagles or other gold coins minted at Philadelphia from 1862 through autumn 1878 were paid out at par; such pieces were stored by the Treasury and were available only by paying a premium.

Estimated Total Population (Mint State). 120 to 180. This is considerably the scarcer of the two date varieties. Most are in lower Mint State levels, but choice and finer examples are seen with some regularity.

Estimated Total Population (Circulated Grades). 250 to 400. Very Fine and Extremely Fine are the typical grades.

Die Data. *1873, Close 3, four-digit date logotype:* 18 are very close, 87 are widest, and 73 are also wide but not quite as wide as 87. The top interior of the 8 is the same size or slightly larger than the bottom interior of 8. The 7 is narrow. The 3 has small knobs at the top and bottom, fairly close to each other, with the top knob being nearer the central projection than the bottom knob is. The top and bottom of the logotype are *always* stronger, while it is lighter at the center, indicating a "rocking" during the preparation of the 1873 Close 3 logotype in its matrix. This was used on some Philadelphia and all San Francisco dies.

Characteristics of Striking and Die Notes. These are usually well struck. Some slight weakness may appear on the eagle's leg at the left reverse.

Selected Auction Records

Note: Early citations do not mention Close 3 or Open 3; presumably, most of the early listings are for the more plentiful Open 3 variety.

In June 1883 John W. Haseltine's sale of the William J. Jenks Collection had lot 476: "1873 Uncirculated." Realized $3. The June 1941 William Forrester Dunham Collection sold by B. Max Mehl included lot 1972: "1873 Uncirculated, with frosty mint surface. Scarce so choice." Realized $5.

Proofs

Estimated Total Population (Proof). 12 to 15.

Proof Die Data and Notes. Proofs have the date logotype low with the left serif of the 1 (1873) closer to denticles than on any circulation strikes seen.

Selected Proof Auction Records

Thomas L. Elder's March 1911 sale of the William H. Woodin collection included lot 1016: "1873. Proof. Very rare in this state. In this condition not offered in any recent sale." Realized $12.50. In the J.F. Bell Collection in December 1944, Stack's described lot 140: "1873 Brilliant Proof." Realized $25. In the Numismatic Gallery sale of the "World's Greatest Collection" (F.C.C. Boyd Collection, January 1946) Abe Kosoff described lot 141: "1873 Brilliant Proof." Realized $60. In June 1946 in his sale of the William Cutler Atwater Collection. B. Max Mehl offered lot 1977: "1873 Perfect brilliant Proof with sharp wire edge. Just as an illustration of how the values of these gem coins are advancing, it is well to mention that in the Bell Sale a specimen brought only $25, while in a recent sale it brought $60." Realized $42.50. The sale of the Melish and

Hester Collections by Abe Kosoff in April 1956 included lot 1279: "1873 Brilliant Proof, scarce." Realized $160.

VF-20	EF-40	AU-50	MS-60	MS-63	PF-60	PF-63
$500	$515	$525	$545	$1,250	$8,500	$15,000

1873, Open 3

Circulation-Strike Mintage: 122,800 (estimated)

Proof Mintage: None

The more plentiful "3" variety.

The mintage distribution of Close 3 vis-à-vis Open 3 quarter eagles is an estimate by Walter Breen.

No quarter eagles or other gold coins minted at Philadelphia from 1862 through autumn 1878 were paid out at par; such pieces were stored by the Treasury and were available only by paying a premium.

Estimated Total Population (Mint State). 300 to 500. This is the more available of the two date styles. Grades range from MS-60 to choice and gem, with higher level coins being rarer.

Estimated Total Population (Circulated Grades). 450 to 700. Extremely Fine and About Uncirculated are the typical grades.

Die Data. *1873, Open 3, four-digit date logotype:* The 187 is virtually identical to that on the 1873 Close 3 and perhaps completely identical; the final 3 is slightly redesigned, its smaller top knob and larger bottom knob are widely separated, and the right side of the 3 is thick in the center (as opposed to being somewhat "pinched" on the Close 3 variety). This logotype was used on some Philadelphia Mint dies.

Characteristics of Striking and Die Notes. These are usually fairly well struck. Lustrous, satiny surfaces are characteristic of high-grade coins.

Selected Auction Records

Selected circulation strike citations: See the auction records under 1873, Close 3, on the previous page. Close 3 and Open 3 were not differentiated in early sales.

VF-20	EF-40	AU-50	MS-60	MS-63
$500	$515	$525	$550	$825

1873-S, Close 3

Circulation-Strike Mintage: 27,000

Rare in Mint State.

These circulated at par in the West at a time when quarter eagles were not seen in circulation in the East or Midwest.

Estimated Total Population (Mint State). 10 to 15. Most are close to MS-60, although several choice pieces are known.

Estimated Total Population (Circulated Grades). 125 to 175. Very Fine is the typical grade, and any finer than this are very scarce.

Die Data. *1873, Close 3, four-digit date logotype: See the 1873, Close 3, listing.*

Four obverse dies were shipped from Philadelphia to San Francisco in November 1872 in anticipation of the 1873-S coinage. Likely, not all were used.

Characteristics of Striking and Die Notes. These are lightly struck at the centers.

Selected Auction Records

Elmer S. Sears in his 1907 fixed-price list offered lot 328: "1873 San Francisco Mint. Mint mark large and touches figure 1 of fraction. Very Fine. $5."

Elmer S. Sears in his 1907 fixed-price list offered lot 329: "1873 Another, but with smaller mint mark, and not touching figure 1 of fraction. Extremely Fine, with lustre. $7." Malcolm N. Jackson Collection sold in May 1913 by the U.S. Coin Co. included two: Lot 239: "1873-S, S over 1 in fraction. Fine, rare." Realized $3. Lot 240: "1873-S S between 1 and fraction bar. Extremely Fine, rare." Realized $3. The William B. Hale Collection sold by B. Max Mehl in November 1939 included lot 879: "1873-S About Uncirculated." Realized $4.60. In the J.F. Bell Collection in December 1944, Stack's described lot 256: "1873-S Uncirculated." Realized $10. The B.A. Talmadge Collection sold by Numismatic Gallery in October 1951 included lot 1261: "1873-S About Uncirculated." Realized $12.25.

VF-20	EF-40	AU-50	MS-60	MS-63
$500	$550	$975	$2,000	$6,500

1874

Circulation-Strike Mintage: 3,920

Proof Mintage: 20

Scarce in any grade.

No quarter eagles or other gold coins minted at Philadelphia from 1862 through autumn 1878 were paid out at par; such pieces were stored by the Treasury and were available only by paying a premium.

Estimated Total Population (Mint State). 25 to 40. These are very scarce in all circulation-strike grades, but of these, a fair number are in Mint State. Qualities range from MS-60 upward to gem, with most being on the lower end of the scale. This is the first of the low-mintage dates of the era that is reasonably available in Mint State, although in absolute terms such pieces are rare.

Estimated Total Population (Circulated Grades). 60 to 90. Extremely Fine and About Uncirculated are the typical grades.

Die Data. *1874 four-digit date logotype:* The 18 are close, and the 87 and 74 are wider and each about the same distance. The top and bottom interior space of the 8 are about the same size; the 8 leans slightly right. The 4 leans slightly right, with a heavy upright and no crosslet on crossbar; the right end of the crossbar ends at about the same distance as the lower right serif; the lower right serif is heavier than the lower left serif. This was used on all dies.

There is a raised rust lump on the earlobe.

Characteristics of Striking and Die Notes. These are usually well struck and prooflike.

Selected Auction Records

Dr. George W. Massamore's sale of the Washington Collection in December 1884 included lot 952: "1874 Extremely Fine lustre." Realized $4.30. Thomas L. Elder in his sale of the Robert J. Bouvier Collection, September 1939, described lot 1477: "1874 Fine. Very rare." Realized $4.75. The June 1941 William Forrester Dunham Collection, sold by B. Max Mehl, included lot 1973: "1874 Uncirculated, with bright mint luster. Quite rare, especially so choice." Realized $8.50. The sale of the Philpott and Zander Collections by Mehl in November 1945 included lot 1123: "1874 Uncirculated with semi-Proof surface, but shows slight cabinet friction. Very scarce." Realized $9.

The New Netherlands June 1957 sale of Eliasberg duplicates included lot 642: "1874. Very Fine or better. Only 3,920 business strikes made. None in the Mason Williams, Green auctions, among others. these can only go up in value, considering the low numbers issued." Realized $25.

Proofs

Estimated Total Population (Proof). 12 to 15.

Proof Die Data and Notes. There is no raised rust lump on the earlobe. There are denticles missing on either side of star 5 (cf. Akers, 1975).

Selected Proof Auction Records

Note: The following is a small selection from Proof citations over the years. Certain of these "Proofs" may have been prooflike circulation strikes.

Thomas L. Elder's March 1911 sale of the William H. Woodin collection included lot 1017: "1874. Brilliant Proof. Extremely rare in this preservation, and seldom offered. Adams does not list it." Realized $40. Malcolm N. Jackson Collection sold in May 1913 by the U.S. Coin Co. included lot 160: "1874 Extremely Fine, Proof surface, rare." Realized $5. In the J.F. Bell Collection in December 1944, Stack's described lot 141: "1874 Brilliant Proof." Realized $80. In the Numismatic Gallery sale of the "World's Greatest Collection" (F.C.C. Boyd Collection, January 1946) Abe Kosoff described lot 142: "1874 Brilliant Proof." Realized $100. In June 1946 in his sale of the William Cutler Atwater Collection, Mehl offered lot 1978: "1874 Perfect brilliant Proof, sharp edges. Limited coinage. Very rare. Recent record, $100." Realized $80. The catalog of the New Netherlands November 1956 sale of the Thomas L. Gaskill Collection described lot 326: "1874 Choice and brilliant Proof. Very rare date, unusually rare

Proof; just 3,920 normally coined plus 20 Proofs. As a Proof, as rare as the 1875. Ex Col. Green, via Jim Macallister." Realized $235.

VF-20	EF-40	AU-50	MS-60	MS-63	PF-60	PF-63
$500	$550	$650	$2,000	$6,000	$8,500	$17,500

1875

Circulation-Strike Mintage: 400

Proof Mintage: 20

Famous low-mintage rarity. A quarter eagle classic.

No quarter eagles or other gold coins minted at Philadelphia from 1862 through autumn 1878 were paid out at par; such pieces were stored by the Treasury and were available only by paying a premium. The circulation strikes of this year seem to have attracted no particular notice at the time, and they were probably paid out by the Treasury in or after December 1878 when gold, silver, and paper money achieved parity for the first time since late December 1861.

Estimated Total Population (Mint State). 2 to 4. These are exceedingly rare. The mintage of the 1875 quarter eagle amounted to just 420 coins totally—the same mintage as for gold dollars this year—divided into 400 circulation strikes and 20 Proofs. Circulation strikes were not saved deliberately by numismatists, while Proofs were. In his study of the quarter eagle series in 1975, David Akers was able to find 24 appearances of circulation strikes over a long period of years—no doubt this included duplicate appearances of the same specimens. *Just two of these were described as Uncirculated.* One of those coins was the Bass Collection II coin. It seems quite obvious that while Proofs are wonderful rarities and are seldom seen, Mint State circulation strikes are rarer yet.

Estimated Total Population (Circulated Grades). 40 to 60. Typical grades are Extremely Fine and About Uncirculated. It is likely that many of the several dozen pieces listed in catalogs over the years as "former Proofs" or "impaired Proofs" were made as prooflike circulation strikes. The relatively high survival rate of this date is due to the activities of New York City dealer Thomas L. Elder, who beginning in the first decade of the twentieth century circulated lists of scarce coins to bank tellers, who found many pieces.

Die Data. *1875 four-digit date logotype:* The 18 are very close, the 87 are slightly wider but still close, and 75 are significantly wider; the bases of 75 are lower than bases of 18. The top and bottom spaces of the 8 are about equal, and the 8 leans slightly right. The 5 slants slightly to the right, has a very prominent flag which extends virtually to the right side of the numeral, and has a very heavy lower right curve; the ball is small and somewhat irregular in shape and is distant from the upright. This logotype was used on all dies for both mints.

On circulation strikes, the date logotype is centered; the tip of the 5 is distant from the neck truncation.

Characteristics of Striking and Die Notes. These are usually well struck, with prooflike fields.

Selected Auction Records

Note: Surprisingly, there have been quite a few auction sales over the years, a few of which are given here.

In June 1883 John W. Haseltine's sale of the William J. Jenks Collection had lot 477: "1875 Uncirculated. Proof surface." Realized $3.90. B. Max Mehl in his February 1921 sale of the Dr. G.F.E. Wilharm Collection described lot 109: "1875 Uncirculated with considerable Proof surface. Excessively rare, only 420 coined. Cost $50." Realized $41. J.C. Morgenthau & Company's September 1935 sale of the Harrie B. Price Collection included lot 233: "1875 Very Fine. Extremely rare, only 420 having been struck." Realized $83.

Proofs

Estimated Total Population (Proof). 12 to 15. John Dannreuther estimates 16 to 20. This is a landmark date, and thus choice pieces have been featured when they have appeared in auction sales over the years. *Many* more coins have been listed as impaired Proofs over the years, and no doubt some of these would better be called prooflike circulation strikes (or else the mintage figure of 20 for Proofs is incorrect; alternatively, some are restrikes, as has been suggested now and again).

Proof Die Data and Notes. The date logotype is positioned to the right, with the upper right of the 5 (1875) very close to the neck truncation.

All Proofs have numerous tiny *raised* die lines in the obverse field and also slight bulging of the obverse die, as made (the bulging is noticeable when a coin is turned at an angle to the light, and the light is reflected into the observer's eye). These die characteristics are rarely mentioned, and it is likely that some catalogers have mistakenly considered them to be hairlines (such as from cleaning).

Selected Proof Auction Records

Note: The following is a selection from Proof citations over the years. Certain of these "Proofs," especially those that were circulated or impaired, may have been prooflike circulation strikes (which are rarer than Proofs). More citations are given than usual—in view of the immense fame of the 1875 date. Similarly, long (or longer) listings could be given for many other rare Proofs of the 1860s and 1870s.

Dr. George W. Massamore's sale of the Washington Collection in December 1884 included lot 964: "1875 Proof." Realized $8. Elmer S. Sears in his 1907 fixed-price list offered lot 331: "1875 Extremely Fine. Practically Uncirculated. Has been a Proof. Excessively rare, as but 420 were struck and nearly all collectors need this date. $50." The June 1941 William Forrester Dunham Collection, sold by B. Max Mehl, included lot 1974: "The 1875 quarter eagle in Brilliant Proof. Magnificent perfect brilliant Proof, bold impression with complete sharp wire edge on both sides. This coin, as the other gold denominations of this year in this Collection are from a Proof set purchased by Mr. Dunham in 1906. Here's one coin the rarity of which has not been appreciated. Only 420 specimens were struck in all. Just how many Proofs were struck, I do not know, but I doubt if more than five per cent were Proofs. We find some of the greatest collections that have been sold in the past fifty years, did not have this coin in brilliant Proof. The Hale Collection, which was in course of formation for over forty years, did not have any kind of a specimen. I consider this coin, in brilliant Proof condition, almost as rare as any quarter eagle. The price at which it is listed in the *Standard Catalogue*, that of $150, is but a small part of its real value. I consider it worth at least double its listed price." Realized $177.50. In the J.F. Bell Collection in December 1944, Stack's described lot 142: "1875 Brilliant Proof. An absolutely Perfect gem in every respect. Only 420 were struck, records as high as $250 at private sale." Realized $235. This coin later appeared in the November 1956 sale of the Thomas L. Gaskill Collection as lot 327: "1875 Almost fully brilliant Proof; tiny (easily removable) reverse tarnish mark. One of the most highly prized rarities of the series; only 400 coined, and 20 Proofs, but seldom seen except in Proof or impaired Proof. The *Guide Book* figure of $325 is much too low for today's market, as that is precisely what the WGC example realized, ten years ago. Atwater's brought $360, various private records have approximated as much. Generally found mishandled; a clean Proof of this date should be worth about $500." Realized $400.

In the Numismatic Gallery sale of the "World's Greatest Collection" (F.C.C. Boyd Collection, January 1946) Abe Kosoff described lot 143: "1875 Brilliant Proof. Very rare. This date is still not fully appreciated for its rarity, especially as a brilliant Proof. In the 'old days' of the Dunham sale it sold from $177.50." Realized $325. In June 1946 in his sale of the William Cutler Atwater Collection. B. Max Mehl offered lot 1979: "1875. Perfect brilliant Proof gem. Bold impression, with raised borders and wire edge. As perfect a specimen of this rarity as could possibly exist. A total of only 420 specimens were minted in all, of which number, of course, only a fraction were struck in Proofs, probably not more than thirty or forty, and of that number probably only about one-half exist today. Only an Extremely Fine specimen in my Roach Collection brought $210. . . . Another rarity with a bright future for advancement in value." Realized $365. Mehl's Will W. Neil Collection, June 1947, included lot 2450: "The extremely rare 1875 quarter eagle, 1875 $2.50 gold. Originally purchased by Mr. Neil as a brilliant Proof. The coin is a Proof, but not in full brilliancy, the field shows slight cabinet friction. However it is a choice and desirable specimen of this rarity, of which only 420 specimens were minted in all. Steadily advancing in value. Just about doubled in value in the past four or five years. Even in the period of time from 1946 to 1947, it advanced 100% in catalog listing. In my sale of the Atwater Collection, in June of 1946, when this coin cataloged for $150, it brought $365. This coin now catalogs for $300. One of the rarest of all quarter eagles." Realized $187.50. Mehl's sale of the Jerome Kern Collection, May 1950, included lot 64: "1875. The Extremely rare 1875 quarter eagle. Perfect brilliant Proof, wire edge. Only 420 minted in all. Probably only a small fraction of that number in existence today. The specimen in my sale of the Atwater Collection brought $365. A coin that is certainly destined to steadily advance in value, as it is really one of our rarities, especially in this beautiful state of preservation." Realized $275.

VF-20	EF-40	AU-50	MS-60	PF-60	PF-63
$7,000	$12,000	$15,000	$30,000	$35,000	$65,000

1875-S

Circulation-Strike Mintage: 11,600

Scarce in any grade.
Very rare in Mint State.

These circulated at par in the West at a time when quarter eagles were not seen in circulation in the East or Midwest.

Estimated Total Population (Mint State). 6 to 10. These are mostly at the low end of the Mint State scale. Very rare.

Estimated Total Population (Circulated Grades). 125 to 175. Very Fine and Extremely Fine are the typical grades.

Die Data. *1875 four-digit date logotype: See the Philadelphia Mint listing for this year.*

The Old Reverse hub is used. On the obverse the date logotype is punched left and high; the 5 (1875) is distant from the neck.

The edge reeding is more widely spaced than on the Philadelphia Mint quarter eagles of this year.

Characteristics of Striking and Die Notes. Most, but not all, are lightly struck at the centers.

Selected Auction Records

Thomas L. Elder's March 1911 sale of the William H. Woodin collection included two: Lot 1080: "1875-S. Silver alloy, closed S. Fine. Very rare." Realized $2.70. Lot 1081: "1875-S. Yellow, gold. The S open. Extremely Fine, with luster. Very rare." Realized $7.75. In the J.F. Bell Collection in December 1944, Stack's described lot 257: "1875-S Brilliant Uncirculated." Realized $15.50. The catalog of the New Netherlands November 1956 sale of the Thomas L. Gaskill Collection described lot 328: "1875-S. Bright, lustrous Uncirculated, with full, frosty mint surface. Sharp and bold; almost in the 'superb' class, in spite of hardly visible 'cabinet friction' in spots. Rare, small coinage of 11,600. Superior to the Atwater, Memorable, Dr. Green, Menjou, Graves, Smith, Melish and other examples; the AU specimen in the WGC auction commanded $33 a decade ago." Realized $47.50.

A Long Island, New York, collector is said to have amassed 18 or more examples of this issue, ranging in grade from Very Good to Mint State.[109] This, of course, is a numismatic accumulation or group, not an old-time hoard.

VF-20	EF-40	AU-50	MS-60	MS-63
$500	$515	$650	$3,500	$7,250

1876

Circulation-Strike Mintage: 4,176
Proof Mintage: 45

Scarce in any grade.
Very rare in Mint State.

No quarter eagles or other gold coins minted at Philadelphia from 1862 through autumn 1878 were paid out at par; such pieces were stored by the Treasury and were available only by paying a premium.

Estimated Total Population (Mint State). 6 to 10. These are seen in various levels of Mint State and are very rare. Apparently, only a few were saved, and these by chance.

Estimated Total Population (Circulated Grades). 70 to 90. Extremely Fine and About Uncirculated are the typical grades. These are very scarce.

Die Data. *1876 four-digit date logotype:* All figures are very closely spaced. The 1 has a lower left serif that is longer than the lower right serif. The 8 has a top interior space that is smaller than the bottom interior space, and the figure leans right. The 6 has a small knob, somewhat irregular in shape, close to but not touching the curve below; it leans very slightly right. This logotype was used on all dies for both mints.

There is a raised "bar" behind the jaw; this is seen on 1876 and 1876-S circulation strikes, and thus on the master die, then transferred to the working dies.

Characteristics of Striking and Die Notes. There is mounding in the date area and some light striking at the centers.

Selected Auction Records

Note: Although most "Selected Auction Records" sections in this chapter contain several examples from a much larger file, the following is a selection from a file of relatively few early listings.

In September 1910 in his sale of the Peter Mougey Collection, Thomas L. Elder described lot 1212: "1876. About Fine. Very rare." Realized $3.10. In June 1935 in the C. Foster Collection, Elder offered lot 2583: "1876 Fine, Rare. Small coinage." Realized $5.50. In Sale 359, January 1936, J.C. Morgenthau & Co. included lot 106: "1876 Extremely Fine. Scarce." Realized $10. Stack's in November 1947 offered lot 902 in the sale of the Mason Williams Collection: "1876 Extremely Fine." Realized $11.

Proofs

Estimated Total Population (Proof). 20 to 25. As can be seen for various Proof quarter eagles, the estimated survivors vis-à-vis the Mint's production records can vary considerably percentage-wise.

Proof Die Data and Notes. The date logotype is centered; the 1 (1876) is midway between the neck and the denticles.

Selected Proof Auction Records

Note: Certain of these "Proofs" may have been prooflike circulation strikes (which are rarer than Proofs).

Thomas L. Elder's March 1911 sale of the William H. Woodin collection included lot 1019: "1876. Brilliant Proof. It has not been offered singly in any of the large sales."[110] Realized $9.25. (The larger sale often included full gold Proof sets.) B. Max Mehl in his February 1921 sale of the Dr. G.F.E. Wilharm Collection described lot 110: "1876 Sharp brilliant Proof. Very rare, seldom offered." Realized $7.35. The June 1941 William Forrester Dunham Collection sold by Mehl included lot 1975: "1876 Brilliant Uncirculated, with semi-Proof surface. Listed at $30 in Proof." Realized $10.50. In the J.F. Bell Collection in December 1944, Stack's described lot 143: "1876 Brilliant Proof gem." Realized $55. In the Numismatic Gallery sale of the "World's Greatest Collection" (F.C.C. Boyd Collection, January 1946) Abe Kosoff described lot 144: "1876 Brilliant Proof." Realized $60. The catalog of the New Netherlands November 1956 sale of the Thomas L. Gaskill Collection described lot 329: "1876 Desirable, mostly brilliant Proof. Almost full wire edge. Greatly underrated; only 4,176 business strikes, 45 Proofs struck. Records, at private sale, to $125." Realized $100.

VF-20	EF-40	AU-50	MS-60	MS-63	PF-60	PF-63
$600	$675	$1,000	$3,250	$7,500	$7,500	$15,000

1876-S

Circulation-Strike Mintage: 5,000

Second lowest S-Mint $2.50 gold coin mintage.
Scarce in any grade.
Very rare in Mint State.

This year marked the second-lowest mintage among quarter eagles from the San Francisco Mint. These circulated at par in the West at a time when quarter eagles were not seen in circulation in the East or Midwest.

Estimated Total Population (Mint State). 5 to 7. These are very scarce. Only a few *different* coins have appeared over the years. As of 1975 David W. Akers had seen only two or three. Certification populations continue to expand year by year as examples are resubmitted, then resubmitted again, giving the misleading impression that more and more are being discovered! Known Mint State specimens are concentrated toward the lower end of the Mint State scale.

This issue is important as the final condition rarity in the quarter eagle series. Although certain later dates are elusive in Mint State—this being true of some of the low-mintage years in the 1880s—no later variety equals the elusive quality of the 1876-S.

Estimated Total Population (Circulated Grades). 75 to 100. Very Fine and Extremely Fine are the typical grades, although About Uncirculated coins appear with some frequency.

Die Data. *1876 four-digit date logotype: See the Philadelphia Mint listing for this year.*

There is a raised "bar" behind the jaw; this is seen on 1876 and 1876-S circulation strikes, and thus on the master die, then transferred to the working dies. The Old Reverse hub is used, this being its last use in the quarter eagle series.

Walter Breen (monograph, 1964) states that "one pair of dies only made and used; reverse always weak." However, this does not seem to explain the use of the Old Reverse hub, which had not been produced at the Philadelphia Mint since circa 1860, nor the notations in literature of upright S as well as slanting S mintmark varieties (*e.g.*, 1921 Langenfelder and 1932 Taylor auction listings).

Characteristics of Striking and Die Notes. These are seen weak at the centers.

Selected Auction Records

In June 1883 John W. Haseltine's sale of the William J. Jenks Collection had lot 478: "1876-S Uncirculated." Realized $3.50. Thomas L. Elder's March 1911 sale of the William H. Woodin collection included lot 1082: "1876-S. The S high, above 1, and large. Fine. Very rare, coinage very limited." Realized $2.50 (face value). The Malcolm N. Jackson Collection sold in May 1913 by the U.S. Coin Co. included lot 242: "1876-S Very Fine and very rare." Realized $3. The William B. Hale Collection sold by B. Max Mehl in November 1939 included lot 880: "1876-S Very Fine. Scarce." Realized $6.30. In the J.F. Bell Collection in December 1944, Stack's described lot 258: "1876-S Brilliant Uncirculated." Realized $20. The sale of the Philpott and Zander Collections by Mehl in November 1945 included lot 1226: "1876-S Extremely Fine with mint luster. Scarce." Realized $5.50. In the Numismatic Gallery sale of the "World's Greatest Collection" (F.C.C. Boyd Collection, January 1946) Abe Kosoff described lot 260: "1876-S Extremely Fine." Realized $19. In June 1946 in his sale of the William Cutler Atwater Collection, Mehl offered lot 2090: "1876-S Semi-Proof. Nearly equal to a brilliant Proof. Rare in any condition, as a total of only 5,000 were minted. Catalogs at $22.50 in Uncirculated. This specimen certainly worth much more." Realized $11.25. The catalog of the New Netherlands November 1956 sale of the Thomas L. Gaskill Collection described lot 330: "1876-S. Fully Very Fine. Rare, only 5,000 made. A real 'sleeper,' the second rarest-S Mint quarter eagle. Should be valued at $30. today." Realized $16.

VF-20	EF-40	AU-50	MS-60	MS-63
$500	$550	$1,000	$3,000	$8,500

1877

Circulation-Strike Mintage: 1,632

Proof Mintage: 20

Fascinating low mintage.
Scarce in any grade.
Rare in Mint State.

No quarter eagles or other gold coins minted at Philadelphia from 1862 through autumn 1878 were paid out at par; such pieces were stored by the Treasury and were available only by paying a premium.

Estimated Total Population (Mint State). 14 to 20. These are mostly MS-60 to MS-63, and very rare. "I have never seen an Uncirculated specimen," Walter Breen wrote in his 1964 monograph. However, his surveys were quite limited and, in addition, more specimens have come on the market since that time—especially after the run-up in market prices from the 1970s onward. Today the 1877 is very rare in Mint State but hardly "impossible." In his 1975 study, David W. Akers was able to locate 14 auction listings in Mint State. Referring to all grade levels, he wrote, "The 1877 has one of the lowest mintages of any date in the series and so it may come as a surprise to some that it appears at auction more often than many supposedly more common dates."

Estimated Total Population (Circulated Grades). 70 to 95. Most are Extremely Fine or About Uncirculated. Although the mintage of the 1877 is among the lowest in the quarter eagle series, a fair number seem to have been saved, probably including by bank tellers who received Thomas L. Elder's "want list" in the early twentieth century, when such coins could still be found in bank holdings and customer deposits. Still, by any evaluation it is a rare date.

Die Data. *1877 four-digit date logotype:* The date has heavy, thick numerals, giving it a bold appearance. The 18 are very close, 87 are wider, and 77 are in between. The upright of 1 is very thick; the left serif of 1 is nearly twice as long as the right serif, and the right side of the right serif cuts off at an angle. The 8 has top and bottom spaces of about the same size, thick sides, and leans slightly right. The bases of the 7's are slightly lower than the bases of the 18; there are very heavy tops to the 7's and heavy teardrop-shaped bottoms; the second 7 is slightly more deeply punched into the die at its base, making the base appear ever so slightly lower than that of the first 7. This logotype was used on all dies for both mints.

Characteristics of Striking and Die Notes. These are usually well struck, although some show very slight weakness on the eagle's leg at the left reverse. High-grade pieces have prooflike surfaces.

Selected Auction Records

In June 1883 John W. Haseltine's sale of the William J. Jenks Collection had lot 479: "1877 Uncirculated. Proof surface." Realized $3.25. Elmer S. Sears in his 1907 fixed-price list offered lot 338: "1877 Another. Uncirculated. Mint lustre. $15." Thomas L. Elder's March 1911 sale of the William H. Woodin collection included lot 1020: "1877. Uncirculated, with Proof surface and mint luster. Very rare. Coinage very limited." Realized $10. In his sale of the Morris Collection, April 1931, B. Max Mehl described lot 533: "1877 Uncirculated, with Proof surface. Very scarce." Realized $12. The William B. Hale Collection sold by Mehl in November 1939 included lot 796: "1877 Apparently was struck as a Proof, now just about Uncirculated with considerable Proof surface. Quite rare. Listed up to $50 in Proof." Realized $12.75. Mehl's sale of the Jerome Kern Collection, May 1950, included lot 66: "1877 Brilliant semi-Proof. Was purchased by Mr. Kern as a Proof. It probably is a Proof, but I think better to catalog it as a semi-Proof. Catalogs $60 in Proof." Realized $56.

PROOFS

Estimated Total Population (Proof). 15 to 20.

Proof Die Data and Notes. These are from three different die pairs, indicating restrikes. John Dannreuther gives detailed information. This would seem to open the possibility for restrikes of other dates struck from a single die pair, thus helping to explain widely varying survival percentages.

Selected Proof Auction Records

Note: Certain of these "Proofs" may have been prooflike circulation strikes (which are also very rare).

In the J.F. Bell Collection in December 1944, Stack's described lot 144: "1877 Brilliant Proof gem." Realized $62.50. In the Numismatic Gallery sale of the "World's Greatest Collection" (F.C.C. Boyd Collection, January 1946) Abe Kosoff described lot 145: "1877 Brilliant Proof." Realized $70. The sale of the Melish and Hester Collections by Abe Kosoff in April 1956 included lot 1289: "1877 Brilliant Proof, scarce." Realized $130. The catalog of the New Netherlands November 1956 sale of the Thomas L. Gaskill Collection described lot 331: "1877 Superb, brilliant Proof, without the faintest trace of hairmarks or cleaning. Perfection; touch of rev. tarnish. An unimprovable example of one of the most underrated dates. Just 1,632 plus 20 Proofs coined. As rare as any Proof after 1860; as a date, comparable to 1865. This 'gem' is definitely in the $150 class. Ex Brand, Reed." Realized $230.

VF-20	EF-40	AU-50	MS-60	MS-63	PF-60	PF-63
$600	$950	$1,250	$3,000	$9,500	$7,500	$15,000

1877-S

Circulation-Strike Mintage: 35,400

Scarce in any grade.

These circulated at par in the West at a time when quarter eagles were not seen in circulation in the East or Midwest.

Estimated Total Population (Mint State). 50 to 80. Grades run from MS-60 or so, where most are situated, but some exist at the gem level.

Estimated Total Population (Circulated Grades). 150 to 200. Many are at the About Uncirculated level.

Die Data. *1877 four-digit date logotype: See the Philadelphia Mint listing for this year.*

The New Reverse hub was introduced this year (having been in use at the Philadelphia Mint since the late 1850s). There is a very small S mintmark.

Characteristics of Striking and Die Notes. These usually have light striking on the eagle's leg at the left reverse. High-grade coins are often prooflike.

Selected Auction Records

Elmer S. Sears in his 1907 fixed-price list offered two: Lot 339: "1877 San Francisco Mint. Mint mark placed over figure 1 of fraction. Uncirculated. Mint lustre. $5." Lot 341: "1877 Another, with mint mark placed over 2 of fraction. Uncirculated. Scarce. $6." The Malcolm N. Jackson Collection sold in May 1913 by the U.S. Coin Co. included two: Lot 243: "1877-S S between 2 and D. Extremely Fine, scarce." Realized

$2.75. Lot 244: "1877-S, S over I in fraction. Extremely Fine, scarce." Realized $2.75. The William B. Hale Collection sold by B. Max Mehl in November 1939 included a pair: Lot 881: "1877-S, S over 1 of fraction. Extremely Fine." Realized $6. Lot 882: "1877-S, S over 2 of fraction. Extremely Fine." Realized $5.75.

The June 1941 William Forrester Dunham Collection sold by Mehl included lot 1976: "1877-S Brilliant Uncirculated, with Proof surface." Realized $6.50. The sale of the Philpott and Zander Collections by Mehl in November 1945 included two: Lot 1227: "1877-S S directly over 1 of fraction. Uncirculated." Realized $5.50. Lot 1228: "1877-S Another as last and about as choice." Realized $7.10. Mehl's sale of the Jerome Kern Collection, May 1950, included lot 178: "1877-S. Uncirculated, frosty mint surface. Variety with microscopic S over 2 of fraction. Scarce so choice." Realized $31.50. The catalog of the New Netherlands November 1956 sale of the Thomas L. Gaskill Collection described these: Lot 332: "1877-S. Mintmark smaller than on preceding issues; placed to right, between feather and branch. EF plus; not too boldly struck up, but lustrous." Realized $13. Lot 333: "1877-S. Similar. S to left, directly over numeral 1. Brilliant Uncirculated. Very nice, not often seen so. Cheap at $25 in this preservation." Realized $25. Lot 334: "1877-S. Duplicate. Same dies as last. Very Fine. Slightly impaired." Realized $11.

VF-20	EF-40	AU-50	MS-60	MS-63
$500	$515	$525	$650	$2,350

1878

Circulation-Strike Mintage: 286,240
Proof Mintage: 20

First truly common Mint State $2.50 gold coin.

No quarter eagles or other gold coins minted at Philadelphia from 1862 through autumn 1878 were paid out at par; such pieces were stored by the Treasury and were available only by paying a premium. Probably most if not all of the 1878 $2.50 gold coin mintage was paid out at par in or after December 1878.

Estimated Total Population (Mint State). 800 to 1,200. Grades run from MS-60 upward, with most in the MS-60 to MS-63 range. This is the only quarter eagle date after 1853 and before 1893 of which more than a few dozen gem MS-65 or finer specimens are estimated to exist.

Estimated Total Population (Circulated Grades). 2,000 to 3,000. These are very common, mostly Extremely Fine and About Uncirculated.

Die Data. *1878 four-digit date logotype:* The 18 are closely spaced, and the 87 and 78 are farther apart and each about the same distance; the base of 1 is high. The 1 has a thick upright, the lower right serif is thinner than the lower left serif and somewhat defective; the figure leans slightly right. Both 8's have top interior spaces about the same size as the bottom interior spaces; the first 8 leans slightly right, and the second 8 leans more to the right. The 7 has a fairly heavy top, is thinner at the left side than on the right, and is differently styled than that on the 1877; the prominent teardrop base is connected to the top by a point that becomes very small right below the top. This logotype was used on all dies for both mints.

Selected Auction Records

Elmer S. Sears in his 1907 fixed-price list offered lot 342: "1878 Uncirculated. Mint lustre. $3," with Proof surface." Realized $2.50 (face value). Malcolm N. Jackson Collection sold in May 1913 by the U.S. Coin Co. included lot 164: "1878 Uncirculated." Realized $2.75. In the J.F. Bell Collection in December 1944, Stack's described lot 145: "1878 Brilliant Uncirculated." Realized $10. In June 1946 in his sale of the William Cutler Atwater Collection, B. Max Mehl offered lot 1982: "1878 Uncirculated frosty mint surface. Catalogs at $10." Realized $10. In April 1947 in his house organ, *Kelly's Coins and Chatter*, James F. Kelly offered an Uncirculated coin for $10. In the October 1951 sale for the New England Numismatic Association Sale, Stack's described lot 385: "1878 Brilliant Uncirculated." Realized $9.25.

Proofs

Estimated Total Population (Proof). 12 to 15.

Proof Die Data and Notes. The medium date numerals are centered below the neck. This die was only used for Proofs.

Selected Proof Auction Records

In June 1883 John W. Haseltine's sale of the William J. Jenks Collection included lot 480: "1878 Brilliant Proof." Realized $4.50. B. Max Mehl's November 1944 sale of the Fred E. Olsen Collection included 1897: "1878 Brilliant semi-Proof, just about equal to a perfect Proof. Rare." Realized $21. The catalog of the New Netherlands November 1956 sale of the Thomas L. Gaskill Collection described lot 335: "1878 Mainly brilliant Proof. Square borders; partial wire edge Somewhat carelessly handled or cleaned, but still desirable. As an authentic Proof, very rarely offered; many so called are first-strikes. But 20 'yellow' Proof sets of this year were made, and 1878 (in all the old dealer's lists and catalogs) was well known as a 'sleeper' issue of Proof gold. Presumably, many of the 20 struck (of each denomination) remained unsold, and were passed out over the counter in Philadelphia. The best that Col. E.H.R. Green could locate via Macallister. Should be seen!" Realized $77.50.

VF-20	EF-40	AU-50	MS-60	MS-63	PF-60	PF-63
$500	$515	$525	$550	$700	$7,500	$15,000

1878-S

Circulation-Strike Mintage: 178,000

These circulated at par in the West at a time when quarter eagles were not seen in circulation in the East or Midwest (until mid-December of this year).

Dramatic mintmark position variations.

Estimated Total Population (Mint State). 100 to 150. These are plentiful, and most are in the range of MS-60 to MS-63. Gems are elusive.

Estimated Total Population (Circulated Grades). 350 to 500. Most are Extremely Fine or About Uncirculated.

Die Data. *1878 four-digit date logotype: See the Philadelphia Mint listing for this year.*

The New Reverse hub is used. There is a very small S mintmark. At least five[111] various positional differences are known, which range *dramatically* from placement over the 1 in the fraction (1/2) to over the upper left of the D.

Characteristics of Striking and Die Notes. These usually have light striking on the eagle.

Selected Auction Records

Elmer S. Sears in his 1907 fixed-price list offered these: Lot 343: "1878 San Francisco Mint. Mint mark placed over figure 2 and near D of fraction. Uncirculated. $3." Lot 344: "1878 Another, with mint mark placed over dividing line of fraction. Uncirculated. $4." Lot 345: "1878 Another, with mint mark placed over figure 1 of fraction. Uncirculated. Rare. $6." Multiple examples were also offered in B. Max Mehl's February 1944 sale of the Belden E. Roach Collection: Lot 1019: "1878-S Variety with mint letter S over and to right of 1 of fraction. About Uncirculated. Scarce die variety." Realized $7. Lot 1020: "1878-S Variety with slanting mint letter S between 1 of fraction and fraction bar. About Uncirculated." Realized $8. Lot 1021: "1878-S Variety with mint letter S directly over 2 of fraction. Bright Uncirculated." Realized $10.50. Likewise, in the Numismatic Gallery sale of the "World's Greatest Collection" (F.C.C. Boyd Collection, January 1946) Abe Kosoff described multiple examples: Lot 262: "1878-S The S is over the 1 in the fraction 1/2. About Uncirculated." Realized $9. Lot 263: "1878-S The S is between the space over the 2 in the fraction and the D. Extremely Fine." Realized $10. Lot 264: "1878-S The S is more to the right than in the previous type. Very Fine." Realized $9. This variety was a focal point for die varieties. Still more multiples appeared in the April 1956 sale by Abe Kosoff of the Melish and Hester Collections: Lot 1294: "1878-S. S is over the 1. Very Fine." Realized $12.50. Lot 1295: "1878-S. S is over the fraction bar. Very Fine." Realized $12.50. 1296: "1878-S. is over the 2. About Extremely Fine." Realized $14.

VF-20	EF-40	AU-50	MS-60	MS-63
$500	$515	$525	$550	$1,500

1879

Circulation-Strike Mintage: 88,870

Proof Mintage: 30

Available in most grades.

Estimated Total Population (Mint State). 300 to 500. Quite a few of these were saved, probably in the year of issue, for 1879 was the first full year that quarter eagles were available again in circulation, since gold coin payouts were suspended in the final days of December 1861. Gems are readily available.

Estimated Total Population (Circulated Grades). 400 to 600. Extremely Fine and About Uncirculated are the typical grades.

Die Data. *1879 four digit date logotype:* The numerals are heavy. The 18 are close, the 87 are wider, and the 79 are wider yet; the base of the 1 is high, and the lower right base is thinner than the lower left base. The 8 has top and bottom spaces of about the same size (slightly larger on some impressions), and the figure leans slightly right. The 7 is of the same general style as used in 1878; the base is slightly lower than other numerals. The 9 has a somewhat irregular lower right curve, and the ball is fairly close to the curve above it but does not touch; the figure leans to the right. This was used on all dies for both mints.

Characteristics of Striking and Die Notes. These are usually well struck.

Selected Auction Records

Elmer S. Sears in his 1907 fixed-price list offered lot 34: "1879 Uncirculated. Mint lustre. $3." The Malcolm N. Jackson Collection sold in May 1913 by the U.S. Coin Co. included lot 165: "1879 Uncirculated." Realized $2.75. B. Max Mehl in his February 1921 sale of the Dr. G.F.E. Wilharm Collection described lot 113: "1879 Uncirculated. Scarce." Realized $3.40. The sale of the Philpott and Zander Collections by Mehl in November 1945 included lot 1127: "1879 Uncirculated" Realized $9.25. In February 1957 the Stack's sale of the J.W. Schmandt Collection included lot 211: "1879 Originally purchased as a Proof, but in reality a 'first strike.' Brilliant and choice." Realized $60.

Proofs

Deliveries of this issue were reported as follows, as part of full gold Proof sets: These figures come directly from original Mint records as studied by R.W. Julian.[112] Second quarter, 7; third quarter, 4; fourth quarter, 10.

Estimated Total Population (Proof). 17 to 22.

Proof Die Data and Notes. The date is slightly high. There is a lump on the neck above the 8.

Selected Proof Auction Records

Note: Certain of these "Proofs" may have been prooflike circulation strikes. Citations for full gold Proof sets (containing six coins including the $2.50) have been omitted.[113]

In June 1883 John W. Haseltine's sale of the William J. Jenks Collection had lot 481: "1879 Brilliant Proof." Realized $3. The 26th Sale, S.A. Clickner Collection (Dr. George W. Massamore), included Lot 992: "1879 Brilliant Proof. Rare." Realized $2.50 (face value). Elmer S. Sears in his 1907 fixed-price list offered lot 346: "1879 Brilliant Proof. Very rare in Proof condition. $6." In the Numismatic Gallery sale of the "World's Greatest Collection" (F.C.C. Boyd Collection, January 1946) Abe Kosoff described lot 147: "1879 Brilliant Proof." Realized $70. In June 1946 in his sale of the William Cutler

Atwater Collection, B. Max Mehl offered lot 1983: "1879 Perfect brilliant Proof, wire edge. Rare. Seldom offered in Proof. Recent record $70." Realized $72.50.

In the 1930s Fort Worth (Texas) rare coin dealer B. Max Mehl was prominent in Rotary International. A member of the local Rotary Club, Amon G. Carter Sr., was born in 1879 and as a gift, Mehl gave him a quarter eagle of that date. From that point it was a short step for Carter to purchase a rare 1879 $4 gold Stella, then other coins, including the 1822 $5 gold coin from the Dunham Collection sale held by Mehl in 1941. Carter, who was involved in such ventures as Gulf Oil, newspaper publishing, and the formation of American Airlines, would buy from Mehl the unsold remainders of his mail bid sales, as well as individual scarcities and rarities that Mehl recommended. Many of these purchases were kept in the original Mehl auction envelopes and passed to Amon Jr., upon his death. Amon Jr. went on to become an important collector in his own right, especially in the field of paper currency.

VF-20	EF-40	AU-50	MS-60	MS-63	PF-60	PF-63
$500	$515	$525	$550	$800	$7,500	$13,000

1879-S

Circulation-Strike Mintage: 43,500

Last San Francisco Mint $2.50 gold coin. Surprisingly rare in Mint State.

Estimated Total Population (Mint State). 5 to 8. These are surprising and inexplicably rare at the Mint State level, and exceedingly rare at MS-63 or finer.

Estimated Total Population (Circulated Grades). 80 to 120. These are generally available in grades from Very Fine to About Uncirculated, with lower grades being the rule. Unlike its Philadelphia Mint counterpart, the 1879-S circulated widely after it was issued. Over the years Very Fine, Extremely Fine, and About Uncirculated coins have been the norm, even for most "name" collections.

Die Data. *1879 four-digit date logotype: See the Philadelphia Mint listing for this year.*

One obverse die has the logotype punched deeply, more so at the bottom of the figures than at the top, indicating that the punch was not held vertically when the working die was finessed. Some strikings are highly prooflike.

The New Reverse hub is used. At least two reverse dies were used to coin 1879-S quarter eagles, one with a small, wide "S" and another with a small, narrow "S."

Characteristics of Striking and Die Notes. These are usually well struck.

Selected Auction Records

Elmer S. Sears in his 1907 fixed-price list offered two: Lot 348: "1879 San Francisco Mint. Mint mark placed close to 'D' on reverse. Uncirculated. $3.50." Lot 349: "1879 Another, with mint mark placed close to figure 1 of fraction. Uncirculated. $3.50." Thomas L. Elder's March 1911 sale of the William H. Woodin collection included these: Lot 1088: "1879-S. The S short and broad, down between 1 and bar. Uncirculated; rare."

Realized $6.50. Lot 1089: "1879-S. Tall, narrow S, between 2 and D, wide '2½.' Fine." Realized $3.25. Lot 1090: "1879-S. Short, closed S, down between 1 and bar, the '2½' crowded close. Very Fine; rare." Realized $3.25. The Malcolm N. Jackson Collection sold in May 1913 by the U.S. Coin Co. included lot 246: "1879-S Wide 2½. S between 2 and D. Very Fine." Realized $3. Abe Kosoff's April 1956 sale of the Melish and Hester Collections included this pair: Lot 1299: "1879-S. S is over the fraction bar. Very Fine." Realized $13.50. Lot 1300: "1879-S. S is over the 2. Very Fine." Realized $13.

VF-20	EF-40	AU-50	MS-60	MS-63
$500	$515	$550	$1,750	$4,500

1880

Circulation-Strike Mintage: 2,960
Proof Mintage: 36

Scarce in all grades.

Estimated Total Population (Mint State). 30 to 50. These are available enough to make them accessible for the specialist, but sufficiently few that this low-mintage quarter eagle is well known as a rare date. Only a handful exist at MS-65 or finer.

Estimated Total Population (Circulated Grades). 150 to 250. Typical grades tend toward the high end of the range, About Uncirculated and Extremely Fine, and are often prooflike and usually very attractive.

Die Data. *1880 four-digit date logotype:* The digits are more widely spaced than on recent issues; the 18 are close, the 88 are wider (as measured at the closest appearance of the two digits at the bottom), and the 80 are wider yet. The 1 is large and leans slightly right. Both 8's have top interior spaces that are slightly smaller than the bottom interior spaces; the first 8 leans right, and the second 8 appears nearly upright. The 0 leans slightly left, which is a somewhat unusual orientation as logotype figures, when they lean at all, typically lean right (the orientation is best noted by observing the interior of the digit). This logotype was used on all dies.

The date logotype is deeply impressed, seemingly more so to the left than to the right side.

Characteristics of Striking and Die Notes. These are usually well struck and often semi-prooflike or fully prooflike, although some are highly frosty.

Selected Auction Records

In June 1883 John W. Haseltine's sale of the William J. Jenks Collection had lot 482: "1880 Uncirculated." Realized $3.50. Elmer S. Sears in his 1907 fixed-price list offered these: Lot 350: "1880 Uncirculated. Mint lustre. $8." Lot 351: "1880 Another, nearly as fine. $7." The Malcolm N. Jackson Collection sold in May 1913 by the U.S. Coin Co. included lot 166: "1880 Extremely Fine, mint luster." Realized $3.25. In the J.F. Bell Collection in December 1944, Stack's described lot 147: "1880 Brilliant Uncirculated." Realized $17.

Proofs

Deliveries of this issue were reported as follows, as part of full gold Proof sets: These figures come directly from original Mint records as studied by R.W. Julian.[114] First quarter, 17; third quarter, 5; fourth quarter, 10.

Estimated Total Population (Proof). 18 to 22. The demand for Proofs is intense due to the overall low mintage of the date (circulation strikes plus Proofs).

Proof Die Data and Notes. The large date numerals are centered below the neck.

Selected Proof Auction Records

Note: Certain of these "Proofs" may have been prooflike circulation strikes.

Thomas L. Elder's March 1911 sale of the William H. Woodin collection included lot 1023: "1880. Brilliant Proof. Very small coinage and rare. Davis Sale." Realized $7.25. B. Max Mehl in his February 1921 sale of the Dr. G.F.E. Wilharm Collection described lot 114: "1880 Uncirculated, Proof surface, nearly equal to a Proof. Rare 2996 coined." Realized $7. The June 1941 William Forrester Dunham Collection sold by Mehl included lot 1979: "1880 Bright semi-Proof. Rare. Very limited coinage. Listed at $22.50 in Proof." Realized $6.50. In the Numismatic Gallery sale of the "World's Greatest Collection" (F.C.C. Boyd Collection, January 1946) Abe Kosoff described lot 148."1880 Brilliant Proof." Realized $40. The sale of the Melish and Hester Collections by Abe Kosoff in April 1956 included lot 1301: "1880 Brilliant Proof." Realized $120.

VF-20	EF-40	AU-50	MS-60	MS-63	PF-60	PF-63
$500	$550	$650	$1,500	$3,750	$6,500	$12,500

1881

Circulation-Strike Mintage: 640

Proof Mintage: 51

Remarkably low mintage. Important rarity.

Estimated Total Population (Mint State). 3 to 5. In Mint State the 1881 is a formidable rarity. Apparently, no more than a handful were deliberately saved by numismatists, as Proofs were readily available. In his 1975 study David W. Akers was able to locate only *one* auction appearance of a Mint State coin and had never seen one personally! However, since 1986 over a dozen have been certified in Mint State. The reader may form his or her own opinions, but it seems likely that resubmissions (due to the value of this particular date) and, possibly, liberal grading have inflated the figure.

Estimated Total Population (Circulated Grades). 35 to 50. Well represented in auction citations (only a few given here, however), but rare when you want to find one! As David Akers points out, some—possibly most—Extremely Fine and About Uncirculated coins are impaired Proofs. During the early twentieth century Thomas L. Elder offered these in a number of his sales, probably through banking connections—as he was also prominent in circulated $1 and $3 pieces; probably, he alerted bank tellers to keep a weather eye out for rare dates such as the 1881 quarter eagle.

Die Data. The digits are bold and closely spaced. The date is fairly large and fills most of the space between the neck truncation and the denticles.

Characteristics of Striking and Die Notes. These are very sharply struck and typically seen with prooflike surfaces, this being true, of course, for impaired Proofs offered as circulation strikes and of actual circulation strikes as well.

Selected Auction Records

Elmer S. Sears in his 1907 fixed-price list offered lot 353: "1881 Uncirculated or nearly so, with bloom. $15." Thomas L. Elder in his September 1910 sale of the Peter Mougey Collection seems to have over-estimated lot 1221: "1881. Uncirculated, Proof surface. Very rare. Entire coinage only 680! pieces. Sufficiently rare to bring $25." Realized $8.50. The sale of the Philpott and Zander Collections by B. Max Mehl in November 1945 included lot 1129: "1881 About Uncirculated with brilliant luster. Rare. Only 680 struck. Catalogs at $30 in Uncirculated." Realized $21. In June 1946 in his sale of the William Cutler Atwater Collection, Mehl offered lot 1985: "1881 Only 2,996 minted in all. Not in the Bell Collection. Recent record $40 with complete wire edge. A total of only 680 specimens minted, and, of course, only a fraction of that number in Proof. Record $80. Should be in the $100 class." Realized $80. The grade was not stated, but was possibly a Proof.

Proofs

The mintage figure of 51 was located by Walter Breen as part of the chief coiner's records at the Mint.[115]

In his 1988 *Encyclopedia*, Walter Breen reported that "specimens of the later years 1878–1907 are always available for a price, partly because British, French, and Swiss banks yielded numerous Uncirculated coins during the two decades following World War II. This had the unexpected side effect of making rare dates like 1881 and 1885 easier to locate than some larger mintages of earlier years." No such quantity of 1881 and 1885 quarter eagles has been confirmed.

Estimated Total Population (Proof). 22 to 28. The low survival rate is unexplained. The rarity of this issue as a date, and the general unavailability of Mint State coins, has made Proofs in especially strong demand.

Proof Die Data and Notes. On Proofs the date logotype is deeply punched into the die, and about centered. Breen (1977, 1989) notes that some light *die* polish areas at BER in LIBERTY and near and below the ear are markers of authentic Proofs.

Selected Proof Auction Records

Note: Certain of these "Proofs" may have been prooflike circulation strikes (which are rarer than Proofs).

In June 1883 John W. Haseltine's sale of the William J. Jenks Collection had lot 483: "1881 Brilliant Proof." Realized $3.50. Elmer S. Sears in his 1907 fixed-price list offered lot 352: "1881 Brilliant Proof. Very rare in any condition, as but 680 are said to have been coined, and a very small part of these as Proofs. $25." Thomas L. Elder's March 1911 sale of the William H. Woodin collection included two Proofs: Lot 1024: "1881. Brilliant Proof. Very rare. Entire coinage only 680 pieces, making it of sufficient rarity to bring $50." Realized $12.50. Lot 1024a: "1881. Brilliant Proof. Rare." Realized $12.75. In the J.F. Bell Collection in December 1944, Stack's described lot 148: "1881 Brilliant Proof gem, only 680 minted. Rare." Realized $80. In the Numismatic Gallery sale of the "World's Greatest Collection" (F.C.C. Boyd Collection, January 1946) Abe Kosoff described lot 149: "1881 Brilliant Proof. Scarce." Realized $70.

VF-20	EF-40	AU-50	MS-60	MS-63	PF-60	PF-63
$2,500	$3,250	$5,500	$10,000	$20,000	$6,500	$13,500

1882

Scarce in all grades.

Circulation-Strike Mintage: 4,000
Proof Mintage: 67

Estimated Total Population (Mint State). 50 to 75. Many have appeared on the market over the years, including in "name" collections. Only a handful exist at MS-65 or finer.

Estimated Total Population (Circulated Grades). 150 to 200. Most are in higher grades such as About Uncirculated or Extremely Fine, less often Very Fine.

Die Data. *1882 four-digit date logotype:* The date is in fairly heavy numerals, the 18 are closest, the 88 are wider, and the 2 is slightly wider yet, low, and leans to the right. The 1 is heavy, with the lower right serif thinner than the lower left serif. Both 8's have top interior spaces the same size or perhaps slightly larger than the bottom interior spaces; both lean slightly right, with the second 8 leaning ever so slightly more than the first 8. The 2 has a very small knob attached by a thin line to the heavy curve to the right, the knob is distant from the diagonal, and the base of the digit is heavy. This logotype was used on all dies.

Circulation strikes: The date logotype is deep in the die. This die was used to make Proofs and also circulation strikes, the latter having extensive prooflike surfaces.

Characteristics of Striking and Die Notes. These are usually well struck. Circulation strikes are often highly prooflike, closely resembling Proofs. Most probably, certain early auction citations for "Proofs" were in fact prooflike circulation strikes (author's opinion; also Akers, 1975). However, frosty circulation strikes also exist.

Selected Auction Records

The sale of the Philpott and Zander Collections by B. Max Mehl in November 1945 included lot 1130: "1882 Brilliant Uncirculated. Very scarce." Realized $12.60. Mehl's Will W. Neil Collection, June 1947, included lot 2456: "1882 Brilliant Uncirculated with semi-Proof surface. Very scarce date in choice condition." Realized $17.25. In April 1959 the Robert H. Pelletreau Collection sold by Stack's included lot 338: "1882 Brilliant Uncirculated gem. Proof-like surface. Very scarce." Realized $61.

Proofs

Estimated Total Population (Proof). 25 to 33. Again, the low survival rate is unexplained.

Proof Die Data and Notes. At least two obverse dies were used to strike Proofs. One has the date logotype deep in the die (and was also used to make circulation strikes); a frosty patch occupies about half of the top loop in the first 8 (1882). Another has the logotype shallow in the die and in a slightly lower position.

Selected Proof Auction Records

Note: Certain of these "Proofs" may have been prooflike circulation strikes.

In June 1883 John W. Haseltine's sale of the William J. Jenks Collection had lot 484: "1882 Brilliant Proof." Realized $3. Thomas L. Elder's March 1911 sale of the William H. Woodin collection included lot 1025: "1882. Brilliant perfect Proof. Very scarce in this condition, and coinage of Proofs this year was very limited." Realized $5. In the J.F. Bell Collection in December 1944, Stack's described lot 149: "1882 Brilliant Proof gem." Realized $32. B. Max Mehl's sale of the Jerome Kern Collection, May 1950, included lot 71: "1882 Perfect brilliant Proof. Only forty proofs minted. Worth more than its record of $35." Realized $32. The sale of the Melish and Hester Collections by Abe Kosoff in April 1956 included lot 1303: "1882 Superb brilliant Proof." Realized $105.

VF-20	EF-40	AU-50	MS-60	MS-63	PF-60	PF-63
$500	$515	$550	$1,250	$2,750	$4,500	$9,500

1883

Circulation-Strike Mintage: 1,920

Proof Mintage: 82

Rare in all grades.
Especially rare in Mint State.

Estimated Total Population (Mint State). 12 to 20. Most are in lower Mint State levels for reasons that are unknown today. Gems are exceedingly rare or possibly even non-existent.

Estimated Total Population (Circulated Grades). 90 to 130. Extremely Fine is a typical grade.

Die Data. *1883 four-digit date logotype:* The 18 are very close, the 83 are nearly as close, and the 88 are close (but farther than the other spacings). The top and bottom interiors of the 8's are about the same size. The first 8 leans slightly right, and the second 8 leans more to the right. The 3 leans right and has a larger top knob, an irregular and smaller bottom knob, and has a base slightly lower than the other figures. This logotype was used on all dies.

Circulation strikes: The date logotype is slightly high (as determined by the position of the 1).

Characteristics of Striking and Die Notes. These are usually well struck.

David W. Akers (1975): "Many deceptive first strikes exist, and some such specimens have been offered as Proofs both at auction and privately. This has given rise to the erroneous conclusion that the 1883 is more common as a Proof than it is as a business strike. This is not at all true and genuine Proofs are really very rare."

Selected Auction Records

Note: Mint State specimens are conspicuously absent from early auction offerings (because some were cataloged as Proofs?).

Elmer S. Sears in his 1907 fixed-price list offered Lot 357: "1883 nearly Uncirculated, with bloom. $5." Thomas L. Elder in his sale of the Robert J. Bouvier Collection, September 1939, described lot 1479: "1883 Very Fine. Only 1,960 struck. Very Rare." Realized $5.50. The sale of the Philpott and Zander Collections by B. Max Mehl in November 1945 included lot 1131: "1883 Extremely Fine with bright luster. Very scarce." Realized $15. Mehl's Will W. Neil Collection, June 1947, included lot 2457: "1883 Uncirculated with semi-Proof surface. Scarce. Catalogs $40 in Proof." Realized $26. The catalog of the New Netherlands November 1956 sale of the Thomas L. Gaskill Collection described lot 343: "1883 Extremely Fine. Very sharp, fairly clean, reddish toning. Unusually rare, only 1,920 business strikes. First non-Proof we have handled." Realized $41.

Proofs

Estimated Total Population (Proof). 35 to 45. This is a low percentage survival rate. Proofs are in special demand due to the low related circulation strike mintage and the rarity of high-grade Mint State coins.

Proof Die Data and Notes. The date logotype is fairly well centered, with the 1 (1883) midway between the neck and the denticles (while on circulation strikes it is slightly high).

Selected Proof Auction Records

Note: Certain of these "Proofs" may have been prooflike circulation strikes (which are rarer than Proofs.

Elmer S. Sears in his 1907 fixed-price list offered lot 356: "1883 Brilliant Proof. Extremely rare. $8." Thomas L. Elder's March 1911 sale of the William H. Woodin collection included lot 1026: "1883. Brilliant Proof. Only a dozen or so struck in Proof condition. Rare. Realized $6.50. In the J.F. Bell Collection in December 1944, Stack's described lot 150: "1883 Brilliant Proof gem." Realized $35. In the Numismatic Gallery sale of the "World's Greatest Collection" (F.C.C. Boyd Collection, January 1946) Abe Kosoff described lot 151: "1883 Brilliant Proof." Realized $50. The sale of the Melish and Hester Collections by Abe Kosoff in April 1956 included lot 1304: "1883 A beautiful brilliant Proof." Realized $95.

VF-20	EF-40	AU-50	MS-60	MS-63	PF-60	PF-63
$1,000	$1,750	$3,250	$6,000	$12,500	$4,500	$9,500

1884

Circulation-Strike Mintage: 1,950

Proof Mintage: 73

Scarce in all grades. Rare in Mint State.

Estimated Total Population (Mint State). 20 to 30. Historically, Mint State coins have come on the market less often than Proofs. Some are prooflike, while others have a generous amount of mint luster, but most are at lower Mint State levels—quite like the 1883 quarter eagles in this regard. These are exceedingly rare at MS-65 or finer, and virtually unobtainable.

Estimated Total Population (Circulated Grades). 80 to 110. About Uncirculated is the typical grade encountered. As is the case with other low-mintage quarter eagles of this era, the 1884 was on the "want list" that New York City dealer Thomas L. Elder circulated to bank tellers in the early twentieth century, resulting in many pieces being saved from bank holdings and customers' deposits.

Die Data. *1884 four-digit date logotype:* The 18 are fairly close, the 88 are about the same distance, and the 84 are extremely close and on some impressions actually touching. The 1 is large; the lower left and right serifs are more normal than on certain earlier issues, but the serif on the left is tapered to a sharper point than the serif on the right. The interiors of both 8's are slightly smaller at the top; both 8's lean slightly right. The 4 has a heavy upright, leans slightly right, has no crosslet to the crossbar, and the right side of the crossbar extends about the same distance as the lower right serif. This logotype was used on all dies.

On circulation strikes the left edge of the serif of the 1 is to the right of a denticle space.

Characteristics of Striking and Die Notes. These are usually well struck.

Selected Auction Records

Elmer S. Sears in his 1907 fixed-price list offered lot 358: "1884 Uncirculated. Mint lustre. Rare. $6." The William B. Hale Collection sold by B. Max Mehl in November 1939 included lot 799: "1884 Uncirculated, with semi-Proof surface; highest portions show slight cabinet friction. Rare. Listed up to $20 in Proof." Realized $11.50. The catalog of the New Netherlands November 1956 sale of the Thomas L. Gaskill Collection described lot 344: "1884 Brilliant Uncirculated. Partial wire edge. Barely in the 'gem' class. On a par with the 1883; only 1,950 regularly coined. Much rarer than the Proof of this date, which is valued to $100." Realized $50. In April 1959 the Robert H. Pelletreau Collection sold by Stack's included lot 340: "1884 Uncirculated. Proof-like surface." Realized $87.50.

Proofs

Estimated Total Population (Proof). 35 to 45. This is a low percentage survival rate.

Proof Die Data and Notes. On Proofs the left edge of the serif of the 1 (1884) is to the left of a denticle space.

Selected Proof Auction Records

Note: Certain of these "Proofs" may have been prooflike circulation strikes.

Thomas L. Elder's March 1911 sale of the William H. Woodin collection included lot 1027: "1884. Brilliant Proof. Of rarity equal to the last, and coinage of both Proofs and regulars not over 2,000 pieces." Realized $7.25. B. Max Mehl in his February 1921 sale of the Dr. G.F.E. Wilharm Collection described lot 118: "1884 Brilliant Proof. Extremely rare in Proof condition. Cost $20 in 1914." Realized $8. Mehl in his February 1921 sale of the Dr. G.F.E. Wilharm Collection described lot 2773: "$2.50 1884 Proof. Very rare. Small coinage. High auction record." Realized $4.10. In the J.F. Bell Collection in December 1944, Stack's described lot 151: "1884 Brilliant Proof gem." Realized $25. The sale of the Melish and Hester Collections by Abe Kosoff in April 1956 included lot 1305: "1884 Brilliant Proof." Realized $95.

VF-20	EF-40	AU-50	MS-60	MS-63	MS-64	PF-60	PF-63
$500	$515	$800	$2,000	$3,500	$6,500	$4,500	$9,500

1885

Circulation-Strike Mintage: 800

Proof Mintage: 87

Very low mintage.
Rare in all grades.

Estimated Total Population (Mint State). 30 to 45. Exceedingly rare and virtually unobtainable at MS-65. Most Mint State coins are at lower levels, this being a general characteristic of quarter eagles of the era. Presumably, numismatists who wanted specimens for their cabinets obtained Proofs, and circulation strikes were ignored.

Estimated Total Population (Circulated Grades). 75 to 105. Most are in higher grade levels such as Extremely Fine and About Uncirculated.

Die Data. *1885 four-digit date logotype:* The figures are large and heavy, fairly widely spaced, with the tops of the 88 lower than the 1 and 5. The 18 are close, the 88 are wider, and the 85 are about as close as the 18 or even slightly closer. The 1 has a thick upright, and the lower left serif is rounded, with the lower right serif slightly smaller and somewhat squared off. The interiors of the 8's are somewhat irregular, seemingly with the top slightly smaller (but that may vary on uncertain impressions); both lean slightly right, the second 8 more so. The 5 leans slightly right and has a ball close to the upright but not touching. This logotype was used on all dies.

On circulation strikes the left edge of the serif of the 1 is about at the center of a denticle.

Characteristics of Striking and Die Notes. These are usually well struck. Circulation strikes are often prooflike.

Selected Auction Records

Thomas L. Elder's November 1920 sale of the R.V. Mathieu and E.B. Townsend Collections included lot 2186: "1885 Only 887 pcs struck. Very rare and seldom seen, should bring $25." The catalog of the New Netherlands November 1956 sale of the Thomas L. Gaskill Collection described lot 345: "1885 Marked 'former Proof,' this looks to us like a lightly handled first-strike. With almost full original sharpness. RRR as a non-Proof; just 800 struck. Like 1881, one of the rarest dates in the entire series, and completely unappreciated. Potentially worth to three figures! Speculators take note." Realized $82.50. In April 1959 the Robert H. Pelletreau Collection sold by Stack's included lot 341: "1885 Uncirculated. Proof-like surface. A most underrated coin. Only 887 coins struck." Realized $167.50.

Proofs

Estimated Total Population (Proof). 35 to 45, many of which are impaired. It can be theorized that Proofs that had been "spent" were picked out of circulation by sharp-eyed bank tellers and numismatists in the early twentieth century, when it was realized that 1885 is a rare *date.* The same can be said for most other Proofs of this era. There is a low percentage survival rate.

Proof Die Data and Notes. On Proofs the left edge of serif of the 1 (1885) is left of the center of a denticle. On the reverse of the Proof die there are some horizontal lines *within* the top of the vertical spaces in the shield.

Selected Proof Auction Records

Note: Certain of these "Proofs" may have been prooflike circulation strikes (which, if anything, are probably rarer than Proofs).

Elmer S. Sears in his 1907 fixed-price list offered lot 359: "1885 Brilliant Proof. Very rare. $8." Thomas L. Elder's March 1911 sale of the William H. Woodin collection included lot 1028: "1885. Brilliant Proof. As a coinage of only 887 pieces is recorded for this year, while the coinage of Proofs was not over 25, this may be considered a rarity." Realized $14.75. The Malcolm N. Jackson Collection sold in May 1913 by the U.S. Coin Co. included lot 171: "1885 Brilliant Proof, extremely rare." Realized $8.25. In June 1946 in his sale of the William Cutler Atwater Collection, B. Max Mehl offered lot 1989: "1885 Perfect sharp brilliant Proof. Only 887 specimens minted. Very rare. not often obtainable. Record $85. This gem is certainly destined to become at least a $100 coin in the very near future." Realized $57.50. The sale of the Melish and Hester Collections by Abe Kosoff in April 1956 included lot 1307: "1885 Brilliant Proof, choice and rare." Realized $125.

VF-20	EF-40	AU-50	MS-60	MS-63	PF-60	PF-63
$950	$2,000	$3,000	$5,500	$10,000	$5,000	$9,000

1886

Circulation-Strike Mintage: 4,000
Proof Mintage: 88

Rare in all grades.

During this era the Treasury Department had no need for gold $2.50 or $3 pieces for depositors or circulation, but circulation strikes were made, in addition to Proofs, "enough to prevent overvaluation from immediate rarity."[116] In other words, the mintage quantity given above was to shortstop dealers and collectors from making a profit on current coinage.

Estimated Total Population (Mint State). 40 to 60. About the best grade that can be found is MS-64, and these are exceedingly rare. Most are in the MS-60 to MS-62 range.

Estimated Total Population (Circulated Grades). 100 to 140. Most are in high grades such as Extremely Fine or About Uncirculated.

Die Data. *1886 four-digit date logotype:* The date is in heavy numerals. The 18 are close, and the 88 and 86 are significantly wider, each with about the same spacing. The 1 leans slightly right. The top and bottom interiors of the 8's are ever so slightly smaller than the bottom interior. The 6 has an imperfectly round ball close to but not touching the curve below it; the numeral leans slightly right (best determined by the orientation of the bottom interior); the base of the 6 is slightly low. This logotype was used on all dies.

Proofs and circulation strikes are from different dies, each having slightly different date logotype positions.

Characteristics of Striking and Die Notes. These are usually well struck. Circulation strikes are often highly prooflike.

Selected Auction Records

Elmer S. Sears in his 1907 fixed-price list offered lot 361: "1886 Uncirculated. Mint lustre. $5." The Malcolm N. Jackson Collection sold in May 1913 by the U.S. Coin Co. included lot 172: "1886 Extremely Fine, scarce." Realized $3. B. Max Mehl in his February 1921 sale of the Dr. G.F.E. Wilharm Collection described lot 120: "1886 Bright Uncirculated. Very scarce." Realized $4.10. The sale of the Philpott and Zander Collections by Mehl in November 1945 included lot 1134: "1886 Brilliant semi-proof. Light nick on obverse." Realized $5.50. In April 1959 the Robert H. Pelletreau Collection sold by Stack's included lot 342: "1886 Uncirculated gem. Scarce." Realized $47.50.

Proofs

Estimated Total Population (Proof). 35 to 45. This is a low percentage survival rate.

Proof Die Data and Notes. The large date numerals are centered below the neck. A new reverse die was used (for more details of all Proof dies, see the Dannreuther text).

Selected Proof Auction Records

Note: Certain of these "Proofs" may have been prooflike circulation strikes.

Thomas L. Elder's March 1911 sale of the William H. Woodin collection included lot 1029: "1886. Brilliant Proof. Very few struck in this condition. Rare." Realized $4.50. The William B. Hale Collection sold by B. Max Mehl in November 1939 included lot 800: "1886 Brilliant Proof; wire edge. Very rare in Proof. Worth far more than its listed price of $15." Realized $10.50. In the J.F. Bell Collection in December 1944, Stack's described lot 153: "1886 Brilliant Proof gem." Realized $25. In the Numismatic Gallery sale of the "World's Greatest Collection" (F.C.C. Boyd Collection, January 1946) Abe Kosoff described lot 154: "1886 Brilliant Proof." Realized $27.

VF-20	EF-40	AU-50	MS-60	MS-63	PF-60	PF-63
$500	$515	$550	$1,250	$3,500	$4,500	$9,500

1887

Circulation-Strike Mintage: 6,160
Proof Mintage: 122

Rare in all grades.

During this era the Treasury Department had no need for gold $2.50 or $3 pieces for depositors or circulation, but circulation strikes were made, in addition to Proofs, "enough to prevent overvaluation from immediate rarity."[117]

Estimated Total Population (Mint State). 40 to 60. Most are MS-60 to MS-62, an unexpected circumstance for a quarter eagle of this era. About the best grade that can be found is MS-64, and specimens truly in this category are seldom seen, although MS-63 coins are available (perhaps suggesting that any piece offered as MS-64 should be examined to see if it might better be called MS-63).

Estimated Total Population (Circulated Grades). 80 to 100. Extremely Fine and About Uncirculated are the typical grades. This issue is scarcer than the mintage suggests.

Die Data. *1887 four-digit date logotype:* The date is large, thus fitting snugly in the space allotted between the bust and denticles. The top of the 1 is high; the 18 are close, the 88 are wider, and the 87 are about as close as the 18. The 8's have top interiors that are slightly smaller than the bottom interiors, and both lean very slightly to the right. This logotype was used on all dies.

Characteristics of Striking and Die Notes. These are generally sharp, except for some weakness at certain stars on the obverse. Circulation strikes are often prooflike.

Selected Auction Records

B. Max Mehl in his April 1937 sale of the George M. Agurs Collection included lot 120: "1887 Uncirculated, with Proof surface." Realized $6.30.

Proofs

Estimated Total Population (Proof). 50 to 65. This is a low percentage survival rate.

Proof Die Data and Notes. The large date numerals have the 1 tightly spaced. A slight notch is in the denticle below that digit.

Selected Proof Auction Records

Note: Certain of these "Proofs" may have been prooflike circulation strikes.

Thomas L. Elder's March 1911 sale of the William H. Woodin collection included lot 1030: "1887. Brilliant Proof. All Proofs in the 1880s are rare." Realized $4.80. The William B. Hale Collection sold by B. Max Mehl in November 1939 included lot 801: "1887 Yellow gold. Brilliant Proof. High wire edge, especially on reverse." Realized $10.25. The June 1941 William Forrester Dunham Collection sold by Mehl included lot 1986: "1887 Brilliant semi-Proof; almost equal to a brilliant Proof. Very scarce. Listed at $15 in Proof." Realized $5.60. In June 1946 in his sale of the William Cutler Atwater Collection, Mehl offered lot 1991: "1887 Only 2,996 minted in all. Not in the Bell Collection. Recent record $40. My theory of the value of these coins I believe is correct, as is evidenced by the constant advancement in the prices they bring at auction. In the Fall of 1944 a specimen of this date brought $16, but another specimen offered a few months ago brought $30 at auction. Almost 100% increase in less than two years." Realized $32.50. The sale of the Melish and Hester Collections by Abe Kosoff in April 1956 included lot 1309: "1887 Brilliant Proof." Realized $70.

VF-20	EF-40	AU-50	MS-60	MS-63	PF-60	PF-63
$500	$515	$525	$800	$1,500	$4,500	$9,500

1888

Circulation-Strike Mintage: 16,001

Proof Mintage: 97

Scarce in all grades.

Estimated Total Population (Mint State). 225 to 300. MS-62 to MS-64 ranges are typical, with a *true* MS-65 being exceedingly rare.

Estimated Total Population (Circulated Grades). 300 to 450. Most are in About Uncirculated preservation, and often very attractive. Extremely Fine coins are not as available, and lower-grade pieces are few and far between.

Die Data. *1888 four-digit date logotype:* The date logotype is slightly smaller than that used in 1887, and thus more pleasing in proportion. The 18 are close, and both pairs of 8's are wider and about the same distance apart. The top interiors of each of the three 8's are about the same size or perhaps ever so slightly smaller than the bottom interiors. The second 8 leans perceptibly to the right. This logotype was used on all dies.

On at least one circulation strike die the logotype was deeply punched.

Characteristics of Striking and Die Notes. These are usually well struck. On circulation strikes, surfaces range from lustrous (usually) to prooflike (the latter usually lack mirror surface within the shield stripes on the reverse).

Selected Auction Records

The Malcolm N. Jackson Collection sold by the U.S. Coin Co. in May 1913 included lot 174: "1888 Uncirculated." Realized $2.75. In February 1921 B. Max Mehl's sale of the Dr. G.F.E. Wilharm Collection described lot 122: "1888 Uncirculated. Scarce." Realized $3.75. Lot 121 in Mehl's December 1928 sale of the Titus, Johnson, and Reamer Collections included Lot 121: "1888 Uncirculated." Realized $4. In the Numismatic Gallery's August 1942 ANA sale lot 276 was described: "1888. Uncirculated." Realized $7. M.H. Bolender's 194th Sale, September 1958, described this: Lot 383: "1888 brilliant Unc., some Proof surface. Small coinage." Realized $23.50.

Proofs

Estimated Total Population (Proof). 40 to 50. This is a low percentage survival rate.

Proof Die Data and Notes. The medium date numerals are centered below the neck. The tops of two 8's protrude from the denticles below the date, from a stray impression from the four-digit logotype. This die was only used on Proofs.

Selected Proof Auction Records

Note: Certain of these "Proofs" may have been prooflike circulation strikes. Citations for full gold Proof sets (containing six coins including the $2.50) have been omitted.[118]

Elmer S. Sears in his 1907 fixed-price list offered lot 364: "1888 Brilliant Proof. $6." Thomas L. Elder's March 1911 sale of the William H. Woodin collection included lot 1031: "1888. Brilliant Proof. Rare." Realized $5.25. The June 1941 William Forrester Dunham Collection sold by B. Max Mehl included lot 1987: "1888 Yellow gold. Perfect brilliant Proof. Rare. Listed at $15 and certainly worth it." Realized $14.25. In the J.F. Bell Collection in December 1944 Stack's described lot 155: "1888 Brilliant Proof gem." Realized $27.50. In the Numismatic Gallery sale of the "World's Greatest Collection" (F.C.C. Boyd Collection, January 1946) Abe Kosoff described lot 156: "1888 Brilliant Proof." Realized $30. The sale of the Melish and Hester Collections by Abe Kosoff in April 1956 included lot 1311: "1888 Superb brilliant Proof." Realized $80.

VF-20	EF-40	AU-50	MS-60	MS-63	PF-60	PF-63
$500	$515	$520	$550	$900	$4,500	$8,500

1889

Circulation-Strike Mintage: 17,600
Proof Mintage: 48

Scarce in all grades.

Estimated Total Population (Mint State). 175 to 250. MS-62 to MS-64 coins come on the market with some regularity. *True* MS-65 coins are great rarities. This continues the trend of the decade; collectors who wanted an example of the date ordered Proofs, and circulation strikes were ignored.

Estimated Total Population (Circulated Grades). 200 to 300. Most are in such grades as About Uncirculated and Extremely Fine.

Die Data. *1889 four-digit date logotype:* The numerals are widely spaced, the 18 are wide but closer than any of the others, the 88 are wider, and the 89 are widest. The 1 is large and with the lower part heavy. The top interiors of both 8's are ever so slightly smaller than the bottom interiors; both lean slightly right. The 9 has a small ball close to but not touching the curve above; the figure leans slightly right (best determined by the orientation of the upper interior). This logotype was used on all dies.

On Proofs the 1 (1889) is centered between the neck and the denticles. On at least one circulation strike die the 1 is low and closer to the denticles.

Characteristics of Striking and Die Notes. Usually well struck. Circulation strikes usually have frosty surfaces.

Selected Auction Records

Elmer S. Sears in his 1907 fixed-price list offered lot 367: "1889 Uncirculated. Mint lustre. $3.50." The Malcolm N. Jackson Collection sold in May 1913 by the U.S. Coin Co. included lot 175: "1889 Uncirculated." Realized $2.75. The June 1955 New Netherlands sale of the Dr. Clarence W. Peake Collection included 484: "1889. Uncirculated. Not entirely sharp, but brilliant. But 17,600 made for circulation." Realized $12. Lot 217 in the February 1957 Stack's sale of the J.W. Schmandt Collection had this description: "1889 Uncirculated. Last year of issue." Realized $70.

Proofs

Although the facts are not known, it probably was the case that by 1889 the Mint was tired of striking Proofs on speculation, keeping them in drawers (awaiting buyers), and then melting or spending unsold pieces. The production quantity of 48 pieces for 1889 may have represented the *true demand* for Proof gold coins of this era. If so, it might be logical to assume that the Proof mintage of the year before, 97 (or 92) pieces, may have yielded sales only in the range of perhaps 48 to 50 coins. Further, perhaps there was a demand for slightly more than 48 pieces, and the Mint realized that, after all, it was a good idea to strike more and then see how many would be sold (for in the next year, 1890, the coinage quantity rebounded). Facts are few and ideas are many.

Estimated Total Population (Proof). 18 to 25. This is a low percentage survival rate despite the lower mintage.

Proof Die Data and Notes. The date logotype is centered, and the 1 (1889) is about equidistant from neck and denticles.

Selected Proof Auction Records

Note: The following is a small selection from Proof citations over the years. Certain of these "Proofs" may have been prooflike circulation strikes.

Elmer S. Sears in his 1907 fixed-price list offered lot 366: "1889 Brilliant Proof. $6." Thomas L. Elder's March 1911 sale of the William H. Woodin collection included lot 1032: "1889. Brilliant Proof. Rare." Realized $5.40. B. Max Mehl in his

February 1921 sale of the Dr. G.F.E. Wilharm Collection described lot 123: "1889 Yellow gold, brilliant Proof. Rare in Proof condition." Realized $4.15. In the Numismatic Gallery sale of the "World's Greatest Collection" (F.C.C. Boyd Collection, January 1946) Abe Kosoff described lot 157: "1889 Brilliant Proof." Realized $35. The sale of the Melish and Hester Collections by Abe Kosoff in April 1956 included lot 1312: "1889 Superb brilliant Proof." Realized $85.

VF-20	EF-40	AU-50	MS-60	MS-63	PF-60	PF-63
$500	$515	$520	$550	$950	$4,500	$8,500

1890

Circulation-Strike Mintage: 8,720
Proof Mintage: 93

Scarce in all grades.

This is the first year of the era in which gold dollars were not struck, that denomination having been discontinued in 1889. Henceforth, quarter eagles would be saved in larger numbers by the general public and would take the place of gold dollars for gift and souvenir purposes.

Estimated Total Population (Mint State). 140 to 200. Nearly all are in grades below MS-65, with MS-62 and MS-63 being about par when a nice specimen is offered.

Estimated Total Population (Circulated Grades). 150 to 225. Most are in high grades such as About Uncirculated.

Die Data. *1890 four-digit date logotype:* The figures are fairly widely spaced, the 18 and 90 are closest, and the 89 are slightly wider apart. The 1 is large and with the base low. The upper interior of the 8 is slightly smaller than the bottom interior; the figure leans slightly right. The 9 has a ball close to and typically touching the curve above it; the figure leans slightly right (best determined by the orientation of the top interior). The 0 leans sharply right (as best seen by the interior orientation). This logotype was used on all dies.

On one circulation strike (Bass II) the date is deeply punched and centered. At the upper right of the field area within the shield there is a raised *die scratch* that looks like an after-the-fact scratch, except that it is characteristic of all specimens seen.

The date logotype on Proofs is slightly lower than on circulation strikes, but the difference is only noticeable upon close examination.

Characteristics of Striking and Die Notes. These are usually well struck. Circulation strikes range from frosty to prooflike.

Selected Auction Records

Elmer S. Sears in his 1907 fixed-price list offered lot 369: "1890 Uncirculated. Mint lustre. $4.50." The Malcolm N. Jackson Collection sold in May 1913 by the U.S. Coin Co. included lot 176: "1890 Uncirculated, Proof surface." Realized $2.75. The William B. Hale Collection sold by B. Max Mehl in November 1939 included lot 804: "1890 Bright

Uncirculated." Realized $6.30. In October 1958 Stack's sale of the S.E. Goldsmith Collection included lot 1626: "1890 Brilliant Uncirculated. Scarce." Realized $30.

Proofs

Estimated Total Population (Proof). 35 to 45. This is a low percentage survival rate.

Proof Die Data and Notes. The date logotype on Proofs is slightly lower than on circulation strikes, but the difference is only noticeable upon close examination.

Selected Proof Auction Records

Note: Proof listings are very extensive, representing a much smaller number of different coins coming on the market multiple times. Cited here are representative listings.

Elmer S. Sears in his 1907 fixed-price list offered lot 368: "1890 Brilliant Proof. Scarce. $7." B. Max Mehl in his February 1921 sale of the Dr. G.F.E. Wilharm Collection described lot 124: "1890 Perfect brilliant Proof. Rare." Realized $4.75. In the Numismatic Gallery sale of the "World's Greatest Collection" (F.C.C. Boyd Collection, January 1946) Abe Kosoff described lot 158: "1890 Brilliant Proof." Realized $32.50. In June 1946 in his sale of the William Cutler Atwater Collection, Mehl offered lot 1994: "1890 Perfect brilliant Proof. Wire edge. Recent record $32.50. More than a 50% increase in value less than two years." Realized $33.50. The sale of the Melish and Hester Collections by Abe Kosoff in April 1956 included lot 1313: "1890 Brilliant Proof." Realized $70.

VF-20	EF-40	AU-50	MS-60	MS-63	PF-60	PF-63
$500	$515	$520	$650	$1,500	$4,500	$8,500

1891

Circulation-Strike Mintage: 10,960
Proof Mintage: 80

Scarce in all grades.

Estimated Total Population (Mint State). 130 to 200. Most specimens range from MS-60 to MS-63. At the MS-65 level the 1891 is especially hard to find.

Estimated Total Population (Circulated Grades). 200 to 300. These figures may be conservative; David W. Akers (1975) stated that in his experience the 1891 is even rarer than the lower-mintage 1892.

Die Data. *1891 four-digit date logotype:* The digits are very widely spaced. The 18 are closest, but still with generous spacing, while the 89 are very wide and the 91 are slightly wider yet. The lower right serif of the 1 is smaller than the lower left serif. The top interior space of the 8 is slightly smaller than the bottom interior space. The 9 has a small, imperfectly formed ball separated from the curve above; the top interior leans slightly right. The final 1 leans slightly right. This logotype was used on all dies.

On Proofs the 1 (1891) is close to the denticles; on circulation strikes it is higher.

On Breen-6310, the Doubled Die reverse has the elements of the die doubled on the right side of the coin; circulation strikes only.

Characteristics of Striking and Die Notes. These are usually well struck. Surfaces of circulation strikes range from frosty to prooflike, often the latter.

Selected Auction Records

Elmer S. Sears in his 1907 fixed-price list offered lot 371: "1891 Uncirculated. Mint lustre. $3." The Malcolm N. Jackson Collection sold in May 1913 by the U.S. Coin Co. included lot 177: "1891 Uncirculated, Proof surface." Realized $2.75. The William B. Hale Collection sold by B. Max Mehl in November 1939 included lot 805: "1891 Uncirculated." Realized $7. The sale of the Philpott and Zander Collections by Mehl in November 1945 included lot 1139: "1891 Brilliant semi-Proof, almost equal to a Proof." Realized $15.50. The catalog of the New Netherlands November 1956 sale of the Thomas L. Gaskill Collection described lot 351: "1891 Just about Perfect. Clean and lustrous, much original surface remaining. Limited issue of 10,860." Realized $17.

Proofs

It is possible that not all were distributed.

Estimated Total Population (Proof). 30 to 40. This is a low percentage survival rate.

Proof Die Data and Notes. On Proofs the 1 (1891) is close to the denticles; on circulation strikes it is higher.

There is a small "notch" in the upright near the base of the first 1; the second 1 is without the "notch." The 91 digits are double punched, with only the vertical stem of the 1 appearing (without any traces of serifs). Vestigial traces of repunching are also seen under the 8. (Bass III coin). It is reported that on some, only the second 1 is repunched.

Selected Proof Auction Records

Note: Proof listings are very extensive, representing a much smaller number of different coins coming on the market multiple times. Cited here are representative listings.

B. Max Mehl in his February 1921 sale of the Dr. G.F.E. Wilharm Collection described lot 125: "1891 Yellow gold. Perfect brilliant Proof. Rare." Realized $4.50. In the J.F. Bell Collection in December 1944, Stack's described lot 158: "1891 Brilliant Proof gem." Realized $25. In the Numismatic Gallery sale of the "World's Greatest Collection" (F.C.C. Boyd Collection, January 1946) Abe Kosoff described lot 159: "1891 Brilliant Proof." Realized $25. The sale of the Melish and Hester Collections by Abe Kosoff in April 1956 included lot 1314: "1891 Brilliant Proof, gem." Realized $85.

VF-20	EF-40	AU-50	MS-60	MS-63	PF-60	PF-63
$500	$515	$520	$550	$1,450	$4,500	$8,000

1892

Circulation-Strike Mintage: 2,440

Proof Mintage: 105

Rare in all grades.

Estimated Total Population (Mint State). 80 to 120. Most are in lower Mint State levels. *True* MS-65 specimens are exceedingly rare.

Estimated Total Population (Circulated Grades). 100 to 150. Most are About Uncirculated, followed by Extremely Fine. Lower-grade coins are few and far between.

Die Data. *1892 four-digit date logotype:* The numerals are widely spaced. The 18 are closest, and the 89 and 92 are significantly wider and each about the same distance. The top and bottom interiors of the 8 are about the same size; the figure leans slightly left, an unusual leaning direction. The 9 leans slightly right (best determined by the orientation of the interior); the ball is very close to the upper curve and touches on some impressions. The 2 has a ball separated from the diagonal; the upper right and base of the digit are thick. This logotype was used on all dies.

On Proofs the date is slightly higher than on circulation strikes, with the 2 (1892) closer to the neck than to the denticles. On circulation strikes the 2 is centered between the neck and denticles.

Characteristics of Striking and Die Notes. These are usually well struck. The surfaces of circulation strikes range from frosty to highly prooflike (including within the shield stripes on the reverse).

Selected Auction Records

The William B. Hale Collection sold by B. Max Mehl in November 1939 included lot 806: "1892 Brilliant Uncirculated. Rare date. Listed at $12.50 in Very Fine condition." Realized $12.75. The sale of the Philpott and Zander Collections by Mehl in November 1945 included lot 1140: "1892 Brilliant Uncirculated. Rare date. Catalogs $20 in Uncirculated." Realized $18.50. The catalog of the New Netherlands November 1956 sale of the Thomas L. Gaskill Collection described lot 352: "1892 A splendid, extra brilliant 'gem.' The finest non-Proof of this rare date that we have seen. Very rare, only 2,440 (and 105 Proofs) made; much rarer in this preservation than in Proof. The latter were saved. Indeed, they were made to be saved. The survival of Mint State examples is largely a matter of chance, and survival of one like this, absolutely free of handling marks, is almost unheard of. Easily a $50 coin; should be worth a great deal more." Realized $41. In April 1959 the Robert H. Pelletreau Collection sold by Stack's included lot 348: "1892 Brilliant Uncirculated, some Proof surface. A very scarce coin. Only 2545 coins struck." Realized $78.

Proofs

In the March 1900 issue of *The Numismatist*, less than a decade after the coin's striking, Augustus G. Heaton commented that $2.50 coins dated 1892 were scarce and that $20 coins of the same year were rare.

Estimated Total Population (Proof). 45 to 55. This is a low percentage survival rate. Most specimens are in lower Proof ranges.

Selected Proof Auction Records

Note: Proof listings are very extensive, representing a much smaller number of different coins coming on the market multiple times. Cited here are representative listings.

The Malcolm N. Jackson Collection sold in May 1913 by the U.S. Coin Co. included lot 178: "1892 Brilliant Proof." Realized $4. In the J.F. Bell Collection in December 1944, Stack's described lot 159: "1892 Brilliant Proof gem. Scarce." Realized $37.50. In the Numismatic Gallery sale of the "World's Greatest Collection" (F.C.C. Boyd Collection, January 1946) Abe Kosoff described lot 160: "1892 Brilliant Proof." Realized $50. In June 1946 in his sale of the William Cutler Atwater Collection, B. Max Mehl offered lot 1996: "1892 Perfect brilliant Proof. Quite rare. Small coinage, only 2545 minted. In the Fall of 1944 a specimen of this coin in Proof condition brought $37.50, but a similar specimen sold at auction recently for $50." Realized $42.

VF-20	EF-40	AU-50	MS-60	MS-63	PF-60	PF-63
$500	$515	$520	$900	$2,500	$4,500	$8,000

1893

Circulation-Strike Mintage: 30,000
Proof Mintage: 106

Common.

Estimated Total Population (Mint State). 600 to 900. MS-64 and MS-65 coins are encountered more often than for any other quarter eagle date up to this point.This is the first date since 1878 in which MS-65 coins exist to the extent of over 20 examples, although in relation to the demand for them, an MS-65 1893 is certainly a rare prize.

Estimated Total Population (Circulated Grades). 500 to 800. Most are in higher levels such as Extremely Fine and, in particular, About Uncirculated.

Die Data. *1893 four-digit date logotype:* The numerals are spaced fairly wide. The 18 are close, the 89 are widest, and the 93 are in between. The top interior of the 8 is smaller than the bottom interior; the 8 leans very slightly right. The ball of the 9 is close to the curve above and touches on some impressions; the digit leans slightly right. The 3 has a heavy right side, and the upper ball is slightly flattened at the end and quite close to the center projection of the numeral; the lower ball is significantly larger and farther away from the center projection; the 3 leans slightly right and the base is slightly low. This logotype was used on all dies.

On Proofs the 1 (1893) is closer to the denticles than to the neck. On circulation strikes the 1 is higher.

Breen's *Encyclopedia* notes this for Proofs (Breen-6314, "Repunched Date"): "Partly double-punched date. Lower knobs of 93 just left of 93." However, the Childs Collection coin (Bowers and Merena, August 1999), lot 625, showed repunching on *all four* digits, including the base of the original numeral 1, upward to the left from the existing 1 in the date, and the remains of an 8 within the lower loop of the 8. The remnants of the 1 and the details within the lower loop of the 8 must have faded from the die as the mintage of this date progressed, with later examples simply showing doubling at the 9 and 3.

Characteristics of Striking and Die Notes. These are usually well struck. Circulation strikes range from frosty (usually the case) to somewhat prooflike.

Selected Auction Records

The Malcolm N. Jackson Collection sold in May 1913 by the U.S. Coin Co. included lot 179: "1893 Uncirculated." Realized $2.75. The William B. Hale Collection sold by B. Max Mehl in November 1939 included lot 807: "1893 Uncirculated; frost mint surface." Realized $5.25. In October 1951 the Numismatic Gallery sale of the B.A. Talmadge Collection included 1153: "1893 Uncirculated, choice." Realized $11. In June 1955 the New Netherlands sale of the Dr. Clarence W. Peake Collection included 486: "1893. Uncirculated. Considerable mint frost. Uncommon." Realized $14.

Proofs

Estimated Total Population (Proof). 45 to 55. This is a low percentage survival rate.

Proof Die Data and Notes. A specimen in the Bowers and Merena Rarities Sale, January 2003, displayed the date logotype low and to the left, with the lower left of the 1 accommodated by a slight indentation in the denticles. The lower left of the 9 and 3 are repunched, and traces of repunching are visible within the 8.

Selected Proof Auction Records

Note: Proof listings are very extensive, representing a much smaller number of different coins coming on the market multiple times. Cited here are representative listings.

In the J.F. Bell Collection in December 1944 Stack's described lot 160: "1893 Brilliant Proof gem." Realized $17.50. The sale of the Philpott and Zander Collections by B. Max Mehl in November 1945 included lot 1141: "1893 Brilliant Proof, as all are." Realized $17.50. In the Numismatic Gallery sale of the "World's Greatest Collection" (F.C.C. Boyd Collection, January 1946 Abe Kosoff described lot 161: "1893 Brilliant Proof." Realized $25 Mehl's Will W. Neil Collection, June 1947, included lot 2467: "1893 Perfect brilliant Proof, wire edge. Record $25." Realized $26.

VF-20	EF-40	AU-50	MS-60	MS-63	PF-60	PF-63
$500	$515	$520	$550	$1,250	$4,500	$7,500

1894

Circulation-Strike Mintage: 4,000

Proof Mintage: 122

Scarce in all grades.

Estimated Total Population (Mint State). 150 to 225. Although many choice, attractive examples exist, at the *true* MS-65 level the 1894 is a rarity.

Estimated Total Population (Circulated Grades). 150 to 250. Extremely Fine and About Uncirculated are the typical grades.

Die Data. *1894 four-digit date logotype:* the 18 have medium separation, the 89 are wider, and the 94 are close. The top interior of the 8 is slightly smaller than the bottom interior; the figure leans slightly right. The ball of the 9 is close to and touches the upper curve on many if not most impressions; the figure leans slightly right. The upright of the 4 is heavy, and there is no crosslet on the crossbar; the figure leans very slightly right. This logotype was used on all dies.

The logotype is deeply punched into the die. It is about centered at the left, but a tight fit. On Proofs the 1 (1894) is close to the denticles; on circulation strikes the 1 is higher.

Characteristics of Striking and Die Notes. These are usually well struck. Surfaces range from frosty to semi-prooflike.

Selected Auction Records

Elmer S. Sears in his 1907 fixed-price list offered lot 377: "1894 Uncirculated. Mint lustre. $4." Sale No. 359 held by J.C. Morgenthau & Co. in January 1936 included lot 117: "1894 Uncirculated." Realized $10. Lot 22 in Wayte Raymond's January 1939 mail bid sale included this: Lot 22: "1894 Uncirculated." Realized $6.75. The William B. Hale Collection sold by B. Max Mehl in November 1939 included lot 808: "1894 Brilliant Uncirculated; almost equal to a Proof. Very scarce." Realized $6.

Proofs

Estimated Total Population (Proof). 60 to 75. This is a low percentage survival rate.

Proof Die Data and Notes. A small, raised bump (or *wart*, as Breen calls it) is seen on Miss Liberty's chin. This is a noted diagnostic for authentic Proofs of this date.

Selected Proof Auction Records

Note: Proof listings are very extensive, representing a much smaller number of different coins coming on the market multiple times. Cited here are representative listings.

The Malcolm N. Jackson Collection sold in May 1913 by the U.S. Coin Co. included lot 180: "1894 Brilliant Proof." Realized $3.75. B. Max Mehl in his February 1921 sale of the Dr. G.F.E. Wilharm Collection described lot 129: "1894 Brilliant Proof. Rare." Realized $5. In the J.F. Bell Collection in December 1944, Stack's described lot 161: "1894 Brilliant Proof gem." Realized $23. In the Numismatic Gallery sale of the "World's Greatest Collection" (F.C.C. Boyd Collection, January 1946) Abe Kosoff described lot 162: "1894 Brilliant Proof." Realized $25. The sale of the Melish and Hester Collections by Abe Kosoff in April 1956 included lot 1318: "1894 Superb brilliant Proof." Realized $70.

VF-20	EF-40	AU-50	MS-60	MS-63	PF-60	PF-63
$500	$515	$520	$750	$1,450	$4,500	$7,500

1895

Scarce in all grades.

Circulation-Strike Mintage: 6,000

Proof Mintage: 119

Estimated Total Population (Mint State). 160 to 220. Mint State Liberty Head quarter eagles are readily available. However, MS-65 specimens are rarities.

Estimated Total Population (Circulated Grades). 175 to 300. *Extremely Fine* and About Uncirculated are the typical grades.

Die Data. *1895 four-digit date logotype:* The numbers are fairly widely spaced, the 18 are closest, the 89 are wider, and the 95 are widest. The top and bottom interiors of the 8 are about the same size; the figure leans almost imperceptibly right. The 9 has a ball close to the upper curve and touching on many if not most impressions; the figure leans slightly right. The 5 is of the upright style and leans slightly right, with an irregularly formed ball very close to and on some impressions touching the upright above it. This logotype was used on all dies.

There are minor date logotype position variations.

Characteristics of Striking and Die Notes. These are usually well struck. Surfaces range from frosty (usually) to prooflike.

Selected Auction Records

The William B. Hale Collection sold by B. Max Mehl in November 1939 included lot 809: "1895 Sharp Uncirculated, bright luster." Realized $5.50. In October 1951 the sale of the B.A. Talmadge Collection by Numismatic Gallery included lot 1155: "1895 Uncirculated, choice." Realized $12.50. The catalog of the New Netherlands November 1956 sale of the Thomas L. Gaskill Collection described lot 355: "1895 Brilliant Uncirculated. Just short of perfection, like the '93 above. Rare, only 6,000 coined. Should be a $25 item!" Realized $23.

Proofs

Estimated Total Population (Proof). 55 to 70. This is a low percentage survival rate.

Proof Die Data and Notes. The medium date numerals are centered below the neck. The knob on the 8 touches the curve above it. The ball of the 5 is spaced from the element above it. The numerals are widely spaced.

Selected Proof Auction Records

Note: Proof listings are very extensive, representing a much smaller number of different coins coming on the market multiple times. Cited here are representative listings.

The Malcolm N. Jackson Collection sold in May 1913 by the U.S. Coin Co. included lot 181: "1895 Brilliant Proof." Realized $3.50. In the J.F. Bell Collection in December

1944, Stack's described lot 162: "1895 Brilliant Proof gem." Realized $22. In the Numismatic Gallery sale of the "World's Greatest Collection" (F.C.C. Boyd Collection, January 1946), Abe Kosoff described lot 163: "1895 Brilliant Proof." Realized $30.

VF-20	EF-40	AU-50	MS-60	MS-63	PF-60	PF-63
$500	$515	$520	$575	$1,100	$4,500	$7,500

1896

Circulation-Strike Mintage: 19,070

Proof Mintage: 132

Slightly scarce.

Estimated Total Population (Mint State). 450 to 700. Most collections have had an example in Mint State. MS-65 specimens are scarce, but many dozens exist.

Estimated Total Population (Circulated Grades). 300 to 500. These are seemingly scarcer than Mint State examples. Extremely Fine and About Uncirculated are the typical grades.

Die Data. *1896 four-digit date logotype:* The date is widely spaced. The 18 are closest, the 89 are very wide, and the 96 are in between. All figures lean slightly right. The top interior of the 8 is about the same size or perhaps slightly smaller than the bottom interior. The 9 has a ball close to the upper curve and touching on many if not most impressions. The 6 is from a different punch (not an inverted 9) and has a ball distinctly far from the curve. This logotype was used on all dies.

At least two different date logotype positions are known on circulation strikes.

Characteristics of Striking and Die Notes. Usually well struck. Surfaces range from lustrous (mostly) to prooflike.

Selected Auction Records

Elmer S. Sears in his 1907 fixed-price list offered lot 381: "1896 Uncirculated. Mint lustre. $3." The William B. Hale Collection sold by B. Max Mehl in November 1939 included lot 810: "1896 Uncirculated." Realized $5.50. The catalog of the New Netherlands November 1956 sale of the Thomas L. Gaskill Collection described the following coin: "Free from blemishes, except for a very faint 'pinpoint' scratch on Liberty's neck. Only 'crank' cataloguers (we are proud of the term) could find anything wrong with this beauty!" Realized $16.

Proofs

Estimated Total Population (Proof). 60 to 75. This is a low percentage survival rate. Typical grades are PF-60 to PF-63. Finer specimens are in the minority.

Proof Die Data and Notes. The medium date numerals are centered below the neck. The numerals are widely spaced.

Selected Proof Auction Records

The Malcolm N. Jackson Collection sold in May 1913 by the U.S. Coin Co. included lot 182: "1896 Brilliant Proof." Realized $3. In the J.F. Bell Collection in December 1944, Stack's described lot 163: "1896 Brilliant Proof gem." Realized $19. B. Max Mehl's Will W. Neil Collection, June 1947, included lot 2470: "1896 Perfect brilliant Proof. From my sale of the Colwell Collection in 1923. Record $26." Realized $30. The sale of the Melish and Hester Collections by Abe Kosoff in April 1956 included lot 1320: "1896 Superb brilliant Proof." Realized $65.

VF-20	EF-40	AU-50	MS-60	MS-63	PF-60	PF-63
$500	$515	$520	$550	$800	$4,500	$7,500

1897

Plentiful.

Circulation-Strike Mintage: 29,768

Proof Mintage: 136

Estimated Total Population (Mint State). 700 to 1,100. Probably 50 to 100 exist at MS-65 or finer, certainly a scarce issue in comparison to those of the next decade. Most pieces are in lower ranges from MS-60 to MS-63.

Estimated Total Population (Circulated Grades). 1,000 to 1,400. Most are Extremely Fine or, in particular, About Uncirculated.

Die Data. *1897 four-digit date logotype:* The 18 have medium separation, the 89 are widest, and the 97 are slightly closer than the 18. The top and bottom interiors of the 8 are about the same size. The 9 has a ball close to and touching the curve above on most impressions; the numeral leans slightly right. This logotype was used on all dies.

Characteristics of Striking and Die Notes. These are usually well struck. Surfaces are usually frosty and lustrous, although a few are partially prooflike.

Selected Auction Records

Elmer S. Sears in his 1907 fixed-price list offered lot 383: "1897 Uncirculated. Mint lustre. $3." Wayte Raymond in his fixed-price list of March 1911 offered this: "1897 Uncirculated, brilliant Proof surface. $3." In April 1949 *Kelly's Coins and Chatter* included this: "1897 Uncirculated. $12.50." The Numismatic Gallery sale in October 1951 of the B.A. Talmadge Collection included two: Lot 1157: "1897 Uncirculated." Realized $16. Lot 1158: "Another 1897. Extremely Fine." Realized $13. The price differential between Mint State and Extremely Fine was still narrow, but would change dramatically in the next decade.

PROOFS

Estimated Total Population (Proof). 55 to 70. This is a low percentage survival rate. Typical grades are PF-60 to PF-63. Finer specimens are in the minority.

Proof Die Data and Notes. The die has two tiny dots at the center of the ear (cf. Breen-6318).

Selected Proof Auction Records

The Malcolm N. Jackson Collection sold in May 1913 by the U.S. Coin Co. included lot 183: "1897 Brilliant Proof." Realized $3. B. Max Mehl in his February 1921 sale of the Dr. G.F.E. Wilharm Collection described lot 132: "1897 Brilliant Proof, yellow gold, partly wire edge. Very scarce." Realized $4. In the J.F. Bell Collection in December 1944, Stack's described lot 164: "1897 Brilliant Proof gem." Realized $20. The sale of the Melish and Hester Collections by Abe Kosoff in April 1956 included lot 1321: "1897 Brilliant Proof. What a beautiful series these make!" Realized $65.

VF-20	EF-40	AU-50	MS-60	MS-63	PF-60	PF-63
$500	$515	$520	$550	$700	$4,500	$7,500

1898

Circulation-Strike Mintage: 24,000
Proof Mintage: 165

Slightly scarce.

Estimated Total Population (Mint State). 600 to 900. Probably 50 to 100 exist at MS-65 or finer, making this a scarce issue in terms of the demand for such specimens.

Estimated Total Population (Circulated Grades). 600 to 900. Extremely Fine and About Uncirculated are the typical grades.

Die Data. *1898 four-digit date logotype:* The date is in bold figures, the 18 have medium separation, the 89 are wider, and the 98 are wider yet. The first 8 leans slightly right; the top interior space is slightly smaller than the bottom interior space. The ball of the 9 is slightly irregular in shape, and a hair's breadth from the curve above (it may touch on some deep impressions). The second 8 is vertical or ever so slightly left in its orientation. This logotype was used on all dies.

As of the 1980s, the original four-digit date 1898 logotype punch was still on hand in the Engraving Department at the Philadelphia Mint.

Characteristics of Striking and Die Notes. These are usually well struck. Surfaces are usually lustrous, but a few are partially prooflike (certain citations given on the following page reflect that some are so prooflike that in the past they have been bought as Proofs).

Selected Auction Records

In March 1938 B. Max Mehl included lot 234 in his sale of the Samuel H. McVitty Collection: "1898 Uncirculated, frosty mint surface." Realized $4.20. The October 1951 Numismatic Gallery sale of the B.A. Talmadge Collection included lot 1159: "1898 Uncirculated, choice." Realized $10.50.

Proofs

Estimated Total Population (Proof). 75 to 95. This is a low percentage survival rate. The typical grades are PF-60 to PF-63. Finer specimens are in the minority.

Proof Die Data and Notes. The medium date numerals are slightly to the right of center with the final digit close to the truncation point of the neck. The numerals are widely spaced.

Selected Proof Auction Records

The Malcolm N. Jackson Collection sold in May 1913 by the U.S. Coin Co. included lot 184: "1898 Brilliant Proof." Realized $3. The June 1941 William Forrester Dunham Collection sold by B. Max Mehl included lot 1997: "1898 Perfect brilliant Proof." Realized $6.25. In the Numismatic Gallery sale of the "World's Greatest Collection" (F.C.C. Boyd Collection, January 1946) Abe Kosoff described lot 166: "1898 Brilliant Proof." Realized $27.50. Mehl's sale of the Jerome Kern Collection, May 1950, included lot 88: "1898 Perfect brilliant Proof. Record $27.50." Realized $25.

VF-20	EF-40	AU-50	MS-60	MS-63	PF-60	PF-63
$500	$515	$520	$550	$675	$4,500	$7,500

1899

Circulation-Strike Mintage: 27,200
Proof Mintage: 150

Plentiful.

Estimated Total Population (Mint State). 600 to 800. These are seemingly scarcer than generally realized, based upon historical data. However, enough pieces exist that the specialist will have no trouble locating one, especially at levels in and around MS-60 to MS-62. Gems are quite rare. Probably only 50 to 90 exist MS-65 or finer.

Estimated Total Population (Circulated Grades). 650 to 950. Over the years many important collections have lacked Mint State examples and have included pieces at the About Uncirculated (in particular) level.

Die Data. *1899 four-digit date logotype:* The 18 have medium separation, the 89 are wider, and the 99 are in between. The 8 has top and bottom interior spaces that are about the same size. The 9's are from the same digit punch, with a ball very close to the curve and touching it on many if not most impressions. This logotype was used on all dies.

Characteristics of Striking and Die Notes. These are usually well struck. Surfaces are usually lustrous, rarely prooflike.

Selected Auction Records

The sale of the Philpott and Zander Collections by B. Max Mehl in November 1945 included lot 1147: "1899 Uncirculated, frosty mint surface." Realized $11.25. In April 1949 *Kelly's Coins and Chatter* offered this: "1899 Uncirculated. $12.50." The catalog of the New Netherlands November 1956 sale of the Thomas L. Gaskill Collection described lot 358: "1899 Brilliant Uncirculated. Exceptionally clean, approaches superb. Moderate coinage. . . . Records to $20." Realized $16.

Proofs

Estimated Total Population (Proof). 90 to 100. This is a low percentage survival rate, but better than many others of the decade. Typical grades are PF-60 to PF-63. Finer specimens are in the minority.

Proof Die Data and Notes. Two pairs of dies were used.

Selected Proof Auction Records

The Malcolm N. Jackson Collection sold in May 1913 by the U.S. Coin Co. included lot 185: "1899 Brilliant Proof." Realized $3. The June 1941 William Forrester Dunham Collection sold by B. Max Mehl included lot 1998: "1899 Perfect brilliant Proof." Realized $6.25. The sale of the Melish and Hester Collections by Abe Kosoff in April 1956 included lot 1323: "1899 Brilliant Proof." Realized $70.

VF-20	EF-40	AU-50	MS-60	MS-63	PF-60	PF-63
$500	$515	$520	$550	$675	$4,500	$7,500

1900

Circulation-Strike Mintage: 67,000
Proof Mintage: 205

Very plentiful.

Estimated Total Population (Mint State). 1,500 to 2,000. Probably about 10% of these are gems (MS-65).

Estimated Total Population (Circulated Grades). 1,500 to 2,000. Extremely Fine and About Uncirculated are the typical grades.

Die Data. *1900 four-digit date logotype:* The 19 are wider than any other digit pair, the 90 are closest, and the 00 are in between; The 19 are high, and the bases of 00 are slightly lower. The 1 is large. The 9 has a ball close to and touching the upper curve on many if not most impressions. Both 0s lean slightly right. This logotype was used on all dies.

On circulation strikes as well as Proofs the date logotype is impressed deeply into the die.

Characteristics of Striking and Die Notes. These are usually well struck and with frosty surfaces.

Selected Auction Records

Elmer S. Sears in his 1907 fixed-price list offered lot 389: "1900 Uncirculated. Mint lustre. $3." The June 1941 William Forrester Dunham Collection sold by B. Max Mehl included lot 1999: "1900 Light yellow gold. Perfect brilliant Proof; unusually bold impression." Realized $9.50. Mehl's Will W. Neil Collection, June 1947, included lot 2474: "1900 Uncirculated, frosty mint surface. Catalogs $10." Realized $10.

Proofs

Estimated Total Population (Proof). 120 to 140. This is a higher than usual survival rate. Although most survivors grade from PF-60 to PF-63, higher level specimens come on the market with regularity.

Proof Die Data and Notes. *The* 19 (1900) is slightly repunched.

Selected Proof Auction Records

The Malcolm N. Jackson Collection sold in May 1913 by the U.S. Coin Co. included two: Lot 186: "1900 Brilliant Proof." Realized $2.75. Lot 186a: "1900 Brilliant Proof." Realized $2.75. It is seen that 13 years after this variety was minted, the market premium was very slight. In the J.F. Bell Collection in December 1944, Stack's described lot 167: "1900 Brilliant Proof gem." Realized $15. The sale of the Melish and Hester Collections by Abe Kosoff in April 1956 included lot 1324: "1900 Brilliant Proof." Realized $50.

VF-20	EF-40	AU-50	MS-60	MS-63	PF-60	PF-63
$500	$515	$520	$550	$625	$4,500	$7,500

1901

Circulation-Strike Mintage: 91,100
Proof Mintage: 223

Very plentiful.

Estimated Total Population (Mint State). 1,600 to 2,000. Probably about 10% of these are gems (MS-65).

Estimated Total Population (Circulated Grades). 2,000 to 2,500. Extremely Fine and About Uncirculated are the typical grades.

Die Data. *1901 four-digit date logotype:* The 19 have medium spacing, and the 90 and 01 are wider and each about the same distance. The bases of the 1's are lower than the bases of 90. The ball of 9 is very close to and usually touching the upper curve. This logotype was used on all dies.

One circulation strike die has signs of repunching at the bottom of the last digit; these are seen with some frequency.

Characteristics of Striking and Die Notes. These are usually well struck and with frosty surfaces.

Selected Auction Records

The William B. Hale Collection sold by B. Max Mehl in November 1939 included lot 815: "1901 Uncirculated." Realized $4.50. The June 1941 William Forrester Dunham Collection sold by Mehl included lot 2000: "1901 Perfect brilliant Proof; wire edge." Realized $6.50. The catalog of the New Netherlands November 1956 sale of the Thomas L. Gaskill Collection described lot 360: "1901 Brilliant Unc. just about a 'gem.' Traces of (easily) removable tarnish." Realized $16.

Proofs

Estimated Total Population (Proof). 135 to 155. This is one of the more available dates of the era. Typical grades are PF-60 to PF-63. Finer specimens are in the minority.

Proof Die Data and Notes. Raised die lines are within the vertical shield stripes.

Selected Proof Auction Records

The Malcolm N. Jackson Collection sold in May 1913 by the U.S. Coin Co. included lot 187: "1901 Brilliant Proof." Realized $2.75. In the J.F. Bell Collection in December 1944, Stack's described lot 168: "1901 Brilliant Proof gem." Realized $18.50. The sale of the Melish and Hester Collections by Abe Kosoff in April 1956 included lot 1325: "1901 Brilliant Proof." Realized $50.

VF-20	EF-40	AU-50	MS-60	MS-63	PF-60	PF-63
$500	$515	$520	$550	$625	$4,500	$7,500

1902

Common.

Circulation-Strike Mintage: 133,540

Proof Mintage: 193

Estimated Total Population (Mint State). 2,500 to 3,500. Probably about 10% of these are gems (MS-65).

Estimated Total Population (Circulated Grades). 3,000 to 4,500. Extremely Fine and About Uncirculated are the typical grades.

Die Data. *1902 four-digit date logotype:* The 19 have medium separation, and the 90 and 02 are wider and each about the same distance apart. The ball of the 9 is close to the curve above and touches on many if not most impressions. The 0 slants slightly to the right (as evidenced by the orientation of the center). The 2 has a ball distant from the diagonal, the upper right of the figure is heavy, and the base goes thinner as it tapers to the point at the lower right. This logotype was used on all dies.

One variety of circulation strike has the bottom of the date in higher relief, from the four-digit logotype being put more deeply into the working die on the bottom than on the top.

Characteristics of Striking and Die Notes. These are usually well struck and with frosty surfaces.

Selected Auction Records

B. Max Mehl in his February 1921 sale of the Dr. G.F.E. Wilharm Collection described lot 137: "1902 Uncirculated." Realized $3.50. The June 1941 William Forrester Dunham Collection sold by Mehl included lot 2001: "1902 Perfect brilliant Proof; raised borders." Realized $6.25. Uncirculated. Unusually choice. Marked $17." Realized $16.

In the early 1980s hundreds of choice and gem Mint State quarter eagles of each date 1902 to 1907 from the Virgil Brand estate were sold to the MTB Banking Corporation, which sold them to various clients.[119]

Proofs

Estimated Total Population (Proof). 110 to 130. Another readily available date (in the context of Proof coinage). Typical grades are PF-60 to PF-63. Finer specimens are in the minority.

Proof Die Data and Notes. Beginning in 1902, and lasting to the end of the design type in 1907, Proof Liberty quarter eagles have a reflective finish, unlike the Proof quarter eagles of 1901 and earlier which tend to have frosted motifs set against mirror fields.

Selected Proof Auction Records

The Malcolm N. Jackson Collection sold in May 1913 by the U.S. Coin Co. included lot 188: "1902 Brilliant Proof." Realized $2.75. This was part of a complete 1902 gold Proof set offered individually. In the J.F. Bell Collection in December 1944, Stack's described lot 169: "1902 Brilliant Proof gem." Realized $17.50. In the Numismatic Gallery sale of the "World's Greatest Collection" (F.C.C. Boyd Collection, January 1946) Abe Kosoff described lot 170: "1902 Brilliant Proof." Realized $20.

VF-20	EF-40	AU-50	MS-60	MS-63	PF-60	PF-63
$500	$515	$520	$550	$625	$4,500	$7,500

1903

Circulation-Strike Mintage: 201,060

Proof Mintage: 197

Common.

Estimated Total Population (Mint State). 6,000 to 9,000. Probably about 10% to 15% of these are gems (MS-65). A visitor's guide to the Philadelphia Mint, published in 1903, commented that quarter eagles were the most popular denomination that was purchased by tourists and others who toured the Mint, seemingly being more popular than the inexpensive Indian cent. The guide stated that no visit would be complete without the purchase of such a coin. At the time, upwards of 50,000 visitors per year thronged through the Mint, although it seems likely that only a minority carried away quarter eagles.

Estimated Total Population (Circulated Grades). 5,000 to 8,000. Extremely Fine and About Uncirculated are the typical grades.

Die Data. *1903 four-digit date logotype:* The 19 are more widely separated than in recent years, the 90 are wider yet, and the 03 are wide, but closer than any of the other pairs. The bases of 1 and 3 are lower than 90. The ball of the 9 is small and very close to the upper curve. The 0 leans slightly right. The 3 has a heavy right side, a small top ball, and a larger bottom ball, both balls being about the same distance from the center projection. This logotype was used on all dies.

The date logotype positions vary.

Characteristics of Striking and Die Notes. These are usually well struck and with frosty surfaces. The 1903 is often seen with copper toning spots (not unusual for quarter eagles of this era, but seemingly mentioned quite often in connection with 1903).

Selected Auction Records

B. Max Mehl in his February 1921 sale of the Dr. G.F.E. Wilharm Collection described lot 138: "1903 Uncirculated." Realized $3.50. The sale of the Philpott and Zander Collections by Mehl in November 1945 included lot 1151: "1903 Uncirculated, frosty mint surface." Realized $8.50. The catalog of the New Netherlands November 1956 sale of the Thomas L. Gaskill Collection described lot 362: "1903 Brilliant Uncirculated. Like the '98 and 1901. These beautiful little coins will never be cheaper!" Realized $16.

Proofs

Estimated Total Population (Proof). 110 to 135. Typical grades are PF-60 to PF-63. Finer specimens are in the minority.

Proof Die Data and Notes. The date logotype is boldly entered into the die and low, almost touching a denticle to the left. There are two die pairs, the second with the date slightly higher.

Proofs were struck from dies in which the recesses (e.g., the portrait of Miss Liberty) were also lightly polished, more so than on the 1902. Thus, Proofs of this date do not have cameo or frosty central motifs. Many if not most specimens have copper toning spots due to an improper mix of the alloy, a situation seen on many circulation strikes as well.

Selected Proof Auction Records

The Malcolm N. Jackson Collection sold in May 1913 by the U.S. Coin Co. included lot 189: "1903 Brilliant Proof." Realized $2.75. In the J.F. Bell Collection in December 1944, Stack's described lot 170: "1903 Brilliant Proof gem." Realized $15. The sale of the Melish and Hester Collections by Abe Kosoff in April 1956 included lot 1327: "1903 Brilliant Proof." Realized $45.

VF-20	EF-40	AU-50	MS-60	MS-63	PF-60	PF-63
$500	$515	$520	$550	$625	$4,500	$7,500

1904

Circulation-Strike Mintage: 160,790
Proof Mintage: 170

Common.

Estimated Total Population (Mint State). 4,000 to 6,000. Probably about 10% of these are gems (MS-65).

Estimated Total Population (Circulated Grades). 4,000 to 5,500. Extremely Fine and About Uncirculated are the typical grades.

Die Data. *1904 four-digit date logotype:* The 19 have medium spacing, the 90 are slightly wider, and the 04 are very close and almost touching. The ball of the 9 is close to and usually touching the top curve. The 0 leans slightly right and its interior is long and elliptical. The 4 has a heavy upright, no crosslet, and the crossbar extends nearly as far right as the lower right serif; the figure leans slightly right and the base is slightly low. This logotype was used on all dies.

Multiple dies were used. One has the date logotype slightly low and punched into the die in medium depth.

Characteristics of Striking and Die Notes. These are usually well struck and with frosty surfaces. Often with copper toning or spots, but not as endemic as for 1903.

Selected Auction Records

The William B. Hale Collection sold by B. Max Mehl in November 1939 included two: Lot 818: "1904 Uncirculated, with brilliant luster. Far more rare than is generally known. One of the really scarce later dates." Realized $4.50. This is an unexplained comment about this date being rare, which it is not; nor was it considered rare by anyone else in the 1930s. Lot 818-A: "1904 The excessively rare variety with *plain edge.* Uncirculated, with full mint luster. I believe this is the first specimen I have seen or handled. It is certainly a distinct variety of this scarce date. And while I would not say that it is unique, but certainly of the greatest rarity." Realized $7.10. A mint error, and very rare as a mint error. Mehl's Will W. Neil Collection, June 1947, included lot 2478: "1904 Uncirculated, full mint luster. Catalogs $10." Realized $10.

Proofs

Estimated Total Population (Proof). 100 to 125. Breen (Proof coin *Encyclopedia*, 1977, 1989) notes that this date is "more often than not nicked and scratched and/or cleaned." If this means that most are impaired, this has no modern verification.

Proof Die Data and Notes. Proofs were struck from dies in which the recesses (*e.g.*, the portrait of Miss Liberty) were also lightly polished, but not as heavily polished as on 1903 Proofs.

Some Proofs (e.g., Auction '90, Superior, Lot 1270) have frosty motifs that under magnification show engraving lines and swirls.

Selected Proof Auction Records

The Malcolm N. Jackson Collection sold in May 1913 by the U.S. Coin Co. included lot 190: "1904 Brilliant Proof." Realized $2.75. In the J.F. Bell Collection in December 1944, Stack's described lot 171: "1904 Brilliant Proof gem." Realized $17.50. The catalog of the New Netherlands November 1956 sale of the Thomas L. Gaskill Collection described lot 363: "1904 Fully brilliant Proof. not quite of 'gem' quality; a pinpoint flan chip upon the obverse (at the 13th star) as made. Rare; 170 Proof impressions taken from the dies. Now valued to $55." Realized $62.50.

VF-20	EF-40	AU-50	MS-60	MS-63	PF-60	PF-63
$500	$515	$520	$550	$625	$4,500	$7,500

1905

Circulation-Strike Mintage: 217,800

Proof Mintage: 144

Common.

Estimated Total Population (Mint State). 5,000 to 7,000. Probably at least 10% of these are gems (MS-65).

Estimated Total Population (Circulated Grades). 5,500 to 8,000. Extremely Fine and About Uncirculated are the typical grades.

Die Data. *1905 four-digit date logotype:* The 19 have medium spacing, the 90 are widest, and the 05 are in between. The ball of the 9 is close to and usually touches the top curve. The 0 leans slightly right. The 5 is of the upright type, with a small ball distant from the vertical element above it. This logotype was used on all dies.

Characteristics of Striking and Die Notes. These are generally well struck and very frosty. Some have lightly struck denticles at the upper right of the reverse.

Selected Auction Records

B. Max Mehl in his February 1921 sale of the Dr. G.F.E. Wilharm Collection described lot 140: "1905 Uncirculated." Realized $3.50. The sale of the Philpott and Zander Collections by Mehl in November 1945 included lot 1153: "1905 Uncirculated, frosty mint surface." Realized $7.75. The sale of the Melish and Hester Collections by Abe Kosoff in April 1956 included lot 1329: "1905 Uncirculated, choice." Realized $16.

Proofs

Estimated Total Population (Proof). 95 to 120. The typical grades are PF-60 to PF-63. Finer specimens are in the minority.

Proof Die Data and Notes. Proofs were struck from dies in which the recesses (*e.g.*, the portrait of Miss Liberty) were also lightly polished. Thus, Proofs of this date do not have cameo or frosty central motifs. Proofs often have orange or coppery toning.

Selected Proof Auction Records

Elmer S. Sears in his 1907 fixed-price list offered lot 398: "1905 Brilliant Proof. $4." In the Numismatic Gallery sale of the "World's Greatest Collection" (F.C.C. Boyd Collection, January 1946) Abe Kosoff described lot 173: "1905 Brilliant Proof." Realized $20. B. Max Mehl's sale of the Jerome Kern Collection, May 1950, included lot 95: "1905 Perfect brilliant Proof. Struck in yellow gold. Catalogs and has a record of $20." Realized $21.

VF-20	EF-40	AU-50	MS-60	MS-63	PF-60	PF-63
$500	$515	$520	$550	$625	$4,500	$7,500

1906

Circulation-Strike Mintage: 166,330

Proof Mintage: 160

Common.

Estimated Total Population (Mint State). 4,500 to 6,000. Probably at least 10% of these are gems (MS-65).

Estimated Total Population (Circulated Grades). 5,000 to 8,000. Extremely Fine and About Uncirculated are the typical grades.

Die Data. *1906 four-digit date logotype:* The 19 and 90 have medium spacing, and the 06 are very slightly closer, the spacing being generous in any event and giving the logotype a balanced appearance. The ball of the 9 is close to and usually touching the curve above. The 0 slants right. The ball of the 6 is very close to and typically touching the curve below; the 6 slants right. This logotype was used on all dies.

Characteristics of Striking and Die Notes. These are usually well struck and very frosty.

Selected Auction Records

Elmer S. Sears in his 1907 fixed-price list offered lot 401: "1906 Uncirculated. Mint lustre. $3." The June 1941 William Forrester Dunham Collection sold by B. Max Mehl included lot 2005: "1906 Perfect brilliant Proof; yellow gold." Realized $6.25. The catalog of the New Netherlands November 1956 sale of the Thomas L. Gaskill Collection described lot 365: "1906 Brilliant Uncirculated. Full mint frost. Like all of these underrated so fine." Realized $15.

Proofs

Estimated Total Population (Proof). 100 to 120. Typical grades are PF-60 to PF-63. Finer specimens are in the minority.

Proof Die Data and Notes. On Proofs the date logotype is high.

The obverse has the portrait lightly polished in the die on some Proofs; others are fully frosty in the nineteenth-century style. The reverse has a frosty eagle and motifs set against mirrored Proof fields.

Selected Proof Auction Records

The Malcolm N. Jackson Collection sold in May 1913 by the U.S. Coin Co. included lot 192: "1906 Brilliant Proof." Realized $2.75. Proof. Very scarce in Proof." Realized $6.50. In the J.F. Bell Collection in December 1944, Stack's described lot 173: "1906 Brilliant Proof gem." Realized $17.50. B. Max Mehl's sale of the Jerome Kern Collection, May 1950, included lot 96: "1906 Perfect brilliant Proof. Yellow gold. Catalogs $20 and certainly worth it." Realized $21.

VF-20	EF-40	AU-50	MS-60	MS-63	PF-60	PF-63
$500	$515	$520	$550	$625	$4,500	$7,500

1907

Circulation-Strike Mintage: 336,294

Proof Mintage: 154

Most common Coronet quarter eagle.

Estimated Total Population (Mint State). 7,500 to 10,000. Probably at 10% to 15% of these are gems (MS-65). This is the most plentiful of all Liberty Head quarter eagles in Mint State, a fact derived from a combination of its being the highest mintage issue among later dates, the pieces not circulating extensively in their time, quarter eagles not being called in as part of the 1933 Gold Order, and their popularity with the public as souvenirs.

Estimated Total Population (Circulated Grades). 7,000 to 9,000. Extremely Fine and About Uncirculated are the typical grades.

Die Data. *1907 four-digit date logotype:* The numerals are nicely balanced. The 19 have medium spacing, the 90 are farthest apart, and the 07 are in between. The base of 1 is very heavy at the left and right serifs. The knob of the 9 is close to and typically touching the curve above; the figure leans slightly right. The 0 leans slightly right. The base of the 7 is slightly low. This logotype was used on all dies.

Several minor logotype variations exist among circulation strikes, including repunchings. One die has a small extension on the bottom of the 7. Another has the base of the 7 triple-punched. On another die the 1 touches a denticle. On another the date logotype is low and punched into the working die more deeply at the bottom of the date than at the top.

Characteristics of Striking and Die Notes. These are usually well struck and with frosty surfaces.

Selected Auction Records

The William B. Hale Collection sold by B. Max Mehl in November 1939 included lot 821: "1907 Uncirculated. Last year of the Liberty head type." Realized $5. The sale of the Melish and Hester Collections by Abe Kosoff in April 1956 included lot 1331: "1907 Last year of the brilliant Proofs." Realized $50. The catalog of the New Netherlands November 1956 sale of the Thomas L. Gaskill Collection described lot 366: "1907 Last year of the type. Brilliant Uncirculated. Should bring about $16.50." Realized $15.

Proofs

Estimated Total Population (Proof). 80 to 100. The typical grades are PF-60 to PF-63. Finer specimens are in the minority.

Proof Die Data and Notes. The medium date numerals are slightly to the right of center with the final digit close to the truncation point of the neck. The numerals are widely spaced.

Selected Proof Auction Records

The Malcolm N. Jackson Collection sold in May 1913 by the U.S. Coin Co. included lot 193: "1907 Brilliant Proof." Realized $2.75. In the J.F. Bell Collection in December 1944, Stack's described lot 174: "1907 Brilliant Proof gem." Realized $17.50. In June 1946 in his sale of the William Cutler Atwater Collection, B. Max Mehl offered lot 2011: "1907 Last year of the Liberty head type quarter eagle. Perfect brilliant Proof gem. Quite rare, and apparently a 'sleeper.' In 1944 a similar specimen brought $17.50 at auction, but in the meantime collectors who study not only the trend but also the rarity of these coins woke up, and when a specimen was offered in January of this year, it brought no less than $47.50, and the cataloger valued it at $82.50." Realized $40. Mehl said more in his February 1947 sale of the W. Geiss Collection, lot 1522: "1907 brilliant Proof. Quite rare. As stated in my catalog of the Atwater Sale, I consider this coin a 'sleeper.' Although a specimen brought only $17.50 in 1944, but in my sale of the Atwater Collection, last June, it brought $40 and I think it is worth much more." Realized $15.25.

VF-20	EF-40	AU-50	MS-60	MS-63	PF-60	PF-63
$500	$515	$520	$550	$625	$4,500	$7,500

12
Indian Head $2.50 Gold Coins (1908–1929)

Indian Head (1908–1929)

Designer: *Bela Lyon Pratt.* **Weight:** *4.18 grams.* **Composition:** *.900 gold, .100 copper.* **Diameter:** *18 mm.* **Edge:** *Reeded.* **Mints:** *Philadelphia, Denver.*

The Story of the Unusual 1908 Design

In 1905 noted American sculptor Augustus Saint-Gaudens was commissioned by President Theodore Roosevelt to redesign the American coinage from the bronze cent to the gold double eagle. Work was begun, and by mid-1907 designs were largely completed for the $10 and $20 denominations. Unfortunately, the artist had been stricken with cancer, and on August 3, 1907, he died, not living to see his $10 and $20 coins reach circulation.

The $2.50 and $5 gold denominations had not been redesigned by this time, although some sketches had been made. Dr. William Sturgis Bigelow, a friend of President Roosevelt, proposed a coinage of intaglio or recessed design for the quarter and half eagles and suggested that Boston sculptor Bela Lyon Pratt was the man to do the work. On behalf of Roosevelt, Bigelow engaged Pratt to prepare models in the early part of 1908. No public announcements were made, and collectors and the public were generally unaware of the progress being made. In fact, in August it was suggested in *The Numismatist* that the quarter eagle would copy the familiar $10 and $20 motifs created by the late Augustus Saint-Gaudens, which were released in autumn 1907:

> No quarter eagles bearing date of 1908 had been coined, and it is not believed that any of the old type will again be struck. Dies for new design quarter eagle and half eagle have been in preparation for several weeks. The character of the new designs cannot

> be definitely stated, as information from several different sources disagreed. One states the $2.50 and $5 will both be the same design as the Saint-Gaudens $10, and others state that they will be like $20, and a third asserts they will be a combination of both.

Perhaps in the offing were miniature versions of Saint-Gaudens's work.

NEW QUARTER EAGLE AND HALF EAGLE DESIGNS APPEAR

The facts were different and were disclosed to collectors in the November 1908 issue of *The Numismatist:*

> That which has been anticipated for months is now a fact that a decidedly new and novel departure in United States coinage appears in the new type $2.50 and $5 gold pieces which were just issued—the first was in November. The great novelty in the new coins is that the design is incuse, instead of being raised or embossed, as is the general coinage in the world.
>
> The planchets are not milled, the field from edge to edge being one flat surface with a design struck in, or sunk. The periphery (so-called edge) is reeded. At last we have the features of a real Indian on our coinage. The central design on the obverse presents in profile the strong features of the male Indian, with long extending and wide full feathered headdress. The design of the reverse is the much commented upon eagle that appears on the Saint-Gaudens $10 piece. The incuse design, even on the smaller planchets, emphasizes or magnifies the characteristics of this muchly feathered and greatly criticized bird. Those who appreciate an innovation certainly have it in the new coins. General comments on the issue will be welcomed from our contributors.

The December 1908 issue of *The Numismatist* began with an article by Howland Wood on the new $2.50 and $5 gold coins. Among other comments, he stated:

> The new gold half and quarter eagles are out. To most people these came unheralded and with very little warning. The public press has very little to say about them though they depart much more from the accepted standards than the Saint-Gaudens pieces did.
>
> The chief departure from the world's accepted standards of how money should be made is a treatment of the background or field. Heretofore the field of the coin has been the most depressed part, while the design has stood out in more or less greater relief. On these new coins the background has become the foreground and is now in the same plane with the highest part of the relief. The design is formed by countersinking into the field. The idea of depressing the design below the face of the coin originated with Dr. William S. Bigelow of Boston, who commissioned Mr. Bela Lyon Pratt, a noted Boston sculptor, to make the designs.

THE DESIGN

The obverse of the Pratt quarter eagle, known as the Indian Head type, features an incuse or recessed area in which there is a relief portrait of an Indian chief facing left, with the incuse word LIBERTY above, six incuse stars to the left and seven to the right, and the date below, also incuse.

The reverse shows a recessed area with an eagle (inspired by the Saint-Gaudens $10) in relief perched on a branch or log, with incused inscriptions including UNITED STATES OF AMERICA above, E PLURIBUS UNUM to the left, IN GOD WE TRUST to the right, and the denomination expressed as 2½ DOLLARS below.

The dates were part of the master die, and thus all working dies had the date numerals in the same position. Beginning with 1908 and continuing through the rest of the series, date position varieties no longer occur.

Curiously and illogically, when mintmarks were added to certain issues, commencing with the 1911-D, the D mintmark was raised on the coin and protruded above the plane or flat area of the field, becoming the only projecting relief area on the coin! Apparently, it was too much trouble to have the mintmark incuse. This is probably just as well, for one can imagine a proliferation of phony mintmarks made for collectors by punching D letters into the fields of 1911 Philadelphia Mint coins to create "1911-D" rarities!

As mintmarks were punched into each die by hand, positions can vary slightly.

Official Statement about the New Design

The *Annual Report of the Director of the Mint*, fiscal year 1908, included this:

> Early in the present year while the President was explaining to Dr. William Sturgis Bigelow the mechanical difficulties met with in the effort to bring to success the double eagle and the eagle of the Saint-Gaudens designs, especially that referring to the commercial desire that the coins should stack or pile to a uniform height, Doctor Bigelow became impressed with the idea that a high or strong relief of design on a coin could be obtained by depressing the design below the face or field of the coin, instead of raising it, as was being done in all coinage operations, thereby the field being flat and uniform in thickness would insure a stacking, and would permit of the pieces being piled to a uniform height.
>
> In all other coins the wear comes on the highest point of the relief. In these, the flat surface takes the wear and protects the relief, which is depressed below it, the shape of the depression following the outline of the relief. This system of countersinking a relief is one of it. It has been little used in modern times except in Japan, where it finds a restricted application chiefly in wood carving. It has never been applied to coins in modern times. The idea of so applying it was Doctor Bigelow's. Acting upon his own responsibility, he asked Mr. Bela Lyon Pratt, an artist of St. Botolph Studios, Boston, to make an experimental design to illustrate the principle. This model was submitted to the President, and the practicality of this new idea in coinage appealed so strongly to him it was decided that the experiment of making a coin on this principle should be made. The design of a real Indian Head, with war bonnet of feathers, was adopted for the obverse side, and the President selected the design of a real eagle, standing for the reverse side; and Mr. Pratt was commissioned to prepare models for the engraver of the United States Mint at Philadelphia for the striking of the coins. This coinage was commenced in November of the present year.

> That the artist in producing faithful representations of both the real Indian and the real eagle has reached a remarkable degree of success, persons familiar with those subjects must attest. The engraving work, executed by Mr. Charles E. Barber, engraver of the United States Mint at Philadelphia, is remarkably fine and sharp in detail, showing consummate skill and an artistic hand.

William Sturgis Bigelow and Bela Lyon Pratt

Born in Boston in 1850, William Sturgis Bigelow was the son and grandson of two of that city's most prominent physicians. Following family tradition, he studied medicine, graduating from Harvard Medical School in 1874, after which time he went to Europe for five years and studied under prominent professors and doctors in Germany and Austria.

After his return he established a private laboratory for bacteriology in Boston. This proved to unstimulating to Bigelow's active mind, so he joined the Massachusetts General Hospital as a surgeon. By 1882 he realized that his life interest lay in another direction, so he journeyed to Japan and spent seven years there studying philosophy, religion, and language, and amassing a glorious collection of art that later became the property of the Boston Museum of Fine Arts, thus giving the institution the world's most prominent holdings in that area.

Bigelow formed a friendship with Theodore Roosevelt and corresponded and visited on many occasions. The president often sought his advice on political and artistic matters. Bigelow's thoughts concerning the Russo-Japanese War were taken into consideration, and, for example, when Charles L. Freer in 1905 offered to give his sizable art collection to the United States government, plus $500,000 to construct a suitable building, Roosevelt suggested that Dr. Bigelow be sent to examine the art. So, it was perhaps natural that Bigelow's thoughts concerning coinage received Roosevelt's immediate and close attention and consideration.

It was reasonable that Bigelow would commission his friend and fellow Bostonian Bela Lyon Pratt to execute his novel coinage ideas.

Pratt, born in 1867, studied at the Yale School of Fine Arts. In 1887 he went to New York, where he studied under Augustus Saint-Gaudens at the Art Students' League. Saint-Gaudens was so impressed with Pratt that he signed Pratt as an assistant in his private studio. Following the suggestion of his mentor, Pratt went to Paris in 1890 to study under Falguière and Chapu. In the École des Beaux Arts he was foremost in his class, earning several awards. Returning to America in 1893, he sculpted two gigantic groupings for the World's Columbian Exposition. In the same year he became an instructor at the Boston Museum School of Fine Arts, in which capacity he remained until his death in 1917.

Works by Pratt include a medal commissioned by Harvard University alumni for President Charles William Eliot, the Yale bicentennial medal, a figure for the Sears Monument (Cambridge, Massachusetts), numerous large sculptures for the Library of Congress, and many other busts, sculptures, and medallions. Statues of nude young women were a particular interest, with one winning a silver medal at the Pan-American Exposition in Buffalo in 1901. At the Panama-Pacific International Exposition in San Francisco in 1915, Pratt's exhibit of 17 pieces of sculpture earned a gold medal. Work was accomplished at his Boston studio, with summers spent at his home in North Haven, Maine.

Mint Director Leach Reminisces

Frank A. Leach, a Californian who served as director of the Mint from September 1907 through November 1909 (one of the most dynamic periods of change in United State coinage design history), gave his memories of the 1908 coinage event in a book, *Recollections of a Newspaperman*, published in 1917:

> Originally it was the intention to give the $5 and $2.50 pieces the same design as that used on the double eagle or $20 piece, but before the final action to that end was taken President Roosevelt invited me to lunch with him at the White House. His purpose was to [have] me meet Dr. William Sturgis Bigelow of Boston, a lover of art and a friend of the President, who was showing great interest in the undertaking for improving the appearance of American coins, and who had a new design for the smaller gold coins. It was his idea that the commercial needs of the country required coins that would 'stack' evenly, and that the preservation of as much as possible of the flat plane of the piece was desirable. A coin, therefore, with the lines of the design, figures, and letters depressed or incused, instead of being raised or in relief, would meet the wishes of the bankers and business men, and at the same time introduce a novelty in coinage that was artistic as well as adaptable to the needs of business.
>
> The President adhered to the idea that the high relief afforded greater possibilities of artistic results, and referred to the beauties of the ancient gold coins. Unquestionably he was correct in this opinion, but I called his attention to the fact that he and the other promoters of the new coinage were trying to do more than the ancient Greek artists and coiners had found possible, and that the Greeks had only been able to produce a high relief on one side of their coins, while we were endeavoring to give a high relief on both sides. We had in a way succeeded, for by use of a medal press we had outdone the Greeks. But the uncompromising demands of trade would not tolerate even the one-sided coins of ancient Greece. The President expressed surprise at my statement, and at once sent a messenger to his room for a beautiful example of Grecian work in the shape of a gold coin of the days of Alexander the Great. Of course, he found one side quite flat, while the other side was in high relief.
>
> I enjoyed my luncheon. It was as simple and devoid of ceremony as a lunch would be in the home of any well-to-do family. Mrs. Roosevelt, a lady friend, and a federal judge, an old-time friend of the President were also at the table. It so happened that it was the anniversary day of April 1865, of the surrender of the judge as a Confederate army officer in the closing days of the Civil War. As might be imagined, it put the judge in a reminiscent mood. He was an excellent talker and interested us all. One of his remarks was that no one could tell what would happen in life. "The day I surrendered as a Confederate soldier I little expected to stretch my legs under a dining table in the White House, as guest of the President. Why, I remember I was so dejected on that occasion that an aged friend of mine said to me, 'You think you and this country are going to hell on a toboggan, but that is all wrong.' So I found out."
>
> It was after lunch and we had excused ourselves from the others that the question as to the new design for the half and quarter eagles took place. The discussion ended

by the president authorizing Dr. Bigelow and me to go ahead and produce some trial pieces after the suggestions of the doctor. Bela L. Pratt, an artist of high repute in Boston, was selected to make the models for the designs, which were to be a faithful copy of an Indian head and the eagle with shortened legs. The models and dies were not finished until sometime in September. When the trial pieces were produced I was pleased with their appearance, for the nationality was so plainly stamped on the coin that it needed no lettering to tell anybody in any part of the world that it had been issued by the U.S. of America. It pleased the President, and he at once gave the official approval necessary for the adoption of the design. Soon after, the new coins were minted and placed within the reach of the public.

Considerable criticism followed the appearance of the new design. The depressed or incused idea of portraying the figures, device, etc. was unfavorably received, while the faithfulness of the designs to the objects represented, as artistic work, was very generally commended. Confirming the truth of the old saying, "there is nothing new in the world," we found, in looking over some authorities on ancient coinage, that almost the very first attempt at making coins was by depressing or incusing the designs. This issue finished the work of changing the designs of the gold coins.

S.H. Chapman, Coin Design Critic

On December 7, 1908, S. Hudson Chapman, the well-known Philadelphia coin dealer, wrote to Theodore Roosevelt to express his displeasure at the new half eagle and quarter eagle—perhaps this being a part of the "considerable criticism" mentioned by Leach:

> It was the hope of everyone that when our new coinage appeared we would have one of great beauty and artistic merit. But the new $5 and $2.50 gold pieces just issued totally lack these qualities, and not only those of beauty, but actually miss the practicability to which every effective beauty in relief has been sacrificed.
>
> The idea of Dr. William S. Bigelow, of Boston, to sink the whole relief below the flat surface of the coin causes it to appear like a design merely incised in the blank, and precludes entirely the effect of miniature bas-relief.
>
> The head of the Indian is without artistic merit, and portrays an Indian who is emaciated, totally unlike the big, strong Indian chiefs I have seen in real life. The treatment of the head is crude and hard, with sharp, abrupt outlines, as if carved by a mere metal chaser; and on the reverse is a reproduction of the Saint Gaudens' eagle, which represents not our national bird (the white-headed eagle—commonly but erroneously called the bald headed eagle—which has no feathers on its feet), but resembles more closely the golden eagle, which is also indigenous to Europe.
>
> The placing of the design below the surface of the flan, with deeply incised outlines, gives the effect of having been engraved into the metal, and can, therefore, be closely imitated by any metal chaser with the graver, without dies or moulds. And I am certain that if this had been suggested to the Secret Service officials it never would have been issued by the Treasury Department, and the issuance ought to be immediately stopped and the coins recalled, for everyone will be in danger of the imitations.
>
> The sunken design, especially the deeply sunken portion of the neck of the Indian, will be a great receptacle for dirt and conveyor of disease, and the coin will be the most unhygienic ever issued.

> The principal claim put out for this coin, and which, according to the claim, would appear to be the most important any design can have, is that it will stack. But, alas! even this is not obtained by this means, for I have before me a stack of twenty pieces—$100 the stack used by cashiers, and it is the most tottering stack of modern coins, rocking to a great degree, and when the table is jarred about four times the upper coins slide off.
>
> They will fall when carried on a bank tray. It is well known that you cannot strike a lot of flat blanks and get them perfectly true. As a connoisseur remarked to me, 'Coins should be like a table, which we do not make with a flat bottom, but with feet to stand upon, and this result in coins can and always has been obtained by a flat rim.'
>
> And then the new coins, being thinner, as the metal is taken up by the full field, they do not make stacks equal in height to the old, and when mixed with the other issue cause the piles to be of unequal height, and the cashier cannot use the height of a stack as a test of count, but must sort this issue out.
>
> The criticism from the bankers is that the first model of the $10 and $20 pieces did not stack firmly should not cause the Mint officials to throw all other considerations to the winds, for the firmness in stacking a coin, as stated above, could be obtained by the use of a sufficiently wide and high rim.
>
> These coins will be a disgrace to our country as a monument of our present ideas of art as applied to coinage.
>
> As compared with those of recent issues of European countries, not to mention the beautiful works of the ancient Greek coin engravers, it is an utterly miserable, hideous production, and let us hope that its issue will not be continued and that it will be recalled and remelted.
>
> I would suggest as a means of obtaining a competent committee to pass upon designs for coinage, that in the future all designs for coinage be submitted to the American numismatic societies. For instance: the American Numismatic Society of New York, and the American Numismatic Association. The matter would then be weighed by men who have devoted their lives or leisure to the study of the art of coinage from the earliest period to the present time, and thus, having a complete purview of the subject, they would be able to judge of the merits of the coins offered, and if such course were adopted we would be saved the mortification of seeing generally the worst designs accepted and the taste of our people degraded, instead of elevated, by the coinage passing through their hands.

The Chapman letter was forwarded to Bigelow, who provided the president with a defense:

> Some of Mr. Chapman's criticisms are well founded, others less so. He says that sinking the relief below the surface makes it look like an incised design and precludes the effect of a bas-relief. This is hardly correct, as Mr. Chapman can readily see for himself in photographs of the Egyptian sculptures. The bas-relief effect is accentuated and not diminished by the shadow of the sharp outline.
>
> He says that the head of the Indian is "without artistic merit and portrays an Indian who's emaciated, totally unlike the big, strong Indian chiefs as seen in real life." The answer to this is that the head was taken from a recent photograph of an

> Indian whose health was excellent. Perhaps Mr. Chapman has in mind the fatter but less characteristic type of Indian sometimes seen on the reservations.
>
> The matter of the eagle was thoroughly threshed out at the time of the issue of the Saint-Gaudens coin. That design proved to be an absolute correct representation of the white-headed American eagle, except that the head was, perhaps intentionally, a little small and the leg feathers a little heavy. Both these criticisms Mr. Pratt has met in the present design. Mr. Chapman says that the American eagle has no feathers on its feet. This statement is true, but not exactly new.
>
> "The placing of the coin below the surface of the flan with deeply incised outlines gives the effect of having been engraved into the metal and can, therefore, be closely imitated by any metal chaser by the graver without dies or moulds." This criticism can hardly be taken seriously. If a forger were going to engrave anything he would not waste his labor on a single coin. It would be as easy to engrave a die as coin of any issue.
>
> "The sunken design will be a great receptacle for dirt and conveyor of disease, and the coin will be the most unhygienic ever issued." This remains to be seen. The question of hygiene has more relation to silver coins than gold, as they find their way into dirtier pockets. A dirty gold coin would be an anomaly. I have never happened to see one.
>
> What Mr. Chapman says in regard to the fact of the coins not stacking is perfectly true. I noticed it as soon as they were issued and called Mr. Leach's attention to it.[1] It proved to be due to an accidental warping of the steel die in hardening. Mr. Leach tells me that it can and will be avoided in the future.
>
> "Coins should be like a table, which we do not make with a flat bottom, but with feet to stand upon, and this result in coins can and always has been obtained by a flat rim." This is true, and it is exactly the principle on which the present issue is made. The flat rim extends from the edge of the coin to the edge of the design.
>
> The thickness of the coins after striking depends on the amount of metal displaced by the die. A stronger relief would give greater thickness. I agree with Mr. Chapman that it would be well if all the coins in circulation were of the same thickness.

Apparently Bigelow prepared texts for two letters for Roosevelt to send to Chapman, one perhaps being sharper than the other, for a letter from Roosevelt to Bigelow, December 12, 1908, relates:

> I have your letter of the 12th, with enclosures. If you will return Mr. Chapman's letter to me so that I may have his address I shall send him the letter that you designed to have sent him; and oh, how I would have liked to send him the other letter, which you did not design to have sent him!

From the viewpoint of today, certain of Chapman's criticisms seem to have been well founded. Circulated examples of the Pratt design do indeed accumulate dirt in the crevices. The design, not popular with the public, might have been better had those familiar with coinage been consulted. But then, as now, numismatists' opinions, if solicited (which they rarely are), are most always ignored. Theodore Roosevelt himself looked upon ancient coins and determined that American coinage designs were pale by comparison. Any Mint official, member of Congress, or anyone else involved with coinage production has but to study past coins—as indeed S. Hudson Chapman did as his life's work—to determine which coins have artistic merit and which do not.

While art is often in the eye of the beholder, numismatists in general have felt that many of America's most beautiful coins exist only in pattern form—the 1879 Schoolgirl dollar and the 1882 Shield Earring dollar, both by George T. Morgan, being but two of many examples.

Mintage Notes, Circulation Strikes

Two mints were employed to strike a total of 15 varieties in the Indian Head quarter eagle series. Examples were produced at the Philadelphia Mint from 1908 through 1915 and again from 1925 through 1929. The Denver Mint, which had opened for business in 1906 but which had not coined the $2.50 denomination, struck Indian Head quarter eagles in 1911, 1914, and 1925.

In each instance except one, mintages amounted to hundreds of thousands. The solitary exception was the 1911-D, which was coined to the extent of 55,680 and came to be known by numismatists as the key issue.

The total of circulation strikes minted was 7,250,261, of which probably 10% to 20% survive today in the aggregate.

Proofs

Sand Blast Proofs were made at the Philadelphia Mint 1908 and 1911 to 1915, and Satin Finish Proofs were produced in 1909 and 1910, partly in response to complaints by numismatists, especially members of the New York Numismatic Club. The production of both types of Proofs was somewhat erratic, and the appearances of the finishes can differ slightly.

This account from *The Numismatist*, October–November 1910, reflects the limited use of the quarter eagle at that time and its proposed discontinuation:

> **$2½ Gold Pieces To Be Issued in Proof Only.**
>
> We are advised by the Director of the Mint that it is the present policy of the department to suspend the coinage of $2.50 gold pieces for circulation, but they will continue to be struck to fill orders for Proof coins.
>
> Few practical purposes have been served in recent years by this coin, which since 1889 has been our smallest gold piece for circulation. In the Western States where gold is used to the exclusion of paper money, the $2.50 is considered undesirable on account of its size.
>
> Considerable quantities of $2.50 gold pieces have been struck each year for several decades, the coinage being near the close of the year and to meet the demand for gift purposes during the holiday season. The department has found that within a few weeks following the holiday season the greater portion of the $2.50 pieces that had been issued during preceding weeks found their way back to the various sub-treasuries, and for which there are no demand until the next season. It is probable that the quarter eagle will continue to be issued in Proof until an Act of Congress designates otherwise. Proofs only have been struck dated 1910.

This caused a rush to buy Proofs to fill in date sets, as it seemed that no circulation strikes would be available. Accordingly, 682 Proofs were made—far and away a record for any Proof quarter eagle of any date and type. *Renaissance of American Coinage 1905–1908*, by Roger W. Burdette, gives much information on Proofs, including internal Mint correspondence including continuing awareness of complaints from collectors. Sand Blast Proofs were made individually by blasting sand particles on the surfaces of circulation strikes and varied in appearance and quality, depending upon the operator of the sand blasting equipment.

CIRCULATION STRIKES RESUMED

Circulation strikes were issued later in the year 1910 and continued intermittently through 1929.

Beginning about 1920, quarter eagles were no longer seen in circulation and were not generally available for face value at banks, even on a limited basis. Bankers who had supplies often charged a small premium for them. The use of Indian Head quarter eagles had never been widespread, and about the only areas in which they were seen with regularity in commerce—such as in restaurants, saloons, and the mercantile trade—was in the Rocky Mountain districts.

More information about the scarcity in circulation of quarter eagles during the 1920s is given in the general introduction of this book.

In 1929 quarter eagle coinage was suspended. Most were melted during the 1930s, although enough remained in public hands that it does not strain credulity to suggest that at least 20% remain of the various issues of the 1920s, most particularly of the last issue, 1929.

COLLECTING COMMENTS

The type set collector can easily find examples of the Indian Head quarter eagle in grades from Very Fine to About Uncirculated for the early range of dates 1908 to 1915 and Mint State for the later dates 1925 to 1929. Uncirculated pieces of all 1908 to 1915 varieties are scarce, and some such as 1914 are especially so. Gem Mint State coins are elusive for the years from 1908 through 1915 but are somewhat available, although hardly common, for the later 1925 to 1929 range. The scarcity of higher grade pieces is explained not by the mintages, which in most instances were generous, but by the format of the coin. The field of a typical coin, exposed to wear and other effects, acquired marks quickly, and even storage in a mint bag was apt to reduce the grade of a piece below the Uncirculated level.

A survey of old-time collections coming on the market since the 1970s will reveal that such grades as MS-60 to MS-63 were the rule for the grades of the quarter eagles therein. This is because in the old days "Uncirculated" was simply "Uncirculated," and once an acceptable piece was acquired, that was it. There was no poring through stocks of coins to upgrade an MS-63 to an MS-64, then to an MS-65. In fact, numbers were widely not used for gold coins until the 1970s, and interpretations were apt to be wildly different even after that time.

Certification data are useful in a *relative sense*, this being especially true of MS-64 or finer coins and of Proofs. In lower Mint State levels as well as for circulated grades, except for the rare 1911-D, the data do not reflect the quantities extant, for there has been little commercial advantage to certifying such pieces.

Proofs are all rare and exist in small proportions to their original mintages, which were low to begin with. Particularly attractive are the special Roman Finish Proofs of 1910 and 1911. In the early years of my coin business there was very little demand for Proof Indian Head quarter eagles, as the Sand Blast issues in particular were viewed as being unattractive in comparison to lustrous Mint State coins. In the late twentieth century that changed, and today Proofs are highly sought.

Grading Standards

1911-D. Graded MS-64.

MS-60 to 70 (Mint State). ***Obverse:*** On MS–60 to 62 coins there is abrasion in the field, this representing the highest part of the coin. Abrasion is also evident on the headdress. Marks and, occasionally, a microscopic pin scratch may be seen. At MS-63, there may be some abrasion and some tiny marks. Luster is irregular. At MS-64, abrasion is less. Luster is rich. At MS-65 and above, luster is deep and frosty. No marks at all are visible without magnification at MS-66 and higher. ***Reverse:*** At MS–60 to 62, there is abrasion in the field, this representing the highest part of the coin. Abrasion is also evident on the eagle's wing. Otherwise, the same comments apply as for the obverse.

1911-D. Graded AU-55.

AU-50, 53, 55, 58 (About Uncirculated). ***Obverse:*** Friction on the cheek is very noticeable at AU-50, progressively less at higher levels to AU-58. The headdress shows light wear, most evident on the ribbon above the forehead and on the garland. Luster is minimal at AU-50 and scattered and incomplete at AU-58. Nicks and contact marks are to be expected. ***Reverse:*** Friction on the wing and neck is very noticeable at AU-50, increasingly less at higher levels to AU-58. Otherwise, the same comments apply as for the obverse.

EF-40, 45 (Extremely Fine). ***Obverse:*** Light wear characterizes the portrait and headdress. Luster is gone. Marks and tiny scratches are to be expected, but not distracting. ***Reverse:*** Light wear is most evident on the eagle's head and wing, although other areas are lightly worn as well. Luster is gone. Marks and tiny scratches are to be expected, but not distracting.

1911-D. Graded EF-40.

VF-20, 30 (Very Fine). ***Obverse:*** Many details of the ribbon above the forehead and the garland are worn away. Many feather vanes are blended together. The field is dull and has contact marks. ***Reverse:*** The neck and the upper part of the wing show extensive wear, other areas less so. The field is dull and has contact marks.

1912. Graded VF-20.

Indian Head quarter eagles are seldom collected in grades lower than VF-20.

PF-60 to 70 (Proof). ***Obverse and Reverse:*** At PF-60 to 63, there is light abrasion and some contact marks; the lower the grade, the higher the quantity. On Sand Blast Proofs these show up as visually unappealing bright spots. At PF-64 and higher levels, marks are fewer, with magnification needed to see any at PF-65. At PF-66, there should be none at all.

1913, Sand Blast Finish. Graded PF-66.

1908

Circulation-Strike Mintage: 564,821

Proof Mintage: 236

Estimated Total Population (Mint State). 5,000 to 7,500. *Estimated population MS-65 or finer:* 600 to 1,000, handily ranking it as the most available of the earlier dates (1908–1915) at the gem level.

Regarding quantities certified, these are skewed toward the mid-range Mint State grades such as MS-62 to MS-65, while in reality many more MS-60 coins exist than, for example, MS-63 specimens. However, there has not been the economic incentive to certify lower range pieces. Among all early-date (1908–1915) Indian Head quarter eagles, the 1908 wins hands-down as the most available in Mint State. Many seem to have been saved as the first year of issue, and others were set aside by chance.

Estimated Total Population (Circulated Grades). 15,000 to 25,000. Most are in higher grades such as Extremely Fine or About Uncirculated. These are very common (in the general class, which includes 1908, 1911, 1912, 1913, 1914-D, and 1915); among these early dates, the 1908 is the most plentiful of all.

Characteristics of Striking and Die Notes. Many if not most have light striking on the higher parts of the eagle; the eagle is in relief within its recess; that is, the eagle itself is below the field of the coin, but it has its own relief; it is not a shell.

Selected Auction Records

A selection of early listings reflects that 1908 was of generic interest until modern times, although this date was often selected for type sets as the first year of the type.

In May 1915 B. Max Mehl's catalog of the B.W. Smith Collection included this description of lot 286: "1908 New type with Indian head. Rev. eagle. Entire design incused (stamped in). About Uncirculated." Realized $3. In October 1951 the Numismatic Gallery sale of the B.A. Talmadge collection included two: Lot 1170: "1908 First year of Indian Head type. Uncirculated." Realized $5. Lot 1171: "Another 1908. Very Fine." Realized $6. In the absence of historical information, some such price differences are beyond knowing today. The answer is that the majority of buyers simply wanted "nice" examples, and an Extremely Fine or About Uncirculated coin would do just fine. Louis E. Eliasberg Sr. did not upgrade his coins. Those he acquired from the Clapp Collection via Stack's in 1952 included choice and gem pieces from connoisseurs John M. Clapp and his son John H. Clapp. Those he acquired elsewhere were in a combination of grades. Among my customers in the early days, the two main condition-conscious collectors of gold coins were Emery May Holden Norweb and John J. Pittman, later joined by Harry W. Bass Jr. Beginning about the 1970s and accelerated with the inception of PCGS and NGC in the late 1980s, countless buyers became very condition conscious. As is well known, today among Indian Head quarter eagles as well as most other types, a Gem Mint State coin can sell for many multiples of an Extremely Fine or About Uncirculated example.

Sand Blast Proofs

Sand Blast Proofs, sometimes called Matte Proofs, were available from the Philadelphia Mint in November 1908.

Estimated Total Population (Proof). 80 to 100. This is a low percentage survival rate. These are the more available issue among Proof quarter eagles of 1908 and 1909. This seems to have been the only year in which there was a significant interest in acquiring Proof examples of the type. Examples appear on the market with frequency.

Proof Die Data and Notes. Proofs of this date are generally called "Matte Proofs," or given the alternate spelling "Sandblast Proofs." The surfaces of the coins are minutely etched, appearing sandblasted (the actual method for making certain *medals* at the time), or pickled, giving the coins the appearance of butterscotch-colored sandpaper. Marks or breaks in the surface appear as bright spots or flecks. Matte Proof quarter eagles have "sharp" border edges, one way to tell an authentic Matte Proof from a post-Mint privately made "Proof." One in-person examination of a Matte Proof is worth many words, but this description may give a general idea.

Proofs of 1908 are slightly darker in hue than are those of later years.

Selected Proof Auction Records

In May 1913 the U.S. Coin Co.'s sale of the Malcolm N. Jackson Collection included lot 194: "1908 'Sand blast Proof.'" Realized $2.75. In February 1921 the catalog of B. Max Mehl's sale of the Dr. G.F.E. Wilharm Collection described lot 143: "1908 New type with large Indian head, Liberty above, date below, 13 stars. Reverse eagle standing, E. Pluribus Unum to left, In God We Trust to right, 2 ½ Dollars below; United States Of America above. The entire design stamped in. Sand blast Proof. (Dull finish). Rare." Realized $5.25. In June 1941 Mehl's sale of the William Forrester Dunham Collection included lot 2007: "1908 First year of the Indian head type. Reverse, eagle. The entire design incused, or stamped in. Sandblast Proof. Perfect, with wire edge. Quite scarce. Listed at $10." Realized $6.75. In June 1946 Mehl's sale of the William Cutler Atwater Collection included lot 2012: "1908. The new type adopted in this year. Indian head. Reverse, standing eagle. Same type as the half eagle of this year with the exception, of course, the value reading 2½ DOLLARS below eagle. Sandblast Proof. Very scarce, far more so than it is generally known. Although the coin is listed at $15, I consider it much under-rated. This coin has a recent record of $20." Realized $18.50.

VF-20	EF-40	AU-50	MS-60	MS-63	PF-60	PF-63
$475	$500	$525	$550	$950	$4,500	$10,250

1909

Circulation-Strike Mintage: 441,760

Proof Mintage: 139

Estimated Total Population (Mint State). 2,000 to 3,000. *Estimated population MS-65 or finer:* 250 to 450.

Estimated Total Population (Circulated Grades). 8,000 to 12,000. These are very common, but not among the several most common in the Indian series. The 1909 and 1910 are slightly less available than the 1908, 1911, 1912, 1913, 1914-D, and 1915. However, there are more than enough to permit interested collectors to locate an example easily.

Characteristics of Striking and Die Notes. These are usually well struck.

Selected Auction Records

In February 1921 the catalog of B. Max Mehl's sale of the Dr. G.F.E. Wilharm Collection described lot 145: "1909 Uncirculated." Realized $3.70. Lot 1808, as described in Stack's May 1945 sale of the George H. Hall Collection: "1909 Uncirculated." Realized $7.50. The Marmaduke Fox Collection sold by M.H. Bolender in March 1951 included lot 1188: "1909 Uncirculated." Realized $7.10.

Satin Finish Proofs

These are sometimes called *Roman Finish Proofs*.

Estimated Total Population (Proof). 60 to 90. This is a low percentage survival rate. It is doubtful if even half the Proof mintage was sold. David Akers (1975) suggests that in the era in which they were issued, many may have been confused in appearance with circulation strikes and may have been spent.

Proof Die Data and Notes. Proofs of 1909 and 1910 are of the satiny *Roman Finish* style and have a bright yellow coloration quite unlike the other Matte Proofs of the Indian Head series. The *Roman Finish* surfaces are intermediate between matte and satin in finish, more closely resembling a Mint State coin than those Proofs with the unmistakable matte finish of other dates in the series. This finish is beautiful to view today, but only in recent decades has it been studied and discussed in print (most notably in Breen's Proof coin *Encyclopedia*, 1977 and 1989).

According to Breen (Proof coin *Encyclopedia*) the term *Roman Gold Finish* has been in use since the early 1940s, although the exact source for the term was unknown to him. Wayte Raymond used to refer to Proof coins with this finish as "brilliant matte Proofs."

A few of the 1908 Sand Blast Proof–style pieces are known for 1909. These are not well differentiated in auction listings.

Selected Proof Auction Records

In May 1913 the U.S. Coin Co.'s sale of the Malcolm N. Jackson Collection included lot 195: "1909 Proof." Realized $3. In his sale of the Morris Collection, April 1931, B. Max Mehl described lot 558: "1909 Type as last. The new style Proof, not brilliant as issued. Very scarce." Realized $3.25. "New style" refers to the satiny surface. In his November 1939 sale of the William B. Hale Collection, Mehl described lot 823: "1909 Proof. Quite rare in Proof. Listed at $10 and certainly worth it." Realized $7.10. In the Numismatic Gallery sale of the "World's Greatest Collection" (F.C.C. Boyd Collection, January 1946) Abe Kosoff described lot 177: "1909 Matte Proof." Realized $20. Mehl's sale of the Jerome Kern Collection in May 1950 included lot 99: "1909. New style Proof between a sandblast and brilliant. Wire edge. Very scarce. Only a limited number of proofs struck. Only 139 specimens. Record $20." Realized $18. In April 1956 Abe Kosoff's sale of the Melish and Hester Collections included lot 1338: "1909 Proof. The Roman Gold finish." Realized $32.50.

VF-20	EF-40	AU-50	MS-60	MS-63	PF-60	PF-63
$475	$500	$525	$550	$1,250	$4,000	$11,500

1910

Circulation-Strike Mintage: 492,000

Proof Mintage: 682

Estimated Total Population (Mint State). 2,000 to 3,000. *Estimated population MS-65 or finer:* 350 to 400. True gems must be considered to be very rare in the context of the demand for them. On the other hand, pieces grading MS-60 or so are readily acquired.

Estimated Total Population (Circulated Grades). 10,000 to 15,000. These are very common, but not among the several most common in the Indian series. The 1909 and 1910 are slightly less available than the 1908, 1911, 1912, 1913, 1914-D, and 1915. With well over 10,000 circulated examples in existence, this date is easy to acquire.

Characteristics of Striking and Die Notes. These are often lightly struck at the centers.

Selected Auction Records

Stack's May 1945 sale of the George H. Hall Collection included lot 1810: "1910 Uncirculated." Realized $7.50. B. Max Mehl's sale of the Jerome Kern Collection in May 1950 included lot 100: "1910 Perfect Proof as last. Very scarce. Record over $20." Realized $21. In April 1956 Abe Kosoff's sale of the Melish and Hester Collections included lot 1341: "1910 Uncirculated." Realized $10.

Satin Finish Proofs

These are sometimes called *Roman Finish Proofs.*

As noted under "Proofs" in the introductory material on page 365, it was stated that no circulation strikes would be made this year. This caused a rush by collectors to buy Proofs to obtain an example of the date. It is unexplained why so few Proofs remain in proportion to the mintage.

Estimated Total Population (Proof). 90 to 125. Of the two "Roman Finish" dates, 1909 and 1910, the 1910 is the more often seen, but examples are rare.

Proof Die Data and Notes. Nearly all Proofs of 1909 and 1910 are of the Satin Finish–style and had have a bright yellow coloration quite unlike the other Matte Proofs of the Indian Head series. A few of the Sand Blast Proof–style coins are known and are exceedingly rare.

Selected Proof Auction Records

In May 1913 the U.S. Coin Co.'s sale of the Malcolm N. Jackson Collection included lot 196: "1910 Proof." Realized $3. The Stack's sale of the J.F. Bell Collection in December 1944 included lot 177: "1910 Sand Blast Proof." Realized $15. In June 1946 B. Max Mehl's sale of the William Cutler Atwater Collection included lot 2014: "1910 Same style Proof as last. Perfect. So-called 'matt' Proof. Recent record $20." Realized $21. In April 1956 Abe Kosoff's sale of the Melish and Hester Collections included lot 1340: "1910 Proof. Roman Gold finish." Realized $35.

VF-20	EF-40	AU-50	MS-60	MS-63	PF-60	PF-63
$475	$500	$525	$550	$850	$4,000	$10,000

1911

Circulation-Strike Mintage: 704,000
Proof Mintage: 191

Estimated Total Population (Mint State). 4,000 to 6,000. *Estimated population MS-65 or finer:* 225 to 375.

Among old-time collections that have come to the auction forum, when Mint State coins are encountered, they are apt to be MS-60 to MS-62.

Estimated Total Population (Circulated Grades). 15,000 to 25,000, mostly Extremely Fine and About Uncirculated. These are very common (in the general class, which includes 1908, 1911, 1912, 1913, 1914-D, and 1915).

Characteristics of Striking and Die Notes. The 1911 is usually well struck.

Selected Auction Records

In February 1920 S.H. Chapman's sale of the Gilbert D. Kingman Collection included lot 878: "1911 Indian Head. Plain edge. Rare." Realized $4. In March 1951 the Marmaduke Fox Collection sold by M.H. Bolender included lot 1191: "1911 P mint. Uncirculated." Realized $6.75. In April 1956 Abe Kosoff's sale of the Melish and Hester Collections included lot 1343: "1911 Uncirculated." Realized $11.

Sand Blast Proofs

These are sometimes called *Matte Proofs*. It is doubtful if even half the Proof mintage was sold.

Estimated Total Population (Proof). 90 to 110.

Proof Die Data and Notes. The Proofs commencing with this year are of the Matte Proof style, similar to that used in 1908 but now of a slightly paler hue. Considering the relative beauty of the Satin Finish, it remains a mystery why the Mint reversed to the Sand Blast Proof style.

Selected Proof Auction Records

In May 1913 the U.S. Coin Co.'s sale of the Malcolm N. Jackson Collection included lot 197: "1911 Sand blast Proof." Realized $2.75. In June 1941 B. Max Mehl's sale of the William Forrester Dunham Collection included lot 2010: "1911 Sandblast Proof, perfect. Very scarce." Realized $7.25. The Stack's sale of the J.F. Bell Collection in December 1944 included lot 178: "1911 Sand Blast Proof." Realized $13. In April 1956 Abe Kosoff's sale of the Melish and Hester Collections included lot 1342: "1911 Matte Proof." Realized $40.

VF-20	EF-40	AU-50	MS-60	MS-63	PF-60	PF-63
$475	$500	$525	$550	$800	$4,500	$11,000

1911-D

Circulation-Strike Mintage: 55,680

The first specimen was struck on April 18, 1911. This was the first time in history that the Denver Mint struck the $2.50 denomination.

Key issue in Indian Head series. "Weak" and "strong" D mintmark differences.

Estimated Total Population (Mint State). 300 to 500, mostly at the low end of the scale. Mint State specimens are very scarce in proportion to the great demand for them. *Estimated population MS-65 or finer:* 50 to 75 using today's grading interpretations; there were probably fewer than 20 using the grading interpretations of circa 1990.

Regarding value, consideration must be taken of the "strong D" mintmark, which is more desirable, vs. the "weak D," which is less so. Certification is of no help in determining the rarity or availability of strong vs. weak D coins, as only in recent times has the strength of the D been mentioned. Often, someone with a "weak D" piece will avoid certifying it, as the "weak D" notation is viewed as a negative.

It is further significant to note David W. Akers' commentary of 1975, when an MS-63 would have been exceptionally notable: "Most known specimens are circulated and truly Choice Uncirculated examples are rare."

Percentage-wise relative to the quantity extant, more 1911-D quarter eagles have been certified, by far, than of any other variety of the Indian Head type. This is for two reasons: First, many dangerous counterfeits exist, and the certification services will encapsulate only the pieces they believe to be genuine. Second and most important, the 1911-D is a scarce and valuable issue at all grade levels.

Many counterfeits exist, most being made by adding a D to a 1911 Philadelphia Mint coin. These lack the evidence of a wire rim on the obverse (see "Die Data," below).

Suggestion: When buying a 1911-D, cherrypick for a "strong D" specimen.

Estimated Total Population (Circulated Grades). 1,500 to 2,500, mostly Extremely Fine, less often lower (VF) or higher (AU). These are usually seen with a weak D. Over a long span of years, most gold coin collections, *including some of the most important ones,* have had 1911-D quarter eagles in these grades.

Die Data. The examples are from a die with a "strong D," with the mintmark punched deeply into the die, and a "weak D," with the mintmark lightly impressed. On the obverse there is always a wire rim at the border from about 12 o'clock to 3 o'clock.

Characteristics of Striking and Die Notes. Most have the mintmark D weakly defined, although this is only *rarely* mentioned in catalog descriptions. On the other hand, specimens with sharp mintmarks are often noted as such. Some have light striking in the feathers on the Indian's headdress and the feathers on the eagle on the reverse. The majority of 1911-D quarter eagles have a partial wire or knife rim on the obverse, varying in position (see citations on the following page). This was caused by metal squeezing upward in a space between the outside of the die and the collar.

Selected Auction Records

The sale of the Philpott and Zander Collections by B. Max Mehl in November 1945 included lot 1231: "1911-D First year of issue. Uncirculated. Very scarce." Realized $13.50. In the Numismatic Gallery sale of the "World's Greatest Collection" (F.C.C. Boyd Collection, January 1946) Abe Kosoff described lot 266: "1911-D Uncirculated. Scarce." Realized $25. Mehl's sale of the Jerome Kern Collection in May 1950 included lot 181: "1911-D. First year of issue. Uncirculated. Very scarce; more so than is generally known. Catalogs $20 but a specimen in my Atwater Sale, in 1946, brought $21." Realized $26. In January 1951 *Kelly's Coins and Chatter* offered this: "1911-D Gem Uncirculated. $30."

VF-20	EF-40	AU-50	MS-60	MS-63
$2,600	$3,300	$4,000	$5,500	$11,000

Note: Values are for coins with bold mintmark; weak D pieces are worth less. Beware of counterfeits.

1912

Circulation-Strike Mintage: 616,000
Proof Mintage: 197

Estimated Total Population (Mint State). 2,500 to 3,500. *Estimated population MS-65 or finer:* 175 to 200. This is a major rarity in gem preservation.

Curiously, the 1912 is often priced as a "type," even though, for example, it is far rarer in MS-65 than a 1908 (also priced as a "type," as the 1908 should be). At the MS-65 level the 1912 is scarcer than the 1914 (however, in terms of Mint State coins in lower levels, the 1914 is rarer).

Estimated Total Population (Circulated Grades). 14,000 to 24,000, mostly Extremely Fine and About Uncirculated. These are very common (in the general class, which includes 1908, 1911, 1912, 1913, 1914-D, and 1915).

Characteristics of Striking and Die Notes. The 1912 is usually well struck.

Selected Auction Records

In June 1942 B. Max Mehl's sale of the Col. J.A. Porter Collection included lot 1139: "1912 Uncirculated." Realized $4.65. In October 1951 the Numismatic Gallery sale of the B.A. Talmadge collection included lot 1178: "1912 Uncirculated." Realized $7. In April 1956 Abe Kosoff's sale of the Melish and Hester Collections included lot 1348: "1912 Uncirculated." Realized $9.

Sand Blast Proofs

These are sometimes called *Matte Proofs*.

Estimated Total Population (Proof). 75 to 95. This is a low percentage survival rate, as is true of other Proofs of the era.

Proof Die Data and Notes. The surface on 1912 Sand Blast (or Matte) Proofs is very finely grained, in contrast to the coarse grain used on Sand Blast Proofs of 1908 and 1911.

Selected Proof Auction Records

In May 1913 the U.S. Coin Co.'s sale of the Malcolm N. Jackson Collection included lot 198: "1912 Sand blast Proof." Realized $2.75. Thomas L. Elder's June 1935 sale of the Wendell C. Foster Collection included this description of lot 2799: "1912 Sandblast Proof. Very rare." Realized $5. The sale of the J.F. Bell Collection in December 1944 included lot 179: "1912 Sand Blast Proof." Realized $13. In June 1946 B. Max Mehl's sale of the William Cutler Atwater Collection included lot 2016: "1912. Sandblast Proof, but of a rather brighter finish. Wire edge. Very scarce, more so than the other dates of this type." Realized $21.

VF-20	EF-40	AU-50	MS-60	MS-63	PF-60	PF-63
$475	$500	$525	$550	$1,300	$4,500	$11,000

1913

Circulation-Strike Mintage: 722,000
Proof Mintage: 165

Estimated Total Population (Mint State). 2,750 to 4,000, mostly at lower levels. *Estimated population MS-65 or finer:* 250 to 350.

Estimated Total Population (Circulated Grades). 15,000 to 25,000, mostly Extremely Fine and About Uncirculated. These are very common (in the general class, which includes 1908, 1911, 1912, 1913, 1914-D, and 1915).

Characteristics of Striking and Die Notes. The 1913 is usually well struck.

Selected Auction Records

In February 1921 the catalog of B. Max Mehl's sale of the Dr. G.F.E. Wilharm Collection described lot 150: "1913 Uncirculated." Realized $4. In his November 1939 sale of the William B. Hale Collection, Mehl described lot 827: "1913 Sandblast Proof." Realized $9.50. In April 1956 Abe Kosoff's sale of the Melish and Hester Collections included lot 1351: "1913 Uncirculated." Realized $11.

Sand Blast Proofs

These are sometimes called *Matte Proofs*.

It is likely that most pieces were not sold.

Estimated Total Population (Proof). 65 to 90.

Proof Die Data and Notes. Breen called the surface on the 1912 and 1913 issues a "fine sandblast finish."

Selected Proof Auction Records

In May 1915 B. Max Mehl's catalog of the B.W. Smith Collection included this description of lot 288: "1913 Sand blast Proof. Rare." Realized $2.85. In his sale of the Morris Collection, April 1931, Mehl described lot 561: "1913 Sand-blast Proof." Realized $4.50. The Stack's sale of the J.F. Bell Collection in December 1944 included lot 180: "1913 Sand Blast Proof." Realized $13. In the Numismatic Gallery sale of the "World's

Greatest Collection" (F.C.C. Boyd Collection, January 1946) Abe Kosoff described lot 181: "1913 Matte Proof." Realized $20.

VF-20	EF-40	AU-50	MS-60	MS-63	PF-60	PF-63
$475	$500	$525	$550	$800	$4,500	$11,500

1914

Circulation-Strike Mintage: 240,000

Proof Mintage: 117

Scarce date.

Estimated Total Population (Mint State). 750 to 1,250, a small figure in comparison to other Philadelphia Mint quarter eagles of the Indian Head design. Most of these are in low Mint State levels. In lower Mint State grades, the 1914 is the second rarest of all Indian Head quarter eagles, exceeded only by the 1911-D. *Estimated population MS-65 or finer:* 80 to 120. This is a major rarity in MS-65.

Interestingly, at the MS-65 level, the 1914 is *not* the rarest Philadelphia Mint coin of the type; the 1914-D is rarer. As with other quarter eagles, grading interpretations seem to have inched upward over the years. Thus, an MS-65 coin would have been viewed as very rare in the 1980s but would not attract wide attention today.

Estimated Total Population (Circulated Grades). 3,000 to 5,000, mostly in grades from Very Fine to About Uncirculated, with Extremely Fine being the norm. As the lower mintage figure suggests, the 1914 is scarcer than other Philadelphia Mint coins of the type. However, there are still enough around to supply the needs of specialists and other interested buyers, and the 1914 usually trades as a common date or at a "type" price.

Characteristics of Striking and Die Notes. Most are well struck, although some have slight weakness at the highest point of the eagle's wing. Such can be determined only upon personal observation, as certification service data and virtually all catalog and price listings are silent on the subject.

Selected Auction Records

In his sale of the Morris Collection, April 1931, B. Max Mehl described lot 562: "1914 Uncirculated." Realized $3.50. The Stack's May 1945 sale of the George H. Hall Collection included lot 1815: "1914 Uncirculated." Realized $7.50. In April 1956 Abe Kosoff's sale of the Melish and Hester Collections included lot 1353: "1914 Uncirculated, scarce." Realized $16.

Sand Blast Proofs

These are sometimes called *Matte Proofs*.

Estimated Total Population (Proof). 55 to 75. Proofs are very rare. The demand for them in the modern market may be accentuated by the fact that high-grade circulation strikes are rarer for 1914 than for any other Philadelphia Mint date of the design.

Proof Die Data and Notes. Matte Proofs of 1914 and 1915 have an especially coarse, "sandpaper-like" finish.

Selected Proof Auction Records

In his November 1939 sale of the William B. Hale Collection, B. Max Mehl described lot 828: "1914 Sandblast Proof." Realized $7.35. The Stack's sale of the J.F. Bell Collection in December 1944 included lot 181: "1914 Sand Blast Proof." Realized $15. In the Numismatic Gallery sale of the "World's Greatest Collection" (F.C.C. Boyd Collection, January 1946) Abe Kosoff described lot 182: "1914 Matte Proof." Realized $20.

VF-20	EF-40	AU-50	MS-60	MS-63	PF-60	PF-63
$475	$500	$550	$650	$2,250	$4,500	$11,750

1914-D

Circulation-Strike Mintage: 448,000

Estimated Total Population (Mint State). 3,000 to 4,500. While one might expect that the 1914-D would be a rarity in Mint State, examples are seen with some regularity. However, most extant Mint State coins are in lower levels such as MS-60 to MS-63. *Estimated population MS-65 or finer:* 75 to 100. At the MS-65 level, the 1914-D is the second rarest Indian Head quarter eagle (the 1911-D being the rarest).

Estimated Total Population (Circulated Grades). 8,000 to 12,000, mostly Extremely Fine and About Uncirculated. These are very common (in the general class, which includes 1908, 1911, 1912, 1913, 1914-D, and 1915).

Characteristics of Striking and Die Notes. These are often lightly struck on the reverse at the eagle's leg and higher parts of the wing, sometimes from bulged dies. On some, the D mintmark is filled at the center and appears as a "blob." The striking quality of the 1914-D is below par and is the least satisfactory of any issue in the early 1908 to 1915 series. Thus, some discrimination is advised when selecting a specimen, as certification holders do not mention quality, and one MS-63 specimen (for example) can be beautiful and the another quite unattractive.

Selected Auction Records

In his November 1939 sale of the William B. Hale Collection, B. Max Mehl described lot 887: "1914-D Uncirculated. Scarce." Realized $7.25. Mehl's February 1944 catalog of the sale of the Belden E. Roach Collection described lot 1023: "1914-D Uncirculated. Scarce." Realized $10.50. The Stack's sale of the J.F. Bell Collection in December 1944 included lot 263: "1914-D Brilliant Uncirculated." Realized $10. In the Numismatic Gallery sale of the "World's Greatest Collection" (F.C.C. Boyd Collection, January 1946) Abe Kosoff described lot 267: "1914-D None minted in 1912, 1913. Uncirculated." Realized $10.

VF-20	EF-40	AU-50	MS-60	MS-63
$475	$500	$525	$550	$1,100

1915

Circulation-Strike Mintage: 606,000

Proof Mintage: 100

Final early Indian Head issue.

Estimated Total Population (Mint State). 3,000 to 4,500. *Estimated population MS-65 or finer:* 300 to 450. In gem grade the 1915 is quite rare in comparison to the demand for it.

Estimated Total Population (Circulated Grades). 12,000 to 16,000, mostly Extremely Fine and About Uncirculated. These are very common (in the general class, which includes 1908, 1911, 1912, 1913, 1914-D, and 1915).

Characteristics of Striking and Die Notes. These are sometimes seen with areas of light striking on the eagle.

Selected Auction Records

In the May 1945 sale of the George H. Hall Collection, Stack's said this for lot 1817: "1915 Uncirculated." Realized $7.50. In October 1951 the Numismatic Gallery sale of the B.A. Talmadge collection included lot 1183: "1915 Uncirculated." Realized $6.75. In May 1957 the Stack's sale of that date included this coin: "1915 Brilliant Uncirculated." Realized $13.50.

Sand Blast Proofs

These are sometimes called *Matte Proofs*.

Estimated Total Population (Proof). 50 to 60. This is the rarest of all Proofs in the Indian Head series.

Proof Die Data and Notes. Matte Proofs of 1914 and 1915 have an especially coarse, "sandpaper-like" finish.

Selected Proof Auction Records

In his sale of the Morris Collection, April 1931, B. Max Mehl described lot 563: "1915 Sand-blast Proof. Scarce." Realized $4.50. In his November 1939 sale of the William B. Hale Collection, Mehl described lot 829: "1915 Sandblast Proof. Last year of the Proofs." Realized $8.50. The Stack's sale of the J.F. Bell Collection in December 1944 included lot 182: "1915 Sand Blast Proof." Realized $16. In the Numismatic Gallery sale of the "World's Greatest Collection" (F.C.C. Boyd Collection, January 1946) Abe Kosoff described lot 183: "1915 Last year of Proofs. Matt." Realized $25.

VF-20	EF-40	AU-50	MS-60	MS-63	PF-60	PF-63
$475	$500	$525	$550	$850	$6,000	$12,000

1925-D

Circulation-Strike Mintage: 578,000

Estimated Total Population (Mint State). 12,000 to 16,000, most of which are in the MS-60 to MS-63 range. Examples that have fields with very few microscopic marks are hard to find. *Estimated population MS-65 or finer:* 800 to 1,200.

The auction record for the past several decades, as available on the Internet, shows that MS-63 is about par for specimens of this date in the finer collections, these having been collected before the emphasis was on minute grading differences. I am not aware of any old-time numismatist who, having an MS-63 coin, would seek an MS-65 as a replacement. This comment has nothing to do with the desirability of MS-65 coins, which, of course, are more desirable than MS-63s; it is simply a reflection of the trends of years ago vs. those of today. Now, buyers are number-conscious.

Estimated Total Population (Circulated Grades). 7,000 to 10,000. These are very common.

Characteristics of Striking and Die Notes. The 1925-D is usually very well struck, although a few have light impressions at the high points of the Indian head. Some were struck from bulged dies, creating weak areas at the centers. Some have a weak D mintmark, and on a few the D seems to be missing altogether, yielding what appears to be a "Philadelphia Mint coin."

Selected Auction Records

In his November 1939 sale of the William B. Hale Collection, B. Max Mehl described lot 888: "1925-D About Uncirculated, with luster. These are the only three dates minted at this mint." Realized $5. Mehl's February 1944 catalog of the sale of the Belden E. Roach Collection described lot 1024: "1925-D Uncirculated." Realized $6.75. The Stack's sale of the J.F. Bell Collection in December 1944 included lot 264: "1925-D Brilliant Uncirculated." Realized $11. In the Numismatic Gallery sale of the "World's Greatest Collection" (F.C.C. Boyd Collection, January 1946) Abe Kosoff described lot 268: "1925-D Last year of issue. None minted between 1914 and 1925. Uncirculated." Realized $12. In October 1951 the Numismatic Gallery sale of the B.A. Talmadge collection included two: Lot 1184: "1925—Denver. Uncirculated." Realized $8.25. Lot 1185: "Another 1925-D. About Uncirculated." Realized $6.50.

VF-20	EF-40	AU-50	MS-60	MS-63
$475	$500	$525	$550	$675

1926

Circulation-Strike Mintage: 446,000

Estimated Total Population (Mint State). 10,000 to 14,000, mostly in levels from MS-60 to MS-63. *Estimated population MS-65 or finer:* 1,000 to 1,400.

Auction data of the past 20 years suggest that MS-63 is about par for a choice specimen in an old-time collection. See comments under 1925-D, on previous page.

Estimated Total Population (Circulated Grades). 5,000 to 8,000. These are common in high circulated grades such as About Uncirculated and, to a lesser extent, Extremely Fine. Anything less is rare (but who cares?).

Characteristics of Striking and Die Notes. The 1926 is nearly always seen well struck.

Selected Auction Records

In June 1941 B. Max Mehl's sale of the William Forrester Dunham Collection included lot 2016: "1926 Uncirculated." Realized $4.75. The Stack's sale of the J.F. Bell Collection in December 1944 included lot 183: "1926 Brilliant Uncirculated." Realized $8. In the Numismatic Gallery sale of the "World's Greatest Collection" (F.C.C. Boyd Collection, January 1946) Abe Kosoff described lot 184: "1926 Uncirculated." Realized $11. In October 1951 the Numismatic Gallery sale of the B.A. Talmadge collection included three: Lot 1186: "1926 Uncirculated." Realized $5.25. Lot 1187: "Another 1926. Very Fine." Realized $5.85. Lot 1188: "Same, 1926. Very Fine." Realized $5.75.

VF-20	EF-40	AU-50	MS-60	MS-63
$475	$500	$525	$550	$675

1927

Circulation-Strike Mintage: 388,000

Estimated Total Population (Mint State). 8,000 to 12,000. *Estimated population MS-65 or finer:* 700 to 950.

Similar to earlier coins of this decade, the 1927 is common in Mint State, with most pieces in the range of MS-60 to MS-63. The auction record shows that MS-63 is about the norm for fine collections gathered years ago.

Estimated Total Population (Circulated Grades). 3,500 to 5,500. These are common in high circulated grades such as About Uncirculated and, to a lesser extent, Extremely Fine.

Characteristics of Striking and Die Notes. These are usually well struck.

Selected Auction Records

In June 1941 B. Max Mehl's sale of the William Forrester Dunham Collection included lot 2017: "1927 Bright Uncirculated." Realized $4.75. The Stack's sale of the J.F. Bell Collection in December 1944 included lot 184: "1927 Brilliant Uncirculated." Realized $8. In the Numismatic Gallery sale of the "World's Greatest Collection" (F.C.C. Boyd Collection, January 1946) Abe Kosoff described lot 185: "1927 Uncirculated."

Realized $9. The Will W. Neil Collection sold by Mehl in June 1947 included lot 2491: "1927 Uncirculated, frosty mint luster." Realized $7.75.

VF-20	EF-40	AU-50	MS-60	MS-63
$475	$500	$525	$550	$675

1928

Circulation-Strike Mintage: 416,000

Estimated Total Population (Mint State). 10,000 to 14,000, mostly in the MS-60 to MS-63 range. *Estimated population MS-65 or finer:* 500 to 800.

Estimated Total Population (Circulated Grades). 4,000 to 6,000. These are much scarcer than Mint State, not that it makes any difference. They are common in any event. Most circulated pieces are at the About Uncirculated level.

Characteristics of Striking and Die Notes. Most are well struck, but some have weak or irregularly raised borders.

Selected Auction Records

In April 1956 Abe Kosoff's sale of the Melish and Hester Collections included lot 1363: "1928 Uncirculated." Realized $10. The Stack's sale of the J.F. Bell Collection in December 1944 included lot 185: "1928 Brilliant Uncirculated." Realized $8.35. In the Numismatic Gallery sale of the "World's Greatest Collection" (F.C.C. Boyd Collection, January 1946) Abe Kosoff described lot 186: "1928 Uncirculated." Realized $10. The Will W. Neil Collection sold by B. Max Mehl in June 1947 included lot 2492: "1928 Uncirculated. These catalog at $10." Realized $7.85.

VF-20	EF-40	AU-50	MS-60	MS-63
$475	$500	$525	$550	$675

1929

Circulation-Strike Mintage: 532,000

Although all of the 532,000 pieces were probably distributed through banks, anyone asking for one was apt to be greeted either with the comment, "We don't have any," or the news that a few had been saved by tellers and were available as a "favor" for a small premium, say for $3 instead of $2.50. Thus, from the outset the 1929 quarter eagle was scarce in circulation.

Estimated Total Population (Mint State). 13,000 to 16,000. These were saved in vast quantities by the public. *Estimated population MS-65 or finer:* 300 to 500.

This is far and away the most common Mint State quarter eagle of any design or date. It is exceedingly plentiful in Mint State, with most pieces being in the MS-60 to MS-63 range and occasionally in MS-64, but, as noted, not often in MS-65. It may be well worth considering that as this text is being prepared, MS-65 is a rare grade for the 1929, but if grade interpretation inflation continues and some of today's MS-64 coins are regraded as MS-65, the *apparent* (but not real) population of MS-65 coins could multiply many times over, as MS-64 coins exist in very large quantities.

Estimated Total Population (Circulated Grades). 5,000 to 8,000. Extremely Fine and About Uncirculated coins became that way not from being in circulation, but from being mishandled by those who acquired them as souvenirs.

Characteristics of Striking and Die Notes. No one rule suffices for all. Some are struck from bulged dies. Others, the majority, are well struck.

Selected Auction Records

In his sale of the Morris Collection, April 1931, B. Max Mehl described lot 564: "1929 Last year of issue. Uncirculated. Scarce and in demand." Realized $2.90. The Stack's sale of the J.F. Bell Collection in December 1944 included lot 186: "1929 Brilliant Uncirculated." Realized $8. The sale of the Philpott and Zander Collections Mehl in November 1945 included lot 1167: "1929 Last year of issue. Uncirculated." Realized $7.75.

VF-20	EF-40	AU-50	MS-60	MS-63
$475	$500	$525	$550	$675

APPENDIX

A

Pattern $2.50 Gold Coins

In the American series, pattern coins tell the story of what might have been in coinage, but wasn't. Such coins include ideas that were proposed by congressmen, citizens, or Mint officials, made into coins, examined and considered, then rejected. In addition, many pieces, actually the majority, were secretly produced by Mint officials for private sale to numismatists.

All told, over 1,800 different varieties of pattern coins exist from 1792 to date. These are usually classified by Judd numbers, from J. Hewitt Judd, M.D., *United States Pattern, Experimental and Trial Pieces*, published by Whitman. By use of these numbers, the shorthand notation such as J-189 is the key to the date, denomination, variety, metal, and other aspects. Saul Teichman's www.uspatterns.com website contains many pictures and much useful information.

Patterns, first made at the Philadelphia Mint in 1792, were produced intermittently until about 1836, after which time activity increased dramatically through 1885. Then followed a period of sparse activity until 1896, when many patterns were produced, though few of the quarter eagle denomination.

New design concepts were usually done on higher denominations. Most pattern quarter eagles are not of new motifs but rather are strikings in off-metals such as copper and aluminum from dies used to strike Proofs. As mentioned, nearly all of these were made secretly at the Mint, up to 1885, and benefited Mint officials. Details are given in the Judd book. These and others are described in order by years.

Note: Pattern coins are shown larger than actual size.

J-23a

1796 Judd 23a. Although this is listed as a pattern, it is a private restrike made years later from rusted dies. It has a partially reeded edge and is made using white metal. It is believed to be unique.

J-49

1831 J-49. Regular dies were struck on a silver dime planchet. This is likely a mint error, not a pattern or coin struck for numismatists. Two are known, of which one is well-worn.

1833 J-49a to 49f. Regular circulation-strike dies were used to make regular coins, but for these, experimental alloys were used. Each has a reeded edge. No examples have been traced today. See listings below and on the following page.

The Coinage Act of June 28, 1834, sought to return gold coins to general circulation by modifying their authorized weight so they could circulate at par. In anticipation of the revised coinage standard, Director of the Mint Samuel Moore sent a report to the speaker of the House of Representatives on January 11, 1833, suggesting alloys for the new gold coins. Moore apparently sought to have some silver incorporated, and related:

> A gold coin alloyed with about one-twelfth of its weight of silver and copper combined resists the effects of attrition, at least as effectually as any other proportion, the purpose of exhibiting the degree of approximation of the color of fine gold produced by various proportions of silver and copper employed as an alloy of gold coin, a number of specimens of the quarter eagle are forwarded with the report, to which the House is respectfully referred. (The numbers are designated by minute points impressed on the reverse of each coin above the head of the eagle.)
>
> No. 1 consists of 61 7/8 grains of pure gold, being the quantity at present required in the quarter eagle.
>
> No. 2 contains 61 7/8 grains of pure gold and 5 5/8 grains of alloy, making 67 1/2 grains, the weight of a quarter eagle of our present standard. The alloy in this specimen consists of silver alone.
>
> No. 3 is of the same weight and fineness as No. 2, but alloyed with silver and copper in equal proportions.
>
> No. 4 is of the same weight and fineness as the preceding, but alloyed wholly with copper.
>
> No. 5 weighs 66 grains, of which 59.4 consist of pure gold and 6.6 grains of alloy, which alloy consists of silver and copper in equal proportions.
>
> No. 6 is of the same weight and fineness as the preceding, but alloyed with silver and copper in the proportion of one part of the former to two parts of the latter.
>
> The first four specimens are of the intrinsic value of our present quarter eagle.
>
> The fifth and sixth are conformable to the coinage in which the eagle would contain 264 grains of standard gold, consisting of 237.6 grains of pure gold and 26.4 grains of alloy.

1833 J-49a. No. 1 in the Moore list given above. Pure gold. 61 7/8 grains.

1833 J-49b. No. 2 in the Moore list. Gold with silver as an alloy. 67 1/2 grains.

1833 J-49c. No. 3 in the Moore list. Gold alloyed with silver and copper, the last two metals in equal proportions. 67 1/2 grains.

1833 J-49d. No. 4 in the Moore list. Gold alloyed with copper, *the standard composition for regular issues. Not a pattern, but listed here as part of the suite of other pieces, for reference.* 67 1/2 grains.

1833 J-49e. No. 5 in the Moore list. Gold alloyed with silver and copper, the last two metals in equal proportions. 66 grains.

1833 J-49f. No. 6 in the Moore list. Gold alloyed with silver and copper, with one part silver and two parts copper. 66 grains.

J-110a

1846 J-110a. Bearing the date 1846, this is a curious piece struck in copper that has about the diameter of a quarter eagle, with the obverse and reverse of an 1846 die pair, but then with the reverse additionally overstruck with a 1846 *half eagle* die. It was first described by New Netherlands Coin Company in the August 1952 ANA sale, lot 4478.

J-137

(1852) Related to the quarter eagle is gold dollar pattern J-137. *Obverse:* USA above, 1852 below. Otherwise, the design is blank. This was a simple, hastily made die to test the concept. *Reverse:* A circular laurel wreath. This pair of dies was never intended for regular coinage. It was used to strike gold impressions of a larger diameter than currently in use, perforated so that the value of gold could be maintained in a larger format coin. Two examples are known, one using an already struck 1846 quarter eagle and the other on an 1859 quarter eagle as the planchet. These were made at a later date for collectors. Gold. Plain edge.

J-151

(1853) In the meantime at the Mint, experiments continued with producing a new format of cent pieces to replace the cumbersome copper "large" cents that had been the standard for many years. To test various metal concepts, an existing quarter eagle die of 1853 (this being of about the correct diameter desired for the experiment) was employed in combination with a possibly newly created reverse die, with an open wreath enclosing the words ONE / CENT. The design was too widely spaced apart with an open space at the center, and obviously made in haste.[1] Pieces were struck in various alloys, generally known as "German silver," this being a term for metal of silvery color, with nickel, copper, and other metals, but lacking precious silver. J-149 was struck with a content of 40% nickel, 40% copper, and 20% zinc; J-150 was made of 30% nickel, 60% copper, and 10% zinc; and J-151 was struck in 40% nickel, 60% copper. Apparently, some were made in "60% nickel, the remainder copper."[2] Elemental analysis of the cent patterns of this year suggests that at best, the stated metal percentages were approximate. For collectors, novodels were created by combining the obverse of the 1850 perforated cent die (J-119) with the reverse of the 1853 (J-149).[3]

J-189

1857 J-189. *Obverse:*
The head of Liberty is facing left, with a coronet inscribed LIBERTY, essentially the same style as later used on the regular nickel three-cent pieces of 1865. There are 13 stars around and the date 1857 below (the same die was used to strike J-186 with a cent reverse). *Reverse:* An eagle is at the center with wings outstretched and a shield on its breast, holding an olive branch and three arrows. UNITED STATES OF AMERICA / 2½ D is inscribed around the border. Obverse die varieties exist. Copper. Reeded edge.

J-270

1860 J-270. Among the patterns of 1860 is an anomalous quarter eagle combining an obverse die dated and used in 1857 for a cent and a new quarter eagle reverse with a wreath around the border enclosing the inscription 2½ / DOLLARS / 1860, creating a *most curious* item of numismatica—one with a date on each side and with the dates being different! *Obverse:* From the Liberty Head die dated 1857 (used in 1857 to strike the J-186 cent). *Reverse:* A pattern die with the wreath enclosing 2½ / DOLLARS / 1860. This fantasy muling with two different dates is an unusual situation even among numismatic delicacies. Copper. Reeded edge.

J-281

1861 J-281 and 282. 1861 $2.50 regular dies. J-281: Silver.[4] Reeded edge. J-282: Copper. Reeded edge.

J-439

1865 J-439. 1865
$2.50 regular dies. J-439: Copper. Reeded edge.

J-542

1866 J-542. 1866 $2.50 regular dies. This may be a mint error. Nickel. Reeded edge.

J-595

1867 J-595. 1867 $2.50 regular dies. Copper. Reeded edge.

J-595

1868 J-654. 1868 $2.50 regular dies. Aluminum. Reeded edge.

J-770

1869 J-769 to 771. 1869 $2.50 regular dies. J-769: Copper. Reeded edge. J-770: Aluminum. Reeded edge. J-771: Nickel. Reeded edge.

J-1026

1870 J-1026 to 1028. 1870 $2.50 regular dies. J-1026: Copper. Reeded edge. J-1027: Aluminum. Reeded edge. J-1028: Nickel. Reeded edge.

J-1164

1871 J-1164 to 1166. 1871 $2.50 regular dies. J-1164: Copper. Reeded edge. J-1165: Aluminum. Reeded edge. J-1166: Nickel. Reeded edge.

J-1230

1872 J-1230 to 1232. 1872 pattern $2.50 dies. In 1872 Chief Engraver William Barber created a series of pattern silver and gold coins. The gold had a new portrait of Miss Liberty. The reverse employed the "Amazonian" motif of an eagle holding the shield; this was used on silver and gold coins. J-1230 to 1232: *Obverse:* Barber's Liberty Head is facing left, with the headband inscribed LIBERTY and tresses flowing down to the right. *Reverse:* Barber's standing eagle with talons holding shield. UNITED STATES OF AMERICA / 2 1/2 DOL. is written around the border. J-1230: Gold. Reeded edge. J-1231: Copper. R Reeded edge E. J-1232: Aluminum. R Reeded edge E. These were produced in secret and sold privately by Mint officials.

J-1234

1872 J-1233 and 1234. 1872 $2.50 regular dies. J-1233: Copper. Reeded edge. J-1234: Aluminum. Reeded edge.

J-1334

1873 J-1333 and 1334. 1873 $2.50 regular dies, Close 3. J-1333: Copper. Reeded edge. J-1334: Aluminum. Reeded edge.

J-1434

1875 J-1434 and 1435. 1875 $2.50 regular dies. J-1434: Copper. Reeded edge. J-1435: Aluminum. Reeded edge.

J-1480

1876 J-1480 and 1481. 1876 $2.50 regular dies. J-1480: Copper. Reeded edge. J-1481: Aluminum. Reeded edge. (Not confirmed to exist today.)

J-1566

1878 J-1566 and 1567. 1878 pattern $2.50 dies. *Obverse:* The Liberty head by Morgan, with its hair combed back and held by a ribbon; a band extends back from the forehead inscribed LIBERTY. Around the border is written E PLURIBUS UNUM / 1878. *Reverse:* The eagle with drooped wings, holding an olive branch (with seven leaves) and three arrows. Around the border, UNITED STATES OF AMERICA / 2½ DOLLARS. The head seems to be too large for the field, the design is hardly finessed, and the widely spaced motto, typically a minor part of any coin design, is placed in a very prominent position here. J-1566: Gold. Reeded edge. J-1567: Copper. Reeded edge.

1884 J-1734. 1884 $2.50 regular dies. Copper. Reeded edge.

J-1752

1885 J-1752. 1885 $2.50 regular dies. Aluminum. Reeded edge. With the arrival of a new Mint director, the secret production of patterns for private sales to numismatists ended.

1908 J-1922: 1908 pattern Indian Head dies by Bela Lyon Pratt. *Obverse and reverse:* This pattern is similar to the adopted design, but with its details not as sharp. Ten pieces were said to have been supplied to President Theodore Roosevelt, examined, then returned to the Mint for remelting. None are known today. Gold. Reeded edge.

APPENDIX B

$2.50 Gold Coins in Treasure Finds

Buried treasure! Pirate gold! Treasures have always been a fascinating part of American lore and history. Over a long period of time, thousands of ships have been lost in American waters (over 6,000 on the Great Lakes alone) and many more in the oceans. While the typical vessel carried iron ore, passengers, coal, or even ice, nearly all had some money aboard. Some, such as those related to the California Gold Rush, carried substantial amounts of gold coins and ingots. The SS *Central America*, lost at sea in 1857, carried the greatest Gold Rush fortune to the bottom of the sea.

Starting in the 1950s, the writer kept a file on treasures. This information has been used in several books, most recently, *Lost and Found Coin Hoards and Treasures: Illustrated Stories of the Greatest American Troves and Their Discoveries*. Most treasures of gold coins consisted mainly of double eagles, the largest circulating denomination. Many also had some quarter eagles. Selected finds are given here.

SS *New York*

Constructed in 1837 at the yard of William H. Brown on the East River, New York City, the SS *New York* was a side-wheel steamship with auxiliary sails, a class of vessel generally known as a steam packet. The *New York* made her first voyage on June 15, 1837, going into service carrying passengers, cargo, and mail on the coastwise route connecting New York City to Charleston, South Carolina. In January 1846 the *New York* was sold to Captain John D. Phillips and went to the Gulf of Mexico. By that time the maritime business in the Gulf was very competitive.

On Saturday, September 5, 1846, the SS *New York* departed Galveston at four-thirty in the afternoon carrying 30 passengers and a crew of 23. At the helm was the owner of the ship, Captain John D. Phillips, a seasoned commander. The load was far short of capacity, foretelling a pleasant voyage with more than usual attention from the crew. Fare was $15 for cabin passage, less for steerage. Money in the estimated amount of $30,000 to $40,000 was aboard, although no authoritative figures were ever published. This consisted of gold and silver coins and, it is likely, many bank notes. We know that among the cargo was a woodworking machine. Probably there were barrels and crates of other goods as well, normal for the route, although one later account stated the hold was empty.

The weather had been foggy and rainy for nearly three weeks, and at departure time a light haze covered the harbor. The ship steamed out of Galveston Bay and headed to the open sea, with no indication of anything unusual. This changed, the seas became rough, and the ship cast anchor. There was a lull the next morning, and on Sunday at 10 o'clock the anchor was weighed and the ship continued its course. Onward to New Orleans, never mind the slight delay. Throughout Sunday the storm worsened, and the ship was tossed about even more violently. The passengers huddled and tried to cheer each other. Surely the winds would subside and the sea would become quiet. Then on to New Orleans, as planned. This did not happen. The worst was yet to come. About midnight or within an hour afterward, a cable snapped, and part of the structure gave way on the starboard side. Water rushed into the hold, the boiler fires were extinguished, and for the first time, passengers seriously feared for their lives.

Into the night men manned pumps, but to no avail. Early the next morning the ship sank, while some deck parts and the wheelhouse floated away. Survivors included 19 passengers and 18 crew, including the captain. Lost were 11 passengers and 8 crew.

Years later, Avery Munson, of New Iberia, Louisiana, who loved scuba diving and exploring the sea, wondered whether there might be any historical accounts of lost ships with treasure aboard within each reach of this port. For several years he combed old newspapers and other accounts. Lightning struck! He found the telltale comment in the *Daily Picayune* of September 10, 1846. With this as a beginning, he enlisted several friends, forming a group of four styling themselves as the Gentlemen of Fortune, including Craig DeRouen and the husband-and-wife team of Gary and Renée Hebert.

The SS *New York*.

The team studied newspaper articles, survivor accounts, charts, and underwater data. The Gulf of Mexico is a center for offshore oil rigs, and much mapping had been done. They consulted shrimp fishermen and others familiar with the Gulf to seek clues and ideas. The group took measurements and made estimates. Finally, in early 2005 they had their "eureka!" moment: The ship's bell was found. In due course their ownership was successfully registered in a federal court, no other claims arose, and recovery commenced. In time the author's book, *The Treasure Ship S.S. New York: Her Life and Loss, 1837–1847*, was published and drew nice reviews. The most important coins were auctioned by Stack's.

An 1836 quarter eagle from the SS *New York* treasure.

The following quarter eagles were included, with grades given by NGC:

1835 AU details; 1836 AU details (3), AU-55, AU-58, Unc. details, MS-61 (2), MS-62 (2); 1839-O AU-55, MS-62; 1843 Large Date, Plain 4 MS-62; 1843-C Large Date, Plain 4 AU details; 1843-O AU details (3), AU-58, MS-60 (4), MS-61 (7), MS-62 (2), MS-63 (2), MS-64 (2); 1844-D AU-53, AU-58; 1845-D MS-64; and 1846 MS-61.

SS *Central America*

In the annals of undersea treasure hunting for United States coins, the saga of the SS *Central America* is an adventure to end all adventures. Its final chapters are still being written in our own time. The author's book, *A California Gold Rush History: Featuring the treasure from the S.S. Central America*, is a definitive study of the ship and the treasure and is recommended to anyone interested in the adventure and saga. In 2019, with Dwight N. Manley, I wrote a sequel, *America's Greatest Treasure Ship: The SS Central America. The Second Treasure-Finding Journey*. Accordingly, only a synopsis is given here.

In San Francisco on August 20, 1857, more than 400 people who had booked passage on the Pacific Mail Steamship Line's SS *Sonora* hastened aboard the vessel. The destination was Panama, to be followed by a train trip across the Isthmus, then a connecting passage on another ship at Aspinwall (today known as Colon) for the Atlantic run. Accompanying the passengers were over 100 bags of mail and a cargo of gold registered at over $1.2 million, consigned by nine major shippers including Wells, Fargo & Co. The ultimate destination of the travelers and cargo was New York City. In addition to over $1.2 million in gold listed on the manifest, many passengers had their own treasures, variously estimated to average from about $1,000 to $5,000 per person. When added to the commercial cargo, the total came to well over $2 million. The *Sonora* landed at Panama, and in time the passengers and cargo traveled 48 miles on the Panama Railroad to Aspinwall.

Ahead was the final leg of the trip to New York City, about 2,000 miles, taking less time than the Pacific part of the journey. On Thursday afternoon, September 3, 1857, passengers continuing from California plus others picked up at Panama were greeted at the dock at Aspinwall by Capt. William Lewis Herndon as they boarded the SS *Central America* for the passage to New York.

Once comfortably settled in their cabins and berths, the nearly 600 passengers and crew members aboard the *Central America* looked forward to their voyage, traveling at slightly over 12 miles per hour, with a scheduled stop in Havana. Matters turned for the worse as the ship headed northward. A fierce hurricane arose, the ship foundered, and by Saturday morning, September 12, there was no hope for survival. Women and children were able to escape on lifeboats to a nearby sailing ship. At eight in the evening the ship was lost, sinking 2,700 feet to the sea floor. Many passengers survived by clinging to floating debris, but most perished.

Fast forward to the twentieth century. In Columbus, Ohio, scientists Tommy Thompson, Barry Schatz, and Bob Evans became part of the Columbus-America Discovery Group, backed by regional financiers. Studies were made of newspaper accounts, sea charts, and other information. After several years of effort, the ship was found on the ocean floor, off of the coast of South Carolina. When gold was brought ashore, excitement prevailed! The scene changed, with multiple challengers claiming shares. The complex matter was finally solved in 1999, when an agreement was reached and the court awarded the finders 92.4% of the treasure and the claimants the remaining part. Dwight N. Manley and his California Gold Marketing Group wrote a check to pay off the Christie's loan and other obligations and to settle all claims. Then began a marketing program that lasted several years. The "Ship of Gold" display, featuring a replica of the side of the ship, was a sensation at several conventions. *Coin World* in 2000 called it the Story of the Year. It was not long before all coins and ingots were sold. The vast inventory of coins included these quarter eagles: 1834, 1843-O, 1845, 1846, 1846-O, 1847-O, 1850 (2), 1851 (11), 1852 (2), 1853 (3), 1854, 1855, 1856-S (8, and to the insurers 1), and 1857-S.

Only a small part of the wreck had been explored by the time the Columbus-America Discovery Group left the site in 1991—likely the safe room or purser's room—but much more remained untouched. The Common Pleas Court of Franklin County, Ohio,

Loss of the SS *Central America*, September 12, 1857.

appointed Ira Owen Kane, a prominent attorney and businessman, as the official receiver for Recovery Limited Partnership (RLP) and Columbus Exploration LLC, with James Henson also on the team. Under the direction of the court, to maximize the assets for the benefit of the investors and creditors, Kane began plans to revisit the SS *Central America* to resume recovery operations. The United States District Court of the Eastern District of Virginia confirmed RLP as the salvor in possession of the SS *Central America* in 2014. This was done under contract with Odyssey Marine Exploration, and more coins and ingots were found, a smaller quantity than on the first recovery. Bob Evans, who had been the lead scientist in the first recovery, was in charge of the second exploration as well.

These quarter eagles were included: 1834 Classic Head (4), 1835, 1836 (10), 1838 (2), 1839-D, 1842-D, 1842-O, 1843 (5), 1843-C, 1843-D (3), 1843-O (9), 1844-C, 1845 (4), 1846, 1846-D (2), 1846-O (2), 1847-C (2), 1847-D (2), 1847-O (4), 1848-C, 1849, 1850 (15), 1850-D, 1850-O (4), 1851 (53), 1851-D, 1851-O (5), 1852 (59), 1852-O (4), 1853 (41), 1854 (10), 1854-O (9), 1855, 1856 (4), 1856-O, 1856-S (70), 1857, and 1857-S (49).

William and Mary

In the early 1970s hundreds of $20 gold coins came on the market. Prominent among them were 1855-S and 1856-S coins with very lightly etched surfaces from the action of fine sand particles, otherwise appearing to be Mint State. The 1856-S pieces were the most numerous. Many of these were sold through WorldWide Coin Investments of Atlanta and were said to have been from a "sunken treasure ship off the coast of Florida." However, the principals of WorldWide, John Hamrick and Bob Harwell, did not know where the pieces had been salvaged, as they had been acquired via an intermediary. The writer handled dozens of double eagles (but no other denominations) obtained from that source. I advertised them in *Coin World* and offered them privately. They sold quickly. Their history remained a mystery with many theories.

In 2009 in *Numismatic Finds of the Americas*, John M. Kleeberg provided answers in an extensive narrative including the following information:

In the spring of 1857, $23,000 in coins was withdrawn from the Sub-Treasury in Charleston, South Carolina, to pay government troops fighting in the Third Seminole War. The money was put aboard the *William and Mary*, in the custody of Army paymaster Major Jeremiah Yellot Dashiell. At the outlet of the Indian River between Vero Beach and Fort Pierce, Dashiell took the funds with him aboard a small boat that left the *William and Mary* and headed to Fort Capron. The boat capsized, and the bag containing the coins was lost in the swirling sand.

In the spring of 1963 James Robert Gordy, age 16, and Albert N. Ashley were skin diving and fishing for crawfish on the coast at Fort Pierce. They were surprised to find a number of coins. James's father, Kenneth F. Gordy, applied to the Florida Internal Improvement Fund for the right to register the find and take possession of the coins. The State of Florida agreed and was to receive a 25% share. The finders reported in September 1964 that they had retrieved 225 silver coins and 477 gold coins since July of that summer. They did not disclose that in 1963 they had salvaged 2,682 gold coins, for a total of 3,264 for the two years.

This remained a secret until 1968, when the finders quarreled and sued each other in the Circuit Court of Saint Lucie County. Finally, on April 12, 1972, an agreement was reached whereby coins remaining at the Saint Lucie County Bank would be divided, with 45% split between the James R. Gordy and Albert N. Ashley (nothing to Gordy's father) and 45% going to the State of Florida. Of these coins, 114 were sold to WorldWide Coins for $101 each on or about June 23, 1972, per the scenario described above. Remaining by that time were 195 gold coins, including these few quarter eagles: 1843-O, 1851-O, 1852, 1854 (2), 1855, and 1856.

Details concerning the complete finds of 1963 and 1964 are unavailable. John Kleeberg learned this regarding the quarter eagles: 787 were found and 137 reported to the state, with dates ranging from 1834 to 1856. It is likely that some lightly etched quarter eagles on the market are from this source.

Gold Hidden in a Baltimore Cellar

On August 31, 1934, two young boys, described as poor and underprivileged, were playing in the cellar of a house at 132 South Eden Street, East Baltimore, owned by sisters Elizabeth H. French and Mary P.B. Findlay and rented by the mother of one of the boys.[1] Henry Grob, age 15, and his companion, Theodore Sines, 14, came upon a cache of gold coins. After a brief discussion as to what should be done, the lads took the treasure to the local police station and turned the find over to the authorities. Later that evening, the boys said that they had "held out" some of the pieces, and these were subsequently added to the first group. One *Baltimore Evening Sun* article put the amount as 3,556 coins with $11,424 face value. All were dated before 1857.

Multiple claims were filed for ownership. For the rest of 1934 and into May 1935 the matter was in the courts. Judge Eugene O'Dunne of the Second Circuit Court of Baltimore eventually awarded proceeds from the entire find to the two teenagers, negating an offer by the two ladies who owned the house to give the boys 50%. During the litigation, all parties agreed that the coins could be sold at auction.[2] The sale was held on May 2, 1935, at the Lord Baltimore Hotel downtown, with Perry W. Fuller serving as auctioneer. About 100 attended, including a few out-of-town dealers and many local curiosity seekers. The major buyer was Thomas L. Elder, who came from New York City. Grouped into 438 lots and casually described (most pieces were simply called "very fine") in a printed catalog, the hoard realized $19,746.15.

Leonard Augsburger, author of *Treasure in the Cellar*, a book about the find, created an inventory that included these $2.50 gold coins: 1834 Classic Head (2), 1836 (5), 1839-D, 1843, 1843-O (4), 1843-C, 1845 (2), 1847-O, 1848-D, 1850 (3), 1851 (5), 1852 (11), 1853 (14), 1854 (7), 1855 (3), and 1856 (4).

The Merkers Kaiseroda Mine Treasure

During World War II, under orders from Nazi leadership, primarily Hermann Goering and Heinrich Himmler, conquered people and nations were systematically stripped of art, gold, and other valuables.[3] On April 4, 1945, the Third Army, 90th Infantry Division took the village of Merkers, a few miles inside the border in Thuringia, Germany.

Stolen treasure in the Kaiseroda Mine.

On the morning of the sixth, Pfc. Clyde Harmon and Pfc. Anthony Kline, U.S. military policemen, stopped two women on a road outside Merkers. Since both were French displaced persons and one was pregnant, the MPs decided rather than to arrest them, to escort them back into the town. On the way, as they passed the entrance to the *Kaiseroda* salt mine in Merkers, the women talked about gold that the Germans had stored in the mine—so much gold, they said, it had taken the local civilians and displaced persons who were used as labor seventy-two hours to unload it.[4]

When American soldiers entered the Kaiseroda mine, they discovered a room 75 feet wide and 150 feet deep. The floor was covered with more than 7,000 numbered bags. Each bag contained gold bars or gold coins. The gold amounted to nearly 250 tons. Paper money was in bales and amounted to 98 million French francs and 2.7 billion Reichsmarks. Suitcases contained jewelry, dental fillings, and other valuables stolen from individuals. In other mine passages were 400 tons of fine artwork stolen from museums and individuals throughout Europe.

Analysis of the inventory committee records and reports by Roger W. Burdette revealed that United States gold coins were contained in 738 bags. This amounted to 1,022,919.67 troy ounces of fine gold, or 1,136,577.41 troy ounces of standard 0.900 fine coin gold, representing approximately $21,145,630 at face value. Further analysis broke down the U.S. gold coins by denomination and showed that most of the coins were double eagles. No determination of dates or mintmarks was possible, since this information was not recorded during inventory.

The quantities of U.S. gold coins in the hoard included 12,714 quarter eagles.

A Society Lady's Security

In early 1933 the United States government placed stringent restrictions on the ownership of American gold coins.[5] Hearing rumors to this effect, a prominent Eastern lady, possibly with the cooperation of her mother, decided to acquire and set aside some pieces for the comfort and financial security they seemed to represent in that troubled economic time.

Years later her heirs enlisted numismatist David Enders Tripp to assist with their sale into the numismatic market. This was a valuable informational find for scholars, as it shows typical gold coins that could be acquired at banks in early 1933. The earlier-dated coins were for the most part worn, while some of the later pieces were gem Mint State. The following quarter eagles were included:

1843-O (2), 1845, 1845-O (2), 1846-O (2), 1847-O (2), 1850 (4), 1851 (7), 1852 (14), 1852-O (2), 1853 (19), 1854 (7), 1854-O (2), 1855 (2), 1856 (8), 1857, 1857-S, 1859, 1859-S, 1861 (15), 1862, 1871-S (2), 1873 (12), 1878 (21), 1878-S (8), 1879 (13), 1879-S (3), 1879 (13), 1879-S (3), 1887 (2), 1890 (4), 1893 (2), 1895, 1896 (2), 1897 (2), 1898 (3), 1899 (6), 1900 (12), 1901 (22), 1902 (23), 1903 (48), 1904 (43), 1905 (56), 1906 (56), 1907 (88), and 1908 (51).

COINS FOUND IN MONTANA

In 1975 Wayne Miller was a fledgling in the coin business in Helena, Montana.[6] He would become well known in the field, particularly so with his landmark *Analysis of Morgan and Peace Dollars*, released in 1976, followed by *The Morgan and Peace Dollar Textbook*, published in 1982. As to a treasure, he relates the story:

> I received a telephone call from a couple who had some coins for sale. They invited me to their home in the Helena Valley. As I parked my car I noticed a most unusual dog houseit consisted of three bales of hay! The husband was an ex-Marine in Army fatigues, over six feet tall. His wife was Chinese and at least a foot shorter. . . . The wife said that for many years her family would put extra money into a jar. What I was looking at was pocket change from 1916 to 1948. No one in the family was numismatically knowledgeable; no effort was made to find or save anything rare, or unusual . . . My generous offer for their 1,500 coins delighted them. They thought that the most they would be able to get would be twice their face value!
>
> About six months later the couple brought in their gold coins. Included were about 20 $20 double eagles, 50 $10 pieces, 90 $5 coins, and 200 $2.50 pieces. Most of these were quite nice. There were also about 100 gold dollars, but most had been damaged or used as jewelry, including about 30 that had been holed and put on a chain. The gold coins realized another $15,000 for the owners. Of course, the coins were worth a lot less in 1975 than they would be today . . . I waited for the next call. But I never saw either of them again. Too bad—I had come to expect the unexpected from this unusual couple.

APPENDIX C

$2.50 Gold Coins in the News

The following is a selection of news articles featuring or mentioning quarter eagles over a long period of time. Included are accounts of counterfeiting. Lightly edited and excerpted. Headlines are those originally used.

Quarter Eagles in Circulation

August 20, 1834, *Evening Post* (New York City). The new Classic Head coins had been authorized by the Act of June 28, 1834:

> **Quarter Eagles**
>
> The half eagles are circulating extensively, and are eagerly sought after and received by all classes. There is not, we verily believe, a word of truth in any of the stories got up by the mercenary tools of the bank in relation to the coinage.
>
> Our correspondents are inquiring for quarter eagles. They ask us why coin of this denomination is not issued. All we have been able to discover is, that, as we are informed, the die sinker of the mint has been industriously employed upon the dies, but without being able yet to complete the quarter eagle die. It is again demanded by the public why, if one artist cannot do the necessary business in time, another is not immediately employed? We are unable to give a satisfactory reply.—*Philad. Paper.*

September 25, 1834, *Macon* (Georgia) *Weekly Telegraph*. The new coins had reached circulation:

> **Quarter Eagles**
>
> This beautiful coin, fresh from the mint, made its appearance among us some days since. It will constitute the most important, and far the most convenient part of our circulating medium. We have been fortunate enough to get hold of some dozen of them, and any bank partisan who *really* wishes a sight of them, and who will call on us, and promise not to get into a *furious* passion, shall be gratified. *Delaware Watchman.*

September 26, 1834, *Gloucester* (Massachusetts) *Democrat*:

Gold Quarter Eagles

We have been much gratified to see some of the new gold quarter eagles, in this city yesterday. They are broader than the old ones, and hence more convenient—and are well calculated, in their flight over land, to carry terror and panic into the hearts of the Bank editors and Bank partisans—while their yellow harvest and solid worth, will cheer and delight the honest farmer and mechanic. *Globe.*

October 10, 1834, *Painesville* (Ohio) *Telegraph*, exchange item, taking issue with the Jackson administration's financial policies:

The Gold Humbug

The *Washington Globe* expresses its gratification at *seeing* some of the new gold quarter Eagles in that city, and observes in relation to them, that "They are broader than the old one, and hence more convenient, and are well calculated, in their flight over the land, to carry panic and terror into the hearts of the Bank editors and bank partisans; while their yellow harvest hue and solid worth will cheer with delight the honest farmer and mechanic."

This is a fair specimen of the *fustian* with which the Jackson papers throughout the country regale their readers on the subject of the new gold coin. From a perusal of their papers one would be led to believe that gold was to be had in abundance for the mere asking, and without an equivalent being required for it. Now the truth is, that so very few of these new quarter eagles "in their flight over the land" have found a resting place in this section of the Union, we should be inclined to doubt their existence altogether if we did not occasionally hear of one being seen perched on the finger of some lucky office-holder, who exhibited it as a decoy to catch the gulls of the party.

A person from this county called at the Commonwealth Bank, one of the Government pets in Boston, a few days since, to obtain the money due on several pension certificates. His request for a little gold could not be granted! The Administration, which we are told has created such a profusion of gold that it "flows upon the Mississippi in a stream," could not spare the poor Revolutionary pensioner a few quarter eagles, the "yellow harvest hue" of which would have "cheered with delight" the war worn veteran, and caused him to thank his stars that he had been spared to witness the return of the "golden age!!"

Of all the *humbugs* invented by the Jackson party to delude the people, and sustain themselves in power, this golden humbug is certainly the most ridiculous. The idea of the General Government attempting to introduce a hard money currency to the exclusion of paper is perfectly absurd, so long as each of the 24 states of the Union can establish Banks and create paper money to an unlimited extent without asking leave of Congress.

Notwithstanding the golden streams that flow in other parts of the country, about which we *learn* so much, it is certain that but little of the new coin is found in this state—excepting in the columns of the Jackson papers. A small supply may be expected previous to the election in November The *panic* and *terror* it will *carry into the hearts* of the Whigs will no doubt be pro-di-gious!

April 18, 1840, *Alexandria* (Virginia) *Gazette*:

Thirty Dollars Reward

Was left in the Water Closet, on board the Steamboat Phoenix, on Thursday afternoon, the 16th instant, during her last trip from Washington, a small SILK PURSE, with a small steel clasp, (broke.) It was tied with small linen string, and contained one hundred and sixty-two and a half dollars in gold, consisting of 30 half eagles, 3 quarter eagles, and 1 guinea. The finder will confer a great favor, and receive the above reward, by leaving it with Capt. Wilson, of the Steamboat Phoenix. The loser thinks it probably that he came out previous to the boat's leaving the wharf at Washington.

December 14, 1866, *Manitowoc* (Wisconsin) *Pilot*:

Treasure Trove

A Rich Deposit in a Bank of Earth—A Cairo dispatch tells the following story:

In the washed banks of a ravine, which juts into the Mississippi river a few miles below Wolf Island, there was, a few days ago, discovered by a Missouri hunter, a keg which the finder at first regarded as a keg of powder, but, on attempting to remove it from its resting place, he found it defied his efforts. He thereupon employed a hatchet which he carried in his belt, and dashing the head of the keg, was both astonished and gratified at a shower of gold and silver coin that fell with a musical jingle all around him. The keg contained $30,000 in eagles, $650 in half eagles, $350 in quarter eagles and $170 in silver. There was nothing in or on the keg to indicate who buried it there, or when it was buried. From appearance, however, it is believed that it was placed there at the outbreak of the rebellion.

December 12, 1916, *Los Angeles Times*:

Chrismastide "Gold Rush" On

NEW YORK, Dec. 11 (AP)—Wall street's annual "gold rush" has begun.

Stacks of gold pieces in the $2.50, $5, $10 and $20 denominations are now leaving the vaults of the New York Federal Reserve Bank by the truckload, bound for country and city banks which will supply the stream of gold coins that pour into Christmas stockings and gift envelopes.

Every year at this time the New York and other Federal Reserve banks have watched a growing flood of gold pieces pour forth, and then suddenly, after the holidays, pour back and become a part of the bank reserves until another Christmas rolls around.

Officials at the Chase National Bank estimate that between $80,000,000 and $90,000,000 in gold coins will be withdrawn from the banks of the country this year, probably setting a new high record. Last year it was estimated that $75,000,000 in gold was put into circulation at this time. In New York alone, it is expected that between $15,000,000 and $20,000,000 will be distributed this year.

For the first time in years the United States Treasury has minted a limited amount of new $2.50 gold pieces as its contribution to the holiday movement. In former years the demand for these coins was so great that the commanded a premium of 25 and 50 cents. They are rarely seen in circulation except around the holiday season. Despite the addition of newly minted gold, the New York Federal

Reserve Bank has less than 100,000 of these "quarter eagles" available to meet the demand of the banks in this district and will be obliged to make allotments in order to insure their equitable distribution.

The peak of the public demand for gold coins will be reached in the three days immediately preceding Christmas, when tellers in the banks of the country will be kept busy passing them out, along with other money in the form of Christmas bonuses. Most of the gold, as well as the currency, will be returned by the middle of January, but bank officials have noted that the number of coins coming back is always smaller and that only a few of the quarter eagles get back into circulation. Even the savings banks, which are the first banking destination of many Christmas gold pieces, handle few of the $2.50 pieces. . . .

April 15, 1933, *Register-Republic* (Rockford, Illinois):

Quarter eagles had the queer faculty of disappearing. Each year banks would put in great stocks of them for men and women who wished to give gold for Christmas—gold in minimum quantity. Bright young nephews and nieces with shining faces would receive them with thanks. And that would be the end of the quarter eagles. The banks would never get them back. Where they went, no one knows. Disappearing quarter eagles is one of the minor mysteries of American economics. . . .

NOT MADE AT THE MINT!

April 5, 1816, *Susquehanna Democrat* (Wilkes-Barre, Pennsylvania):

American Eagle Debased!

Counterfeit pieces in imitation of quarter eagles, having got into circulation, it would be well for the public to be ware. They are larger than the real ones, and are dated 1803.[1]

May 30, 1843, (Bennington) *Vermont Gazette*:

Beware of Counterfeits

A large number of counterfeit Mexican dollars and American quarter eagles have been seized by the Police, and it is feared that more of this currency is afloat. The Mexican dollars are well executed, (the die being perfect.) but may be detected by the peculiar greasy feeling that distinguishes counterfeit coin. The quarter eagles are of too light weight to deceive any one accustomed to handle the genuine mint drops.

September 26, 1843, *Hampshire Gazette* (Northampton, Massachusetts):

Counterfeit Coin

Twenty-five and ten cent pieces, gilded over by a new process, are in circulation as half and quarter eagles.

June 25, 1844, *Times-Picayune* (New Orleans):

We hear that there is a considerable quantity of counterfeit money in circulation, imitations of the quarter eagles coined at Dahlonega, Ga. The coiner of that mint has given a description of one piece submitted to him, which we copy for the benefit of those dealing in gold. The counterfeits are, of course, considerably underweight.

This piece purported to be struck at the mint in this place in 1843, the date was evidently made twice on the die; the first, being too much to the right, was defaced, and the second punched in on the erasure, which gave an indistinctness to the figures; the impression on both sides had the appearance of being rounded, as the dies had been made by casting, or by some other process, from a correct coin, the beaded and blank borders were equal to the coin struck at the mint; the milling on the edge was defective, and appeared as though the lines were nearly filled up; each quarter eagle issued from the mint contains sixty-four and a half grains, but this piece was found to weigh only forty and a half grains; on cutting the edge with a knife, and applying acid, it was shown to be composed of brass, (a composition of zinc and copper) and gilt either by the electro-galvanic process, or by the ordinary modes of gilding, as the acid would not affect any part but where the surface was removed; the appearance as to color was tolerably good, sufficiently so to pass readily along with genuine coin that are a little worn.

July 9, 1844, *Centinel of Freedom* (Newark, New Jersey):

Counterfeit Gold Coin

The coiner at the mint at Dahlonega cautions the public against counterfeit quarter eagles which are in circulation. They purport to have been struck at the mint in that place in 1843.

Each quarter eagle issued from the mint contains sixty-four and a half grains, but these are found to weigh only forth and a half grains. On cutting their edge with a knife and applying acid, they were shown to be composed of brass (composition of zinc and copper) and gilded either by the electro galvanic process, or by the ordinary modes of gilding, as the acid would not affect any part but where the surface was removed. The appearance as to color was tolerably good.

March 16, 1847, *Portland* (Maine) *Weekly Advertiser*:

Counterfeit Coin

A systematic attempt seems to have been made within a few days past, both in this city and the neighboring towns, to pass the new emission of counterfeit quarter eagles. Several were passed in Charlestown yesterday, and one or two in this city. In one case, however, the counterfeit was detected as soon as offered, but before the guilty party could be secured, he has left the store, at the very top of his speed. From the miserable execution of the counterfeit, and the difference in its weight as compared with the genuine, it would seem difficult for anyone who had the least experience, to be deceived by it. *Boston Traveller, 12th.*

August 30, 1847, *Philadelphia Inquirer*:

A new emission of counterfeit quarter eagles is 'about.' Their date is 1844, and their execution is so good that they have even been received in banks.

January 25, 1848, *Easton* (Maryland) *Star*:

Counterfeits

The *New York Tribune* says: One of the most ingenious counterfeits we have ever seen has just been discovered. It purports to be a quarter eagle of the N. Orleans

Mint, dated 1843. It is of full weight and good color, and was pronounced genuine by the best judges of specie in Wall Street. It was sent to the Philadelphia Mint for examination, and after being subjected to the usual tests it was there also pronounced a genuine quarter-eagle. Exposed to a powerful microscope, not the slightest difference could be discovered between it and a genuine coin of the New Orleans Mint, except that the edge was slightly more rounded, which might have been occasioned by wear. Upon being sawn in two, however, it was discovered to be a mere shell of gold, the interior being filled with silver. The gold was worth $1.25, leaving a good profit to the maker.

Suspicion was excited in regard to this piece by its ring, which was peculiar; but other quarter-eagles which were genuine were found to possess the same peculiarity. So perfect a *fac simile* is this counterfeit that it would seem that there is no safety in receiving gold coin unless each piece is tried with the file—all other tests fail against this fraud. We understand that a half eagle of the same character has been received at the Philadelphia Mint from the New Orleans Mint, and that eagles have been detected which have been *sweated* so as to be worth but $9. The discovery of the above counterfeits has created a considerable excitement among the banks and specie dealers, as no one knows how much of the false coin is stowed away in his bags.

February 10, 1848, *Boston Evening Transcript*:

Counterfeit Gold Coins

The direction of the United States Mint, in a letter to the superintendent of the branch mint at New Orleans, speaks of the counterfeit half and quarter eagles, which have been detected in circulation, as "remarkable and dangerous imitations of the true coin." He says none of the original dies can have been used by the counterfeiters, and it must therefore be supposed, either that they have the services of a most skillful engraver, or have possessed themselves of a dangerous process, recently discovered in England, for making very perfect dies of cast iron, which are *fac similes* of the original medal or coin.

May 29, 1849, *Portland* (Maine) *Weekly Advertiser*:

A Counterfeiter Arrested

This morning, a dentist of this city, Joshua R. Russell, was arrested for passing counterfeit quarter eagles, in different stores in this city. Upon being arrested, there was found at his office, fifteen dollars of counterfeit paper money—consisting of two 5's on the Connecticut River Bank, and a 3 and a 2 on another bank—very badly executed; also several counterfeit gold pieces, and a case of gold pencils, probably stolen. He was arrested by officers Fuller and E.L. Shed. The dentist fought like a tiger, but was finally taken to jail, to be examined this afternoon. *Lowell Courier, 18th.*

November 17, 1849, *Sandusky* (Ohio) *Register*:

A Counterfeiter Caught

A fellow residing in Norwalk by the name of Nelson Recktor from some circumstances became suspected of counterfeiting by the U.S. marshal, Mr. G.A. Jones of

Mt. Vernon. To make assurance doubly sure, the marshal disguised himself, pretending to be a blackleg, and thus won the confidence of Recktor, who showed him his dies, his press, his galvanic apparatus, and quantities of bogus. The marshal purchased some four or five hundred dollars of half and quarter eagles of him, for the purpose of making the thing sure.

Recktor in some of his confidential revelations implicated a half brother of his, named Ellis, and night before last both of the scamps were arrested in a ball-room in Norwalk, where they were "tripping the light fantastic toe," and to-day leave for a boarding house in Columbus, where they are lodged at the expense of the state. We understand that this Recktor has been for a long time very flush of money without any visible means of support. He would make his bogus of some base metal and gild them by a galvanic process, thus making a very dangerous counterfeit.

November 30, 1849, *Norfolk* (Dedham, Massachusetts) *Democrat*:

Counterfeiters Caught

Two men, who had lived for some months in a very retired way near Norwalk, Huron County, (Ohio.) were recently surprised by the police, and found to be pretty extensive manufacturers of counterfeit coin. They had dies and machinery for the production of eagles, half and quarter eagles, and silver coin. Three gangs of counterfeiters have, within a month past, been broken up in Ohio, in the same manner.

December 19, 1849, *Alexandria* (Virginia) *Gazette*:

The *New Orleans Picayune* states that $337.50 in counterfeit quarter eagles were found recently on a trader in that city, who, however, cleared himself by proving that he had received them in good faith. They were sent to the Branch Mint and found to be made of the kind of brass called Prince Rupert's metal—a bright colored alloy consisting of two parts of zinc to one of copper.

February 26, 1851, *Daily Missouri Republican* (St. Louis):

Arrest of Counterfeiters

Two men, calling themselves William Baker and George Ferguson, were arrested at Port Deposit, on the 7th instant, on the charge of passing counterfeit gold coin. They were fully committed by Justice Orr, and lodged in the Elkton jail the same night by office Stephenson. Two hundred and forty dollars, in half eagles and quarter-eagles, dated 1843, were found upon them. They stated they were from Philadelphia- one was about 25 years of age, the other about 40.

March 13, 1851, *Republic* (Washington D.C.):

A New Kind of Bell-Metal

The Boston *Journal* states that, some three or four years since, two young men were convicted, in the municipal court, and sentenced to the State prison, for passing counterfeit quarter eagles. After serving a portion of their sentence they were pardoned, and ever since have, so far as is known, been good citizens. While under arrest they disclosed to Mr. Gustavus Andrews, keeper of Suffolk jail, a spot where a large number of the counterfeit coins were deposited, and which were subsequently recovered by Mr. Andrews, and, in due time, Mr. Andrews delivered the "bogus" to the sheriff of the county.

After the conviction and sentence of the two young men, and supposing that the "bogus" might contain a small portion of gold, the district attorney suggested that the Commonwealth should have the benefit of it. Accordingly, it was agreed that it should be tested, and, upon a given day, it was delivered to Mr. Newell Harding, the well-known silversmith in Court Square, who melted it, and run it into a solid bar. The bar was then placed in the hands of an experienced chemist, who fully tested it, and found that *gold was not* one of its component parts. The bar, and the result of the test, were returned to the sheriff, together with a bill from the chemist of $2.50 for services rendered.

Finding that the "bogus bar" was likely to remain to the end of time wholly useless, Mr. Andrews applied for and received it. The idea struck him that a "dinner bell" would be of service at the new jail, which was now nearly ready for occupancy; and he accordingly took the bar to a foundry, where a small portion of "bell metal" was added to it, and the whole cast into a large-sized "dinner bell," the tone of which is far superior to that of many which are in daily use in the city. For the purpose of giving the origin of the "fine-toned bell," which had had thus procured, to posterity, Mr. Andrews caused the following inscription to be engraved upon it, viz:

"Manufactured from 660 counterfeit quarter eagles, February 19, 1851. Gustavus Andrews, Boston."

The bell is now among the many curiosities in Mr. Andrew's collection, at the jail office.

January 27, 1852, *Easton* (Maryland) *Star*:

Counterfeit Gold Coin

Counterfeit quarter eagles are in circulation in Savannah. The piece is described as being composed of some hard metal which has the color and ring of silver, but is easily distinguished by its glossy brightness. It has been cast in a mould and has the milled edge. It may be easily detected by the roundness of its imprint, and the oily feeling which it has when pressed between the fingers. It purports to be of the coinage of 1847.

November 23, 1852, *State Gazette* (Trenton, New Jersey):

Another Charge of Counterfeiting

Isaiah O. Eakins and Mary Ann Eakins, his wife, were on Saturday brought before Charles F. Heazlitt, Esq., U.S. Commissioner, charged with making and passing counterfeit gold coins of the United States, in the similitude of quarter eagles. From the testimony, it seems that the defendants visited a man, named Ferdinand Vollyers, and showed a sample of spurious quarter eagles, which they could sell at $30 for a $100. The husband paid the first visit, and left one as a sample. The next day the wife came and left another as a sample, and pressed him to purchase. He refused, but made an arrangement to meet her the next night at Franklin Square and Seventh Street. He met her and was shown several hundred of these pieces. He did not purchase, but discovered that the defendants lived in Pegg Street, in the Northern Liberties. Witness then took the two sample pieces to Lieut. Carpenter, of the Northern Liberty Watch, who arrested both the defendants. Isaiah Eakins also showed the witness a counterfeit Mexican dollar, and told him he could sell him a keg of silver, and said they had sent a number of barrels of it to Texas and Mexico. The defendants admitted to the witness that the quarter eagles were counterfeit, and said that they knew men who had made a fortune passing such coin. Another witness was examined, who testified that Isaiah wanted to sell him some of the coin. The defendants were held in $3000 each to answer the charge of making and passing, at the present term of the Court. J.G. Michener, Esq., appeared for the defendants, and R.P. Kane, Esq. for the United States. *Ledger.*

August 11, 1853, *Daily Republic* (Washington, D.C.):

"Stuttering" Johnson, the Counterfeiter

The examination of Joseph H. Johnson, whose arrest in New York we noticed, and in whose possession about $2,000 in counterfeit bills of the denomination if $5, on the Fallkill Bank, Poughkeepsie, New York, and $1,000 in counterfeit gold eagles, half-eagles and quarter-eagles were found, was taken on Saturday before Justice Bogart. The prisoner stated that he was a native of Pennsylvania, a tailor by trade, and was not guilty of any crime; that he had been sent on from Philadelphia to trap some parties who were here engaged in passing the money, and that the money found upon him was sent to him to enable him to find out the counterfeiters, and that he should have found them but that he himself was trapped. The magistrate did not believe his story, and locked him up for trial. In addition to the above charge, the United States marshal has issued a warrant charging him with counterfeiting United States coin. *Philadelphia Register.*

November 7, 1854, *Centinel of Freedom* (Newark, New Jersey):

A large amount of counterfeit quarter eagles are in circulation, and so well executed as to deceive any one. They are made from a genuine New Orleans Mint die, stolen some years since, and bear the "O" under the talons of the eagle. Prof. John Torrey, assayer, has analyzed the coin, and finds that it is made of a casing of pure gold, filled with silver, and probably with platina, to increase the weight. The weight is 60 5–10 grains, which is only four grains light, and the coating of gold weighs 80 1–10 grains. It is therefore worth $1.17 in gold, and 8 cents in silver, or $1.25 in raw material, besides the labor of making.

November 9, 1854, (Hannibal) *Missouri Courier*:

Counterfeit Quarter Eagles

Two counterfeit quarter eagles have recently been taken at the New York Post Office. They are thus described by the *Journal of Commerce*:

"It is made from a genuine New Orleans Mint die, stolen some years since, and bearing the 'O' under the talons of the eagle. Professor John Torry, assayer here, has analyzed the coin, and finds that it is made of a casing of pure gold, filled with silver, and probably with platina, to increase the weight. The weight is 60 5–10 grains, which is only four grains light, and the coating of gold weights 30 1–10 grains. It is therefore worth $1.17 in gold, and eight cents in silver, or $1.25 in raw material, besides the labor of making. The maker and vendor could not, therefore, realize more than $1 each, which would seem too small profit, except, that the counterfeit is so well done that there is but little risk of detection.

September 5, 1855, *Albany* (New York) *Evening Journal*:

Great Haul of Counterfeit Money

Yesterday we noticed the arrest of a man named John Rhodes, on a charge of burglary and grand larceny. Since then we have learned some facts in relation to his arrest, which prove him a fit candidate for State Prison. This forenoon he was brought before Judge Parmelee, at the Court of Session, and plead guilty to the charge—which is, of robbing a store in the town of Berlin several months ago. He seems to have acted thus at the advice of his friends, in order to keep out of the clutches of officers who have been on his track for some time past for counterfeiting. Rhodes is a married man and resided in Berlin, where he has a wife and two children.

Officers Kipp and Phillips (after he was committed to jail) immediately repaired to the house of Rhodes, and while searching for counterfeit coin, finally discovered about $1,000 in spurious dollars and quarter eagles in a shot bag concealed in a trunk, which they took possession of. Thus by pleading guilty to a charge on which he was indicted some time ago, he will probably escape with a lighter punishment than is arrested for counterfeiting. His sentence has been suspended for the present. *Troy Budget.*

October 25, 1856, *Alexandria* (Virginia) *Gazette*:

Dangerous Counterfeits

There seems to be circulating in the city at present, a considerable quantity of counterfeit gold coin purporting to be quarter and half eagles. Two of the latter were received yesterday by a gentleman at the cattle show grounds in exchange for a Virginia bank bill. Both are dated 1851, and exceedingly well executed; although being lighter and softer to the touch than the genuine coin, are easily distinguished by the careful observer. Quarter eagles of a base issue have also been received during the week by two retail houses on Baltimore street. There is evidently in the city a party from the eastern cities engaged in passing off bogus coin during the exciting scenes of the cattle show week. *Balt. Sun.*

October 2, 1857, *New Albany* (Indiana) *Daily Ledger*:

Samuel Sheeley, a wealthy and well known farmer of Hamilton County, Ohio, was arrested on Tuesday evening on a charge of counterfeiting. Six bogus quarter eagles and two $20 counterfeit notes were found in his possession. He endeavored to bribe the officer who arrested him, but was handcuffed and taken to the Cincinnati jail. He has a large family.

September 7, 1858, *Portland* (Maine) *Weekly Advertiser*:

Look Out For Them

Counterfeit quarter eagles, extremely well executed, and likely to deceive even good judges of money, are in circulation. They have none of the greasy feeling which is the usual characteristic of base coin, and the only way to which they can be detected is through the brittleness of their material. By throwing them down smartly they will shiver like glass.

July 11, 1859, *Philadelphia Inquirer*:

A Postmaster Charged with Counterfeiting

A great deal of excitement has been created in New Brighton, by the arrest of Mr. J. Glass, Postmaster at that place, on a charge of counterfeiting. United States Marshal Campbell was led to suspect that Glass dealt in counterfeit money, and he accordingly lost no time in making arrangement for ascertaining whether a report so prejudicial to the character of the accused, was correct. The person so instructed played his role to admiration. Part of the money which was received from Glass was found to be counterfeit, and the Marshal's suspicions being now almost reduced to absolute conviction, he visited New Brighton with his deputies and arrested the prisoner.

His house was subsequently searched, and several bogus "quarters," "halves," gold dollars, quarter eagles, and half eagles, found secreted in the different rooms. Two hundred dollars in counterfeit bank bills were also found in his house. It was made up of notes on the Chemung and York County Banks, N.Y., so well executed that a person familiar with bills of this character only would be likely to detect them. Glass was brought to the city last evening, and taken before U.S. Commissioner Bailey for examination. He waived a hearing, however, and was discharged on $1500 bail for his appearance at Court. Previous to his arrest, Mr. Glass bore an excellent character abroad, and stood high in the estimation of the community. He is a married man, and is possessed of a large amount of property.

For some time back officer Hackett of Ravenna has been very active in picking up counterfeiters. From certain papers, which fell into his possession, he was led to believe that Glass was connected with a gang of Ohio counterfeiters, whose capture he was instrumental in effecting; so determined to satisfy himself of the fact, he came to New Brighton and laid his plans for acquiring the information he desired. Calling on Glass, he purchased five dollars' worth postage stamps, and received in change, a small amount of bogus. So the matter came as described above. *Pittsburg Evening Chronicle.*

October 22, 1859, *Public Ledger* (Philadelphia):

Charge of Conspiracy

Yesterday, Henry Moulton was before Recorder Enue, on the charge of conspiracy to defraud. It was alleged that Moulton represented to the prosecutor that he would furnish him with four hundred dollars in counterfeit quarter eagles, for two hundred dollars, the counterfeits to be of such a character that it would be impossible to detect them. As a specimen of the counterfeits a genuine quarter eagle was shown. The two hundred dollars were paid, but the pretended counterfeits were not furnished. Moulton was held to answer. The prosecutor does not seem to care about his part in the transaction being known.

June 27, 1860, *Nevada* (California) *Democrat*:

A Gang of Counterfeiters Arrested

A dispatch from San Andreas says that Constable Denning, while executing a search warrant for stolen goods, on the 26th inst., in a cabin about half a mile from that place, made a discovery of moulds, metal, and unfinished counterfeit coin. The officers succeeded in arresting nine of the parties concerned. The counterfeits are eagles, half eagles, quarter eagles, half dollars and quarters. The dies of the quarters and quarter eagles were found, and also a quantity of tin, acids, etc.—almost a whole laboratory. It is stated that under Sheriff Thorn had been aware of the proceedings of the gang for some time, and was only waiting for further developments to make a descent upon them. It is regretted that the exposition was made so soon, as there were others residing in different parts of the county who might also have been arrested. The names of those arrested are, Thomas Gants, S.E. Tilton, J.J. Holmes, L. Wendell, J. Smallwood, and three others. One of them wishes to turn State's evidence.

July 21, 1860, *Columbian Register* (New Haven, Connecticut), exchange from the *Journal of Commerce*:

Counterfeit Coins

The whole country is flooded with counterfeits of gold and silver coin, and unless something is done to arrest the growing evil, the rogues will have it all their own way. Formerly a pair of scales and a bottle of nitric acid were all that was necessary to enable any receiver of money to detect the bogus coin, while an expert would separate the genuine from the counterfeit by the very touch and ring of the piece. Science and skill have changed all that; and now the experts are themselves at fault, while the common people are altogether at the mercy of the manufacturer of bogus coin.

Up to a recent period the most dangerous fraud in circulation was made from a genuine die, fitted to strike quarter eagles from the mint at New Orleans. It bore the date of 1854, if we remember rightly; and the pieces were made of composition metal handsomely plated, and coined in this stolen die. That was followed by the practice of splitting the gold dollar, taking out about sixty cents of its value, and soldering the shell together again. Then came the sawing into the edge of a piece, generally a half or quarter eagle, cutting two-thirds of the way through, and afterward filling up the coin, re-milling and gilding the edge. The latest and most skillful of these frauds is perpetrated, as far as detected chiefly with the eagle. The piece is split into three parts, or at least the two outside shells containing the impression are separated from the centre. The latter is forfeited to the operator and its place supplied by a filling of platina to which the outsides are fastened, the edges being re-milled and handsomely plated. This is so well done, that very few experts, outside of the two accomplished testers of coin employed at the office of the Assistant Treasurer, can detect the cheat.

The ten dollar piece under this management loses about $5.50 of its gold, and remains equally good for general circulation. The fact that this is done at all, is proof that it is carried on upon a large scale; for the exquisitely fine machinery and the skill and science necessary to success, could not be profitably employed except in the conduct of an extensive business. The pieces are full weight, and except through the wonderful instinct of here and there a rare expert, they cannot be detected, as they answer all tests that do not involve the breaking or cutting of the coin. There must be, at this moment a large number of them on deposit in our banks, and in almost every bag of coins one or more of these, or other similar frauds, may be discovered, while the number of bad pieces offered at the Sub-Treasury has sometimes amounted to fifty or sixty dollars in a single package of five thousand. . . .

April 25, 1862, *San Francisco Bulletin*:

Look Out for the Bogus Quarter Eagles

A bogus quarter eagle has been shown us which looks so like the genuine that it was accepted at one of our banks without suspicion until a second handling. It bears date of 1847, is lighter yellow color than most of our San Francisco coinage, and is sufficiently well executed to deceive unless narrowly examined. Closer scrutiny shows the lines not so distinct and clear as in the genuine, and the first S in "States" of the legend is badly formed. Weighed, its lightness would detect it. A sharp acid discovers that the coin is silver, thinly coated with gold, probably by the electrotype process. As it lacks the "S" under the eagle which our branch mint stamps, it was doubtless made in the East, to imitate a Philadelphia coin. There is so little bogus money in this country that a bad coin may travel through scores of honest hands before it is stopped. Look out for bogus quarter eagles, then, and be sure that they have the true ring. The gentleman who finds himself stuck with this silver quarter-eagles received it from a Chinaman.

July 14, 1875, *Weekly Republican* (Scranton, Pennsylvania):

Capture of Counterfeiters in California

The Treasury Secret Service division at Washington, has received information of the arrest at Oroville, California, of Motroni Sebastiano and Augustine Buszzi, two members of the notorious Marysville gang of counterfeiters. These men were in Oroville during the session of the Democratic convention, and took advantage of the crowded condition of the saloons to pass bogus quarter eagles. They disposed of ten before arousing suspicion, and when a local officer apprehended Sebastiano only one piece was found in his possession.

An operative of the Secret Service, after a diligent search, discovered Buszzi asleep at 4 o'clock in the morning under a tree. A search of his pockets brought to light fifteen base quarter eagles. The prisoners were taken to Marysville, near which town the manufactory was located. It was a one story and a half frame structure, facing a slough which runs into the Feather river and close to a dense swamp. In this house were found fifty unfinished quarter eagles, just as they had left the moulds, a quantity of used and unused crucibles, ladles and bottles of various acids, etc. The two men were taken to San Francisco, and after a preliminary examination before U.S. Commissioner Obeirne, were committed in default of bail for trial.

December 1, 1879, *Government Counterfeit Detector* (Philadelphia):

Quarter Eagle

Authorized to be coined, act of April 2, 1792.

Weight, 67.5 grains; fineness, .916 2/6; value, $2.50.

Deviation of weight allowed in coinage, 0.25 grains.

Deviation of fineness allowed in assay, .002; lowest, .899; highest, .901.
Coinage commenced, 1796.
Weight changed, act of June 28, 1834, to 64.5 grains.
Fineness changed, act of June 28, 1834, to .899.225.
Fineness changed, act of January 18, 1837, to .900.
Least legally current weight, 64.18 grains.
Total amount coined to close of fiscal year ended June 30, 1878, $26,933,600.

COUNTERFEITS.- The quarter eagle although too thin and small for sawing and filling has, however, been mutilated, bored and stuffed by another process; also extensively counterfeited in various ways. Nearly all counterfeit quarter eagles are too light, and experts could detect the fraud by hefting them, even in the dark. Such a piece, dated 1846, has been made weighing but forty-eight grains, instead of the 64.5 grains of the true coin.

February 16, 1887, *New York* (New York City) *Herald*:

Counterfeit Quarter Eagles

PHILADELPHIA, Feb. 15. 1887.—The United States Mint here to-day secured a counterfeit two dollar and a half gold piece of 1852, for which it has been in quest for years for the purpose of completing its cabinet. It was presented to Superintendent Fox by L.H. Taylor & Co., the bankers, who got it in a ten thousand dollar lot from the Sub-Treasury yesterday. The assayer declared it one of the most dangerous bogus gold coins ever made. "It contains only twenty-seven cents worth of gold." he said, "yet its weight is that of the real article to a hair, its size is exactly the same, save that the genuine coin is slightly thinner at the middle than the counterfeit, and it has the true ring of the pure metal. I readily recognized it by the head upon it. That style head and Liberty was not stamped upon the two and a half pieces of 1852."

January 30, 1894, *Cleveland* (Ohio) *Leader*:

Gold and silver coin counterfeits are of course much easier of detection than are spurious bills. Although the reproduction of outward form is often perfect, the unerring scale points out lightness within. When suspicion of coin is aroused reference to scales may be quickened by knowledge of the dates that most often appear on counterfeits. They are for the double eagle, $209, 1850, '51, '80, '84. The eagle &10, was extensively counterfeited prior to 1805. The most common dates for the bad coins of this denomination as 1801, '02, '10, '41, '47, '49, '52, '55, '58, '61, '71, '75, '79, '80, and '81. With the half eagle the usual dates for the counterfeits are 1800, '03, '21, '37, '38, '43, '44, '45, '47, '48, '51, '53, '55, '56, '57, '60, '61, '62, '69, '72, '75, '80, '81, '82, and '85. The seldom seen $3 piece is extensively counterfeited. In the quarter eagles, $2.50, the years most often met with are 1843, '44, '46, '51, '52, '53, '54, '55, '57, '58, '61, and '62. The gold dollars from counterfeiters' dies bear the dates 1851, '52, '53, '54, '56, '57, '60, and '61. Various dates up to 1873 appear on spurious standard silver dollars, and since 1878 every year appears. In half-dollars and quarters all dates have been counterfeited, but the latest dates of the former are the most deceptive.

APPENDIX

D

Error $2.50 Gold Coins

Over the 134-year history of the gold quarter eagle, the U.S. Mint and its branch locations struck millions of the $2.50 coins. Inevitably, a few errors occasionally escaped inspection and entered circulation. These mistakes and varieties are often eagerly sought by collectors.

Examples of quarter eagle error coins are given here.

Note: Error coins are shown larger than actual size.

Defective Die

A coin that has raised metal from a large die crack or small rim break. Coins that show evidence of light die cracks, polishing, or very minor die damage are generally of little or no value.

This 1851 Liberty Head quarter eagle features a die break on the obverse at 9 o'clock. Graded AU-58, it sold for $312 at a March 2020 Stack's Bowers auction.

Off Center

A coin that has been struck out of collar and incorrectly centered, with part of the design missing. These are misstruck coins that were made when the planchet did not enter the coinage press properly. Coins that are struck only slightly off center, with none of the design missing, are called broadstrikes (see the next category).

The 1912 Indian Head quarter eagle pictured here is struck 5% off center and graded AU-58. It sold for $1,527.50 at the June 2012 Stack's Bowers Baltimore auction, with the following listing: "Bright honey gold with lively luster. Struck off-center to 2 o'clock, the rim through BERTY and a few of the following stars, rim broad from 6 to 11 o'clock. On the reverse, the rim intersects the bottom details of the denomination. No edge reeding. Both neat and rare at the same time."

Broadstrike

A coin that was struck outside the retaining collar that still has the full design showing, unlike off-center strikes, above. When coins are struck without being contained in the collar die, they spread out larger than normal pieces.

This 1855 quarter eagle, graded MS-63, sold for $26,400 at the August 2021 ANA auction. The auction listing read, in part: "Failing to properly seat itself within the collar, the planchet on which this 1855 quarter eagle was struck instead lay atop the collar. The resulting impression from the dies, while imparting full detail to all design elements, caused the planchet to spread out, which is most readily evident as crescents of unstruck planchet along the upper left obverse and lower left reverse. . . . Extraordinary rarity and impressive Mint State preservation that is sure to result in spirited competition among advanced Mint error enthusiasts."

Lamination

This flaw occurs when a fragment of metal has peeled off the coin's surface because a foreign substance, such as gas oxides or dirt, was trapped in the strip as it is rolled out to the proper thickness. Lamination flaws may be missing or still attached to the coin's surface.

The 1904 Liberty Head quarter eagle, graded MS-62, has a lengthy lamination on the reverse of the coin. It was described as "sharply defined with pleasing color in a medium-gold hue." At the June 2011 Stack's Bowers Baltimore auction, it sold for $373.75.

The rare date 1909-O Indian Head quarter eagle shows lamination on the upper right of the obverse and is graded AU-55. It sold for $4,112.50 at the August 2017 ANA auction.

Brockage

A mirror image of the design is impressed on the opposite side of the same coin. These errors are caused when a struck coin remains on either die after striking, and it impresses its image into the next unstruck planchet, leaving a negative or mirror image.

The 1904 Liberty Head quarter eagle shown here is an example of both a partial brockage and a broadstrike error. Graded MS-66, it sold for $13,800 as part of the C.B. Slade Jr. Estate, June 2010.

WRONG PLANCHET

A coin that is struck on a planchet intended for another denomination or of the wrong metal. The coin shown here is a 1906 Indian Head cent struck on the planchet of a Liberty Head quarter eagle.

This coin appeared in *100 Greatest U.S. Error Coins* (2010) by David J. Camire, Fred Weinberg, and Nicholas P. Brown. The authors stated the following about this rare error:

> To hold in your hands and see with your own eyes a gold Indian Head cent is an event most coin collectors have never had the opportunity to experience. Only five genuine examples have been confirmed in the past 50-plus years. There is mention of three or four additional gold Indian Head cents, but it's been impossible to verify and authenticate these others. One or two of those reported may be gold plated, some other type of error, or just plain counterfeit.
>
> Speculation abounds as to the origin of the gold Indian Head cents. Due to the extra care that was taken at the Mint when accounting for precious metals, it is difficult to believe that a gold planchet intended for a Liberty Head $2.50 gold piece accidentally ended up in the tote bin or collar for Indian Head cents. Were these pieces struck deliberately, perhaps for Colonel Green, who owned all five specimens of the 1913 Liberty Head nickel? Today, the reason for their existence—just like the reason for the existence of those famous 1913 nickels—is unimportant compared to the fact that such a rare off-metal wrong-planchet error striking even exists.

APPENDIX

E

Counterfeit $2.50 Gold Coins

Gold coins of all denominations are popular targets for counterfeiters, but this is especially true for quarter eagles. The Anti-Counterfeiting Task Force (ACTF) of the Industry Council for Tangible Assets (today known as the National Coin & Bullion Association) conducted a 2018 survey of dealers, which showed that quarter eagles were the most commonly encountered counterfeits among pre-1933 gold coins.

Of the 363 dealers the ACTF surveyed, 42% had been offered a fake quarter eagle, compared to 36% who had been offered counterfeit half eagles and even fewer who had encountered fake gold dollars, eagles, and double eagles.

In a 2009 article for Professional Coin Grading Service, veteran grader Mike Sargent said that 40% of the counterfeit gold coins submitted to PCGS for authentication are Indian Head quarter eagles. He added that there are obvious reasons why counterfeiters gravitate toward smaller denominations like gold dollars and quarter eagles:

> First of all, one does not need a whole lot of gold to make these small coins, allowing the counterfeiter to sell fakes at a lower price point to unsuspecting buyers. Also, these counterfeits sell for the highest premium above their intrinsic gold value when compared to any other series of gold coins.
>
> For the most part, these four series of coins [gold dollars, Indian Head quarter eagles, $3 gold coins, and Indian Head half eagles] tend to have the largest ratio of design element-to-field, making it more difficult for proper authentication. The open fields on larger coins make it more difficult to hide depressions, tooling and inadequate luster, thus making authentication easier. Every single date in the $2½ Indian series exists as a counterfeit. In fact, PCGS once received a complete set of fakes in a custom holder, quite an achievement by an unwitting collector!

Improvements in coin-production technology and online selling platforms have made it easier than ever to create and sell convincing counterfeit coins and coin holders. If you plan to collect quarter eagles, it's important to know how to protect yourself from the ever-increasing volume of fakes being produced.

In the fourth edition of *Cash in Your Coins*, Beth Deisher says that buying from reputable dealers, especially if they offer guarantees that their coins are genuine, is a good way to avoid risky purchases. Be careful when buying through social media or online platforms like eBay, Craigslist, Facebook, Amazon, Alibaba, DHgate, and Wish.com. Beware of coins offered "as-is," with no guarantee of authenticity or refund policy.

Counterfeits produced in China are particularly common:

> On January 24, 2020, the Department of Homeland Security issued a 54-page report ("Combating Trafficking in Counterfeit and Pirated Goods") noting that the majority of fake and imitation products seized by U.S. Customs and Border Protection (CBP) during the past two decades arrived from China

Deisher also offers this sage advice: "Always remember: If the price is too good to be true—significantly below market price—it's probably counterfeit."

If you are able to handle a coin in person before buying, measuring its diameter, thickness, and weight can help to weed out counterfeit quarter eagles.

Quarter Eagle Dimensions and Specifications				
Date	Weight (Grams)	Tolerance	Diameter (mm)	Composition
1796–1808	4.374		~20.65	.9167 gold, .0833 copper and silver
1821–1827	4.374		~19.05	.9167 gold, .0833 copper and silver
1829–1834	4.374		~18.28	.9167 gold, .0833 copper and silver
1834–1836	4.180	0.008	~17.48	.8992 gold, .1008 copper and silver
1837–1839	4.180	0.016	~17.48	.900 gold, .100 copper and silver
1840–1907	4.180	0.016	17.98	.900 gold, .100 copper and silver
1907–1929	4.180	0.016	17.78	.900 gold, .100 copper

Closely inspect the surfaces of the coin, as some counterfeits will show distinctive markings. In the *United States Gold Counterfeit Detection Guide*, Bill Fivaz discusses some of these characteristics that may appear on inauthentic coins. These include color, mushy or sunken letters, spikes, tool marks, surface bubbles, greasy luster, and harsh cleaning, among others.

If you want to learn more about identifying counterfeit gold coins, Fivaz gives more detail and images of these "rules of thumb" in *United States Gold Counterfeit Detection Guide*. The book also devotes a chapter to quarter eagles, with close-up images of counterfeit coins and notes on the telltale signs that gave them away.

When viewed close-up, the pimply surface of this 1850-D quarter eagle makes it obvious that the "coin" is a cast counterfeit.

These small spikes near the denticles of this 1898 Liberty Head quarter eagle are a sign that the coin is a fake.

Notes

Chapter 1

1. No contemporary account of this event has been found.

Chapter 2

1. The totals in the 1934 *Report* do not necessarily agree with other figures and totals in the same issue of the *Report*. Moreover, there may be instances in which coins reserved for the Assay Commission were not counted (although for most years they were), that special presentation strikings may not be included for years prior to 1860 and for some later years as well, etc. Certain Charlotte and Dahlonega Mint daily records (as preserved in the National Archives) differ from published *annual* totals. Certain mintages are not recorded at all, including 1841 Philadelphia and 1845 New Orleans. Thus, these figures, while they appear to be precise, must be regarded as approximate.
2. Wire rims are called "fins" at the mints today. For many years in numismatics, these were called wire *edges*, but in recent times it has been realized that wire *rim* is more correctly descriptive.
3. Letter, January 4, 2000.

Chapter 4

1. *Varieties of United States Quarter Eagles*, 1964, p. 9. Breen was simply stating his opinion or giving a theory. No Mint records have been located to support such a procedure, although the process seems likely. The *business strike* term is a Breenism and has no counterpart in coinage records. The better term is *circulation strike*.

Chapter 5

1. This dime is not part of the collection today.

Chapter 7

1. Spelled Scott in Philadelphia directories of the time; spelled Scot on an image of George Washington that he engraved for a print and by the Mint payroll clerk. Scot is the form most often used in later numismatic texts.
2. The coin was actually from a relapped version of the same die; see Bass-Dannreuther for details.
3. David J. Davis, Russell J. Logan, Allen F. Lovejoy, John W. McCloskey, and William L. Subjack, *Early United States Dimes 1796–1837*, p. 42, is the source for "JR" numbers, now adapted and paraphrased; Bass-Dannreuther numbers added.
4. David J. Davis, Russell J. Logan, Allen F. Lovejoy, John W. McCloskey, and William L. Subjack, *Early United States Dimes 1796–1837*, pp. 45 and 47.
5. The 1802 dime has the same general size proportions.
6. David J. Davis, Russell J. Logan, Allen F. Lovejoy, John W. McCloskey, and William L. Subjack, *Early United States Dimes 1796–1837*, pp. 56 and 61.
7. *Ibid.*, pp. 57 and 65.
8. *Ibid.*, pp. 57 and 65.
9. *Ibid.*, p. 66.
10. *Ibid.*, p. 71.
11. *Ibid.*, p. 71.
12. *Ibid.*, p. 71.
13. *Ibid.*, p. 71.
14. Mehl had not bothered to consult current reference books.
15. The collection was hardly "the world's greatest," but it did include many great coins.
16. The term *Proof* was used to describe *every* gold coin in this early sale; at the time, there were no grading standards. Probably, this would be equivalent to About Uncirculated or Mint State today. Thus, it is classified here with circulation strikes.
17. The term *Proof* was used to describe *every* gold coin in this early sale; at the time, there were no grading standards. Probably, this would be equivalent to About Uncirculated or Mint State today. Thus, it is classified here with circulation strikes.
18. Charles Bell, who for a time served as governor of New Hampshire.
19. Although one more edition of the *Standard Catalogue* appeared after this description was written, no "greatly revised" version was ever created. The reference work had been first published by Wayte Raymond in 1934. A lot of the information intended for the revised *Standard Catalogue* found its way into to Scott's 1971 *Encyclopedia*, by Don Taxay.

Chapter 9

1. Although it may seem unnecessary to describe die details if only one die is known for the date, the listing of such characteristics will aid the specialist who may search for new die varieties, if such exist.
2. 1988 *Encyclopedia*, p. 489.
3. The Mint Cabinet was not formed until June 1838, at which time Adam Eckfeldt provided certain specimens of numismatic interest that he had saved since the time of minting, acquired in bullion deposits, or otherwise located.
4. The Brand journals are now in the library of the American Numismatic Society.
5. Noted as "Proof, cleaned" in the *Sylloge*. In the nineteenth century the curators of the Mint Collection cleaned the *silver* coins several times but, fortunately, spared most of the gold coins—the present specimen being an unhappy exception.
6. The Garrett correspondence was preserved by The Johns Hopkins University until 2000, then transferred to the American Numismatic Society Library, New York City. This quotation and certain others here were used in the 1982 book, *United States Gold Coins: An Illustrated History*.

Chapter 10

1. As printed in *The American Sentinel*, August 22, 1834.
2. For Senator Benton of Missouri. Coins minted during this era were sometimes called "Bentonian currency" as well.
3. This feature is seen more prominently on 1834 reverse die D.
4. These extended lines also can be seen on *certain* states of 1834 reverse die B, but are not as prominent as on 1834 reverse die D.
5. In 2019 Mark Borckardt attributed all Classic Head quarter eagles with photos appearing in the Heritage Permanent Auction Archives, the Stack's Bowers archives, and the Goldberg archives, a total of more than 4,000 individual auction appearances.
6. Haynor numbers are from Daryl Haynor's book on Classic Head quarter eagles and half eagles, *United States Classic Gold Coins of 1834-1839*. The book compiles notes from John McCloskey with additional information of his own, and HM numbers representing Haynor and McCloskey.
7. Under high magnification, on high-grade pieces very *faint* traces of other lines can be seen above stripes 5 and 6.
8. The tip of the arrow may appear to be slightly separated on certain die states and strikings.
9. The description of the die crack is from the Eliasberg specimen; the crack does not extend farther downward than the upper left serif of the 7.
10. These repunchings may fade in later strikings (cf. Breen, *New Varieties of $1, $2.50 and $5.00 United States Gold*, 1968, p. 6).
11. For example, the lower interior opening on the digit 8 used for 1838 dies has a very small central opening, and if it had been used, it would be visible within the rather large opening at the bottom part of the present 9. Similarly, there are no other 1839 dies from *any* mint that have a reasonable chance of being an 1839, 9 Over 8, overdate.
12. Or January 23, 1839 (cf. Clair M. Birdsall, p. 91).
13. Data in this paragraph adapted from Clair M. Birdsall, *The United States Branch Mint at Dahlonega, Georgia*, Table VI, from R.W. Julian's research in the National Archives.
14. Woodward did not look through many catalogs, it seems.
15. From his description of lot 1719 in the Pittman II sale, mentioned on page 132.
16. Report of the Secretary of the Treasury Levi Woodbury, December 6, 1836, printed in *Niles' Weekly Register*, December 17, 1836 (also see notes under "1836" in appendix C).
17. *Encyclopedia*, 1988, p. 491.
18. Clair M. Birdsall, *The United States Branch Mint at Charlotte, North Carolina*, p. 70.
19. Dr. John W. McCloskey, letter, January 4, 2000.
20. Clair M. Birdsall, *The United States Branch Mint at Charlotte, North Carolina*, p. 70.
21. However, on page 76 of his text, Birdsall gives a different total: 18,173.
22. Dr. John W. McCloskey, letter, January 4, 2000.
23. Clair M. Birdsall, *The United States Branch Mint at Dahlonega, Georgia*, p. 21.
24. Clair M. Birdsall, *The United States Branch Mint at Dahlonega, Georgia*, p. 21.

25. Dr. John W. McCloskey, letter, January 4, 2000.
26. House of Representatives; 26th Congress; 1st Session; Executive, Doc. No. 92.
27. *Annual Report* for 1839; see expanded information in Chapter 2 on the history of the New Orleans Mint.
28. *Walter Breen's Complete Encyclopedia of U.S. and Colonial Coins*, 1988, p. 495.

Chapter 11

1. *Walter Breen's Complete Encyclopedia of U.S. and Colonial Coins*, 1988, p. 210, quoting Alexandre Vattemare, 1861.
2. Or, in some instances, circulation strikes may have been made first, after which the dies were polished to make Proofs; for some quarter eagles of the 1820s and 1830s the production sequence is not known.
3. This survey is cited in the introduction to $20 double eagles.
4. Clair M. Birdsall, *The United States Branch Mint at Charlotte, North Carolina*, p. 71, from individual delivery records.
5. Figure from the superintendent. The coiner's figures, not verified, were: November, 4,250; December, 1,644.
6. Clair M. Birdsall, *The United States Branch Mint at Dahlonega, Georgia*, p. 21.
7. Adapted from Clair M. Birdsall, *The United States Branch Mint at Dahlonega, Georgia*, Table VI, from R.W. Julian's research in the National Archives; also Birdsall, pp. 56 and 80.
8. *Walter Breen's Complete Encyclopedia of U.S. and Colonial Coins*, 1988, p. 495.
9. A related situation exists for the 1873 $3, for which the Mint Report mentions only Proofs, although it is obvious that at least a few hundred were produced for circulation.
10. For information on market cycles see the author's *The Expert's Guide to Collecting and Investing in Rare Coins*.
11. Mehl seems to have kept extensive records on the 1841, but he did not choose to reveal more than sketchy details of extant pieces of which he was aware. He overlooked certain nineteenth-century citations, which was and still is not unusual for later catalogers, as early sale listings by Cogan, Woodward, et al., are not easy to find, often are not illustrated, and usually include only terse descriptions. Mehl's 1940 description seems to have been the foundation for certain later listings by others, most notably the 1946 "World's Greatest Collection" specimen (cataloged by Abe Kosoff).
12. The Dunham coin is said to have been stolen in 1964 (cf. Commentary in the Stack's offering of lot 865 in the James A. Stack Sr. Collection, October 1994).
13. These notes and the following registry are adapted by the author from Mark Borckardt's study published in the Bowers and Merena catalog of the Columbia Collection, November 1998.
14. It was popular years ago for numismatists to refer to the Philadelphia Mint as either the "parent mint" or the "mother mint." Such terminology is not often seen today. The "private collector in Connecticut" was none other than Joseph C. Mitchelson, later mentioned by Mehl (1940 et seq.). In 1911 Mitchelson passed away and his collection went to the State of Connecticut through terms of his will. Mitchelson's collection is now housed in a special room and vault at the Connecticut State Library in Hartford.
15. Interestingly, Stack's offering of the James A. Stack Sr. Collection coin in 1994, lot 865, used the term "Little Princess" multiple times, including in the headline, but did not credit the firm with originating the nickname.
16. Information adapted from the Mark R. Borckardt study for the Columbia Collection specimen and the present writer's expansion of the information for use in the Harry W. Bass Jr. Collection Part II offering of an 1841 quarter eagle in 1999.
17. Earlier, under the 1829 quarter eagle, it is noted that, seemingly, more Proofs than usual were made this year, which was the inauguration year for President Andrew Jackson. Coincidence? Perhaps.
18. Through the efforts of David and Susan Tripp as intermediaries, the Garrett records and correspondence were transferred in 2000 to the American Numismatic Society, New York City, joining the Virgil M. Brand archives, which had been transferred to the ANS a few years earlier (through the Brand heirs, the Tripps, and the present writer).

19. Jacob Shapiro, a.k.a. Jacob F. Bell, of Chicago; his son David Shapiro was later a founder of the RARCOA dealership and was active in the Professional Numismatists Guild.
20. Jerome (David) Kern, 1885–1945, was one of America's leading composers. Today he is remembered for *Showboat*, *Roberta* (with the song, "Smoke Gets In Your Eyes"), and other shows and melodies. His collection was auctioned by B. Max Mehl in 1950.
21. For a while the Numismatic Gallery had two offices as the facility at 42 East 50th Street, New York City, was maintained; later, operations were consolidated on the West Coast.
22. Recollection of Abner Kreisberg to the author, circa 1978.
23. Per later recollection of Abe Kosoff.
24. Adapted from Clair M. Birdsall, *The United States Branch Mint at Dahlonega, Georgia*, Table VI, from R.W. Julian's research in the National Archives.
25. Details in Clair M. Birdsall, *The United States Branch Mint at Dahlonega, Georgia*, p. 91.
26. Clair M. Birdsall, *The United States Branch Mint at Dahlonega, Georgia*, p. 23.
27. Clair M. Birdsall, *The United States Branch Mint at Dahlonega, Georgia*, p. 56.
28. Mehl must not have looked very far in his library!
29. Actually, in 1908.
30. Silas C. Stevens, who was especially active in the last decade of the nineteenth century and the first decade of the twentieth. At one time Theophile E. Leon, who became a "scout" for Virgil M. Brand, worked for Stevens. When the sale of the 1893 Isabella quarters at the World's Columbian Exposition fell short of expectations, Stevens bought thousands of remainders.
31. Cataloger Walter Breen seems to have overlooked the high-grade About Uncirculated coin sold a few years earlier in 1950 in Mehl's Golden Jubilee Sale, Lot 31, but he did have Mehl's Dunham catalog on hand to consult. Somehow, the several other auction offerings of higher grade pieces were also disregarded.
32. In his 1988 *Encyclopedia* Breen noted that these two pieces were "in private collections."
33. Clair M. Birdsall, *The United States Branch Mint at Charlotte, North Carolina*, p. 72; information from the coiner's records.
34. The coiner's report noted that 1,901 coins were returned to the treasurer for remelting, for they were considered unacceptable for circulation. Just eight coins were found to be satisfactory. Later, Director R.M. Patterson used the figure of 1,905 coins returned, with just four being acceptable, this being incorrect.
35. Adapted from Clair M. Birdsall, *The United States Branch Mint at Dahlonega, Georgia*, Table VI, from R.W. Julian's research in the National Archives.
36. For details see appendix C.
37. Clair M. Birdsall, *The United States Branch Mint at Charlotte, North Carolina*, p. 72; information from the coiner's records.
38. Birdsall: "Crosslet 4 head die and tail die both cracked during run. Not used again."
39. Adapted from Clair M. Birdsall, *The United States Branch Mint at Dahlonega, Georgia*, Table VI, from R.W. Julian's research in the National Archives.
40. This information differs from that in the "Mint Register of Dies" in the National Archives and is from Clair M. Birdsall, *Dahlonega*. Breen's data (*Encyclopedia*, 1988) differ: "2 obverses, 5 reverses shipped between December 22, 1842 and January 17, 1843."
41. Clair M. Birdsall, *The United States Branch Mint at Dahlonega, Georgia*, p. 57.
42. Clair M. Birdsall, *The United States Branch Mint at Dahlonega, Georgia*, p. 57.
43. Clair M. Birdsall, *The United States Branch Mint at Charlotte, North Carolina*, p. 73; information from the coiner's records. There was no 1844 coinage after the fire of July 27.
44. Mulford B. ("Britt") Simons, from Pennsylvania, was one of the most widely admired and respected of professional numismatists in the 1970s. Unfortunately, he died from an addiction that was beyond his control. His passing was widely mourned.
45. Adapted from Clair M. Birdsall, *The United States Branch Mint at Dahlonega, Georgia*, Table VI, from R.W. Julian's research in the National Archives.
46. In this and other years, and at various mints, there was no strict attention paid

to the date of the obverse die used in a given calendar year; thus, as R.W. Julian has pointed out in several other contexts, mintage figures based on calendar years do not necessarily reflect the actual number of coins dated that year. This same comment could be made for other copper, silver, and gold issues of the era.

47. Clair M. Birdsall, *The United States Branch Mint at Dahlonega, Georgia*, p. 27.
48. Adapted from Clair M. Birdsall, *The United States Branch Mint at Dahlonega, Georgia*, Table VI, from R.W. Julian's research in the National Archives.
49. Description from the Bass Collection Part II coin, lot 376.
50. Clair M. Birdsall, *The United States Branch Mint at Dahlonega, Georgia*, p. 58.
51. From research by R.W. Julian in the National Archives.
52. Breen picks up the Mehl comment, which by then had become fact, or at least conventional wisdom.
53. Seemingly not so, for a reading of the Bell description indicates that it was in a higher grade and not scratched.
54. In 1999 the present writer "rediscovered" the situation and gave it some publicity in the Bass II catalog, not being aware at the time of the New Netherlands prior publication.
55. Clair M. Birdsall, *The United States Branch Mint at Charlotte, North Carolina*, p. 73; information from the coiner's records. The Charlotte Mint, rebuilt after the fire of July 27, 1844, did not again produce coins until October 1846, when half eagles were coined; quarter eagles were first coined in December.
56. Dr. John W. McCloskey, letter, January 4, 2000.
57. Adapted from Clair M. Birdsall, *The United States Branch Mint at Dahlonega, Georgia*, Table VI, from R.W. Julian's research in the National Archives.
58. This is a very significant comment by cataloger Walter Breen (edited by John J. Ford Jr.) as it calls attention to "imperfect punches" and credits this punch (for just one four-digit punch was used) for making a die that resembled an overdate. However, this landmark comment was later forgotten.
59. Clair M. Birdsall, *The United States Branch Mint at Charlotte, North Carolina*, p. 74; certain figures include some coins reserved for the Assay Commission.
60. Adapted from Clair M. Birdsall, *The United States Branch Mint at Dahlonega, Georgia*, Table VI, from R.W. Julian's research in the National Archives.
61. Breen noted that the first piece was described in the New Netherlands sale of the Gaskill Collection, Sale 48, lot 249.
62. "Touted" was a favorite Breen word, implying some sort of misdoing on the part of anyone suggesting that an 1848 CAL. quarter eagle was rare. In the same description, Breen "touts" the coin as "extremely rare AU."
63. The tea caddy has been accepted by most historians, quite possibly incorrectly. "A small chest called a caddy" (nothing about tea), commented the *Washington Union* (as quoted in *Niles' Register*, LXIV, p. 336).
64. At one time the *Guide Book of United States Coins* stated that two Proofs were known, this on the advice of a Midwestern dealer. Later, one of these "Proofs" was inspected by modern students of the series and found to be prooflike Mint State, after which the Proofs were deleted (cf. comment to the author by Kenneth E. Bressett, *Guide Book* editor emeritus).
65. Multiple coins listed under each lot were sold separately. Lot 22 offered 26 individual items including three Gobrecht dollars, a 1792 half disme, this 1848 CAL. quarter eagle, and a "Fragment of the Independence Bell" that sold for 50 cents.
66. Citation furnished to Mark Borckardt by P. Scott Rubin, July 16, 1998. The catalog is now available on the Newman Numismatic Portal.
67. This was in the final year of Chapman's life.
68. Adapted from Clair M. Birdsall, *The United States Branch Mint at Dahlonega, Georgia*, Table VI, from R.W. Julian's research in the National Archives.
69. Comment by John W. McCloskey, as printed by David W. Akers, Pittman II sale, lot 1763.
70. Adapted from Clair M. Birdsall, *The United States Branch Mint at Dahlonega, Georgia*, Table VI, from R.W. Julian's research in the National Archives.

71. This shipment involved three pairs each of quarter eagle and half eagle dies.
72. As quoted by David W. Akers, Pittman II sale, lot 1764.
73. Comment by John W. McCloskey, as printed by David W. Akers, Pittman II sale, lot 1763.
74. Adapted from Clair M. Birdsall, *The United States Branch Mint at Dahlonega, Georgia*, Table VI, from R.W. Julian's research in the National Archives.
75. The diary is preserved in the National Archives. Citations are from an article by Rick Snow in the magazine *Longacre's Ledger*, June 2001.
76. Comment by John W. McCloskey, as printed by David W. Akers, Pittman II sale, lot 1763.
77. Adapted from Clair M. Birdsall, *The United States Branch Mint at Dahlonega, Georgia*, Table VI, from R.W. Julian's research in the National Archives.
78. Cf. text by Breen under 6214 (*Encyclopedia*, 1988).
79. The term silver alloy was often used by Elder to describe gold coins with a particularly light color. However, while the alloy typically contained some natural silver as an "impurity," the standard and primary metal used in alloying was copper.
80. Breen (*Encyclopedia*, 1988): "Most Uncs. are from a hoard of 5 discovered in May 1986."
81. Also see comment from John W. McCloskey, cited by David W. Akers, Pittman II sale, lot 1774; however, that comment mentions that the C does not touch the fraction bar.
82. Adapted from Clair M. Birdsall, *The United States Branch Mint at Dahlonega, Georgia*, Table VI, from R.W. Julian's research in the National Archives.
83. "Most acceptable" is a curious description for what seems to be a severely impaired coin from a numismatic viewpoint. Few knowledgeable collectors would want a quarter eagle with a solder mark on the portrait of Miss Liberty, or anywhere else on the coin.
84. Taglione, *The Quarter Eagles*, 1986, p. 282.
85. Adapted from Clair M. Birdsall, *The United States Branch Mint at Dahlonega, Georgia*, Table VI, from R.W. Julian's research in the National Archives.
86. Mehl and Sears had been fine friends and business associates. In 1918, when Sears severed his partnership with Wayte Raymond in the United States Coin Company, he announced his retirement from numismatics and stated that his inventory would be sold through Mehl in Texas. This was done via a sale held on October 29 of the same year. However, retired coin dealers often re-emerge on the scene, and in 1921 Sears bought the Manning Collection specimen of the 1804 dollar from Mehl for $2,500, plus a handling fee. On August 25, 1926, Sears, toastmaster at the ANA convention banquet, "introduced little Miss Dana Mehl, who showed us how the Charleston should be danced. As an encore she gave another style of dance, accompanied by a song, one of the lines frequently repeated being something about 'Poor Old Dad,' which showed how badly mistaken a child may sometimes be—that is, if she was referring to Max" (from an account in *The Numismatist*).
87. Also see comment from John W. McCloskey, cited by David W. Akers, Pittman II sale, lot 1774; however, that comment mentions that the C does not touch the fraction bar.
88. Adapted from Clair M. Birdsall, *The United States Branch Mint at Dahlonega, Georgia*, Table VI, from R.W. Julian's research in the National Archives.
89. Knowledge concerning mintmarks was very sketchy at the time, and Heaton was not aware that no 1858-S $2.50 pieces were struck; this comment no doubt prompted what Adams said in 1909.
90. The present author notes lot 1640 in Elder's April 1936 sale of the Walter J. Livingston Collection and lot 339 in J.C. Morgenthau's October 1940 Sale No. 418.
91. Also see comment from John W. McCloskey, cited by David W. Akers, Pittman II sale, lot 1774; however, that comment mentions that the C does not touch the fraction bar.
92. Adapted from Clair M. Birdsall, *The United States Branch Mint at Dahlonega, Georgia*, Table VI, from R.W. Julian's research in the National Archives.
93. Clair M. Birdsall, *The United States Branch Mint at Dahlonega, Georgia*, p. 35.

94. Adapted from Clair M. Birdsall, *The United States Branch Mint at Dahlonega, Georgia*, Table VI, from R.W. Julian's research in the National Archives.
95. An insight into cataloger Breen's very limited use of readily available resources (such as the world's largest American coin library at the American Numismatic Society, in the same city where Breen lived at the time). "Less than half-a-dozen" means no more than five records were known to him. As can be seen from other listings, he did not look very far!
96. As a long-time dealer in gold coins, I have come to know that Very Fine is the standard grade for a San Francisco Mint quarter eagle of this era. When a collection comes to hand, this is the grade expected. On the other hand, Philadelphia Mint coins of the same time period are apt to vary widely in grades and are of a higher average preservation.
97. Adapted from Clair M. Birdsall, *The United States Branch Mint at Dahlonega, Georgia*, Table VI, from R.W. Julian's research in the National Archives.
98. Adapted from Clair M. Birdsall, *The United States Branch Mint at Dahlonega, Georgia*, Table VI, from R.W. Julian's research in the National Archives.
99. The "much inferior specimen" was the recently sold WGC coin, the catalog wording for which seems to have been borrowed in part by Mehl.
100. The first specimen with Type I reverse was reported by Douglas Winter, *Coin World*, October 19, 1983. In *The Quarter Eagles*, 1986, Paul F. Taglione commented: "Very scarce, one of the rarest of all quarter eagles. . . . I know of only 6 in existence. The finest was in Heritage's 1985 Midwinter Sale."
101. In his description of a Proof 1863 $5 in his June 1883 sale of the William J. Jenks Collection, lot 400, John W. Haseltine commented: "I am informed that in this year but 30 quarter eagles, and about the same number of half eagles and three dollar gold pieces were struck. Hence they must be of exceeding rarity." This is a very pertinent comment, for it seems to indicate that Haseltine, whose ties with the Mint were closer than any other dealer of the time, was informed that not all Proof gold coins this year were made in the same quantity. By inference, it is logical to assume that more Proof gold dollars were made (for more exist today) and fewer $10 and $20 pieces.
102. The Garrett correspondence was preserved by The Johns Hopkins University until 2000, then transferred to the American Numismatic Society Library, New York City. This quotation and certain others here were used in the 1982 book, *United States Gold Coins: An Illustrated History*.
103. Repunched mintmark mentioned in Breen's 1964 monograph (in combination with his "low date" [centered date] logotype); not mentioned in his 1988 *Encyclopedia*.
104. Shame on them!
105. Erroneously listed as "reverses" in Mint records.
106. For example, David W. Akers (1875) found 16 auction appearances; Paul F. Taglione (1986) suggested the number was less than 30—which seems to indicate, perhaps, 25 or so.
107. Die description from the Bass II sale coin, lot 568.
108. Walter Breen (*Encyclopedia*, 1988) is more generous and suggests that 15 to 20 Proofs survive.
109. Mark Van Winkle, letter, October 3, 1996.
110. At least not since the Mills sale.
111. Cf. Paul F. Taglione, *The Quarter Eagles*, 1986; Walter Breen stated that just four dies were made and/or are known.
112. R.W. Julian, letter, March 29, 2000. Also, Julian, "Notes on U.S. Proof Coinage II: Gold," *Numismatic Scrapbook Magazine*, February 1967.
113. Many full gold Proof sets for various years of the 1860s onward will be found under citations for Proof $20s.
114. R.W. Julian, letter, March 29, 2000. Also, Julian, "Notes on U.S. Proof Coinage II: Gold," *Numismatic Scrapbook Magazine*, February 1967.
115. Quoted by R.W. Julian, "Notes on U.S. Proof Coinage II: Gold," *Numismatic Scrapbook Magazine*, February 1967. This differs from the official delivery records,

which "record 40 complete gold Proof sets (delivered on February 9) plus 20 gold dollars and 10 three dollar gold pieces."

116. This was stated in the 1887 *Report of the Director of the Mint*.
117. This was stated in the 1887 *Report of the Director of the Mint*.
118. Many full gold Proof sets for various years of the 1860s onward will be found under citations for Proof $20s.
119. John Dannreuther, conversation with the author, January 6, 2000; other sources.

Chapter 12

1. This would seem to indicate that some of the coins of 1908 had warped or distorted surfaces. It seems that Bigelow had seen some of the regular issue ("as soon as they were issued").

Appendix A

1. This same die was used to strike J-124a, listed with the 1850 coinage, but the 1850 coin is possibly a later restrike.
2. James Ross Snowden, *A Description of Ancient and Modern Coins in the Cabinet of the Mint of the United States*, 1860, p. 120.
3. Certain of these were listed in appendix A of the 7th edition of the Judd book, but are listed in the present text under the pattern issues of the year.
4. From circulation strike (not Proof) dies on a dime planchet. Probably a mint error (cf. Saul Teichman).

Appendix B

1. On October 24, 2014, Leonard Augsburger reviewed this section and made extensive changes based upon his research and his book, *Treasure in the Cellar*, 2008.
2. *The Numismatist*, April 1935, page 237, "Baltimore Hoard of Gold Coins to Be Sold at Auction."
3. Adapted from Roger W. Burdette, "U.S. Mint & Nazi Gold, Merkers *Kaiseroda* Salt Mine Treasure," *Journal of Numismatic Research*, Summer, 2013, Issue 3. pp. 53–61.
4. Ziemke, Earl F. *The U.S. Army in the Occupation of Germany 1944-1946*. Center of Military History, United States Army. Washington D.C. 1990. pp. 228–231. The term "salt mine" refers to potassium, sodium, magnesium, and other chemical salts, not just ordinary table salt.
5. Information furnished by David E. Tripp, letter, August 1996; he appraised the coins and assisted in their sale.
6. Adapted from an interview with Wayne Miller conducted by the author in Denver, Colorado, August 16, 1996; reviewed and edited by Wayne Miller, letter, September 26, 1996.

Appendix C

1. These may be brass pieces made by Kettle in England and widely distributed. Kettle also made half eagles.

Style Notes

Some quoted material, including auction descriptions, has been lightly edited to avoid repetition or to simplify. In no instance has the meaning been changed. Listings that simply say *Guide Book* instead of the full title, *A Guide Book of United States Coins*, have been changed to *Red Book*, as there are various Guide Books. Quoted auction prices may or may not represent actual sale prices as many items have been reserved or "bought in." This was a very common practice generations ago, not as much so today. Certain quoted prices are those listed by the auction houses and in some instances may not include a buyer's fee, such as was sometimes charged in the very early days when prices were given as face value, but for which there is little documentation.

Denticle/dentil has been standardized as denticle. Proof when referring to a coin format is capitalized.

Credits and Acknowledgements

A full list of those who have helped build my file of quarter eagle notes over the years would probably include several hundred names. In recent years those who have helped include the American Numismatic Association, American Numismatic Society, Mark R. Borckardt (coauthor of chapter 10), Roger W. Burdette, California Gold Marketing Group, Julia Casey, David Calhoun and the

Harry W. Bass Jr. Foundation, John W. Dannreuther, Richard Doty, Jennifer Dow, Bob Evans, Jeff Garrett, Ron Guth, Daryl Haynor, Wayne Homren, R.W. Julian, Christine Karstedt, John Kleeberg, John Kraljevich, David W. Lange, Dwight N. Manley, John McCloskey, Christopher R. McDowell, Jennifer Meers, John Pack, D. Brent Pogue, Saul Teichman, and Fred Weinberg.

Images are mostly from (alphabetically) Heritage Auctions, the National Numismatic Collection at the Smithsonian Institution (photography by Tom Mulvaney), and Stack's Bowers Galleries. In addition, images are from the author's resource files. Branch Mint 1838 sketches are by George L. Osborn.

About the Author

Q. David Bowers has been in the rare coin business since he was a teenager in 1953, including in later times as a founder of Stack's Bowers Galleries. He is a founding member of the Rittenhouse Society. He has been central in the showcasing at auction the greatest collections ever sold, including those of T. Harrison Garrett (for the Johns Hopkins University), Ambassador and Mrs. R. Henry Norweb, Virgil M. Brand, Louis E. Eliasberg, Harry W. Bass Jr., and D. Brent Pogue—accomplishments unmatched in professional numismatics. The author is a recipient of the Pennsylvania State University College of Business Administration's Alumni Achievement Award (1976); he has served as president of the American Numismatic Association (1983–1985) and president of the Professional Numismatists Guild (1977–1979); he is a recipient of the highest honor bestowed by the ANA (the Farran Zerbe Award); he was the first ANA member to be named Numismatist of the Year (1995); and one of only a few living people enshrined the Numismatic Hall of Fame (at ANA Headquarters in Colorado Springs).

Bowers is a recipient of the highest honor given by the Professional Numismatists Guild and has received more "Book of the Year Award" and "Best Columnist" honors given by the Numismatic Literary Guild than has any other writer. In July 1999, in a poll published in *COINage*, "Numismatists of the Century," Dave was recognized as one of six living people in this list of just 18 names. He was ranked as one of the Top Ten Most Influential People in Numismatics by *Coin World* in 2021. He is the author of over 60 books, including many Whitman titles, hundreds of auction and other catalogs, and several thousand articles including columns in *Coin World* (since 1961, the longest-running column in numismatic history) and *The Numismatist*.

Dave is a trustee emeritus of the New Hampshire Historical Society and a fellow of the American Antiquarian Society, the American Numismatic Society, and the Massachusetts Historical Society. He has been a key consultant for the Smithsonian Institution for decades (beginning with the curatorship of Dr. Vladimir Clain-Stefanelli), the Treasury Department, and the U.S. Mint, and is research editor of *A Guide Book of United States Coins* and editor of *Mega Red*. For many years he was a guest lecturer at Harvard University. This is a short list of his honors and accomplishments. In Wolfeboro, New Hampshire, he is a former member of the Board of Selectmen and is the town historian.

About the Foreword Writer

Mike Fuljenz is a nationally renowned expert in precious metals and coins, and the author of several books on gold coins. His books, commentary, and media appearances have earned a number of awards, including the National Literary Guild's Book of the Year Award. Mike is the president of Universal Coin & Bullion, based in Beaumont, Texas.

About the Coauthor of Chapter 10

Mark R. Borckardt is a senior cataloger and senior numismatist at Heritage Auctions. During his long career in numismatics, he has cataloged many rarities and great collections, including the collections of Harry W. Bass Jr., Louis E. Eliasberg, and Eric P. Newman. Borckardt was inducted to the Rittenhouse Society in 1994. He was named the 2020 Numismatist of the Year by the American Numismatic Association, and was a recipient in 2021 of the Early American Coppers Club's Herbert Silberman Award (granted to only 10 people in the past 40 years).

Selected Bibliography

Adams, Edgar H. and William H. Woodin. *U.S. Pattern, Trial and Experimental Pieces*. New York: American Numismatic Society, 1913.

Adams, John Weston. *United States Numismatic Literature. Volume I. Nineteenth Century Auction Catalogs*. Mission Viejo, CA: George Frederick Kolbe Publications, 1982.

———. *United States Numismatic Literature. Volume II. Twentieth Century Auction Catalogs*. Crestline, CA: George Frederick Kolbe Publications, 1990.

Akers, David W. *United States Gold Patterns*. Englewood, OH: Paramount International Coin Corporation, 1975.

———. *United States Gold Coins: An Analysis of Auction Records, Gold Quarter Eagles*. Englewood, OH: Paramount International Coin Corporation, 1975.

American Journal of Numismatics. American Numismatic and Archaeological Society, later the American Numismatic Society. New York City, NY, and Boston, MA: Various issues 1866 to 1912.

Attinelli, Emmanuel J. *Numisgraphics, or a List of Catalogues in Which Occur Coins or Medals, Which Have Been Sold by Auction in the United States*. New York: 1876.

Bass, Harry W., Jr., and John W. Dannreuther. *Early U.S. Gold Coin Varieties: A Study of Die States 1795–1834*. Atlanta, GA: Whitman Publishing LLC, 2006. Text by Dannreuther from the extensive Bass notes.

Bolles, Albert S. *The Financial History of the United States from 1774 to 1885*. Three volumes. New York, 1879–1894.

Bowers, Q. David. *United States Gold Coins: An Illustrated History*. Los Angeles, CA: Bowers and Ruddy Galleries, 1982; later printings by Bowers and Merena Galleries, Inc., Wolfeboro, NH.

———. *The History of United States Coinage*. Los Angeles, California: Bowers and Ruddy Galleries, Inc., 1979; later printings by Bowers and Merena Galleries, Inc., Wolfeboro, NH.

———. *Abe Kosoff: Dean of Numismatics*. Wolfeboro, New Hampshire: Bowers and Merena Galleries, Inc., 1985.

———. "Collecting United States Gold Coins: A Numismatic History." Chapter in *America's Gold Coinage*, the proceedings of the Coinage of the Americas Conference, American Numismatic Society, November 4–5, 1989. New York City, NY: American Numismatic Society, 1990.

———. *American Coin Hoards and Treasures*. Wolfeboro, NH: Bowers and Merena Galleries, Inc., 1997.

———. *Harry W. Bass Jr. Museum Sylloge*. Wolfeboro, NH: Bowers and Merena Galleries, 2002.

Bowers, Q. David with Mark Borckardt. *Harry W. Bass Jr. Museum Sylloge*. Wolfeboro, NH: Bowers and Merena Galleries, 2002.

Breen, Walter. *Walter Breen's Encyclopedia of U.S. and Colonial Proof Coins, 1792–1977*. Albertson, New York: FCI Press, 1977. Updated edition, 1987.

———. *Walter Breen's Complete Encyclopedia of U.S. and Colonial Coins*. Garden City, NY: Doubleday, 1988.

Burdette, Roger W. *Renaissance of American Coinage, 1905–1908*. Great Falls, VA: Seneca Mill Press, 1906.

Carothers, Neil. *Fractional Money*. New York: John Wiley & Sons, 1930.

Coin World. Sidney, OH: Amos Press, *et al.*, 1960 to date.

Coin World Almanac. Third edition. Sidney, OH: Amos Press, Sixth edition, 1990.

Coinage Laws of the United States 1792–1894. Modern foreword to reprint by David L. Ganz. Wolfeboro, NH: Bowers and Merena Galleries, Inc. 1991

Dannreuther, John W. "James Barton Longacre: A Maligned Artist." Adapted from a Groves Lecture presentation at the American Numismatic Society, New York, April 15, 2000.

———. *United States Proof Coins*. Volume IV: Gold. Gahanna, OH: Kolbe & Fanning Numismatic Booksellers, 2017.

DeLorey, Thomas K. "Longacre: Unsung Engraver of the U.S. Mint," *The Numismatist*, October 1985.

Dickeson, Montroville Wilson. *The American Numismatical Manual*. Philadelphia: J.B. Lippincott & Co., 1859. (1860 and 1865 editions were slightly retitled as *The American Numismatic Manual.*)

Eckfeldt, Jacob Reese and William Ewing DuBois. *New Varieties of Gold and Silver Coins, Counterfeit Coins, and Bullion; With Mint Values*. New York: George P. Putnam, 1851.

Heaton, Augustus G. *A Treatise on the Coinage of the United States Branch Mints*. Washington, D.C.: published by the author, 1893.

Hodder, Michael and Q. David Bowers. *The Norweb Collection: An American Legacy*. Wolfeboro, NH: Bowers and Merena Galleries, Inc. 1987.

Judd, Dr. J. Hewitt. *United States Pattern, Experimental and Trial Pieces*. Racine, WI: Whitman Division of Western Publishing Company, 1959 and later editions (edited by Q. David Bowers, Whitman Publishing, Atlanta, GA).

Julian, R.W. "United States Proof Coinage." Manuscript created in 1980 for *Coins* magazine and published sequentially between September 1980 and December 1982.

Mason's Monthly Illustrated Coin Collector's Magazine. Philadelphia and Boston: Ebenezer Locke Mason. Various issues of the 1860s, 1870s, and 1880s.

McCloskey, John W. Manuscript notes of his studies of Classic Head quarter eagles for use in the present book (typescript dated and signed, November 28, 1999; verified and signed again, July 5, 2007), plus edits and comments on the existing manuscript in 1999 and 2000.

Moran, Michael F., and Jeff Garrett. *1849: The Philadelphia Mint Strikes Gold*. Atlanta, GA: Whitman Publishing, 2016.

NGC Census Report. Sarasota, FL: Numismatic Guaranty Company of America, various issues 1980s to date.

Numismatic News. Krause Publications, Iola, WI. Various issues 1950s to date.

Numismatic Scrapbook Magazine. Lee F. Hewitt, Chicago, IL; Amos Press, Sidney, OH. Various issues 1935 to 1976.

Numismatist, The. Dr. Geo. F. Heath, Farran Zerbe, American Numismatic Association, 1888 to date. Currently published in Colorado Springs, CO.

PCGS Population Report, The. Newport Beach, California: Professional Coin Grading Service, Inc. Various issues, 1980s to date.

Pollock, Andrew W. *United States Pattern Coins and Related Pieces*. Wolfeboro, NH: Bowers and Merena Galleries, 1994.

Raymond, Wayte. *Standard Catalogue of United States Coins and Paper Money* (titles vary). Scott Stamp & Coin Co. (and others): New York, 18 editions 1934 to 1957 editions.

Schein, Allan. *The Gold Indians of Bela Lyon Pratt*. Published by the author, 2016.

Sumner, William G. *A History of American Currency*. New York: Henry Holt and Company, 1874.

Taglione, Paul F. *A Reference to United States Gold Coinage*, Volumes 1–4. Boston, MA: Numismatic Research and Service Corporation, 1986.

United States Mint, Bureau of the Mint, *et al. Annual Report of the Director of the Mint*. Philadelphia, PA; Washington, D.C., c. 1849 to 1890.

Vermeule, Cornelius. *Numismatic Art in America*. 2nd edition. Atlanta, GA: Whitman Publishing LLC, 2007.

Winter, Douglas. *Charlotte Mint Gold Coins, 1838–1861, a Numismatic History and Analysis*. Wolfeboro, NH: Bowers and Merena Galleries, Inc., 1987.

———. *New Orleans Mint Gold Coins, 1839–1909, a Numismatic History and Analysis*. Wolfeboro, NH: Bowers and Merena Galleries, Inc., 1992.

———. *Gold Coins of the Dahlonega Mint 1838–1861*. Dallas, TX: DWN Publishing, 1997.

Yeoman, R.S. *A Guide Book of United States Coins*. Kenneth, E. Bressett, editor. Whitman Publishing Company (and Western Publishing Company, Inc.), Racine, Wisconsin: various editions 1946 to date, current publisher, Whitman Publications, Atlanta, GA, now Pelham, AL.

Index